Challenging Neighbours

Rethinking German and
Dutch Economic Institutions

Springer
Berlin
Heidelberg
New York
Barcelona
Budapest
Hong Kong
London
Milan
Paris
Santa Clara
Singapore
Tokyo

CPB
Netherlands Bureau for Economic Policy Analysis

Challenging Neighbours

Rethinking German and Dutch Economic Institutions

With 40 Figures
and 104 Tables

Springer

CPB Netherlands Bureau for Economic Policy Analysis
P.O. Box 80510
2508 GM The Hague
The Netherlands

ISBN 3-540-63501-7 Springer-Verlag Berlin Heidelberg New York

Cataloging-in-Publication Data applied for
Die Deutsche Bibliothek - CIP-Einheitsaufnahme
Challenging neighbours: rethinking German and Dutch economic institutions; with 104 tables / CPB, Netherlands Bureau for Economic Policy Analysis. - Berlin; Heidelberg; New York; Barcelona; Budapest, Hong Kong; London; Milan; Paris; Santa Clara; Singapore; Tokyo: Springer, 1997
ISBN 3-540-63501-7

Printed in Germany

Hardcover-Design: Erich Kirchner, Heidelberg

SPIN 10547232 42/2202-5 4 3 2 1 0 - Printed on acid-free paper

Preface

This book is an example of CPB-teamwork. It started in autumn 1993 on the initiative of Gerrit Zalm, former director of CPB, currently minister of finance of the Netherlands. The purpose of the project is to increase insights in the German and Dutch economies' strengths and weaknesses, in particular regarding their institutional orders. These insights, in turn, can provide policy options for policy-makers to enhance social innovation: the adjustment of institutions and practices to changing circumstances. The study emphasizes that social innovation is a process of trial and error in which policy-makers face various trade-offs. Hence learning is of paramount importance. That also applies to CPB: the study took a long time to mature, not least because it was an interesting and challenging learning process for its authors. The project leader, George Gelauff, showed considerable 'Ausdauer' in guiding and coaching a changing team through the many ups and downs that came with the process.

In retrospect, three phases can be distinguished in the project. The first phase may be called the exploratory phase. During this phase, almost all divisions of CPB were asked to conduct a comparative analysis in their field. With respect to the choice of focus, they had complete freedom. This phase took about one year and was concluded with an internal workshop where the research output was presented. Results of this phase were laid down in internal papers; some of these were published as CPB-research memoranda (vocational education, agriculture, trade interelationships) or in the annual Central Economic Plan (sectoral structure).

During the second phase, which started at the beginning of 1995, it was decided to focus the study on a number of topics that were considered to be of special interest for Dutch and German policy-makers. Selected topics were the socio-economic order, labour market and social protection, corporate governance and finance of SMEs, R&D policies, and regulation and competition policies. During this phase, lasted until May 1996, the analysis of these topics was deepened. At the same time, work started on the development of an overall analytical framework for the analysis of institutions. Staff members which were involved in this phase were Corina den Broeder (labour market), Philip ten Cate (health care), Theon van Dijk (from February 1996 on R&D policies), George Gelauff (analytical framework, corporate governance and labour market), Larissa van Geijlswijk (electricity and gas markets), Nicole de Jager (small business finance) and Helmer Vossers (from June 1995 at the Dutch Ministry of Finance, on social protection and pensions). Main research products of this period are research memoranda on corporate governance and the labour market, again other results were laid down in internal papers.

The final phase, the actual writing of the book, started in July 1996 and lasted until early July 1997. For this task, the team was temporarily reinforced. The team that wrote the book consisted of Eric Bartelsman (Chapter 14, Health Care), Lans Bovenberg (Chapters 6 and 7, Social Protection and Pensions), Corina den Broeder (Chapters 8, 9 and 10 on the Labour Market and Corporate Governance), Kick Bruin of the Dutch Social and Economic Council (Chapter 12, Regulation and Competition Policies), Theon van Dijk, now at National Economic Research Associates (Chapter 11 and 12, R&D Policies and Regulation and Competition Policies), George Gelauff (Chapters 1, 2, 5, 10 and 11, on Comparing German and Dutch Institutions, the Interplay of Institutions, Socio-Economic Governance, Corporate Governance and R&D policies, respectively), Larissa van Geijlswijk (Chapter 13, Electricity and Gas Markets), Nicole de Jager, now at ING Group (Chapters 3 and 4, Economic Development in Comparison and Structural Comparison; the work on SME finance will be published separately), André de Jong (Chapter 13 and 14, Electricity and Gas Markets, Health Care), Kees van Paridon of the Scientific Council for Government Policy (WRR) (Chapters 3 and 4, Economic Development in Comparison and Structural Comparison). The general direction of the writing of the book was in the hands of Lans Bovenberg, George Gelauff en André de Jong.

Other staff members of CPB that provided support for the production of the book were Ton Brouwer, Adri den Ouden, Maja Verhoeve and Erwin Zijleman (construction of figures), Jacqueline de Haan-Vellinga and Kathy Schuitemaker (secretarial assistance), Gerda Janssen, Luciënne Damshuizer en Aurelia Meershoek-Horbowiec (librarians) and John Koenders and Chris Stoop (reprography).

Finally, I would like to express my gratitude to the many institutions and persons - see the list of acknowledgements - who have provided us with information or have commented on preliminary drafts of chapters of the study. A special word of thanks is due to the Social and Economic Council of the Netherlands and the Dutch Scientific Council for Government Policy for their kind permission to lend out staff members of their institutes to CPB.

F.J.H. Don
Director

Table of Contents

1 Comparing German and Dutch Institutions

What is so challenging about Germany and the Netherlands being neighbours? In terms of arable area (united) Germany is almost nine times the size of the Netherlands, the German population is over five times as large as the Dutch population and the ratio of gross domestic products of the two countries equals a factor six. From another perspective, consumption per capita differs to a much less extent and is in both countries among the highest in the world. Also, macro economic investment ratios are hardly different. So why compare two countries, which apart from size seem to be so much alike? Yet, the structure of the enterprise sector clearly differs, just as several features of the welfare state. Do significant differences exist after all? These and similar questions may arise with a comparative study between Germany and the Netherlands. Accordingly, these considerations constitute the core subject of this introductory chapter.

This chapter focuses on the motivation and the background of the study. Furthermore, it also summarizes the study's main results. Section 1.1 addresses the reasons for a comparative study of German and Dutch institutions. Section 1.2 provides an overview of the contents of the book and presents policy options.

1.1 Motivation

Four questions guide the organisation of the first part of this chapter. Section 1.1.1 asks 'Why a comparative study?'. It considers what can be learned from a comparative economic analysis. Section 1.1.2 poses the question: 'Why focus on institutions?'. It addresses the reasons and limitations behind the principal characteristic of the study: the institutional approach. Section 1.1.3 asks 'Why a qualitative analytical method?' It turns to the motivation for the study's analytical framework, which heavily leans on economic theory. The question 'Why Germany?', is addressed in Section 1.1.4, which discusses the reasons for a comparison between Germany and the Netherlands.

1.1.1 Why a Comparative Study?

Two objectives guide this comparative study of Germany and the Netherlands. The first is to broaden the insight in the German and Dutch economies' strengths and weaknesses, in particular regarding their institutional order. These insights can be relevant for economic policy. The foreign economy may act as a mirror, which enables policy makers to take a fresh look at current domestic practices and institutions, to reappraise their strong points and to think of ways to improve their imperfections. The second objective adds a future orientation. The aim is to shed light on the impact of major demographic, economic, technological and social trends on the institutional order of the two countries. This may contribute to the process of joint learning, so that rather than being overcome by changing circumstances, policy makers can anticipate them pro-actively.

Social Innovation. This study's basic view on the economy emphasizes learning and social innovation in an uncertain and changing environment. Chapter 2 argues that economic agents are boundedly rational, *i.e.* they have a limited knowledge of their environment and an imperfect view of the future. Bounded rationality and an uncertain environment make learning a matter of primary importance. Individuals learn and their collective knowledge base constitutes one of society's most valuable assets. A part of the process of learning concerns reflections of society on its own functioning. These reflections by citizens, politicians, entrepreneurs, or representatives of social organisations on the strong and weak features of the current institutional order steer the process of social innovation: the adjustment of institutions and practices to changing circumstances.

A citation from CPB (1992: 51) illustrates the importance of social innovation:

> 'Lastly, history also teaches that time after time, individuals, firms, sectors and entire economies often push their success formulas too far, for too long. Even when clear signals are sent that limits are being reached, the inability to adjust to new circumstances is often striking. It explains why social innovation has been placed at the heart of the prosperity circle. Especially for developed countries, which are striving for continued economic growth and development, social innovation is extremely important and, as history has shown time and again, very difficult. Failure to achieve it opens the door to institutional sclerosis and ultimately relative economic decline.'

Bounded rationality makes social innovation a process of trial and error. Nobody is able to derive a clear-cut optimal institutional configuration that maximizes social welfare. Frequently, there is also no guarantee that such an optimum exists. Different configurations affect different performance criteria in opposite ways and no strong argument can be given that one of these criteria dominates the others. 'Solving' a problem in terms of one criterium through institutional adjustment may create problems in terms of other criteria. For instance, deregulation may increase incentives and flexibility, but may harm commitment to invest in relationship-specific assets. This points also at the possibility that different institutional orders can co-exist at the same time. By consequence, social innovation largely is a process of trial and error. This makes it more fruitful to think in terms of trade-offs between various performance criteria, than in terms of a unique institutional solution that maximizes social welfare.

A Single Step in Social Innovation. The current study forms part of the trial and error process of social innovation. On the one hand, it aims to contribute to social innovation. It attempts to learn from experiences in Germany and the Netherlands by comparing their institutional orders. On the other hand, of course bounded rationality also applies to the study itself. It cannot pretend to present a final solution on all fields covered. Instead, carrying out the study has been a learning process of its own. As such the study forms no more than a single step in the continuing trial and error process of social innovation. Yet, being part of that process is what makes comparative economic analysis so interesting and rewarding.

1.1.2 Why a Focus on Institutions?

Institutions can be defined as humanly devised constraints that structure human interaction (North, 1994).[1] Institutions range from formal constraints, such as rules, regulations and legislation, to informal constraints such as norms of behaviour. The following chapters address in particular formal constraints, because these are nearest to economic analysis. For instance, topics that arise are labour market regulations, wage bargaining, institutions that affect corporate governance, science and technology policy *etc.*

Institutions Matter. From an economic perspective, institutions matter because institutions affect national welfare and wellbeing, primarily through productivity and employment. For instance, a country's educational institutions may promote human capital formation, which raises labour productivity in the long run. Technology policy may enhance research and development. Labour market regulation, taxation and social insurance influence labour supply and demand decisions and search behaviour of unemployed, and thus affect a country's activity rate, the number of working hours per capita. Of course, many other examples can be given.

Comparison of a broad range of countries provides evidence for the importance of institutions and policies on a country's prosperity (Lal and Myint, 1996; Olson, 1996). In particular, the experiences of those countries with weak institutional orders show that the absence of well-developed institutions severely hamper economic growth and may cause poverty. Olson (1996: 19) concludes:

> . . . 'the large differences in per capita income across countries cannot be explained by differences in access to the world's stock of productive knowledge or to its capital

---

[1] Box 2.1 in Chapter 2 contains a number of definitions of key concepts.

markets, by differences in the ratio of population to land or natural resources, or by differences in the quality of marketable human capital or personal culture. Albeit at a high level of aggregation, this eliminates each of the factors of production as possible explanations of most of the international differences in per capita income. The only remaining plausible explanation is that the great differences in the wealth of nations are mainly due to differences in the quality of their institutions and economic policies.'

Institutions Matter More and More. The above discussion on social innovation already indicated that institutions are also relevant for developed countries that benefit from a more secure institutional order than some developing countries or new market economies. In response to actual economic developments, awareness of the importance of institutions for productivity and welfare increased considerably in recent decades. Stronger international interdependency formed a major driving force, because it diminished nation states' capacity to act in the traditional fields of fiscal and monetary policy.

The 1970s and early 1980s showed the limitations of (uncoordinated) fiscal expansionary policies. During the 1950s and the 1960s, liberalisation of international trade made OECD economies more open (Maddison, 1983: 596). By consequence, a relatively large part of fiscal stimulation leaks away abroad. The failing French fiscal expansion in 1981-82 constitutes a case in point. As a response to increasing international dependence, the shift to supply-side policies in the 1970s in particular turned attention to wage moderation and institutions affecting wage formation (see also Bruno and Sachs, 1985). In his 1976 lecture for the American Economic Association, Lindbeck (1976: 7) emphasized that: 'a successful stabilization policy *in open economies* cannot rely only on aggregate demand policies; relative prices between tradables, non-tradables and labour are also highly relevant'.

The limits of monetary policy became apparent in the 1980s and early 1990s, when liberalisation of financial markets increased international mobility of financial capital. Liberalisation increased the importance of trust in financial markets (Drazen and Helpman, 1988). Stability and adherence to strict policy rules breed trust. Financial markets punish every departure from what they consider solid policy, with rising interest rates and currency depreciation as a result. The Mexican peso crisis forms a recent example. Financial markets strongly discipline governments and monetary authorities. Lawrence *et al.* (1996: 17) write:

'With their expansion and integration, international capital markets place increasing pressure on governments. Under the Bretton Woods system a 5 percent shift in currency values was a major international event. International markets achieve such changes now in a matter of days and sometimes minutes. Markets pass judgement on government actions continuously, judgements that governments ignore at their peril.'

In recent years, national governments increasingly became aware of these constraints and have adapted their policies. More and more they aim at designing a stable macro-economic policy.

In the 1980s and 1990s continuing internationalization intensifies the shift away from macroeconomic fiscal and monetary policy towards policies directed at improving the quality of immobile factors of production and of economic institutions. Mobility of factors of production gains further momentum. Two trends act in a mutually reinforcing way: technologies that decrease the costs of transportation and communication, and further liberalisation of international markets. These trends foster the rise of 'foot-loose' industries, promote intra-industry trade and enhance mobility of factors of production (Lawrence *et al.*, 1996). For instance, European integration offers more possibilities for European citizens to follow a profession outside their native country and companies can shift production abroad more easily. These developments form part of the process of internationalization, the continuing international entwining of economic activities.

Locational Competition. Internationalization underlines the importance of high quality immobile factors of production and institutions to attract mobile factors of production and tie these to a country or a region. Again citing Lawrence *et al.* (1996: 18):

> 'As national differences narrow and the intensity of competition increases, business decisions on where to locate become more sensitive to differences in domestic policies and practices. Paradoxically, the more similar countries are, the more significant their remaining differences become in determining trade and investment flows.'

Therefore, policies that raise the quality of immobile factors of production and of national institutions gain importance and become potentially more effective.

Internationalization implies that to some extent national governments become competitors, whether they like it or not. Enterprises compete on national and international markets. Nation states 'compete' by means of their educational system, their social and physical infrastructure, the tax system, the quality of their government, and their legislative framework. Through the quality of their immobile factors of production and their institutions, nation states may attract financial capital, direct investments by foreign companies and high-qualified labour. This strengthens a nation's knowledge base, increases productivity and improves employment opportunities (compare Siebert, 1995).[2]

---

[2] Note that locational competition concerns only one element of the interaction between institutions and economic performance. In many cases the direct impact of a nation's institutional order on domestic productivity and employment, adhered to above, is more important than locational competition. In this respect the statements of Krugman (1994,

This study can also be seen as part of the process of locational competition. By analyzing the strengths and weaknesses of the two countries' institutional orders, it makes locational competition between Germany and the Netherlands more transparent. This may provide challenges for policy makers to improve upon their neighbour's performance by designing innovative approaches to policy issues. In a world of bounded rationality, competition is an important channel for experimenting and for producing information about what works and what does not work. An assessment of a country's institutional order may indicate topics for further experimentation.

In conclusion, a country's institutional characteristics influence the productivity of domestic enterprises and the attractiveness of a country to foreign enterprises. An economy that fails to secure its attractiveness as an investment site will lose ground and consequently bear high adjustment costs in the future. Loss of access to the global technical knowledge base, falling productivity, and product quality lagging behind on the world market either depresses national welfare and wellbeing or necessitates adjustment processes with high adjustment costs. Preventing such a scenario provides an incentive for countries to learn from each other. This study's benchmarking characteristics may contribute to that learning process.

Limitations of a Focus on Institutions. Of course, this study's focus on institutions entails some limitations. In particular, the analysis generally has a micro-economic orientation, because of the often detailed character of institutions. At the same time, although restricted by internationalization, macro-economic policy remains an important determinant of economic performance. However, no attempt is made to fully review micro- and macro-economic factors and provide a complete assessment of economic performance. This applies also to the impact of macro-economic policies on German unification. Both on macro-economic policy and on German unification, this study refers to the elaborate literature (see for instance Giersch *et al.*, 1992; Sinn and Sinn, 1992; van Ark *et al.*, 1996 and the references cited there).

Another limitation involves the number of institutions and the degree of detail required to perform meaningful comparisons. As shown by the list of contents, the study focuses on the three main markets (labour, capital and goods and services), technology, a number of major institutions that affect these markets (the socio-economic order, social security and pensions), and some illustrative case studies on the product market (electricity, health care).

1996) that countries do not compete for a share on the world market remain all too valid.

1.1.3 Why a Qualitative Analytical Method?

Because of the large effort required to assess the impact of institutions on performance, international comparative analysis of broad sets of institutional arrangements generally involves a trade-off between measurement without theory and theory without measurement. This study is located on the theory side of this trade-off. In particular, it develops an elaborate analytical framework based on theories in institutional economics. The analytical framework introduces four main trade-offs to structure thinking about the impact of institutions on performance and about how changes in the social, technological and international conditions affect a country's institutional order. Therefore, the study complements quantitative benchmarking studies like the recent competitiveness report by the Ministry of Economic Affairs (EZ, 1995). Moreover, the analytical framework suits the mission of CPB to perform independent analyses that are both scientifically sound and relevant to policy making.

The broad range of topics and the qualitative analytical method are challenging and at the same time subject to limitations. Structured thinking about relationships between institutions, performance and trends, poses intellectual and policy challenges. In this respect, Challenging Neighbours constitutes only a first step. Indeed, the qualitative approach, to a certain degree supported by empirical evidence, provides only broad linkages between institutions and performance. Detailed assessments about the quantitative impact of specific institutions on specific performance indicators, like company performance, would require a more focused approach.

Another limitation is that the study takes current institutions as given. Apart from occasional short historical retrospectives, the analytical framework does not attempt to explain the current institutional order in Germany and the Netherlands. Hence, from a historical perspective, Challenging Neighbours presents a static picture. However, with respect to future developments, it offers a more dynamic perspective, because it assesses the impact of important changes in the economic environment on the institutional order.

1.1.4 Why Germany?

From the Netherlands' point of view, Germany is an obvious choice for a reference country.[3] The economies have strong mutual links, *e.g.* in the monetary field and regarding trade, and the performance of the German economy is vital to Dutch

---

[3] The comparison of Germany and the Netherlands is also complementary to the comparative-strength analysis in the long-term CPB(1992) scenario study. In particular, instead of treating the European Union as a single economic block, the present study narrows the focus on countries within the European Union.

economic performance. Also, issues occupying employers, employees and policy makers in the two countries are rather similar, although solutions and ways of approach often differ. Examples here are deregulation initiatives and discussions on the economic structure, known in Germany as the Standort debate. Moreover, despite the geographical proximity, knowledge of the German economy and of German institutions is limited in the Netherlands.

The Social Market Economy. The German economic order by itself justifies a further analysis. A distinct economic model characterizes Germany: the Social Market Economy, which is frequently contrasted with the Anglo-American model. Long-term relationships, quality products, high-skilled labour, elaborate social security, and co-determination are just a few key words associated with the Social Market Economy. Not that long ago many people considered these features to be strong points of an economic model that combined economic vigour with solidarity and consensus. Indeed, the social market economy was said to outperform the Anglo-American model (Albert, 1992). Nowadays different words fill the air: unemployment, poor performance, firms investing abroad, structural rigidities, resistance to change, and political deadlocks. These weaknesses contrast with the flexibility of the Anglo-American model: newly emerging technologies, start-up activity, high employment creation, fast reallocation of labour, physical and financial capital.

Delta. Whereas the popular opinion on the Social Market Economy shifted from a superior form of capitalism to an example of institutional rigidity, an opposite development took place for the Netherlands. Dutch disease turned into the Delta model, delta representing both the geographical position of the Netherlands in the Rhinedelta and the mathematical symbol for change. In the 1970s and early 1980s the Netherlands formed an example of how *not* to deal with stagflation: an expanding welfare state, failing social agreements between unions and employers' organisations, surging unemployment and disability benefits, and widening government budget deficits despite substantial natural gas revenues. Nowadays, foreign commentators praise the cooperation of unions to moderate wages, the structural reforms in welfare state arrangements, product market deregulation, and the recent policy of strict limits on government expenditure instead of the budget deficit. These are sometimes called distinct elements of the Dutch Delta model. The Delta model is said to combine the positive features of the Anglo-American model and the Social Market Economy: flexibility and solidarity.

This study attempts to present a more balanced view on these sometimes rather quickly shifting perceptions on the strengths and weaknesses of the German and Dutch economies. By making a structural comparison between the two countries, it takes some distance from the current stereotypes. Such a comparison scrutinizes the similarities and differences in the ability of the German and Dutch institutional orders to deal with social, demographic and international trends. Delving deeper into specific institutions is a way to arrive at such a more balanced view of the two economies.

The Impact of German Unification. Of course, unification strongly affected the performance of the German economy in the 1990s: it was an exogenous shock that had severe effects on the German economy. The consequences of unification would have posed a huge challenge to any economy and many countries would be in worse shape after a comparable shock than Germany is now. Moreover, the problems caused by unification drew attention away from policy change in other areas. At first, the positive effects of the expenditure boom concealed the need for structural changes, which were required not only by unification but also by the challenges posed by international developments. However, in recent years, rising unemployment, increasing government budget deficits and a higher tax burden have put Standort Germany again at centre stage.

To what extent does unification affect the conclusions from a German–Dutch comparison? In the 1990s, the Dutch reform process, which started after the stagflationary period of the 1970s and early 1980s, gathered momentum, whereas the German economy faced unification. Under these circumstances, a comparison can easily lead to the conclusion that the Dutch economy performs better than the German economy does. How does that affect the results of this study? In many areas, such as corporate governance, health care, or the markets for electricity and gas, unification hardly influences the conclusions, because the analysis focuses on micro-economic institutional arrangements and on sectoral performance.

However, unification plays a role in other areas, for example the socio-economic order, social protection and wage formation. Here, unification provides a test how German institutions perform under severe strain. Large shocks such as unification, may expose rigidities that hamper adjustment in the socio-economic order, the welfare state and wage formation. In that respect, it may be useful for Germany to review the policy errors made in the Netherlands after the oil crises, as well as the lengthy and still ongoing reforms. In the stagflationary period, the Dutch economy got so far out of hand that still substantial adjustments are required to bring economic indicators back to reasonable levels. Nowadays, inactivity is still substantial, income per capita does not stand out favourably in an international comparison, and, although currently falling, government debt remains high.

The review of Dutch policy in the 1970s and 1980s, however, does not mean that the oil price shock in the Netherlands is fully comparable with the unification shock in Germany. Three major differences stand out. First of all, also Germany experienced the oil price hikes. In fact, the direct impact for Germany was even more negative than for the Netherlands, because Germany does not possess substantial natural gas reserves. Secondly, the severe crisis of the welfare state in the Netherlands, as a consequence of the oil price shock, was home-made. It resulted from early but wrong policy reactions to the oil crises. Thirdly, unification appears to be a much larger shock for the German economy. The size of the burden that unification imposes on the German economy, for instance in terms of the financial resources required to restructure the Eastern Länder, exceeds the adverse impulses during the period of stagflation.

Learning. To enhance learning, this study frequently contrasts German and Dutch institutions with those in the United States or the United Kingdom. International trends put the capacity of German and Dutch institutional orders for social innovation to the test, in particular the capacity to tackle economic rigidities. Unification intensifies this process in Germany. If adaptability is higher in the Anglo-American model, much may be learned from these economies. If international trends invoke a shift to the Anglo-American model in the world economy, as is sometimes asserted, knowledge of the distinct features of that model becomes even more relevant. Moreover, putting the differences between Germany and the Netherlands in a proper perspective provides another reason to take the Anglo-American model into consideration.

Finally, note that moderate differences between the German and Dutch institutional orders may enhance mutual learning. Both countries are fairly close in terms of their economic structure and institutions. This serves to increase the practical effectiveness of mutual learning because actual implementation of measures derived from the learning process will not require fundamental change. In general, specific institutions cannot be considered separately but rather must be analyzed in relation to other national institutional arrangements or to cultural characteristics. Thus it is difficult to replace a specific part of legislation from one country by that from another country that is diametrically different. For instance, it would be unlikely that the social security institutions of either Germany or the Netherlands would ever be replaced by those in the United States. However, the practical implementation of social security legislation in Germany may produce interesting policy options for the Netherlands. Implementing policy options from such similar countries can indeed be more effective. This increases the significance of a comparative study of Germany and the Netherlands. Of course the other side of the coin is that the gains of a comparison between rather similar countries may be relatively modest compared to a comparison between more different countries. Therefore, the United States and the United Kingdom frequently act as benchmark countries.

1.2 Structure of the Study and Summary of Policy Options

This section provides an overview of the study and its main policy conclusions. For each chapter, it summarizes the institutional analysis, reviews the impact of trends on the relevant set of institutions and provides policy conclusions. In accordance with the focus of the study on major trade-offs in institutional design, policy conclusions primarily should be regarded as food for thought and not as

Box 1.1 Coordination and trade-offs

Coordination mechanisms *define the type of human interaction:*
- *competition entails rivalry between agents striving for something that not all can obtain,*
- *control entails the power of an agent to take decisions and impose these on others,*
- *common values and norms pertain to congruent sets of preferences within a group of economic agents*
- *cooperative exchange involves bargained consultation and cooperation between a limited number of otherwise independent agents with different preferences.*

Coordination issues *identify four main areas that require coordination:*
- *market power results from economies of scale or collusion,*
- *externalities are interdependencies outside the price system,*
- *specificity concerns investment in relationship-specific assets,*
- *risk sharing deals with fundamental uncertainty.*

Coordination issue	***Relevant trade-off***
market power	*diversity versus scale or scope*
externalities	*experimentation versus certainty*
specificity	*flexibility versus commitment*
risk sharing	*incentives versus solidarity*

precise prescriptions. The complexity of many of the issues touched upon prevents simple solutions.

1.2.1 Chapter 2 The Interplay of Institutions, Trade-offs, Performance and Trends

Where in the present chapter 'Why?' forms the leading question, Chapter 2 focuses on 'How?'. It sets the stage for the study by providing the analytical framework of Challenging Neighbours. It focuses on how institutions might affect economic performance and how long-term social, technological, economic and demographic trends impact the relationship between institutions and performance.

Focusing on trade-offs, this study emphasizes that institutional design is a process of learning by trial and error. The analytical framework starts from an analysis of the main sources of market failure and the main economic coordination mechanisms. The framework identifies four mechanisms to coordinate decisions between economic agents and four major market failures that require coordination. Market failures relate to market power, externalities, specificity, and uncertainty (compare Box 1.1). The four coordination mechanisms are: competition, control, cooperative exchange, and common values and norms. An assessment of strengths and weaknesses of the coordination mechanisms yields four fundamental trade-offs, namely, diversity versus scale or scope, experimentation versus certainty, flexibility versus commitment, and incentives versus solidarity.

The trade-offs show that different institutional orders are feasible, which each feature both strong and weak points. National institutions determine which side of a trade-off features more prominently in a specific country. Since a country's position on each trade-off affects economic performance, this links institutions to performance. The comparative strengths and weaknesses of the coordination mechanisms depend on social, technological and economic conditions affecting the environment in which the institutions operate. Trends changing the environment may shift these conditions.

Conclusions Chapter 2 on Trade-offs in Institutional Design

In a neoclassical world, institutional design boils down to selecting those institutional arrangements that minimize the sum of transaction costs and production costs. In the second-best world of bounded rationality and opportunism of this study, however, the choice between coordination mechanisms to alleviate market failures is not a matter of straightforward calculation. All coordination mechanisms are imperfect and produce transaction costs. Therefore, institutional design consists of a process of trading off various imperfections, of learning by trial and error, and of searching for ways to adjust to changing circumstances. Indeed, institutional design amounts to a process of social innovation.

Path dependency makes institutional design also dependent on history. Shifting between coordination mechanisms is a complex and lengthy process, because institutions are interrelated and rooted in society.

Another complicating factor is that the process of institutional design invokes a commitment problem, which may delay institutional adjustments. Frequently, private agents base their (long-term) decisions on the expectation that institutions remain unchanged. In some respects, institutional adjustment implies that the government reneges on an ex-ante implicit agreement with private agents. This may harm agents' specific investments that were conditional on the ex-ante institutional arrangements. In the eyes of private agents, the government loses reputation when it (frequently) adjusts the institutional environment. Accordingly, the government loses support for its policies. This may explain why adjustment of institutions takes place only after a relatively intense shock or when a process of gradual decline has crossed a certain threshold level.

The impossibility to derive a clear-cut optimal institutional configuration, implies that trade-offs replace solutions. 'Solving' one problem through institutional adjustment may create other problems. Hence, in this international comparative study, it is more fruitful to think in terms of institutions that affect a country's position on various trade-offs than in terms of institutional solutions that maximize some kind of social welfare function.

1.2.2 Chapter 3 Economic Development in Comparison

Nations are often compared on the basis of well known indicators of economic performance, such as the growth of GDP, the unemployment rate, the fiscal deficit, the inflation rate and the balance of payments. Chapter 3 surveys the actual economic performance of the German and Dutch economies during the past decades. It starts by describing the post-war economic development at the macro-economic level. In doing so, it focuses on the six main goals of economic policy, namely economic growth, high employment, low inflation, a solid government budget equilibrium, sustainable development and an equitable income distribution. In addition, the economic consequences of German unification are discussed in more detail.

Conclusions Chapter 3 Economic Development in Comparison

Similar Patterns of Development. Both countries share broadly the same pattern of economic development during the post-war period. Just as most other countries in the industrial world, they first experienced unprecedented growth until 1973, followed by a period of recession between 1973 and 1983, and subsequently signs of recovery after 1983. Besides similar economic growth, other similarities between Germany and the Netherlands should be noticed as well. In particular, both countries featured a strong increase in government expenditures and social security. Also the income distribution developed in more or less the same fashion. After 1980, both countries shared similar monetary goals and policies.

Divergence after 1983. After 1983 and certainly after 1990 developments in both countries increasingly diverged. In the early eighties the economic situation especially in the Netherlands deteriorated seriously. As a result, the willingness to accept painful measures was much stronger than in Germany. Germany's turn came after 1989, when unification impacted Germany's economic performance much more sweeping and enduring than was initially thought. Indeed, the enormous efforts in the new Länder have not yet resulted in a self-sustaining, flourishing economy. On the contrary, the unification revealed that the economic structure of the German economy was not fully prepared to take on this challenge of unification. The 'Standort' debate has gained in urgency.

Differences in Momentum of Change. In the past the German economy was most successful regarding growth, unemployment and inflation. The Netherlands has taken over that position. Still both countries currently do not differ so much in level, but mainly in the rate of change. The Netherlands seems to have been better able in the last decade to adjust its economy to changing external conditions. As the German economy proved more robust in the wake of the oil crises, it had less strong incentives for institutional change in the eighties. After 1989, the unification process posed high demands on the German capacity for adjustment. The initial boom in demand temporarily masked the structural deficiencies, which were revealed only more clearly in the recession of 1992/93. From then, the adjustment process had gained ground. Now Germany faces the challenge to further remedy the deficiencies and adapt to changing circumstances. At the same time the Netherlands should try to keep up its momentum for change, removing old rigidities and avoiding new ones.

1.2.3 Chapter 4 A Structural Comparison

The economic performance of a nation strongly depends on the quality of its institutions. But economic performance depends also on the available economic structure. This structure is the stock of production factors, resulting from investment decisions in the past. The quality and quantity of the stock of production factors determine to a considerable extent the outcome of the economic process. Hence in Chapter 4, the economic structure and its development over time for the two countries is compared in more detail. The topics that are discussed are the natural and geographical conditions, energy and natural resources, the demographic situation and labour supply, the qualitative and quantitative dimensions of the capital stock, the transport and communication infrastructure, the environment and the regional pattern of economic activity. Both countries have experienced major changes in about all the investigated areas.

Conclusions Chapter 4 A Structural Comparison

Structural Shifts in Energy Supply. Germany experienced a decline of its coal production, thereby increasing its dependence on energy imports. The Netherlands, in contrast, was fortunate enough to discover substantial resources of natural gas in Slochteren. On the one hand, this discovery reduced its energy import dependency. On the other hand, it contributed to an unsustainable expansion of the welfare state, which set the stage for a serious crisis at the end of the seventies and early eighties.

Aging Populations. Both countries were and still are confronted with a slowing down of population growth, increasing ageing, and inward migration. This slowing down of population growth and ageing started earlier in Germany than it did in the Netherlands.

Well-educated Populations. Educational qualities of the population are high in both countries, especially in Germany. Although catching-up, the Netherlands is still lagging Germany.

Labour supply: Shifts in Participation. Labour supply has changed in both countries. Whereas older men withdrew from the labour market, younger women entered. Especially the traditionally low rate of labour force participation of Dutch women has increased substantially over the last few decades.

Lagging Investment. After 1973, a relatively low investment rate has constrained the growth of the private capital stock. Also the R&D position and public investments in transport and communication infrastructure have deteriorated. Both governments have started to take action to reverse this trend.

Struggling with Environmental Problems. Both countries have actively tried to reduce the burden on the natural environment. In several areas these efforts have been successful. In other areas, however, for example CO_2 and NO_x emissions, high population density and a rigid economic structure have complicated efforts.

1.2.4 Chapter 5 Governance of the Socio-economic Order: An Economic Perspective

This chapter focuses on institutions that affect the role of the state, divided into the socio-economic order and the political system. It uses the United States as a benchmark. The socio-economic order involves the relationships between the state, representatives of workers and employers, and other societal organisations. In the competitive American model, individual adaptability ranks high while government failure causes scepticism about the efficiency of government intervention. In Germany and the Netherlands, in contrast, cooperation between the state and private agents within an elaborate institutional environment characterize the role of the state.

Despite their similarities viewed from the perspective of the United States, at a closer look the German and Dutch socio-economic orders differ with respect to the role of the government in cooperative exchange. In particular during 1946-1982, but to some extent nowadays as well, formalized policy coordination among government and social partners constitutes an important difference between the Dutch consultation economy and the German social market economy.

In the Netherlands after the Second World War, motivated by the need for solidarity and industrial peace to enhance economic reconstruction, representatives of employees and employers supported the founding of the bipartite Foundation of Labour in 1945, aimed at consultation between employers and employees on labour conditions, and the threepartite Social Economic Council in 1950, aimed at consultation over socio-economic policy. The government favoured the creation of these institutions to increase control over macro-economic variables, in particular to encourage wage moderation in order to enhance economic growth.

In the German social market economy in contrast, the desire to constrain the power of the state and restrict the partisan influence of employers' and employees' organisations on government policy, motivated separate roles for government and social partners. As a result, the German Constitution prohibits active participation of the social partners in public policy formation. At the same time, wage formation is autonomous ('Tarifautonomie'), which implies that unions and employers' organisations bargain over wages without any intervention of the government.

After explaining these models, the chapter reviews the tensions challenging the Dutch and German socio-economic order. On the one hand, these tensions originate in large economic shocks, such as stagflation in the 1970s and 1980s and German unification in the 1990s. On the other hand, tensions stem from gradually unfolding trends in the social, technological en international environment. The final part of the chapter assesses the strengths and weaknesses of the socio-economic order in the light of these trends.

Conclusions Chapter 5 Governance of the Socio-Economic Order

Partial Resemblance of Shocks. To a certain degree, the German position after unification resembles the Dutch position after stagflation in the early 1980s. Both shocks required medium-term moderation of real disposable incomes: in the Netherlands because of terms of trade losses and fast growing labour supply; in Eastern Germany because of a fall in the capital-labour ratio due to excessive scrappage of outdated East-German equipment; in West Germany to pay the price of the restructuring of the East German economy. Socio-economic institutions in both countries failed to internalize the external effects of wage inflation. Moreover, expectations proved difficult to adjust to new circumstances. Accordingly, a vicious circle of rising labour costs, declining employment, rising tax burdens and widening government budget deficits resulted.

Different Timing of Shocks. After a long period of deadlock and social turmoil in the 1970s and early 1980s, the severity of the home-made crisis forced the Netherlands to initiate an economic adjustment process in the 1980s. Consequently, when unification hit the German economy in the early 1990s, the Dutch reform process was already gathering momentum. A stronger separation of the responsibilities of government and the social partners revitalised the coordination mechanism of cooperative exchange in the Netherlands. At the same time, commitment to common goals was strengthened. Once a longer-term common goal had been identified, like the restoration of profitability and employment, the institutional framework facilitated a joint approach to address economic and social issues.

Challenges Facing Germany. The German socio-economic order and political system face strong challenges to set in motion a process of recovery. In the Netherlands it took a considerable period of time before a redefinition of the position of government in the consultation economy revitalized cooperative exchange. The structure of the German socio-economic order and political system demand a large effort to prevent a stalemate from arising. The strong political checks and balances, *i.e.* the formal separation of government and the associations of labour and capital in cooperative exchange, the juridical foundation of the socio-economic order, interlocking federalist relationships and the opposition majority in the Bundesrat, hamper attempts to establish political support and commitment to address nation-wide challenges.

Trends Demand More Flexibility. Social and technological trends cause decentralisation in industrial relations. Internationalisation requires differentiation to meet competitive and institutional conditions on a broad range of international markets. Decentralisation shifts bargaining on labour agreements from national to sectoral levels and from sectoral levels to individual companies. This enables differentiation between sectors and companies to meet trends towards heterogeneity, individualisation and market-oriented technologies.

Policy Conclusions on Governance of the Socio-Economic Order

Advantage of Early Response. The first policy conclusion from the dismal Dutch experience during stagflation is that it may take a joint effort and a long time to turn the vicious circle into a virtuous circle. In particular, if the vicious circle has been allowed to proceed for a long period of time, restoring stock variables like unemployment and government debt to acceptable levels requires much effort. To illustrate, despite prolonged wage moderation, inactivity in the Netherlands still is considerable. Recognizing that paying the price at an early stage will be much cheaper than postponing it, may help to accelerate adjustment.

New Combinations. The main policy conclusion from the trends and shocks would be to look for new combinations of coordination mechanisms at different levels within the socio-economic and political order. New combinations have to identify new positions on the trade-offs that comply with demands from the trends and challenges posed by the shocks, within the boundaries set by key social values. In other words, new combinations should increase flexibility while preserving social cohesion.

New combinations in the Dutch socio-economic order entail a shift towards more advisory cooperative exchange that aims to enhance internal flexibility. At the national level agreements no longer specify a detailed outcome for which the parties involved should strive, but identify common policy interests, specify general guiding lines or define boundary conditions. At the sectoral or firm level employers, unions and the government apply their specific policy instruments to implement the general agreements.

New combinations in Germany entail the challenge to translate the strong checks and balances into a more flexible socio-economic and political order. An interesting question to pursue is to which extent it is possible to strive for advisory cooperative exchange at the regional level. It is frequently stated that the Dutch model only fits a relatively small homogeneous society. Since the Netherlands just as frequently has been pictured as one of the Bundesländer, the question arises whether the model contains any value when applied at the level of individual Länder. Advisory cooperative exchange at the regional level would put the Germany socio-economic order in a favourable position: diversity to accommodate to regional circumstances, experimentation due to stronger competition between Länder, and internal flexibility and commitment due to cooperative exchange within Länder.

Benefits and Costs. Such a model would imply new roles for actors both at the national and the regional level. Less national coordination would reinforce subsidiarity. It promotes external flexibility, experimentation and incentives. These sides of the trade-offs clearly correspond with the shifts demanded by the social and international trends. Yet, less national coordination may entail a cost in terms of commitment, certainty and solidarity. It increases the risk that decentral actors attempt to free ride on national institutions. Hence, new combinations may not only require a shift in authority but also of (financial) responsibility, so that actors at the regional level internalize the consequences of their actions. A new role at the national level for representatives of labour an capital and the government would be to broadly define priority areas and provide general guidelines and recommendations, while leaving it to regional representatives to address these issues in a way most suited to their specific circumstances.

An Example: Wage Formation and Social Security. A new combination would result from a shift of wage bargaining towards more regional differentiation and less national sectoral coordination. Decentralisation of unemployment insurance would support such a process, because Länder representatives of labour and capital would bear the consequences of high wages in terms of higher regional unemployment contributions. In that case, decentral administration of unemployment benefits should concur with budget responsibility. This might imply that financial equalization of social security contributions between Länder only applies if Länder are struck by shocks outside their own span of control.

The Price of More Policy Competition. Diminishing national coordination increases inequality. Consequently, another important role of national actors would be to preserve solidarity, in order to protect citizens against adverse shocks that originate outside their own span of control. A national government needs sufficient leeway to put supra-regional solidarity above regional interests. Unification constitutes a case in point: it not only demands flexibility and diversity but also solidarity. Confining solidarity to outside shocks means that under normal circumstances Germans would have to accept a greater degree of inequality. It seems reasonable to pay this price, because the present situation also produces inequalities, be it of an other nature, which in the long term undermine social cohesion.

No Simple Prescriptions. No blueprint of an optimal socio-economic order that perfectly corresponds to changed conditions can be given. The main purpose of this chapter is to encourage thinking about the complex process of social innovation in the socio-economic order. If some prospects look interesting, experimentation in that direction in specific policy fields seems the proper way to proceed.

1.2.5 Chapter 6 Social Protection

This chapter focuses on social insurance and assistance. Social insurance covers specific contingencies (sickness, disability, old age, and unemployment). Social assistance provides a minimum income floor in the form of means-tested benefits. The chapter deals first with the basic principles of social insurance. Why is social insurance needed? What are the trade-offs that the government confronts in designing social insurance? Subsequently, it describes the features of social protection in Germany and the Netherlands before the Dutch reform process started in the early eighties. It discusses also how the design of the Dutch system gave rise to its failure. This sets the stage for a discussion of the reform process in the Netherlands. Subsequently, the various trends affecting the future of social protection are investigated.

Policy Options for the Netherlands on Social Protection

Better Governance of Social Insurance. The main lesson from Germany for the Netherlands concerns a more efficient governance of the benefit administration. Many reforms have already been implemented or are currently in the process of being implemented. In particular, the Netherlands is introducing various checks and balances in the governance structure of social insurance, in order to enhance the accountability of the social insurance administration. In line with the situation in Germany, the roles, objectives, and responsibilities of the various players have been clarified.

Better Administration of Social Assistance. Also in social assistance is the Netherlands moving in the direction of the German system, by using less detailed regulations to guide the administration of social security at a decentralized level. To reap the benefits of this reform, it is essential that plans proceed to increase the budget responsibility of municipalities, which execute social assistance.

Improve Monitoring of Unemployment Benefits. The number of people claiming unemployment benefits has stayed at a high level while the unemployment rate (i.e.

the people searching for a job) declined. Hence, better monitoring of unemployment benefit recipients seems to be called for.

No Legal Extension of Supplementary Insurance in Sickness Schemes. In the sickness scheme, the Netherlands has gone further than Germany in using financial incentives for employers and introducing competition in insurance. However, some collective wage contracts negotiated at the industry level still force individual employers to take out supplementary insurance from a selected insurance company. This may discourage policies to reduce sickness absenteeism that are tailor-made to each firm. Moreover, it may reduce the competitive pressures on insurance companies. Collective agreements on supplementing statutory benefits are still legally extended to all firms in an industry.

Better Incentives for Efficient Claim Assessment in Disability. The relatively high Dutch replacement rates for social disability (both relative to the corresponding German rate and to the Dutch replacement rates for unemployment) continue to make the disability scheme vulnerable to moral hazard. Although disability benefit claims have fallen in recent years, they started to rise again in 1996. In stemming the inflow into disability schemes, the Netherlands can benefit from the tight claim assessment procedures in Germany, which are based on control and strict regulations. Indeed, in Germany, requests for disability are handled at a lower level and more applicants are refused admittance. One explanation is that insurance doctors refer many applicants to specialists. The Dutch plans for allowing private insurance of disability may help to tighten the claim assessment procedure, which remains in public hands. In particular, insurance companies have clear incentives to fight lax assessments in the courts. In this way, competition can help to break the culture of conflict-avoidance, which has led parties with conflicting interests to shift the burden to the collective pool. This is particularly important in the Netherlands, which lacks the German 'juridical' tradition of stemming inflows into social insurance through strict controls and regulations.

Policy Options for Germany on Social Protection

Moderate Wages and More Flexibility. A well-functioning labour market with a high level of employment is a prerequisite for generous social insurance. Moreover, participation in the labour market should be the preferred route for protecting people against income loss. Hence, inactivity should be combatted by raising employment rather than by reducing effective labour supply.

In this connection, wage moderation yields a double dividend: first, by supporting profitability and investment, increasing the labour-intensity of production, and enhancing international competitiveness, wage moderation enhances employment -- the financial base of the welfare state. Second, it reduces public spending because social benefits are generally linked to wages and because a high level of employment reduces the number of benefit claimants.

To improve overall employment, also a flexible labour market can make an important contribution. A labour market with low entry barriers to outsiders constitutes an important insurance mechanism against the risk of income loss. This is especially so in combination with two-earner families. Hence, partners of breadwinners should be encouraged to seek (part-time) work, in part through arrangements that allow parents to combine child raising and careers. In this way, income insurance is provided through the market and the family.

Stronger Work Incentives in Unemployment Insurance and Social Assistance. The interaction between social insurance and the labour market goes both ways. By encouraging claimants to get back to work, social insurance raises effective labour supply, thereby moderating wages and labour costs. To make the German welfare state a trampoline rather than a hammock, the German system of unemployment insurance may have to provide stronger work incentives. This especially applies to older workers who benefit from rather generous benefits. Indeed, long-term unemployment in Germany is concentrated among older workers, which makes the German welfare state particularly vulnerable to aging.

German single-earners with low incomes and many dependants also feature high replacement rates, reflecting the needs principle of the social assistance system. To alleviate the unemployment trap, the German government has proposed to increase the gap between the local average of low labour incomes and social assistance. However, this proposal has been abandoned.

The duration of unemployment benefits is another important determinant of incentives to actively search for work. In contrast to the situation in the Netherlands, German unemployment assistance benefits are provided for an unlimited period.

Stronger Incentives in Sickness Scheme. Sickpay is particularly generous in Germany. Even overtime pay is compensated during illness. The German government has reduced statutory sick pay to 80 percent of the reference wage but supplementary provisions negotiated by employers and unions continue to supplement benefits to 100 percent. Privatizing the sickness scheme, as in the Netherlands, would imply that employers bear the full cost burden of the effect of generous extra-statutory provisions on the sickness rate. This would encourage employers to reduce these supplementary provisions.

More generally, Germany relies more on control and regulations while the Netherlands has introduced more market elements (and financial incentives) in social security. Germany's emphasis on control and regulations implies that Germany may need to use less financial incentives to stem moral hazard than the Netherlands. Nevertheless, the market-oriented reforms in disability and sickness insurance in the Netherlands may provide a source of inspiration for Germany in reforming its social insurance system.

Unfinished Agenda for Reform of Social Protection in Germany and the Netherlands

Enhancing Employability of Vulnerable Groups. Technological and organization developments increasingly put vulnerable individuals with few marketable skills at risk. To prevent long-run dependency and social exclusion, governments should shift away from passive towards active support. The latter support should strengthen the earnings capacity, skills, adaptability, and employability of vulnerable individuals. Social benefits were originally intended to primarily relieve liquidity constraints by carrying people over relatively short unemployment spells. At the present time, however, structural unemployment and dependency require more active, interventionist policies with conditional and in-kind benefits (e.g. training and other investments in human capital) to avoid social exclusion and to raise labour productivity by building up human capital. By enhancing the employability and earning capabilities of vulnerable individuals with little marketable skills, social insurance addresses social exclusion and family instability at the root.

Conditional transfers based on the transaction principle (i.e. balancing the carrot of the benefit with the stick of certain obligations) can be used to screen claimants, thereby alleviating moral hazard. The obligations imposed on benefit recipients give them a direct interest in improving their circumstances. Moreover, in-kind transfers can link support to activities (such as training, unpaid trial employment, community work) that encourage rather than discourage re-entry into employment.

Wage subsidies or vouchers for the long-term unemployed can be used as a particular form of in-kind benefits aimed at stimulating demand for the low skilled. This demand may be stimulated also by deregulating sheltered sectors. Indeed, more flexible labour and commodity markets help to increase the access of vulnerable groups to work.

More Support for the Young. Preventive measures are most effective if they occur early in life. In this connection, assistance to single parent households is particularly important in order to protect children from the intergenerational transfer of deficits and to prevent passive income support later in life. The shift towards active support at the beginning of the life cycle poses a challenge to governments. Such a policy of social investment and investment in human capital reduces the costs of passive income support only in the future. Hence, in the short run, governments have to pay twice: once for active support of the young and once for passive support of the old, who did not benefit from preventive measures early in life.

More Entrepreneurial Benefit Administration. A shift towards more active labour-market policies involving conditional and in-kind benefits (see below) calls for tailor-made solutions implemented by a decentralized benefit administration that exploits its information advantage about individual circumstances. More generally, a more heterogeneous and diverse population requires more tailor-made and innovative solutions. Accordingly, social security administrations should be transformed from hierarchical bureaucratic organizations to more decentralized, entrepreneurial and customer-oriented bodies. The central government should continue to play an important role in setting the rules of the game, including the levels of compulsory insurance. However, it can delegate the provision of social benefits increasingly to decentralized agencies. In order to provide these decentralized bodies with proper financial incentives, the central government should delegate also (part of) the budget responsibility.

1.2.6 Chapter 7 Pensions

For two reasons pensions are an important topic for this study. First, the German pension system differs substantially from the Dutch one. This increases the scope for mutual learning. Second, both countries will experience rapid aging over the next four decades. This poses serious challenges to the pension systems of these countries. After outlining the theoretical framework, this chapter describes the Dutch and German pension systems as well as their performance. Subsequently, it discusses the trends that affect the future of income support in old age. These trends include financial innovation, international integration, technological change, individualization, a more heterogeneous population, and more heterogeneous tastes and needs. These trends are likely to be as important as aging in determining the future of old-age insurance. The chapter concludes with policy options for old-age insurance in Germany and the Netherlands.

Policy Options for the Netherlands on Pensions

Strengthen the Insurance Element. The Dutch pension system implies a high marginal and average tax wedge, thereby distorting labour supply. Moving away from final-pay to average-pay occupational schemes would reduce the marginal and average wedge by tightening the link between premiums and benefits.

Increase Investment in the Corporate Sector. The system of book reserves implies that German pension savings directly increase the supply of capital to the corporate sector. Dutch pension funds, in contrast, have traditionally invested a large share of their capital in government bonds. More recently, however, Dutch pension funds are increasingly investing in corporate equity. This facilitates the investment of pension saving in high-yielding projects in the corporate sector, enhances capital mobility within the corporate sector, allows a higher expected return over a long horizon, makes the return less sensitive to unexpected inflation, and may help to improve corporate governance. By investing a larger share in venture capital firms, pension funds could contribute to increasing the supply of risk-taking capital for starting entrepreneurs. Alternatively, if the collective part of old-age insurance is reduced (see below), starting entrepreneurs can be allowed to invest a larger share of their previously accumulated pension saving in their own firm. This would also boost the supply of capital to new, growing firms.

More Diversity in the Second Pillar. Increasing the possibilities for firms to opt out of industry-wide pension funds is consistent with the trend towards more heterogeneous preferences, which requires more diversity. Moreover, more opt-out possibilities increase competitive pressures on pension funds to improve their performance. To address these trends, firms could be required to participate in industry-wide pension funds only for pension benefits with lower aspiration levels (especially for middle- and higher incomes, see below).

Offering not only firms but also workers more options to select their own pension fund would meet the trend towards more heterogeneity, which requires tailor-made solutions. However, these individual options may give rise to adverse selection and high transaction and information costs, thereby raising pension costs. Accordingly, more individual options should be introduced carefully, for example by reducing the aspiration level for collective insurance for middle- and higher incomes (see below).

Policy Options for Germany on Pensions

Less Public Insurance. The German welfare state seems especially vulnerable to aging because at present a large part of public transfers accrues to the elderly. Germany therefore may want to gradually reduce PAYG benefits for those earning higher incomes by focusing the public pension scheme more on poverty alleviation. This would yield a better balanced portfolio between funded and PAYG schemes as workers with middle- and higher incomes would substitute private pensions for public PAYG benefits. The first pillar could be financed from general tax revenues rather than payroll taxes. Relying on broad-based taxes paid by the entire population rather than payroll taxes alleviates the tax burden on workers by shifting this burden in part onto those outside the labour force, including the retired with higher incomes. Reducing net public benefits for and increasing taxes on the richer elderly makes the welfare state less vulnerable to the aging process.

More Independent Pension Funds. Occupational pensions in Germany stress commitment at the expense of flexibility. However, various trends, including German unification and increased international financial integration, call for more flexibility. In this context, the case for removing the tax obstacles against setting up independent pension funds is strong. The current system of book reserves discourages the development of modern financial markets, inhibits the efficient allocation of capital across firms, and does not allow pension savings to be diversified. Moreover, it prevents pension saving from benefiting from higher returns and more diversification.

Better Portability of Pension Rights. To enhance flexibility in the German labour market, the vesting period for pension benefits could be shortened. Furthermore, increased portability of pension rights would facilitate labour mobility.

Unfinished Agenda for Pension Reform in Germany and the Netherlands

Less Collective Insurance. In setting the mandatory, collective level of pension insurance, one needs to trade off, on the one hand, providing enough risk sharing and, on the other hand, tuning pensions to individual needs. Setting the mandatory level too low harms inter- and intragenerational risk sharing, may induce workers to exploit means-tested benefits, and may lead to underinsurance due to adverse selection. Setting the level too high, in contrast, results in overinsurance by forcing some households to save more than they would like. The associated implicit tax distorts saving and harms employment.

At the same time, financial innovation and a better educated workforce reduce the need to protect individuals against risks through collective pension insurance. The government could reduce the need for intergenerational risk sharing through collective pension funds further by issuing indexed bonds, which provide insurance against inflation risk.

In both Germany and the Netherlands, the third, voluntary, pillar, which can cater to individual preferences, is small because the mandatory, collective level of pension insurance is quite high. Indeed, as tastes have become more heterogeneous and the mandatory aspiration level has increased in after-tax terms, many workers are likely to have become overinsured. One way to increase the flexibility and personal responsibility in pension insurance would be to reduce high compulsory levels of collective pensions and provide more tax privileges to individual accounts. Such accounts could insure individuals against not only old-age risk but also other human capital risks, such as unemployment and obsolescence of human capital.

Raising the Effective Retirement Age. Encouraging early retirement is an increasingly costly policy. It not only directly reduces labour supply but also harms employment of the younger generations by raising premium and tax rates. In particular, it raises these rates both by narrowing the contribution base and by increasing the required financing for the early retirement benefits.

Indexing the statutory retirement age to life expectancy is the most natural way to insure society against a longer average life of its citizens so that people spend part of their longer life in work and part in retirement. A higher retirement age implies that the human capital embodied in the elderly is used more intensively. By using human capital more equally over various generations, a higher retirement age attacks the potential fiscal and social problems due to aging at the root. The elderly rely less on the solidarity of the young and more on their own human capital. Indeed, labour income of the elderly could become another major pillar of old-age insurance. By keeping older workers longer employed, governments reap a double dividend. The working elderly not only reduce social spending but also broaden the contribution base.

Supplementing Current Reforms. Current reforms do not seem sufficient to significantly raise the effective retirement age. In particular, raising the effective retirement age requires a stronger labour-market position of elderly workers. Employers can be encouraged to employ elderly workers not only by increasing the skills of the elderly but also by tightening rules against age discrimination and by reducing wage costs. To achieve this, age-related pay schemes may have to be reconsidered so that wages can be better adjusted to individual productivity levels. This may also require modification of social security schemes. For example, occupational pension systems and unemployment insurance schemes that link benefits to final pay, discourage gradual retirement through occupational downgrading with lower rates of pay.

Stimulating More Efficient Retirement Decisions. Different people may want to leave the labour force at different times and in different ways. To facilitate efficient decision making by workers with diverse needs and preferences, pension systems should confront potential retirees and their employers with the social costs of retirement. In other words, early and delayed retirement benefits should be actuarially fair.

Various routes for withdrawing from the labour force may be substitutes. Accordingly, in confronting employers and workers with the social costs of early retirement, governments should pursue a comprehensive approach. Various conditional social security benefits, such as unemployment and disability benefits, are subject to moral hazard. As the work force ages, these moral hazard problems become more serious as older workers are subject to higher disability and unemployment risk. These considerations increase the need to reform social insurance along the lines outlined in Chapter 6.

Increasing Labour Supply of the Young. Higher labour supply of the young strengthens the base for financing old-age benefits. One way to accomplish this is to enhance labour supply of vulnerable groups with little marketable skills through a more activating social insurance system. Another way is to increase labour supply of women. There is still considerable scope for women to increase their labour supply. Improved child care, which can be provided by elderly workers, may enhance labour-market participation of women with young children. A higher female participation rate strengthens the labour skills and human capital of women. This allows them to rely less on public transfers when old; an added benefit from the point of view of reducing the claim of old-age pensions on the public budget.

1.2.7 Chapters 8 and 9 Labour Market: Institutional Environment and Institutional Arrangements

Chapters 8 and 9 examine the strengths and weaknesses of German and Dutch labour market institutions in view of current and future economic trends. The American labour market is used as a benchmark. Labour market institutions are broadly defined as arrangements that structure the interactions between individual employers, workers and outsiders. They govern labour relations between employers and employees, managers and employees, and affect the position of outsiders and insiders. Hence, both labour market regulations and cooperative arrangements between (organised) employers and employees are considered.

Chapter 8 starts with the analytical framework. Subsequently, it compares labour market regulations that provide the institutional environment for cooperative exchange and competition on the German, Dutch and American labour markets. Labour market regulations regarding dismissals, working time, short-time work and atypical contracts are explored. Chapter 9 investigates cooperative exchange and competition in labour relationships. It compares systems of collective bargaining, vocational employee training and co-determination.

Policy Options for the Netherlands on the Labour Market

Improve Conditions for Apprenticeships. To encourage Dutch firms to invest more in portable training, two main elements seem important. First, co-financing of workers should be increased, thereby boosting the returns of the firm on apprenticeship training. Collective labour agreements may have to provide more flexibility to adjust apprenticeship wages to training costs and the situation in the labour market. Co-financing of workers is especially important if certificated skills make these skills more easily portable across firms and industries, thereby facilitating job mobility. The other lesson from Germany is that the apprenticeship system should be diverse enough to be attractive for a wide ability range. In particular, in Germany low achievers still have relatively easy access to the system. At the same time, the German system appeals also to high achievers.

More Focused Collective Extension. In Germany, separate collective labour agreements for wages and general labour conditions allow legal extension to be confined to general labour conditions. In the Netherlands, in contrast, collective extension usually relates to an integrated collective agreement, covering both wages and other labour conditions. This allows less scope to deal with firm-specific conditions and preferences. Moreover, compulsory extension is not limited to provisions involving positive externalities across firms, but also restrains competition in wage formation. However, compulsory extension may help to address the hold-up problem associated with firm-specific investments, including search activities.

Policy Options for Germany on Labour Market

More Flexibility. The social and international trends towards individualisation, more volatility, and more heterogeneity suggest that the importance of flexibility will increase. With respect to labour market regulations, the main differences between Germany and the Netherlands are the more extensive use of short-time work in Germany, versus the greater popularity of part-time work and flexibility through flexible contracts in the Netherlands, especially through temporary work agencies. More liberal regulations with respect to the use of flexible contracts in Germany, could increase the access of unskilled workers to the labour market. Moreover, flexible contracts may meet the more heterogeneous needs of employers and workers. Not only a more flexible labour market but also deregulation of sheltered sectors may enhance the access of vulnerable groups to work.

No Short-Time Work for Structural Problems. At present extensive short-time work provisions provide working-hour flexibility in Germany. In practice, the efficiency of short-time work is often doubtful because it can result in a subsidy on loss-making activities, thereby hampering employment flows towards more profitable activities.

Collective Bargaining: More Regional and Firm-Specific Variations. With respect to wage formation, the Dutch system involves a mixture between commitment and flexibility and between centralization and decentralization. Consensus building at the centralized level makes labour relations at the firm level less confrontational, improves the internalization of external effects and strengthens commitment. A number of firm-level agreements can account for firm-specific conditions and preferences, although the general framework for these agreements is still influenced by the central level. In addition, some scope for firm-specific variations in sectoral agreements renders the system of collective bargaining more flexible.

In Germany, sectoral collective bargaining is less strongly influenced by consensus building coordination at a centralized level. This hampers the internalization of external effects and may reduce the sensitivity of wage formation to the unemployment level. Rather, it may induce leapfrogging, by giving leading sectors a large autonomy in collective bargaining. Since Germany is much larger than the Netherlands and hence features more diversity, part of the centralized coordination could occur at the regional rather than the national level. This would allow for more experimentation and diversity as regional actors at the level of the Länder could adjust to regional circumstances. Moreover, the building of consensus tends to be easier at a lower level. In order to ensure that regional agents internalize the effects of their bargain on the unemployment level, the regional level may have to assume a larger budget responsibility for unemployment insurance. The role of the national level would be to provide general guidelines, while delegating more specific issues to the regional level.

Firm-level agreements are currently less popular in Germany than in the Netherlands. Only the trend towards firm-level variation within sectoral agreements, for instance concerning working-time provisions, is similar. The German system thus captures neither the advantages of centralization nor those of decentralized wage bargaining. Hence, more scope for firm-specific and regional-specific variations in sectoral agreements is desirable for in order to arrive at a better mix of the coordination mechanisms of competition and corporative exchange. Various trends, including the need for regional differentiation after German unification, demand more flexibility, diversity, and experimentation in collective bargaining.

1.2.8 Chapter 10 Corporate Governance

This chapter focuses on the institutions that govern stakeholder relationships between management, shareholders and creditors. Two reasons motivate the analysis. First, corporate governance institutions are important to enhance company performance due to conflicting objectives of various agents and the incompleteness of contracts. Second a comparative analysis provides scope to learn about the impact of such institutions because institutions differ across countries.

Policy Options for Germany on Corporate Governance

Replace the Co-determined Supervisory Board. Analogously to the German interlocking politics (Politikverflechtung) in intergovernmental relationships, interlocking checks and balances in corporate governance restrict flexibility and hamper exchange of information. The German supervisory board constitutes the nexus of all checks and balances between the different stakeholders. This combination of the interests of several stakeholders in a single institutional body complicates decision making, tends to narrow the discussion to rather general observations, and hampers exchange of information, because of a fear of loss of confidentiality. A stronger division of responsibilities among the various actors and institutional bodies, such as the works council, may still provide the checks and balances that are required to sustain commitment, while at the same time enhancing incentives and flexibility. Two institutional adjustments seem desirable. First, replacing the co-determined supervisory board and more intensively using supervisory board subcommittees. Second, restricting the voting power of banks, conform current policy proposals, would also contribute to disentangling interlocking checks and balances.

Policy Option for the Netherlands on Corporate Governance

Leave Cooption. To raise the efficacy of Dutch corporate governance in safeguarding the quality of both management board and supervisory board, the influence of shareholders on the supervisory board should increase. A lesson from the German model is to leave cooption and to allow a (substantial) majority of votes in the general meeting of shareholders to replace the supervisory board. To some extent, these adjustments restrict the autonomy of high-quality management boards. Yet, this constitutes a relatively low price for enhancing effective governance, especially because shareholders have less incentives to interfere with the strategies of a high-quality management. These changes would give the Dutch corporate governance institutions a relatively strong centre position on the trade-off between commitment and flexibility; this system would suffer neither from the inefficacy of a co-determined board as in Germany nor from a short-term orientation or frequent hostile takeover practices as in the United States.

1.2.9 Chapter 11 Science and Technology Policy

Over the last years, German and Dutch policy makers have taken a series of initiatives in science and technology policy. In Germany, this is partly the result of the 'Standort' debate, in which the diminishing attractiveness of the German economy as a location for private research activities has been of importance. Furthermore, there is an on-going debate among German economists about the innovative performance of traditional sectors like machinery and chemistry. The aim of this chapter is to put these policy measures into perspective by comparing science and technology policies in Germany and the Netherlands from an institutional point of view. The chapter first presents some theoretical background, stressing the different roles of science and technology for the production of innovations. Next science and technology policies in Germany and the Netherlands are analyzed. Based on a review of relevant trends, mutual policy options are derived.

A General Lesson: the Importance of Trade-offs

Developments in the field of science and technology policy emphasize quality, cooperation and relevance. The most important lesson from the analytical framework is to recognize the existence of trade-offs. To some extent increasing relevance may enhance quality, if a larger share of contract finance urges researchers to leave well-trodden paths and improve quality. Cooperation in multidisciplinary teams may create economies of scale and thus also enhance quality. Yet, trade-offs put boundaries to these synergy effects and require science and technology policy to administer a sometimes delicate balance.

Relevance and quality touch upon the trade-off between flexibility and commitment. Science policy should not lose sight of commitment required to maintain the long-term foundations of the scientific knowledge base by emphasizing relevance too much. In contrast, to some extent, a stronger emphasis on scientific evaluation criteria to enhance quality pushes scientists away from projects and research interests with high (short-term) value for society, because in a number of disciplines the latter type of research operates less at the forefront of scientific evolution.

Multidisciplinary research relates to the trade-offs between flexibility and commitment and between diversity and scale. Cooperative exchange underlies multidisciplinary research. Hence, the motivation of scientists from different disciplines to make their own preferences and methods subservient to the common goal, is crucial to the success of this type of cooperation. However, to some extent that demand is at odds with incentives and quality evaluation within each single discipline. Hence, science policy has to find an adequate position on the trade-off between problems in society that demand a multidisciplinary approach and incentive structures within science.

The lesson not to neglect trade-offs, can be operationalized into a policy option to systematically examine the impact of specific measures on the main policy objectives. This would lower the risk of disappointment when policies meant to improve one objective, worsen another. Against this general background, some more specific policy options come to the fore.

Policy Options for Germany on Science and Technology Policy

Higher education. In the field of higher education the Dutch experience may be of interest to German policy makers. Dutch higher education policy constitutes an interesting experiment to find an adequate balance on the trade-off between diversity and scale and on the trade-off between flexibility and commitment. Autonomy and quality control enhance flexibility, research schools provide a framework to bundle competencies and recent initiatives to establish centres of excellence and top research schools strengthen the position in locational competition between national knowledge bases.

Analogously to the policy options mentioned in Chapter 5, strengthening subsidiarity may promote differentiation and flexibility in German higher education. Diminishing national coordination and a peer review system of quality control may increase experimentation to reduce the length of studies and to curtail the high teaching load. Locational competition between Länder and financial incentives may support this process. An example of a financial incentive is the Dutch system that relates basic funding to the number of students with an enrolment of four years or less.

A smaller teaching load provides room to enhance flexibility and quality of research in higher education. In addition, it may be worthwhile to consider financial incentives that promote the international orientation of science. Shifting some part of basic funding to internationally cooperative research or to visiting scientists may increase exposure to international scientific developments and may give an impetus to quality.

Large Research Centres. Their size makes the large research institutes vulnerable to the risk of becoming locked in technologies of the past. This risk is relevant to Germany in particular, because the large research centres constitute a significant share of the specific knowledge base. Germany applies financial incentives to increase flexibility of the large research institutes and the Blue List institutes. Incentives for the Blue List institutes are strongest because part of their funding has been transferred to the German research council, where they have to compete with universities. That may be a suitable policy option for the large research centres as well.

Policy Options for the Netherlands on Science and Technology Policy

Higher Education. The trade-off in university research between quality and multidisciplinary research needs attention from Dutch policy makers. A tension exists between scientific quality norms in the committees that recognize and evaluate research schools and the objectives of policy makers. If policy makers emphasize relevance and multidisciplinary research, whereas recognition and evaluation committees implicitly or explicitly apply monodisciplinary criteria and emphasize coherency in research programs, individual research groups may face incompatible requirements. The process of trying to comply with these requirements may become time and resource consuming and frustrating.

Peer Review Finance. The organisation of the German system of peer review finance provides an example for the Netherlands. Both countries aim at increasing flexibility and quality by strengthening peer review finance in higher education. Cooperation, technology transfer and relevance increasingly become criteria to assess project proposals. For peer review finance to achieve the objective of flexible adjustment of scientific research to new developments, a flexible financing organisation is essential. Therefore, a successful reorganisation of the Dutch research council is essential to achieve flexibility.

Basic Research Institutes. The German Max Planck Gesellschaft provides an example, both for the Dutch basic research institutes and for the large research centres in the two countries. It not only performs high-quality basic research but also explores new scientific areas and as such is agenda setting for German higher education R&D. Hence, it combines quality and flexibility. Despite its stronger orientation on basic research and the conflict of interests between scientific incentives and market incentives, patenting activity with the Max Planck

Gesellschaft exceeds that of the German large research centres. A flexible set of institutes under a common umbrella organization, supported by special facilities such as Garching Innovation, appears to be a strong asset in the German research infrastructure. On this issue Germany provides an interesting case for the Dutch policy initiatives to concentrate the basic research institutes in a separate and flexible organisation. Of course, the Dutch basic research institutes will never reach the scope and size of their German counterparts, due to the difference in size of the countries.

Large Research Centres. By involving companies and sectoral organizations in the drafting of basic funded programs, the Netherlands more strongly relies on cooperative exchange to adjust the research activities of the large research centres. If the aim is to promote flexibility, the German policy appears more effective and the Netherlands may further consider increasing the share of peer review finance or contract finance for the large research centres.

Point of Attention to Policy Makers in Both Countries

Competition Within the Scientific Research Base. A point of attention for policy makers, related to strengthening incentive structures and a stronger orientation towards societal needs, concerns the transaction costs associated with increasing competition within the scientific research base. Transaction costs not only concern the often substantial costs to draft proposals to apply for funding, but also the costs of lower investments in a specific institute's knowledge base. On the long run this may reduce quality. Hence to some extent policy makers should lean against the winds of internationalization and flexibility to protect sufficient commitment among the scientific research base to maintain a high-quality knowledge base. In addition, policy should guard a level playing field among the research institutes to prevent unfair competition from institutes with a relatively large degree of basic funding.

1.2.10 Chapter 12 Regulation and Competition Policies

The chapter discusses regulation and competition policies in the market for goods and services in Germany and the Netherlands. Current discussions on privatization and market liberalization illustrate the policy relevance of this theme. Germany and the Netherlands have not been leaders in this field, but are catching up. Changes are stimulated by developments in the Anglo-Saxon countries, the creation of an internal European market, technological developments, and modern regulation theory. In Germany, the discussion on these themes is part of the Standort debate, which started already in the early eighties. In the Netherlands, debate on this issue started with the project on market performance, deregulation and quality of legislation.

The chapter assesses the current situation of Germany and the Netherlands. It focuses on the sheltered sectors, where Dutch and German governments are sovereign to create institutions. First, the theoretical motives behind regulation and competition policy are explained. To this end, four market prototypes are distinguished. Second, recent developments in actual (de)regulation and competition policies in Germany and the Netherlands are described. Theory and recent developments are then combined to assess the impact of specific (de)regulation and competition policy measures. Finally, the chapter derives policy options from the experiences in Germany and the Netherlands.

Options Implemented in the Netherlands on Regulation and Competition Policies

Competition Policies. The major policy option the Netherlands could derive from German (as well as the European) practice with respect to competition policies is now being implemented. The new Dutch Competition Act is a close copy of the corresponding German and European provisions.

Organization of Competition Authorities. One of the most marked differences between the European competition policy regime on the one hand and the German scheme on the other, is in their institutional design. According to the Monopolies Commission, the main disparity between German and European competition regimes is in the diverging objectives and, closely linked to these, in their respective institutional structures. Whereas the main objective of German policy is to safeguard competition and to protect the freedom of competitors, in European policy practice an intermingling of competition goals with other social or economic objectives, like for instance industrial policy goals, cannot be excluded. The reason is the absence of a clear and indisputable separation of responsibilities in European competition policy practice.

In the Netherlands a similar issue played a role during the preparations of the New Competition Act. In the initial plans, the new competition authority was semi-autonomous, creating a possibility for active involvement of the Minister of Economic Affairs in individual cases. A lesson from Germany, which is implemented in the mean time, is to make the competition authority more autonomous. Indeed, after three years the new Dutch competition authority will be (almost) completely independent, following the Bundeskartellamt.

Policy Option for the Netherlands on Regulation and Competition Policies

An additional policy option for the Netherlands could be found in the useful task performed by the German Monopolies Commission. This is an independent commission of experts with the task of reporting regularly on the state of development of concentration among enterprises. Every two years it produces a report for publication by the government. It can also at its discretion produce special reports on sectors.

Unfinished agenda for Germany and the Netherlands

Organization of Regulators. Analogously to competition authorities, independence is also desirable for the (future) regulators in Germany and the Netherlands. Neither Germany nor the Netherlands are yet so far in the deregulation process that a complete network of regulators exists, like for example in the United Kingdom and the United States. Following their examples, it seems best not only to make the (future) regulators independent from the now responsible ministries, but also to place them under the competition authorities. In this way knowledge and expertise can be shared and the risk of regulatory capture is smaller. This principle seems to be easier to implement in Germany, where the Bundeskartellamt is already organized mainly along industry-specific departments.

Further Liberalisation. With respect to regulation policy, many other measures still have to be worked out into details. Both Germany and the Netherlands are in the process of implementing European Union directives, mainly aimed at liberalising sectors with a natural monopoly nature. In telecommunications, competition will be intensified by more network competition and a less restrictive concessions policy. Germany is somewhat behind in this respect as German Telecom is one of the few monopolistic operators in Europe that controls the cable TV network. Giving up its dual ownership of both the telephone- and cable-network is a necessary condition for creating competition in the communications industry. With respect to the liberalization of postal services Germany is ahead of the Netherlands. In public transport, competition is practically non-existent in both countries and will be hard to establish without additional government actions. It must be concluded that stimulating competition in these industries is an important challenge in both Germany and the Netherlands. Furthermore, exploring privatization opportunities at the more decentralized government levels should be encouraged. Possible examples are waste management and public housing.

A Level Playing Field for Public and Private Companies. Special attention should be given to initiatives aimed at levelling the playing field of private and public companies in sectors where these are in competition directly or potentially. In the Netherlands the Cohen Committee has recently published a report with a list of proposals to deal with mixed markets of public and private firms. With respect to Germany, for this purpose the OECD recommends to review the overall regulatory structure. It is obvious that a levelling of playing fields of (semi-)public and private firms, where these are in direct competition, is crucial in removing distortions in resource allocation.

In this respect also lower levels of government have a substantial potential for privatization, especially in the fields of housing, utilities and transport. Whereas privatization is proceeding rather steadily at the federal level, action at the Länder and local levels was much more subdued. There are several indications that lower government objects to initiatives aimed at further privatization. First, local governments do not seem to be very eager to place private and public providers of services to municipalities on a more equal basis. Furthermore, Länder governments prove to be slow in introducing European Union directives, aimed at contributing to the internal market, in particular those regarding public procurement.

1.2.11 Chapter 13 Electricity and Gas Markets

Chapter 12 offers a broad overview of competition policy. Chapter 13 analyses this theme in depth for one particular field, namely the Electricity and Gas Markets. This sector provides an excellent illustration of the importance of introducing market forces. For decades it was taken for granted that electricity and gas provision were natural monopolies requiring heavy government intervention. This view is now subject to criticism. With competition the key word, the institutions in these markets are now being reformed in many countries, including Germany and the Netherlands. The overriding aim is to increase efficiency by strengthening competition.

The chapter outlines the shift in thinking on the role of government in natural monopolies. Subsequently, the existing institutions in the German and Dutch electricity and gas markets are examined, as well as the performance of these sectors. Then the current proposals to liberalize the two markets are analyzed. To provide a benchmark, the chapter describes the situation in the United Kingdom, which now has five years of experience with the operation of a highly liberalized electricity market. It also evaluates the state of affairs concerning the liberalization of the European energy market.

Policy Options for the Electricity Market

Policy Options. The conclusion of the analysis is that from the point of view of the functioning of markets, doubts remain about the effectiveness of the reform proposals in Germany and the Netherlands. How can both governments improve the chances for effective liberalization? For Germany policy options are to introduce regulated third-party access, separation of the grids and more contract freedom. With these measures the prospects for competition would be greatly strengthened.

The most effective way to strengthen the forces of competition in the Netherlands on the domestic market would be the conversion of the four existing regional generators into independent production companies. This would open the way for genuine competition between the major domestic generators provided they get a fair start on a level playing field. The separation of the central grid would also follow naturally from this line of argument. Indeed, putting the grid in the hands of one of the generators could easily lead to complaints of unfair competition from the others.

Economies of scale and the competitive position on the European market may constitute arguments to combine the relatively small Dutch generators into a single large-scale production facility. To secure competition this option would more strongly demand effective separation of the grid and independent ownership relations. Moreover, it requires a powerful Supervisory Authority. The Swedish example shows that independent ownership not necessarily requires complete privatisation of the entire energy sector. Therefore, from the perspective of strengthening market forces, separation and full independence constitute policy options that are worthwhile considering.

Policy Options for the Gas Market

Although there are important differences between electricity and gas, for example with respect to storage, there is also one crucial similarity from the perspective of market regulation: the existence of network-characteristics. This would seem to imply two policy conclusions for Germany and the Netherlands, which also came to the fore with electricity: the need to separate the natural monopoly from competition activities and the need for independent supervision. For the same reasons as in the case of electricity, it raises doubts – as part of an exercise to introduce more market forces – to leave the grid in the hands of parties that also have interests in the sale of gas.

Difference in Markets. On further consideration, however, there is one important difference between electricity and gas. First of all, *already now* competition in the European gas market is much more advanced than in the electricity market. because only a few countries in Europe dispose of natural gas resources. At the same time the share of gas in total energy use has continuously risen in the past decades and for the future a further strong increase is expected. This gives the many European countries without major natural gas resources, such as Germany, a strong interest in strengthening free trade and competition in the gas market to secure reliable gas supply at low prices. For these reasons confidence seems justified that the European gas market will be further opened up. From this perspective the steps Germany has taken up to now to liberalize the gas market seem to be modest. Additional policy options to stimulate competition would be the introduction of regulated instead of negotiated TPA and strict unbundling of the networks. A first step would be a no-regret policy option to promote regulated TPA on a European scale to maintain a level-playing field. However, the size of the German market also creates room for more unilateral steps. These initiatives could induce other countries to take the same steps.

Difference between the Dutch and the German case. The position of the Netherlands differs from that of Germany and of other European countries, because it is one of the few European countries with large natural gas reserves. In fact, the Dutch government itself is the *de facto* owner of both these reserves and, through Gasunie, part of the grid. As a result, the Dutch government faces an important trade-off between competition and the rents of natural gas, which largely flow to the central government. What counts, in particular, for the Dutch economy as a whole is the loss of rents from abroad. Strict adherence to the British example by separating the grids will only add to those losses, because it will eliminate also domestic monopoly rents Gasunie gains through the grid. The Dutch government has chosen to accept the reduction of rents from abroad as a result of the internal gas market, but is not prepared to walk in front and lose even more (domestic) revenues for the sake of (international) competition. Given this position, there is only limited room for further liberalization. One option would be to introduce regulated TPA instead of negotiated TPA, but to prevent predatory pricing by foreign suppliers and to create a level playing field, this policy would require similar steps in other countries.

1.2.12 Chapter 14 Health Care

The analytical framework describes two models of health care, managed competition and national health. Subsequently, the chapter discusses the institutional choices that have been made in Germany and the Netherlands with respect to health care financing, delivery systems, and the interactions between payers and providers. The actual performance of the German and Dutch health care systems is evaluated and the effects of emerging trends are briefly reviewed. The final part concludes with policy options for Germany and the Netherlands and provides thoughts on the unfinished agenda.

Policy Options for the Netherlands on Health Care

Although both systems are quite similar and also have moved in the same direction during the last years, some characteristics of the German health care system stand out that provide relevant policy options for the Dutch. Germany does not allow insurer/provider integration as a means of using competitive incentives to curb provider moral hazard. However, the German method of negotiating the relative value scale of provisions among physicians, as well as peer review of budget excessive treatment is a cooperative mechanism that may mitigate the problem somewhat. Nonetheless, the Netherlands cannot look to Germany for lessons from an operative managed care system.

Policy Options for Germany on Health Care

Germany utilizes more specialist and hospital care than the Netherlands. The general practitioner as gatekeeper in the Netherlands has often been credited with screening for over-use. General practitioners in the Netherlands feature among the lowest pharmaceutical prescription rates in OECD countries, and provide treatments for many simple ills rather than referring patients to more expensive secondary care. It may be worthwhile to assess how such a gatekeeper function could be introduced into the German system.

Unfinished Agenda for Health Care Reform in Germany and the Netherlands

Untackled Market Failure. Compared to the United States and the United Kingdom, both health systems performed reasonably well up to now, but not without unremitting policy effort. The systems will come under increased pressure in the years to come because the observed trends are expected to boost demand. This guarantees a continuing public debate on how to strike a balance between affordability, accessibility and quality; as well as on which coordination mechanisms should be used to manage the health care system.

From the perspective of the analytical framework the main market failure that both countries have not tackled so far is moral hazard from the side of the provider. Both models of health care, managed competition as well as national health, address this market failure. However, the managed competition model scores better in aligning the private incentives of providers with desired behaviour than the national health model does. Because moral hazard toward over-provision is the key market failure that goes unchecked in Germany and the Netherlands, it is a logical step to first explore the scope for more managed competition in the system. More competition also yields more diversity and experimentation, which would fit nicely with a number of trends, such as a more heterogenous population and the radical character of technological change. More managed competition would come at a price, however. Specifically, the diversity brought about by more managed competition implies more differences in service levels, in other words more inequality. Whereas vulnerable groups may benefit from enhanced efficiency, they may gain less than other groups.

Experimentation. On balance, the price of more managed competition does not seem high enough to obstruct more experimentation with managed competition. In view of the strong preferences for equal treatment in Germany and the Netherlands, it is suggested to start with a *limited* experiment, also because managed competition entails sailing into untested waters. Various experiments would be possible. We suggest to start with the introduction of managed competition in the private insurance sector and leave the sickness funds and special insurance schemes unchanged, at least initially. Chapter 14 contains an outline for such an experiment.

Impact. If effective, managed competition could remove the most important market failures in private health care. Hence, consumer preferences and costs would be better reflected in delivery. We cannot be sure, however, that the rise in health care expenditures will be contained under managed competition. But this will no longer be perceived as a social problem because it would truly reflect consumer preferences.

Furthermore, managed competition could change the incentive structures for technological change in medicine. Instead of a focus on high cost - low benefit solutions, it could turn medical research towards more cost-effective treatments. For Germany and the Netherlands, however, this effect is probably quite small, because medical R&D in these countries accounts for only a small part of global R&D in this field. Finally, managed competition for private insurance could create opportunities for experiments and new ideas about insurance and medical care more generally. If successful, these ideas could be applied to the sickness funds as well.

2 The Interplay of Institutions, Trade-offs, Performance and Trends

Where in the previous chapter 'Why?' formed the leading question, this chapter focuses on 'How?'. Chapter 1 examines why a comparative study is worthwhile, why institutions matter, why an analytical approach is useful and why Germany constitutes an important reference country. This chapter presents the analytical framework. It centres on the questions how institutions might affect economic performance and how long-term social, technological, economic and demographic trends influence the relationship between institutions and performance. Formal institutions, i.e. rules, regulations or policies, are the main focus of the study (Box 2.1).

Since economic science has no univocal theory of economic development, no clear-cut analytical framework exists that links institutions and performance. Recent comparative studies handle the analytical framework in various ways. Porter (1990) developed a system to assess national competitive advantage in an industry depending on a firm's strategy and structure, its cluster of related and supporting industries, its factor conditions and its demand conditions. Mayes and Hart (1994) apply the Structure, Conduct, Performance model of Schmalensee (1989). In this model variables related to market structure, like available technologies or seller and buyer concentration, determine market conduct, *i.e.* the behaviourial rules followed by agents who operate on the market. Comparison of market conduct to ideals like perfect competition yields the possibility to assess market performance. In another approach, CPB (1992) distinguishes three views on economic development, *viz.* a neoclassical, Keynesian and Schumpeterian perspective, and assesses strengths and weaknesses of world regions on aspects derived from these perspectives. Finally, the EZ (1995) applies a broad set of quantitative indicators in a benchmarking study on the competitiveness of the Dutch economy compared with four other countries, including Germany.

Focusing on trade-offs, this study emphasizes that institutional design is a process of learning by trial and error. Instead of presenting an optimal set of institutions, trade-offs occupy a central place. Trade-offs show that different feasible institutional orders exist, which each have their strong and weak points. Moreover, the balance between strengths and weaknesses shifts under the influence of trends. Section 2.1 presents the foundations of the analytical framework. In passing, it also explains the structure of the remainder of this chapter.

Box 2.1 Definitions of main concepts

Coordination mechanisms *define the type of human interaction:*
- *competition entails rivalry between agents striving for something that not all can obtain,*
- *control entails the power of an agent to take decisions and impose these on others,*
- *common values and norms pertain to congruent sets of preferences within a group of economic agents*
- *cooperative exchange involves bargained consultation and cooperation between a limited number of otherwise independent agents with different preferences.*

Coordination issues *identify four main areas that require coordination:*
- *market power results from economies of scale or collusion,*
- *externalities are interdependencies outside the price system,*
- *specificity concerns investment in relationship-specific assets,*
- *risk sharing deals with fundamental uncertainty.*

Institutions *are the humanly devised constraints that structure human interaction. They are either formal or informal:*
- *formal institutions consist of formal constraints, e.g., policy rules, regulations, laws, constitutions, contracts, property rights, bargaining agreements,*
- *informal institutions concern informal constraints, e.g., norms of behaviour, conventions, self imposed codes of conduct.*

Institutional change *concerns the evolution of institutions through time:*
- *institutional design is the process of constructing and adjusting formal institutions*
- *evolution of informal institutions is the (gradual) process of changing norms of behaviour, conventions, etc.*

Conditions *are the characteristics of the environment that affect coordination:*
- *social, e.g., heterogeneity of social groups, individualisation, emancipation,*
- *technological, e.g., tacitness, complexity,*
- *(international) economic, e.g., internationalisation, liberalisation, emerging regions,*
- *demographic, e.g., age structure of the population.*

Trends *concern changes of conditions that persist for a certain period of time.*

Sources: North (1994), Streeck and Schmitter (1991), de Jong (1989)

2.1 Foundations

This section pays attention to two aspects of the analytical framework: its general structure and the behaviourial assumptions. Section 2.1.1 presents the structure of the analytical framework. It shows the relationships between the framework's main components and sketches its basic philosophy. Section 2.1.2 turns to behaviourial assumptions. It compares neoclassical rationality with bounded rationality and opportunism that feature prominently in Transaction Costs Economics.

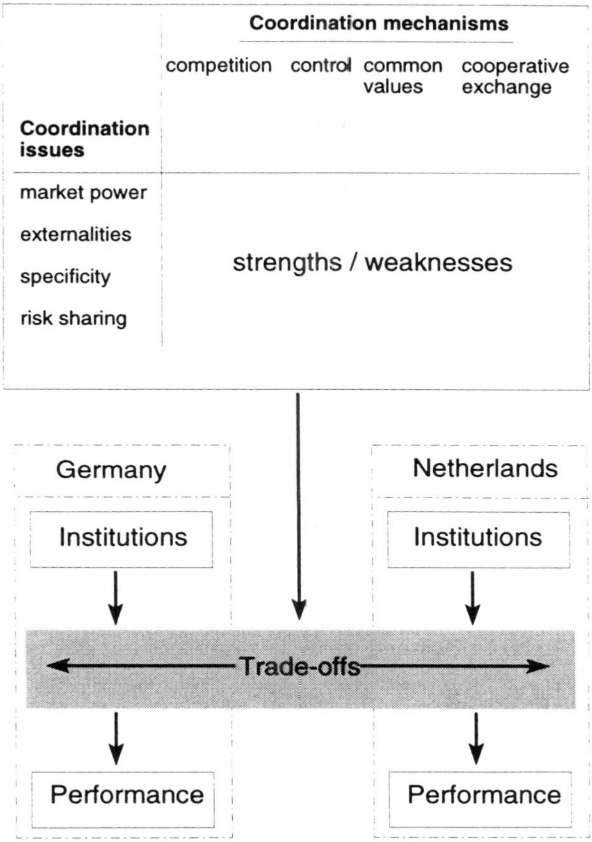

Figure 2.1 A framework to analyze the interplay of institutions and performance

2.1.1 General Structure

The construction of the framework starts from an analysis of four main sources of market failure and of four main economic coordination mechanisms (see Box 2.1 for the main concepts used). The first building block, on the vertical axis of the matrix in Figure 2.1, identifies four coordination issues, which correspond to four types of market failure: market power, externalities, specificity and risk sharing. Section 2.2 reviews the specific features of these four main types of market failure.

Market failure implies that coordination by the invisible hand may have to be replaced by other means of coordination. Therefore, the second building block, on the horizontal axis of the matrix in Figure 2.1, analyses four coordination mechanisms for interaction between economic agents. It emphasizes that government intervention through control is not the only answer to the failures of the competition. Government intervention can also fail and in some cases may even aggravate market failure. Therefore, in some cases two other coordination mechanisms may be important: common values and norms, and cooperative exchange. Section 2.3 reviews the general features of each of these four coordination mechanisms.

A comparative strength analysis of the coordination mechanisms applied to each of the four coordination issues, results in a four fundamental trade-offs (Section 2.4). Each coordination mechanism has its distinct strengths and weaknesses in addressing the coordination issues (the matrix in Figure 2.1). From these strengths and weaknesses four main trade-offs come to the fore that link institutions and performance. National institutions influence which side of a trade-off features more prominently in a specific country (the lower part of Figure 2.1). Since a country's position on the trade-off affects economic performance, trade-offs provide a link between institutions and performance. For instance, the flexible US labour market enhances allocation of labour from companies in declining industries to those in expanding industries. At the same time it may hamper investment by workers in firm-specific knowledge because they risk losing their investment on future dismissal. Hence, institutional diversity makes performance characteristics differ across countries. Performance feeds back to institutions when it invokes institutional adjustment.

Trends may also invoke institutional adjustment (Section 2.5). The comparative strengths of the coordination mechanisms manifest themselves differently under different social, technological and economic conditions. For instance, competition may be more appropriate in a heterogeneous society, and common values and norms more easily develop in a homogeneous society. It will be clear that trends directly affect these conditions, which feeds forward into the relative strengths and weaknesses of the coordination mechanisms. This might invoke a shift in the position of a country on a trade-off, and through changing performance characteristics feed back into institutional adjustments.

2.1.2 Bounded Rationality, Opportunism and Transaction Costs

The rational economic agent of neoclassical theory does not need many institutions. Secure property rights and a well-functioning market mechanism come a long way to achieving efficient allocation and welfare maximization. Equipped with full rationality and perfect foresight, guided by the invisible hand of the market mechanism, people choose those actions that in equilibrium appear to be in their common interest. Pareto efficiency defines the common interest: a reallocation can make nobody better off without making somebody else worse off. Moreover, contracts are comprehensive, *i.e.* contracts specify all parties' obligations in all possible future states of the world to the full.

Bounded Rationality. Why is it so difficult to find the neoclassical economic agent in everyday life? Ample examples exist of economic agents who make systematic reasoning errors, not only in complex decision problems, but also in relatively simple experimental situations (Conlisk, 1996: 670). From an economic perspective, the reason for systematic errors follows from the basic postulate underlying economics: scarcity. 'Human cognition is a scarce resource' (Conlisk, 1996: 686). It takes time and effort to review and weigh various options, and to take a decision. In other words, deliberation entails costs, so that people economize on deliberation. In principle, they would be able to oversee all relevant contingencies, to assign probabilities to each of these contingencies and to take a fully informed decision or to write a comprehensive contract. However, it would be irrational to act in such a way. For many contingencies, the probability that they arise is so small that considering them is not worth the time and effort. In other cases, reviewing contingencies in full detail would require so much time that the window of opportunity to take a decision would have been missed.

Economizing on deliberation costs explains why people generally apply heuristics, *e.g.* rules-of-thumb, to deal with decision problems. Heuristics mean that people are boundedly rational (compare Box 2.2).[1] 'Heuristics are rational in the sense that they (. . .) avoid deliberation costs, but boundedly rational in the sense that they often lead to biased choices' (Conlisk, 1996: 676). Accordingly, economic agents possess only limited knowledge of their environment and the actions of other agents. Information asymmetries exist between economic agents and foresight is imperfect.

Bounded rationality necessitates learning and innovation. People improve their heuristics by learning, which is also a costly process that commands scarce resources. Learning not only takes place individually but also socially. This study may act as an example: its purpose is to learn from experiences in Germany and the Netherlands by comparing their institutional order.

Opportunism. Opportunistic behaviour concerns 'self-interest seeking with guile' (Williamson, 1985). Magill and Quinzii (1996: 14) define *opportunism* as follows: 'an agent is said to be opportunistic if the choice of his actions is based

---

[1] Simon (1947, 1957) laid the foundation for the analysis of bounded rationality in economics. Bounded rationality and opportunism are central concepts in Transaction Cost Economics founded by Coase (1937) and substantially elaborated by Williamson (1975, 1985). Lazonick (1991: 206-227) provides a brief overview of the main concepts of Transaction Costs Economics and a discussion of its strengths and weaknesses. Conlisk (1996) contains an elaborate survey of bounded rationality in economics. Chapter 1 of Magill and Quinzii (1996) also contains an introduction on the topics addressed in this section. Dixit (1996) applies these concepts to politics in a Transaction Costs Politics framework.

Box 2.2 Bounded rationality, opportunism and transaction costs

Bounded rationality:
- *to economize on deliberation costs people apply heuristics, e.g. rules-of-thumb,*
- *heuristics imply boundedly rationality: economic agents possess only limited knowledge of their environment and the actions of other agents and hold an imperfect view of the future.*

Opportunism concerns:
- *self-interest seeking with guile,*
- *self-interest transgressing social values and norms.*

Transaction costs are:
- *the costs of arranging a contract ex ante,*
- *and monitoring and enforcing it ex post.*

Bounded rationality and opportunism cause ex-ante transaction costs:
- *gathering information on environment and future contingencies,*
- *signalling one's own intentions and competence to potential contracting partners,*
- *screening the other party's competence,*
- *searching for alternatives,*
- *negotiating and drawing-up contracts.*

Bounded rationality and opportunism cause ex-post transaction costs:
- *monitoring costs,*
- *costs of enforcement: bargaining, verification and litigation,*
- *costs of protection against third-party encroachment,*
- *potential costs of default or bankruptcy.*

Source: Eggertsson (1990), Magill and Quinzii (1996)

exclusively on his self-interest and is not influenced by a desire to respect social norms'. Therefore, opportunism may result in 'incomplete or distorted disclosure of information, especially calculated efforts to mislead, distort, disguise, obfuscate or otherwise confuse' (Williamson, 1985). Of course few people are completely opportunistic. Moreover, countries may differ in the extent to which opportunistic behaviour is socially and morally acceptable.

Transaction Costs. Bounded rationality and opportunism cause transaction costs. Transaction costs are 'the costs of arranging a contract ex ante and monitoring and enforcing it ex post, as opposed to production costs, which are the costs of executing the contract' (Matthews, 1986).

Ex-ante transaction costs comprise the costs of gathering information on the relevant conditions affecting the transaction and of future states of the world that may impact the gains of the transaction.[2] Examples concern the selection procedure in hiring new employees or reviewing guarantee conditions in a purchase agreement. In particular if transactions contain a substantial amount of bargaining, an economic agent must spend time and effort to signal his intentions and reliability to potential contracting partners. At the same time the agent must screen the other party's competence as well. Ex-ante transaction costs also include a process of searching for alternative transaction parties. Finally after parties have reached an agreement-in-principle, they have to devote resources to negotiate, itemize and write possibly detailed actions in complex contracts.

Ex-post transaction costs consist of the private and social costs of monitoring, enforcement and possible default. During the contracting period parties have to monitor each other's actions to guard against opportunism. Information asymmetries may considerably complicate monitoring activities and raise related transaction costs. Enforcement of a contract may invoke new negotiations or even legal steps if negotiation does not succeed. Enforcement may also include the protection of property rights against third parties. Protection of brand names or copyrights against illegal imitation falls under the latter category. Costs may arise from default or bankruptcy when the contract breaks down. Social transaction costs are the costs of maintaining a legal system to monitor and enforce contracts and resolve disputes.

Bounded rationality, opportunism and the related transaction costs make it infeasible to design comprehensive contracts (Hart, 1995: 22-23; Milgrom and Roberts, 1992: Ch. 5; Kay, 1993: 55; MacLeod, 1995: 20). Bounded rationality means that contracts cannot specify all parties' obligations in all possible future states of the world to the full. Contracting parties face difficulties to develop a common language to unambiguously define the terms of a contract. Parties fail to write a contract that is interpretable and perfectly enforceable in court. By consequence, contracts usually only specify general objectives, bounds on actions to be taken, division of power to act, dispute-resolution mechanisms, *etc.*. Opportunism creates the risk that parties exploit the incompleteness of contracts. Without opportunism incomplete contracts would not pose many problems, since parties still would act trustworthy and would aim at a mutually beneficial outcome. In contrast, opportunism makes the reliability of the other party's actions *a priori* uncertain, which substantially raises both ex-ante and ex-post transaction costs.

---

[2] Conlisk (1996: 690) considers costly deliberation and costly information gathering as two joint inputs in 'producing' a decision. Transaction costs include the costs of collecting information, but also contain various other costs components (compare Box 2.2). Therefore, this framework focuses on deliberation costs and transaction costs as the two main cost categories in coordinating decisions among economic agents.

2.2 Coordination Issues: Four Types of Market Failures

For several fundamental reasons markets may fail as a coordination mechanism. Four types of market failures constitute the points of departure for this study's analytical framework (compare Box 2.1). Sections 2.2.1 and 2.2.2 discuss the first two types of market failures, which already arise in the static world of spot markets. They consist of the well-known cases of monopoly power, due to strategic behaviour or increasing returns to scale, and of externalities, due to transaction costs or non-excludability. Sections 2.2.3 and 2.2.4 turn to the third and fourth type of market failure, which in a dynamic context deal with specificity and uncertainty, respectively.

2.2.1 Market Power

Market power forms a textbook case of market failure. It may result from deliberate action of economic agents, for instance through collusion, or from increasing returns to scale in production technology or information technology that lead to a natural monopoly. Compared with perfect competition, a firm with market power is able to create rents by constraining supply. The allocative inefficiency of market power creates a cost to society. Lack of competitive pressure may also lead to managerial complacency. Few incentives for monopolies to reduce costs, introduce new products or implement process innovations, generate dynamic inefficiencies (compare Armstrong *et al.*, 1994).

In contrast, in a natural monopoly economies of scale and scope may create dynamic efficiencies, which may require concentration. Energy distribution grids are well-known examples. In these cases regulation attempts to control the adverse effects of monopoly, while preserving the positive effects of economies of scale and scope.

Non-rival goods are a specific type of goods that generate increasing returns in production. Use by one agent of a non-rival good does not limit the use by other agents. Technologies are non-rival goods: once a technological design has been created it can be used many times without requiring additional inputs (Romer, 1990). If a production process depends on rival inputs (labour, capital) with constant returns to scale and on non-rival inputs (technological design), increasing all inputs by the same percentage generates a more than proportional increase in output (Romer, 1990: 75, 76). In other words, non-rivalness implies increasing returns to scale.

2.2.2 Externalities

Basically, externalities correspond with missing markets. Externalities are interdependencies between individual preferences or activities that are outside the price system and therefore not fully discounted in individual decisions. Myles

Box 2.3 Rivalness, excludability, externalities and types of goods

	Excludable	*Non-excludable*
Rival	*private goods*	*common property*
Non-rival	*club goods*	*public goods*
	Lower ⟸ *Externalities*	⟹ *Higher*

Source: World Bank (1994: 25)

(1995: 313) defines: 'An externality is present whenever some economic agent's welfare (utility or profit) includes real variables whose values are chosen by others without particular attention to the effect upon the welfare of the other agents they affect'. By consequence, the market will provide an inefficiently low amount of goods that involve positive externalities (education, infrastructure networks), whereas it provides too many goods that involve negative externalities (pollution, resource depletion). If a market would exist for the relevant good, the price mechanism would achieve efficient allocation.

Non-excludability can be regarded as a type of externality (compare Box 2.3). If agents value a good positively, non-excludability implies that no economically feasible way exists to exclude non-payers from consumption of that good. All agents benefit from a non-excludable good once it has been produced. Supply of non-excludable goods and services is vulnerable to free-rider behaviour. Monitoring activity forms a case in point. Take the example of a group of individuals, who lend money to a firm. If monitoring the firm entails costs and if monitoring information is not excludable, each single lender is inclined to free ride on the others' monitoring activity.

In many cases transaction costs or other types of market failures prevent a detailed definition of property rights that make individual economic agents internalize externalities. If a specific externality involves many agents, like CO_2 emissions by motor cars, the transaction costs of negotiating property rights preclude the emergence of a market for pollution rights. 'In many cases it seems likely that the welfare loss due to waste of resources in organising the market would outweigh any gains from having the market' (Myles, 1995: 325). If the number of agents is relatively small, transaction costs of organising a market may be less of a problem, but by definition these cases violate the assumption of competitive behaviour. Hence, production or information monopolies prevent competitive equilibria to arise.

Types of Goods. Box 2.3 shows how (non-)excludability and (non-)rivalness delineate four types of goods (World Bank, 1994). *Private goods* are both rival and excludable. Consumption by one consumer reduces the supply to others and a consumer can be prevented from consumption. For instance, although construction and maintenance of an energy distribution grid entails economies of scale, access to the grid is excludable and therefore can be provided through the market. *Club goods* are excludable but non-rival. Drivers can be excluded from access to a toll road, but an additional car does not prevent others from using the road, provided the road is not congested. A *common property* is rival but non-excludable. Examples concern a water basin, the quantity of a species of fish in the ocean, clean air in urban areas or a congested urban road. Common property is vulnerable to the tragedy of the commons: everyone has an incentive to exploit it, but no-one has an incentive to care for it.

Non-rivalness and non-excludability characterize a *public good.* Hence, public goods combine the two types of market failures described above: they give rise to market power and externalities. Public provision forms the textbook solution to the existence of public goods. National defence is a well-known example. In the subsequent analysis public goods are not addressed separately because the discussion of market power and externalities largely covers public goods as well.

2.2.3 Specificity: The Hold-up Problem

The third type of market failure originates in the context of specificity from contracting problems caused by changing bargaining power in the course of time.[3] This contracting problem, the hold-up problem, emerges if contracting parties substantially invest in relationship-specific assets, characterized by sunk costs and contracts are incomplete.[4] Once the relationship-specific investment has been made, the investing party can be forced to accept a worsening in the terms of the relationship, because the investment cannot be put to an alternative use without substantial losses. This reduces the investing party's ex-post bargaining power. By consequence, the investing party has been held up (Milgrom and Roberts, 1992: 136, 307; Armstrong *et al.*, 1994: 138). Of course the investing party is aware of the possibility of ex-post opportunism. Therefore, if the party that benefits

[3] The market failures of specificity and uncertainty (see next section) can also be considered as specific types of externality. In this view, externalities associated with specificity arise from missing markets for commitment and externalities associated with uncertainty arise from missing securities markets. However, because specificity and uncertainty take a central place in this study, they are treated separately.

[4] Sunk costs are costs that are irrecoverable once made (see Box 12.1). Hence, the sunk costs of the investment are lost if the asset is excluded from its major use. Transaction Costs Economics uses the term 'asset specificity'. The degree of asset specificity is defined as the fraction of the value of the asset which is lost if the asset is excluded from its major use (Milgrom and Roberts, 1992: 307). If two parties both make relationship-specific investments their assets are co-specialized, *i.e.* the two assets are most productive when used together and are of little value separately. Asset specificity often originates in ex-ante transaction costs. Once one has paid all the ex-ante transaction costs, these costs are sunk.

from the investment cannot convince the investing party of its commitment to keep to the initial agreement, the fear of becoming vulnerable to ex-post opportunism can induce the investing party to abstain from profitable investments. As a consequence, welfare improving value creation has been curbed.

An example of the hold-up problem concerns investment in relationship-specific equipment by a supplier and a procuring firm (Hart, 1995: 27).[5] Ex ante, the parties agree on a division of costs and revenues of an investment to be made by the supplier in machinery and technology, which is tailored to the requirements of the procuring firm. The supplier runs the risk that after it has made the investment, the procuring firm uses its ex-post higher bargaining power to force down the price of products delivered by the supplier. Therefore, it will be less inclined to engage in relationship-specific investment. Depending on the division of costs and revenues in the initial agreement, ex-post the balance may also turn out to the disadvantage of the procuring firm, for instance if it becomes highly dependent on the products delivered by the supplier. This example illustrates the crucial features of the hold-up problem: assets are relationship-specific so that at least a part of the investment costs are sunk, ex-ante bargaining power differs from ex-post bargaining power and no credible commitment can be given that parties will keep to the initial agreement because contracts are incomplete and parties may act opportunistically.

2.2.4 Uncertainty: Risk Sharing

In theory, the existence of uncertainty does not contradict a neoclassical equilibrium, but the assumptions required to derive an equilibrium are hardly tenable in reality. Introduction of security markets for each future state of the world forms a theoretical solution to establish a neoclassical equilibrium in an uncertain environment (see for instance Myles, 1995: 202).[6] However, introducing a set of securities that covers every relevant future state of the world would entail prohibitively high informational requirements and would create excessively high transaction costs. The absence of complete securities markets creates a market

---

5 Kay (1993: 53) presents several other examples of potential hold-up situations derived from business practice.

6 A security bears a predetermined income if the relevant state of the world does occur and nothing otherwise. Introduction of security markets differs from devising a complete set of contingent markets. A system of contingent markets requires markets for all products in all possible future states of the world. Security markets separate the intertemporal allocation of income from the allocation of income over products. Therefore, the number of markets associated with introduction of securities equals the sum of the number of products and the number of relevant states of the world, whereas with contingent markets it equals the product of those two numbers. Both solutions produce exactly the same equilibrium outcome (Myles, 1995: 202).

failure: 'in general when risk markets are incomplete and information is imperfect, markets are not constrained Pareto optimal: the invisible hand does not work. There exist market interventions, which respect the limitations on information and risk distribution opportunities, which can make everyone better off' (Stiglitz, 1991: 22).

In a world characterized by bounded rationality and opportunism, the private insurance market encounters four types of problems: costs of information, interdependent risks, adverse selection and moral hazard. *Costs of information* are part of the transaction costs of private insurance contracts. Due to fundamental uncertainties some risks are difficult to calculate, like the effects of unemployment caused by an adverse macro-economic shock. In addition, several of the transaction costs in Box 2.2 apply to insurance contracts, both for the insurer and for the insured. Moreover, often information on risk characteristics is nonrival. By consequence, economies of scale may constitute an additional market failure in risk sharing.

Interdependent risks affect many agents at the same time. Pooling of interdependent risks works out detrimental for an insurance company, because these risks do not cancel each other. This is one of the reasons why insurance companies do not insure natural disasters, the consequences of inflation, or unemployment.

Unobservable characteristics underlie *adverse selection.*[7] Adverse selection may occur if one party in a transaction does not hold sufficient information on the others' characteristics and it is not in the interest of the other party to reveal that information. People who are bad risks are not inclined to reveal that to the insurance company, but are eager to buy insurance. By consequence, the pool of insured people will contain a relatively high share of risk-prone people, which drives up insurance premium rates. This sets in motion a process of adverse selection. Because of the relatively high premium rates, some people with a low risk profile refrain from insuring themselves. Hence, the share of risk-prone people in the pool of insured rises further. Again premium rates increase, which drives more less-risky individuals out of the market, *etc*. In the end adverse selection causes under-insurance. The process restricts insurance possibilities for people with a low risk profile: the good risks. Good risks would be willing to buy insurance if premium rates were more in accordance with their risk characteristics.

Adverse selection problems are important when information asymmetries between the insured and the insurer are large. Information asymmetries are less relevant either if both the company and the insured are ignorant of the risk characteristics or if the company can obtain much information on private risk profiles. In the first case the insured and the company are both behind the

[7] Akerlof (1970) introduced the concept of adverse selection in an analysis of the market for 'lemons'. For a basic introduction on adverse selection and moral hazard see for instance Stiglitz (1993: 153-158).

Rawlsian 'veil of ignorance'. Adverse selection does not occur because individual risk characteristics are not manifest and both the insurer and the insured are unaware of bad or good risks. The main problem here is that often entering into an insurance contract is impossible when people are still behind the veil of ignorance (Sinn, 1995: 8). Personal abilities are only unknown in early childhood or even before birth, but young children cannot decide to buy insurance and legal and moral restrictions prevent parents to bind their children to an insurance contract that requires them to spend a considerable part of their future income on insurance premiums. At the age that people can personally decide to take up insurance most of the veil of ignorance has been lifted.

The second option, *i.e.* insurance companies gathering more information on personal risk characteristics, may bring about considerable transaction costs. Several instruments enable companies to obtain more information or attract good risks. Examples are medical tests, advertising, and signalling methods like coinsurance.[8] However, the costs embedded in these screening and signalling activities only serve to prevent adverse selection and therefore can be considered as part of the transaction costs of providing insurance through competition.

Unobservable actions underlie *moral hazard*. Insurance lowers incentives to avoid the risks people are insured for. To a certain degree, increased risk taking is a positive effect of insurance (Sinn, 1995). It encourages people to engage in risky activities that may benefit society, such as moving to a new job, inventing new products or starting a business. However, if insurance provides too much protection, it erodes all caution and fosters too risky activities. People may even engage in rent seeking activities to exploit informational asymmetries. In those cases moral hazard curbs the effectiveness of insurance. Drivers who are insured against car accidents drive less carefully. In particular, moral hazard is likely to appear when the insured can easily influence their risk characteristics without being observed by the company. For instance, a high insurance benefit in case of unemployment would reduce the incentive to search for an new job. The person involved could easily pretend to search for a job actively, while in practice performing hardly any effort at all.

2.3 Four Coordination Mechanisms

Section 2.2 identifies four types of market failures. Traditionally, market failure forms an argument for government intervention.[9] However, Section 2.3.1 below

---

[8] People who opt for high coinsurance signal the insurer that their risk profile is relatively low. Hence, the insurer can offer them lower premium rates.

[9] Of course, social considerations form an other reason for government intervention. Examples are income redistribution through social security or housing subsidies for low-income earners. Also merit goods may require government intervention

argues that government intervention does not constitute an universal remedy. On the contrary, recent insights emphasize government failure and state that in some cases government intervention may even aggravate market failure. Therefore, institutional design requires a balanced view of the strengths and weaknesses of both market and government. Section 2.3.2 further reviews these strengths and weaknesses by focusing on the two coordination mechanisms that underlie the market and government intervention: competition and control. In addition it examines two additional coordination mechanisms: common values and norms, and cooperative exchange. Section 2.3.3 discusses how institutional design involves choosing among these coordination mechanisms. This sets the stage for Section 2.4 which applies the four coordination mechanisms to the four coordination issues identified in Section 2.2.

2.3.1 Government Intervention and Government Failure

In various ways the government can intervene to deal with market failure. Regulation or even public ownership can control private monopoly power in natural monopolistic markets, while competition policy guards against the creation of monopoly rents through collusion. Positive externalities may ask for government provision or subsidisation (education, infrastructure), whereas negative externalities (pollution, resource depletion) require regulation or taxation.

Furthermore, in a world characterized by bounded rationality and opportunism, many aspects of government intervention lower transaction costs in the private sector of the economy (Chang, 1994: 49). The government lowers private transaction costs by instituting and enforcing a system of property rights, by striving for macroeconomic stability and by facilitating the solution of coordination problems between private economic agents. In the absence of well-defined property rights, individual contracting costs would be substantial. Preventing expropriation or rent abrogation would require a considerable amount of resources. Recall the reform process to a market economy in former centrally planned economies, or the situation in some less developed countries. A regulatory system conducive to macroeconomic stability saves resources needed to hedge against price or exchange rate volatility or saves inventory costs. Technological standards or technological quality requirements are examples of government imposed norms or standards that save transaction costs in private coordination.

However, next to market failure also government failure exists (see for instance Wolf, 1993). Direct government intervention does not have to be superior to the market, if the government faces comparable limitations as the market, such as bounded rationality and opportunism. Because it lacks price signals, the government may have less information than the market, which may make the consequences of government failure worse than those of market failure (compare Dasgupta, 1991: 82). In other words, in these cases the transaction costs of government intervention outweigh the transaction costs of market coordination.

Government intervention may generate transaction costs through the potentially high costs of gathering information by the government, through rent seeking behaviour by the private sector and through compliance costs. Rent seeking brings about social costs when agents engage in unproductive activities to capture artificial rents created by government policies. Compliance costs pertain to the direct costs imposed on economic agents to comply with government regulation. Examples are administrative costs or costs of juridical procedures linked to government regulation. In particular for small and medium-sized companies compliance costs may entail a substantial burden.

Additional transaction costs result from distortions in the intentions of government policies. From inside the government, bureaucrats may exploit their informational advantage over politicians and pursue their own interests, for instance by aiming at budget maximization or at power maximization.[10] Moreover, strong outside interest groups may bias government activities towards their own objectives. For instance, regulatory capture theory analyzes how producer interest groups 'capture' a regulatory agency and design regulation at the industry's advantage. Policy then restricts entry in a specific industry, diverts subsidies to specific companies or sets a lower limit to product prices.[11] Olson (1982) shows that powerful organized interest groups may harm economic efficiency, except when they become sufficiently encompassing so as to internalize the external effects of their behaviour (Crouch, 1993: 9; van Waarden, 1997).

2.3.2 Main Features of the Coordination Mechanisms

This section generalizes the previous discussion of market failure and government intervention in two ways. Firstly, it uses a somewhat more abstract approach by analyzing competition and control as the coordination mechanisms underlying market coordination and government intervention. Secondly, it adds two coordination mechanisms: common values and norms, and cooperative exchange. These entail additional ways to respond to market failure and contain their own strength and weaknesses (see Box 2.4 for an overview). In some respects these coordination mechanisms improve upon competition or control, in other ways they perform less adequately.

Analysis of four abstract coordination mechanisms enables a separation between the coordination mechanisms and the economic agents that use the coordination mechanisms in real world situations. For instance, it would be erroneous to identify

[10] Tirole (1994: 13) underlines the opposite possibility. Government officials refuse new assignments and oppose maximization of their agency's size because new tasks expose their low abilities.

[11] See Laffont and Tirole (1993: Ch. 11) for a formal treatment of regulatory capture in an agency-theoretic framework.

Box 2.4 Four coordination mechanisms and their potential strengths and weaknesses

	Competition	*Control*
Applied in	*market*	*legislation, court order, army, Fordist company*
Potential strengths	*allocation, information dissemination, incentives, experimentation, individual freedom*	*enforcement, certainty, policy implementation*
Potential weaknesses	*rent seeking, transaction costs, commitment, income distribution*	*incentives, rent-seeking, information and compliance costs, capture by interest groups, individual freedom*
	Common values and norms	*Cooperative exchange*
Applied in	*family, volunteer group, church, team, NGO*	*research joint venture, supplier relationship, industrial relations*
Potential strengths	*motivation, commitment, internal flexibility*	*mutual learning, incentives, internal flexibility*
Potential weaknesses	*free riders, external rigidity, lack of privacy*	*enforceability, abuse of cooperation, external rigidity*

government activity completely with coordination through control. At times the government operates on the market and in a number of countries cooperative exchange makes up a considerable part of the policy instruments of the government.[12] Different coordination mechanisms can even operate simultaneously in one organisation: in some of its internal coordination a company can apply control principles, whereas in other instances it may resort to cooperative exchange or competition.

Competition. Competition entails rivalry between agents striving for something that not all can obtain. Competition means coordination by the invisible hand. Under ideal circumstances competition achieves efficient allocation, adequately conveys information through price signals and provides incentives for individual

[12] Therefore, the discussion of government failure in Section 2.3.1 talks about government intervention, i.e. that part of government activity that uses control as a coordination mechanism.

flexibility. Moreover, competition is anonymous, which promotes individual freedom and privacy.

Section 2.2 argues that under less favourable circumstances competition fails. Market power and risk sharing may result in rent seeking. For some types of externalities, high transaction costs may preclude competition. Commitment to keep to long-term agreements is weak. Finally, competition may produce a socially or politically unacceptable distribution of income.

Control. Control entails the power of an agent to take decisions and impose these on others. Control not only pertains to government intervention. Other examples are court orders or an army. Companies may also apply principles of control. For instance, control features extensively in the traditional Fordist hierarchical company (Best, 1990).

In several ways strengths and weaknesses of control constitute the mirror image of competition. Control provides certainty: participants need not perform long search actions or make large costs to guard against opportunism of others. Furthermore, policy design and policy implementation are relatively easy in a control situation. Compared to cooperative exchange (see below), control does not require consultation of many different parties and extensive bargaining.

Section 2.3.1 also illustrates the drawbacks of control. Control takes away incentives and may invoke rent-seeking behaviour. Compliance costs and the costs of gathering information may be prohibitive to exercise control effectively. Controllers may give in to interest groups or may pursue private interests, which distorts the intentions of control measures. Evidently, control curbs individual freedom.

Common Values and Norms. Common values and norms pertain to congruent sets of preferences within a group of people. Common values and norms form the guiding coordination principles within a community. Various types of communities exist, ranging from a family to a club, a church, a volunteer group or a team of people working towards a common goal. Repeated interaction promotes spontaneous solidarity, consensus, and common values and norms in a community. Dasgupta (1991: 75, 79) interprets social norms as implicit social contracts to cooperate, embedded in customs and rituals and resulting from repeated interaction. If people are not extremely myopic, it is in the self-interest of each member of the group to keep to the norms, in other words the norms are self-enforcing. Common values and norms diminish the incidence of opportunistic behaviour between members of a group.

Effective coordination based on common values and norms coincides with a strong motivation and high commitment of individual members of a community to achieve their common goal. Moreover, under favourable conditions the absence of strictly formalized agreements and the high degree of consensus promote flexible adjustment to changing circumstances, within the existing relationship.

When conditions turn out unfavourable, coordination through common values and norms and solidarity may become unstable. Common values and norms and solidarity may take a long time to develop, but can be destroyed quickly. In particular when circumstances change rapidly, social norms may cease to be adequate, information asymmetries intensify and the ability of members of the group to monitor behaviour of others declines (compare Dasgupta, 1991: 76). Free riders threaten the internal coherence and consensus within a community. Members may take advantage of information asymmetries by pretending to act in the interest of the community, while in reality they pursue their own goals and exploit the solidarity of other members (moral hazard).

Two additional potential disadvantages of coordination by common values and norms exist. External rigidity can be considerable, in other words it may be very difficult to leave the community and build relationships with other agents. In addition, compared to the more anonymous coordination in a market environment, members of a community lack privacy.

Cooperative Exchange. In several ways cooperative exchange takes an intermediate position compared to the other coordination mechanisms. It involves bargained consultation and cooperation between a limited number of otherwise independent parties with different preferences (see also Streeck and Schmitter, 1991; Kay, 1993). Parties may be private firms, but also interest organisations or even the government. Besides the issues that parties cooperate upon, the mutual relationship on other issues does not have to be cooperative but may even be competitive. Some concrete examples clarify these points.

In the field of product design, a supplier and a procuring corporation can enter into a cooperative-exchange arrangement (compare Best, 1990). In contrast to a competitive relationship, which concentrates on detailed specifications of standardized components and processes in the production chain, a cooperative-exchange arrangement focuses on design and interaction between suppliers and procuring firms. A procuring firm does not confront suppliers with detailed specifications of the products required and subsequently asks for tenders. Instead it submits the functions a product should serve to a supplier together with a considerable amount of technological information on the production process in which the product of the supplier has to be incorporated. The supplier offers a prototype design and the two firms enter in several rounds of consultations until the required product has been developed. Analogously, companies enter a cooperative-exchange relationship when they start a research joint venture.

Cooperative exchange also takes place on a more aggregated level. Industrial relations constitute a well-known example of cooperative exchange between interest associations. In countries with industrial relations on a sectoral or national level, peak organisations of labour and capital interact in a close and highly structured, bargained and cooperative way. Unions and employers' organisations bargain about wages but may cooperate on the organisation of a vocational training program.

Covenants about environmental objectives are the subject of a cooperative-exchange relationship between the government and private firms.

Under favourable circumstances cooperative exchange combines the advantages of competition and of common values and norms. Compared to both a market relationship and unilateral control, cooperation generally implies that parties become more knowledgeable about each others' situation: the flow of information between the parties increases (McMillan, 1995). Mutual learning raises the quality of their combined activity and improves the effectivity of their relationship. At the same time the competitive aspect of cooperative exchange provides incentives to stay alert and innovative, to exploit market opportunities and to quickly adjust to a changing environment. In addition, the non-formalized character of the relationship facilitates adjustment, because it does not require the reformulation of contracts or respecification of directives, which may both involve time-consuming procedures (compare Kester, 1992: 28).

The supplier relationship again serves as an example to clarify these advantages of cooperative exchange. Consultation and cooperation with a limited number of suppliers serve several purposes for the procuring firm. It enhances learning processes and improves the problem-solving capabilities of the firm by exploiting detailed technological knowledge of suppliers. This decreases product development times, improves product quality and raises efficiency in production. The supplier can improve its technological knowledge base and raise the quality of its products because it learns from the technological know-how of the procuring company and from the feedback on its prototypes and design given by the procuring company. Improving product quality not only is advantageous to the relationship with the procuring firm, but also strengthens the competitive position of the supplier on the market.

Of course less advantageous features also exist. To some extent cooperative exchange is vulnerable to the potential weaknesses of coordination based on common values and norms. A party may exploit information asymmetries or may abuse the cooperative stance of the other party. In addition, cooperative exchange can turn into collusion when the parties use their relationship to restrict entry in the relevant market. In contrast to the internal flexibility of cooperative exchange, *i.e.* the ability of parties to quickly adjust the subject matter of their cooperation, external rigidities may arise. Switching between partners is more difficult and sometimes the cooperative-exchange relationship takes precedence over market opportunities (McMillan, 1995: 231). A supplier may have to forgo profitable market demand to meet demand by a procuring firm with which it maintains a relationship.

2.3.3 Institutional Design: Trade-offs Replace Solutions

So far this chapter has identified four coordination issues and four coordination mechanisms. In this framework, institutional design can be regarded as the selection of a set of institutions that supports the coordination mechanism that is most appropriate to resolve or reduce the problems associated with a specific coordination issue (compare Box 2.1 and Figure 2.1).

The choice between coordination mechanisms is hardly a straightforward calculation. All coordination mechanisms are imperfect and give rise to transaction costs. In a neoclassical world the solution would be to select those institutional arrangements that minimize the sum of transaction costs and production costs. However, in a second best world of bounded rationality and opportunism, generally no clear-cut optimum exists. Moreover, even if a solution existed nobody would be able to locate it. Therefore, institutional design consists of a process of trial and error and of searching for ways to adjust to changing circumstances.

This path dependency makes institutional design also dependent on history. Shifting between coordination mechanisms is a complex and lengthy process, because institutions are interrelated and rooted in society (see also van Waarden, 1997). Thus it is difficult to replace a specific part of legislation from one country by that from another country with a largely different institutional order.

Another complicating factor is that the process of institutional design contains a hold-up problem of its own, which may delay institutional adjustment. From a transaction-cost politics perspective, institutions follow from a cooperative-exchange agreement between private agents and the government.[13] Frequently, private agents base their (long-term) decisions on the expectation that institutions will remain unchanged (Dixit, 1996: 57). Therefore, in some respects, institutional adjustment means that the government reneges on an ex-ante agreement with private agents. This may harm specific investments that were conditional on the ex-ante institutional arrangements. In the eyes of private agents, the government loses reputation when it frequently adjusts the institutional environment. By consequence, government loses support for its policies. This helps to explain why adjustment of institutions only takes place after a relatively intense shock or when a process of gradual decline has crossed a certain threshold level (compare Dixit, 1996: 67-71).

The impossibility to derive a clear-cut optimal institutional configuration, means that trade-offs replace solutions. 'Solving' one problem through institutional adjustment may create other problems. Hence, in this international comparative study it is more fruitful to think in terms of institutions that affect a country's

---

[13] This meta hold-up problem also points to a dual role of the government in this analysis. The direct role of the government concerns the government policies to reduce a market failure that have been mentioned above. The 'meta' role pertains to designing institutions that support one of the coordination mechanisms. For instance, the government can design and maintain a system of property rights that supports competition. Generally, distinguishing the two roles poses no difficulties, but at times it is useful to keep the distinction in mind.

position on various trade-offs than in terms of institutional solutions that maximize some kind of social welfare function.

2.4 Issues and Mechanisms Combined: Trade-offs

To analyze in more detail the trade-offs that exist in the process of institutional design, this section contains a *comparative strength analysis* of the four coordination mechanisms applied to the four coordination issues identified in Section 2.2. The first two coordination issues, discussed in Section 2.4.1 and 2.4.2, relate to (technical) characteristics of goods and services: increasing returns to scale and externalities. Section 2.4.3 turns to intertemporal coordination associated with relationship-specific investments. Section 2.4.4 analyzes how the coordination mechanisms deal with uncertainty.

Trade-offs follow from the way the various coordination mechanisms address the coordination issues. Applied to a single coordination issue, each of the four coordination mechanisms features specific strengths and weaknesses. Criteria to assess these strengths and weaknesses build on the assessment in Box 2.4. For each coordination issue one dominant trade-off emerges. Because this framework distinguishes four coordination issues, four trade-offs can be derived, which provide the crucial link between institutions and performance.

The manifestation of the strong and weak points of the coordination mechanisms also depends on the conditions that apply in a certain country at a certain point in time. For instance, in a highly volatile environment competition may outperform control or cooperative exchange. Therefore, the assessments below end with a short review of the relevant conditions that influence the trade-offs between coordination mechanisms.

2.4.1 Market Power

Different coordination mechanisms entail different options to reduce the welfare loss due to market power (see Box 2.5).[14] Enhancing *competition* means creating markets. For example, anti-trust policy fights collusion and improves market performance. It may also prohibit companies that obtain large market sizes due to increasing returns: the case of the break-up of AT&T into several Baby Bells in the United States is a much cited example (see for instance Stiglitz, 1993: 459). Besides the potential strength of contending the adverse effects of collusion, market creation may fit consumer preference for diversity. Less economies of scale or

---

[14] For each type of market failure Box 2.5, Box 2.6, Box 2.7 and Box 2.8 highlight the main strengths and weaknesses of the various coordination mechanisms. More detailed assessments can be found in the text. Coordination principles that are not or only partially relevant for a specific type of market failure, are not included in the text and the boxes.

scope forms a potential disadvantage of market creation (Armstrong *et al.*, 1994: 106). These economies are best exploited by one or a few firms, so promoting entry lowers the gains from economies of scale or scope.

The most drastic *control* way to deal with market power is nationalization. However, generally nationalisation does not solve managerial complacency and political objectives may dominate efficiency objectives. Therefore, governments more frequently apply regulation to control natural monopolies.

Nowadays regulatory innovation and technological change provide opportunities for *unbundling*, *i.e.* the separation of activities in which economies of scale are important from those in which they are not (World Bank, 1994: 53, 54). For instance, unbundling separates the construction and maintenance of an energy distribution grid from the provision of services through the grid, whereas previously a large public monopoly performed both activities. Competition enhances efficiency in the provision of services, while a regulated natural monopoly enables a separate company to reap economies of scale in exploitation of the grid. Another example concerns the separation of railway track maintenance from railway operations. Unbundling not only applies vertically but also horizontally, for instance when different companies provide freight railway transport and passenger transport. Regional differentiation constitutes another case of horizontal unbundling, which facilitates regulation because it enables performance comparison between regions.

Next to economies of scale, also economies of scope confine unbundling. Economies of scope exist when a single provider is more cost effective in the provision of two or more services than separate companies that each produce a single service. Economies of scale or scope particularly occur in cases of horizontal unbundling. Regionally separated companies will perform some activities separately that would invoke proportionally less costs if combined.

Bundling frequently also involves cross-subsidization. For instance, a company charges identical prices for customers in remote areas and for customers for which connection to a service network is relatively cheap. In these cases unbundling makes different lines of business more transparent and more clearly identifies the extent of subsidies. However, a drawback of unbundling may be that making subsidies explicit diminishes political support for these subsidies and as a consequence reduces solidarity in society.

The Trade-off between Diversity and Scale or Scope. Market power creates a trade-off between diversity on the one hand and exploiting economies of scale or scope on the other hand. Box 2.5 shows that competition promotes diversity but may prevent companies from benefiting from economies of scale. Analogously, static efficiency from competition has to be weighted against the dynamic efficiency gains from economies of scale or scope.

Box 2.5 Market power: main strengths and weaknesses of coordination mechanisms

Activity	*production, product supply*
Characteristics	*increasing returns to scale, non-rivalness*
Market failure	*monopoly rents, managerial complacency*

Coordination mechanism	*Implementation*	*Potential weaknesses*	*Potential strengths*
Competition	*anti-trust policy*	*economies of scale and scope*	*diversity*
Control	*nationalisation, regulation*	*diversity*	*economies of scale and scope*

→ *Trade-off:* ***diversity ⇔ scale or scope***

Conditions. The discussion above shows that technological characteristics of goods and services are important factors that influence market power. Economies of scale and scope in production may create natural monopolies. In contrast, economies of scale may be less relevant for products that can easily be differentiated. In addition, for goods and services that are not directly linked to a specific location, openness of an economy reduces market power because it enlarges the relevant markets.

2.4.2 Externalities

Externalities correspond with missing markets. Section 2.2.2 already indicated that only in specific cases creating competition through *market creation* constitutes a way to resolve externalities. If fishing technology becomes more efficient or the number of fishermen increases, overfishing of a lake can be prevented by granting a single individual the right to fish (see Stiglitz, 1993: 590). In other cases increasing excludability lowers externalities and strengthens private competition. For instance, patents reduce spill-overs of technological knowledge and increase competition in research and development.

Taxes, subsidies and tradeable permits are *market-oriented* instruments that the government can use to have private agents internalize externalities. Negative externalities ask for taxation or tradeable permits, subsidization makes private agents internalize positive externalities. Possibilities for experimentation constitute the main advantage of addressing externalities while preserving competition. Given the incentives provided by taxes or subsidies or within the national or supranational ceilings set by tradeable permits, private agents are free to select their most appropriate course of action. The many actions taken by a large number of private parties provide room for experimentation, which fosters innovative ways to deal

Box 2.6 Externalities: main strengths and weaknesses of coordination mechanisms

Activity	*production, product supply, negotiation*
Characteristics	*externalities, non-excludability*
Market failure	*inefficient allocation, transaction costs*

Coordination mechanism	*Implementation*	*Potential weaknesses*	*Potential strengths*
Competition	*market creation, taxes, subsidies*	*certainty*	*experimentation*
Control	*public provision, regulation ownership*	*experimentation*	*certainty*
Cooperative exchange	*intermediary, covenants, encompassing interest groups*	*enforcement, certainty*	*commitment, accountability*
Common values and norms	*information*	*enforcement*	*commitment*

→ *Trade-off:* ***experimentation*** ⇔ ***certainty***

with externalities.

The *control* approach applies coercion to internalize the externalities. The government provides goods or regulates production. Control prevents the free-rider consequences of non-excludability, because the government makes participation obligatory. Ownership is a potential control solution to externalities between private agents. A merger internalizes externalities between firms (Myles, 1995: 346). If several externalities exist between firms, ownership is counterproductive because it would create inefficiently large conglomerates that would also obtain market power.

Compared with competition, control provides more certainty as to the degree and the way externalities are internalized. For instance, at the micro level regulations can specify in detail the bounds on emissions of pollutants and the technologies to reduce emissions. Of course, this type of control limits possibilities for experimentation. In addition, various forms of government failure and rigidities constitute potential weaknesses of public provision or regulation.

Delegation of decision power, encompassing interest groups and covenants constitute ways through which *cooperative exchange* (partly) internalizes externalities, while at the same time retaining market incentives. Delegation of decision power provides a rationale for the existence of firms that act as intermediaries or representatives for a group of private agents. For instance, banks as delegated monitors solve the free-rider problem of monitoring borrowers by a large group of individual lenders (Van Damme, 1994: 20). Since individual lenders are free to select the bank they prefer and banks compete on the financial market, these kinds of activities can be interpreted as a form of cooperative exchange. Encompassing interest groups can internalize the external effects of their agreements on the economy. In their wage negotiations national unions and employer's organisations take the employment effects of their wage agreements into account, whereas atomistic wage bargaining disregards possible unemployment effects. Compared to regulation, covenants between government and private firms involve a more flexible way to tackle externalities, because firms retain considerable freedom to choose how to reach the agreed targets. Commitment, accountability and credibility are strong features of addressing external effects through cooperative exchange.

If consumers buy products that save energy or that contain less packing material, voluntarily separate waste, or reduce driving speed to curtail emissions of pollutants, they have internalized externalities through *common values and norms*. The government attempts to influence values and norms by providing public information. Once values and norms have settled, commitment to adhere to the internalized objectives is one of their strong points. However, their voluntary character restricts enforcement.

The Trade-off between Experimentation and Certainty. Instruments that enhance internalization of external effects in a competitive environment support experimentation and innovation. Reacting to incentives, private agents choose the most appropriate way to deal with externalities. Control limits possibilities for experimentation, but provides more certainty. Cooperative exchange and common values and norms are in between these two cases. Commitment to address externalities may be relatively high and room for experimentation exists. Their voluntary character makes enforcement more difficult and the outcome less certain.

It should be noted that externalities pertain to a broad range of topics in this study. Not in all cases the trade-off between various coordination mechanisms closely fits with experimentation versus certainty. In those cases a separate more suitable interpretation has been chosen.

Conditions. Discussing market power and externalities, which conditions favour which coordination principle? Consumer preferences and technological characteristics constitute the main conditional variables. Homogeneous preferences, a relatively small population, little mobility and risk aversion support cooperative exchange and control, whereas competition performs better in a heterogeneous, large, mobile and risk taking society. Cooperative exchange works best in a society in which encompassing interest associations can rely on a relatively homogeneous rank and file. In that case interest associations can more easily guide their members and enforce an agreement. Risk aversion raises the demand for government protection. If citizens worry about the state of the environment and the consequences of pollution on their individual well-being, they support government environmental policies.

Cooperative exchange and control also perform well, if economies of scale characterize technology. Economies of scale may ask for collective action of a group of companies to set standards, start a research joint venture if R&D costs exceed the financial capabilities of an individual firm, *etc*. In contrast, small-scale technologies support product differentiation in an environment of competition. Non-excludability in technology, *i.e.* large spill-overs, can be handled in two ways. In a control approach, the government may embark on technological missions to compensate for the low incentives of private agents to engage in R&D. Private incentives are low because private agents can appropriate only a small part of the revenues. The other approach is to reinforce competition by increasing excludability, for instance through a strong patent system.

2.4.3 Relationship-specific Investments

How do the four coordination mechanisms deal with the hold-up problem, described in Section 2.2.3? In other words, to what extent and in which way do they encourage parties to keep to ex-ante agreements and thus support relationship-specific investments?

Competition. As may be clear from the discussion in Section 2.2.3, pure market competition characterized by short-term contracts is vulnerable to the hold-up problem. Making *ex-ante payments* forms a market-oriented way to support specific investments by realigning ex-post and ex-ante bargaining powers (see Box 2.7). The party that ex-post loses bargaining power strengthens its position by requiring an ex-ante payment from the party that might renege on the agreement (taking hostages). Collateral in a lending agreement is a straightforward example. Financial constraints are the main reason why ex-ante payments are only effective in some cases. Start-up firms cannot provide collateral. The magnitude of sunk costs may inhibit the use of collateral, for instance when a producer considers building an electricity power plant (Armstrong *et al.*, 1994: 138). Also workers, especially if they are poor, are unable to supply sufficient funds that may act as ex-ante payment.

Another market-oriented instrument to align incentives between parties is to *reallocate revenues*. Aligning incentives would lower the possibility of opposing interests and as a consequence would reduce the risk of opportunistic behaviour. Management compensation in the form of stock options is the paramount example: it aims at more closely aligning management and shareholder incentives (Blair, 1995: 87-92). However, doubts exist as to the effectiveness of this instrument (see Gelauff and den Broeder, 1996: 39). Moreover, aligning incentives does not guarantee long-term investments, incentives can also concur at a short-term orientation.

Therefore, the main potential weakness of competition is the market failure incorporated in the hold-up problem: too little commitment which results in

Box 2.7 Specificity: main strengths and weaknesses of coordination mechanisms

Activity	*investment in relationship-specific asset*
Characteristics	*specificity: sunk costs* *time: ex-post bargaining power differs from ex-ante bargaining power*
Market failure	*risk of ex-post reneging curbs relationship-specific investments*

Coordination mechanism	*Implementation*	*Potential weaknesses*	*Potential strengths*
Competition	*ex-ante payments, reallocate revenues*	*commitment*	*external flexibility*
Control	*ownership*	*flexibility*	*enforcement*
Common values and norms	*reputation*	*enforcement,*	*commitment*
Cooperative exchange	*monitoring, co-determination, restrict freedom to act, covenants, delegation*	*flexibility, enforcement*	*commitment, internal flexibility*

→ *Trade-off:* ***external flexibility ⇔ commitment***

Definitions

External flexibility: *the ability of economic agents to switch between relationships.*

Internal flexibility: *the ability of parties to adjust the contents of their implicit agreement within an existing relationship.*

underprovision of welfare-improving relationship-specific investments. But then again, market coordination also entails some strong features: flexible adjustment and efficient allocation. Flexible reallocation of labour, physical and financial capital promotes moving labour and capital out of declining sectors into promising new sectors. It also allows swift adjustments to economic shocks. Market-oriented institutions that support external flexibility, *i.e.* the ability to quickly switch between relationships, also promote opportunities for innovations to prove themselves on the market. This improves the orientation of technological knowledge to new opportunities or shifting consumer preferences. It also creates chances to exploit first-mover advantages. Hence, institutions that support competition promote external flexibility and efficient allocation, but diminish commitment and the potential for investments in relationship-specific assets.

Control. In some cases, *ownership* forms an effective control measure to tackle the hold-up problem through enforcement. If relationship-specific assets fall under common ownership the incentive to renege on the initial arrangement vanishes. In terms of the supplier-user example the ownership solution implies vertical integration, *i.e.* the procuring firm acquires the supplier (Hart, 1995: 33). Vertical integration increases the incentives of the procuring firm to invest in technological know-how and product development with the acquired firm (the former supplier), since there is no risk that these will be expropriated after the investment has been completed. These investments are fully under the procuring firm's control.

In particular when economies of scale exist and sunk costs are large, ownership may be a feasible alternative. Armstrong *et al.* (1994: 138) analyze the relationship between electricity generation and electricity distribution. Economies of scale exist in both activities. With two separate firms performing these tasks, investment in a power plant or in a distribution network becomes vulnerable to the hold-up problem. Vertical integration can overcome that problem. A hold-up situation can also arise between a public regulatory agency and a regulated utility (Armstrong *et al.*, 1994: 86, 139). The firm is vulnerable to changes in regulations or in environmental standards once it has made an investment. Here, 'vertical integration' comes down to public ownership.

Ownership also entails some substantial disadvantages or can even be infeasible. Coordination through ownership is inflexible, in particular when economies of scale or scope are less dominant. It is hard to imagine that for each transaction with some substantial investment characteristic a firm will acquire a supplier and that it will outsource the acquired supplier when production processes change or more attractive suppliers appear on the market. Moreover, economic agents may not be wealthy enough to purchase the other party. In other cases, the ownership solution is not feasible. In particular, potential hold-up problems in labour relationships have to be solved in a different way, simply because a firm cannot own a worker.

Common Values and Norms. If relationships cover a sufficiently long period of time in which similar agreements have to be made repeatedly, *reputation* may become important as a coordination mechanism and common values and norms may develop (Dasgupta, 1991: 79). Common values and norms support commitment to keep to ex-ante agreements. For instance, if a procuring firm reneges on an initial agreement with a supplier, the supplier will not invest in future relationship-specific assets any more. Reneging by the procuring firm is a signal to other suppliers as well not to engage in a future cooperative arrangement with that firm. Hence, the reputation of the user is harmed and it forgoes the benefits of dedicated supplier relationships.

Yet, a long-term relationship purely based on common values and reputation is highly vulnerable to opportunistic behaviour. By consequence, these relationships quickly become unstable, in particular when economic agents operate in a competitive environment that changes frequently. In such an environment bargaining is part of the mutual interaction and common values cannot be the sole coordination mechanism.

Cooperative Exchange. Taking an intermediate position between competition and common values, cooperative exchange is well-suited to reduce the intensity of the hold-up problem. Just as well-developed markets and well-defined property rights support competition, cooperative exchange requires governance institutions that commit parties to keep to initial agreements. Box 2.7 lists various ways to support cooperative exchange in practice. Enhancing *monitoring* capabilities of parties, precludes opportunistic behaviour. For instance, representation of block shareholders on the board of directors improves the effectivity of direct shareholder monitoring of management and reduces the scope for managerial opportunism. Employee *co-determination* rights enable employees to monitor management and to partly control managerial decisions that might hamper relationship-specific investment by employees. *Rules* that restrict the freedom to act can also compel parties to keep their initial agreements. For example, dismissal protection regulation lowers the threat of employers to lay-off employees if they do not accept lower wage growth than initially agreed upon. *Covenants* constitute an additional instrument to reach an agreement that leaves enough room to adjust to specific circumstances, but commits parties to a long-term objective.

Another type of institution concerns *delegation* of bargaining power to a higher level of authority. Individual parties cannot use a change in their ex-post bargaining power to renegotiate an agreement if bargaining power is out of their direct control (Hartog and Teulings, 1996). For instance, sectoral wage bargaining strengthens commitment and reduces the hold up problem. Individual workers and employers have a negligible influence on wages during periods of renegotiation because they have delegated their bargaining authority to higher level unions and employers' organisations. Moreover, the scope to adjust wages to specific shocks that affect the ex-post bargaining position of individual workers or firms disappears or is left to a higher level.

The strong feature of cooperative exchange is that it supports commitment. Commitment manifests itself in relationship-specific investments in technology, financial capital, physical capital and human capital. Cooperative exchange also supports internal flexibility, *i.e.* the ability of parties to adjust the contents of their implicit agreement to changing circumstances. Workers will be more inclined to invest in firm-specific human capital and adjust their skills to new technologies applied in the firm, suppliers invest in technologies tailored to the needs of the procuring firm, financiers engage in long-term relationships with companies *etc.*

External rigidities and the risks of unprotected and unbalanced specificity constitute the main potential disadvantages of coordination of specific investments by cooperative exchange. Because of *external rigidities*, separation of contracting partners is difficult with cooperative exchange compared to market relationships. For instance, in a financial system characterized by long-term relationships unprofitable investment projects may not be terminated quickly enough.

Caballero and Hammour (1996a, 1996b, 1996c) analyze the general equilibrium *risks* of specific investments that cannot be contractually or institutionally protected against ex-post rent appropriation by one of the parties involved. On the one hand, institutions that support cooperative exchange will protect relationship-specific investments. On the other hand, because protection hardly ever is complete, the scope for unprotected specificity increases if cooperative exchange is applied extensively. An intuitively appealing way to tackle this incomplete protection situation is to balance specificity, *i.e.* to equalize the assets both parties invest in the relationship. With zero net specificity the ex-post incentive to renege vanishes. However, in practice balancing may be difficult to achieve and balancing is vulnerable to changes in the external environment that shift bargaining power. Compared to the case with full protection, in general equilibrium potential rent appropriation due to unprotected and unbalanced specificity may result in: underutilization of factors of production, rationing of the appropriating factor in production, too low a level of scrapping of production units, and an asymmetric response to a symmetric shock (Caballero and Hammour, 1996c). Hence, insufficient protection of specificity entails substantial risks.

The Trade-off between External Flexibility and Commitment. Box 2.7 shows that coordination of actions in the field of relationship-specific investments entails a trade-off between external flexibility and commitment (compare Dixit, 1996: 62). In a competitive environment, little protection of specificity results in relatively low levels of commitment and of specific investments. Enhancing commitment through institutions that support cooperative exchange, control or common values and norms, raises specificity but reduces external flexibility.

Note that support of specificity generally lowers external flexibility but may increase *internal* flexibility. Shifting labour between companies or sectors may be more difficult but employees may be more inclined to switch between jobs within a company or to adapt to new technologies of production processes in a firm. Therefore an alternative interpretation of the trade-off is between external and internal flexibility.

Still another interpretation in terms of insurance of specific investments against adverse shocks, concerns the trade-off between risk spreading and risk reduction. Risk *spreading* coincides with low specificity and high external flexibility under coordination through competition. In a competitive environment individuals hedge against the adverse effects of creative destruction by investing in general skills and by flexibly changing occupations. In contrast, cooperative exchange, control and common values *reduce* the risks of expropriation of relationship-specific assets by limiting external flexibility. Job security encourages workers to invest in firm-specific human capital because it reduces the risk of opportunistic appropriation by employers of the rents on human capital.

Conditions. The extent to which the strengths and weaknesses of the coordination principles manifest themselves depends on the social, technological and economic conditions that exist in a country. With respect to *behaviourial* characteristics, the strong points of competition are especially important in a society characterized by individualism, heterogeneous preferences and a high rate of time preference (compare Kay, 1993: 60). Decentralized decisions in a market oriented environment can account for heterogeneous conditions and preferences. Heterogeneous preferences also make it costly to delegate decision power or to reduce the freedom of choice. A high rate of time preference relatively strongly discounts the benefits of relationship-specific investments and thus favours competition. In contrast, homogeneous preferences, collectivism and a low rate of time preference support commitment.

Technological characteristics that favour competition are codified knowledge, small-scale technologies and rapidly changing technologies. Strong codification creates large knowledge spill-overs which make it difficult to sustain long-term R&D relationships, both between suppliers and procuring firms and in research joint ventures. In contrast, tacit knowledge supports these technological long-term relationships. Economies of scale or scope in technology increase the returns on technological cooperation and promote cooperative exchange. This is especially relevant for firms in well-established industries with incremental technological change, characterized by diffusion of technological innovations in existing production processes. In these companies the risk profile of new investment projects can be assessed relatively easily, consensus exists as to the appropriate way to run the firm and good governance can assure successful outcomes of investment projects. Here, cooperative exchange is conducive to more complex relationship-specific technologies. If technologies change rapidly or if technological change is discontinuous, competition performs relatively well, because relationship-specific knowledge ages rapidly.

Competition also thrives in a volatile *economic* environment. Volatility requires flexible adjustments of factors of production at a decentralized level, in particular if shocks are highly firm-specific. The advantages of cooperative exchange are more important in markets characterized by imperfect competition, for instance as a result of sunk costs, and in an environment with stable economic conditions at the firm level.

2.4.4 Uncertainty and Risk Sharing

Risk sharing among individuals provides a way to diminish the effects of uncertainty. Sharing can be achieved through competition when private companies offer insurance, through control when the government makes insurance compulsory and through common values and norms when social groups take care of less privileged members. This section addresses the potential strengths and weaknesses of these coordination principles in dealing with risk sharing.

Competition. The fundamental failures of insurance markets identified in Section 2.2.4 imply that private insurance through market intermediaries can only partially

Box 2.8 Uncertainty: main strengths and weaknesses of coordination mechanisms

Activity	*adverse shock (creative destruction)*
Characteristics	*uncertainty, information asymmetries*
Market failure	*information costs, interdependent risks, adverse selection, moral hazard*

Coordination mechanism	*Implementation*	*Potential weaknesses*	*Potential strengths*
Competition	*insurance market*	*solidarity*	*variety, incentives*
Control	*social security, uniform conditions*	*incentives*	*solidarity*
Common values and norms	*private-group charity*	*enforcement, privacy*	*in-group solidarity*

→ *Trade-off:* ***incentives*** ⇔ ***solidarity***

provide protection against risks. In cases were market failures do not dominate, variety forms the basic strength of private insurance (see also Box 2.8). Variety first of all involves the freedom of economic agents to opt for insurance or not and to select the insurance company they prefer. In many cases agents can also influence the conditions of their insurance contract: they may bear a part of the risk themselves or they may choose the most appropriate insurance package from a range available on the market. Competition may also provide incentives to diminish moral hazard and to efficiently administer insurances.

Lack of solidarity forms a potential weakness of competition in risk sharing. The failures of insurance markets, in particular interdependent risks and adverse selection, are most manifest for those risks that ask for solidarity among people. Examples are adverse macroeconomic shocks, unemployment, *etc.*

Control. Control measures can reduce some of the problems of private insurance. To a certain extent, uniform conditions diminish the information costs problem of private insurance. By stating rules for uniform conditions in insurance contracts the government lowers the information costs of private insurance. Uniform conditions make contracts more transparent and facilitate the comparison of products of different companies, which lowers transaction costs and enhances competition. A disadvantage of uniform conditions is that they run counter to consumer preference for variety.

With interdependent risks the government can act as an insurer of last resort, even after the adverse event (Don and Besseling, 1996). Compulsory taxes or premiums extend coverage and contributions from the group of people directly involved to the entire population or a large part of the population. As such it provides insurance, for instance against natural disasters or against inflation in pension contracts. Macroeconomic stabilization policy also is an example of a public insurance policy.

By making insurance compulsory, the government can also address adverse selection problems or lower the transaction costs of excessive signalling. Social security is a well-known case in point. Compulsory collective unemployment insurance eliminates the possibility that private insurance companies will attract good risks and the collective insurance fund or the government ends up with all the bad risks. As such, compulsory insurance promotes equity and solidarity (compare Box 2.8).

Moral hazard is more difficult to control. Collectivization does not solve moral hazard, in fact it often aggravates it by eliminating competition. Due to the lack of competition, incentives for administrators to cope with moral hazard are low. Costs can be shifted relatively easily into higher contributions, because insured persons cannot turn to competing firms that charge lower contributions. Only a strong monitoring technology can alleviate moral hazard. However, since information asymmetries can be substantial, monitoring can never be perfect. A collective unemployment insurance may oblige unemployed people to apply for jobs, but the insurance fund can never properly monitor the way a person behaves at an interview.

Collective insurance promotes solidarity. Compulsory participation either forces all participants to pay for a stronger monitoring technology to diminish moral hazard or it forces them to pay for the additional expenses related to moral hazard. These costs are accepted to preserve the insurance scheme and to promote solidarity in society. Solidarity involves a redistribution between the lucky, *i.e.* people with many talents and favourable circumstances, and the unlucky, *i.e.* people with less talents or misfortune in life. Solidarity also applies between generations (Bovenberg and Van der Linden, 1996). Public pay-as-you-go pension systems involve intergenerational risk sharing, which protects the income of the old through premiums payed by the young. Changes in premium rates allow a (partial) shift of macroeconomic shocks from the elderly to the young, which can be efficient because the young are generally better able to adapt to changes in wealth.

In contrast, collective insurance lowers incentives, may invoke political risks, or may entail improper cross-subsidization between social groups or economic sectors. The lack of competition reduces incentives for search activities, mobility or effort by economic agents. Some well-known examples refer to the labour market, where social security affects incentives to participate, search for a job, and prevent shirking. The political risk concerns the possibility that a political majority may decide to diminish or end social security provisions (see Bovenberg and Van der Linden, 1996). Cross subsidization takes place when the banking sector subsidizes the construction sector through a uniform premium for disability insurance. The implicit solidarity in cross-subsidization sometimes is intended, but sometimes it is not. In either case, it affects allocative efficiency.

Common Values and Norms. Common values and norms provide insurance for members of social groups when group members help and support each other. Traditional forms of charity by churches or the well-to-do, or mutual assistance in ethnic groups are examples. Common values and norms in homogeneous groups reduce the incidence of moral hazard. In-group solidarity constitutes a strong point of common values and norms in dealing with uncertainty. If group characteristics are difficult to define, this coordination mechanism becomes vulnerable to adverse selection. Lack of privacy, arbitrariness and inequality between groups are other potential disadvantages.

The Trade-off between Incentives and Solidarity. The main trade-off that arises in cases of risk sharing is between incentives and solidarity (compare Box 2.8). This trade-off essentially contrasts the lack of insurance through competition with compulsory risk-sharing through control. In most of the cases that concern solidarity between lucky and unlucky or between elderly and young, interdependent risks and adverse selection preclude market insurance. Social security provides compulsory insurance, which can insure interdependent risks and which diminishes adverse selection but does not resolve moral hazard. Compulsory insurance brings about costs of moral hazard and reduces incentives for economic agents. These have to be traded against more solidarity in society.

Conditions. Heterogeneous societies, which emphasize individual freedom and where economic agents appreciate risk-taking, promote an institutional order in which financial incentives play an important role. Solidarity among members of a group is also hard to maintain in a heterogeneous and quickly changing society. In contrast, if equity considerations and risk aversion characterize preferences, demand for solidarity arises.

2.5 The Impact of Trends on Institutions

Trends may invoke institutional adjustment. The analysis in Section 2.4 shows that the comparative strengths of the four coordination mechanisms manifest themselves differently under different conditions. Trends shift these conditions, which might cause a shift in the position of a country on a trade-off. The resulting change in performance characteristics may evoke institutional adjustments.

To illustrate, this section briefly reviews the influence of three (groups of) trends on the trade-offs: social, technological and economic trends. It contains a positive analysis, *i.e.* it tries to assess which shifts in trade-offs trends will induce, not which actions should be taken to counteract the influence of a trend. The final paragraph briefly touches upon the latter, normative, strategic questions. Moreover,

Table 2.1 Illustrations of the impact of trends on the trade-offs

Trade-off: Trend	diversity ⇔ scale or scope	experimentation ⇔ certainty	ext. flexibility ⇔ commitment	incentives ⇔ solidarity
Preferences				
– more heterogeneity	⇐	⇐	⇐	⇐
– individualisation		⇐	⇐	⇐
– sustainability	⇒	⇒	⇒	⇒
Technology				
– less tacit		⇐	⇐	
– entrepreneurial firm	⇒		⇒	
International economy				
– higher mobility	⇒	⇐	⇐	⇐
– more competition	⇐	⇐	⇐	⇒

the section does not aim to present a complete review of all possible interactions but rather to illustrate some of the shifts that might occur (see Table 2.1 for a summary). Subsequent chapters that deal with specific institutions discuss the impact of trends on institutions in more detail and pay more attention to institutional adjustments that may be needed to respond to a particular trend.

Social Trends. Social trends pertain to individual preferences. Increasing heterogeneity in society, individualisation and increased awareness of the need for a sustainable development are important social trends. More *heterogeneity* coincides with a broader range of quickly changing tastes, which shifts the trade-offs towards more competition. It asks for more diversity, experimentation, and external flexibility and hampers solidarity because it increases information asymmetries.

Individualisation shifts three of the four trade-offs towards more competition, the impact on the trade-off 'diversity versus scale or scope' is unclear. Because it lowers the capacity of encompassing interest groups to discipline individual members, individualisation reduces certainty . It also reduces commitment to achieve common goals. Moreover, individualisation decreases demand for collective protection, because more emancipated consumers obtain individual forms of protection through private insurance, higher mobility or private lawsuits.

The greater awareness of *sustainability* creates shifts in the opposite direction. People pay more attention to environmental issues and long-term environmental risks. In particular broad-scale or even world-wide environmental policies create large markets with the potential to achieve economies of scale. Environmental concerns ask for more internalization of external effects, hence for more certainty.

Long-term concerns require more commitment to invest in assets that yield revenues in the long run. Furthermore they raise demand for world-wide and intergenerational solidarity to obtain collective protection against future shocks.

Technology and Organization. The spread of information technology increases spill-overs and makes technologies *less tacit.* For instance, computer-aided engineering offers possibilities to design new products by the combination of modules available in libraries of blue-prints (Carlin and Soskice, 1997: 68). To some extent the stock of codified knowledge may replace firm-specific human capital and may enable companies to quickly design new products or processes. Larger spillovers associated with codified knowledge create strong incentives for firms to exploit first-mover advantages and quickly bring new products to the market. In addition, driven by quickly changing consumer tastes and increasing competition on product markets, technological development is shifting from large-scale R&D projects towards more small-scale market-oriented projects.

Less excludability reduces the returns on private sector R&D and lowers private investment in R&D. This intensifies the externality problem that lies behind the trade-off between experimentation and certainty and induces a shift towards more competition. In addition, spillovers require more external flexibility because first-mover advantages become more important and aging of technology is more rapid.

In contrast, the emergence of the *entrepreneurial firm* provides opportunities for cooperative exchange. Trends away from Fordist large-scale factories towards new forms of coordination within companies, between companies, and between companies and the government, produce a company as a learning organisation (see Table 2.2). Moreover, it results in strategies based on flexible specialisation or high quality incremental innovation (Piore and Sabel, 1984; Katzenstein, 1989; Best, 1990; Streeck, 1995; Carlin and Soskice, 1997). Learning, continuous incremental innovations, internal flexibility and cooperation constitute an approach to deal with a quickly changing technological environment, which differs from small-scale market-oriented projects. Moreover, cooperative exchange enables entrepreneurial companies to meet idiosyncratic requirements of procuring companies (Carlin and Soskice, 1997). Therefore, in an environment were technology becomes less tacit, tacitness that remains is very important. Incremental innovation in the entrepreneurial firm is more conducive to economies of scale in R&D and requires more commitment to support relationship-specific investments.

International Economy. In the world economy several trends are important, *viz.* internationalization, liberalisation and deregulation, and emerging regions in Asia and Eastern Europe (CPB, 1992; Kennedy, 1993; Wright and Jacquemin, 1993; de Jong and Don, 1995). The impacts of these trends run largely parallel and point in two directions: more openness causes a higher mobility of factors of production and stronger competition. Openness and international *mobility* expand relevant markets and create increasing returns to scale and scope. International mobility

Table 2.2 The entrepreneurial versus the Fordist hierarchical firm

	Entrepreneurial firm	Fordist firm
Strategy	innovation in product, process or organization	minimizing costs through continuity in production and design
Innovation	marginal adjustments, persistence to detail at every activity level	radical structural change, large R&D budget, large staff of engineers
Organisation	flexibility at micro level	rigid
Learning	perpetual problem solving at every activity level	centralized, minute subdivision of labour
Economies of time	process time reduction, fast implementation of new product designs	mass production, throughput
Suppliers	cooperative exchange, information exchange	price competition or hierarchical control (vertical integration)
Institutions	enable cooperative exchange and learning (RJV, education), encourage industrial restructuring	promote competition: anti trust, sector regulation
Industrial policy	universal or sector specific, boundary conditions	firm specific, support specific companies

Source: Best (1990)

reduces the efficacy of national control measures to diminish external effects, which induces a shift towards experimentation. National governments become more constrained by international product and financial markets. Mobility also creates outside options, which makes long-term commitments less easy to sustain. It reduces solidarity, because it undermines the social insurance contract and creates adverse selection problems (Sinn, 1995: 10).

Stronger competition raises diversity because more players appear on the market. It also creates more volatile markets and more firm-specific shocks, which entails a tendency towards experimentation and external flexibility. More volatility and more firm-specific shocks increase the demand for solidarity.

Strategy. What is the appropriate response to a trend: follow it or fight it? Should a country adjust its institutional order in the direction of the trend or should it strengthen institutions that counteract the trend? Following it and adapting to the trend may be useful when the trend is unavoidable and taking an alternative course would entail high costs. Fighting it may be useful to preserve highly valued social achievements or to improve competitiveness by exploiting and enhancing country-specific comparative advantages. No general answers can be given to these questions without delving deeper into specific institutions. That forms the subject matter of most of the following chapters.

3 Economic Development in Comparison

The economic performance of a nation strongly depends on the working of its institutions. The preceding theoretical chapter analyzed how institutions can affect the economic performance of an economy and how long-term social, technological, economic and demographic trends could influence the relationship between institutions and performance. In Chapters 5 till 14 this relationship will be analyzed in much more detail.

But economic performance also depends on the available economic structure. This structure is the stock of production factors, resulting from investment decisions in the past. This stock involves the population and labour force, the investments in knowledge, technology, machinery, buildings and infrastructure, and the environmental qualities. The quality and quantity of the stock of production factors determine to a considerable extent the outcome of the economic process. Hence in Chapter 4 the economic structure and its development over time for the two countries will be compared in more detail.

Before that, however, a brief overview will be given of the actual economic performance of the two economies in the recent past. The interplay of economic institutions and economic structure ultimately determines the economic performance. Hence, differences in economic performance can throw light on the quantity and quality of the stock of production factors and on the way the economic institutions influence the economic process. Furthermore, public attention on economic development is mainly directed at the outcome of the economic process.

This chapter deals with the results the economic process has generated in both economies. It starts with a description of the post-war economic development at the macro-level, concentrated on the four main goals of economic policy, namely economic growth, low unemployment, low inflation and a solid government budget. Here also the economic consequences of German unification will be touched upon. Next certain topics are discussed in more detail, like the government budget, international economic relations, monetary policy, income distribution and consumption.

Table 3.1 Average annual growth rates for GDP and GDP per capita, 1950-1994

	Growth rate GDP				Growth rate GDP per capita			
	D	NL	WE	USA	D	NL	WE	USA
1950-1960	8.2	4.6	4.9	3.3	7.1	3.3	4.1	1.6
1960-1973	4.3	4.8	4.5	4.4	3.5	3.6	3.7	3.1
1973-1983	1.6	1.6	1.9	2.2	1.7	0.9	1.6	1.1
1983-1994	2.7	2.5	2.5	2.8	1.9	1.9	2.4	1.8

Notes: D = West-Germany, NL = Netherlands, WE = Western Europe, USA = United States. Data for Western Europe range till 1992.

Source: Maddison (1995)

3.1 Economic Development at the Macro Level

3.1.1 Economic Development during 1950–1973: 'The Golden Age'

The economic development of the Western world after 1945 can be roughly divided in two periods. Until 1973 nearly all countries experienced a prosperous development with unprecedented growth rates, while after 1973 oil crises and structural deficiencies resulted in a disappointing pattern of economic development, with low growth, high unemployment, large deficits and high inflation. Only at the end some signs of improvement can be observed.

This pattern is reflected by Table 3.1 which shows the growth rates for GDP and GDP per capita in Western Germany, the Netherlands, Western Europe and the United States for four periods between 1950 and 1994. As can be seen, Western Germany and the Netherlands did not deviate from the common pattern.

When the growth rates of GDP within each single period are considered, it appears that before 1960 the growth rate of Germany has been substantially higher than that of the Netherlands or Western Europe. Substantial population growth, a relatively new and large capital stock (even taking into account the war-destruction), the successful introduction of a new currency and the acceptance of the concept of 'Soziale Marktwirtschaft' all contributed to the 'Wirtschaftswunder'. But the growth rates after 1960 indicate that from that time onwards Germany had become a 'normal' economy. Unification in 1990 has further reduced the German GDP growth rate, which now refers to total Germany. For the period from 1994 till 1997 GDP of total Germany is expected to grow by 2.1 percent per year, while this is 2.8 for the Netherlands and 2.7 for the United States (CPB, 1997).

GDP per Capita. Figure 3.1 compares the relative level of GDP per capita in Western Germany and the Netherlands with the United States for the period 1950-

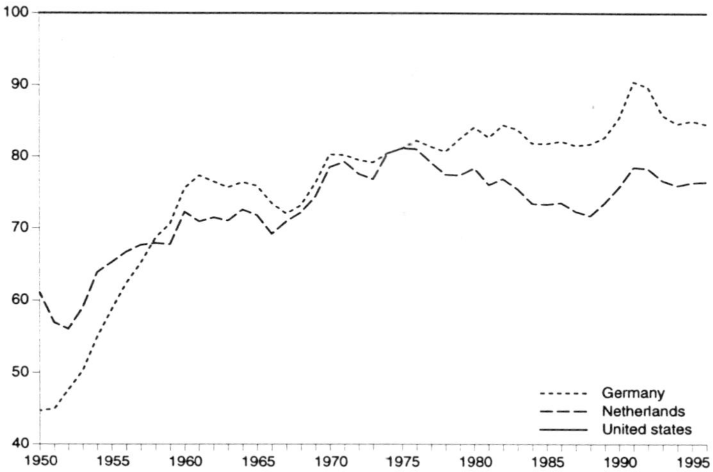

Figure 3.1 GDP per capita in West-Germany and the Netherlands relative to the United States, 1950-1995

1995. With regard to the Dutch development, it has to be taken into account that the population growth in this country was substantially higher than in Germany. Since 1960, Germany had a population increase of 17 percent, the Netherlands of 32 percent. The consequence has been that even though GDP had grown more in the Netherlands (+176 percent) than in Germany (+167 percent), the GDP per capita increase in the Netherlands (109 percent) was lower than in Germany (+129 percent). The relative decline for the Netherlands, especially after 1973, is related to the decline in labour participation (see Section 3.2).

3.1.2 Economic Development during 1973–1983: Stagflation

In 1973 the world economy was hit by a strong increase in oil prices. That event marked the end of an era of unprecedented economic growth. However, already before 1973 certain indicators showed less desirable outcomes. Inflation was increasing, also due to high wage increases. Government expenditures increased in most countries. Once the oil prices increased, growth stagnated and unemployment increased. A number of countries, including the Netherlands, reacted by a Keynesian demand policy, but they found that this medicine did not have substantial influence any more on economic growth and unemployment. At the same time, government expenditures increased and inflation soared. Economic policy seemed to have lost control. Germany had the same experience around 1978. This situation has been titled as stagflation. It took some time before these structural changes were acknowledged by the relevant actors and translated into

Box 3.1 Wages in German and Dutch manufacturing industry

During the 1970s, wage growth in Germany and the Netherlands exceeded the European average. Since then, both countries attempted to moderate wage costs, but this effort has been more successful in the Netherlands (Verdonk and Wiggers, 1994). As a result, the current wage level in Dutch manufacturing industry now equals 4/5 of the (western) German level, whereas Dutch labour productivity in the manufacturing industry exceeds the German level (CPB, 1996). Also from a European perspective, German labour costs per unit of production have become extremely high. This has caused a loss of the German market share on the European export market (CPB, 1996).

To measure the impact of wage bargaining, the wage income share is a better measure than unit wage costs, because the latter are strongly influenced by the value of the exchange rate (Köddermann, 1996). An analysis of the wage income share for the total economy shows that German values for the total economy are not alarming, since they are currently roughly in line with those in other countries (Köddermann, 1996). This is related to the relatively high labour productivity in the German services sector. In the manufacturing industry, in contrast, the wage income share has considerably increased. It is now much higher than the Dutch level. Hence, both abundant wage growth and the appreciation of the DM contributed to the loss of the German market share in the European export market (CPB, 1996).

Figure *Wage income share manufacturing*

more appropriate policies.

Table 3.1 shows that especially the Netherlands was hit by these crises. The revenues of the natural gas resources were mostly used for consumption, not for investment. Furthermore, the Dutch government felt less pressure to adjust its expenditures. On the contrary, expenditures were heavily increased, in particular

Table 3.2 GDP volume growth rates in Germany, the Netherlands, the United Kingdom, Sweden, European Union and the United States, 1973-1996

	D	NL	GB	S	EU	USA
1973-1983	1.6	1.7	1.1	1.5		2.1
1983-1990	3.1	3.1	3.2	2.5	3.0	3.5
1990-1996	1.4	2.2	1.4	0.6	1.5	2.0

Notes: D = (West-)Germany, NL = the Netherlands, GB = United Kingdom, S = Sweden, EU = European Union, USA = United States. German data for the first two sub-periods, 1980-1985 and 1985-1990, refer to West-Germany. For the third period, the data are for united Germany.

Source: OECD, Economic Outlook no. 60, data on diskette

for social insurance. Because wage rate increases remained high, firms were faced with low profits (see Box 3.1). The competitiveness of the exposed sector was threatened. Employment growth was minimal. With an increasing population, this implied a strong decline in participation. The Dutch relative position for GDP per capita declined till about 1988, as can be seen in Figure 3.1. The relative position of Germany towards Western Europe did hardly change in that period.

After the second oil crisis the economic problems increased even more. Especially in the Netherlands the cabinet had no room left for manoeuvre. Political parties, social partners and also the public in general now became aware of the new situation. This resulted in important political changes, with Christian-Democrats leading new cabinets in both countries to face these difficulties. In 1982 Helmut Kohl became the successor of Helmut Schmidt. Ruud Lubbers in the same year started as head of government in the Netherlands with a severe and unpopular austerity policy. Both government leaders stayed in power for a very long time. Lubbers became the longest ruling prime minister in the Netherlands, and resigned only in 1994. In October 1996 Kohl became the longest ruling *Bundeskanzler* in German history. Figure 3.1 reveals that after 1988 the Dutch economy started an upward movement. So did West-Germany after 1990. The difference between the two countries, in favour of Germany, has declined slightly.

3.1.3 Economic Development during 1983–1996: Recovery and Unification

After the heavy economic recession of the early 80s, it took some time for the OECD countries to recover. The United States then had the highest economic growth. Table 3.2 shows that after 1983 there was a renewed momentum in many countries. The United States could retain its high growth pattern. Especially Germany seemed even more competitive than before, with all economic indicators at record levels. It could meet any challenge, so it seemed. And that challenge

Box 3.2 Relatedness between the German and Dutch Economy

Apart from the high degree of coherence in the monetary field through the EMS, also the real economy of western Germany and The Netherlands appears to show strong links[1]. The figure below shows the yearly GDP growth rates. The German and Dutch economies are closely related, both with regard to the timing and to the extent of business cycle fluctuations. For example, in comparison to the G7, these countries went through a stronger recession in the beginning of the eighties and showed a less pronounced upswing thereafter. Similarly, the upturn after the flattening of growth in the mid-eighties started at a later stage than in the G7, but was likewise stronger as a consequence of the demand expansion after the German unification.

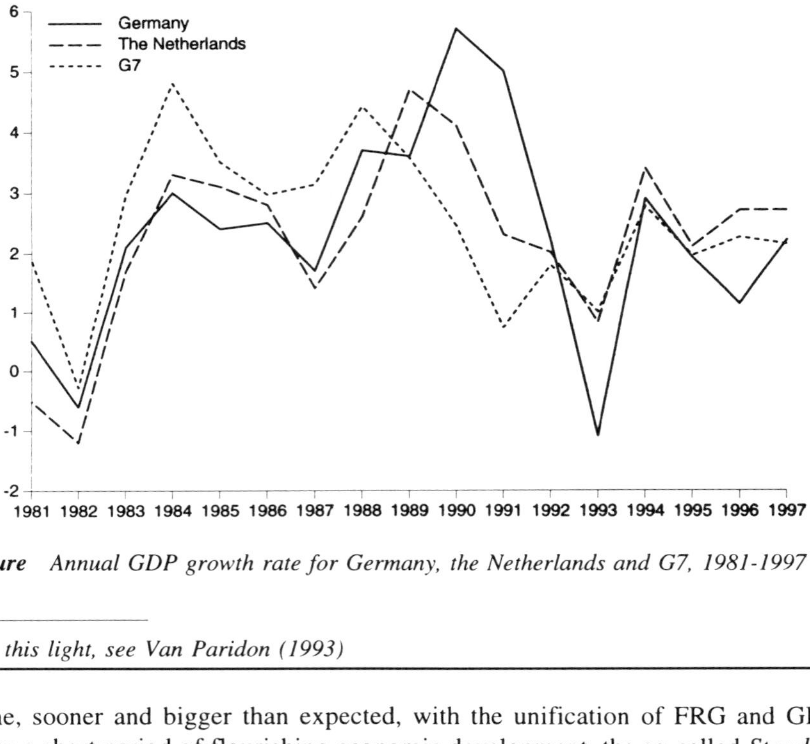

Figure *Annual GDP growth rate for Germany, the Netherlands and G7, 1981-1997*

[1] *In this light, see Van Paridon (1993)*

came, sooner and bigger than expected, with the unification of FRG and GDR. After a short period of flourishing economic development, the so-called *Standort*-problems did show up again, even stronger than before. Since then the German economy is struggling to recover. At the same time, the Netherlands have gone through a long period of wage moderation (see Box 3.1), expenditure cuts and institutional adjustments of all kind. This has resulted in a remarkably strong employment growth and the restoration of a more healthy budgetary position. The Dutch miracle or *Modell Holland* has recently become quite popular. The difference between the Dutch and German growth rate of about 0.8 percent point

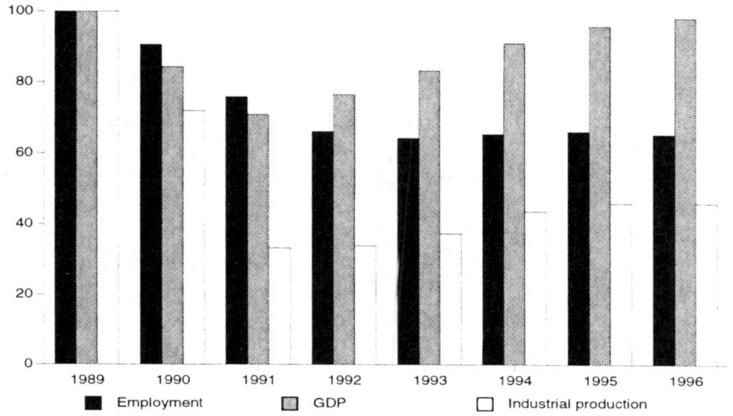

Figure 3.2 Economic development of the new Länder, with 1989 = 100

is noteworthy. While until the early 90s the Dutch economy followed closely the business cycle of Germany, also due to the strong economic ties between the two countries; thereafter more divergences occurred (See Box 3.2).

German Unification. In 1989/1990 Western Germany was confronted with a long-desired, but at the same time completely unexpected event, namely the unification with the German Democratic Republic. The flight of people, the lack of political support from the Soviet Union and above all the complete economic breakdown did melt away the political power of the SED-regime[1]. The fall of the Berlin Wall, at november 9th 1989, meant the final breakthrough. In a few months time the GDR broke down completely. At July 1st 1990 the Monetary, Economic and Social Union started, and at October 3rd 1990 Germany was again united and sovereign. The economic and financial consequences of this treaty have been enormous, and much more enduring than Bundeskanzler Kohl and many others in 1990 had estimated.

Whereas the GDR was often seen as a relatively strong economy, the introduction of the DM and of free market competition have had devastating effects, as can be seen in Figure 3.2. Industrial production broke down, because the consumers in the new Länder changed to the long preferred Western products, and existing markets in Eastern Europe disappeared. Through the Treuhand the German government tried to privatise the stock of state-owned firms and other assets as quickly as possible, to improve the country's competitiveness. However, with obsolete

---

[1] See Van Paridon (1995) and De Jager (1994) for a description of this breakdown, and Sinn and Sinn (1992) for a thorough description of the unification process.

Table 3.3 Economic growth, employment and unemployment in West- and East-Germany, 1991-1997

	GDP growth		Employment growth		Unemployment rate		Budget deficit
	West	East	West	East	West	East	
1991	5.0	-11.1	2.5	-15.7	6.1	11.2	3.3
1992	1.8	7.6	0.9	-12.8	6.5	15.6	2.8
1993	-1.9	8.2	-1.5	-2.8	8.1	15.9	3.5
1994	2.2	9.9	-1.1	1.7	9.2	14.6	2.4
1995	1.6	5.3	-0.6	1.1	9.3	14.7	3.5
1996	1.3	1.3	-1.0	-1.2	10.1	16.7	3.9
1997	2.5	2.5	-0.2	0.0	10.4	16.5	2.9

Note: Data for 1997 are estimates of the German government

Source: Sachverständigenrat (1996) and BMWi (1997)

machines, low-quality products, inefficient organisation and without the experience of competition, the GDR firms had no real chance. The consequence was heavy restructuring and, in many cases, the closing down of whole factories. Employment broke down, from 10 million in 1989 till hardly 6 million in 1993. Especially the manufacturing sector was hit hard: in a few years time manufacturing production declined by 80 percent. The result was a strong increase in unemployment. Strong wage increases amplified the problems. From the early beginning, firms in the new Länder have been handicapped, not only by the strong DM, but also by the high wage costs per unit of product. In manufacturing, these costs were 20 percent higher than in West-Germany, itself already an expensive place to produce. Initially, inflation was soaring, mainly due to price increases for non-market goods - housing, energy, transport -, but it was quickly brought under control. With relatively low incomes, tax revenues were also low. To finance Länder and communities, private and public investment projects, and the various social security arrangements, yearly about DM 150 billion was transferred from West to East, about 50 percent of Eastern GDP. Box 3.3 portrays this situation.

Table 3.3 contains data for economic growth, employment growth, the unemployment rate and the budget deficit for the period 1991-1997, for both parts of Germany. It shows that after the dramatic breakdown a strong recovery occurred in the new Länder, that slowed down again in recent years. The unemployment rate remained very high. Furthermore, both in the old and new Länder employment growth was very disappointing. Finally, whereas in 1989 the budget balance was positive, the situation worsened afterwards. The conclusion is that unification certainly left many marks on the German economic performance since 1990.

Box 3.3 Skewed demand problems in the new Länder

The economy of the new Länder has not been self-supporting yet. Total domestic demand has so far been much bigger than domestic production. The current account has been extremely negative. This was possible only because of a huge flow of transfers from the old to the new Länder, partly to private consumers through social security funds, partly to public authorities and partly to private investors through all kinds of investment-inducing subsidies. In total, the amount of transfers between 1991 and 1996 come close to DM 1000 billion.

Table *Composition of demand for East- and West-Germany, 1994*

	East	*West*	*Germany*
		% of GDP	
Domestic demand	*176.0*	*92.1*	*99.5*
Private consumption	*78.4*	*55.2*	*57.2*
Public consumption	*36.2*	*18.2*	*19.8*
Gross investment	*61.4*	*18.7*	*22.5*
Exports	*24.0*	*36.1*	*25.1*
Imports	*100.5*	*25.5*	*29.0*

Why did not domestic industry and services take full advantage of the demand potential? First, there is a lack of demand for domestic products in both home and foreign markets.[1] *The imports-to-GDP ratio remains at about 100 percent, a very high figure compared with the 25 percent in western Germany. Moreover, investments were hampered by poor marketability of products, insufficient management skills, a poor infrastructure, administrative delays, unsettled property claims, and a pollution clean-up burden (OECD, 1993). The second reason for the difficult economic situation of the new Länder is the wage costs per unit of production. This is about 35 percent higher in the new Länder, compared with the old Länder.*[2] *This has been another significant barrier to investments. Despite the fact that the wage/productivity ratio is likely to improve in the future (as unions moderate wage claims in order to secure employment), the continuing large cost gap and the recession in the west can be expected to depress investment growth. In addition, financial government support will probably be reduced because of tight budgetary conditions. The great dependence on the west German economy and on public transfers, makes the eastern German economy vulnerable to unfavourable developments in both.*

---

[1] *It appeared that the internal demand for domestic production largely came from the portion of private sector demand that could not be satisfied abroad.*

[2] *In 1996 East German wages were 80 percent of the western German average, whereas productivity, approximated by nominal GDP per worker, was only 58 percent of the western level.*

Table 3.4 Productivity growth in (West-)Germany, the Netherlands, the United Kingdom, Sweden, European Union and United States, 1973-1996

	D	NL	GB	S	EU	USA
1973-1983	1.9	1.8	1.6	0.7		0.4
1983-1990	1.9	1.2	1.4	1.6	2.0	1.1
1990-1996	2.5	0.7	2.2	2.7	2.0	0.9

Explanation: See Table 3.2.

Productivity level and development over time. The productivity development of the respective countries is inversely related to their GDP growth pattern. Table 3.4 gives the productivity growth rates for the same group of countries as above. Those countries with higher GDP growth rates, like the Netherlands and the United States, saw relatively low productivity growth rates. Slower growing economies like Germany and Sweden saw instead an increase in their productivity growth rates. This difference can be partly caused by structural characteristics; Germany for instance has a bigger share of more productive manufacturing sectors, the Netherlands of less productive services. Some observers like Kleinknecht (1994) have argued that the slow Dutch productivity growth is directly related to the wage moderation policy that has been pursued since 1982.

Even though the productivity growth has been relatively low, the Dutch economy is still one of the most productive ones in the OECD. According to calculations by Pilat (1996), only the United States currently has a higher productivity level. Table 3.5 shows the results for certain OECD countries, with the Dutch level fixed at 100, for GDP per hour worked and for value added in manufacturing per hour worked. Both indicators reveal a similar pattern. Between 1960 and 1985 the Netherlands realised a remarkable progress in value added in manufacturing per hour worked; only Japan performed better. After 1985 Dutch productivity growth was lower than that of its competitors, but so far it still outperforms most other economies. The relative productivity level of Germany has shown a decline between 1960 and 1973; thereafter it stabilized compared with the Netherlands.

Conclusion. While initially the economic development of Germany and the Netherlands remained more or less similar, with the Netherlands around 1981 in a more problematic role, since 1990 the pattern has been increasingly diverging. Gradually the Netherlands have been able to improve its overall economic performance. German economic development has become much more problematic, also because of the economic consequences of unification.

Table 3.5 Productivity levels per hour worked in some OECD countries, relative to the Netherlands

	Manufacturing				Total
	1960	1973	1985	1995	1994
The Netherlands	100	100	100	100	100
Germany	110	86	81	84	82
United States	197	113	93	104	92
United Kingdom	89	61	56	72	74
Sweden	98	90	82	94	68
Japan	38	55	64	75	61

Source: Pilat (1996)

3.2 Labour Market Performance

Unemployment. The high and sofar still increasing unemployment rate is often seen as one of the clearest signs that the German economy currently is in trouble. Figure 3.3 shows the development over time for both Germany and the Netherlands. Until 1992 the unemployment rate in Germany was lower than in the Netherlands. After 1985 the difference declined considerably. With unification, German unemployment went up strongly, especially in the new Länder. There unemployment rose to unprecedented levels, early 1997 even to 18 percent. The

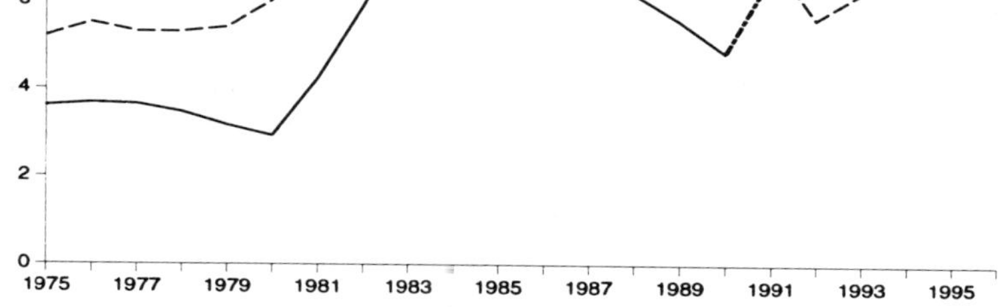

Figure 3.3 Standardised unemployment as a percentage of labour supply

Table 3.6 Types of unemployment

	Standardised unemployment	Youth / adult[a]		Unskilled / skilled[b]	Long-term[c]	
	1996	1979	1995	1994	1983	1995
	in %	ratio		ratio	in %	
USA	5.4	2.81	2.69	4.3	23.9	17.3
GB	8.2	2.85	2.10	3.3	65.7	60.7
D	9.0	1.48	1.10	2.8	65.8	65.4
NL	6.3	2.79	2.10	1.9	69.2	74.4
S	9.2	3.57	2.33	5.4	24.9	35.2

[a] OECD (1996a: 187). Ratio of youth unemployment against adult unemployment. Youth unemployment: 15 to 24 years. Adult unemployment: 25 years and over.
[b] Ratio of unemployment for unskilled against unemployment of skilled. Unemployment rates. USA, GB, S: OECD (1996a: 165), males. D: 1989. Abraham and Houseman (1993: table 11), males, Fachhochschule versus no qualification. NL: 1990. (CPB, 1994: 23), males and females, primary versus higher educated.
[c] OECD (1996a: 202). % of total unemployment with a duration of 6 months and over.

Dutch unemployment level declined considerably after 1992. The difference has increased till about 4 percentage-points in favour of the Netherlands. However, it has to be acknowledged that the hidden unemployment is quite high in the Netherlands. When disability and early retirement schemes are taken into account, the OECD arrives at an unemployment rate of about 25 percent (OECD, 1996b: 41).[2]

Table 3.6 reveals certain characteristics of the unemployment situation in a number of countries. Germany has a low youth unemployment rate, while the Netherlands is about average here. Both Germany and the Netherlands do show a relatively low unemployment rate for the unskilled, but high shares for long-term unemployed.

Employment Growth. Both countries have shown a strong decline in their employment rate between 1970 and 1985 (Figure 3.4). The consequences were especially harsh for the Netherlands, while here the employment rate was already much lower than in Germany. However, after 1985 the Dutch labour market performance improved considerably, due to a combination of high employment growth and a declining increase of the potential labour force. The Dutch employment growth has been as high as in the United States, as can be distilled

[2] Similar calculations for Germany are not available.

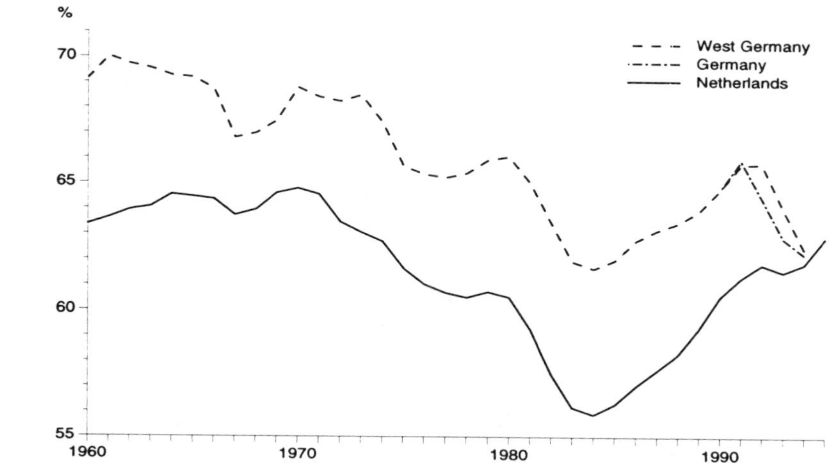

Source: Statistisches Bundesamt, CPB (1996; Wildcat & CEP96), CBS

Figure 3.4 Employment rate for Germany and the Netherlands, 1960-1995

from Table 3.7. This strong employment growth has led to a reduction in unemployment and a strong increase in labour participation. At the same time the employment growth in Germany, and in the European Union in general, has been on the whole negative.

Table 3.8 compares the labour market performance of these countries. Both Germany and the Netherlands do have a slightly bigger potential labour force, i.e. the share of the population between 15 and 65 is higher. Their actual use of that potential is, however, much lower. Both the gross and net participation rate, calculated in persons, are 3 to 10 percent-points lower than in the other three countries mentioned here, with the Netherlands 3 percent-points behind Germany.

Table 3.7 Employment growth in Germany, the Netherlands, United Kingdom, Sweden, European Union and United States, 1973-1996.

	D	NL	GB	S	EU	USA
1973-1983	-0.3	-0.1	-0.5	0.9		1.7
1983-1990	1.2	1.9	1.8	0.9	1.1	2.4
1990-1996	-1.1	1.5	-0.8	-2.0	-0.5	1.1

Explanation: See Table 3.2.

Table 3.8 Indicators of labour market activity, most recent data

	USA	GB	D	NL	S
			in %		
Potential labour force[a]	65.3	64.8	68.6	68.7	63.7
Participation rate[b]	77.8	74.3	70.9	67.1	78.3
Unemployment[c]	5.5	8.7	8.2	6.5	9.2
Employment rate[d]	73.5	67.8	65.1	62.7	71.1
	in hours per year				
Working hours per employee[e]	1747	1683	1590	1447	1544
Working hours per head[f]	1279	1119	995	897	1085

[a] 1993. Share of population aged 15-64 (mid-year estimates). Data for Germany refer to total Germany. Source: OECD (1995a).

[b] 1995. Sum of total employment and standardized unemployment as a share of the potential labour force.

[c] 1995. Source: CPB (1997: 198-199); OECD (1996a: 198). Standardized unemployment rate.

[d] 1995. Total employment divided by the population 15-64. Source: OECD (1995b: 204); for the Netherlands: CPB (1997: 184-185). Data for Germany refer to total Germany.

[e] 1994. Yearly actual working time per employee (in Sweden per person in employment) in 1994. Sources: For GB, D and NL.: Eurostat (1996); Unpublished updates of "Working Time in the European Union - Estimated Annual Working Time", For US and S: OECD (1995b: 208).

[f] 1994. Yearly actual working time per head 15-64.

Part-time Labour. Furthermore, the Netherlands has a high share of part-time labour, both for men and women. Remarkably, the acceptance of this situation has been higher in the Netherlands than in any other European country[3]. As a consequence the employment rate, calculated in labour years, is relatively low in the Netherlands. Both Germany and the Netherlands also have rather low working hours, per employee and per head, which in case of the Netherlands can be partly explained by the high share of part-time labour. The average Dutch employee works 380 hours per year less than an American one, a difference of about 30 percent.

[3] At the question why people were working part-time the answer on the reason 'Could not find a full-time job' was lower in the Netherlands than elsewhere, and on the reason 'Did not want a full-time job' higher than in any other European country. This observation holds both for men and women (Eurostat, 1996: 138-139).

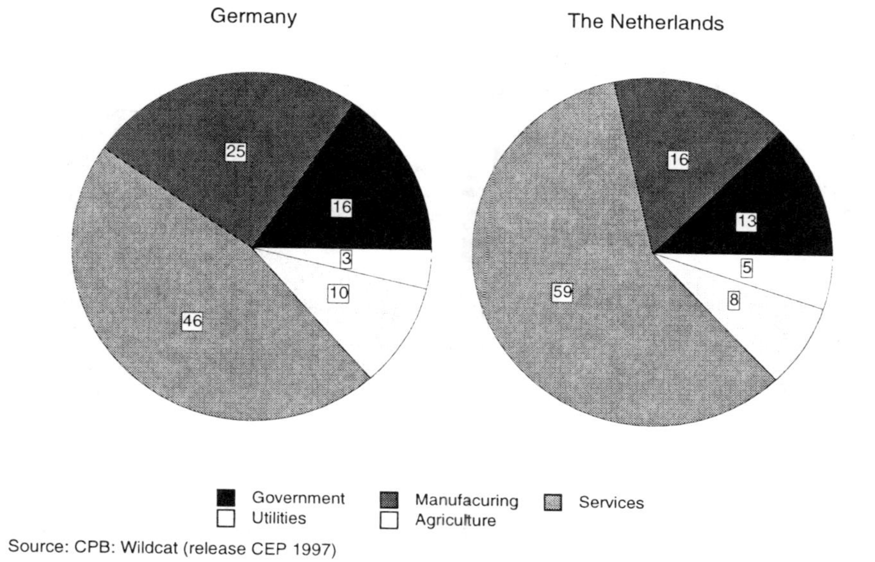

Figure 3.5 Sectoral employment distribution in Germany and the Netherlands, 1995

Sectoral Structure. Figure 3.5 shows that in 1995 the German economic structure is still relatively manufacturing-oriented. Its employment distribution being characterised by a higher share of services, the Dutch economic structure has been more adjusted to services. The share of government employment is slightly higher in Germany than in the Netherlands.

Conclusion. The conclusion must be that the labour market performance of both countries since 1980 has been sub-optimal, certainly in a more global perspective. Unemployment increased considerably, and so did long-term unemployment. It has become a major socio-economic problem. Especially in Germany employment growth has been very weak. After 1991 the employment has declined considerably. The Netherlands have been able to improve its employment growth performance considerably after 1983. The employment growth has resulted in lower unemployment and a higher labour participation. Still, the Dutch labour market situation is difficult. Hidden unemployment is still high. So in both countries an unfinished agenda for labour market reform exists. In chapter 9 the labour market institutions of both countries will be discussed in more detail.

3.3 The Public Sector

Government Expenditures. In international comparisons, both Germany and the Netherlands show a strong government involvement in the national economy, when

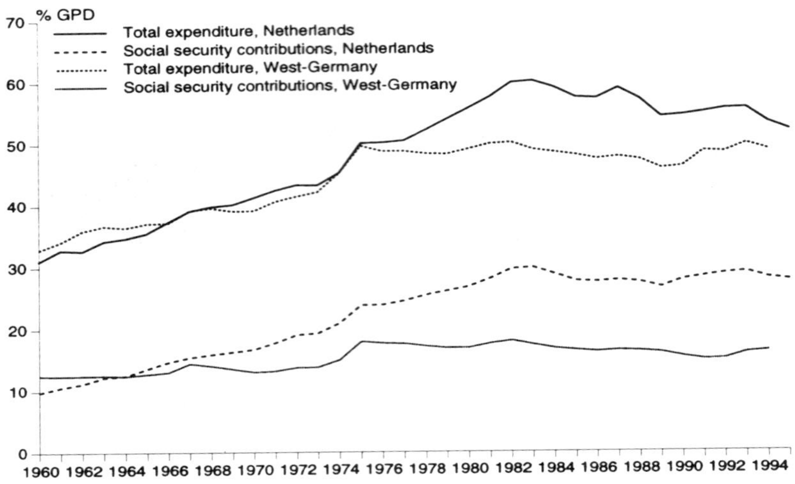

Figure 3.6 Total government expenditure and social security outlays in Germany and the Netherlands

measured by the share of government expenditures in GDP. In 1996, this share is for both countries about equal, 49 percent for Germany and 49.9 percent for the Netherlands. In the United Kingdom the share amounts to 41.9 percent, in the United States 33 percent (OECD, 1996c: Annex table 28).

Both countries initially followed the same pattern of increasing government expenditures, as can be distilled from Figure 3.6, but after 1975 the increase continued for the Netherlands. In Germany the level stabilized more or less. In recent years both countries showed renewed convergence, due to the austerity policies of the Netherlands and the impact of unification on the government budget in Germany.

This different pattern over time for government expenditures shows up also in the budget deficit. While Germany had a much lower deficit in the 80s, the Netherlands has been able in recent years to bring down its deficit considerably. Figure 3.7 shows that after the 1990 unification process German government could not prevent a strong rise of its budget deficit, manoeuvring itself in a difficult position for the Economic and Monetary Union (see also Table 3.2).

A closer look at the standardised components of government spending (Table 3.9) shows that the differences between the two countries currently are rather limited. In both the Netherlands and Germany in 1996 social security formed the biggest spending category. In contrast to OECD statistics, in Table 3.9 the German expenditures exceed those of the Netherlands. The reason is an upward correction of the German figures to account for the fact that in Germany social security expenditures are given as net figures, while in the Netherlands these expenditures

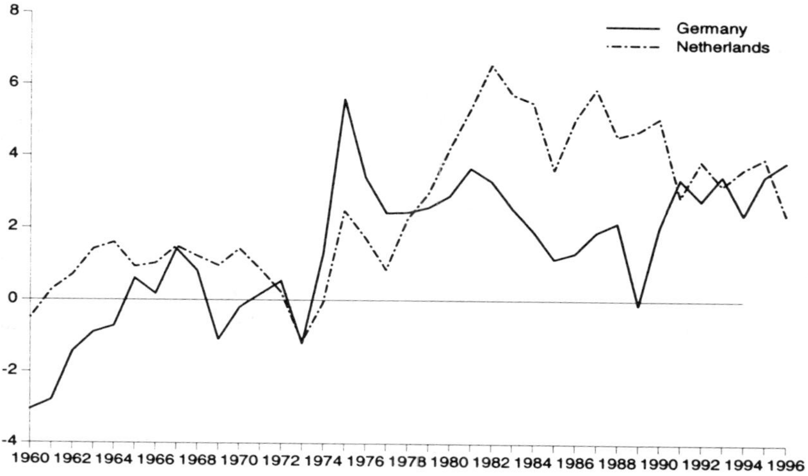

Figure 3.7 Government budget deficit in Germany and The Netherlands, 1960-1994

are presented as gross figures, so including taxes and premiums paid on social security benefits. Table 3.9 shows that in Germany government consumption is higher. The other elements are more or less equal. When the revenue side of the government account is considered, it can be concluded that both governments finance their disbursements in about the same way. In both countries, about halve of total spending is financed by taxes and approximately one third by social security premiums. Non-tax revenues are about 5 percent of total receipts. The financial means necessary to finance the remainder are obtained by borrowing.

Table 3.9 Components of the government budget in 1995 in percentages of GDP

Disbursements	D	NL	Revenues	D	NL
Compensation of employees	9.0	11.6	Direct and indirect taxes	24.3	26.0
Non-wage government consumption	3.5	5.1	Soc. security contributions	20.9	17.2
Income transfers	27.8	22.4	Property income	1.2	2.9
Subsidies	2.2	1.9	Other government receipts	1.1	0.8
Interest payments	4.8	6.0	Net lending	4.1	4.0
Property and entrepreneurial income	1.1	0.8			
Net fixed capital formation	1.5	1.4			
Total	51.6	51.4	Total	51.6	51.4

Source: Van de Hoef and Ter Rele (1996).

Table 3.10 Gross social security expenditures as a percentage of GDP, for Germany, Netherlands, France, United Kingdom and EU-12, 1993.

	D	NL	F	GB	EU-12
Total	31.0	33.6	30.9	27.8	28.8
Sickness	8.3	7.4	8.2	5.3	7.0
Disability	3.6	7.5	2.4	3.4	3.1
Pensions	9.5	10.6	11.3	11.1	10.5
Widows and orphans	3.2	1.8	2.2	0.3	2.3
Family and children	2.5	1.8	2.9	3.1	2.3
Unemployment and labour market	3.0	3.1	2.6	2.0	2.6
Other expenditures	1.0.	1.3	1.5	2.4	1.1

Source: Eurostat (1995)

Social Security. Government expenditures for social security are an important element of the total government budget, as was made clear in Table 3.9. Employers and employees also have additional arrangements. Together the social security expenditures account for about one third of GDP. In 1970 these expenditures were about 20 percent, but they increased strongly in the 70s. In the 80s the percentage more or less stabilized in both countries, with the Dutch percentage slightly higher. After 1990 these expenditures rose quickly in Germany due to unification, and started to decline in the Netherlands.

Table 3.10 shows the gross expenditures for the various social security arrangements for Germany and the Netherlands, as well as for France, the United Kingdom and the European Union average (12 member-states) for 1993. The differences between the countries are relatively small. Even for the United Kingdom these expenditures are about 28 percent of GDP.

Certain arrangements, like those for sickness, pensions, and unemployment and labour market, do show about the same level of expenditures in the countries mentioned. For arrangements regarding widows and orphans and for family and children, bigger differences can be observed. For instance, Germany pays 3.2 percent of GDP to widows and orphans, the United Kingdom only 0.3 percent. The latter country disburses family and children with 3.1 percent of GDP, the Netherlands with 1.8 percent. The biggest difference, however, arises with disability. Here the Netherlands has a special position, with expenditures for disability 2.5 to 3 times higher than in the other countries mentioned here. It is therefore not surprising that the adjustment of the social security system in the Netherlands started with the disability law. This law has been drastically adjusted since then, which has resulted in a reduction of the number of dependent people, but still the level is very high.

Table 3.11 Tax receipts and tax structures in certain OECD-countries, 1995

	D	NL	GB	USA	J	OECD
			% of GDP			
Tax receipts	39.3	45.9	34.1	27.6	27.8	38.4
			share of total tax receipts (%)			
Personal income	26.5	20.3	27.6	35.7	22.8	27.5
Corporate income	2.9	7.3	8.0	8.9	14.8	7.5
Social security	37.0	33.8	17.3	24.1	31.5	22.5
Taxes on goods and services	28.7	25.8	35.3	17.9	15.5	31.9
Other taxes	5.0	12.9	11.7	13.3	15.3	10.6

Source: OECD (1997a).

Taxes and Tax Wedge. Government expenditures and social security payments are made possible through taxes and premiums. As Table 3.11 illustrates, both Germany and particularly the Netherlands do have relatively high taxes. Both countries are above OECD average, while the United Kingdom and certainly the United States and Japan are far below that average.

Table 3.11 also gives the distribution of the tax receipts among the several sources. This distribution is rather similar for the countries mentioned here, although each country has its own characteristics. The United States has a relatively high share for its personal income tax, Japan for its corporate income tax, Germany for social security premiums, and the United Kingdom for taxes on goods and services. The Dutch pattern equals more or less the average pattern. In the last decade both the German and Dutch government have come up with proposals to reduce taxes and to simplify the system. These efforts, described in Box 3.4, have not been fully successful so far.

Besides the overall tax rate, the so-called tax wedge is an important factor for the functioning of the labour market. The average wedge influences the overall labour costs, the marginal wedge indicates which share of additional labour revenues are falling to the person involved. According to a recent study by the OECD, the direct tax wedge on labour costs for Germany is about 42 percent, comparable to France and Italy, but mich higher than in Japan, the United Kingdom, the United States and Canada (see Leibfritz *et al.*, 1997: Fig. 8) For the Netherlands this wedge is even higher than for Germany. For the marginal tax rate the situation is about the same. Also here Germany and the Netherlands score relatively high, compared with the Anglo-saxon countries, with the German level slightly higher than the Dutch one.

Conclusion. After the strong increases in government expenditures, both Germany and the Netherlands had to accept the necessity of applying a policy of austerity.

Box 3.4 Tax reform in Germany and the Netherlands

After the drastic tax changes in the United States and the United Kingdom in the early 80s, Germany and the Netherlands followed a few years later. In Germany the then existing tax system was adjusted and taxes were lowered in three steps, starting in 1987. Before, however, the last step was made, the whole situation changed because of the unification. Even though this last step was implemented, the German government was forced to introduce a special tax - the so-called solidarity tax rise - to finance the extra expenditures. This special tax was thought to be temporarily. After a year it was abolished, but 18 months later the tax was reactivated. Currently, the German government has to decide when this tax will be abolished again or when it will be lowered. In January 1997 the same government came up with new proposals to adjust the tax system, by reducing the minimum (from 19 till 15) and maximum (from 53 till 39) rates and by broadening the tax base. According to governmental calculations, the overall tax reduction would be about 30 billion DM, about 1 percent of GDP. Compared with the earlier tax adjustment, with a net reduction of about 2.5 percent of GDP, this new adjustment is relatively small. Whether it will be implemented, is not sure yet. Government and opposition are currently struggling to see if a compromise is possible. Corporate taxes are a different story. Even though nominal corporate tax rates in Germany are higher than in the Netherlands or the United Kingdom, the effective tax rate is lower, due to the many ways to reduce the tax base. The German government has come up with proposals to reduce these tax rates as well or to abolish them even (Gewerbesteuer). In the most recent proposals, however, the initial reductions have been curtailed, while at the same time the possibilities to carry forward losses or, in emergencies, to set losses against profits have been diminished considerably.

In 1986 the so-called Oort-Commission came up with proposals to adjust the Dutch tax system. Several goals could be distinguished: to reduce both the maximum tax rate and the number of tax brackets, to combine taxes and premiums for national insurances and to simplify the existing system of tax deductions. The first two elements were more or less realised, but it was not possible to scrap or reduce the deduction system. To find a way out here, the so-called Stevens-Commission came up with new proposals, but again they were not accepted. More details about these proposals and about their estimated impact can be found in Gelauff (1992).

Germany seemed to have an easier task, with a lower level of expenditures and a smaller deficit. At a rather moderate pace cuts in expenditures were realised. In the late 80s, Germany even realised a surplus on its government budget. With the unification and its economic aftermath, the perspectives changed dramatically. Government expenditures rose dramatically, and the budget deficit increased. Efforts to cut expenditures have not been as successful as expected. The Netherlands had to apply a much more drastic austerity policy. It took 15 years before a more stable situation - with a deficit below the EMU-criterion and a declining debt-ratio - could be realised. Both countries do now have about the same level of government expenditures as a percentage of GDP. The situation seems slightly in favour of the Netherlands, because the budget deficit is lower and prospects for further reduction are brighter.

3.4 Foreign Trade

For both Germany and The Netherlands, foreign trade in goods and services is of great importance for their economic well-being. In international perspective, both are open economies. Due to its small size the Dutch economy is more open than the German one. In 1995 exports of goods and services as a percentage of GDP amounted to 53 percent for the Netherlands and 23 percent for Germany. For western Germany alone this figure was 35 percent, indicating how difficult the foreign trade relations in the new Länder have developed so far (see European Commission, 1995: Table 38). Both countries are important players on the world market. Germany takes second position, with a share of about 10 percent of total world exports and imports. Only the United States has a bigger share. With some minor ups and downs, Germany has realised this share already for the last 15 years. The Netherlands takes the seventh position on the world export list, with a share of around 3.5 percent.[4] Dutch foreign trade contains a slightly higher share for services in total exports than Germany: 17.6 percent against 12.5 percent. This appears to be in line with the sectoral structure of the Dutch economy. Dutch imports contain a slightly lower share of services (15.2 %) than Germany's imports (20.8 %) (CPB: Wildcat, 1997). Both countries have been able to realise a major surplus on their current account. The Netherlands still has this position, but the German position changed dramatically after unification. Since 1991 the German current account balance is negative.

Table 3.12 Composition of German and Dutch foreign trade of goods, 1992

	Germany		The Netherlands	
	Imports	Exports	Imports	Exports
	% of total trade			
Agricultural products and raw materials	14	7	17	26
Energy	8	1	9	10
Industrial products, of which:	78	92	74	64
intermediary goods	37	45	37	35
consumer goods	29	27	25	21
investment goods	12	20	12	8

Source: CPB: Wildcat; De Graaf and Noordman (1995).

[4] See OECD (1996b: Annex table 46). The figure for the Netherlands is based on own calculations.

Table 3.13 Technological contents of German and Dutch foreign trade in industrial products, 1992

	Germany		The Netherlands	
	Imports	Exports	Imports	Exports
		%		
Low-tech	33	21	33	39
Medium-tech	39	48	38	37
High-tech	28	31	29	24

Source: De Graaf en Noordman (1995).

Composition of Foreign Trade. Greater differences between the two countries are found in the composition of their foreign trade in goods. Table 3.12 reveals that German exports are much more oriented towards industrial goods, more specifically investment goods. Dutch exports have relatively high shares for agricultural products and energy (see Box 3.5). Within the industrial products, there is a higher share for intermediary products and consumer goods. The composition of imports is more or less similar for the two countries.

Table 3.14 Export destinations and import origins for Germany and the Netherlands, 1995

	Exports of		Imports to	
Export destinations/import origins	D	NL	D	NL
		%		
Germany	0.0	28.6	0.0	23.4
Netherlands	7.5	0.0	8.6	0.0
France	11.7	11.1	10.8	7.4
United Kingdom	8.1	9.7	6.4	10.1
Italy	7.6	5.6	8.4	3.6
Belgium-Luxembourg	6.5	12.9	6.6	11.8
EU-15	57.7	79.4	55.5	66.2
Other Western Europe	11.7	3.5	7.2	3.8
United States	7.3	3.6	6.8	8.0
Japan	2.5	1.0	5.3	3.3

Source: CBS (1997), Deutsche Bundesbank (1996).

Box 3.5 Agriculture: Differences between Germany and the Netherlands

Germany and the Netherlands currently differ greatly in the production and trade of agricultural products. That difference cannot be explained by disparities in natural resources. Both countries enjoy a temperate climate, have a fertile soil, without the need to irrigate or the threat of inundation. The agricultural sector in both countries has been treated more or less similar in the last 35 years, due to the common market for agricultural products (CAP) within the European Union.

The differences have a longer history. Time has left its marks on the structure of German agriculture. The dominant position of industry and the power of the Prussian landlords led to a situation in which farmers were protected against cheap imports to ensure domestic food supply and to slow down the steady migration to urban areas. Many farmers were poor and lack of funds hampered a complete adjustment to modern developments. Even with the CAP this situation still exists. Food processing is still mainly oriented toward the home market, rather than toward export possibilities, with specialisation in meat and dairy products, cereals, and beverages. Whereas farms in West Germany are rather small, those in the new Länder are relatively big. After unification their situation has drastically changed. Large subsidies of the German government and the EU have promoted structural adjustment. If this reform proves to be successful, Germany could become a net exporter of cereals, and more self–sufficient in dairy products. On the cereal market, this could even undermine the strong French export position within the EU. This likely increase of self-sufficiency is reflected in a more favourable attitude of the German government towards free trade. However, the lack of processing capacity is considered to be an important bottleneck in the development of agricultural production in East–Germany.

The Dutch agricultural sector has taken a different road. The favourable geographical position has been an important source of comparative advantage in trade. During the crisis in the last quarter of the 19th century due to falling world market prices for cereals, restructuring rather than protection was seen as a permanent solution. The resulting rise in production, notably livestock and horticulture, and the success of the triptych research, development and instruction has led to a modern and highly productive agricultural sector, which rapidly adopts new technologies. This is also an important settlement motive for processing industries. The consequence has been that the Netherlands has specialised in animal products and in products of the horticultural sector. The large export shares of vegetables and fruits on the one hand and flowers and plants on the other can be attributed directly to this highly productive and innovative sector. Finally, the large share origin of the relevance of coffee and chocolate products and tobacco manufactures can be traced both to the favourable geographical position and to Dutch colonial history.

Source: Folmer (1995)

The same pattern exists with the technological contents of the foreign trade in industrial products. While the technological contents is about equal in imports (see Table 3.13), the technological content of the exports of both countries differs considerably. German export are much more oriented towards medium- and high tech industrial products, while Dutch exports in industrial products exhibit a high share in low-tech products. Inside Europe, Germany is the leading country for high-tech products, but according to a recent study the world-wide position of Germany has weakened after 1992. Japan and the United States have increased their lead (BMBF, 1997).

Export Destinations. Not only do the Netherlands and Germany differ in the composition of their foreign trade in goods, they also have a different distribution regarding the destinations of exports and origins of imports. Table 3.14 shows that the Netherlands have a much more skewed distribution, both for exports and imports. Germany alone is responsible for about 25 percent of Dutch foreign trade; the biggest three trade partners of the Netherlands account for 48 percent of the foreign trade. The most important trade partner for Germany is France, with a trade share of about 11 percent. The Netherlands is in third place, with a share of about 8 percent. Table 3.14 moreover shows that the greater part of the foreign trade of both countries is with other EU countries.

Conclusion. Foreign trade is of great importance for both economies. Germany has a stronger position in industrial products, while the Netherlands has relatively big shares in agricultural and energy exports. Until 1990, both economies could realise major surpluses on the foreign account. Due to the unification, after 1990 Germany witnessed a considerable decline on the foreign account. The Dutch position, however, improved even further. In the mutual relationship it was shown that western Germany is a more important trade partner for the Netherlands than vice versa, indicating that Dutch export performance and therefore its economic development is more sensitive to fluctuations in western Germany's demand than the other way around.

3.5 Monetary Policy

One of the typical characteristics of Germany is the support of the population for their currency, the DM, and for the independent position of the German central bank, the Deutsche Bundesbank, in striving for its main policy goal, namely stabilizing the value of the DM. The discussion on the EMU has taught that most other countries in Europe do not share these values in the same way and are therefore more reluctant to accept similar conditions within the EMU. No doubt the Netherlands comes closest to the German position among the EU-countries. The Dutch do not have the same anti-inflationary bias as the German population, but it is commonly accepted that De Nederlandsche Bank, the Dutch central bank, has shown after 1979 the same strong preference for low inflationary policies as the Bundesbank. The Dutch central bank has been as independent as the Bundesbank in realising its goals and selecting its policies and instruments; it could be given recommendations by the minister of finance, but this instrument was never used.

Table 3.15 Average annual inflation rates in (West-)Germany, the Netherlands, United Kingdom, Sweden, European Union and the United States, 1973-1996

	D	NL	GB	S	EU	USA
1973-1983	4.8	6.5	13.4	11.0		7.7
1983-1990	1.6	1.2	5.0	6.9	4.8	4.0
1990-1996	3.0	2.3	3.9	4.1	3.8	2.8

Explanation: See Table 3.2.

Stable Exchange Rate Between Dutch Guilder and Deutsch Mark. For De Nederlandsche Bank a stable exchange rate between the two currencies, the Dutch Guilder (Dfl) and the DeutschMark (DM), has been always of great importance. In the years of stability under the Bretton-Woods agreement this policy did not cause much trouble. Because of the higher inflation rate in the Netherlands in the 60s and 70s, it was inevitable to devalue the Dfl against the DM, even though the Dfl revalued against most other major currencies in that same period. After the breakdown of Bretton Woods, intra-EEC arrangements were negotiated to create a stable currency area in the EEC. Due to major disparities in inflation, the system could hardly function. In the 70s the Dfl had to be devalued against the DM several times.

EMS. Around 1974 the Bundesbank chose for a stricter monetary policy to reduce the German inflation as much as possible. The Bundesbank has realised an unprecedented record in bringing down the inflation. This example was so attractive that other central banks started to use the Bundesbank monetary policy as a guide for their own monetary policies. De Nederlandsche Bank was one of the first. From 1979, with the start of the European Monetary System, the main policy goal of the Dutch central bank was to peg its currency to the DM, hoping that the ensuing monetary policy would help to bring down Dutch inflation to (the lower) German level. Table 3.15 shows the fruits of this policy. For the whole period, the overall inflation has been even lower than in Germany. Of course, the successful wage moderation policies in the Netherlands have also contributed greatly.

More and more countries inside the EMS have since 1979 chosen for the same option, to bind their currency to the DM to bring down in inflation. Not without success, as history has shown. In the late 80s inflation went down in about all EU-member states and exchange rates were stabilized. It seemed that without much debate the European Union had entered a situation with stable exchange rates. Why not make the next step, so it was thought, and create a new currency area, with one European currency and an European Central Bank? This was considered to be the final step in the completion of the internal market. Backed by renewed economic growth it became possible to negotiate the Treaty of Maastricht including an Economic and Monetary Union. The events in 1992 and 1993 made clear how

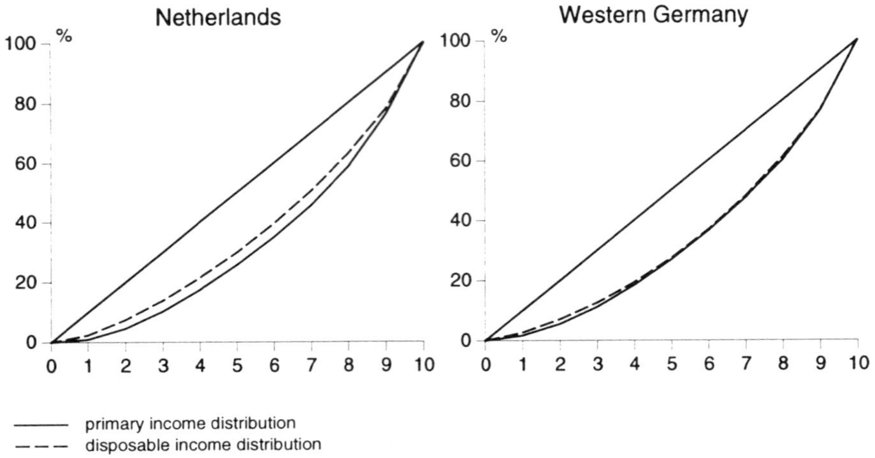

Source: De Kam and Allers (1993)

Figure 3.8 Primary and disposable income distribution in western Germany and The Netherlands

difficult it was to keep the exchange rates with all the EMS partners stable. Even in these turmoils, however, the exchange rate between DM and Dutch guilder remained completely unchanged.

3.6 Distribution of Income and Consumption

Income Distribution. Both in the Netherlands and Germany the primary income distribution of employees is considerably skewed, slightly more so in the Netherlands: in this country the top 30% income groups account for 53.5 percent of total primary income, against 50.6 percent in Germany. For the self-employed, the income distribution in Germany is less equally distributed, compared with German employees and with the Dutch self-employed. Because self-employed only make up a small share of the total economically active population,[5] the overall primary income distribution is more equal in Germany than in the Netherlands (De Kam and Allers, 1993).

The secondary income distribution results after redistribution through social security and income taxation (see for instance OECD, 1995c). The figures include the total population, hence not merely the active population. It follows that, except

[5] Self-employed make up 10.7 percent of the active population in Germany, and 8.9 percent in The Netherlands.

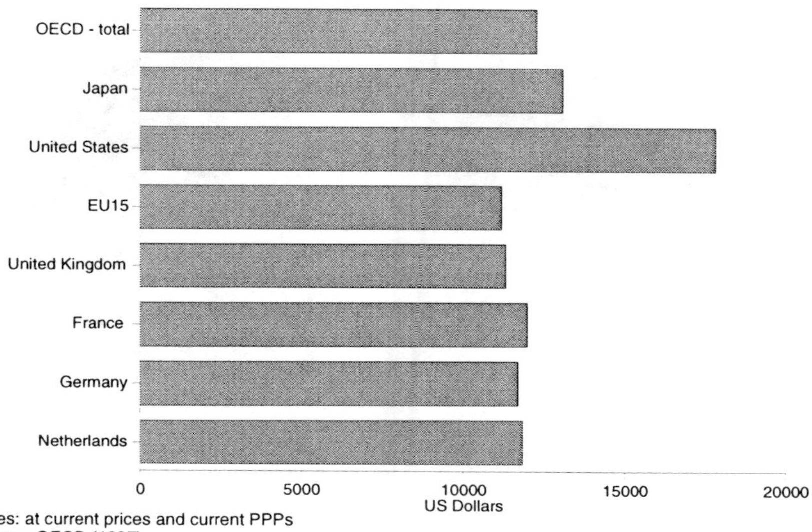

Notes: at current prices and current PPPs
Source: OECD (1997)

Figure 3.9 Private final consumption per head at current prices and current PPP's, 1995

for the first 10% income group, the secondary income distribution is more even in the Netherlands than in western Germany. Considering the relatively greater inequality for the primary income distribution, this reflects the far-reaching role of the Dutch government in redistributing income.

The importance of income redistribution is shown in Figure 3.8 which depicts the Lorentz curves for Germany and the Netherlands. These represent cumulative shares in total primary income and secondary income of the 10 percent groups making up the active population. Since the Dutch Lorentz-curve depicting the disposable income distribution deviates less from the diagonal than its German equivalent, the Dutch income distribution is more equal than the German. The gap between the curves representing the primary and secondary income distribution reflects the larger role of the Dutch government in redistributing income.

When the development over time is analyzed, it can be observed that from 1950 till 1983/84 the income distribution has become more equal in both countries (see for instance OECD, 1995c). Thereafter, however there are indications that the trend started to reverse, albeit only little. In both countries the social security incomes increased less than wages. In the Netherlands the inflow of new people on the labour market, often in part-time jobs, also meant an increase of people with a relatively lower income.[6]

---

[6] See SCP (1996). See also WRR (1996) for a different perspective on the income distribution development.

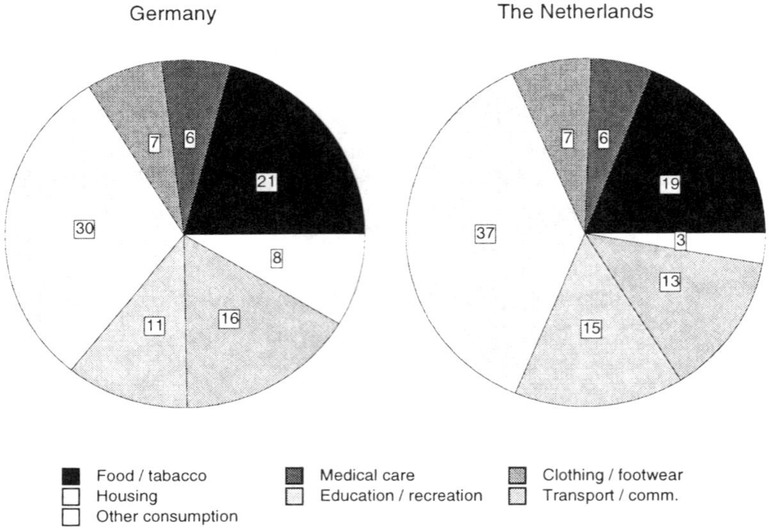

Source: CBS(1997:T19), Statistisches Bundesamt (1996:T24.8)

Figure 3.10 Private consumption by type in Germany and the Netherlands, 1994

Consumption. Figure 3.9 shows that in 1995 private consumption per head at purchasing power parity was about equal in Germany and the Netherlands, namely \$11700 and \$11900 respectively. This in turn is only little above the European Union average of \$11200. In the past the consumption per head in West-Germany was about 8 to 10 percent higher than in the Netherlands, but because of unification - now including 15 million extra people with a much lower income - this difference nearly disappeared. These results seem to conflict with the relatively high productivity level in the Netherlands, which was shown by Table 3.5. However, as pointed out in Section 3.2, the high share of part-time labour and low participation rate in the Netherlands reduce the total number of hours worked and so the income per head of the population.

Figure 3.10 makes visible that the composition of private consumption does not differ greatly between Germany and the Netherlands. In both countries, the residual category "other consumption" (comprising consumer durables such as household appliances and furniture, all goods and services for leisure activities and beverages and tobacco) takes up the largest share of the household budget –about one-third. With 18% in both countries, expenses for housing, such as rents, maintenance and heating and lighting charges, are the second biggest spending category.

For other products, the consumption patterns differ somewhat. Whereas in Germany relatively more is spent on medical care, and on transport and communications, spending on account of food takes up a larger share in the Netherlands. In this light, it is noted that expenditure on medical care and on education comprises government as well as private outlays because of differing national practices regarding the financing of these services.

3.7 Conclusion

This chapter has dealt with the overall post-war development of Germany and the Netherlands, with emphasis on recent developments and recent events like unification, and on certain subjects - labour market performance, public sector, foreign trade, monetary policy and income distribution.

Both countries have more or less followed the same pattern of economic development. Just as so many other countries in the western world, they first went through a period of unprecedented growth till 1973, then a period of recession and even crisis between 1973 and 1983, and after 1983 signs of recovery. Whether we are at the edge of a new prosperity period, is still difficult to say. After 1990 Germany's economic performance was strongly influenced by the unification, more sweeping and enduring than initially thought. So far the enormous efforts in the new Länder have not yet resulted in the creation of a self-sustaining, flourishing economy.

Both countries saw in the 60s and 70s a strong increase in the size of government expenditures and social security. After 1983 the Netherlands have been more successful in reducing the government expenditures. Their income distribution was also more or less the same. After 1980 they both had similar monetary goals and policies. Until 1983 they showed about the same pattern of employment growth and unemployment. After 1983 and certainly after 1990 increasing differences could be observed.

In line with the divergent employment pattern, a change in order between Germany and the Netherlands has occurred in recent years. While in the past the German economy was the most successful one regarding growth, unemployment and inflation, in recent times the Netherlands has taken over that position. Notions like 'Holland-model' or 'Dutch model' have entered the headlines. Of course, the impact of unification should not be neglected in that respect.

All in all both countries do not differ so much in level, but much more in the rate of change. The Netherlands seems to have been better able in the last decade to adjust its economy to changing conditions than the German economy. Again, the impact of unification is certainly important here, but it seems that this difference in adjustment capacity, in favour of the Netherlands, started earlier and has a broader scope. Unification initially masked this situation, but after a few years that same unification process had revealed the structural deficiencies very clearly. Now Germany faces the challenge to further remedy the deficiencies and adapt itself to changing circumstances. At the same time, the Netherlands should try to keep its momentum for change, removing old rigidities and avoiding new ones.

4 A Structural Comparison

The economic performance of a country depends on the way the existing institutions do stimulate or curb economic initiatives to optimize the use of the available resources in the national economy. Certain structural resources are 'god'-given: natural conditions like climate and geomorphology, the presence or lack of natural resources and the availability or absence of natural ways of transport - seas, lakes, rivers -, belong to this category. Other resources are also 'god-given', but their value or character has changed due to human intervention: the environmental situation is a good example. Most other structural resources, however, are the inheritance of past investment decisions, in buildings, machinery, education, technological knowledge and transport infrastructure. Together they constitute the economic and natural structure of a country, determining to a considerable extent the maximal production possibilities of a country. Extending or adjusting that structure is an essential but at the same time slow process; essential because it determines the future production possibilities and hence the economic performance of a country, slow because of the time-consuming character of investment and its gradual impact on the existing stock for the different categories mentioned.

This chapter describes the different structural characteristics of the German and Dutch economy. Subsequently, the natural and geographical conditions, energy and natural resources, the demographic situation and labour supply, the qualitative and quantitative dimensions of the capital stock, the transport and communication infrastructure, the environment and the regional pattern of economic activity will be discussed. The first elements are more or less exogenous, the last elements are determined by (deliberate) decisions made in the past by the different actors.

4.1 Geographical Conditions

The current geographical conditions of a country depend on historical, political and natural factors. Historical and political factors have been decisive for the current size, as well for its positioning among other nations. Natural factors have shaped the geographical conditions, like the location on a continent, the accessibility to open sea or to rivers, the fertility of the soil, the level of hilliness, and the existing climate. These geographical conditions can strongly influence the economic

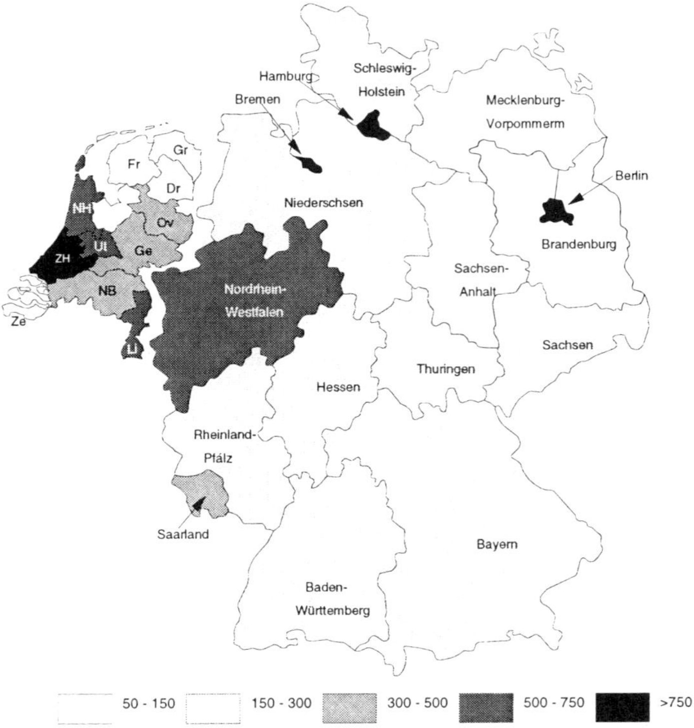

Figure 4.1 Population density in Germany and The Netherlands by Länder and provinces

potential of a country. Technological progress has increased the possibilities to upgrade that potential.

Germany. The total land area of Germany is approximately 357000 square kilometres, whereas the total surface area of the Netherlands amounts to roughly 41500 square kilometres. Germany is about 8.6 times bigger than its north-western neighbour. Figure 4.1 visualises the relative size of Germany and the Netherlands, as well as the population density by Länder and provinces. Germany has also more neighbours, namely nine. The Netherlands has only two neighbouring countries, Belgium and Germany.

Although Germany is a large country, it certainly is not the biggest in Europe. Leaving Russia aside, Germany is smaller than France (552000 km^2) and Spain (505000 km^2). About 70 percent of the total surface is situated in the western part of the country. Topographically three major zones can be distinguished: the north German flatland, which contain a substantial number of lakes and wetland; central Germany, with hills and mountains rising to an elevation of 1000 metres; and a mountainous southern area with hills, large lakes and the Alps with elevations of up to 3000 metres. Half of Germany's total surface area is utilised for agricultural purposes. Roughly 30 percent of the area consists of forest, whereas 12 percent is used for housing and traffic. The remaining area is covered by water, wetland and undisturbed land (OECD, 1993).

The Netherlands. The Netherlands is a very flat country, part of the same North-German flatland mentioned above. There are just occasional hills in the southern and eastern parts. As in Germany, utilisation of land in the Netherlands is primarily for agricultural purposes: 59 percent of the total area. Wooded areas are more scarce than in Germany, taking up 10 percent of the total surface area. Space for housing and traffic amounts to approximately 8 percent and about 17 percent consists of water. The remainder refers to natural sites and non-classified areas (CBS, 1997).

Natural water-routes, forming part of the natural infrastructure and hence of endowments, are important characteristics of the landscape in both countries. With around 700 kilometres, the Rhine and the Elbe are the longest navigable rivers in Germany (Statistisches Bundesamt, 1995). Altogether, leaving man-made waterways such as channels aside, Germany counts 2900 kilometres of water-routes. Besides through its position along the North Sea, the importance of waterways in the Netherlands appears from the fact that the total number of navigable kilometres on natural water-routes amounts to 1300 (Eurostat, 1993b).

4.2 Energy Resources and Energy Use

Earlier it was mentioned that this chapter deals with structural, slowly adjusting characteristics. Still, major changes may occur, as this paragraph will reveal. The energy landscape has changed dramatically over the last 40 years, in both countries. In the 50s the German economic development was strongly dependent on and favoured by an abundant supply of coal. Its dependence on foreign imports was relatively small. At the same time, the Netherlands was strongly dependent on energy imports, having hardly any domestic energy resources available. Then, several important changes occurred: on the European continent coal production became increasingly uncompetitive, the importance of natural oil increased immensely, and in the Netherlands natural gas was discovered in Slochteren. How did both countries deal with these changes?

Even though coal has lost its dominant position in total German energy use, it still is the primary natural resource for Germany, taking up about 57 percent of Germany's total energy production and 3.9 percent of the world production of coal (EZ, 1993). Moreover, Germany has a relatively modest production of crude oil and natural gas.[1] About 57 percent of the total German energy supply is imported.

---

[1] Germany has also a modest production of iron ore and mineral salts.

This share has increased, also because domestic production decreased by 28 percent between 1984 and 1994 (OECD, 1996a). Germany is almost entirely dependent on foreign oil sources. It is, however, nearly self-sufficient in coal. With 81 Mtoe the bulk of domestic production refers to coal (57%), which is Germany's major primary energy source. Furthermore, Germany generated about 39 Mtoe of nuclear energy (28%) and approximately 14 Mtoe of gas (8%). The remaining 6 percent referred to the production of crude oil, solid fuels other than coal, and hydro energy. The energy Germany imports, mainly consists of crude oil and petroleum products. Moreover, it imports some gas.

The discovery of the Slochteren gas[2] brought about major changes in the Dutch economy: Dutch coal production was deliberately stopped around 1966, and energy-intensive economic activities in agriculture and manufacturing (petrochemical industries) boosted because of low gas prices. Natural gas became about the sole energy source in domestic consumption. The presence of natural gas allowed the Dutch to refrain from using nuclear energy. Gas currently takes up about 92 percent of the total Dutch energy production, with beneficial consequences for the environment. This production is about 3.3 percent of the world gas production in 1990 (EZ, 1993). In 1993 the proven reserves did allow a current yearly production of 62.9 Mtoe to continue for another 28 years (BP, 1994). Apart from natural gas, the Netherlands extracts crude oil – particularly in offshore (North Sea) activities. With 3.4 Mtoe in 1992, Dutch oil production is just below German levels; on a global scale this production is unimportant.[3]

Table 4.1 gives the main characteristics of the energy supply and production for both countries. The differences are clear. In Germany coal and to a much lesser extent nuclear energy are important for the energy supply, in the Netherlands natural gas has an outstanding position. This is certainly the case for the domestic production. Table 4.1 also reveals the differences in energy consumption. The German energy intensity per million persons in 1994 amounted to 4.13 Mtoe. In terms of GDP, measured in billion 1994 PPP dollars, energy intensity in Germany amounted to 1.39 Mtoe in 1991. Both figures are higher in the Netherlands. Per million persons the Dutch energy intensity was 4.58 Mtoe, per billion GDP in 1994 PPP dollars 1.77 Mtoe. Furthermore, the decline in energy intensity between 1984 and 1994 has been much stronger in Germany than in the Netherlands (OECD, 1996a).

Conclusion. Both Germany and the Netherlands have been confronted with major changes in their energy situation. Especially Germany shows how strongly an economic structure can be determined by the presence of natural resources, and how difficult it is to amend this structure once economic or technological

[2] The Netherlands also exploits important sources on its part of the North Sea.

[3] The Netherlands also produces sand and grit as well as salt.

Table 4.1 Total Primary Energy Supply (TPES) and Domestic Energy Production (DEP) for Germany and the Netherlands, 1994.

	Germany		the Netherlands	
	TPES	DEP	TPES	DEP
Total (in Mtoe)	336	143	70	66
per million persons	4.13	1.75	4.58	4.28
per billion GDP, in 1994 PPP dollars	1.39	0.59	1.77	1.66
Fuel mix (in %)				
– oil	40	3	37	7
– coal	29	57	13	0
– natural gas	18	10	47	91
– nuclear energy	12	28	1	2
– other sources	1	3	2	1

Source: OECD/IEA (1996)

developments affect the comparative advantage of these resources. Production and employment declined in the German coal industry, creating major economic and social problems in specific regions. Germany also became increasingly dependent on energy imports. The Netherlands, in contrast, could profit from the discovery of natural gas, financially and environmentally, but also here certain negative consequences appeared. First, the gas revenues stimulated government expenditures, mostly for consumption purposes. This did not improve the country's competitiveness. Second, the abundant supply of natural gas (at low prices) stimulated the growth of energy-intensive sectors. Even though natural gas is relatively clean, it still puts a burden on the environment. Once energy supply should become less abundant and/or available only at higher prices, a painful adjustment process may result, similar to that in the German coal industry.

The lesson is clear. The presence of natural resources can be useful for the economic development of a region, but the resulting specialisation can become a serious handicap once technological, economic or natural changes undermine the comparative advantage of the available energy resource.

4.3 Demography

The demographic situation of a country at a certain point in time is the outcome of a complex process of human decisions, health conditions, natural disasters, and of historical political and military events, here and (in the case of migration) elsewhere. Volume and composition of the population influence the economic potential of a country to a considerable extent, in particular through the determination of potential labour supply.

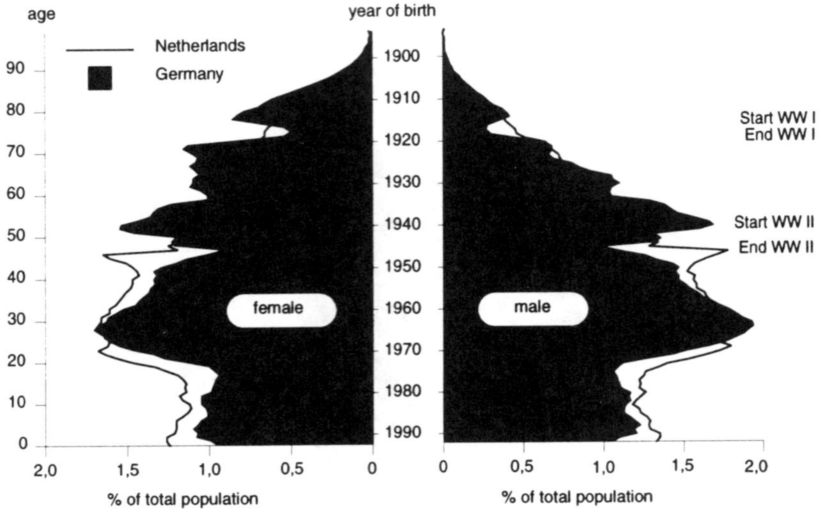

Source: Eurostat (1994 a)

Figure 4.2 The age pyramids of Germany and the Netherlands in 1992

Population: Size, Growth and Age. Of the 81.5 million inhabitants Germany counted in 1994, 81% lived in the western part of the country[4]. Despite the negative *natural* population growth, the total population in the old Bundesländer grew by 7% as from 1980, as a consequence of the influx of immigrants, the many new arrivals from East Germany before and since unification and asylum seekers. To indicate, in the period 1989-1994 the net influx was about 3.4 million people, whereas the total population increased in that same period with about 2.9 million. The population in the new Bundesländer (15.5 million in 1994) decreased by 7% since 1980, a decrease which occurred almost entirely after 1988. Altogether, the total German population increased by 4.2% since 1980. The current German demographic situation is influenced by the Second World War, as can be seen in Figure 4.2. The age groups around 75 and 50 show a much smaller share than the surrounding age groups.

In 1994, the Dutch population amounted to 15.3 million[5]. Living at a small area, this implies that the Netherlands is a densely populated country. Here 366 inhabitants live per square kilometre against 223 in Germany.[6] Since 1980, the

[4] All data for Germany are from Statistisches Bundesamt (1996).

[5] All Dutch data are from CBS (1997).

[6] West Germany is more densely populated than the eastern part (254 against 150 inhabitants per square kilometre).

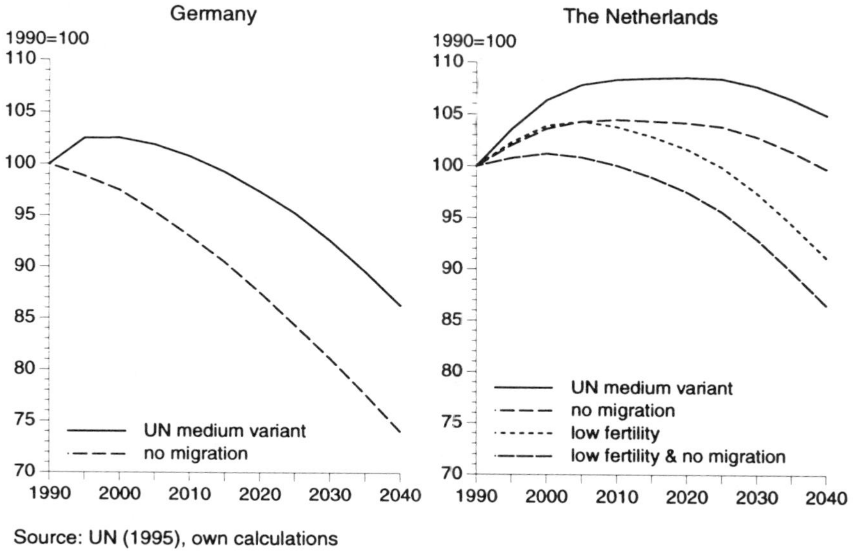

Figure 4.3 Population development for Germany and the Netherlands under different assumptions, 1990-2040

Dutch population has increased by 8.9%, more than double the growth rate of Germany. About half of it was due to natural population growth. The Dutch population is relatively young. It therefore comprises relatively more persons in their fertile ages (see hereafter). The other half is caused by immigration. The Netherlands too was confronted with a net influx of people. In the period 1989-1994 the net migration to the Netherlands was 317 thousand persons.

The demographic prospects for both countries are similar in pattern, but divergent in timing. Both Germany and the Netherlands are heading for a decline of their total population, but Germany will reach this situation much earlier, somewhere around 2000. For the Netherlands this turnaround will arrive around 2020. Figure 4.3 shows these demographic prospects. The population decline would start earlier and would be stronger, if immigration would be absent or (in the Dutch case) if the fertility rate in that country would be at the same (lower) level as in Germany.

Like most other developed economies, the German and Dutch population are subject to a process of ageing: the share of the juvenile generation declines (dejuvenation), the share of the elderly generation rises (greying). In 1990 the young-age dependency ratio (children under 15 as a share of the population aged from 15 to 65 years) was 27 percent in the Netherlands and 24 in Germany. Since 1950 a remarkable decline occurred. Then this ratio was 47 for the Netherlands and 35 for Germany. The greying of the population can be distilled from the old-age

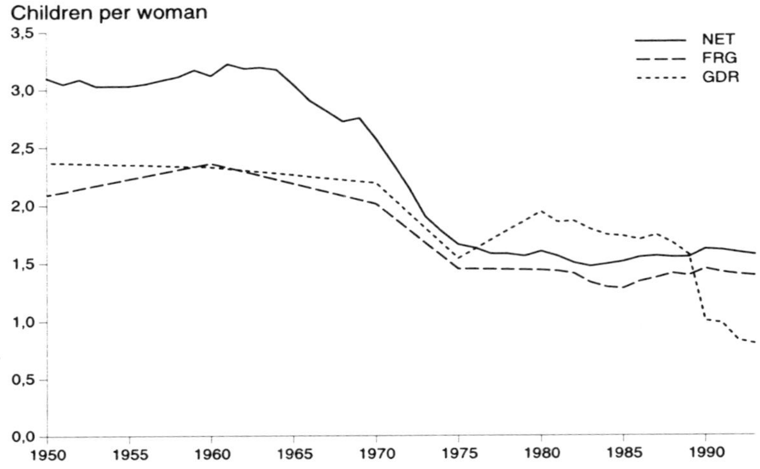

Source: BiB (1994), CBS (1994c)

Figure 4.4 Total fertility rates for FRG, GDR and the Netherlands, 1950-1993

dependency ratio (people above 64 as a share of the population between 15 and 65). Here Germany with 22 percent is ahead of the Netherlands (19%). The processes of dejuvenation and greying started later in the Netherlands than in Germany, but it ran at a much faster pace. This was caused by the influence of the size and length of the baby-boom between 1945 and 1960 and by the collapse in the late 60s, early 70s of the rate of child-bearing. Figure 4.4 shows the development of the fertility rate for the period 1950-1993, for both the FRG and the GDR and for the Netherlands.[7] Figure 4.4 moreover points to the recent plunge in the East German fertility rate: since German unification the number of births has halved. The all time low fertility rate of 0.8 reflect the dramatic changes in the new Länder, with clear demographic repercussions (see for instance Witte and Wagner, 1995).

The expectations for the dependency ratios are shown in Figure 4.5. Till about 2015 the young-age dependency will continue its decline, whereafter a recovery is expected. Around 2040 this ratio could show about the same level as today. The old-age dependency rate shows a strong and even increasing growth during the whole period till 2040. Only at the end there are indications of a slow-down. At that moment this ratio is around 50 percent, indicating that for every two persons between 15 and 65 there is one person above 64.

[7] Another striking difference between German and Dutch women is the age of child-bearing-women. In the Netherlands the mean age of women is 29.7 years against 27.8 years for German women.

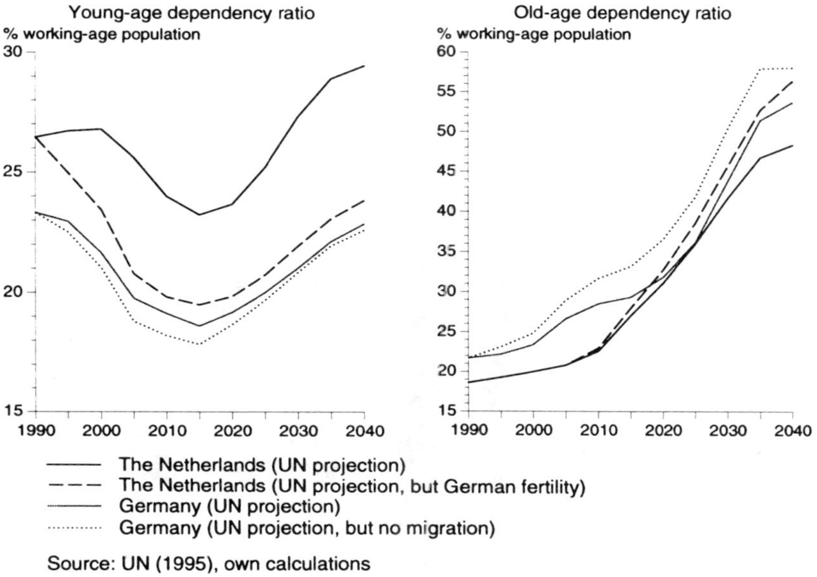

Figure 4.5 Development of the dependency ratios for Germany and the Netherlands under different assumptions, 1990-2040

Ethnological Composition. Another change in the demography of both countries is the change in the ethnological composition of the population. In 1994 about 7 million people in Germany were counted as foreigners, about 8.6 percent of total population. In the Netherlands the number of foreigners is 780 thousand, about 5 percent of total population. However, these national data are based on different definitions of nationality.[8] There are much stricter rules for foreigners to apply for the German nationality than for the Dutch nationality. In 1994 26 thousand foreigners (0.03 percent of total population) got the German nationality[9], in the Netherlands that number was 49 thousand (or 0.3 percent). In the Netherlands, the number of foreigners, born in a foreign country or, if born in the Netherlands, child of a father or mother born elsewhere, is much higher than 780 thousand, namely 2.6 million. About half of them, 1.3 million or 8.5 percent of total population, are from a non-OECD country. This last figure is comparable with the

---

[8] Since 1994 it is allowed in the Netherlands to have two nationalities. Especially the number of Turks has declined drastically, from 203 thousand in 1994 till 154 thousand in 1996.

[9] Another 230 thousand got the German nationality because they were treated as Aussiedler, for which the possibility exists of 'Anspruchseinbürgerung'.

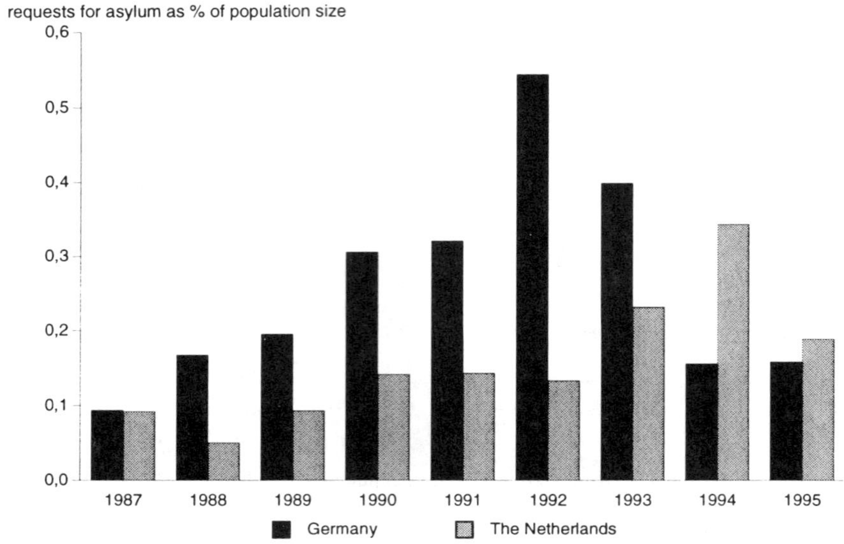

Figure 4.6 Requests for asylum, 1987-1995

German one.

Over the past few years, both Germany and the Netherlands have seen a great influx of asylum seeking people. Figure 4.6 shows that in the late 80s this influx was still low. After the fall of the Berlin wall and the ensuing political unrest in Eastern Europe, the immigration towards Germany boomed till unprecedented levels. After a long and difficult debate it was decided to apply stricter rules for asylum applications. Thereafter the influx in Germany declined considerably. Now the Netherlands was confronted with a strong increase. In absolute terms this influx was much lower than for Germany, but Figure 4.6 reveals that taking into account the much smaller population in the Netherlands, the Dutch influx in 1994 was not so much behind the German influx in its top year 1992.

Labour Supply and Level of Education. In the preceding chapter the labour market situation in both countries was already dealt with. In addition to the material presented there, here data for the labour supply according to age group will be given. Table 4.2 shows that the employment/population ratios in Germany and the Netherlands for the age-groups below 45 are about the same as in the other countries mentioned here, but that above that age the ratios for these two countries are much lower. In these age groups ample room exists for both countries to raise the employment. By doing so the dependency of this group on social security could be reduced.

Table 4.2 Employment/population ratios by age group, 1994

Age group	D[a]	NL	GB[a]	S	USA
15-24	52.2	55.4	58.8	41.5	58.2
25-34	72.1	76.8	74.1	75.6	78.3
35-44	76.1	74.9	79.1	84.4	81.1
45-54	72.2	67.5	76.5	85.9	78.6
55-64	33.6	29.1	46.6	64.1	54.6
> 65	2.9	0.0	5.2	9.2	13.5

[a] Data for Germany and the United Kingdom refer to 1993.

Source: Own calculations based on data from OECD (1996c).

One related aspect deserves some more attention here, namely the level of education of the population. In the preceding chapter it was shown that the productivity level in the Netherlands, expressed as GDP per hour worked, was remarkably high, higher than in Germany. A high productivity level depends not only on a sufficient capital stock and R&D knowledge, but also on the educational level of the labour force. The German labour force has a high educational attainment level, related to the extensive apprenticeship system. Only the United States scores better. The Dutch educational attainment level, in contrast, lags behind that in the four countries of reference (see Figure 4.7).

The current unfavourable position of the Netherlands is caused by the relatively late process of catching up in educational enrolment. In 1960 only 17% of Dutch 18 year old youngsters followed education, compared to 27% in Germany (CBS, 1993; Fischer *et al.*, 1993). Between 1985 and 1992, the enrolment of 18-year old youngsters in Germany remained at a constant level, whereas the Dutch enrolment rate continued to increase considerably during the 1980s. At the beginning of the 1990s, Dutch educational enrolment reached German levels (De Jager, 1996). Enrolment in upper secondary education is almost as high as in Germany. Total enrolment in tertiary education is also similar, although the average age of students in Germany is higher than in the Netherlands. This implies that the educational attainment level of both countries will converge (De Jager, 1996).

Quality of Education. The quality of education is difficult to compare across countries[10], since available indicators such as class-size or teacher characteristics are not satisfactory. Scores on international tests, measuring scientific and reading performance, provide some information on the quality of the system. The results

[10] See on this issue for instance Bottani (1995).

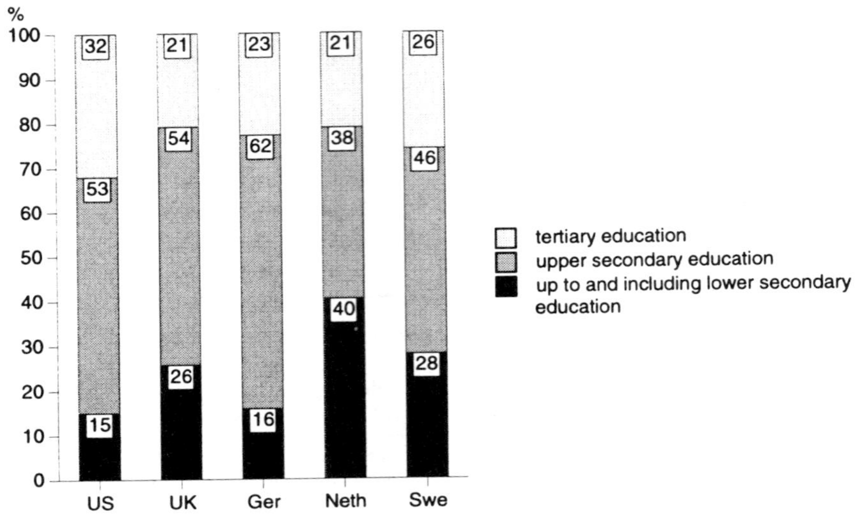

Figure 4.7 Educational level of the population 15-64, 1994

of six international science tests, administered by the International Association for the Evaluation of Educational Achievement between 1963 and 1991, report a good performance of Dutch and German pupils on science subjects, and worse results of American students (Hanushek and Kim, 1995). In a recent study students in 41 nations were compared on mathematics and science (The Economist, 1997). With South-East Asian countries in first positions, the Netherlands gained a 9th place for mathematics and a 6th place with science, being about first among the industrialized countries. Germany came at 23rd respectively 19th place. The United States were even lower. With all reservations, the conclusion can be that the Netherlands has been able to improve its performance, but that the German development seems to be less favourable than often is thought.

Conclusions. Both Germany and the Netherlands are confronted with important changes in the demographic situation. These changes are related to size, ageing, and ethnographic composition. Both countries are approaching the moment when the number of people will start to decline. That moment is much nearer for Germany than for the Netherlands. In fact, if there had not been a net influx of foreign people, Germany would have been already over the hill. In the near future a decline of the German population seems inevitable, while the Netherlands will go the same way, with some delay. At the same time the processes of dejuvenation and greying will continue and, in the case of greying, even gain in importance. Again, Germany is ahead of the Netherlands. The resulting decline in the potential labour force and the strong increase in the number of elderly will have important consequences for the economic development of both countries. This regards economic growth, composition of demand, labour supply, and the financing of pensions and health care. The third change is related to the ethnographic composition. To a certain extent the influx of foreigners can delay the decline in size and mitigate the processes of dejuvenation and greying. However, this group poses different problems, related to their difficult entry at the labour market, their relatively low level of education, and more generally with societal integration.

4.4 Capital Stock and Investment

After natural resources and human capital, business capital is the third type of production factor addressed in this chapter. Here, the concept of business capital transcends the traditional definition of cumulated investment in physical capital consisting of equipment, buildings and means of transportation. Besides expanding productive capacity by investing in physical capital, firms create intangible capital as a resource base to enhance their competitiveness. Investment in intangible capital includes spending on research and development (R&D), outlays on intellectual property rights like patents and licences, investments in technical know-how, marketing, advertising and efforts in product design. More and more, both knowledge related intangible capital and human capital are considered to be decisive factors for firms from countries relatively well endowed with these factors of production, to compete in the world economy. Therefore, with respect to business capital this section starts with an overview of some indicators of physical and intangible investments in Germany and the Netherlands. Next, internationalization of investment will be touched upon by examining direct foreign investments by German and Dutch enterprises. Finally, attention will be paid to regional investment patterns in Germany to give an impression of the position of future German growth centres relative to the Netherlands.

Physical Capital. At first sight, the similarities between the two countries do prevail also in the area of physical business capital. The relative size of this stock compared with their respective GDP is almost identical. In 1992 the German physical capital stock was 3.6 times the size of GDP, the Dutch equivalent 3.7 times. The similarity also exists with the current level and the development over time of the investment ratios in the two countries, as a share of GDP. Table 4.3 reveals that both Germany and the Netherlands have had above OECD-average investment ratios in GDP, but that after 1973 that positive margin disappeared. The United Kingdom and the United States had a much lower ratio, both before and after 1973.

Figure 4.8 gives more information for both countries on the sectoral level. Here the differences between the two countries are more pronounced. Over a longer period of time, the Dutch growth rates of the investment volume are relatively high

Table 4.3 Gross fixed capital formation as a percentage of GDP, 1960-1994

	D	NL	GB	US	EU	OECD
1960-1973	24.6	25.6	18.3	18.4	23.3	22.1
1973-1983	21.0	21.0	18.4	19.3	22.0	22.3
1983-1990	19.9	20.3	18.1	18.5	20.0	20.9
1990-1994	22.3	20.0	16.5	16.3	19.9	20.3

Source: OECD (1996d).

in agriculture and in manufacturing. German investment growth has been high in the service sector, compared to the Netherlands. In each sub-period distinguished, the overall Dutch growth rate was higher than that in Germany. Both countries followed more or less the same pattern of development over time, with high growth rates before 1973, a steep decline afterwards and recovery after 1983.

Intangible Capital. So far attention was given only to physical capital. However relevant such attention was in the past, in the current situation it is essential to broaden the scope by paying sufficient notice towards 'intangible capital', the domain of knowledge creation, diffusion and application. A more qualitative analysis of the existing stock, mainly with regard to new technologies, computers, robots, Computer Integrated Manufacturing (CIM) and medical technologies, shows that both countries have been able to adjust their stock to a significant extent (see Box 4.1).

In contrast to hardware spending per capita, which is of a similar magnitude in the two countries, Dutch software spending per capita of 160 dollars in 1991 has substantially exceeded German software spending of 110 dollars per capita in that same year (OECD, 1994c).[11] The OECD average equalled 140 dollars per capita. In the range of OECD countries, the Netherlands occupies the fourth position after Switzerland, The United States, and Sweden; Germany is twelfth in row. As for intangible investments in advertising, German enterprises spent $ 206 per capita in 1992, while Dutch firms spent $ 158 per capita (WEF, 1994). With these figures Germany and the Netherlands are tenth and seventeenth respectively, in a ranking led by Switzerland and the United States. Expenditure on advertising of $ 330 per capita in these two leading countries is double the amount spent in the Netherlands.

R&D Efforts. Besides the above scant material on software and advertising spending, comparative information on intangible capital is primarily available for research and development (R&D) by enterprises. R&D investments as a percentage

[11] These are 1991 figures, converted using PPPs.

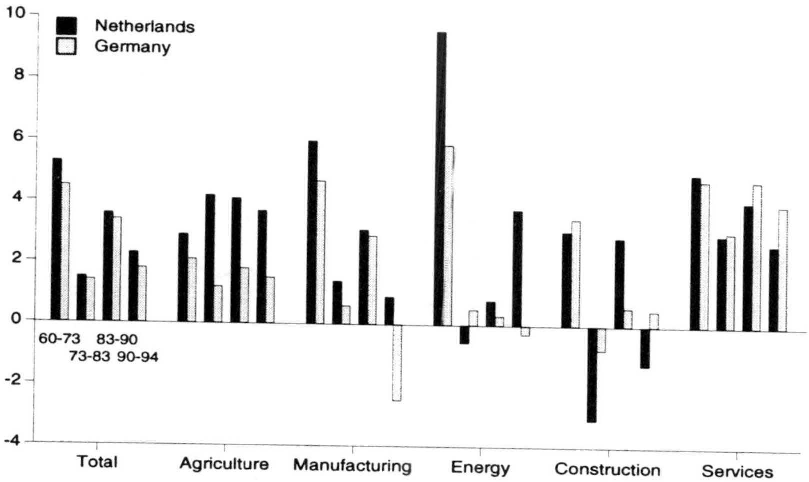

Source: Stat. Bundesamt. Volksw. Gesamtr. (national accounts); CBS, Nationale rekeningen (national accounts)

Figure 4.8 Growth rates of investment volume in Germany and The Netherlands, 1960-1990

of GDP in the Netherlands are low compared to Germany. Figure 4.9 shows that, starting at an almost common level of 1.2 % of GDP at the beginning of the 1970s, the German R&D investment ratio rose steadily to 2% of GDP in 1989, while the Dutch R&D investment ratio levelled off to 1% of GDP during the 1970s and the first half of the 1980s, only to rise to 1.3% in 1988.[12] According to Slabbers and Verspagen (1994) this diverging development between Germany and the Netherlands until 1988 can be partly attributed to the difference in sectoral structure, with the Dutch economy being service-intensive and therefore R&D-extensive. Since the end of the 1980s R&D investment ratios are declining in many OECD countries. The fall has been substantial both in Germany and the Netherlands. In view of the already low level of enterprise R&D, the decline in the Netherlands is striking. When the broader concept of intangible investments is used - besides investments for R&D expenditures for education, licensing, software and marketing -, the Dutch position improves considerably. For 1992 the Netherlands takes the fourth position among 10 leading OECD-countries, while Germany takes

[12] The increase of R&D investment over 1985-1988 is caused by the construction of some large laboratories for research into microprocessors and high-quality chemical products in these years. Conventions on R&D statistics require registration of the expenses for these laboratories in the year they have been installed. Therefore, the 1985-1988 figures are biased upwards and the fall after 1988 is relatively large compared to the case in which these expenses are spread over time (CPB, 1994).

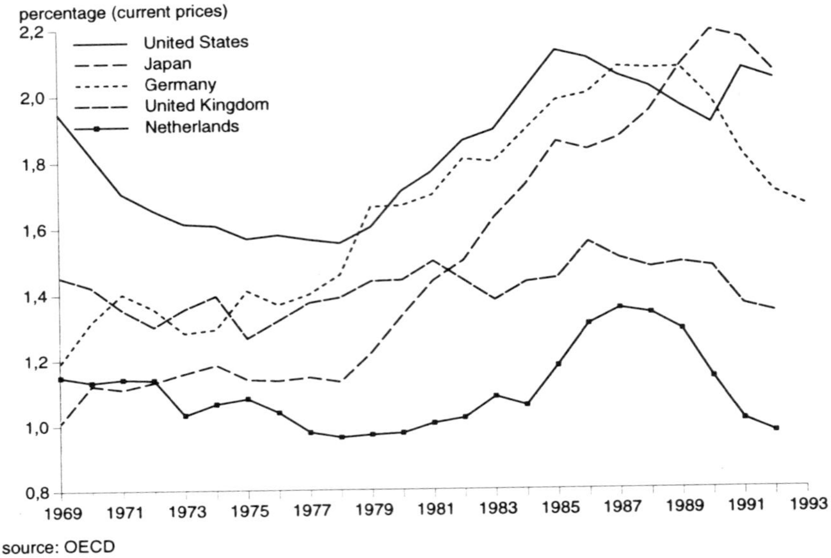

Figure 4.9 R&D investment by enterprises as a percentage of GDP, 1969-1993

the last position. When educational expenditures are left out, Germany climbs back to the third position (CPB, 1996).

Falling R&D intensity since 1988 is partly associated with restructuring activities and reorganizations within the five biggest Dutch multinational enterprises: AKZO, DSM, Philips, Shell and Unilever. These adjustments were aimed at realising a higher research efficiency and at an intensified market orientation (see CPB, 1994, and Minne, 1995)[13]. In 1987 these five enterprises accounted for 66% of total enterprise R&D investments in the Netherlands, in 1992 their share has fallen to 50%.[14] At the same time Dutch SMEs were able the increase their R&D-efforts. In terms of GDP this implies a fall from 0.9% to 0.5%. Especially drastic cost reductions and reorganizations by Philips account for the substantial drop in R&D

---

[13] While R&D investments of the five large Dutch multinationals fell substantially in the home country, these companies' R&D investments outside the Netherlands showed no decline over 1987-1992.

[14] Both in Germany and The Netherlands R&D is primarily performed by large enterprises. The share of small and medium-sized enterprises in total R&D expenditure in both countries is about 15%, while the share of SMEs in employment is 60% in Germany and 70% in The Netherlands (European Network for SME Research, 1994).

Box 4.1 On the diffusion and application of information and communication technologies

In the field of general computer know-how and in the use of information technology, the position of Germany and of the Netherlands is largely comparable. Hardware spending per capita (OECD, 1994c), number of computers per person and computer power per capita (WEF, 1994) are of a similar magnitude in the two countries. In a survey held in 41 countries the two countries belong to the group where computer literacy among employees and strategic exploitation of information technology in enterprises was relatively high (WEF, 1994). The use of robots in manufacturing differs, however, between the two countries. In 1992 the number of robots per 10,000 manufacturing workers equalled 14 in the Netherlands and 49 in Germany (WEF, 1994). Germany was only outperformed here by Sweden and Japan. Robots are applied predominantly in the automobile industry, in which Germany has a strong position.

In addition to the general view on the diffusion of information technology and mechanization, the application of Computer Integrated Manufacturing (CIM) technologies has been considered. CIM pertains to the integration of all streams of information between the various activities in enterprises related to production (EZ, 1991). CIM lowers costs, increases productivity, shortens product cycles and improves quality by working simultaneously on design, construction, production planning and production. In 1991 90% of the German firms in the investment goods sector could point at at least one computer aided activity. Computerization of production processes has increased in Germany, in particular within large enterprises. In Germany CIM can be found mainly in the electronics, furniture, machinery and processing industry sectors. In contrast to Germany, the application of CIM in the Netherlands is still largely experimental. Explanatory factors for these differences are the lower degree of automation in Dutch manufacturing, also due to the different sectoral structure, the difficulty to quantify the positive effects of CIM, which significantly influences Dutch management decision making, and the smaller scale of Dutch supply companies (Minne, 1992).

expenditures.[15] Domestic R&D investments of a number of Dutch medium sized enterprises in these years decreased as well. In addition, the share of enterprise R&D commissioned by foreign firms fell from 8.5% in 1982 to 2.4% in 1991, which is in contrast to the development in other European countries. In Germany the corresponding share showed an increase from 1.4 to 3.1%. Together with the low level of R&D investment, these observations point in the direction of a weak competitiveness of the Netherlands in the field of enterprise R&D. According to Minne (1995) R&D performed by Dutch enterprises still is relatively expensive despite the wage moderation policies since the early 80s.

[15] In 1988 R&D investments by Philips of 2100 million guilders consisted of nearly 60 % of R&D expenditure by the five large enterprises (*f*3535 million). In 1993 after a cutback in R&D expenditure of almost a quarter to *f*1550 million, the share in the total of *f*3250 million fell to 48% (see Minne, 1995).

R&D reorganization is not a specifically Dutch, but rather a European phenomenon. In Germany too, the fall of R&D investments did raise concern about the position of their R&D-intensive enterprises on the world market. However, because of the large R&D share of the five Dutch multinational enterprises, their R&D behaviour induced large fluctuations in national R&D investments. The bigger size of the German economy prevented a similar major decline in that country. Furthermore, enterprise R&D costs divided by total R&D personnel in Germany are lower, in particular current non-labour outlays.

It is difficult to observe whether the reorganisations have been successful. An, admittedly weak, indicator of that success is the number of patent applications at the European Patent Office. Over the period 1988-1992 the number of German applications showed no significant fall, while those from the Netherlands increased considerably (Minne, 1995). However, the Dutch figures may be biased by the fact that they also contained applications for R&D departments of foreign subsidiaries of Dutch firms.

On balance, both German and Dutch R&D-intensive enterprises are engaged in a process of reorientation towards raising R&D productivity and tying R&D efforts closer to consumer tastes. Compared with their German counterparts, Dutch enterprises are handicapped by their higher cost levels and by the substantially lower level of R&D investment as a percentage of GDP.

Sectoral Structure. The sectoral structure of both economies has changed considerably in the last decades. Table 4.4 makes clear that both economies have seen a decline in agriculture and manufacturing, and a strong increase in production value in services. That process of deindustrialization has been stronger in the Netherlands than in Germany. While the Netherlands is already a service-oriented economy, Germany still has a much more manufacturing oriented economic structure. This remark is not only relevant for the production value; also for employment the same pattern can be observed, as Figure 3.5 makes clear. At the same time, it has to be recognised that the interrelationships between manufacturing and services have increased, for instance because of increased outsourcing activities.

Another characteristic of the economic structure is the size distribution of the firms. Table 4.5 reveals that the number of big firms, i.e. those with more than 500 employees, is similar in Germany and the Netherlands. The share of small firms is slightly bigger in the Netherlands. Medium-sized firms have a bigger share in Germany. More differences exist in the employment distribution according to size. In the Netherlands many more people do work in small firms, while German employees are more employed in bigger firms. The average number of employees per firm is 15 percent higher in the Netherlands than in Germany. Another observation is that the firm dynamics, the birth and death of firms, in the period 1986-1991 was about three times stronger in Germany than in the Netherlands (see Suijker).

Table 4.4 Structure of production for Germany and the Netherlands, shares in value added, 1960 and 1993/4

	The Netherlands		Germany	
	1960	1994	1960	1993
	% of value added			
Agriculture	9.7	4.5	6.5	1.4
Manufacturing	33.4	21.5	42.0	32.8
incl. metal	12.6	8.4	20.8	18.4
Energy	6.9	8.3	8.9	5.4
Construction	8.2	6.7	8.6	7.4
Services	43.2	63.9	35.9	59.5
incl. trade	18.0	17.4	15.5	12.8

Note: Because the value added of interest margins is negative, the shares of these sectors do not add up to 100 percent.

Source: CPB, own calculations.

Foreign Direct Investments. A country's attractiveness as an investment location can be derived from the volume of foreign investments a country can attract. Such investments can create new production facilities and employment. Less positive is the popular judgment about outgoing foreign direct investment. This outgoing stream is seen as eroding domestic production and employment. Such investments do strengthen, however, the competitiveness of the firms involved, and may support the existing employment. That certainly is the case for those investment activities aiming at facilitating market expansion abroad. Moreover, foreign direct investments are a channel for international dissemination of knowledge.

Table 4.5 Number of firms and employment according to firm size, 1993

	The Netherlands		Germany	
	Number	Employment	Number	Employment
Total	419	43[illegible]9	2291	20420
	% of total			
0-9	89.9	27.9	88.1	18.8
10-99	9.0	25.8	11.0	26.8
100-499	0.9	18.8	0.8	16.9
> 500	0.2	27.5	0.2	37.5

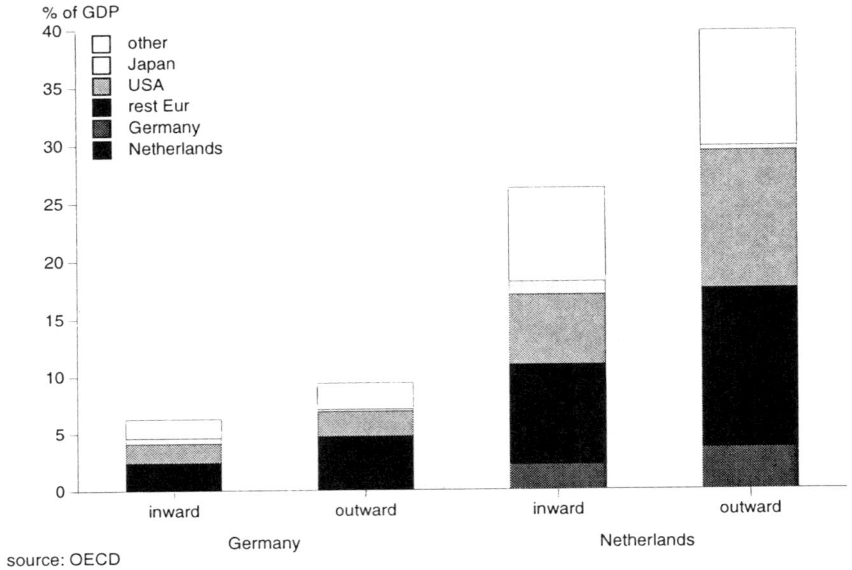

Figure 4.10 Foreign direct investment position of Germany and the Netherlands in 1992

Figure 4.10 shows the foreign direct investment position of Germany and the Netherlands. Amounting to almost 40 and 30 percent of GDP respectively, both inward and outward directed assets of the Netherlands considerably exceed German assets. The sizable international investment positions are a manifestation of the openness of the Dutch economy and the large share of multinationals in the enterprise sector.[16] In particular the relatively small amount of (inward) foreign physical assets invested in Germany raised concern with German policy makers about the attractiveness of Germany as an international investment location (BMWi, 1995). About 50% of (outward) foreign assets from German and Dutch enterprises has been invested in other European Unions countries, followed by the United States as the second important region.

Both the share of Germany in the outward investment stock of the Netherlands and the Dutch share in the German inward investment stock in Figure 4.10 show that the Netherlands is an important investor in Germany. Dutch enterprises

[16] Although it may be one of the relevant factors, the size of an economy is not the single explanatory factor for international differences in FDI. Over 1980-1990 outward direct investment flows exceeded 2% of GDP in the United Kingdom, Switzerland, Sweden and the Netherlands, amounted to about 1% of GDP in Australia, Belgium, Canada, Finland, France, Germany, Japan and Norway, and were about 0.5% of GDP or below in Austria, Denmark, Italy, Portugal, Spain and The United States (OECD, 1992).

Box 4.2 Foreign direct investments: background

Foreign direct investments (FDI) has contributed to the economic development in the post war period by enhancing capital formation and industrial development. During the late 1950s and 1960s FDI growth equalled twice the high growth rate of the world economy. Stagflation in the late 1970s and early 1980s manifested itself in a slowdown of foreign investment. During the second half of the 1980s FDI strongly accelerated. In the period 1983-1990 the annual nominal growth rate of FDI equals 26%, compared to 9% for international trade. In the nineties a new slowdown occurred. Both trade and FDI grew yearly with 4.5 % in the period, 1990-1995 (OECD, 1996b).

A number of factors account for the high growth rate of FDI since the mid-1980s. Positive prospects for international investments arose from the economic recovery and structural reform in OECD countries. The process of internationalization made an increasing number of firms expand their activities towards foreign markets. This process has been enhanced by technological developments, in particular information and communication technologies. In addition, more enterprises opted for investment in foreign countries instead of exporting from their home base. On the one hand, new technologies provided opportunities to benefit from the international division of factors of production, in particular in countries with low labour costs. On the other hand enterprises invested abroad to be closer to their consumers. Increased diversity and swift changes in consumer demand as well as the need to provide after sales services required production, design and distribution to be closer to the market. A final factor is the more positive attitude towards FDI by governments, who became aware of the importance of access to technology and know-how of foreign firms and removed impediments to inward FDI.

FDI is only partly associated with physical investments because it also includes cross-border mergers and acquisitions. The latter component increased considerably in the 1980s. The merger and acquisition activity was partly driven by the factors mentioned above, partly a reaction to challenges presented by political and economic integration. In Europe the process towards the single market is the obvious example.

Source: OECD (1992), OECD (1994b), Dicken (1986).

provide 18% of total foreign physical capital in Germany. These are all manufacturing enterprises, predominantly in the chemical, oil and electronics industry. The Netherlands is a less significant investment location for German assets abroad. The share of German assets in the Netherlands is only 8%, two third of this is invested in the services sector and one third in manufacturing. There is a clear relationship between trade pattern and direct investment contents.

Foreign direct investments facilitate the international transfer of knowledge by establishing contacts with sometimes considerably different technologies, consumer tastes and markets in other regions. From this point of view the outward orientation of the Dutch enterprise sector may be regarded as a counterbalance to the relatively disappointing domestic R&D situation described above. However, Slabbers and Verspagen (1994) cite research on innovation and learning, which indicates the importance of domestic R&D to benefit fully from technological developments abroad. Hence, the weak position of Dutch domestic R&D should not be neglected.

The Dutch outward orientation can also be found in intangible foreign investment data on the technology balance of payments.[17] In 1991 the overall balance of payments for foreign patents, licenses, trademarks, designs, inventions, know-how and closely related technical services by German and Dutch enterprises amount to minus 0,1% and 0,2% of GDP respectively (OECD, 1994a). This difference is less pronounced compared to the physical investment positions.

Conclusion. Before 1973 the growth of physical capital investments was much higher than afterwards, and other countries did much better in the period after 1973. On the whole the Dutch economy showed a weak position regarding the amount of domestic R&D activities. While Germany performed better in their R&D efforts, the Germans in turn had problems to attract sufficient foreign direct investment. Here the Netherlands did much better. At the list of top foreign investors, Dutch firms quite frequently appear. A special factor for the Netherlands has been the major impact of just five major multinational companies on the R&D investments of the whole economy; in certain years they allowed for about 80 percent of the total national effort.

4.5 Transport and Communication Infrastructure

Investment in Infrastructure. In a time of increasing internationalisation of about all economic activities, the quantity and quality of the transport and communications infrastructure is of great importance for the current and future performance of a national economy. Without adequate investments in infrastructure national competitiveness could be severely threatened.[18]

Accessibility by Road. Both Germany and the Netherlands are well accessible by road. The Netherlands and to a lesser extent Germany do have a high density in road infrastructure (length of road infrastructure divided by area). The area of Nordrhein-Westfalen and the contiguous provinces of Gelderland, Brabant and Limburg belong to the best accessible regions in Europe. However, these indicators presume unhindered road traffic. In reality, traffic congestions have become much more frequent. Both countries show a high degree of capacity utilisation: realised distance divided by length of total infrastructure (see EZ, 1995). It is therefore not surprising that they are strongly hit by congestion. Furthermore, certain densely populated areas like the Randstad in the Netherlands and the Ruhr and Munich area in Germany are hit even more strongly. Because transport activities are relatively more important for Dutch national economic performance, traffic

---

[17] Technology balance of payments data strongly underestimate the actual flows of knowledge, because they only measure flows accompanied by monetary payments.

[18] Most of the information of this paragraph is distilled from Brus (1996).

congestions are a bigger problem here. Therefore, Dutch road traffic scores lower in international comparison than that of Germany.

Accessibility by Rail. The same relative quality judgement is given to rail traffic. The accessibility by rail is better for Germany than for the Netherlands, due to the more dense rail infrastructure, and its stronger emphasis on long-distance freight transport by rail. This last element is related to the differences in country size and the presence of a competitive railway industry.

Accessibility by Inland and Sea Shipping. The accessibility by inland shipping is better for the Netherlands, due to its natural situation. The quality of this transport modality has also contributed to the outstanding position of the Rotterdam harbour, the biggest harbour in the world and also the biggest 'German' harbour. In 1995 the Rotterdam harbour had 42 percent of the total transshipment of the nine major harbours between Le Havre and Hamburg. Antwerp, at second place, realised 15 percent. Hamburg, with 10 percent, and Bremen, with 4 percent, are lagging far behind. Rotterdam especially has a strong position for oil and other bulk products. It also belongs, together with Hamburg and Antwerp, to the most efficient container harbours, the sector with the highest growth expectations. Rotterdam has gained this position because of its excellent accessibility for sea-traffic, with a short distance to the sea, very deep water, no locks and an excellent supply of harbour facilities. The German harbours face strong handicaps in accessibility. The consequence is that the costs of calling are the lowest in Rotterdam and much higher for Hamburg and Bremen. When Rotterdam is set at 100, Bremen scores 230 and Hamburg 2?4. At the same time, it has to be noted that Rotterdam is less diversified and so more dependent on its harbour than Hamburg.

The position of a harbour does not only depend on its accessibility for sea-traffic, but also on the quality of its hinterland connections. Here again Rotterdam scores very favourably, with a strong emphasis (58 percent) on the inland shipping modality, particularly for the international flows. Traffic by road counts for 38 percent, traffic by rail only for 4 percent. These percentages are about opposite for Hamburg and Bremen. Here traffic by rail has a share of about 46 percent, by road of 41 percent and by inland shipping of only 14 percent. That relatively high share for rail in German harbours is related to the lack of adequate inland waterways in the postwar Federal Republic. Rail infrastructure provided the alternative. The use of this transport mode was further stimulated by the existence of subsidised prices.

Accessibility of Air Traffic. Both countries have a major international airport, namely Frankfurt am Main for Germany[19] and Schiphol for the Netherlands. The growth of air traffic has been very impressive in recent years, both for passengers and for freight. So far, both airports have been able to meet this increase in demand. But for the near future, certain limitations are arising, mainly connected to available space, noise and other environmental aspects. According to some scenarios, already in 2005 maximum capacity for both airports could be reached. The attractiveness of an airport depends on its position in the country, on its hinterland connections, and on its position in the world wide hub and spoke system. Frankfurt seems to be in a more advantageous position for its accessibility and hinterland, both nationally and internationally. Less clear is its positioning on the world air traffic market. Here the bigger airport, namely Frankfurt, seems in a more advantageous position, but due to an earlier liberalisation of its air traffic Schiphol still is in a position to overcome its disadvantage.

More generally, both sea and air traffic are currently in a turbulent phase of increasing scale. In that process the bigger harbours or airports are in a better position to survive. A fewer number of ports will remain in a central position. In this respect Rotterdam seems better positioned than other harbours, and Frankfurt appears to lead in air ports. Whether this outcome will be realised depends, however, also on investment activities to keep the mainports attractive and to contain factors like congestion or environmental pollution, that could hamper that development. These activities should not be confined to investment in physical infrastructure alone. Clustering of logistic activities and deregulation and liberalisation of transport activities could also contribute.

Telecommunications. For telecommunications infrastructure, the Netherlands seems currently in a better position. First costs for calling are much lower (50 percent) than in Germany. Second, the number of connections per capita is higher in the Netherlands. And finally, the Netherlands seems to be further advanced the process of liberalising its telecommunications market. Recently, German firms have become more active here. It is expected that at 1st january 1998 the German telecommunications market will be fully liberalised. The expectations for both countries are that the costs for calling will decline considerably and that the supply of telecommunication services will increase.

Conclusion. For a remarkably long time both Germany and the Netherlands have paid little attention to their infrastructure. Investments in road infrastructure, in harbours and inland waterways, and in airports did not equal the strong increases

[19] Germany has furthermore a number of medium-sized airports like Düsseldorf and Munich.

in demand. Investments in public transport were even lower, sometimes below the level of replacement. The consequence has been that both in quantitative and qualitative terms the available infrastructure has not been able to contribute optimally to economic development. With the increased congestion on all forms of infrastructure, and in the light of the new requirements of globalisation, this attitude has started to change. For Germany unification meant another incentive. Investment in infrastructure now has a much higher preference. In both countries major programmes are set up to reduce the main bottlenecks and to meet the new demands.

4.6 Environment

In both Germany and the Netherlands (the deterioration of) environmental qualities has been a major topic in the public debate and in politics. This attention is strongly related to the population density, the level and structure of economic development and the relative value citizens from both countries have placed upon a clean and safe environment. Both countries show a relatively high level of expenditures for pollution control, as compared with other OECD countries. They are also below-average on certain pollution indicators, like industrial waste per unit GDP or municipal waste pro capita. On the other side, they both are above-average with respect to the use of nitrogenous fertilizers and pesticides. This short overview will focus on the emissions of CO_2, SO_2 and NO_x. At the end some remarks on waste production are given.

CO_2 Emissions. Emissions of CO_2 from energy use in Germany fell from 1114 millions of tons in 1980 to 897 millions of tons in 1994, representing an about 19 percent reduction, according to Figure 4.11. This reduction was solely due to the decreased CO_2 release of stationary sources, which took place despite growth in both industrial output and electricity generation, since emissions from mobile sources grew from 1980 till 1993 from 137.8 to about 184.6 millions of tons. This growth in transportation took place in both the old and the new Länder. However, in Western Germany the fall in emissions from stationary sources exceeded the rise in emissions from transportation. Per capita emissions amounted in 1992 to 11.5 ton in all of Germany and to 11.3 and 12.5 ton in its western and eastern parts, respectively. From 1980 to 1994, CO_2 emissions from energy use rose in the Netherlands by 8.2 percent: from 159 to 172 million tons. This was accounted for by the huge increase in emissions by mobile sources and by energy transforming industries, such as electricity and heat plants and refineries, despite the cut back in releases by the industrial sector and the sum of the agricultural, commercial and residential sectors. Finally, both per capita and GDP ratios are lower in western Germany than in the Netherlands (OECD, 1995; Statistisches Bundesamt 1995, 1996; CBS, 1997).

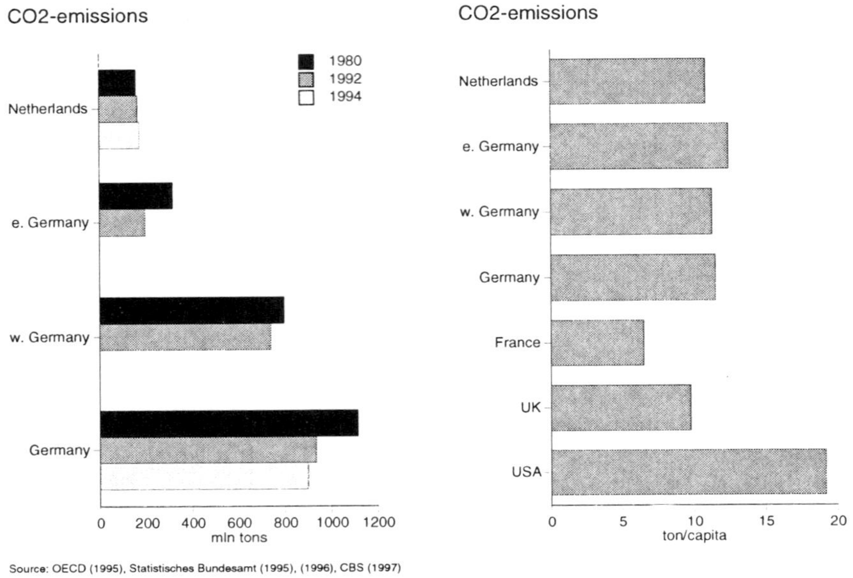

Figure 4.11 CO_2-emissions in millions of tons and ton per capita in 1992

SO_2 Emissions. Figure 4.12 shows that, during the last decade, SO_2 emissions in Germany declined by 60 percent: from 7.5 million tons in 1980 to 3.0 million tons in 1994. Most of this reduction was achieved in the old Länder due to the installation of desulphurisation equipment in power plants, improved energy efficiency and conversion to gas. Until 1990 emissions actually grew in the new Länder, mainly as a consequence of increases in production and the lack of pollution controls. In 1992 the new Länder accounted for 77.5 percent of total SO_2 emissions. From 1990 onwards, however, emissions of SO_2 have been declining steadily. Per capita emissions for total Germany amounted to 48.0 kilogram in 1992, with 13.4 kg per head in western Germany and 193.1 in eastern Germany. In the Netherlands, SO_2 emissions were reduced even more over the past decade: from 0.5 million tons in 1980 to 0.15 million ton in 1994, representing an about 70 percent reduction (OECD, 1995; Statistisches Bundesamt 1995, 1996; CBS, 1997).

NO_x Emissions. Emissions of nitrogen oxides (NO_x) have, as can be learned from Figure 4.13, declined by about 35 percent in Germany: from 3.4 million tons in 1980 to 2.2 million tons in 1994. Since emissions in the new Länder have only started a slow decline from 1990 onwards, the declining trend in NO_x emissions in overall Germany can largely be attributed to the decline in the old Bundesländer. For the greater part this trend can be attributed to the installation of catalytic converters in passenger cars and to NO_x reduction systems in power plants. In the

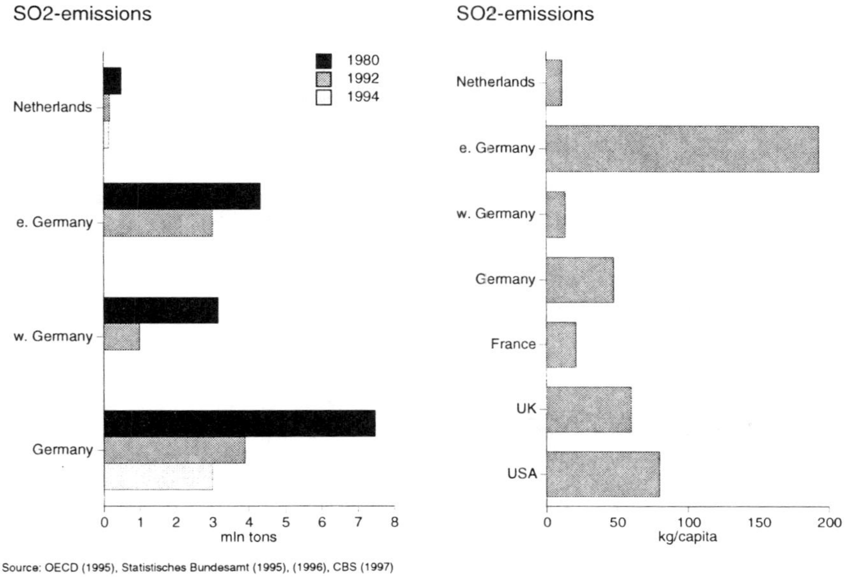

Figure 4.12 SO_2-emissions in millions of tons and kg per capita in 1992

new Länder NO_x emissions per capita are still lower than in western Germany. In the Netherlands, where the declining trend started in 1988, NO_x emissions decreased by 8 percent from 1980 till 1994, which contrasts poorly to the 17.1 percent reduction achieved in western Germany from 1980 till 1992. However, for Western Germany this reduction can be seen as a catching-up process since per capita emissions in 1992 turned out equal in both countries (OECD, 1995; Statistisches Bundesamt 1995, 1996; CBS, 1997).

Waste Production. Germany's industry produces almost twice as much waste as its Dutch counterpart: in 1994 it 59 kg/$1000 GDP in Germany against 32 in the Netherlands. The OECD average was 88 kg/$1000 in 1994, the OECD-Europe average 54. However, the amount of municipal waste per capita in the Netherlands is much higher (500 kg per head) than in Germany (360 kg per head).[20] The OECD average is 500 kg per head, the OECD-Europe average is only 400 kg per head.

[20] Industrial or production-related wastes include wastes from energy and water supply, construction, mining, manufacturing and hospitals. Municipal wastes concern household wastes, bulky wastes (*e.g.* old refrigerators) and commercial wastes (similar to household wastes).

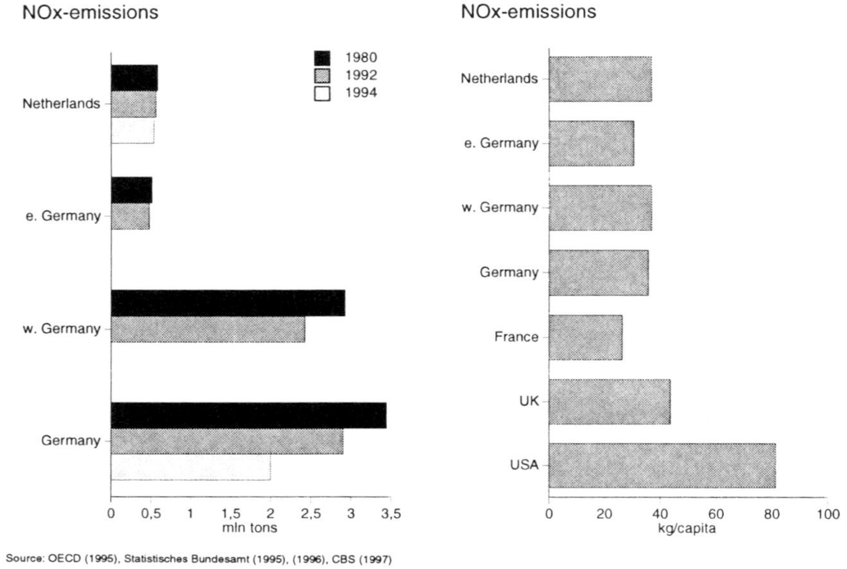

Figure 4.13 NO_x-emissions in millions of tons and kg per capita in 1992

Conclusions. To realise a cleaner and safer environment, both Germany and the Netherlands have been very active in the last decades. In certain areas, like the reduction in SO_2-emission, they have succeeded quite well. In other areas, however, both countries have been confronted with more difficulties. Even though emission reduction policies on the whole have been successful, the expected decline in emissions did not appear, because of the strong growth of production or consumption. One can only say that without such environmental policies the situation would have been worse.

4.7 Regional Patterns: Shifts in German Growth Centres

Germany has gone through some major changes in regional growth patterns, a long-term change of the centre of gravity to the south, and a recent, much more drastic change, the unification. The change in Germany towards the South has been present in the whole after-war period. In 1953 the income per capita for Nordrhein-Westfalen was 20%-points above average and for Bayern 17 %-points below average, in 1990 the first state was now 4%-points below average, the second 4 %-points above. After 1990, however, this southern movement has come more or less to a standstill.

This break after 1990 is strongly connected with the second change mentioned, namely the reunification of Germany. Suddenly, the country had 5 additional Länder, with a much lower GDP per capita. In 1991 their level was about 64 %-

points below German average. In the meantime, this situation has improved considerably, but in 1995 these eastern states were still 43 %-points below average. All the West German states are above average. An inverse relationship can be observed between the GDP per capita level and the unemployment rate. Especially the eastern states have shown a high level of unemployment.

The consequence of both changes have been a gradual moving-away of the German centre of gravity from the Netherlands. The German growth centres have been gradually moving south, and in recent years also eastward. Although the two Länder closest to the Netherlands, Niedersachsen and Nordrhein-Westfalen, are still large in terms of economic activity, their relative importance is declining. To keep their market share Dutch exporters should operate more on the faster growing, but also more distant German markets.

4.8 Conclusions

This chapter dealt with several structural characteristics of the German and Dutch economy. Both countries have gone through major changes in about all the areas investigated here. Successively the main conclusions are repeated here.

Germany saw the decline of its coal production and the increased dependence on energy imports. The Netherlands was luckier by finding natural gas in Slochteren which reduced its energy import dependency, but had also negative consequences for Dutch competitiveness. Both countries were confronted with a slow down of the population increase, with an increasing ageing and with the inflow of sizeable groups of foreigners. This slow down and ageing started earlier in Germany than in the Netherlands. The educational qualities of the population and hence of the potential labour force are high in both countries. Again Germany has so far had the lead, but also here the Netherlands seems to come closer. Labour supply has changed in both countries. There has been a significant decline for older men, and a strong increase for younger females. Especially Dutch females have changed their labour market behaviour.

Both countries have taken an active stance to reduce the burden on the environment. In certain areas, like the CO_2 reduction in Germany, the results were considerable, but in many cases these efforts have not been that successful yet, due to the high population density, the existing economic structure and the increase in production and consumption activities. Furthermore, Germany has experienced a moving of the economic centre of gravity towards the south, and in recent years to the east.

In the preceding chapter, it was concluded that the economic performance of both countries, after a long period of unprecedented growth, has slowed down after 1973. This change was also visible with the structural characteristics. Before 1973 private and public investments were relatively high, thereafter they slowed down considerably. Whether increasing structural problems caused a worsening in economic performance or that the causality runs the other way, is an issue that cannot be resolved here. Clear is that both economies could no longer cope adequately with adverse shocks. The jump in oil-prices, however strong its impact was, was not the real cause. Structural changes had occurred, but went more or less neglected. New competitors, new products, new technologies threatened existing production and employment facilities. Markets for products and production factors had lost much of the early post-war dynamism. Besides increasing regulation, it could be observed that both the German and Dutch society had realised such a strong growth in income and wealth that its inhabitants had become much more risk averse, less able to adjust themselves to the new challenges. Once the economic performance worsened after 1973, it became even more difficult to bring about these changes.

It took more than one decade to accept the lesson that continuous economic growth requires sufficient and timely changes. Because in the Netherlands the economic situation was really problematic in the early 80s, there the pressure to accept drastic and sometimes painful measures was stronger than in Germany, which experienced a less dramatic economic performance at that time. The difference in phasing and in harshness of policy measures between the two countries provides a valid explanation for the differences in economic performance in the last ten years. But another factor has to be added, namely the impact on the German economy of the unification. Even though the German economic performance seemed excellent around 1989, the underlying economic structure was not adequately adjusted yet to the new challenges. The unification initially masked this situation, but after a few years that same unification process had revealed the structural deficiencies very clearly. Now Germany faces the challenge to further remedy the deficiencies and adapt itself to changing circumstances. At the same time, the Netherlands should try to keep its momentum for change, removing old rigidities and avoiding new ones.

The following chapters will deal with the way the big question - how to deal with changing circumstances, new challenges and necessary adjustments - has been answered in both Germany and the Netherlands on a number of important markets, and which role actors, actions and institutions have played in that respect.

5 Governance of the Socio-economic Order: An Economic Perspective

After a presentation of indicators on welfare and wellbeing and a review of factors of production in the previous two chapters, this chapter marks the shift to the analysis of institutions. It focuses on institutions that affect the role of the state, divided into the socio-economic order and the political system, using the United States as a benchmark. The socio-economic order pertains to the relationships between the state, (representatives of) labour and capital and other social organisations.

Compared with the following chapters that deal with specific sets of institutions, this chapter is more on a meta level. It turns to the institutional environment and political processes that guide the development of specific institutional arrangements. By consequence, it directly touches upon the strong and weak elements of the German and Dutch economic models. As indicated in Chapter 1, the popular view on these models changed considerably in recent years: Dutch disease turned into Delta and the Dutch consultation economy turned from a liability into an asset. In contrast, perceptions on the German social market economy drifted away from vigour and solidarity towards structural rigidity and resistance to change. The aim of this chapter is to review these popular perceptions from a meta level as well. Popular perceptions frequently to a considerable extent result from rough insights and recent information on the short-term economic situation. Instead it may be more fruitful to look at structural factors that underlie the socio-economic order and political system in Germany and the Netherlands and analyze how these affect adaptability to change.

This chapter aims to address the socio economic order and politics from an economic-theoretical perspective. Of course a thorough discussion of these subjects may easily exceed the space available in one chapter. Also the subjects can be approached from many different scientific backgrounds (history, political science, sociology) and within these sciences various angles can be taken. Therefore, in line with the entire study this chapter's economic-theoretical perspective hopes to contribute some building blocks to the trial and error process of social innovation (compare Chapter 1). Yet, that may be fruitful to add depth to popular perceptions.

From an economic perspective, two different models characterize the role of the state in the United States compared to Germany and the Netherlands. In the United States the role of the state is limited, to a large extent it leaves adjustment to private actors and to market processes. In the competitive American model individual adaptability ranks high and government failure causes scepticism about government intervention in the economy. In Germany and the Netherlands, cooperation and negotiation between the state and private agents within an elaborate institutional environment characterize the role of the state. Collective adaptability plays a distinct role. Social security protects workers against the most severe consequences of the process of creative destruction. In the cooperative German and Dutch models, the state is more actively involved in economic adjustment.[1]

The structure of this chapter is as follows. Section 5.1 starts with a review of the main features of the socio-economic order in the United States, Germany and the Netherlands. To present a stylized analytical background and to provide a historical dimension, the comparison focuses on the main features of the socio-economic order in Germany and the Netherlands. These features fitted in well with social, technological and economic conditions in the post-war golden age (1948-1973). Yet, many of these still play an important role today: changes in the socio-economic order develop only gradually. In a comparable approach, Section 5.2 presents some highlights of the political system in the United States, Germany and the Netherlands.[2] Subsequently, Section 5.3 reviews tensions that create challenges for reform in the Dutch and German socio-economic order. These tensions on the one hand comprise the effects of large economic shocks, such as stagflation in the 1970s and 1980s and German unification. On the other hand, tensions follow from gradually unfolding trends in the social, technological en international environment of the two countries. The assessment in Section 5.4 addresses the strengths and weaknesses of the institutions that affect the role of the state in the light of the challenges facing the two countries.

5.1 The Socio-economic Order

From the perspective of the United States, many common features characterize the role and position of the state in Germany and the Netherlands. In recent decades,

---

[1] In a third model, which may be called the control model, the state relatively strongly directs economic development by means of active industrial policy, supported by macroeconomic policy and education. The state develops a coherent vision of the future that provides a focal point for economic agents to organize their activities. France is a European example, but the model also applies to Asian newly industrialising countries such as South Korea or Singapore (see Chang and Rowthorn, 1995). This model will not be discussed in detail.

[2] Of course another a well-known difference between the role of the state in United States compared with Germany and the Netherlands concerns the extent of social protection. The next chapter addresses social security and the welfare state.

a sceptical view on the role of government and an emphasis on individual freedom characterize the United States (CPB, 1992a: 57-63).[3] Public expenditure, social security outlays and taxes are among the lowest in the industrialized world, whereas market incentives and property rights are well developed. Extensive reliance on litigation and the predominant role of price competition characterize the United States as a low-trust society (Casson, 1991). In contrast, Germany and the Netherlands feature a more positive attitude towards government and cooperation. Public opinion is less convinced of government failure and more inclined to cooperation (Mansbridge, 1994).

This section analyzes the main features of the socio-economic order. Because of the similarities between Germany and the Netherlands from the perspective of the United States, Sections 5.1.1 and 5.1.2 first describe and compare the main features of the socio-economic order in the competitive United States model vis-a-vis the cooperative German and Dutch model. Section 5.1.3 reviews the conditions that support the cooperative and the competitive model and explains why in particular the cooperative model flourished during the post-war period 1948-1973. More specific differences between the German socio-economic order, known as the social market economy,[4] and that in the Netherlands, known as the consultation economy, constitute the subject matter of Section 5.1.4.

5.1.1 A Competitive and a Cooperative Model

The United States. Competition and control form the two main coordination mechanisms in the socio-economic order of the United States: the state applies control to safeguard competition. As a result of an individualistic ethic and a sceptical view on the role of government, the United States is characterized by a

---

[3] Distrust of government intervention in particular is high among authors in the individualistic-contractarian school of thought (Von Mises, Nozick, Hayek, Friedman and Buchanan), who confine the functions of the state primarily to the enforcement of the law and of private contracts and to the provision of public goods and services, like national defence. In all other cases government intervention is not legitimate since it violates individual freedom. For more details and references see the review of the literature of state intervention in Chapter 1 of Chang (1994).

[4] Müller-Armack coined the phrase 'social market economy'. In the 1920s and 1930s neoliberal economists, Von Mises, Rüstow and Röpke, and during and shortly after the Second World War representatives of the Freiburger Schule, Böhm and Eucken, laid the foundations for the philosophy behind the social market economy. Their personal views and the practical implementation of the social market economy by Ludwig Erhard after the Second World War have been described extensively in the literature (see for instance Giersch *et al.*, 1992; Lampert, 1992; Hamel, 1994; Watrin, 1994; Schlecht, 1990 and references cited there). Box 5.4 below contains a short review of the historical foundations of the social market economy.

Box 5.1 The United States government between private interest and public purpose

Shifts between emphasis on private interest versus public purpose characterize politics in the United States. In the nineteenth century the cycle covered democratization in the 1830s (public purpose), government domination by slaveholders in the 1840s and 1850s (private interest), abolition of slavery in the 1860s (public purpose), followed by a 30 year period of conservative rule (private interest). The start of the twentieth century witnessed a shift in politics to the public purpose in the two decades of the Progressive Era, during which Theodore Roosevelt and Woodrow Wilson democratized American institutions. In contrast, Republican restoration during the New Era of the 1920s stressed free market and free trade. Coolidge and Hoover advocated a self regulating economy led by the free market in which the sole task of government is to provide favourable conditions for private enterprise.

The social deprivation of the Great Depression inspired Franklin Roosevelt's New Deal, which forms the strongest case of public-purpose policy in the United States. The broad-based policy package ranged from reform of the financial system to restore the banking system, public provision of employment, social security measures to support the unemployed, support and planning of agriculture and manufacturing. Roosevelt aimed at collaboration between government, industry and agriculture to fight deflation, unemployment and falling real incomes. He considered it the duty of government to secure the people's right to employment, medical care, education and a reasonable standard of living also in case of sickness and old-age.

After the 1950s in which conservatism, the cold war, strong anti-communism and private interest dominated politics, the 1960s started out as the time of Kennedy's New Frontier and Johnson's Great Society. Kennedy rejected the idea of the national government as an intruder or adversary. His administration tackled unemployment with tax reductions, investment tax credits and worker training programs. Wage-price guideposts were meant to control inflation. Johnson continued Kennedy's war on poverty. Remarkably, the Nixon administration proposed a guaranteed minimum income and indexed social security benefits. However, the 1960s and 1970s ended in turmoil with the Vietnam war, violent protest, deceleration of economic growth and Watergate.

By the end of the 1970s the perception of government intervention changed again. In 1978 the Democrat Carter stated that the government cannot set goals, define a vision, eliminate poverty, reduce inflation or save the cities. During the Reagan administration in the 1980s scepticism of government assumed an even stronger ideological component: 'Government is not the solution to our problem, government is the problem.' Ideology strongly advocated private initiative, individual freedom, incentives and small government. Cuts in public spending, tax reduction, welfare reform and deregulation appeared high on the agenda. The public budget deficit soared. By the end of the 1980s concerns arose about the quality of US primary and secondary education, about low investments in physical infrastructure and about the lack of institutions that encourage cooperation.

Source: Adams (1977), Schlesinger (1986), Dertouzos et al. (1989), CPB (1992a)

relatively small government sector. An important task of the state is to provide public goods, including protection of atomistic market relationships, *i.e.* to secure property rights and to endorse the enforcement of formal contracts. Box 5.1 shows that in the course of time the emphasis on private interest versus public purpose shifted in the United States. In the 1980s public policy centres on safeguarding individual freedom and is alien to cooperation (Therborn, 1992: 30; Kenworthy, 1996: 57). Moreover, the American Constitution strongly protects individual rights and strictly separates legislative, executive and judiciary bodies. Individuals and organisations have wide-ranging possibilities to gain protection and exercise their rights through private lawsuits.

The state achieves its aim to protect competition and universal individual rights through strict application of control measures. American public authorities 'implement regulations rather formally and inflexibly and are unwilling to take account of specific circumstances of individual firms' (Van Waarden, 1997: 64). Transgressors face heavy fines. Authorities in the United States strongly advocate a uniform treatment of all citizens and organisations, *i.e.* they apply rules and regulations in a similar way to all agents involved. Negotiations with individual agents to take account of their specific situation arouse suspicion. The risk of being summoned to appear in court on the accusation of unequal treatment, may well strengthen these policies.

Strict enforcement and control make relationships between the state and business adversarial (Van Waarden, 1997: 56, 65; Katzenstein, 1989: 348). In a sense, a competitive struggle to weaken and reinforce regulation marks the relationship between business and government. From the perspective of American companies, the state primarily functions as a regulator. Strict and inflexible enforcement of regulations arouses resistance. Companies oppose regulatory measures and try to appeal to specific decisions in court. Companies also try to influence government through extensive lobbying activities and may even persuade a regulatory agency to design regulation at the industry's advantage (regulatory capture). This feeds the perception of interest associations as rent seekers and invokes further calls for strict enforcement of regulations. Hence, government and business are engaged in a low-trust relationship, in which actions of one party reinforce antagonism on the side of the other party.

Germany and the Netherlands. In Germany and the Netherlands cooperative exchange guides coordination in relationships between the state and representatives of labour and capital.[5] Naming already illustrates the difference with the competitive American model: in the German and Dutch model organisations of

---

[5] In the socio-economic order cooperative exchange concerns bargained consultation and cooperation between peak associations of labour and capital, and in some cases also the government.

Box 5.2 Why does cooperative exchange fit in the social market economy?

The founding principles of the German social market economy contain a high degree of liberalism. They emphasize the free market economy as the dominant economic order, since the market economy promotes individual freedom and self-realization. Individual freedom requires both safeguards against government coercion and against concentration of economic power in the hands of companies or pressure groups. Moreover, the philosophy behind the social market economy stresses thinking in terms of institutional spheres ('Denken in Ordnungen'). This explains why some of the founders of the postwar German socio-economic order are known as Ordo-liberals (Giersch et al., 1992: 26, n30).

An important question is how to reconcile these liberal features with cooperative exchange, which also occupies a prominent place in the German socio-economic order. Two partly overlapping interpretations come to the fore, one stresses historical undercurrents, the other focuses on congruent factors between the main principles of the social market economy and the cooperative model.

The historical interpretation draws on the roots of the German socio-economic order. Box 5.4 shows that the liberal character of the social market economy can be understood from experiences in twentieth century German history. However, Crouch (1993) and Lehmbruch (1996) argue that cooperative exchange has even deeper roots (compare Box 5.3 for the Dutch case). In the sixteenth and seventeenth century the German Empire never became an absolutist state. By consequence, it did not solve the religious conflict between Catholicism and Protestantism by privileging one of them, but by designing cooperative institutions based on the principle of joint representation (Lehmbruch, 1996). Moreover, before Germany became a unitary state under Prussian domination in 1870, its constituent territories developed institutions that built on medieval guild structures instead of confronting these. Even after 1870 the authoritarian government of the Second Empire shared political space with cartels as associations of interests. During the 1890s, expanding social-democratic trade unions used existing representational institutions, such as elected boards that managed local sickness funds, to establish their position in the socio-economic order (Crouch, 1993: 307, 322, 323). These factors underscore Streeck's (1995) proposition that the German postwar economic order constitutes a historical compromise between postwar liberal capitalism and more ancient christian-democratic and social-democratic countervailing forces.

Possibly as a result of these historical undercurrents, several features of the cooperative model, expounded in Section 5.1, fit in the principles of the social market economy. In the cooperative model, interest associations partly obtain a public authority status. In other words, they become 'Ordnungsfaktoren' in the social market economy. Furthermore, sharing political space restricts the power of the state. At the same time, cooperative exchange controls the impact of interest groups on the state by structuring their mutual relationships. In these respects, Lehmbruch (1995) also alludes to the congruence between cooperative and federalist elements in the German socio-economic order. However, handing over public authority to interest associations reduces democratic accountability. Finally, in so far as it gives a voice to representatives of labour, the cooperative model touches upon the social aspects of the social market economy.

labour and capital are often called social partners. Central or sectoral interest organisations have a solid historical foundation in Germany and the Netherlands (compare Box 5.2 and Box 5.3), whereas they are much less prominent in the United States. For example, no central employers organisation exists in the United States (Therborn, 1992: 30). German and Dutch interest organisations not only negotiate wages, but also perform other socio-economic roles. German peak organisations of employers and workers are involved in the organisation of the vocational education program (see also Chapter 9). In both countries the social partners perform a role in the practical implementation and supervision of social security (see Chapter 6). Lehmbruch (1996) refers to German health care institutions as an example of successful cooperative exchange (see also Chapter 14).

In the cooperative model, the state shares political space with interest associations in a structured way (Crouch, 1993). In specific policy fields, the state provides an institutional environment in which cooperative exchange can function. For instance, German and Dutch institutional arrangements support cooperative exchange by imposing compulsory membership of interest associations, like in German health care, or by legally extending agreements between interest associations to non-affiliated actors. In addition, in some policy fields interest associations obtain independent authority. For example, German 'Tarifautonomie' strongly curbs the impact of the state on wage formation (see Chapter 9). Also the German state shares authority with peak organisations in designing the vocational training curriculum. In the United States, the market orientation and the legal tradition geared to safeguarding individual freedom counteract these types of *formalized* political power of interest associations.

5.1.2 The Two Main Models Compared

What light can the analytical framework of Chapter 2 shed on the two models? In general, the main characteristics of the models described above show that the competitive model focuses governance on the market failures associated with market power and public goods, whereas the cooperative model also takes into account specificity and returns to scale. More specifically, differences between coordination through competition and control in the competitive model and coordination through cooperative exchange in the cooperative model suggest the presence of trade-offs that affect the performance of the socio-economic order.

To identify the relevant trade-offs a distinction has to be made between the level of private economic actors and the level of the state, in particular the executive branch. Trade-offs differ between these levels. In addition, in order to properly analyze the cooperative model a third intermediate level has to be taken into consideration, because this model embodies three types of relationships. Chapter 9 elaborates on the first of these: bargained interaction between peak level and sectoral organisations. Here the focus is on the two other types of relationships: the

Box 5.3 The roots of the Dutch socio-economic order

An underlying reason for the Dutch inclination towards cooperative exchange is that the establishment of a unitary state in the Netherlands took a relatively long period of time. In the 16th and 17th century, in contrast to other states, the Netherlands did not abandon the corporatist order of the previous era. When countries like France or Spain changed to centralized absolute monarchies, in the Dutch Republic the seven Provinces kept substantial autonomy. Only in 1803-1813, the French occupation established a unitary state with a centralized administration in the Netherlands.

The 'school issue' of 1878 initiated the emergence of confessional political parties and together with the response to working class protest laid the foundations of pillarization. Calvinists and Roman Catholics strongly opposed the rather general humanist and Christian values taught in public schools and required the government to subsidize their private schools. To substantiate their demands, they founded their own political parties. Protests against poor working conditions during industrialisation fostered socialism. To safeguard their workers from socialist influence, Calvinists and Catholics established their own unions next to the socialist trade union. Subsequently, also employers' organisations became organised along the cleavage lines between Calvinists, Catholics and Socialists.

In the 1910s the consociational model of democracy crystallized in the Netherlands. The consociational model forms an alternative to the Westminster majoritarian model of democracy and rest on the fact that strong cleavages are conducive to political stability in pluralistic societies. Strong cleavages anchor political parties' electorates and enable party leaders to partly accommodate their interests to those of other parties while forming coalitions.

Consociationalism developed into extensive pillarization when in the 1920s and 1930 each subculture established and expanded its own social organisations in the fields of politics, industrial relations, education, health care, culture, housing, and social security. Pillar organizations not only became distribution channels for government funds but also became involved in policy formation and policy implementation.

Initiated by mass unemployment during the Great Depression, ideas on industrial organisation converged between Catholics and Socialists, which laid the foundation for the Dutch socio-economic order after the Second World War. Based on the principle of subsidiarity (see Box 5.5), Catholic ideas on decentralized industrial councils stressed the autonomy of lower level social organs, legalized by the state. The fear of losing workers to socialism shifted the Catholic view from organic bottom-up growth of socio-economic institutions towards a larger degree of state intervention to fight unemployment. After the failed revolution of 1918, Socialists favoured state intervention to direct the economy, culminating in the 1935 Plan of Labour. In addition, Socialists proposed a system of industrial boards with a public legal status in an attempt to gain support from the Catholic working class. The convergence of Catholic and Social Democrat ideas led to a so-called Roman-Red coalition in 1939 and prepared the emergence of a socio-economic order based on cooperative exchange after the Second World War. Hence, in contrast to the social-democratic Nordic model, the Dutch model descends from both Christian Democracy and Social Democracy.

relationship between an association and its members, and the relationship between an association and the state. Table 5.1 below summarizes the basic trade-offs that come forward in this section.

Trade-offs at the Private Level. In the competitive model individual actors and society as a whole benefit from flexibility and diversity in the economy. The economic order provides many possibilities to satisfy individual preferences and to adjust behaviour to changing circumstances. Incentives keep agents alert and active.

Compared to the competitive model, cooperative exchange restricts the capacity to act of individual members of an association. In a well-functioning cooperative model, associations are strong enough to effectively defend and implement the result of their agreements among their members. Moreover, their legal position shields associations from outsiders that may free ride on their agreements or may jeopardize their agreements, for instance by undercutting a wage bargain (compare Geelhoed, 1996b: 26). By consequence, compared to the American model, individual members forego part of their discretion to pursue short-term gains (Hemerijck, 1992: 44; Streeck and Schmitter, 1991: 232, 237).

However, cooperative exchange entails also advantages for individual members. By getting organised, members may be able to better protect their interests. Unions strengthen the power of workers against individual employers, employers unite in employers' organisations to counteract union power. Social security reinforces collective protection in Germany and the Netherlands. In the United States, flexibility and legal action provide some degree of protection for individuals and organisations, but collective protection is much weaker. By consequence, the German and Dutch socio-economic orders promote solidarity, whereas in the United States incentives play a more dominant role.

In Germany and the Netherlands, members of associations may benefit also from specific investments that would not emerge in a competitive relationship. Reducing individual ex-post bargaining options by delegating bargaining power to higher level associations, prevents individual parties to renege on ex-ante agreements and promotes long-term relationship-specific investments. Individual members are more committed and less vulnerable to opportunistic behaviour of other parties.[6] To illustrate, both employees and owners in a company may benefit from a higher amount of firm-specific human capital. In contrast, the American model provides more flexibility for individual workers or companies to adjust to specific circumstances. Adjustment processes may entail a fast writing off of specific investments. Foreseeing this risk, private actors will be less inclined to make specific investments. As such, the German and Dutch socio-economic orders

[6] Chapter 9 more elaborately addresses these issues.

Table 5.1 Trade-offs related to the socio-economic order

	United States	Germany, Netherlands
Private agents	*competition*	*cooperative exchange*
– protection	incentives	solidarity
– bargaining level	flexibility	commitment
– combined action	diversity	scale or scope
Government	*control*	*cooperative exchange*
– policy implementation	enforcement	commitment
– policy differentiation	scale	diversity
– interest groups	certainty	internalisation

promote commitment among private agents, whereas the American model promotes flexibility.

In addition, members of German and Dutch associations may gain from economies of scale and scope. Branch organisations and employers' organisations enable companies to cooperate in common advertising campaigns, to reach agreements on technological standards, to facilitate diffusion of knowledge, or to formulate and enforce quality norms (Weder and Grubel, 1993). Unions and employers organisations combine expertise in designing and administering vocational training programs (compare Chapter 9). Of course, compared to the competitive United States model, combined action implies that individual companies have less opportunities to develop specific products or processes. Hence, where cooperative exchange in Germany and the Netherlands enables the exploitation of economies of scale or scope, the American socio-economic order promotes diversity.

Trade-offs at the Level of the State. Just as cooperative exchange restricts the capacity to act of the members of an association, it restricts also the capacity to act of the state. By granting associations independent authority, the state loses the possibility to intervene in specific policy fields. In addition, not only an interventionist government foregoes part of its discretion in formulating policy and policy objectives, cooperative exchange affects also the intentions of a non-interventionist state because it diminishes market interaction and individual freedom.

Besides restricting government policy, rigidities and mixed responsibilities in the cooperative model may raise transaction costs. The deliberation process often is lengthy and may produce second-best compromise solutions (CPB, 1992b: 96; SER, 1992: 115). The division of responsibilities between participants is not always clear. In particular, the democratic accountability of associations is low (Skidelsky, 1995: 23). Their autonomy may make it a tedious process to adjust their behaviour towards changed circumstances that are outside the scope of their current bargaining interests but that affect the position of society as a whole or of the government. The performance of the Dutch socio-economic order in the 1970s forms a case in point (see Section 5.3.1).

So the question arises, why would the state share political space with interest associations? In other words, why does cooperative exchange constitute a reasonable alternative for the government to the combination of competition and control?

A first part of the answer, is that the above advantages of cooperative exchange for members of the associations also comprise advantages from a social welfare point of view. If people are relatively risk-averse, the political process will favour institutions that promote solidarity. The welfare-enhancing returns on relationship-specific investments may induce the government to institutionally support commitment. Analogously, promoting economies of scale or scope may improve welfare as well. Thus, to raise national welfare the government may strive for solidarity, commitment and returns to scale or scope.

A second part of the answer is that cooperative exchange forms a transaction costs effective coordination mechanism to reach those objectives. Solidarity, commitment and economies of scale require a certain degree of cooperation and collective action. As described above, atomistic competition does not support these objectives. At the other extreme, cooperative exchange may also outperform government intervention. Cooperative exchange strengthens commitment and credibility in the relationships between individual members, the associations and the government. Compared to the government, associations are closer to their members, are more knowledgable of their members' situation and preferences, can communicate propositions to their members by taking recourse to a common set of values and perceptions, and are able to react more quickly to changes in the position of their members. Therefore, associations are more accountable to their members compared to the government, which implies that the credibility of their actions is higher (Streeck and Schmitter, 1991; compare also CEPR, 1993). The state may well be able to formulate the same policy as the outcome of the bargain between the interest associations, but enforcing the policy will be more difficult. Because the state has a broader set of objectives than the relatively homogeneous associations, the credibility is lower that the state's policy has fully taken the interests of the members of the association into account. Moreover, compared to the associations, members face more difficulties to monitor the state and steer its actions towards their intentions, which also lowers credibility.

These reasons strengthen commitment in a socio-economic order based on cooperative exchange. On the other side of the trade-off, enforcement constitutes the strength of the competitive model. The experience in the United States teaches that a considerable amount of control is needed to protect competition in a strongly competitive economy. In the United States the enforcement of control measures tends to be relatively strict and inflexible to prevent abuse. The discussion above shows that enforcement in the cooperative model may pose problems. Hence, the competitive and cooperative model are on two sides of the trade-off between enforcement and commitment (see Table 5.1).

In addition, other improvements to policy effectiveness comprise a benefit of sharing political space with interest associations (see also SER, 1992: 114–118). Although policy formulation may require more time, the government is able to implement a policy relatively fast by appealing to the social responsibilities of the social partners. Compared to strictly enforced uniform control measures, government policies may differentiate more between separate associations. At a lower level, the associations have some leeway to closer accommodate different preferences among their members. Moreover, in formulating its policy the government may also gain from the varied expertise of interest associations. Thus, government policies benefit from diversity in the cooperative relationship with the associations. In contrast, control in the American model enables the exploitation of economies of scale: similar treatment of all agents involved requires uniform policy measures. Hence, as shown by Table 5.1, with respect to policy differentiation a trade-off between scale and diversity arises.

Furthermore, a structured relationship between the state and a limited number of encompassing interest associations reduces the probability that lobbying by a multitude of small interest groups affects government policy in an obscure way. Actions of small scale interest groups may invoke negative external effects on society. Encompassing associations are large enough that the results of their actions feed back into their own preferences. Because they internalize the external effects of their actions, this steers their actions closer to the common good. The competitive model aims at certainty by applying strong control measures to curb lobbying activities of a multitude of interest groups. Hence, the position of the American socio-economic order is closer to certainty, whereas internalization characterizes the German and Dutch model.

The trade-offs in Table 5.1 explain the at first sight paradoxical position of government in the competitive model. On the trade-offs the American socio-economic order is closer to enforcement, scale and certainty, *i.e.* on the opposite side of flexibility, diversity and experimentation. These features are required to support a private economic order that stands out on flexibility, diversity and incentives. Table 5.1 also makes clear that the position of private agents and the position of the state in the cooperative model are less far apart.

5.1.3 Social, Technological and International Conditions

The strengths and weaknesses of the competitive and the cooperative model depend on the social, technological and international economic environment of the socio-economic order (see Table 5.2). The cooperative model performs well in a social environment characterized by stable and homogeneous preferences, by homogeneous social structures, and by risk aversion. Stability and homogeneity strengthen

Table 5.2 Conditions supporting the competitive and cooperative model

	Competitive model	Cooperative model
Preferences	quickly changing	stable
	heterogeneous	homogeneous
	risk taking	risk averse
Social structures	heterogeneous	homogeneous
Technology	radical	incremental
(International) economy	stable	volatile
	homogeneous	diverse

the bond between associations and their members.[7] In contrast, heterogeneity and quickly changing preferences are more conducive to the competitive model. Heterogeneity makes it more difficult for large interest associations to represent the preferences of all its members. The lack of homogeneous social structures facilitates free rider behaviour by individual members, which threatens cohesion of the associations. In addition, risk aversion fits with solidarity and collective protection offered by the cooperative model, whereas a preference for risk taking is closer to the incentive structures provided by the competitive model.

Radical technological innovations and a volatile (international) economic environment also bring the strengths of the competitive model to the fore. Section 2.4.3 argues that competition fits in well with quickly changing new technologies, whereas cooperative exchange supports incremental technological development in relatively well-known technologies. The flexibility of the competitive model enables quick adjustment to a volatile environment. In contrast, a stable economic environment makes it more easy for interest associations to foresee the outcome of their negotiations and to reach an agreement and thus supports the performance of the cooperative model.

These conditions show why the German and Dutch model suited the post-war period well.[8] In essence, the period 1949-1973 showed a virtuous circle in which stable conditions supported cooperative institutions and the building of cooperative institutions strengthened economic stability. The main type of conditions conducive to cooperative exchange included stable and homogeneous preferences, catching-up of technology, and a fast growing international economy. The 'reconstruction mentality' after the Second World War and the homogeneous social structures of the 1950s and early 1960s established relatively uniform and stable preferences. The experience of the Great Depression and Second World War may have

---

[7] Compare the discussion on the Dutch consociational model of democracy in Box 5.3.

[8] For more details on Germany and the Netherlands see for instance Giersch *et al.* (1992), de Wolf and Driehuis (1980), van der Wee (1983), Hemerijck (1992), van Ark *et al.* (1996).

generated risk aversion and a demand for solidarity. Catching-up of technology also demands cooperative exchange. High growth of world markets and the liberalisation of international trade created returns to scale and scope. Cooperative exchange facilitated companies to reap the revenues from scale and scope.

Institutions established during this period substantially contributed to economic stability (van der Wee, 1983: 48). International trade liberalisation and cooperation promoted an almost uninterrupted growth of world trade. The expansion of social security together with the system of progressive income taxes contributed to income stability over the business cycle. A higher share of cyclically less sensitive government expenditure in domestic absorption also dampened aggregate demand fluctuations. Hence, institutions contributed to an economic environment in which cooperative exchange could flourish.

In contrast, conditions in the United States to a larger extent supported the competitive model. The American society is much more pluriform and heterogeneous than society in most European countries, including Germany and the Netherlands. The American 'frontier mentality' more closely fits in with an environment of risk taking and incentives. The United States is strong in technological development through radical innovations, which also concurs with the competitive model.

5.1.4 The Social Market Economy and the Consultation Economy Compared

Despite their similarities viewed from the perspective of the United States, on a closer look the German and Dutch socio-economic orders differ with respect to the role of government in cooperative exchange. In particular during 1946-1982 but to some extent nowadays as well, formalized policy coordination among government and social partners constitutes an important difference between the Dutch consultation economy and the German social market economy. The latter model features more separate roles of private and public actors.

In the Netherlands after the Second World War, motivated by the need for solidarity and industrial peace to enhance economic reconstruction, representatives of employees and employers supported the founding of the bipartite Foundation of Labour in 1945, aimed at consultation between employers and employees on labour conditions, and the threepartite Social Economic Council in 1950, aimed at consultation over socio-economic policy.[9] Until 1995, a legal obligation existed

[9] The 1950 legislation established the Social Economic Council as the peak organisation of the Statutory Trade Organisation ('Publiekrechtelijke Bedrijfsorganisatie'), an elaborate system of vertical commodity boards and horizontal industrial boards. Because initiatives to structure the economy through commodity boards and industrial boards failed, the main task of the Social Economic Council shifted to an advisory council to the government on socio-economic policy (Hemerijck, 1992: 151).

for the government to consult the Social Economic Council on issues of socio-economic policy. The government favoured the creation of these institutions to increase control over macro-economic variables, in particular to stimulate wage moderation in order to enhance economic growth.

In contrast, the desire to constrain the power of the state and restrict the partisan influence of employers' and employees' organisations on government policy, motivated separate roles of government and social partners in the social market economy. After the Second World War, the German socio-economic order lacks formal consultative institutions (Slomp, 1990: 129). The German Constitution prohibits active participation of the social partners in public policy formation. Wage formation is autonomous ('Tarifautonomie'), which means that unions and employers' organisations bargain over wages without any intervention of the government (Lampert, 1992: 240). 'The state was regarded as a possible danger to society and democracy rather than as a partner in bargaining. It was better, many agreed, to keep the state at a distance' (Slomp, 1990: 129). The experience with the impact of 'cartels of employees and employers' (Watrin, 1994: 19) on government during the Weimar Republic formed another reason for independent wage bargaining (compare Box 5.4).

Experiments with formalized concertation between government and representatives of labour and capital were short-lived in Germany. In 1967 the Minister of Economics Schiller initiated the Concerted Action: regular meetings between representatives of government, the Bundesbank, the social partners and economists (Giersch *et al.*, 1992: 148; Smyser, 199[illegible]: 19). Aim of the Concerted Action meetings was to guide the participants on the levels of wages, prices and investment that were most suited from an economic perspective. As such, the meetings remained within the boundaries set by the Constitution (see also Geelhoed, 1996b: 23). This is manifest also from other characteristics of the Concerted Action. Coordination concerned only the provision of information, parties did not conclude any formal agreements and the meetings were not institutionalized in a specific organisational model like the Dutch Foundation of Labour and the Social Economic Council. The meetings were not very successful. Already in 1970 and 1971 representatives of labour and capital hardly responded to the guidance given and in 1977 unions quit Concerted Action.

Commitment versus Flexibility. The stronger interaction between the associations and government policy in the Netherlands involves government more closely in the bargaining process. In times that the model operates well, this constitutes a way for the government to steer bargaining towards the common good. It strengthens commitment between the government and the social partners and raises the prospects that the social partners internalize the external effects of their actions. However, three-party cooperative exchange complicates the bargaining process and may hamper enforcement of the agreements. Deliberately or not, the two other bargaining partners may collude against the government. Another disadvantage is

Box 5.4 Historical foundations of the social market economy

The basic principles of the social market economy can be traced to German history and the interpretation of history by the founders of the social market economy. According to this interpretation, private economic power eroded the liberal economy of the German Reich of 1871. In the absence of policies to preserve competition, monopolies and cartels rose to economic power and gained political influence as well. By the end of the 1870s, Bismarck changed German economic policy from liberal to protectionist. In 1897, the Supreme Court formally allowed cartels, which legalised the German cartel economy.

Money creation by the government-controlled Reichsbank contributed to the early 1920s hyper inflation. The central bank largely financed the First World War government expenditure by issuing notes, leading to a sixfold increase of cash in circulation. After the war, the government financed the large reparation payments imposed on Germany also by monetary expansion. Inflation surged from 70% in 1919 to $4 * 10^{12}\%$ *by November 1923 until a currency reform and the establishment of a independent central bank restored monetary confidence in November 1923. The hyper inflation struck many German families, for instance by sweeping away life-long savings.*

After the First World War, the weak governments of the Weimar Republic further interfered with the free market economy by giving in to private-interest groups calling for restrictions of competition. As a result of the compulsory arbitration procedure, government policy on the labour market got stuck between contrasting claims by employers' interest groups and unions. Compulsory arbitration by the Federal Ministry of Labour was intended as a procedure of last resort to settle industrial disputes, but instead induced the parties to strongly hold on to their bargaining positions and speculate on a favourable outcome of arbitration. The arbitration process created lengthy procedures and worsened industrial relations, since generally at least one party disapproved the compulsory agreements. Inefficiencies caused by lobbying interest groups distorted the economy and delayed the recovery from the Great Depression. Moreover, the absence of a separation between economic and political influence laid the foundations of the Nazi regime, characterized by total concentration of economic and political power.

From the second half of the 1930s onwards, the Nazis increased government influence on the economy. Expansionary policy, successful in 1932 and 1933 to end the Great Depression, continued for too long and required additional government intervention through price and wage controls to check inflation. Nationalist goals legitimized centralization and eventually fully degenerated into warfare. During the Second World War the German economy more and more changed into a centrally planned system.

The above experiences provided just as many lessons for the founders of the social market economy. The experience in the Bismarck era teaches that a strong state must protect competition. The period of hyper inflation underscores the need of an independent central bank. Social deprivation caused by the Great Depression and hyper inflation calls for social security to protect against creative destruction and to prevent a political backlash. The Weimar Republic shows that government must be impartial and must resist becoming involved in partisan interests of pressure groups, which calls for 'Tarifautonomie'. The Third Reich learns that strong checks and balances within government must control the power of the state.

Source: Giersch et al. (1992: 27, 28), Owen Smith (1994: 4), Paqué (1996: 99)

that involvement in cooperative exchange reduces the flexibility of government policy. In times of crisis government involvement reduces its capacity to formulate policy independently from the interest associations. The government may face sincere difficulties to counteract the influence of associations if substantial shifts in policy are needed. Hence, in times of crisis flexibility of the German government regarding issues under its jurisdiction exceeds that of the Dutch government, because of the former's independent position in the socio-economic order. Of course, total adaptability then strongly depends on the flexibility of German government itself and of the political system (see Section 5.2). Moreover, regarding issues outside its jurisdiction, of which wage formation is of primary importance, the German government lacks any formal influence whatsoever.

5.2 The Political System

The political systems in the United States, Germany and the Netherlands contain various checks and balances. This section reviews some institutions that affect these checks and balances and assesses the position of the political systems mainly on the trade-off between flexibility and commitment and to some degree also on the trade-off between diversity and scale. Flexibility entails the ease to adjust policy to changing circumstances. Commitment concerns the ability of different parties to pursue a common policy and to hold on to that policy even when opportunities arise to reap short-term political gains. Diversity entails the possibility to meet individual or regional political aspirations. Scale refers to partisan loyalty facilitating united actions by political parties.

Section 5.2.1 addresses some important features of the American political system. Section 5.2.2 compares German political institutions and their performance in practice with the United States. Section 5.2.3 positions the Dutch political system vis-a-vis the German system. Section 5.2.4 concludes by putting the three systems in the perspective of the trade-off between flexibility and commitment.

5.2.1 Main Features of the American Political System

Politics in the United States is polarized. In the American two-party system executive power lies in the hands of one political party. Alesina and Rosenthal (1995: Ch. 2) contest the view that this system entails a tendency for political parties to move towards the middle of the political spectrum. Instead they present theoretical arguments and empirical evidence that support the polarization view: presidential candidates and senators tend to take relatively extreme positions. Alesina and Rosenthal (1995) argue that voters prefer moderate policies. To achieve moderate policies, voters divide power by granting the executive and legislative branches of government to different parties. If one party holds the White House, voters bring about moderation by handing Congress to the other party. The midterm cycle, *i.e.* the congressional elections that take place at midterm of the presidency, constitutes an important institution for voters to divide power.

Depending on the circumstances, flexibility to adjust policy to changing circumstances constitutes an advantage or a disadvantage of the American political system. A newly elected president may bring about a relatively strong shift in policy, in particular during the first period in office. Policy changes are relatively easy if the new president can rely on a majority in Congress. Yet, even without such a majority, weak partisan loyalty provides opportunities to realize desired policy changes. In Germany and the Netherlands representatives mainly consider themselves as members of their political party and promote the viewpoints of that party. In contrast, in the United States dedication of individual representatives to the electorate in their state of origin may exceed partisan loyalty, in particular if specific items on the policy agenda strongly affect the home state. An example concerns the implementation of the 1981 tax reduction plans by the Reagan administration. To persuade a sufficient number of Democrats, who occupied a majority in Congress, to support the tax reduction bill, the administration granted concessions to each of the individual representatives. Concessions generally consisted of specific benefits for the home state of the representatives, like tax relief for oil industry in Texas, support for cultivation of peanuts in Georgia, etc. These concessions substantially raised the impact of the tax reduction bill on the federal budget.

A lack of commitment and a lack of stability are disadvantages of the weak partisan loyalty in American politics. The American political system not only is diverse and flexible but may also generate fragmentation (Katzenstein, 1989: 348). Developing a coherent view and reaching consensus on a suitable policy is time-consuming, because of the constitutional fragmentation and geographical dispersion of power (Nye, 1990: 220). Struggles for control between the executive branch and the legislative branch, weak party loyalties of representatives, and the strength of pressure groups contribute to oscillations and inconsistencies in policy. The failure of legislation on health care reform during the first term of the Clinton administration shows that weak partisan loyalty may undermine the position of a President with a majority in Congress. Political appointments of a considerable number of civil servants for a relatively short period of time, weaken the ability of the executive branch to pursue a constant policy. Moreover, fragmentation provides opportunities for powerful single-issue pressure groups to influence policy formation.

5.2.2 Germany vis-a-vis the United States

The German political model contains some broad similarities with that in the United States. Yet, on the two trade-offs distinguished here, substantial differences exist.

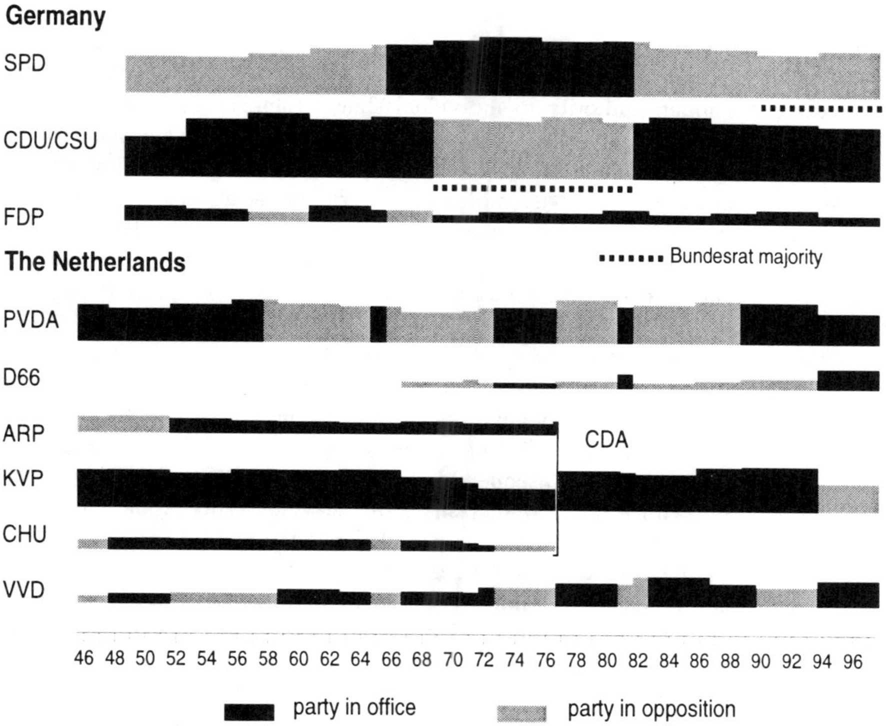

Figure 5.1 The German and Dutch political landscape

Similarities: Political Parties and Federalism. In two respects the German political system resembles that of the United States. Firstly, the presence of two large political parties makes the political landscape resemble the American two party model. In each election for the Bundestag since 1950, the Christian Democratic CDU/CSU party obtained between 40% and 50% of the votes.[10] Votes for the Social Democrats, the SPD, ranged in the order of 30% to 45%. Except for the grand coalition of CDU/CSU and SPD in 1966-1969, German governments generally consisted of a coalition of one of these two large parties with the liberal FDP, which obtained between 5 and 12% of the votes (see

---

[10] For the data until 1992 see for instance Gabriel and Brettschneider (1992: 596), recent data can be found on the websites of the German and Dutch Parliament.

Figure 5.1).[11] Hence, comparable to the United States either one of the two large parties holds office.

Secondly, like the United States, Germany is a federal state. The German federal order delegates much authority to individual states (Länder) and municipalities (Gemeinden), guided by the principle of subsidiarity (see Box 5.5). German Länder exercise primary powers in areas such as education, environment, cultural affairs, law enforcement and the supervision of local government (Katzenstein, 1987: 16). In addition, the Länder control a major part of the bureaucracy. The German Constitution strongly divides authority between the federal government and the Länder to prevent the disastrous centralization of power that took place during the Third Reich (compare Box 5.4).

German federalism entails some checks and balances, which are comparable to the American midterm cycle. Alesina and Rosenthal (1995: 254) refer to a study by Brady *et al.* (1992), which analyzes how German voters can balance the national government through Land elections. Frequently, a German governing coalition loses votes in the subsequent Land elections and is re-elected during national elections with a much higher share of the votes. This is similar to the American midterm cycle. Land elections may balance the national government in three ways. They may create legislative majorities by the opposition party at the Land level. This establishes a counterweight to the national government, because of the substantial autonomy of the Länder. Furthermore, a shift in votes at Land elections may signal voters' discontent to the parties holding national government. Finally, Land elections may reinforce the position of the opposition party in the Bundesrat, the national assembly of state representatives. In particular, if the opposition obtains a Bundesrat majority, this considerably restricts the room for manoeuvre of the federal government.[12]

Differences: Consensus and Incremental Change. Although voters may balance political parties in a comparable way in the United States and Germany, several features of the German political system create a stronger tendency to consensus and incremental change than in the United States. Firstly, in contrast to the conclusions of Alesina and Rosenthal (1995) about polarization in the United States, Katzenstein (1987: 39) explains that the structure of German political

---

[11] Two minor exceptions to this pattern existed in the 1950s. During 1953-1957 also the Deutsche Partei (DP) and the Bund der Heimatvertriebenen und Entrechteten (BHE) were part of the CDU/CSU and FDP coalition. The 1957-1961 government consisted of a coalition of the CDU/CSU with the DP. Since the early 1960s the DP and BHE failed to reach the electoral threshold.

[12] In 1969–1982 the opposition Christen Democrat Party (CDU) controlled the Bundesrat, since 1990 the Social Democrats (SPD) hold a majority in the Bundesrat under a CDU/FDP government.

Box 5.5 Subsidiarity

The subsidiarity principle states that higher level authorities should perform only those tasks that lower level authorities cannot perform efficiently (Schlecht, 1990: 154). In the German social market economy, subsidiarity defines the division of responsibilities between government and the market, between government and citizens, between national government and international organisations and between the federal government, the states and the municipalities.

Applied to government involvement in markets, according to the subsidiarity principle 'governments carry out a selection of activities that cannot be provided efficiently through private competition and abstain from those areas in which private competition works' (Sinn, 1996). Concerning the relationship between government and citizens, subsidiarity primarily applies to social security. In principle the government must provide social security only for those risks and emergencies for which private insurance is impossible (Hamel, 1994: 112).

Subsidiarity also guides the German position in international organisations, in particular in the European Union. Germany emphasizes that the EU should perform only those tasks that individual member states cannot perform themselves and considers subsidiarity as an important counterbalance against centralization of power in the EU administration (Schlecht, 1990: 154). This view has been brought forward in the European Summit declarations of Birmingham and Edinburgh in 1992, and Amsterdam in 1997.

In the Netherlands the subsidiarity principle guided the emergence of Roman Catholic ideas on corporatism at the end of the 19th century (see Box 5.3).

---

parties encourages centrist political solutions. The two main parties both consist of strong rightist and leftist wings that cause both parties to move to the political centre. More importantly, the need to form coalitions with the FDP to obtain a Bundestag majority, reinforces centrist tendencies of governments (see also Lehmbruch, 1995). Although the FDP represents only some 10% of the votes, it plays a pivotal role in the formation of a new government, since it represents votes that decisively affect electoral results. Switching alliances by the FDP to accommodate a changing public mood, caused the shifts between CDU/CSU and SPD governments, depicted in Figure 5.1. Since the FDP needs to emphasize its distinct characteristics to survive, it will be inclined to take a relatively independent position from its coalition partner, creating a centrist tendency in government. Another difference with the United States is that in Germany coalitions also feature frequently at the Land level. During 1949–1982, over 70% of the governments of German Länder consisted of coalitions (see Table 1-2 in Katzenstein, 1987: 40).

Secondly, partisan loyalty prevents fragmentation and instability. Cooperative exchange within political parties and a common party standpoint in the political debate is common for Europe. Hence commitment and stability feature more prominently in the European political system than in the United States. As a result, reaching consensus within the party may be time consuming, but this process contributes to unity of policy. Moreover, once a consensus has been reached, decisions can be taken quickly if a party holds a majority in Parliament.

The third centrist tendency follows from German federalism. The strength of German federalism resembles that of the United States, but its cooperative character creates a distinction between the two nations. German layers of government to a large extent share power, whereas the United States model formally separates the powers of the federal and state governments (Katzenstein, 1987: 46). In the United States the federal government and the states each cover specific policy fields, which they administer largely independently from each other. In contrast, in Germany on most major policy initiatives the Bundestag must reach an agreement with the Bundesrat. Federal, Land and local governments cooperate horizontally and vertically in bilateral or multilateral policy networks. In addition, Länder bureaucracies administer many federal programs, whereas financially the Länder depend on federal tax revenues.[13] The German system of intergovernmental relationships bears the name cooperative federalism or interlocking politics (Politikverflechtung). Analogous to the socio-economic order, cooperative exchange guides German federalism, whereas American federalism more strongly builds on competition between states and federal control.

Germany's cooperative federalism promotes political consensus and limits large scale institutional and political change (Katzenstein, 1987: 57; 1989: 336; Streeck, 1995). In particular if the opposition holds a Bundesrat majority, strong tendencies towards consensus exist. Consensus strengthens commitment but reduces flexibility. For instance, in practice redistribution of budgets between Länder and the federal government proves difficult. Often, if the federal government wants to advance its own priorities, it must provide additional finance (Katzenstein, 1987: 52). By consequence, the German federal model takes a position between the United States and the French model. The United States occasionally features substantial shifts in policy, for instance in 1981. In France deadlocks in intergovernmental relations may occur (Katzenstein, 1987: 57). In between these two models, the German system of intergovernmental relations promotes incremental change.

Fourthly, stable government bureaucracies and institutional linkages of government with private economic organisations also promote incremental change. Because political appointments of civil servants are uncommon in Germany, the executive branch is less fragmented compared to the United States. Institutionally embedded politics provide a framework to develop a coherent vision, but hamper restructuring of institutions and social engineering. Being part of institutional

---

[13] In 1989, expenditure by the Länder equalled 9% of GDP, whereas tax revenues directly collected by the Länder equalled almost 2% of GDP. Vertical tax transfers from the federation to the Länder made up the difference. The system of vertical tax equalization operates fixed revenue quotas for income taxes and corporate taxes, whereas the distribution of value-added tax revenues is subject to annual negotiations. Besides vertical tax equalization, also some horizontal equalization between Länder takes place to equalize living conditions. For more detail on both systems see Owen Smith (1994).

networks makes it difficult for political groups to contemplate restructuring the socio-economic order. Discussing institutional restructuring in Germany, Katzenstein (1989: 353) states: '.... the effort to think of new ways of organizing politics is stymied by the heavy hand of West German institutions which make "thinking the unthinkable" so difficult'.

The strong legal foundations of the social market economy and the possibility to test economic policy proposals in court against the Constitution constitute a fifth factor conducive to incremental change. It creates a relatively juridical policy debate in Germany. The German Constitutional Court has stated that the Constitution does not explicitly opt for a specific economic order, such as the social market economy (Lampert, 1992: 98).[14] Hence, the legislator is free to design an appropriate economic policy, under the condition that the policy must comply with the Constitution. The latter condition creates the possibility to test policy proposals against the Constitution. The Constitutional Court acts as the final arbiter of disputes between the federal executive and the Bundestag, between the federal government and the Länder, between different Länder, and between other courts (Katzenstein, 1987: 18). The Constitutional Court has played a central role in several large political issues in Germany. For instance, it ruled on such diverse issues as national television networks, party financing, admission to university, foreign policy, abortion and codetermination.

Not only the Constitution, but also the large amount of complex state regulations contributes to juridification of the German politics and society. Juridification makes Germany an even bigger litigation society than the United States. 'The city state of Hamburg alone provides work for more judges than all of England, while Germany as a whole employs about as many as the litigation-mad US with three times more inhabitants' (Klau, 1997). Strong emphasis on juridical consequences of economic policy proposals may produce rigidity in economic policy formation.

5.2.3 The Netherlands

Figure 5.1 shows that the Dutch political landscape substantially differs from that in Germany. Where coalitions between one large party and the FDP characterize Germany, Dutch coalition governments often consist of three or even four parties. The catholic KVP, party usually together with the protestant ARP and CHU parties, (with which it merged in 1977 to from the Dutch Christian Democratic Party (CDA)), constituted a steady factor in Dutch politics until 1994. In 1994 an unprecedented 'purple' coalition consisting of Social Democrats (PvdA), leftwing liberals (D66) and rightwing liberals (VVD) took office.

---

[14] The social market economy observes the requirements on the socio-economic order imposed by the Constitution, but it does not follow unequivocal from the Constitution. Other models might also comply with the Constitution.

Coalitions. In particular in the past, Dutch political parties' electorates were relatively stable, which enabled the formation of coalitions without the fear that a party would lose a large part of its electorate (compare Box 5.3). In recent times social trends towards heterogeneity make the political cleavages less profound. Nevertheless, coalition governments remain, since no single party is large enough to obtain an absolute majority. In the period after the second World War, the largest party in an election for the Dutch Lower House obtained no more than 35% of the votes. In the 1994 elections the electorate of the four large parties further converged: PvdA obtained 24% of the votes, CDA 22%, VVD 20% and D66 16%. Coalitions generally demand strong partisan loyalty.

The Netherlands lacks strong institutional feedbacks that generate a divided government like the position of president and Congress in the United States or the position of Länder governments or the Bundesrat in Germany. Although representatives from Dutch provinces elect the Dutch Upper House, the involvement of the Upper House in day-to-day politics is less strong. In contrast to the Lower House, the Upper House has no right of initiative and no right of amendment. The main task of the Upper House is to verify whether new bills are compatible with existing legislation. In the Netherlands the main checks and balances follow from the composition of a government coalition itself, based on the position of parties in the Lower House. By consequence, elections for the Lower House and subsequent cabinet formation take a crucial place in Dutch politics.

Coalition agreements play an important role in creating commitment among Dutch coalition parties. Extensive negotiations after general elections precede the formation of a new government, and at times result in long formation periods. Once a coalition agreement has been arranged and the new government has been installed, the agreement retains a central position during the entire period of office. It contains the result of a process of giving and taking by each of the coalition partners on many policy issues and forms a point of reference when decisions have to be made or when new developments require an answer. The difficulty of adjusting parts of the coalition agreement without bringing the entire agreement up for discussion and even the existence of the coalition itself, explains why interim adjustments are hard to achieve.

Commitment and Flexibility. Broad coalitions, the function of coalition agreements, the central position of the Christian Democratic party and relatively frequent changes of coalition partners create a centrist tendency and incremental change in Dutch politics. Broad coalition governments avoid sharp partisan changes and face difficulties in dealing with large shocks or in taking tough measures. Alesina and Rosenthal (1995: 248) cite some theoretical and empirical studies that show how coalition governments may delay adjustment. If a budget deficit arises after an adverse shock, each member of a coalition will try to prevent that the fiscal burden affects the social group it represents. Since no party is large enough to impose its policy proposals, a deadlock may result until the costs of further delays become so high that measures cannot be avoided. Empirical studies show that after the oil shocks of the 1970s single party or two-member coalitions more easily adjusted than large coalition governments. The central role of the coalition agreement strengthens commitment of the parties involved to maintain their agreed policies. However, it also reduces flexibility because parties have an important incentive not to change policies. As such, the coalition agreement strengthens the tendency towards incremental change in Dutch politics.

In contrast, the emphasis on economic analysis compared to legal discourse, combined with a relatively pragmatic attitude to policy adjustments, may make economic policy formation relatively more flexible in the Netherlands. Compared to the German juridical policy debate, in the Netherlands the role of formal economic analyses in policy preparation makes the debate more oriented towards economic issues and in a certain sense more technocratic. Occasionally, specialists from political parties, unions or employers' organisations even discuss equations from economic models as part of the economic policy debate. The juridical consequences of changes in economic policy play a secondary role.

5.2.4 Conclusion

Although at first sight the institutional characteristics of the German political system parallel those in the United States, the performance in practice resembles the Netherlands. On the trade-off between flexibility and commitment, the American political system balances on the edge of flexibility and fragmentation. In contrast, in Germany the internal organisation of political parties, coalitions, cooperative federalism, stable bureaucracies and linkage with private organisations cause a movement to the political centre and create incremental policy change. Broad coalition governments produce comparable tendencies in the Netherlands, yet a more technocratic and pragmatic policy debate promotes flexibility compared to the juridical debate in Germany.

A difference between Germany and the Netherlands concerns the timing of policy adjustments. The absence of checks and balances from federalist institutions and the importance of coalition agreements imply that in the Netherlands the period of formation of a new government constitutes the most important time to adjust policies or to implement new initiatives. Because of less strong coalition agreements, in Germany more flexibility exists between coalition partners to adjust their policies during the period of office. The strength of the opposition at decentral levels determines whether these adjustments can be implemented smoothly or not. If the opposition holds a strong majority in Länder governments a prolonged period of negotiation may result. These negotiations resemble Dutch coalition talks but may converge more slowly, because the parties do not face the need to form a government together.

5.3 Challenges for Reform

This section turns to tensions that created and still create challenges for reform in the Dutch and German socio-economic order. Tensions on the one hand comprise the effects of large economic shocks, such as stagflation in the 1970s and 1980s and German unification. These tensions form the subject matter of Section 5.3.1. On the other hand, Section 5.3.2 addresses tensions that follow from gradually unfolding trends in the social, technological en international environment of the German and Dutch economies.

5.3.1 Shocks: Stagflation and Unification

Stagflation Reforms the Dutch Model. All over the OECD stagflation characterized 1973-1982, yet stagflation struck the Dutch economy very hard. In contrast to the virtuous circle of 1948-1973 and partly caused by institutional characteristics of the welfare state (see Chapter 6), the Netherlands was caught in a vicious circle of rising labour costs, falling labour participation, rising public expenditure, rising public deficits, rising burden of taxes and social security contributions resulting in a further increase in labour costs, etc. Already during the 1960s and early 1970s Dutch real wages 'surged ahead of the north-west European average' (van Ark *et al.*, 1996: 296). Public expenditure soared from 31% of GDP in 1960 to 60% in the early 1980s, largely caused by rising income transfers and interest payments. Inactivity not only concerned unemployment but also the number of disability benefit recipients, which swelled more than four fold over 1970–1985 (van Ark *et al.*, 1996: 319).[15] The government could partly finance public expenditure from rising revenues from exploitation of the Dutch natural gas reserves that were linked to rising oil prices. Nevertheless, the burden of taxes and social security contributions as well as the public deficit strongly increased.

During the stagflationary period, the Dutch socio-economic and political order failed as an effective device for crisis management (compare Hemerijck, 1992: 25).[16] In the period 1973-1982 unions and employers' organisations failed to reach successful agreements in the Foundation of Labour and disagreed in the Social Economic Council on the goals of economic policy, while economic growth stagnated and unemployment surged. Also the government appeared incapable to

---

[15] Disability insurance contained some attractive features for employers and employees, in particular a high benefit until retirement of 80 percent of wages until 1985 and of 70% thereafter (see also Chapter 6). Dutch disability insurance contains a substantial share of hidden unemployment.

[16] See Figure 5.2 for a schematic representation of the shifts in the position of the United States, Germany and the Netherlands on the trade-off between flexibility and commitment and the extreme sides of this trade-off.

```
                 fragmentation------flexibility--------commitment------stalemate

1948-1972                          US              G  N
1973-1982                   US                     G          N
1983-1989           US                             G    N
1990-                          US                  N       G
```

Note: G = Germany; N = the Netherlands; US = the United States

Figure 5.2 Position of politics on the trade off flexibility–commitment

formulate an effective response, despite several studies that accurately analyzed the situation. Several factors contributed to the failure: inertia in three-party cooperative exchange, union-member militancy that reduced the capability of peak-level unions to reach agreements, institutional linkage of public-sector wages and social security benefits to private-sector wages, the difficulty for all actors to revise their perceptions and expectations after the prosperous 1960s, the sequence of shocks to the economic system that turned policy formation into shooting at a moving target, and the natural gas revenues that created a misplaced feeling of budgetary security. In addition, openness made the Dutch economy very vulnerable to shocks in the world economy and high birth rates in the 1950s boosted labour supply during the 1970s. In isolation, most of these factors were not unique for the Netherlands, yet in combination they largely explain the lamentable performance of the Dutch economy.

From the end of 1982 onwards the new Dutch government broke the deadlock by taking a more independent position in Dutch cooperative exchange (Hemerijck, 1992: 183-190). It initiated a policy of budgetary restraint and delinked public sector wages and social security benefits from wage agreements in the private sector, without consulting the social partners. Moreover, it exerted considerable pressure on the social partners to reach a bipartite agreement to moderate wages. The government altered the bargaining situation so that social partners could not shift the costs of stagflation on to the government, but had to internalize the external effects of wage inflation. With almost 10% of the labour force unemployed, another 14% on disability benefits, 6% on sickness benefits, and expectations diminished by some ten years experience of crisis, the bargaining position of the unions became very weak. By consequence, wage moderation resulted, supplemented by a government reduction of minimum wages and a reduction of benefit levels from 80% to 70% of gross wages. Prolonged real wage moderation combined with rapid productivity growth substantially reduced unit labour costs in the 1980s.

Stagflation led to a major internal reform of the Dutch socio-economic order: existing institutions were given an new interpretation. Government policy shifted from cooperative exchange to a certain degree of control at the moment when the Dutch political system is most flexible, *i.e.* when the new government took office.

Already at the time of its installation in November 1982, the centre-right government took the decisive steps that changed the socio-economic order (Hemerijck, 1992: 183-190). The more independent position of the government strengthened cooperative exchange between the social partners and increased flexibility. The character of the relationship between government and social partners changed from bargaining over mutual concessions, like trading tax reduction for wage moderation, to the development of common policy orientations. The 1980s and 1990s witnessed a number of successful bilateral agreements between the social partners. In contrast to the failed attempts at detailed, broad 'social accords' in the 1970s, the agreements from the 1980s and 1990s contain non-binding qualitative recommendations on specific topics like youth unemployment or minimum wages. The better delineation of responsibilities also increased democratic accountability.

In contrast, the German performance during stagflation was less pronounced (compare Carlin, 1996). Although the German economy has not been spared elements of sclerosis (Giersch *et al.*, 1992: 213-220), higher flexibility compared to the Netherlands and more appropriate macro-economic policies did not necessitate institutional adjustments in the German socio-economic order and contributed to the relatively stable performance of West German industry in the 1970s and 1980s. German institutions that foster long-term relationships enhanced quick diffusion of core technologies through all industrial sectors, incremental improvements of products and production processes, and flexible specialisation (Katzenstein, 1989: 317-328). Flexible specialisation means that German firms specialized in high quality products to avoid price-competitive market segments (see also Streeck, 1995).

A disadvantage of the relatively modest adjustment was that, compared to their competitors, German manufacturing firms could maintain their export position only by paying a price in terms of relative profitability vis-a-vis other EU countries (CPB, 1996: 161-167; Carlin and Soskice, 1997: 60). In the 1980s manufacturing firms in other EU countries, including the Netherlands, used widening profit margins to improve their profitability, which deteriorated during the 1970s. However, in contrast to other EU countries, to maintain its export position German manufacturing could not improve its profitability. As a result German manufacturing stood less well-prepared for the challenges of the 1990s.

Unification Increases Strain on the German Model. Unification put considerable pressure on the German socio-economic order.[17] With unification all relevant

[17] This section only briefly touches upon unification from the perspective of its impact on the socio-economic order. Sinn and Sinn (1992) contains a thorough review of the unification process, the arrangement of property rights, privatisation and wage strategies. See also Chapter 3.

West-German actors, including the political opposition and representatives of labour and capital, approved the transfer of the entire western socio-economic order to the East (Streeck, 1995). The transfer of institutions prevented a lengthy process of institution building that currently requires much effort in other transition countries and levelled the institutional playing field between the western and the eastern part of united Germany. Beside these advantages, the rigidities of the western socio-economic order constituted a major disadvantage (Giersch *et al.*, 1992: 268). The extensive framework of regulations and lengthy administrative procedures limited flexible reallocation of labour, physical capital and finance, required for East-German restructuring.

At first, unification strengthened the West-German socio-economic order, however, after the initial boom it added severe strain to the German model (Lehmbruch, 1996). In March 1990 unions and employers' organisations proposed to transfer the western model of industrial relations to the east. Subsequently they advocated modernization of East-German industry and succeeded in quickly raising East-German wages in order to prevent low-wage competition by eastern firms (Sinn and Sinn, 1992: 166). The consequences of restructuring and wages that considerably exceeded productivity were high unemployment in East Germany, very large financial transfers to finance social security and infrastructure investment, and associated rising budget deficits and taxes. High negotiated wage increases in 1995 led to a crisis in the metal employers' organisation, with member firms leaving the organisation. Weakening of employers' organisations reduced the probability to arrive at a peak level agreement to tackle the problems associated with unification (Lehmbruch, 1996). The unions' 'Bündnis für Arbeit' proposal failed and the government initiated a reform process with its 'Program for growth and employment' and subsequent proposals for tax reform. However, political and social opposition makes implementation very difficult.

5.3.2 Social, Technological and International Trends

Besides the impact of major economic shocks, gradually unfolding trends in the social, technological and international environment may pose challenges and opportunities to the German and Dutch socio-economic and political order. This section reviews the shifts that major trends generate on the position of Germany and the Netherlands on the relevant trade-offs, against the background of the American model (see Table 5.1 for an overview of the trade-offs).

Social Trends. Increasing heterogeneity and individualism in society push the position of countries on the trade-offs towards the strong features of the American model (see Table 5.3). Trends in European countries towards heterogeneous preferences, towards less respect for authority and towards more open procedures, reduce the capacity of interest associations to guide their members and to enforce an agreement. Hence, a less homogeneous rank and file of associations and a declining ability of associations to internalize external effects cause shifts from commitment and certainty towards flexibility and experimentation. Moreover, the capability of interest associations to protect their members or to provide them with advantages of collective action declines when the preferences of members are more disparate or change quickly (Geelhoed, 1996a). Accordingly, the position on the incentives-solidarity trade-off shifts towards incentives.

In the political sphere, increasing heterogeneity reduces the effectiveness of government policies targeted at specific homogeneous groups in society (Skidelsky, 1995: 125; Dixit, 1996: 111; Geelhoed, 1996a). Hence, the larger demand for tailor-made solutions shifts the position on the flexibility-commitment trade-off towards more flexibility. Heterogeneity and individualism also manifest themselves in less partisan loyalty. Steadily declining membership of political parties illustrates the weaker support of political parties by active members. Less stable voter preferences may increase the number of floating votes at elections. Less partisan loyalty causes a shift from scale towards diversity.

Growing awareness of sustainability and concerns about the quality of life form two trends that to some extent counter the tendency towards the American model. In particular world-scale environmental problems, like the greenhouse effect, create political demands for international and intergenerational commitment. Crime, violence and ethnical tensions raise concerns about the quality of life. On the one hand these developments raise calls for more control measures by governments and induce a shift away from the permissive society towards the American model. Yet, on the other hand they ask for international cooperation. In addition, relationships with ethnic minorities may benefit from cooperative exchange to address problems in a cooperative way.

Technology and Organization. Technological developments provide challenges and opportunities for the German and Dutch models. Challenges originate from information technology and a stronger market orientation of R&D. The spread of information technology makes technologies more codified, increases spillovers, creates incentives for firms to exploit first-mover advantages and quickly bring new products to the market (compare Section 2.5). An economic environment characterized by competition and external flexibility supports these trends. In such an environment the role of the state is limited to promoting competition and preventing rigidities in the socio-economic order that may hamper quick adjustment by companies to market opportunities. Since the United States model promotes competition and external flexibility, it appears better prepared to exploit these trends.

The emergence of the learning entrepreneurial firm provides opportunities for an institutional order based on cooperative exchange. Learning, continuous incremental innovations, internal flexibility and cooperation constitute a different approach to deal with a quickly changing technological environment. This calls for a socio-economic order and government policies that support internal flexibility and

Table 5.3 Impact of trends on the role of the state

Trend	Position on the trade-off shifts towards	Model US	Model GN
Social			
Cooperative exchange			
– more heterogenous rank and file	external flexibility	+	–
– more divers interests	experimentation	+	–
– more preferences for freedom to choose	incentives	+	–
Politics			
– less common values	external flexibility	+	–
– less partisan loyalty	diversity	+	–
– more awareness of sustainability	commitment	–	+
– concern about quality of life	commitment	–	+
Technology and firm organization			
– more codified and market oriented	external flexibility	+	–
– emergence of the entrepreneurial firm	commitment, internal flexibility	–	+
International economy			
– opting out potential	external flexibility	+	–
– national combined action less rewarding	diversity	+	–

long-term relationships, in other words it shifts the position on the trade-off towards commitment and internal flexibility.[18]

International economy. Internationalization affects the institutional foundations of a socio-economic order based on long-term relationships. Increased international mobility of production factors raises possibilities for parties to renege on an agreement and as such weakens commitment and aggravates the hold-up problem. International institutions that support long-term relationships are largely absent, because the market-oriented United States economic order plays an important role in the international economy and because institutions building is considerably more difficult on an international level. The link with national interest associations weakens for companies that increasingly operate on foreign markets and few international counterparts exist. This shifts the position on the flexibility–commitment trade-off towards external flexibility. Moreover, combined action through national interest associations, for instance through common advertising or national R&D cooperation, becomes less rewarding for companies operating on world

[18] Note the difference between internal and external flexibility. Chapter 2 explains that the hold-up problem generates a trade-off between external flexibility and commitment. Commitment and long-term relationships are also conducive for internal flexibility. Hence, the trade-off can also be stated in terms of external versus internal flexibility.

markets. Hence, from the point of view of the national socio-economic order the weight of diversity increases at the cost of scale or scope. From the perspective of institutional support for long-term specific investments, the national level constitutes a more suitable degree of decentralisation. Therefore, internationalisation favours the United States socio-economic order above the German and Dutch model (Pekkarinen *et al.*, 1992: 17; Streeck, 1995; Lehmbruch, 1996).

5.4 Policy Conclusions

Current and past developments pose some huge challenges to the German and Dutch socio-economic orders. Tendencies towards more heterogeneous and individualistic societies, information technology and internationalization affect both the social market economy and the consultation economy. On top of that, unification puts additional stress on the German model. Streeck (1995) even doubts whether German economic institutions are able to withstand these pressures. Does the above comparison provide any policy conclusions that substantiate or qualify this statement?

Shocks. Although caused by completely different developments and with higher intensity (compare Section 1.1.4), to some extent the German position after the unification shock parallels the Dutch position after stagflation in the 1980s (compare Figure 5.2). Both shocks required medium-term moderation of real disposable incomes: in the Netherlands because of terms of trade losses and fast growing labour supply; in Eastern Germany because of a fall in the capital-labour ratio due to excessive scrappage of outdated East-German equipment (see Sinn and Sinn, 1992: 166); in West Germany to pay the price of the restructuring of the East German economy. Socio-economic institutions did not internalize the external effects of wage inflation: in the Netherlands because of inert tripartite bargaining relationships and because of shifting power from peak-level unions to lower levels; in Germany because West-German peak organisations of labour and capital shared a common interest to raise East-German wages and a counterweight from East-German employers' organisations did not exist (Sinn and Sinn, 1992: 167). Moreover, in Germany shifting power from peak-level employers' organisations to lower levels, weakened the bargaining strength of the organisations. In both countries expectations also proved difficult to adjust to the changed circumstances. A vicious circle of rising labour costs, unemployment, rising tax burdens and increasing government budget deficits resulted.

The severity of the home-made crisis and the policy errors during the stagflationary period forced the Netherlands to initiate an economic adjustment process in the 1980s. Consequently, when unification hit the German economy in the early 1990s, the Dutch reform process was already gathering momentum. The different timing of the shocks forced the Netherlands into a structural reform process at an earlier stage. Cooperative exchange revitalised in the Netherlands through a stronger separation of the responsibilities of government and social partners. Reduced involvement of social partners in government policy to some extent moved the consultation economy towards the social market economy. However, because the institutional framework had not been abolished, some degree of commitment remained. Once a longer-term common goal had been identified, like the restoration of profitability and employment in the Foundation of Labour agreement of November 1982, the institutional framework and the participants' experience with consultation facilitated a combined approach to address economic and social issues (Rinnooy Kan, 1993: 40).

The main policy conclusion for Germany from the dismal Dutch experience during stagflation is that it may take a combined effort and a long period of time to turn the vicious circle into a virtuous circle. In particular, if the vicious circle has been allowed to proceed for a long period of time, restoring stock variables like unemployment or government debt to acceptable levels requires much effort. For instance, despite prolonged wage moderation, inactivity in the Netherlands still is considerable. A socio-economic order based on cooperative exchange requires consensus and commitment to address these challenges and to pay the price, not least in terms of less real disposable income growth. Recognizing that paying the price at an early stage will be much cheaper than postponing it may help to accelerate adjustment.

The German socio-economic order and political system face strong challenges to set in motion a process of recovery. In the Netherlands it took a considerable period of time before a redefinition of the position of government in the consultation economy revitalized cooperative exchange. The structure of the German socio-economic order and political system demand a large effort to prevent a stalemate from arising. The strong checks and balances, *i.e.* the formal separation of government and the associations of labour and capital in cooperative exchange, the juridical foundation of the socio-economic order, interlocking federalist relationships and the opposition majority in the Bundesrat, hamper attempts to establish political support and commitment to address nation-wide challenges.

Therefore, two alternative scenarios come to the fore. Firstly, a stalemate in German social and political relations generates a development that parallels the Netherlands in the 1970s and 1980s. This scenario eventually leads to costly adjustment. Alternatively awareness of the severity of the situation, possibly deepened by the example of the Dutch experience, generates broad social support for a policy of real disposable income restraint. The latter scenario will demand substantial internal flexibility of the German social market economy, its political actors and not least the German population at large.

Trends. From the overview in Table 5.3 of the impact of trends on the role of the state, increasing flexibility in the German and Dutch models appears inevitable. In particular concerning the socio-economic order, the social and international trends unequivocally require shifts towards external flexibility, experimentation, diversity and incentives, whereas technological trends provide a mixed picture. In the political sphere a more balanced picture arises in which commitment countervails diversity and external flexibility.

Does a greater demand for flexibility necessitate a shift towards the American socio-economic order? To some extent indeed it does. Social and technological trends cause decentralisation within industrial relations. Internationalisation requires differentiation to meet competitive and institutional conditions on a broad range of international markets. Decentralisation shifts bargaining on labour agreements from national to sectoral levels and from sectoral levels to individual companies. This enables differentiation between sectors and companies to meet trends towards heterogeneity, individualisation and market-oriented technologies (SER, 1992: 114; Albeda, 1993: 27; Chapter 9). Decentralisation diminishes the scope for central agreements between social partners and between social partners and the government.

Yet, exploiting and revitalizing one of the strong features of cooperative exchange may offer a solution that differs from a total shift towards the American socio-economic order. That strong feature concerns internal flexibility. If internal flexibility to some degree replaces external flexibility in making the unavoidable shift towards differentiation and decentralisation, cooperative exchange can be a valuable asset in the socio-economic order. However, it should be a form of cooperative exchange tailored to the constraints imposed by the trends.

In the Netherlands several developments in the socio-economic order contribute to this emphasis on internal flexibility. The 1992 agreement in the Social Economic Council (SER, 1992) has been a major step towards these developments (see also Rinnooy Kan, 1993: 45). Revitalizing internal flexibility rests on three cornerstones: a clear division of responsibilities between government and social partners, consultation to identify important areas that require policy action, application of specific policy instruments to implement these actions by each of the actors on their specific area of responsibility.

SER (1992: 119) specifies the following division of responsibilities concerning the main policy areas related to the socio-economic order. Wage negotiations and agreements concerning conditions of employment are a primary responsibility of the social partners. Fiscal and monetary policy concerns the primary responsibility of the government. Employment and labour market policies are a joint responsibility. Concerning the independent responsibilities of social partners and government the Dutch situation closely resembles Germany. Joint responsibility for labour market policy differs from the strong separation of responsibilities in the German constitution.

The renewed contents of consultation marks a shift towards internal flexibility. Consultation changes from result-oriented bargaining to enabling agreements that identify common policy interests, specify general guiding lines or define boundary conditions. Agreements no longer specify a detailed outcome for which the parties involved should strive, like a specific level of wages and taxes that should reduce unemployment to a certain number. Instead they contain qualitative recommendations on specific topics like training, youth unemployment or minimum wages (compare Section 5.3.1).

Each of the three parties, *i.e.* employers' organisations, unions and the government, applies its specific policy instruments to implement the general enabling agreements. The phrase 'policy instruments' should be seen in a broad perspective. Generally, central organisations only recommend or try to convince sectoral organisations or individual companies to implement certain measures.

The above adjustments shift the Dutch socio-economic order towards a relatively unambitious 'advisory consultation economy' (Albeda, 1993). Weak enforcement forms a disadvantage of the largely voluntary character of recommendations. However, the formalized process of information exchange and the development of common strategies on a central level enables parties to strengthen commitment. Moreover, it lifts consultation above short-term issues and directs it at subjects that are of major importance to the long-term viability of the Dutch economy. And of course crucially from the perspective of the trends, it strengthens internal flexibility of the socio-economic order, because it enables adjustment of the agreements to specific circumstances at decentral levels.

New Combinations. Do these adjustments in the Dutch socio-economic order, *i.e.* a shift towards more advisory cooperative exchange that aims to enhance internal flexibility, constitute a policy option for Germany? The main policy conclusion would be to look for new combinations of coordination mechanisms at different levels of government. New combinations have to identify new positions on the trade-offs that comply with demands from the trends and from unification, within the boundaries set by key social values. In other words, new combinations should increase flexibility while preserving social coherence.

New combinations in Germany entail the challenge to translate the strong checks and balances into a more flexible socio-economic and political order. An interesting question to pursue is to which extent it is possible to strive for advisory cooperative exchange at the regional level. It is frequently stated that the Dutch model only fits a relatively small homogeneous society. Since the Netherlands just as frequently has been pictured as one of the Bundesländer, the question arises whether the model contains any value when applied at the level of individual Länder. Advisory cooperative exchange at the regional level would put the Germany socio-economic order in a favourable position: diversity to accommodate to regional circumstances, experimentation due to stronger competition between Länder, and internal flexibility and commitment due to cooperative exchange within Länder.

Such a model would imply new roles for actors both at the national and the regional level. Less national coordination would reinforce subsidiarity. It promotes external flexibility, experimentation and incentives. These sides of the trade-offs clearly correspond with the shifts demanded by the social and international trends. Yet, less national coordination may entail a cost in terms of commitment, certainty and solidarity. It increases the risk that decentral actors attempt to free ride on national institutions. Hence, new combinations may not only require a shift in authority but also of (financial) responsibility, so that actors at the regional level internalize the consequences of their actions. A new role at the national level for representatives of labour an capital and the government would be to broadly define priority areas and provide general guidelines and recommendations, while leaving it to regional representatives to address these issues in a way most suited to their specific circumstances.

Wage formation and social security constitute an example. A new combination would result from a shift of wage bargaining towards more regional differentiation and less national sectoral coordination.[19] Decentralisation of unemployment insurance would support such a process, because Länder representatives of labour and capital would bear the consequences of high wages in terms of higher regional unemployment contributions. In that case, decentral administration of unemployment benefits should concur with budget responsibility. This might imply that financial equalization of social security contributions between Länder only applies if Länder are struck by shocks outside their own span of control.

Diminishing national coordination increases inequality. Consequently, another important role of national actors would be to preserve solidarity, in order to protect citizens against adverse shocks that originate outside their own span of control. A national government needs sufficient leeway to put supra-regional solidarity above regional interests. Unification constitutes a case in point: it not only demands flexibility and diversity but also solidarity. Confining solidarity to outside shocks means that under normal circumstances Germans would have to accept a greater degree of inequality. It seems reasonable to pay this price, because the present situation also produces inequalities, be it of an other nature, which in the long term undermine social cohesion.

No Simple Prescriptions. No blueprint of an optimal socio-economic order that perfectly corresponds to changed conditions can be given. The main purpose of this chapter is to encourage thinking about the complex process of social innovation in the socio-economic order. If some prospects look interesting, experimentation in that direction in specific policy fields seems the proper way to proceed.

---

[19] More detail on these issues can be found in Chapter 6 and 9.

6 Social Protection

Reform of social protection has played a central role in revitalizing the Dutch consultation economy. Compared to other European countries, the Netherlands was forced to start reforming its social protection system already at a relatively early stage, namely in the beginning of the eighties. At that time, a number of adverse macro-economic shocks to a system with generous and open-ended benefits as well as lax administrative controls had set in motion a vicious circle of an increasing number of benefit recipients and an erosion of employment. After doubling in the seventies from 0.6 million in 1970 to 1.3 million in 1980, the number of benefit recipients under the age of 65 (recomputed to full-year benefits) continued to rise rapidly at the time. Initially, the rising financial burden of inactivity was stopped through lower benefit rates, while the ratio between benefit recipients to those employed stayed more or less constant. Only recently did more fundamental reforms succeed in reducing the number of benefit recipients (see Figure 6.1).

The Dutch case may be particularly interesting from a German point of view because the heavy burden of German unification has given rise to a vicious circle of an increasing number of benefit recipients, rising spending on social protection (see Figure 6.2) and weak employment performance, which to some extent resembles the one suffered by the Netherlands in the early eighties.

This chapter focuses on social insurance and assistance. Social insurance covers specific contingencies (sickness, disability, old age, and unemployment). Old-age insurance is covered in Chapter 7. Social assistance, which acts as insurance of last resort, provides a minimum income guarantee in the form of means-tested benefits.[1]

The rest of this chapter is organized as follows. Section 6.1 deals with first principles. Why is social insurance needed? What are the trade-offs that the

---

[1] In addition, public provision and regulation of child-care, education, training, health care, and old-age care can be viewed as social insurance in-kind. Moreover, governments mitigate income risks through redistributive taxation (see, e.g., Varian, 1980). In-kind provision may help to alleviate moral hazard associated with cash transfers (see Blomquist and Christiansen, 1995). Furthermore, child-care provisions may encourage labour supply, thereby alleviating labour-market distortions.

government faces in designing social insurance? Section 6.2 describes the features of social protection in Germany and the Netherlands before the Dutch reform process started in the early eighties. It discusses also how the design of the Dutch system gave rise to its failure. This sets the stage for the reform process in the Netherlands, which is discussed in Section 6.3. Section 6.4 investigates various trends affecting the future of social protection. Against the background of these trends and the reform process in the Netherlands, Section 6.5 discusses various policy options for Germany and the Netherlands.

6.1 Theoretical Framework: Market Failures and Trade-offs

After introducing the concepts of contingencies and insurance, Section 6.1.1 explores the failures of the competitive coordination mechanism in providing insurance against social risks. Section 6.1.2 then investigates how other coordination mechanisms, and in particular the control mechanism in the form of mandatory social insurance, can alleviate the various failures of the private insurance market. By identifying the drawbacks of the control mechanism, Section 6.1.3 outlines various trade-offs affecting the choice between mandatory social insurance and voluntary private insurance. The impact of the external conditions on these trade-offs is analyzed in Section 6.1.4. The Dutch experience has demonstrated that the institutional framework for administrating social insurance plays a crucial role in affecting the efficiency of social insurance. Accordingly, Section 6.1.5 discusses separately the governance structure of the benefit administration.

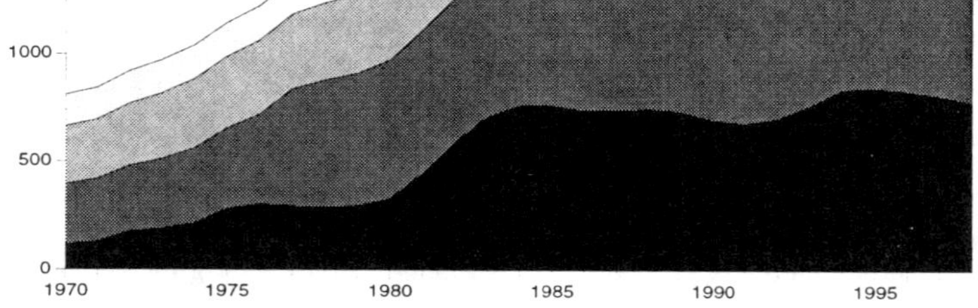

Figure 6.1 Number of benefit recipients below 65 years in the Netherlands, 1970-1998

6.1.1 Social contingencies: the Logic and Failure of Market Insurance

Contingencies. If risk averse individuals are subject to random events, they might want to pool the risks associated with these events. Indeed, an insurance company can be viewed as a collection of risk averse individuals who share risks. In particular, rather than being concentrated among a few unlucky individuals who are hit by an adverse event, the damage caused by that event is spread over all individuals who participate in the insurance pool. In this way, the lucky individuals assist the unlucky ones. Risk-averse individuals find insurance particularly attractive if the concerned contingencies involve high costs but occur only with low frequency. If the random event involves only low costs or occurs frequently, an individual is likely to prefer to bear the risk himself so as to save on transaction costs.

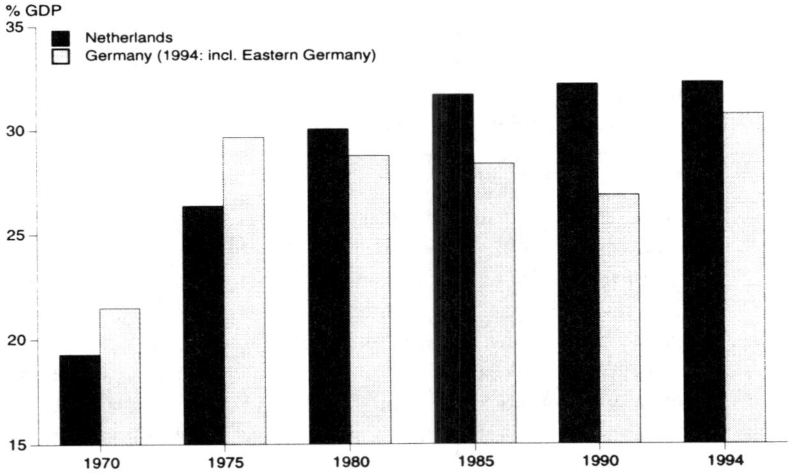

Source: Eurostat (1994) and SB (1996)

Figure 6.2 Spending on social protection[a] in Germany and the Netherlands

---

[a] As defined in the social security protection of Eurostat. This definition is quite broad and includes spending on social insurance and assistance, health and supplementary pension. Hence, it includes private social expenditures that are provided collectively. Furthermore, the definition, which involves before-tax spending, does not correct for differences in tax treatment of social benefits across countries. The Netherlands taxes social benefits more heavily than Germany does. This difference in tax treatment accounts for about 3 percentage points of the difference in (before-tax) expenditure shares across the two countries in 1990. This correction, however, leaves the development of the difference in expenditure shares through time largely unaffected.

Market Insurance. The private insurance market with voluntary insurance of individuals and competitive insurance companies can provide insurance against certain types of random events. In particular, the random events should be independent among the individuals, the probability distribution of the risks needs to be known to the insurance company, and the insured should not know the outcome of the event when he concludes the contract. This Section outlines how these conditions may fail in the case of the social risks of unemployment, illness, and disability.

Interdependent Risks. The private market cannot provide insurance against interdependent risks. A risk is interdependent if the insured event hits a lot of the insured at the same time. In that case, the insurance company cannot use the law of large numbers to spread risks over the insured population. Various macroeconomic risks, like unemployment, fall in this category.

Fundamental Uncertainty. Private insurance companies can not calculate actuarially fair premiums if the probability distribution of the insured event is not known. This is the case if fundamental uncertainty in the sense of Knight (1921) is present. Certain contingencies, like depressions, wars, natural disasters, and financial crisis, may not even be foreseen.

Information Costs. Private insurance often involves high transaction costs associated with the gathering of information on the features of the insurance contract and those of the insured. These ex-ante transaction costs (see Box 2.1 in chapter 2), which involve searching, screening, and signalling, originate in asymmetric information about the features of the contract parties, who may act in an opportunistic fashion. To illustrate, driven by competitive forces, the insurer may try to attract only the good risks through various screening procedures (so-called cream skimming). Moreover, insurees may engage in signalling activities to convince the insurer that they are good risks. Low risks may decide not to insure themselves at all. This leaves the insurance company with only the bad risks. This process of adverse selection may break down the insurance market altogether.[2] In particular, the markets for sickness and disability insurance are vulnerable to adverse selection.

Solidarity. As a result, high-risk groups find it difficult or impossible to find insurance on the private market. Following the philosopher Rawls, solidarity with high risk groups can be viewed as a form of insurance after the insured fact has

---

[2] Cream skimming and adverse selection are related to the business stealing effect, which is discussed in the chapter on competition policy and gives rise to excessive competition and entry.

occurred (see also Sinn, 1995). When a risk-averse individual does not yet know the outcome of an event (i.e. when the individual is still behind the so-called veil of ignorance and thus does not know whether he/she is handicapped or chronically ill), he/she can conclude an insurance contract to reduce risk. After the information about the outcome of the insured event has become available, the insurance company redistributes resources from the lucky to the unlucky individuals. What is insurance *ex ante* becomes solidarity *ex post*. However, many high-risk groups were never in a position to insure themselves behind the veil of ignorance because that veil had already been lifted when they reached adulthood and could conclude an insurance contract.

Impact of market failures. Leaving insurance to the free market not only results in a lack of solidarity with vulnerable groups but also fails to provide adequate insurance to more affluent groups. This under-insurance resulting from the breakdown of the insurance market is due to interdependent and difficult to calculate risks and high transaction costs, which are in part associated with asymmetric information.

Insurance through other coordination mechanisms. In addition to the competitive coordination mechanism in the form of competitive insurance companies, other coordination mechanisms may provide insurance. To illustrate, the institutions of the family and the corporation, which correspond to the coordination mechanisms of common values and norms and cooperative exchange, may help to insure social risks. Members of family and other voluntary associations and communities can insure each other against individual-specific shocks. As regards corporations, the owners insure workers by keeping wages and employment relatively stable through the business cycle. In this way, firm-specific shocks are absorbed by those who can diversify their claims on the capital market rather than by workers, who can not diversify their human capital.[3] Corporations can provide also mandatory sickness and disability insurance to its employees in order to alleviate adverse selection.

The failure of other institutions. As institutions offering insurance, the family and the corporation suffer from various imperfections so that they, like the free market, cannot offer adequate insurance to all individuals. The family, for example, is quite a small pool in which to share risks. Hence, the family can benefit from the law of large numbers only to a limited extent. Moreover, various single people cannot draw on the family to pool risks. Finally, the family is vulnerable to the risk of

---

[3] As part of the competitive coordination mechanism, a flexible labour market together with general skills (i.e. low asset specificity of human capital) protects workers against firm-specific shocks by allowing workers to quickly find jobs in other firms.

breakdown, leaving vulnerable individuals uninsured. Similarly, various people, including the unemployed, the self-employed, and employees working in small corporations, do not have access to insurance provided by corporations.

6.1.2 The Logic of Social Insurance

Mandatory insurance. The failures of other coordination mechanisms in providing adequate insurance provide the logic of using the control mechanism as an insurance device. The government has special powers of compulsion so that it can use the coordination mechanism of control. Accordingly, it can enforce mandatory collective pooling of risks through social insurance and assistance. The rest of this section describes how the government can address various failures of the insurance market by enforcing risk pooling through mandatory social insurance.

Interdependent risks and fundamental uncertainty. Through its powers to enforce compulsory taxes and premiums, the government can provide insurance after the insured fact has occurred. This allows for the insurance of risks that cannot be calculated ex ante. Moreover, by relying on compulsion rather than the law of large numbers, the government can insure interdependent risks. For example, the government can share unemployment risks intertemporally through public debt policies. In this way, the government forces lucky generations to pay for unlucky ones.

Information Costs. Mandatory pooling of risk through social insurance is a way to reduce the transaction and information costs associated with voluntary insurance. This use of control as the coordination mechanism in effect exploits the economies of scale in gathering information. In particular, individuals can delegate the gathering of information about the features of the insurance contract to a higher level. Hence, this information needs to be gathered only once.

Social Benefits of Solidarity. The government can enforce solidarity of low-risk with high-risk groups, even after the veil of Rawls has lifted.[4] In this way, a social insurance system may benefit the economy through a number of channels. In particular, by contributing to a more equal distribution of income and wealth, social insurance gives the unlucky and the poor a clear stake in society. The social contract implicit in social insurance underpins the legitimacy and stability of

---

[4] Another advantage of mandatory insurance is that it prevents individuals from taking out inadequate insurance so as to exploit the income guarantee provided by social assistance and other means-tested benefits.

property rights and the market process, thereby reducing crime and enhancing mutual trust.[5]

Social insurance also legitimizes the processes of creative destruction and resource reallocation that characterize a dynamic market economy by protecting the victims of these processes. To illustrate, unemployment insurance reduces the political pressure to protect declining sectors by maintaining the incomes of laid-off workers. Furthermore, it may contribute to a flexible labour market and the access of outsiders to jobs by facilitating the removal of employment protection. In this way, unemployment insurance ensures that insurance is not provided in particularly inefficient ways.

Unemployment insurance allows liquidity constrained individuals to continue to search for an efficient job match and to invest in marketable skills rather than being forced to take the first available, possibly inefficient, job offer. In this way, the welfare state improves the allocation of human capital and enhances labour productivity. Social insurance may also encourage people to take on more socially beneficial risks, e.g., by investing in firm specific human capital, engaging in entrepreneurial activities, and experimenting and specializing more generally (see Sinn, 1995).

6.1.3 The Trade-Offs

The Coordination Mechanisms in Terms of Exit Barriers. One can interpret the various coordination mechanisms in terms of exit barriers. The control mechanism does not allow exit. Hence, assets are fully specific to the pool in which risks are shared. Without the option of leaving the pool, voice rather than exit is the governance structure. Accordingly, insurance is provided through the political process. The competitive mechanism, in contrast, allows for free exit. The threat of opting out imposes discipline and provides incentives to produce efficiently, engage in innovation by experimenting, and respond flexibly to changing consumer needs. Indeed, through the governance structure of exit, the competitive mechanism provides information about preferences, cost structures, and new, improved insurance methods. However, free exit makes the competitive mechanism vulnerable to adverse selection, the opting out of good risks, and the strategic use of information resulting in high transaction costs. In terms of exit barriers, cooperative exchange and common values and norms are in between the

[5] For example, long-run contracts can be more easily enforced if contract partners have sufficient funds to make ex-ante payments to address the hold-up problem. Indeed, agents with low incomes tend to suffer more from liquidity constraints than others. Hence, a more equal distribution of income and wealth can boost growth by enhancing the ability of people to invest through improved access to credit markets.

mechanisms of control and competition, with common values and norms being closer to control and cooperative exchange being closer to competition.

The control mechanism, while helping to address market failures, suffers from a number of drawbacks. This gives rise to a number of trade-offs between government and market failures.

Scale versus Variety. Compulsory insurance can not tune the level and nature of the insurance to the preferences and behaviour of the individual. This yields a trade-off between variety (under voluntary insurance) and scale (under compulsory insurance).[6]

Transaction Costs. Another disadvantage of the control mechanism is that, in selecting the level of provision and regulation, the political system suffers from various imperfections, including rentseeking and lobbying activities. For example, the power of the government to redistribute income may induce various pressure groups to wage wasteful distributional battles. Moreover, to avoid abuse of its powers of compulsion, the government subjects itself to regulations as well as various checks and balances. This reduces the ability of the government to flexibly respond to changing needs. The associated transaction costs of an imperfect political process must be compared with the transaction and information costs implied by imperfect insurance markets and other institutions providing insurance.

Market versus Political Risks. The political system determining the insurance level may create risks as the government cannot commit future voters to present arrangements and cannot perfectly anticipate future developments. This gives rise to a trade-off between market risk (under the competitive coordination mechanism) and political risk (under control).

Legislative rigidities (e.g. involving constitutional constraints) are one way to commit future governments to an implicit long-term contract between present and future generations. These rigidities hamper the government's ability to flexibly adjust its policy. Hence, in designing checks and balances, society faces a trade-off between commitment and flexibility.

Solidarity versus Incentives. Mandatory social insurance is vulnerable to unintended behavioral reactions. In particular, employees, employers, and social

---

[6] This trade-off is discussed in general terms in Section 2.4.1. This trade-off can be stated also as a trade-off between *under*insurance (under voluntary insurance) and *over*insurance (under compulsory insurance).

security officers reduce efforts to avoid claims on social security. They may also try to obtain resources out of the system, sometimes by outright abuse.[7]

The resulting fundamental trade-off facing the welfare state is that between, on the one hand, risksharing and solidarity, which requires pooling of risks on a large scale, and, on the other hand, incentives on a decentralized level to reduce the claims on the collective pool.[8] This dilemma originates in the lack of information on the central level about the features and efforts of individual agents. This information problem gives rise to moral hazard, i.e. lack of incentives to exert efforts to reduce claims on the collective pool, because the market for such efforts is missing. This makes it difficult for the central authorities to find mechanisms to internalize the adverse external effects from careless decentralized behaviour.

The trade-off between reducing moral hazard and enhancing solidarity and risksharing emerges when selecting the optimal size of the pool within which risks are to be shared. The larger the pool, the more risksharing and solidarity becomes possible. However, a larger, more anonymous, pool tends to exacerbate moral hazard by reducing the incentives and possibilities for monitoring behaviour. In this way, a large pool may erode the norms constraining moral hazard.

The trade-off between risksharing and incentives can be stated in terms of a trade-off between moral hazard and adverse selection. Hidden actions render mandatory pooling vulnerable to moral hazard. Hence, the control mechanism suffers from lack of information about decentralized actions. The free insurance market, in contrast, may give rise to adverse selection and excessive efforts to uncover and disseminate information about risk features. Accordingly, whereas the control mechanism may suffer from lack of information, the competitive mechanism may induce excessive efforts to obtain and disseminate information.

Alternatively, one can view this trade-off as one between solidarity and responsibility. Solidarity through mandatory pooling is more appropriate if individuals cannot affect risk features. If individuals can influence these features (i.e. if they can be held responsible for them), however, collective insurance of these features becomes less attractive.

---

7 Lindbeck (1995) argues that these behavioral responses tend to increase over time as agents learn to exploit benefits only gradually. Moreover, the social norms, values, and habits constraining opportunistic behaviour may erode over time as a greater number of people engage in such behaviour.

8 This trade-off is discussed in more general terms in Section 2.4.4 of Chapter 2. Also market insurance suffers from moral hazard. However, in order to protect their market share, competitive insurance companies face an incentive to combat moral hazard. The government does not face competitive pressures to reduce moral hazard because it can force people to take part in social insurance.

The Trade-Offs. The upper part of Table 6.1 summarizes the various trade-offs in choosing between mandatory insurance through the control mechanism and voluntary insurance through the competitive mechanism. Mandatory social security exploits economies of scale. Moreover, it mitigates adverse selection and transaction costs associated with excessive information gathering. Finally, it facilitates risk sharing and solidarity. The competitive mechanism allows for more diversity, reduces political risk, and contains moral hazard by providing incentives for responsible behaviour.

6.1.4 The Impact of External Conditions

The lower part of Table 6.1 indicates how the merits of mandatory pooling depend on the economic environment. These conditions allow us to explore how trends affecting the economic environment affect the trade-offs between mandatory and voluntary insurance. Moreover, the effects on the trade-offs of international or sectoral differences in the conditions can be determined.

These conditions can be divided into three groups. The first group of conditions determines whether society attaches a high value to insurance and solidarity. In particular, high risk aversion (which is implied by an older population) and a strong preference for equity imply that insurance and solidarity are highly valued. Accordingly, overinsurance through mandatory insurance is less costly than underinsurance through voluntary insurance.

The second group of conditions affects the magnitude of the various market failures. This group thus determines whether the free market (i.e. the coordination mechanism of competition) is able to provide adequate insurance. In particular, heterogeneous risk features and asymmetric information about these features (i.e. hidden information) render insurance markets vulnerable to adverse selection and excessive gathering of information. Moreover, high information costs about individual insurance contracts make such contracts unattractive. Poorly developed financial markets allow neither risksharing nor income smoothing over the life cycle. Correlated shocks do not allow competitive insurance companies to exploit the law of large numbers. Finally, an unstable environment featuring fundamental uncertainty prevents competitive insurance companies from computing actuarially fair premiums.

By impacting the size of the government failures, the third group of conditions determines how the control mechanism of mandatory pooling performs. The first conditions within this group involve the effect of a high level of insurance on the efforts to reduce insurance claims. In particular, risk features that are costly to affect alleviate moral hazard. The same holds true for strong norms and values as well as symmetric information about efforts to reduce insurance claims. Also a low preference for privacy helps to combat moral hazard because it facilitates monitoring of efforts to reduce insurance claims.

Table 6.1 Mandatory versus voluntary insurance

	Mandatory social security	Voluntary insurance
Strengths	Exploiting economics of scale Reducing information costs Facilitating solidarity Facilitating risksharing	Allowing diversity Reducing political risk Reducing moral hazard Enhancing incentives
Conditions		
Conditions Group 1:		
Preferences		
risk aversion	high and homogeneous	low and heterogeneous
preference for equity	high	low
Social conditions		
population	older	younger
Conditions Group 2:		
Risk features	heterogeneous	homogeneous
Information		
information about ex-ante risk features	asymmetric	symmetric
information costs about insurance contract	high	low
Financial markets	not well developed	well developed
Uncertainty		
shocks	correlated	uncorrelated
uncertainty	fundamental	not fundamental
environment	unstable	stable
Conditions Group 3:		
Risk features		
costly to affect	yes	no
Information		
information about effort	symmetric	asymmetric
Preferences		
norms and values	strong	weak
preference for privacy	low	high
preference for freedom to choose	low	high
Homogeneous	yes	no
Elasticity of effort with respect to incentives	homogeneous	heterogeneous
Political process	efficient	inefficient
International mobility	low	high

Other conditions within the third group impact the costs of uniform insurance. In particular, low preference for freedom to choose, homogeneous preferences, and homogeneous elasticities of effort with respect to incentives imply that a uniform insurance package does not violate individual preferences. Furthermore, an efficient political process and homogeneous preferences mitigate the transaction costs of agreeing on a common level of insurance by voice.

Finally, international mobility determines whether the control mechanism of mandatory pooling at the national level is effective in preventing low risks from opting out. Low international mobility implies that low risks can not exit the national pool.

6.1.5 Benefit Administration: Experimentation Versus Certainty

Decentralization. As noted in Section 6.1.3, the welfare state faces the fundamental trade-off between enhancing solidarity and combatting moral hazard. One way to reduce this dilemma is to delegate the administration of social security to decentralized executive organizations with superior information about the behaviour and the features the claimants.[9] However, the superior information of the decentralized administration confronts the central government with another information problem, namely how to ensure that the executive agencies administer social security in the interest of society as a whole. Hence, the central government faces moral hazard of not only insured but also the insurance administration.

Regulation Versus Financial Incentives. The government can affect the administration of social security in two ways: first, direct regulation (through legislation, subsidiary directives, rules etc) supplemented by supervision (i.e. checks and balances) and, second, financial incentives. Regulation is closer to the coordination mechanism of control while financial incentives are closer to that of competition. Whereas regulation restricts the discretionary room of administrators, financial incentives allow for more discretionary decisions of the decentralized authorities.

Various Kinds of Financial Incentives. By employing financial incentives in the provision of mandatory social insurance, the government uses elements from the coordination mechanisms of both competition and control. Financial incentives can be provided in various ways. One way is to provide decentralized executive authorities with a budget. In deciding how to link the budget to actual insurance claims, the government faces a trade-off between incentives and risksharing, which is similar to the trade-off discussed in Section 6.1.3. This dilemma is familiar from the principal-agent literature and originates in asymmetric information about the

[9] More generally, the trade-off can be weakened by enhancing information about the efforts of benefit claimants. Improved monitoring, however, may violate privacy.

efforts of principal. The larger the incentives of the agent (i.e. the administrator) to conform to the objectives of the principal (i.e. the central government), the more risk the agent bears. In particular, the larger the financial responsibility of the agent (because the budget is not or only weakly related to actual claims), the larger the risk that he will be punished for shocks that he cannot affect but that the principal cannot distinguish from reduced efforts by the agent.[10] Indeed, incentives depend to some degree on a lack of security.[11]

The government can go further in using financial incentives by allowing competition between various executive organizations administrating the mandatory, collective insurance. This yields more information about efficiency in insurance administration.[12] However, the transaction costs of selecting a particular executive organization by the group covered by the collective insurance may be quite high as the participants in the collective pool have to reach agreement among themselves about the choice of the executive organization. In reaching this agreement, individuals within the pool have to use voice rather than exit to make their desires known.

A further step in the direction of competition is to allow particular groups to opt out of the collective insurance and to select their own insurance companies.[13] Hence, while these groups are still forced to take out insurance, they are free to select their own insurance company. These insurance companies compete on the level of premiums and non-mandatory benefits. In order to keep premiums low, the companies have a direct interest in executing insurance in an efficient way.

The Trade-Offs. Depending on the size of and the mobility between the pools, competition between insurance companies may give rise to substantial transaction

---

[10] If the principal can find observable indicators correlated with these unobservable shocks, it can reduce this trade-off by using these indicators to adjust the budget for risk factors. The same trade-off between incentives and risksharing emerges in the regulation of monopolies. Indeed, the single administrator can be viewed as a monopoly. With cost plus pricing (which is similar to linking the budget of the benefit administration to actual claims), monopolies face no incentives to reduce their costs. With price regulations (which is similar to fixing the budget independently from actual claims), in contrast, the monopolies bear the risk of changes in costs. In a sense, they have the right on residual returns from cost reductions (see Table 7.1 in Chapter 7).

[11] This trade-off is particularly problematic in the insurance market; strong competition in insurance market may give rise to bankruptcies, thereby hurting the insured.

[12] The government may ask various executive organizations to bid for the right to execute or provide a particular insurance for a pre-determined pool of individuals.

[13] Hence, these groups can use the exit option to discipline the administration of social insurance so that they do not have to rely on the voice option. The alternative options of voice and exit are discussed in the context of corporate governance in Chapter 10. Indeed, corporate governance raises similar issues as the governance of social insurance.

costs associated with signalling and creamskimming. Moreover, it may harm solidarity between groups with various risk features because the resulting actuarially fair premiums erode cross-subsidies across pools. Thus, by relying heavily on financial incentives, the government may encounter the failures of the competitive mechanism described in Section 6.1.1. To enhance solidarity and reduce transaction costs, the government may enforce transfers between low and high risks through special provisions. These solutions result in a mix between the coordination mechanisms of control and competition. Indeed, such a mix may succeed in exploiting the strengths of both coordination mechanisms.

Experimentation Versus Certainty. The alternatives of control and competition to internalize the externalities of decentralized administrative behaviour give rise to another trade-off, namely that between experimentation and certainty.[14] The more discretionary room the principal allows the administrator to exploit its informational advantage, the larger is the risk that administrators deal differently with similar claimants. Indeed, experimentation to some extent requires differences in treatment.[15]

The Conditions. Table 6.2 summarizes the conditions affecting the trade-off between experimentation and certainty. The first group of conditions determines whether the central government can put the behaviour of decentralized administrators in rules that can be easily verified. In particular, regulation is difficult if the central government lacks information about the efforts of the decentralized agencies and does not know what the proper strategy of these agencies should be. Also heterogeneous conditions at the decentralized level complicate the formulation of rules that are tailor-made for each specific situation.

The second group of conditions determines whether the discretionary decision making allowed by financial incentives is important. This decision making is valuable if, first, decentralized efforts are important in coming up with tailor-made solutions for a heterogeneous population and, second, experimentation at the decentralized level generates innovations in monitoring technologies and benefit administration more generally.

The third group of conditions determines whether the additional risks that financial incentives impose on the benefit administration are high and costly. In particular, these risks are not very costly if the benefit administration is risk neutral. These risks do not have to be large if the shocks that the decentralized

[14] This trade-off is discussed in general terms in Section 2.4.2 of Chapter 2.

[15] Another related trade-off facing the central government in affecting decentralized behaviour is that between solidarity and incentives. The more the government relies on financial incentives, the larger the risk that the administrators creamskim the good risks. See Newhouse (1996).

Table 6.2 Financial incentives versus direct regulation in benefit administration

	Financial incentives	Direct regulation
Strengths	Experimentation Tailor-made solutions	Certainty Equal treatment
Conditions		
Information		
information about efforts executive agencies	asymmetric	symmetric
information about proper strategy at decentralized level	asymmetric	symmetric
Insured population	heterogeneous	homogeneous
Benefit administration		
scope for innovation	ample	limited
costs of differentiation	low	high
risk neutral	yes	no
Uncertainty		
shocks	uncorrelated	correlated
shocks	observable at central level	unobservable at central level
Preferences		
preference equal treatment	low	high

administrator cannot affect either are observable at the central level (so that the central level can compensate these shocks by pooling risks across various decentralized administrators) or are uncorrelated so that the administrator benefits from the law of large numbers. Finally, the condition about the preference for equal treatment determines whether the risk of unequal treatment implied by financial incentives is a serious cost for society.

6.2 Social Security in Germany and the Netherlands in the Mid Eighties

This section applies the theoretical framework introduced in Section 6.1 to describe the main features of the social insurance systems in Germany and the Netherlands in the mid-eighties. Since that time, the fundamental features of the German system have remained intact. In the Netherlands, in contrast, reforms have substantially changed the system. These reforms are described in Section 6.3.

The first two sections, which focus on the factors determining the behaviour of the benefit claimants, deal with the trade-offs introduced in Section 6.1.3. In particular, Section 6.2.2 explores the benefit levels. On the one hand, low benefit

Box 6.1 Unemployment insurance and social assistance

Benefit structure. *In both Germany and the Netherlands, the initial period of unemployment is covered by an insurance benefit based on previous earnings, age, and work history.*[1] *After this benefit runs out in Germany, the unemployed receives an earnings-related unemployment assistance benefit, which is based less on the insurance principle and more on need. Indeed, this benefit is not only generally lower than the insurance benefit but also means tested against household income. In Germany, unemployment assistance is granted for an indefinite period to unemployed persons with sufficient work history. The Dutch unemployment insurance benefit, in contrast, is replaced by social assistance after the unemployment spell has lasted 1/2 to 5 years, depending on work history. Whereas the insurance benefit is financed by unemployment contributions, the general tax system funds the social assistance benefits.*

Sanctions. *Unemployment benefits are conditional on being available for work. German courts, however, have interpreted this obligation rather liberally. The number of sanctioned unemployed is very low in Germany.*

Benefit levels. *For an Average Production Worker (APW), the initial replacement rate in the Netherlands is appreciably higher than its German equivalent (see Figures below).*[2] *When the unemployment continues, benefits decline in both countries. In the Netherlands, the drop is slightly steeper, thereby mitigating the initial gap with Germany.*

The benefit structure at a minimum income level differs from that for the APW in two important respects. First, the replacement rates do not taper off much as unemployment spells last longer. Second, replacement rates are higher (see Table below). In the case of a single earner with children, the net benefit in Germany even exceeds the minimum wage.[3]

Social assistance. *German social assistance benefits are more tailored to individual circumstances. In particular, housing costs (including heating costs) are fully covered at the individual level*[4] *while special expenses (on clothing for example) are reimbursed. Moreover, the entitlement increases with the number of children. The Netherlands does not differentiate benefits in this way. Accordingly, benefits for single-earners with many dependents are relatively high in Germany.*

---

[1] *In addition to the statutory unemployment schemes, both countries feature also extra-statutory provisions. These supplementary benefits depend on the company's financial situation and the former employee's length of service.*

[2] *The replacement rate is the ratio between the benefit payment and previous earnings. The computation takes into account rent subsidy, child benefit and any tax implications.*

[3] *A legal minimum wage is absent in Germany; as estimate for the minimum wage the minimum wage for "Angestellten" in the metal industry is used. This wage is relevant for people with low education.*

[4] *The Netherlands provides a separate means-tested housing benefit if rent is below a certain amount. Persons receiving social assistance but not collecting the housing benefit may receive a housing allowance.*

Box 6.1 Unemployment insurance and social assistance (continued)

Table *Replacement rate in unemployment at minimum wage level*

	1984		*1995*	
	G	*NL*	*G*	*NL*
	in %			
Single person	*73*	*85*	*78*	*84*
Single earner	*91*	*98*	*97*	*98*
Single earner with two children	*115*	*98*	*108*	*98*

Source: CPB (1995).

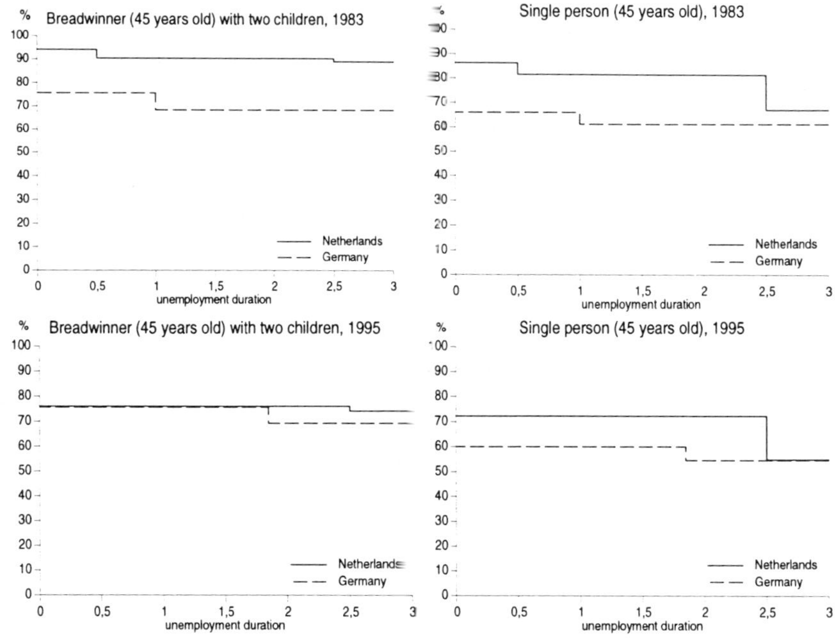

Figures *Replacement rates in unemployment for average production worker*

Source: CPB (1995).

levels alleviate moral hazard by reducing insurance. On the other hand, they imply only limited solidarity. Hence, the benefit level gives an indication of the position of a country on the trade-off between incentives and risksharing (or solidarity). Moreover, if benefits are generous, some workers who are not so risk averse may be overinsured. Accordingly, the insurance level is not tailor-made to the preferences of these workers. A high benefit level thus indicates that a country emphasizes scale rather than diversity on the trade-off between scale and diversity. Section 6.2.3 turns to the monitoring of claimants. By better monitoring claimants, the government alleviates moral hazard, thereby weakening the trade-off between incentives and solidarity. However, monitoring may be costly in terms of violating privacy.

The subsequent sections deal with the way the central government fights moral hazard of the decentralized benefit administration. As described in Section 6.1.5, the government can employ direct regulation, supervision, and financial incentives to ensure that the administrators of social insurance behave in the interests of the central government. Direct regulation and supervision are investigated in Section 6.2.4 and financial incentives in Section 6.2.5. The relative emphasis on these various instruments determines the position of the two countries on the trade-off between experimentation and certainty.

Section 6.2.6 then turns to performance of social insurance. It describes how the Dutch social insurance system interacted with macroeconomic shocks to generate a vicious circle of increasing benefit claimants, higher spending, premiums and labour costs, and employment losses. Subsequently, Section 6.2.7 surveys the development of spending on social insurance in Germany and the Netherlands, concluding that the Dutch social insurance system had become unsustainable by 1983.

6.2.1 Benefit Levels

The benefits for unemployment and disability in the Netherlands tend to be more generous than those in Germany (see Box 6.1, Box 6.2 and Table 6.3). Moreover, Dutch benefits for the social disability scheme, which is especially vulnerable to moral hazard (see also Section 6.2.3 below), are relatively generous compared to the benefits for unemployment and are of longer duration. Generous extra-statutory arrangements supplementing the statutory scheme protect Dutch and German employees from income loss during illness.

6.2.2 Monitoring Claimants

Another way to alleviate moral hazard is monitoring the claimant. As regards disability and sickness, monitoring refers to the strictness of medical checks. As regards unemployment and welfare, it describes how seriously administrative agencies verify the information supplied by the claimants.

Table 6.3 Replacement rate and operation of social insurance, 1983 and 1995

	Germany[a] 1983	Netherlands 1983	Germany[b] 1995	Netherlands 1995
	in %			
Sickness				
replacement rate[c]	100	100	100	100
sickness rate[d]	4.4	7.7	5.1	5.5
Occupational risk				
replacement rate[e]	100	n.a.	100	n.a.
Social risk				
replacement rate[f]	62	84	62	75
requests[g]	2.1	2.1	1.4[h]	1.8
admissions[i]	67.5	94.5	62.1	88.4
invalidity rate[j]	10.3	13.3	5.1	10.1
Unemployment				
replacement rate[k]	68-75	81-89	66-73	66-75

[a] Former West-Germany.

[b] Total Germany, except for replacement rates, which refer to former West-Germany.

[c] In Germany, continued payment of salary for six weeks. After this period 80% of gross wage net, but not exceeding the net wage. In the Netherlands additional benefits to the basic rate of 70% (80% until 1987) of gross wage is usual.

[d] Total benefit years as a percentage of compulsory insured. Source: BFG (1995:31); internet site Bundesministerium fur Arbeit und Sozialordnung; Ctsv (1996: Table 4.2); CBS (1997:36).

[e] In case of full incapacity to work, a pension of 67% of gross income is provided by the employment injuries scheme, supplemented by the invalidity insurance up to 70%. Part of the employment injury benefit is disregarded in the calculation of the supplement, which may cause a replacement rate of more than 100%.

[f] The replacement rate refers to a married couple with two children and one income-earner who started his career at twenty years of age with a salary of 65% of the Average Production Worker (APW). His income was to increase linearly up to 130% of the APW at age 50. However, at age 45 he loses his work capacity (fully). Consequently, his last earned wage amounts to 119% of the APW. The replacement rate in Germany is the social assistance level in relation to the net wage, since for a household of this kind the invalidity benefit is lower than the social assistance level. The replacement rate in the Netherlands involves the initial benefit. In 1995 the standard duration of this benefit is 1½ year at this age, but in many cases additional insurance supplement the follow-up benefit to the same level.

[g] Number of requests for work incapacity benefits as a percentage of the insured workforce, excluding civil servants. Germany: Rentenversicherung, corrected for potential insured, Netherlands: WAO. Source: BMA (1984:T1,T3); BMA (1995:T4,T8,T25); Ctsv (1996: table 5.2); CPB (1996: A7)

[h] Figure refers to 1994.

[i] Allocated benefits for job incapacity as a % of requests, excluding pre-test recovered and civil servants. Germany: Rentenversicherung, Netherlands: WAO. Source: BMA (1984:T3); BMA (1995:T25); Ctsv(1996:T5.2); AAF/AoF (1985:A15); Ctsv(1995:T7.3).

[j] Disability benefit recipients as a percentage of the number insured, excluding civil servants. Germany: Rentenversicherung, excluding potential insured. Netherlands: WAO. Source: BMA (1984:T1); SB (1985:406; 1996:460); internet site VDR; Ctsv (1996:T5.2).

[k] The replacement rate refers to a married couple with two children, one earner 45 years old at the beginning of unemployment and an employment record of 25 years. The higher figure depicts the initial replacement rate, the lower the case of long-term unemployment.

Box 6.2 Disability insurance

The German system distinguishes between disability due to 'occupational' and 'social' risk. The German scheme that insures occupational accidents and illness provides benefits amounting to around 80% of previous earnings in case a person's disability prevents work altogether. However, many disabled workers collect only a partial benefit, depending on the nature of the disability.

In the case of a social risk, the public pensions insurance scheme (Rentenversicherung) provides the benefit. This benefit, in contrast to the benefit in case of occupational accidents, depends on the number of contribution years (actual and allocated) and the average earnings during the working life. Hence, the benefit is contingent on not only disability but also contributions.

In neither Germany nor the Netherlands has parliament regulated the details of the examination process. In Germany, the courts (in particular a landmark ruling by the Federal Social Court) have filled this gap. In the Netherlands, in contrast, the details have been left to the executive agencies. This reflects the different traditions of the two countries. Germany relies more on the legal system while the Netherlands relies more on the discretion of specific groups in society.

Table Replacement rates disability insurance (social risk)

	1984		*1995*	
	G[1]	*NL*	*G*[1]	*NL*
Single person	*48-67*	*80*	*42-59*	*71*
Single earner	*47-57*	*81*	*49-55*	*73*
Single earner with two children	*62-62*	*84*	*62-62*	*75*

[1] *The first number refers to Berufsunfähigkeit, while the second number refers to Erwerbsunfähigkeit. Berufsunfähigkeit and Erwerbsunfähigkeit concern two different types of disability due to social risk (Rentenversicherung). An insured person receives a disability benefit because of occupational unfitness (Berufsunfähigkeit) if illness prevents a person from earning more than half of the usual wage in his or her occupation or a comparable occupation (BMA, 1997c). Labour unfitness (Erwerbsunfähigkeit) applies if an insured person is no longer able to perform any regular work at all. See Box 6.5 for reform measures aimed at abolishing this distinction.*

Source: BMA (1995) and own calculations.

Sickness Scheme. In Germany, the medical verification of sickness absenteeism plays a more important role than in the Netherlands. In particular, on the first day of absence from work, manual workers must obtain a medical certificate from their physician. Non-manual workers must collect such a certificate on the fourth day after falling ill. These certificates, which legitimize the absence from work, contain a prognosis for the probable return to work. If this prognosis turns out to have been too optimistic, the person has to obtain a new certificate. Sickness absenteeism in the Netherlands has traditionally been assessed only on the basis of random checks by so-called 'lay controllers' (see Prins, 1990). This monitoring device, while protecting privacy, is less effective in fighting moral hazard.

Disability Insurance. Also the application procedure for disability scheme is more medically orientated in Germany. The German system distinguishes between disability due to occupational and social risks (see Box 6.2). The Dutch integrated insurance system, which is unique in the world, does not make this distinction. Disability insurance due to occupational risks lends itself well to a detailed description of the insured risk, facilitating direct regulation of the inflow into the scheme. In the case of accident insurance, the insured time frame (i.e. working hours plus travelling time) is an important element. In the case of occupational illness, Germany relies on internationally accepted lists of occupational illnesses. An employee suffering one of the complaints on these lists receives a benefit, regardless of whether the illness in question was contracted at work. This approach yields a direct link between injury and benefit level.

Disability due to social risk is especially difficult to verify because employees with subjective complaints may claim benefits. In this case too, the claim-assessment procedure is more medically oriented in Germany (see Prins *et al.*, 1993). The view of the insurance doctor, who is expected to have good clinical and diagnostic skills, weighs heavily in the whole procedure. Referral to specialists for further medical examinations is common. In the Netherlands the insurance doctor plays a less prominent role in the examination process.

Unemployment Insurance. Germany is quite serious about verifying information applied by claimants. Applicants for unemployment benefits must present their identity cards and income-tax forms and hand over their social insurance cards. The various executive agencies frequently cross-check their computer records. To illustrate, the entire unemployment register is checked against the sickness-fund registers eight times a year (see Buist and Homburg, 1994). In the Netherlands, the privacy of the benefit recipients is more protected, complicating the verification of information.

6.2.3 Regulation and Supervision of the Benefit Administration

Regulation refers to the use of the control mechanism in ensuring that the social security administration acts in the interests of the government. It involves legislation, directives, and rules constraining the discretion of the decentralized administration. Germany used more regulation than the Netherlands in unemployment and sickness. In social assistance, in contrast, the Netherlands relied more on regulation.

Independent supervision was lacking in the Netherlands in the eighties. The social partners (i.e. employers' associations and trade unions), who were closely involved on the operational side, were responsible also for supervision. With social partners administrating social insurance (except for unemployment insurance), the German government either supervises the administration of social insurance directly or delegates this to independent bodies: the Federal Insurance Office (Bundesversicherungsamt) or Federal Audit Office (Bundesrechnungshof). Unemployment insurance is administered by the Federal Labour Office, which is supervised by the social partners and representations from various levels of government. Accordingly, the German system features various checks and balances in the governance structure of social insurance.

6.2.4 Financial Incentives in Benefit Administration

Germany employs financial incentives in the administration of welfare and sickness schemes. The Netherlands, in contrast, did not use these incentives at all.

Sickness Scheme. German employers are financially responsible for the sickness payments during the first six weeks of illness of an employee. Until 1994, most Dutch employers faced little financial incentive to combat sickness absenteeism because benefits for most firms were paid by a sectoral fund. German absenteeism rates due to illness were around 30% lower than Dutch rates until the end of 1993.

Social Assistance. Whereas the Netherlands controls the administration of social assistance through direct regulation, Germany relies also on financial incentives. Indeed, German municipal authorities not only administrate but also finance welfare. Dutch social assistance, in contrast, is almost entirely financed by the central government. Accordingly, municipalities lack financial incentives to limit the number of welfare recipients. To compensate for this, the Dutch central government laid down various administrative rules in great detail. The German federal law does not contain many specific executive or administrative instructions. This has largely been delegated to the states and districts, which actually administrate welfare. Hence, on the trade-off between experimentation and certainty (see Section 6.1.5), Germany stresses experimentation more than the Netherlands does.

6.2.5 The Mechanisms of Failure

The description of the social insurance systems reveals that, compared to the Netherlands, Germany applied more instruments to restrain the inflow of claimants into the social insurance system. The Netherlands provided not only high benefits but also did not seriously monitor the eligibility of claimants for benefits. At the same time, it lacked regulation and independent supervision of the benefit administration and did not employ financial incentives in encouraging decentralized administrators to reduce the inflow and increase the outflow. Hence, the Dutch system did not adequately combat moral hazard of benefit recipients, employers, and the benefit administration. This set the conditions for failure of the system. This failure became apparent only gradually in the late seventies and the beginning of the eighties when the Dutch economy was hit by adverse macroeconomic shocks.

Destabilizing Welfare State. By protecting aggregate demand in an economic downturn, the welfare state was initially perceived as an important automatic stabilizer. The macro-economic experiences in the seventies and eighties of several European countries and the Netherlands in particular showed, however, that the welfare state is not shock proof and may actually contribute to unemployment persistence. In particular, an adverse macroeconomic shock, such as deteriorating terms of trade due to an increase in energy prices, may set in motion a vicious circle between the costs of the welfare state and an erosion of employment, the economic base undergirding the welfare state.

This vicious circle runs as follows: a lower level of economic activity raises inactivity, thereby boosting public spending. To finance the additional spending, tax and contribution rates[16] are raised. The higher tax burden, in turn, depresses labour demand by increasing labour costs. Moreover, it discourages labour supply by reducing after-tax wages. The associated lower level of employment boosts public spending and tax rates further.

This vicious circle is particularly strong if generous and open-ended benefits in combination with lax and inefficient administrative controls fail to encourage benefits recipients to return to work and allow employers to dump low-productive workers in social security schemes (e.g. disability schemes). This process is strengthened further if the increasing number of claimants create a dependency culture by eroding the norms and values that restrain moral hazard of beneficiaries, employees, employers, and administrators.[17] With the welfare state acting as a 'social hammock', a temporary adverse macroeconomic shock may threaten the long-run viability of the welfare state, thereby forcing the government to renege on its previous commitments. In this way, the welfare state becomes destabilizing rather than stabilizing.

Welfare State and Social Exclusion. The welfare state appeared to be counterproductive also in promoting social cohesion, by reducing the access of low-productivity workers to jobs. High taxes and premiums that raise labour costs cut off demand for low productivity workers. At the same time, replacement rates

---

[16] Social security contribution rates, even if based on the insurance principle, are often viewed as taxes. Indeed, mandatory social security typically involves significant cross-subsidies between different risk classes.

[17] See also Lindbeck (1995), who argues that the inertia created by habit and norms imply that disincentives tend to be stronger in the long run than in the short run.

tend to be relatively high at the lower income levels, thereby increasing reservation wages, depressing search intensity, and compressing the wage structure. Hence, the loss of employment will typically be concentrated among low-skilled workers. The prolonged periods of inactivity tend to erode the human capital and working habits of these individuals. This makes the loss of employment for these groups difficult to reverse. The resulting reduced access to work for the low skilled thus contributes to social exclusion of these vulnerable groups. This process of increasing the population of outsiders is strengthened further if administrators face only weak incentives to return benefit recipients back to work.

The Hold-up Problem. Another channel through which social insurance may be counterproductive in generating equity and sharing risks involves the hold-up problem. By giving labour too strong an ex-post negotiating position to extract rents from entrepreneurs, social security may give rise to unemployment of labour as low profitability discourages entrepreneurs from investing. In general equilibrium, the bargaining position of workers is weakened through unemployment (see Caballero and Hammour, 1996). The rationing mechanism of unemployment strengthens the insider-outsider distinction between various workers, thereby increasing the risks facing a given individual.[18]

6.2.6 Performance

The vicious circle described above contributed to the growth of Dutch spending on social insurance. Indeed, overall expenditure on social insurance as a percentage of GDP rose appreciably faster in the Netherlands than in Germany between 1970 and 1990 (see Figure 6.2). Whereas the Dutch ratio was still below the German one in 1970, it exceeded the German ratio by 1980. Dutch social expenditure increased especially rapidly between 1970 and 1983, after which the expenditure to GDP ratio continued to rise at a lower pace until 1994. The German ratio rose until the mid seventies. Subsequently, notwithstanding the aging of the population and the oil price shocks, a small decline set it. However, after German unification in 1990, it started to rise again mainly on account of higher pension payments to older, redundant workers in Eastern Germany.

The more rapid increase in Dutch social spending during the seventies can be attributed primarily to disability insurance. Especially during the second half of the seventies, the number of disability claimants surged. The number of unemployment benefits rose particularly rapidly between 1980 and 1984 (see Table 6.4, Table 6.5 and Figure 6.1).

---

[18] Also hiring and firing costs strengthen the bargaining position of the insiders, thereby further weakening the position of outsiders.

Table 6.4 Increase in social security expenditure ratio, 1970-1983

	Germany[a]			Netherlands		
	ratio increase	vol. increase[b]	price change[c]	ratio increase	vol. increase[b]	price change[c]
	% of GDP	in %	in %	% of GDP	in %	in %
Old age/dependents	2.5	0.4	3.7	1.8	1.7	2.3
Unemployment	1.4	12.0	-1.2	5.1	16.3	3.5
Disability	0.9	2.3	2.2	4.8	9.8	1.6
Family support	0.3	-1.8	5.1	-0.3	-1.0	2.5
Sickness[d]	1.9	0.1	4.5	1.7	0.7	3.7
Total	7.4	1.1	3.5	14.2	4.4	2.4
GDP		2.2	4.9		2.3	6.7

[a] Excluding East Germany.
[b] This corresponds to the increase in the target group. For disability and unemployment, the target group is the number of benefit recipients. For sickness, it is the total population.
[c] Relative to the price change of GDP.
[d] This category includes collective spending on health and sickness related absenteeism from work.

Source: Eurostat (1994).

In the 1980s, as the extension of social security had led to a situation where every working person had to support almost one benefit recipient, consensus emerged in the Netherlands that reform of the social security system was called for. The system had become counterproductive in achieving the objectives for which it was set up. Rather than stabilizing shocks and protecting solidarity, it had resulted in the persistence of employment losses, the reduced access of vulnerable groups to the labour market, and a vicious circle eroding the economic base for providing generous benefits. In reforming its system, the Netherlands could benefit from the experience of its challenging neighbour Germany, which had been able to contain its social spending as a percentage of GDP despite the oil shocks.

6.3 Reforms in the Netherlands

6.3.1 General Reform Strategy

In reforming the welfare state, two broad strategies can be distinguished. The first strategy aims at preserving the European legacy of solidarity as much as possible by fighting moral hazard through a more efficient administration of social benefits. The second strategy, which can be identified with Anglo-Saxon approach, focuses

Table 6.5 Recipients of social protection benefits ('inactive' persons) and employed persons ('active' persons), the Netherlands, 1970-1998

	1970	1975	1980	1985	1990	1995	1996	1997[a]
Social security beneficiaries (in thousands)	2030	2520	3059	3733	3991	4184	4186	4188
Employment (in thousands)	4592	4500	4624	4486	4858	5127	5231	5328
Benefits to employment ratio (in %)	44.2	56.0	66.2	83.2	82.1	81.6	80.0	78.6
Of which:								
Old age and survivor benefits	28.9	32.7	35.4	39.7	40.3	40.6	40.3	40.0
Sickness	3.2	3.5	3.6	3.7	3.8	3.7	3.6	3.5
Disability	9.0	12.8	19.5	21.1	23.4	20.6	19.9	19.7
Unemployment	1.6	4.4	5.2	14.7	11.1	13.6	13.3	12.8
Other social assistance	1.5	2.6	2.4	4.0	3.6	3.2	3.0	2.7

[a] Estimates.

Source: CPB (1997).

on reducing the level of public insurance and widening the income gap between working and nonworking. This implies moving towards incentives and diversity on the incentives-solidarity and diversity-scale trade-offs.

The reform of the Dutch social insurance system, which was initiated in the mid eighties, combines these two strategies: It combats moral hazard of both the insured and the benefit administration. Indeed, the two strategies are to some extent complementary. To illustrate, reducing the level of benefits becomes more effective in decreasing claims on the social security system if the benefit administration is efficient (see also Coe and Snower, 1997). Rather than providing passive income support, the social security system was reformed so as to encourage participation in the labour market. Indeed, unemployment should be combatted through raising employment rather than reducing labour supply. This strategy was executed in different phases.

Cutting Benefits. In the mid eighties, reforms aimed primarily at fighting moral hazard of workers and benefit recipients by reducing the level of benefits. For example, unemployment benefits and statutory disability and sickness benefits were cut in several steps from 80 % to 70 % of final pay during the 1984-86 period. These measures were not very successful in substantially reducing the number of recipients of social insurance benefits, in part because private supplementary arrangements offset some of the cuts in disability and sickness benefits (see Box 6.3). Moreover, minimum benefits fell compared to the average wage level because

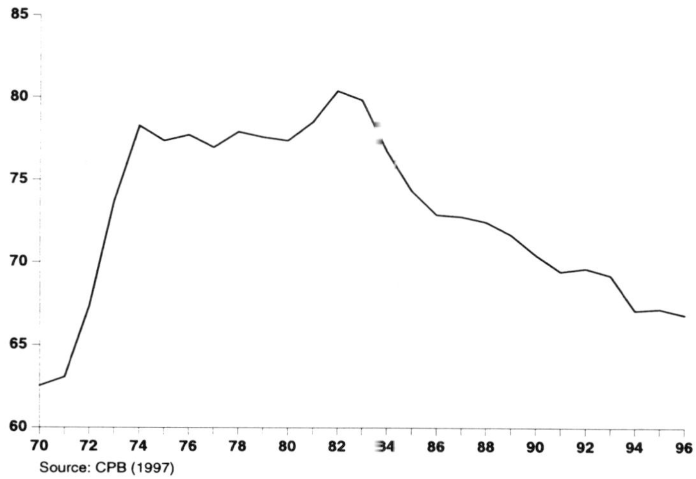

Figure 6.3 After-tax minimum wage to after-tax modal wage, the Netherlands, 1970-1996

the minimum wage, to which these benefits are linked, was frozen in nominal terms or indexed to prices rather than wages in a number of years (see Figure 6.3). Also the link of other benefits to wages was not applied in several years.

Tightening Eligibility. Also other measures were aimed at combatting moral hazard of workers and benefit recipients. In particular, eligibility conditions and monitoring of benefit recipients were tightened by introducing waiting periods before being entitled to benefits[19], tightening the disability and unemployment criteria, and introducing more insurance elements in unemployment insurance (by linking benefits more closely to work history).

Independent Supervision. After the national audit office concluded, and a parliamentary inquiry later confirmed, that the absence of independent supervision had contributed to the unbridled growth of social security outlays, supervision of employee insurances was delegated to an independent body, the Social Insurance Supervisory Commission (CTSV). This body, set up in 1995, was established to introduce more checks and balances and to clarify and separate responsibilities in the governance structure of social insurance.

---

[19] In particular, qualifying conditions for unemployment insurance were tightened in 1991 and 1995. Among other things, the required employment record for wage related benefits was lengthened.

More Efficient Benefit Administration. In the nineties, social insurance was reformed more fundamentally by affecting the behaviour of employers and benefit administrations. In particular, measures were taken to affect the behaviour of employers through financial incentives in the sickness scheme. More recently, reform of the benefit administration was initiated in order to enhance the efficiency of the administrative process. Initially, in accordance with the control mechanism (see Section 6.1.5), more regulations reduced the discretionary room for administrators so as to cut the inflows into the various schemes. Later on, financial incentives were introduced to reconcile discretionary decision making with spending control and an active policy of returning claimants back to work. Moreover, the role of the public sector in executing sickness and disability schemes is being reduced by relying more on competition between private insurance companies and public agencies.

Decentralizing the Administration of Social Assistance. At the same time, the administration of social assistance in the Netherlands is in the process of being reformed in the direction of the German system by relying less on central regulations and more on financial incentives. In particular, the responsibility and discretion of local government is increased while detailed central regulations are being reduced. From 1996 onwards, Dutch municipalities have more discretion to grant supplements to welfare for special cases. The responsibility for financing these supplements will be shifted to the municipalities in 1999. In particular, the budget that the central government provides to the local authorities will depend on other factors than the actual number of welfare claimants. In this way, local communities are rewarded financially if they succeed in getting social assistance claimants into work. This move towards financial incentives in benefit administration follows from the need to tailor to an increasingly heterogeneous population (see Table 6.2).

6.3.2 Sickness and Disability

The most fundamental reforms in the Netherlands involve the sickness and disability schemes. This section elaborates on these reforms.

Cutting Benefits. Initially, measures were largely aimed at combatting moral hazard of the employee. This was accomplished primarily by cutting the statutory benefit rates; benefits were cut from 80 % to 70 % of final pay between 1984 and 1986. In 1993, disability benefits for newly eligible young claimants were reduced further. However, supplementary benefits in collective labour contracts largely offset this reduction in statutory benefits (see Box 6.3).

Tightening Regulation and Improving Monitoring. In the disability scheme, criteria for eligibility were tightened. From 1987 onwards, the labour market

Box 6.3 Effects of lower statutory benefits in the Netherlands

Statutory benefit rates in sickness and disability insurance were sharply reduced in the Netherlands in the 1980s and 90s. Statutory sickness payments were cut from 80% to 70% of earnings in 1985. Disability payments were reduced twice, initially also from 80% to 70% of earnings in 1985 and subsequently in 1993 by making the benefit age-related.

The cuts in the statutory sickness benefits have been fully compensated by supplementary arrangements negotiated by social partners. Similar agreements offset about half of the cuts in statutory disability benefits implemented in 1985 and around three-quarters of the cuts in 1993.

Two factors may have contributed to these offsets negotiated by social partners. First, the government makes collective labour agreements legally binding for all firms in a particular sector. Second, the social partners do not fully internalize the adverse effects of higher benefits on moral hazard because the public statutory scheme pays most of the benefits. The combination of public and supplementary private insurance gives rise to overinsurance (see Teulings and Van der Ploeg, 1993, and Lindbeck, 1994). Free choice yields the optimal insurance contract if an insured can insure his risk at only one insurance company. If the insured has access to more insurance companies, the market yields overinsurance. Indeed, insurers typically demand that the insured does not have contracts elsewhere, realizing that this would reduce the incentives of the insured to prevent the insured event.

By privatizing the sickness scheme and introducing financial incentives for employers in the disability scheme, the government addresses this problem of over-insurance. Employers are fully rewarded for their efforts to reduce insurance claims, either by cutting supplementary benefits or improving working conditions.

situation could no longer be discounted in determining eligibility for disability benefits. In 1993, the legal definition of the appropriate job was widened. With residual earning power determining benefits, people who in the past would have received full benefits now receive only partial benefits. At the same time, the government reduced the discretion of the executive organizations by issuing specific criteria for determining disability and residual earning power. Moreover, a disability benefit is granted for only five years after which the extent of disability and residual earning power is assessed again. For the existing claimants, a program of reassessment was started in 1994.

Introducing Financial Incentives. As far as the sickness scheme is concerned, the first two (small firms) or six (large firms) weeks of sickness have to be paid by the employer, effective in 1994. In 1996, the Netherlands went even further than Germany in using financial incentives for employers by no longer insuring sickness through the social insurance system at all. The employer is legally required to pay 70 % of pay (during the entire first year, after which the disability scheme kicks in). Firms have the option to take out private insurance with premiums differentiated according to actuarial risk.

Financial incentives for employers were introduced also in the disability scheme. A system of bonuses (for reintegration) and penalties (for new disability claims) was introduced in 1992 but repealed in 1995. A new system is due to become effective in 1998. The public system will involve experience rating (on the basis of benefits paid during the first five years of disability). Employers can opt out of this public system (for the first five years of the disability benefit) by either taking out private insurance or taking financial responsibility for statutory benefits. In Germany, contributions to the occupational scheme are differentiated only across sectors. Accordingly, also in the disability scheme do the Netherlands go further than Germany in using financial incentives for employers.

Benefits of Competition. The plans for competition in disability insurance and the privatization of sickness insurance have two primary aims. First, by introducing competition, efficiency gains are expected to be reaped in the implementation and administration of the insurance. Indeed, employers, private insurers, and public administrators face more incentives to return the sick and disabled back to work. Moral hazard is likely to be reduced as competition yields information about efficient cost levels in benefit administration. Organizations that are most successful in preventing disability and encouraging revalidation and reintegration can exploit this as a comparative advantage. Relying on the discipline of the market thus reduces the need for the government to extensively regulate the benefit administration as a monopoly. Instead, the government can rely on the ingenuity, experimentation, and tailor-made solutions of decentralized agencies.

Second, competition ensures that contributions closely match actuarial risks. Hence, employers are directly confronted with the costs and benefits of their actions on these risks; they can no longer shift the costs of their behaviour unto a collective pool. This encourages employers to reduce risks by improving working conditions and by cutting extra-statutory benefits (see Box 6.3). In this latter way, incentives for employers may indirectly enhance incentives for workers as well. By introducing incentives in both the sickness and disability schemes, the employer is responsible for combatting both sickness and disability. Hence, the system transfer between the sickness and disability scheme is eliminated. In particular, industrial insurance boards are no longer encouraged to shift people from the sickness scheme, which is financed on a sectoral basis, to the disability scheme, which is financed nationally (see Box 6.4).

Costs of Competition. Introducing competition in disability insurance does not escape the trade-off between incentives and solidarity and the trade-off between adverse selection (and transaction costs) and moral hazard. In particular, in order to reduce their premiums, employers may try to select the good risks, thereby weakening the labour-market position of vulnerable groups and raising search and transaction costs on the labour market.

Box 6.4 System transfers

A 'system transfer' involves a benefit recipient moving from one benefit scheme to another. These transfers may give rise to two problems.[1] First, the agencies administrating the schemes may not internalize the costs of transferring a claimant to another scheme. Second, system transfers may complicate the process of control because they require the transfer of information.

Two system transfers are important in both countries, namely from unemployment to welfare and from sickness to disability. The first transfer is less frequent in Germany than in the Netherlands because long-term unemployed with sufficient work history in Germany collect unemployment benefits for an unlimited period.

The two countries deal differently with the system transfer from sickness to (social) disability. In Germany, separate independent organizations are responsible. This may reduce inflows into social disability because applicants are examined by administrators that are responsible only for this program.

In the Netherlands, the sickness and disability schemes used to be administered by the same body, namely the industrial insurance board. However, this board was financially responsible for only sickness benefits. Disability benefits were paid out at national level. Accordingly, the board faced a financial incentive to transfer a sick employee from the sickness to the disability scheme.

[1] The WRR (1994) identified these problems.

Several measures alleviate this potential problem. First, a separate insurance for the early handicapped is introduced. Second, various measures strengthen the labour-market position of those with health problems. To illustrate, employers may receive a special budget to cover the additional costs associated with taking on employees with weak health.[20] Third, insurance premiums apply to the pool of workers in any firm. Hence, risks are pooled across all employees. Especially in large firms, improving working conditions are a much more effective method to reduce premiums than selecting employees on the basis of health conditions. Fourth, the premiums for the public scheme are subject to a maximum. This maximum premium is lower for smaller firms.

The Results of the Reforms. The first results of the introduction of financial incentives for employers in sickness insurance introduced in 1994 point to a marked reduction in sickness absenteeism in the Netherlands of about 10 to 15 %. It is too early to judge the effects of fully privatizing sickness insurance in 1996. CPB has estimated that full privatization will result in an additional fall in sickness absenteeism of about 5 %.

---

[20] Furthermore, measures aimed at returning claimants of disability benefits to work have been introduced and, more recently, extended.

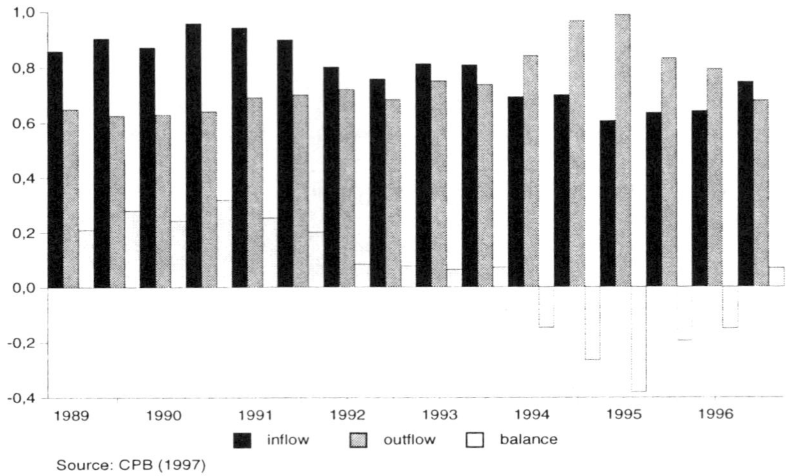

Figure 6.4 Inflow and outflow of disability scheme in the Netherlands (in percent of employment)

The reforms in the disability scheme appear to have led to a one-time downward shift in an upward trend in disability claimants due to the aging of the population. Figure 6.4 shows that the reassessments of the existing claimants, which started in 1994, boosted the flows out of the disability scheme. At the same time, the tighter criteria for eligibility reduced the inflows. More recently, as the program of reassessing existing claimants draws to an end, the number of disability claimants resumed its upward trend. As a percentage of total employment, however, the number of disability claimants continues to fall slightly.

6.3.3 Evaluation

Figure 6.1 and Table 6.5 show that the Dutch reforms, while stemming the rapid increase of benefit recipients in the seventies and early eighties, did not succeed in reversing the rise in claimants under 65 years old until 1994. Due to rapid employment growth, the ratio of benefit recipients to employment (the so-called i/a ratio) started to decline already in 1993. It seems very difficult to reduce the stock of inactive people claiming social insurance benefits once the vicious circle described in Section 6.2.6 has been allowed to reduce the access of vulnerable workers to the labour market.

Table 6.1 indicates that, despite the Dutch reforms, the invalidity rate and the admission rate into disability schemes in the Netherlands still exceed the corresponding rates in Germany. Moreover, Germany has been as successful as the Netherlands in reducing these rates between 1983 and 1995. Only in the sickness scheme, has the Netherlands been more successful in cutting claims.

The fall in invalidity rates in Germany originates mainly in a tightening of eligibility criteria in 1984 (see Frick and Sadawski, 1996). From that time on, one qualifies for (social) disability benefits only if one has worked three years during the five years before becoming disabled. This requirement primarily affects women who have acquired rights in the past but have stopped working regularly. This tightening of disability eligibility rules was mitigated to some extent by a loosening of eligibility rules for the old-age pension scheme.

Another factor behind the fall in German invalidity rates is a loosening of the rules to retire at age 60 after long-term unemployment and an extension of the duration of unemployment benefit payments for older workers (see Riphahn, 1997). Since (social) disability benefits are less generous than unemployment benefits in Germany, there is an incentive to draw on unemployment rather than disability benefits before retirement.

6.4 Trends

6.4.1 German Unification

The burden of unification has turned out to be heavier than expected at the time of the unification, in part because the productivity level of the East German economy was lower than anticipated. In the absence of social consensus about how this heavy burden of unification is to be shared, it has set in motion a vicious circle of tax increases, wage increases, and employment reductions in Germany as a whole (see Section 6.2.6 for a discussion of a similar vicious circle in the Netherlands). The increasing number of recipients of public transfers in combination with a weak employment performance have contributed to increasing concerns about the sustainability of the present German social security system.

After unification, the West German system of social protection was transferred to East Germany, allowing for only small differences in the institutional regulations. The levels of unemployment and social assistance payments set a floor for wages in East Germany. As productivity in East Germany is quite low, many workers would have to accept wages below this floor in order to be competitive with workers in Middle and Eastern Europe. In this way, the German welfare state contributes to poor employment performance in East Germany (see, *e.g.*, Carlin and Soskice, 1997).[21]

German social security spending rose quite dramatically in the 1990s: between 1989-94 the total bill increased by the equivalent of 3.5% of GDP (see Figure 6.2). This spending boost was primarily the result of reunification. Unemployment

---

[21] For a more elaborate analysis of the reasons behind and the effects of high wage settlements in the wake of German unification, see Chapters 3 and 4 of this study and also Sinn and Sinn (1992).

benefits and old-age pensions account for most of the recent increase in German social security spending. East Germany accounts for one fifth of the German labour force but one third of German unemployment. Including hidden unemployment in early retirement and job creation schemes, the unemployment share is even larger.

6.4.2 Higher Demand for Social Insurance

Several trends, which apply not only to Germany but also to the Netherlands and other OECD countries, raise the demands on the welfare state.

Aging. Older people tend to behave in a more risk-averse fashion because they adapt less easily to shocks in income. Hence, the demand for social insurance rises, reflecting a move into the direction of risksharing on the trade-off between risksharing and incentives.

More Risks. Also other trends, which affect the conditions in Table 6.1, may raise the demand for social insurance. These trends[22] include a weakening of other risk-sharing arrangements, such as the firm (offering life-time employment) and the family, and a more volatile and unpredictable economic environment associated with rapid structural change (due to, for example, shorter life cycles of products and production processes and more radical technological innovations). By protecting the victims of this dynamic process of structural change, social insurance may help to legitimize these processes and encourage individuals to take on more risks.

More Income Dispersion. Low-skilled workers with a weak position on the labour market are expected to continue to put a heavy burden on the social security system. The heterogeneity of labour productivity within the population may well rise further as a consequence of internationalization and technological and organizational developments favouring skilled labour with multiple skills (see Snower, 1996).

Organizational developments, which allow employers to better assess individual productivity of workers, increasingly 'select out' individuals whose productivity lies below the minimum income level guaranteed by the welfare state. These individuals with little marketable skills thus increasingly lack access to the labour market so that they become an increasing burden for the welfare state. Also medical technology is likely to reveal more of the actual features and risk characteristics of individuals. Accordingly, both organizational and technological developments increasingly lift Rawls' veil of ignorance. Once this veil has been

[22] For a more extensive description of these trends, see Chapter 2.

Box 6.5 Proposed reforms in German disability insurance

In June 1997 the German government presented a bill to the Bundestag containing reform proposals for the combined disability and public old age insurance (Rentenversicherung). The proposal does not require approval by the Bundesrat. Various motives underlie this and earlier proposals for reform: addressing the consequences of aging, lowering the burden of social security contributions, enhancing labour market performance, and improving possibilities for adjustment to personal circumstances (compare Sachverständigenrat, 1996: Ch. 5). Box 7.2 in Chapter 7 reviews the reforms in the old-age component of the Rentenversicherung.

The reform of disability insurance involves two main elements. Firstly, unemployment risk is eliminated from disability insurance. Due to a court decision, the disability insurance currently covers also unemployment risk. In particular, insured persons who are partly disabled and unable to find a job for the remaining part are entitled to a full disability benefit. After the reform, a person's health status constitutes the only relevant criterium for a disability benefit.

Secondly, the two types of disability benefits within the Rentenversicherung, 'the occupational disability benefit' and 'the labour disability benefit' (see Box 6.2), are abolished. Mainly higher qualified employees benefit from the occupational disability benefit, which implies unequal treatment. Instead, a three-step system will be introduced. People who are able to work only three hours a day receive a full benefit, people who are able to work between three and six hours a day receive a partial benefit, and people who are able to work more than six hours a day receive no benefit at all.

---

lifted, vulnerable groups can no longer insure themselves on the market against low earning capabilities. Moreover, as vulnerable individuals become increasingly trapped in unemployment or low paying jobs while other high-skilled individuals face a very low risk of becoming unemployed, the government can rely less on the insurance principle to ensure solidarity between individuals with different levels of human capital. Hence, protecting individuals with little marketable skills and high risk characteristics thus requires more explicit redistribution through compulsory mechanisms.

If the insured have more information about risk features than insurance companies, more heterogeneous risk features increase the danger that voluntary insurance results in adverse selection and high transaction costs. Also through this channel, a more heterogeneous population may raise the demand for mandatory insurance.

6.4.3 Complications for Social Security

Several trends complicate the provision of generous mandatory social security.

Aging. The aging of the population increases the burden on the welfare state because the welfare state transfers resources away from the young towards the elderly. Whereas population aging thus boosts the demands on the welfare state, the means to satisfy these claims are diminishing as the working population shrinks. This reduces the commitment of younger workers to the intergenerational contract implicit in the current welfare state (see Chapter 7), thereby increasing political risks associated with mandatory insurance.

Aging of the workforce intensifies the moral hazard problems in social insurance because older workers are subject to higher disability and unemployment risk, in part because older workers may be less adaptable. Also through this channel does aging increase the demands on the welfare state.

Political Risks. A more heterogeneous population with diverging risk features increases the redistributive character of the welfare state. To illustrate, compared to skilled workers, unskilled workers face a larger unemployment risk. Hence, unskilled labour is cross-subsidized by skilled labour in unemployment insurance - even if not only premiums but also benefits rise with income. The increasingly redistributive character of the welfare state may well reduce the political support of the middle class for generous social security provisions. By using the governance structure of voice in this way, individuals with a lot of marketable skills may opt out of the social contract with vulnerable groups.

International Mobility. Internationally mobile individuals may opt out of the social contract in an alternative way. In particular, they may use the exit option by moving to countries with a lower level of mandatory social insurance. At the same time, high levels of mandatory social insurance may attract individuals from abroad who are likely to benefit from the system. More generally, increasing mobility across risksharing pools erodes risksharing by allowing the good risks to opt out.

Also international mobility of capital may complicate the provision of social security if social security premiums are shifted forward onto capital. In particular, social security taxes are not paid by employees in terms of lower net wages if effective wage floors constrain the flexibility of after-tax wages. In this way, high social security taxes harm the international competitiveness of domestic firms.

Diversity. A more heterogeneous population complicates the determination of a uniform level of insurance, thereby increasing the transaction costs of the political process. Indeed, it shifts the position on the diversity-scale trade-off towards diversity (see Table 6.1). An increased preference for freedom to choose as a result of more emancipated consumers exerts a similar impact on the position on this trade-off. Moreover, a more heterogenous population makes it more difficult to identify the truly needy (see also Box 7.4 in Chapter 7). This information problem shifts the position on the trade-off between insurance and incentives towards incentives.

More Flexibility. Increased flexibility of labour supply behaviour allows employers and workers to increasingly exploit social insurance provisions. Hence, also this trend moves the position on the trade-off between insurance and incentives towards incentives.

Privacy and Norms. On the one hand, privacy considerations may worsen adverse selection, thereby making mandatory social insurance more attractive. On the other hand, a higher preference for privacy complicates monitoring, thereby shifting the incentive-risksharing trade-off towards incentives. The erosion of common norms that constrain moral hazard has the same effect.

6.4.4 The Impact of Trends on Other Risk-sharing Arrangements

The architects of the modern welfare state, such as Beveridge, stressed that work and the family should be the principal foundation of social welfare. Indeed, a well-functioning labour market, the two-earner family and more efficient capital markets can reduce the need for social insurance provided by the state. This section explores how various trends affect these other risk-sharing arrangements.

Labour Market. An efficient labour market yielding a high level of employment is probably the most important complementary institution to the welfare state. A more flexible labour market with lower entry barriers for outsiders and greater reliance on contract labour, self-employment, part-time employment and job sharing, reduces the risk of long-term unemployment and thus the need for extensive social protection.[23] The same holds true for a less rigid allocation of leisure, education, care, and work over the life cycle. More generally, increased flexibility, mobility, employability (including the capacity to continue to learn), and adaptability are alternative ways to reduce risk (see also Section 2.4.3). Higher labour demand on account of the aging of the labour force can facilitate the role of the labour market in providing insurance. The same holds true for higher labour-force participation of women associated with improved human capital of women. At the same time, however, the weak position of low-skilled individuals reduces the potential role of the labour market in protecting these individuals. Moreover, an older labour force, due to aging, may well be less adaptable.

---

[23] Atkinson (1995) argues that social insurance originated in the emergence of a primary sector with modern employment relationships. In this sector, employers pay an efficiency wage premium because they cannot monitor workers and have to incur search costs to replace existing workers. This wage premium results in workers queuing for these primary jobs. Workers thus are subject to the risk of being unable to find a job in the primary sector. This increases inequities. In this way, information problems increase the need for solidarity enforced by the government.

Capital Market. Improved investment and risk-sharing arrangements on modern capital markets expand the possibilities for private insurance markets. The globalization of capital markets allows insurance companies to spread risks across larger and better diversified pools. Moreover, technological improvements can reduce the costs of information associated with private insurance, thereby reducing transaction costs and mitigating adverse selection and moral hazard.[24] Modern capital markets allow for more income-smoothing during the life cycle, which is presently still undertaken by the welfare state. These trends, facilitating insurance through the free market, shift the position on the diversity-scale trade-off towards diversity.

Family. Another institution for risksharing that can relieve the burden on the welfare state is the family. Families are supported by norms and values and can address the failures of insurance markets. In particular, norms and values prevent low-risk people from opting out of the family pool, thereby avoiding adverse selection. Moreover, family members can easily monitor each other, thereby preventing moral hazard.

The improved labour-market position of women, which is associated with better educational opportunities, has boosted the number of dual income families. In these families, partners can insure each other against temporary income losses. Indeed, as the traditional family with a single breadwinner with a full-time job caring for many dependants becomes less important, the minimum wage and the benefit levels in the social insurance system can be reduced.

On the negative side, however, the organization of the division of tasks within a two-earner family is more complicated than in a family with a single income-earner. This taxes the marriage relationship, thereby contributing to increased divorce risk. Also the reduced access of young men with little marketable skills to the labour market has increased the pressure on the family because it has made these men less attractive marriage partners. These trends increase the number of single-parent families who cannot benefit from risksharing arrangements between partners and are thus particularly vulnerable to poverty. In this way, the inequities between those who do not need the welfare state (i.e. the members of two-earner households) and those who are dependent on it (i.e. the members of single parent households or singles) increases. Accordingly, redistribution in favour of households with only one adult may be called for. This, however, may encourage the break-up of households. Moreover, the government may find it increasingly difficult to identify various types of households in view of the increasing diversity of household types.

---

[24] However, technological developments (e.g. in medical technology) may make information about individual risk features more asymmetric. This would worsen problems of adverse selection.

Table 6.6 Impact of trends on strengths of mandatory and voluntary insurance

	Mandatory insurance	Voluntary insurance
Aging		
More risk averse population	+	-
Smaller contribution base	-	+
More moral hazard	-	+
Economic environment		
More volatile and unpredictable	+	-
More international mobility	-	+
Technology		
Biased against low skilled	+	-
Improved screening	+	-
Social trends		
More heterogenous risk features	+	-
Less common norms	-	+
Preferences		
More heterogeneous	-	+
More preferences for freedom to choose	-	+
More preferences for privacy	-/+	+/-

6.4.5 The Trends: An Overall Perspective

Table 6.6 summarizes the impact of the various trends on the position on the trade-offs affecting the choice between mandatory and voluntary insurance. The table shows a mixed picture. On the one hand, various trends increase the importance of the strong points of the market, namely diversity, experimentation, and incentives. On the other hand, other trends point to the increased importance of solidarity enforced through the control mechanism, because these trends tend to increase inequities.

Also developments in labour and capital markets and the family may increase the stress on the welfare state. On the one hand, more redistribution through compulsory mechanisms is called for to reduce inequities. On the other hand, the political support for these redistributive activities may well fall, as many high-skilled and two-earner households do not need welfare-state benefits but can instead rely on the labour and capital markets and the two-earner family.

German unification yields a similar conflict. On the one hand, it demands more solidarity with vulnerable groups. On the other hand, it requires more flexibility.

Increased flexibility on labour markets is likely to generate similar tensions. On the one hand, to encourage people to take more risks and to legitimize the process of reallocation in an increasingly dynamic and flexible economy, the government may need to provide generous social insurance. On the other hand, the increased flexibility of labour supply behaviour allows employers and workers to increasingly exploit social insurance provisions. Accordingly, the challenge is to find a new mix of the coordination mechanisms of control and competition that exploit the strengths of these coordination mechanisms in the face of these conflicting trends. For many high-skilled and two-earner households, more competitive mechanisms seem to be called for. At the same time, control remains needed to protect and activate vulnerable groups with little marketable skills.

6.5 Policy Options for Reform: The Unfinished Agenda

6.5.1 Policy Options for the Netherlands

The Dutch reforms described in Section 6.3 were largely in line with the lessons from the German experience. The main lessons from Germany for the Netherlands involved a more efficient governance of the benefit administration. Many of the required reforms have been implemented or are currently in the process of being implemented.

Checks and Balances in the Governance of Social Insurance. The Netherlands is introducing various checks and balances in the governance structure of social insurance. This in order to enhance the accountability of the social insurance administration. For instance, in line with the situation in Germany, the roles, objectives, and responsibilities of the various players have been clarified.

Administration of Social Assistance. Also in social assistance is the Netherlands moving in the direction of the German system by using less detailed regulations to guide the administration of social security at a decentralized level. To reap the benefits of this reform, it is essential that plans proceed to make the municipalities, which execute social assistance, responsible for a larger part of the financing. More generally, in the administration of social assistance, several trends shift the trade-off between experimentation and control towards experimentation (see Section 6.5.3 below). Accordingly, also in social assistance, the introduction of more competitive elements is called for. This may enhance cooperation between labour offices and municipalities in helping benefit recipients to find jobs.

Unemployment Insurance. Also in unemployment insurance, better monitoring of benefit recipients seems called for. The recent fall in the unemployment rate in the Netherlands indicates that less people are actively looking for work. At the same time, the number of people claiming unemployment benefits has stayed at a high level (see Figure 6.5). Seen in this light, the low Dutch unemployment rate may be a sign of weakness rather than strength because it indicates that not many people drawing social insurance benefits are actively looking for work. Another complication is the increasing difficulty to separate voluntary from involuntary

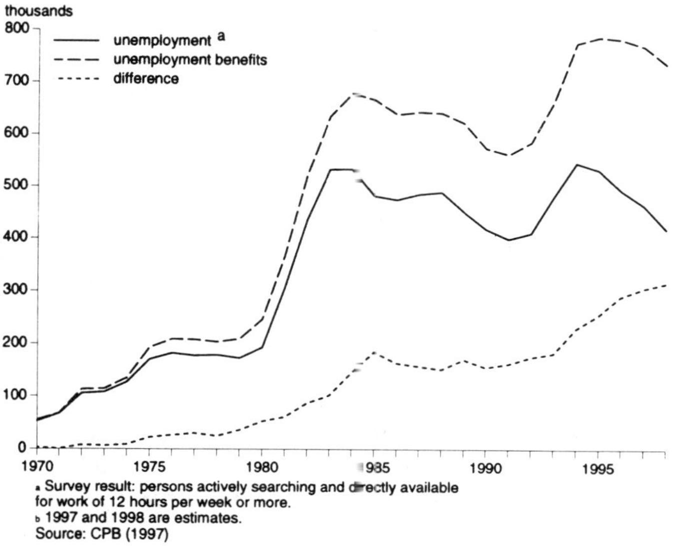

Figure 6.5 Unemployment in the Netherlands, 1970-1998[b]

unemployment, especially for workers with flexible contracts. A more efficient benefit administration aimed at screening claimants and bringing claimants back to work can help to better utilize the human capital of the benefit recipients (see also Section 6.5.3 below). Indeed, stronger work incentives for those claiming unemployment benefits are called for.

Sickness Scheme. Compared to the Netherlands, Germany continues to rely more on stricter medical control in sickness schemes. This different emphasis can be explained by a higher preference for privacy in the Netherlands and a more juridical tradition in Germany.

In the sickness scheme, the Netherlands has gone further than Germany in using elements of competition. However, some collective wage contracts negotiated at the industry level still force individual employers to take out supplementary insurance from a selected insurance company. Collective agreements on supplementing statutory benefits are still legally extended to all firms in the industry.[25]

Disability. The Dutch system of disability insurance, in contrast to the corresponding German system, does not distinguish between social and occupational risks. The relatively high Dutch replacement rates for social disability (both relative to the corresponding German rate and the Dutch replacement rates for unemployment)

[25] This holds true also for supplementary insurance of disability risk.

continue to make this scheme vulnerable to moral hazard. Although disability benefit claims have fallen in recent years, they started to rise again in 1996, as the reassessment program started in 1994 drew to a close. Indeed, the aging of the workforce implies a rising underlying trend, because older people are more likely to claim disability benefits. This is especially so if the claim assessment procedure keeps resulting in the, compared to the German situation, relatively high levels of admissions to the disability scheme.

A tighter claim assessment procedure may help to stem this trend. In stemming the inflow into disability schemes, the Netherlands can benefit from the German emphasis on control and strict regulations. Indeed, in Germany, requests for disability are at a lower level and more applicants are refused admittance (see Table 6.3). One factor in this respect is that insurance doctors refer many applicants to specialists (see Prins *et al.*, 1993). The Dutch plans for allowing private insurance of disability may help to tighten the claim assessment procedure, which remains in public hands. In particular, insurance companies have clear incentives to fight lax assessments in the courts. In this way, competition can help to break the culture of conflict-avoidance, which has led parties with conflicting interests to shift the burden to the collective pool. This is particularly important in the Netherlands, which lacks the German 'juridical' tradition of stemming inflows into social insurance through strict controls and regulations.

6.5.2 Policy Options for Germany

The Labour Market. German unification has shown that the German welfare state is not shock proof. The Dutch experience reveals the importance of breaking at an early stage the vicious circle of less employment and higher inactivity spending, premiums and labour costs. Inactivity should be combatted by raising employment rather than by reducing effective labour supply. A well-functioning labour market with a high level of employment is a prerequisite for generous social insurance. Indeed, participation in the labour market should be the preferred route for protecting people against income loss.

In this connection, wage moderation yields a double dividend: First, by restoring profitability and investment, increasing the labour-intensity of production and enhancing international competitiveness, it protects employment -- the financial base of the welfare state. Second, it reduces public spending because social benefits are generally linked to wages and because the number of benefit claimants is reduced.

To protect overall employment, also a flexible labour market can make an important contribution. A labour market with low entry barriers to outsiders constitutes an important insurance mechanism. This is especially so in combination with two-earner families. Hence, partners of breadwinners should be encouraged to seek (part-time) work, in part through arrangements that allow parents to combine child raising and careers. In this way, insurance is provided through the market and the family.

Unemployment Insurance and Social Assistance. The interaction between social insurance and the labour market goes both ways. By encouraging claimants to get back to work, social insurance raises effective labour supply, thereby moderating wages and labour costs.[26] To make the welfare state a trampoline rather than a hammock, unemployment insurance must provide stronger work incentives. This especially applies to older workers who benefit from rather generous benefits because of the strong insurance element in German unemployment insurance. Indeed, long-term unemployment in Germany is concentrated among older workers, which makes the German welfare state particularly vulnerable to aging.[27] Especially for older workers, the incentives for and obligation to seek work may have to be increased.

Benefit levels in Germany and the Netherlands are rather generous compared to other countries. Although Dutch benefits tend to be higher than German benefits, German replacement rates are higher for some groups. In particular, reflecting the needs principle of the social assistance system, German single-earners with low incomes and many dependants feature high replacement rates (see Box 6.1). To alleviate the unemployment trap, the German government has proposed to increase the gap between the local average of low labour incomes and social assistance. However, this proposal has been abandoned (see OECD, 1996).

The duration of unemployment benefits is another important determinant of incentives to actively search for work. In contrast to the situation in the Netherlands, German unemployment assistance benefits are provided for an unlimited period (see Box 6.1).

Sickness Scheme. Sickpay is particularly generous in Germany. Even overtime pay is compensated during illness. On average, the German sickness rate of the industrial workforce in 1994 was 5.5 percent, a level surpassed only by the Netherlands (see OECD, 1996). The German government has reduced statutory sick pay to 80 percent of the reference wage but supplementary provisions negotiated by employers and unions continue to supplement benefits to 100 percent. Privatizing the sickness scheme, as in the Netherlands, would imply that employers bear the full cost burden of the effect of generous extra-statutory provisions on the sickness rate. This would encourage employers to reduce these supplementary provisions.

---

[26] Another important way to moderate labour costs is to reduce the overall burden of taxes and social security premiums.

[27] In 1995, 40 per cent of the long-term unemployed were over 55 years old (see Carlin and Soskice, 1997).

More generally, Germany relies more on control and regulations while the Netherlands has introduced more market elements (and financial incentives) in social security. Germany's emphasis on control and regulations implies that Germany may need to use less financial incentives to stem moral hazard than the Netherlands. Nevertheless, the market-oriented reforms in disability and sickness insurance in the Netherlands may provide a source of inspiration for Germany in reforming its social insurance system. The proposed Dutch system can be seen as a mix of coordination through control and competition. The statutory benefits are determined by the political process. Moreover, several regulations protect the position of vulnerable groups (see Section 6.3.2). A mix of control and competition may exploit the strengths of both coordination mechanisms, thereby improving the trade-off between moral hazard and adverse selection.

6.5.3 The Unfinished Agenda for Both Countries

Remaining Challenges. Both Germany and the Netherlands are not yet adequately prepared to address the challenges of the 21st century. In addition to the policy options discussed in the previous section, therefore, more reforms are called for. Major remaining policy problems concern the low participation rates of older workers (see Chapter 7) and of workers with little marketable skills. The social insurance system contributes to these low participation rates by providing rather high replacement rates for these groups.

A Broad Strategy. A single solution addressing the various trends is not available. Countries are thus advised to rely on a broad range of measures. Policies are often complementary in the sense that the effect of each policy is greater when it is implemented together with other policies than when it is introduced in isolation (see Coe and Snower, 1997). Employing several instruments is attractive also for political reasons: costs and benefits are spread over several groups. To illustrate, to reduce the claims of low-skilled workers on social security, the government can combine the stick of lower unconditional benefits with the carrot of tax cuts and deregulation of sheltered sectors aimed at raising the demand for low-skilled labour. Most importantly, taking action on several fronts diversifies risks. Indeed, the process of social innovation is a process of trial and error in the face of current problems and newly emerging trends. For lack of space, this chapter cannot fully discuss all elements of such a broad strategy in detail. Instead, it will mention some of the major elements that could be part of such a strategy.

Enhancing Employability of Vulnerable Groups. Technological and organization developments increasingly put vulnerable individuals with few marketable skills at risk. To prevent long-run dependency and social exclusion, the government should shift away from passive towards active support. This latter support should strengthen the earnings capacity, skills, adaptability, and employability of vulnerable individuals. Social benefits were originally intended to primarily relieve liquidity constraints by carrying people over relatively short unemployment spells. At the present time, however, structural unemployment and long-term dependency require more active, interventionist policies with conditional and in-kind benefits (e.g. training and other investments in human capital) to avoid social exclusion and to raise labour productivity by building up human capital. By enhancing the employability and earning capabilities of vulnerable individuals with little marketable skills, social insurance addresses social exclusion and family instability at the root.[28] These interventions thus imply a shift away from remedial to pre-emptive, preventive measures.

Conditional transfers based on the transaction principle (i.e. balancing the carrot of the benefit with the stick of certain obligations) can be used to screen claimants, thereby alleviating moral hazard. The obligations imposed on benefit recipients give them a direct interest in improving their circumstances. Moreover, in-kind transfers can link support to activities (such as training, unpaid trial employment, community work) that encourage rather than discourage re-entry into employment.

Wage subsidies or vouchers for the long-term unemployed can be used as a particular form of in-kind benefits aimed at stimulating demand for the low skilled. This demand can be stimulated also by deregulating sheltered sectors. In these sectors, the unskilled do not have to compete directly with labour in low-wage countries. Moreover, more flexible labour and commodity markets help to increase the access of outsiders to work by reducing entry barriers, which act as implicit taxes on low-skilled work (see also Chapters 8 and 9). Another option in this connection is to reduce (explicit) tax rates on low incomes and unskilled work. However, unless tax rates are cut over a broad range, substantial tax cuts for specific groups may result in high marginal tax rates, thereby distorting the labour market and reducing the incentives to acquire skills. Hence, in order to avoid a low-skill trap, this policy would require a cut in the overall tax burden.

More Support for the Young. Preventive measures are most effective if they occur early in life. In this connection, assistance to single parent households is particularly important in order to protect children from the intergenerational transfer of deficits and to prevent passive income support later in life.

The shift towards active support at the beginning of the life cycle poses a challenge to governments. Such a policy of social investment and investment in human capital reduces the costs of passive income support only in the future.

---

[28] Improving skills helps also individuals who cannot be educated because it reduces the scarcity of skilled labour, thereby improving the relative wage earned by unskilled labour.

Hence, in the short run, governments have to pay twice: once for active support of the young and once for passive support of the old.[29]

Consequences for the Benefit Administration. A shift towards more active policies involving conditional and in-kind benefits calls for tailor-made solutions implemented by a decentralized benefit administration that exploits its information advantage about individual circumstances. More generally, a more heterogeneous and diverse population requires more tailor-made and innovative solutions. Accordingly, social security administrations should be transformed from hierarchical bureaucratic organizations to more decentralized, entrepreneurial and customer-oriented bodies. While the central government is still likely to play an important role in setting the rules of the game and in determining the levels of compulsory insurance, it may actually want to leave the provision of social services and benefits increasingly to decentralized public and private agencies.

The behaviour of the decentralized agencies can by affected by various kinds of financial incentives (see Section 6.1.5). Indeed, as a result of the trends, the trade-off in administrating social insurance between experimentation and certainty is likely to shift towards experimentation (see Table 6.2). To illustrate, if the administration of unemployment benefits is increasingly delegated to decentralized agencies, more of the budget responsibility can be decentralized as well in order to avoid moral hazard of the decentralized agencies. The risks of this strategy of relying on financial incentives are cream-skimming behaviour of the decentralized agencies (they focus on those individuals with good risk features) and unequal treatment of similar people. Accordingly, financial incentives should be complemented by supervision and regulations protecting vulnerable groups. A mix of control and competition may thus exploit the strengths of both coordination mechanisms, thereby improving the trade-off between solidarity and incentives in an environment that calls for more diversity and experimentation.

Continuous Learning. In a dynamic world, a sustainable welfare state requires constant change. Not only do exogenous trends demand adjustments of provisions, also endogenous unintended responses to social insurance systems usually become apparent and fully understood by boundedly rational governments only after some time. In this connection, experimentation by decentralized benefit administrations may help to uncover what works and what does not work.

Reform: Stability versus Commitment. This continuous process of reform involves a trade-off between flexibility (i.e. experimentation), and commitment (i.e. stability and certainty). Stability of social insurance provisions is valuable because

---

[29] For a similar transition problem in the context of old-age insurance, see Chapter 7. See also the discussion of the trade-off between stability and commitment below.

these provisions can be regarded as long-term contracts between the government and its citizens. In order to protect older groups that can not adjust flexibly to changes, reforms may have to be phased in gradually. Accordingly, in reconciling confidence in the contracts with timely adjustments, policy makers should anticipate future trends so that they can timely adjust the welfare state and the mix of various coordination mechanisms in providing insurance. Indeed, sustainable solidarity requires constant adaption to new circumstances. This is the challenge policy makers face. This chapter intends to help policy makers to take up this challenge by exploring both the major forces that impinge on social insurance and the most important trade-offs that policy makers have to confront in designing social insurance.

7 Pensions

For two reasons, old-age insurance is an important topic for this study comparing the institutional framework of the German and Dutch economies. First, the German pension system differs substantially from the Dutch one. This increases the scope for mutual learning. Second, both countries will experience rapid aging over the next four decades. This poses serious challenges to the pension systems of these countries.

The chapter is organized as follows. Section 7.1 outlines the theoretical framework of this chapter. It discusses how market failures in old-age insurance imply a role for the coordination mechanisms of control and corporative exchange. The limitations of these coordination mechanisms, however, give rise to various trade offs, which are affected by the economic environment. Section 7.2 turns to a description of the Dutch and German pension systems. How these systems affect the performance of the two economies is discussed in Section 7.3. Section 7.4 deals not only with aging but also with non-demographic trends that affect the future of income support in old age. These trends include financial innovation, international integration, technological change, individualization, a more heterogeneous population and more heterogeneous tastes and needs. Indeed, these trends are likely to be as important as aging in determining the future of old-age insurance. Section 7.5 combines the current performance of the pension systems discussed in Section 7.3 and the future trends explored in Section 7.4 to arrive at policy options for old-age insurance in Germany and the Netherlands.

7.1 Market Failures and Trade-Offs

7.1.1 Market Failures

The competitive coordination mechanism provides old-age insurance in the form of individual saving schemes. In these schemes, individual retirement benefits are directly related to individual contributions. At any point in time, accumulated capital corresponds to the discounted value of expected future retirement benefits. These individual saving schemes can be provided by the market as defined-contribution (DC) pension plans. These personal pension plans can provide insurance against longevity risk by paying out benefits as annuities.[1] The market, however, suffers from various failures in providing income protection to the elderly. This section discusses these market failures.

Lack of Intergenerational Risksharing. As noted in Chapter 6, the free market cannot provide insurance against major interdependent risks, including investment risks due to depressions, wars, natural disasters, inflation, financial crisis, etc. This is because the market cannot enforce risksharing among non-overlapping generations. In particular, generations that are not yet born cannot commit to a risksharing arrangement. By the time young generations can conclude such a contract, they already have information about the outcome. If they know that they would have to transfer resources to the older generations, the younger generations would choose to opt out by not concluding the contract. Accordingly, the free market cannot benefit from the economies of scope associated with pooling risks across generations.

As a result of this lack of risk pooling, the individual tends to be risk averse when investing pension saving, thereby reducing expected returns. The emphasis on low risk on the trade-off between low risks and high returns thus harms the efficiency of the free market in delivering high expected pension benefits for low premiums.

High Transaction and Information Costs. Another reason for the inefficiency of the free market are the high information and transactions costs associated with concluding individual pension contracts. The market does not benefit from the economies of scope of information gathering and concluding contracts with pre-selected workers. Individual pensions are complex products. Hence, insurance companies providing personal pension schemes may charge more than 25% of the premium as administration costs. Moreover, salespersons may mislead ill-informed customers about the merits of specific DC plans.

Adverse Selection. High information costs about the features of individuals may make the market vulnerable to adverse selection. In particular, adverse selection may prevent individuals with high mortality risk from obtaining actuarially fair insurance against longevity risk.

Myopia and Moral Hazard. Also other factors may result in underinsurance. If individuals are myopic, they may leave insufficient resources for retirement. Also moral hazard may cause rational agents to save inefficiently low amounts for

[1] DC schemes are not redistributive ex ante and are thus actuarially fair. However, if these plans provide annuities, they insure against longevity risk. Hence, these plans redistribute incomes ex post away from short-lived individuals to long-lived ones.

retirement in order to exploit means-tested retirement provisions provided by the state.

Lack of Intragenerational Solidarity. The free market does not provide adequate old-age insurance to vulnerable individuals who do not have sufficient means to save during their working life. As indicated in Section 6.1.2 of Chapter 6, the lack of solidarity with vulnerable groups may not only be undesirable in itself but also harm the economy.

Consequences of Market Failures. The free market thus fails to provide adequate insurance against longevity risk and also other risks in old age due to macroeconomic shocks. This leads to cautious investment behaviour and hence low returns on pension saving. Also high information and transaction costs reduce effective returns and contribute to underinsurance against income risks in old age. Finally, the free market may give rise to old-age poverty, in part because individuals fail to provide sufficient pension savings.

7.1.2 Coordination Mechanisms in Old-Age Insurance

Other coordination mechanisms can help to alleviate the market failures associated with personal pension plans. This section explores how the market failures are addressed by pay-as-you-go (PAYG) systems employing control and defined-benefit (DB) schemes using cooperative exchange.

PAYG Schemes. PAYG schemes pay retirement benefits out of premiums collected on the labour income of the young. PAYG schemes thus can in principle ensure that the standard of living of the elderly is not too far out of line with the incomes of the young. In this way, PAYG systems may prevent large disparities in standards of living between various generations, thereby benefiting solidarity.

PAYG systems employ the coordination mechanism of control to provide insurance against interdependent risks by committing younger generations to a risksharing arrangement (see Gordon and Varian, 1988); by changing the level of compulsory premiums paid by younger workers, PAYG schemes can shift adverse shocks to the young. This intergenerational risksharing aimed at protecting the incomes of the elderly can be efficient because the young are generally better able to adapt to changes in wealth than the old, who feature only limited human capital and a short planning horizon.

PAYG schemes can be seen as part of an implicit social contract between generations. The older generations raise the younger generations, thereby transferring human capital to the young. The elderly provide the young also with public capital goods, such as a clean natural environment, public infrastructure, and most importantly, knowledge. The ideas generated by the older generations enhance the productivity of the young. Indeed, the younger generations stand on the shoulders of the old. In return for this service, the older generations expect the younger generations to transfer part of the return on this investment to them when they have exhausted their human capital in retirement (see e.g. Razin and Sadka, 1995). The market cannot enforce this implicit contract among generations.

Defined Benefit Schemes. DB schemes can be viewed as a mixture of PAYG and DC schemes. DB schemes, which are typically provided as occupational schemes by firms, employ the coordination mechanism of cooperative exchange.[2] Just like DC schemes, DB systems use capital funding. However, in contrast to DC schemes, benefits are based on salary levels during the working life rather than on the discounted value of individual life-time contributions. In order to be able to pay these wage-linked benefits, DB schemes rely not only on the accumulation of financial assets but also on an implicit contract between the partners in the cooperative exchange, namely the firm, its workers, and retirees of different ages. If returns are low and wage increases are substantial, the firm and younger workers transfer resources to older generations.[3] If returns are high, in contrast, these parties benefit from lower pension premiums.

DB schemes thus back up the benefit promise not only by financial assets (as in DC schemes) but also by the market power of the firm and the commitment of future workers to the implicit contract. In particular, a firm can enforce this implicit contract only if it earns rents due to market power so that it can insure the elderly against low returns without being pushed out of the market by young firms that do not have to care for retired workers. Exit barriers for young workers ensure that DB schemes can transfer resources from younger workers to retirees and older workers. If young workers were fully mobile across firms, they could not be committed to the contract with the retired and older workers in their firm; if a firm attempted to tax its younger workers to transfer resources to its retirees, these workers would move to young firms without retirees and older workers. Accordingly, firms can perform the redistributive activities associated with the benefit promise in DB schemes only in less than perfectly competitive product and labour markets.[4]

---

[2] Also the fourth coordination mechanism introduced in Section 2, namely common values and norms, can play a role in providing old-age insurance. To illustrate, families can provide old-age insurance to their older members.

[3] In particular, wage increases result in considerable additional pension obligations with respect to older workers. The costs of these additional obligations are spread over all workers.

[4] Hence, in perfectly competitive markets, government regulations (i.e. the coordination mechanism of control) have to help occupational DB schemes to perform inter- and intragenerational redistribution by making collective labour agreements compulsory for particular sectors. Moreover, to prevent adverse selection, workers in a particular firm must be forced to participate in DB schemes.

Employers may use DB schemes as an instrument to alleviate imperfections in labour markets. Employers often adopt these pension schemes to address labour-market failures associated with asymmetric information and lack of commitment (see Chapter 8). In particular, long vesting periods, limited indexation of pension rights for those who end participation before retiring, and linking retirement benefits to the final wage motivates workers not to shirk (when effort is costly to monitor) and binds workers to the firm (see Lazear, 1986). This reduces costs associated with monitoring, training, hiring, and firing. Moreover, a stronger commitment of the worker to the firm encourages the stakeholders of the firm (e.g., shareholders and workers) to invest in firm-specific capital.[5]

Tax Incentives and Mandatory Insurance. Providing tax incentives for old-age insurance is another way to deal with underinsurance due to myopia and moral hazard in exploiting means-tested provisions. Alternatively, the government may employ control by requiring workers to take out pension insurance. In doing so, the government may leave the individual free to select the insurance company or pension fund. However, to avoid adverse selection, reduce transaction costs, and facilitate intergenerational risksharing, the government may also force workers or firms to pool old-age insurance. Accordingly, workers are required not only to take out pension insurance but also pool their risks.[6]

7.1.3 Trade-Offs

Also the coordination mechanisms of control and cooperative exchange suffer from various imperfections. This section discusses these imperfections and the trade-offs that these imperfections give rise to.

Intergenerational Solidarity versus Incentives in the Labour Market. The intergenerational transfers associated with intergenerational risksharing imply that PAYG benefits are not actuarially fair. Accordingly, for a generation as a whole, the discounted retirement benefits do not match the contributions. This imperfect match between benefits and costs implies that premiums distort labour supply. Voluntary DC schemes, in contrast, do not distort labour supply because they redistribute neither across nor within generations. On the trade-off between

---

[5] In this context, explicit contracts may not be able to deal with the so-called hold up problem, where a mutual advantageous investment does not occur because parties cannot credibly commit to a contract. See Section 2.4.[illegible] in Chapter 2.

[6] Competition between various companies administering the mandatory, collective insurance may still be allowed. For a discussion on various mixes between the coordination mechanisms of control and competition in social insurance, see Sub-section 6.1.5 in Chapter 6.

incentives and solidarity, therefore, PAYG schemes stress solidarity and DC schemes emphasize incentives.

Intragenerational Solidarity versus Incentives on the Labour Market. The labour-market distortions implied by PAYG systems depend on the particular pension and contribution formulas. In setting these formulas, governments face a trade-off between, on the one hand, enhancing labour-market incentives by keeping marginal tax rates at low levels, and on the other hand, establishing intragenerational solidarity by alleviating old-age poverty. Benefit formulas that let benefits rise with life-time earnings curtail marginal tax rates on labour income: if not only contributions but also benefits rise with earnings, incentives to reduce labour supply to the formal sector are mitigated.[7] If retirement benefits are flat or means tested but premiums rise with income, in contrast, pension premiums are very much like a tax distorting labour supply. In this case, however, retirement benefits may be better targeted at alleviating old-age poverty.

Distorting Saving or Labour Supply. Whereas compulsory funded saving schemes for workers alleviate the saving distortion (i.e. workers not saving enough for old age because of moral hazard or myopia), they worsen the labour-supply distortion; even if workers are forced to save part of their labour incomes, they can still escape pension contributions by working less. Moreover, compulsory pension premiums can raise wage costs of low skilled workers, thereby reducing the access of these workers to the labour market. In contrast to mandatory pension provisions, tax incentives do not directly hurt incentives to supply labour. However, tax incentives absorb budgetary means. This may require higher taxes elsewhere, thereby indirectly hurting labour supply.

Intergenerational Solidarity versus Incentives on the Capital Market. The intergenerational risksharing in DB schemes requires some degree of monopoly power for firms and exit barriers for younger workers (see Section 7.1.2 above). Whereas exit barriers and monopoly power allow for intergenerational risksharing, the associated lack of competition harms the incentives of DB schemes to invest their funds efficiently.[8] Hence, a trade-off emerges between, on the one hand,

---

[7] In practice, however, benefit formulas may be non-transparent so that, irrespective of the benefit formula, workers perceive pension contributions as a tax. Labour supply is curtailed also if workers discount future benefits due to myopia or lack of confidence in the sustainability of the pension scheme.

[8] Allowing investment companies to bid for the pension pool may help to alleviate moral hazard associated with monopoly power. However, the transaction costs associated with this bidding process may be quite high.

risksharing and, on the other hand, incentives to reduce moral hazard in investment policy.[9]

Insurance and Risktaking. Introducing competition among pension funds to encourage these funds to reap higher returns may be counterproductive, however. In particular, allowing individuals or firms to opt out of collective pension funds would eliminate intergenerational risksharing. In view of the additional investment risk borne by the individual, pension plans would have to pursue a more cautious investment strategy with a lower expected return. This illustrates the value of social insurance in inducing agents to incur more risk (see Sinn, 1995) and Section 6.1.2 in Chapter 6). This discussion links up also with the trade-off between diversity and scale.

Scale versus Diversity. PAYG schemes, and to a lesser extent DB schemes, require compulsory participation under rather uniform conditions; if individuals were free to opt out and select their own pension (DC) packages, intra- and intergenerational risksharing and redistribution would be eroded. Limitations on individual choice, however, amount to an implicit tax and generate welfare losses.

DC schemes leave more scope for individual choice and can cater better to the specific needs and preferences of each individual participant. However, individual choice implies higher transaction costs and no intergenerational risksharing. Compared to individual DC schemes, compulsory DB schemes involve pre-selected workers, thereby mitigating transaction costs. Moreover, these latter schemes involve more pooling of risks, thereby allowing for more efficient risksharing and thus a higher return. Indeed, a trade-off emerges between exploiting economies of scale and scope (in uniform, compulsory pension plans) and tuning pensions to specific needs through product differentiation (in voluntary personal pension plans).[10]

Political versus Market Risk. Whereas PAYG systems are less vulnerable to investment risk than DC schemes, they are likely to be more exposed to political risk. In particular, the implicit intergenerational contract is vulnerable to the hold-up problem.[11] All generations would benefit from a contract stipulating that the older generations educate the young and bequeath public assets (such as a clean natural environment and knowledge) while the younger generations take care of the

---

[9] This trade-off is similar to the fundamental trade-off between risksharing and incentives facing the welfare state introduced in Section 6.1.3 of Chapter 6. The government can weaken this trade-off through issuing indexed bonds (see also Box 7.3 below).

[10] This trade-off between scale and diversity is discussed in more general terms in Section 2.4.1 in Chapter 2. It emerges also in Section 6.1.3 in Chapter 6.

[11] See Chapter 2 for a discussion of the hold-up problem.

Box 7.1 The Aaron condition

The Aaron condition (see Aaron, 1966) shows how the rate of return on capital, the growth rate of labour productivity, and the growth rate of the labour force affect the relative merits of PAYG versus funded schemes. The long-run return to PAYG schemes depends on the growth rate of labour income determining the growth of the contribution base. The return on funded schemes, in contrast, depends on the rate of return on financial assets. Hence, in the long run, funding can offer higher retirement benefits if the rate of return on financial capital exceeds the growth rate of labour income (i.e. the sum of the growth rate of labour productivity and the growth rate of employment). However, PAYG schemes are always more favourable to the first generation because they can offer pensions benefits without having to build up assets.

The Aaron condition can be interpreted as an arbitrage condition involving the relative returns on human and financial capital. PAYG schemes rely on the human capital of the younger generations. In fact, PAYG schemes make the elderly a direct stakeholder in the human capital of the younger generations. Therefore, PAYG schemes are particularly attractive compared to funded schemes if a high growth rate of wages implies a high return on human capital while financial markets offer only low returns.

The table below compares the average growth rate of wages with the average real return on capital during the seventies and eighties. In contrast to the real interest on government bonds, the return on shares substantially exceeded the growth rate of wages during this period.

Table *Real wage growth contrasted with real returns on capital, selected OECD countries, 1971-90*

Country	*Real wage growth*	*Real average annual return on equities*	*Real average annual return on government bonds*
Canada	*1.1*	*5.0*	*1.1*
Denmark	*2.5*	*9.4*	*4.5*
France	*4.0*	*9.6*	*1.3*
Germany	*3.6*	*9.3*	*2.6*
Japan	*3.0*	*11.2*	*0.0*
Netherlands	*1.4*	*8.6*	*1.8*
Switzerland	*1.8*	*4.7*	*−1.7*
United Kingdom	*2.4*	*10.8*	*1.6*
United States	*0.1*	*5.9*	*1.2*

Source: World Bank (1994).

older generations during retirement by insuring these latter generations against adverse income shocks. However, the younger generations can not credibly commit to such a contract if, when they grow up, they gain in economic and political power at the expense of the older generations. Indeed, when the younger generations are in middle age and have to return the favour to the older generations, they have an incentive to exploit their stronger political and economic position vis-à-vis the older generations by refusing to transfer resources. This incentive is mitigated if they take into account that, by breaking the intergenerational contract, they most probably will have to take care of their own retirement provisions.[12] It is strengthened, however, if the contract becomes more expensive to maintain on account of a high retiree-worker ratio due to aging of the population. Indeed, PAYG systems are vulnerable to demographic shocks (see also Box 7.1 on the Aaron condition).

DC schemes are less vulnerable to political and demographic risks because they feature well-defined property rights on individual pensions. As a mix of DC and PAYG plans, DB schemes suffer from some political risk as individual property rights on assets tend to be ill-defined[13].

Accordingly, PAYG schemes focus on decreasing market risks while DC schemes emphasize the reduction of political and demographic risks.

The Trade-Offs. The upper part of Table 7.1 summarizes the various trade-offs between, on the one hand, voluntary insurance provided through the competitive mechanism in the form of DC schemes and, on the other hand, various restrictions on free choice of pension insurance, which are implied by the coordination mechanisms of control and cooperative exchange in the forms of PAYG and DB schemes. In contrast to mandatory insurance, voluntary insurance enhances incentives to supply labour, allows for diversity, mitigates political and demographic risks, and reduces moral hazard in investment policy. Compared to voluntary insurance, various restrictions on free choice facilitate solidarity and intergenerational risk sharing, encourage risktaking in investing pension saving, reduce transaction costs by exploiting economies of scale and scope, and mitigate adverse selection.

7.1.4 The Impact of External Conditions

Table 7.1 indicates how the merits of mandatory PAYG and DB schemes depend on the economic environment. The first group of conditions, which include risk aversion and a preference for equity, determine whether society attaches a high value to intergenerational insurance and solidarity. Also, a volatile economic environment with large unexpected shocks to the economy-wide returns on human and financial capital implies that agents highly value insurance against these

---

[12] Also intergenerational altruism alleviates this incentive.

[13] Indeed, DB schemes typically involve incomplete contracts combined with the governance structure of voice.

Table 7.1 Mandatory versus voluntary insurance

	Pay-as you go (PAYG) and defined benefit (DB) schemes	Defined contribution (DC) schemes
Strengths	Facilitating solidarity	Enhancing incentives to supply labour
	Exploiting economies of scope	Allowing diversity
	Reducing market risk by facilitating inter-generational risksharing	Reducing political risk
	Facilitating risktaking	Hedging against demographic shocks
	Mitigating adverse selection	Reducing moral hazard in investment policies
Conditions		
Conditions Group 1:		
Preferences		
Risk aversion	high	low
Preference for equity	high	low
Uncertainty		
Uncertainty	fundamental	not fundamental
Environment	unstable	stable
Conditions Group 2:		
Financial markets		
Well-developed markets	no	yes
Indexed bonds available	no	yes
International capital mobility	low	high
Rate of return	low	high
Environment	unstable	stable
Information		
Life expectancy	homogeneous	heterogeneous
Information about life expectancy	asymmetric	symmetric
Information costs about pension contracts	high	low
Individual capacity to understand long-term contracts	low	high
Conditions Group 3		
Labour market		
Labour supply	inelastic	elastic
Marginal tax wedges due to other programs	low	high
Political process	efficient and stable	inefficient and unstable

Table 7.1 Mandatory versus voluntary insurance (continued)

Conditions Group 3: (continued)		
Norms and values		
Intergenerational altruism	strong	weak
Demographics		
Wage growth	high	low
Growth rate labour force	high	low
Participation rate	high	low
Average age population	young	old
Income inequality		
Older generations poor relative to younger generations	yes	no
Preferences for old-age insurance	homogeneous	heterogeneous

How to read this Table:

The upper part of this Table ('Strengths') summarizes the various trade-offs by presenting the strengths of, on the one hand, PAYG and DB schemes (the second column) and, on the other hand, DC schemes (the third column). A strength of PAYG and DB schemes implies a weakness of DC schemes and the other way around. For example, the first row in the second column (under 'PAYG and DB schemes') contains the words 'Facilitating solidarity'. This indicates that, in contrast to DC schemes, PAYG and DB schemes facilitate solidarity. Similarly, the words 'Enhancing incentives to supply labour' in the third column (under 'DC schemes') indicate that DC schemes enhance incentives to supply labour. PAYG and DB schemes do not provide these incentives. The first row of the upper part of this Table thus presents the trade-off between solidarity and incentives to supply labour discussed in Sub-section 7.2.3.

The lower part of this Table ('Conditions') summarizes the impact of the external conditions on the various trade-offs. In particular, it states the conditions under which particular pension schemes are attractive, because these conditions make either the strengths of these schemes important or the weaknesses unimportant. To illustrate, the word 'high' in the second column (under 'PAYG and DB schemes') of the row with 'risk aversion' in the first column indicates that PAYG and DB schemes are attractive if risk aversion is high. The word 'low' in the third column of this row (under 'DC schemes') indicates that DC schemes are attractive if risk aversion is low.

macro-economic risks.

The second group of conditions determines whether the free market fails to provide adequate old-age insurance. In particular, leaving old-age insurance to the free market is unattractive if financial markets are poorly developed so that after-tax returns are low. Moreover, if international capital mobility is low, pension funds can not take advantage of high returns abroad and of international portfolio diversification to hedge risks. Also interdependent risks, which may be due to an unstable macro-economic environment, prevent insurance on competitive markets. Furthermore, asymmetric information about life-expectancy gives rise to adverse selection in annuity markets. Finally, high information costs about individual old-age insurance contracts imply that individuals are easily misled and cannot be trusted to make responsible decisions over a long time horizon.

The third group of conditions determines whether the control mechanism performs well. In particular, control is attractive if labour supply is relatively inelastic while the marginal tax wedges on labour supply implied by other taxes and means-tested programs are relatively low. These latter conditions limit the labour-market distortions due to a departure from actuarially fair premiums. Moreover, a stable and efficient political system as well as strong norms and values of intergenerational altruism undergird a credible commitment to the benefit promise, thereby reducing political risks associated with control. In this connection, DB schemes seem particularly attractive in corporatist settings in which workers trust firms to carry out commitments in implicit contracts.

High wage and population growth makes PAYG schemes less expensive to maintain (see Box 7.1). PAYG schemes are particularly attractive if rapid growth of wages causes the younger generations to be relatively affluent compared to the older generations; many OECD countries introduced PAYG systems after the second world war when the young benefitted from rapid productivity growth while the depression and the war had left many elderly desolate. A low retiree-worker ratio due to a young population makes DB schemes less vulnerable to changes in the rate of return. Hence, a young population combined with rapid wage growth enhances the credibility of the commitment of younger generations and firms to PAYG and DB schemes. Finally, homogeneous tastes for old-age insurance ensure that the welfare losses from uniform, mandatory systems are only small.

7.1.5 Commitment versus Flexibility

The Trade-Off. As noted in Section 7.1.2, firms tend to employ DB schemes to motivate workers and to encourage bonding to the firm. These positive incentive effects, however, come at a price. In particular, limited portability impedes external flexibility in the form of labour mobility across firms. This renders the allocation of labour less efficient. Moreover, final-pay schemes may discourage gradual retirement by reducing the flexibility of wages in old age and providing incentives to employers to lay-off older workers. Furthermore, as pensions are not directly related to premiums paid, premiums may distort labour supply because they are perceived as a tax. Indeed, a trade-off between *static* efficiency (i.e. using the stock of human capital efficiently) and *dynamic* efficiency (i.e. accumulating the stock of human capital) emerges.[14]

By linking retirement benefits to wages, DB schemes provide labour-market incentives but leave workers particularly exposed to individual human-capital and job-mobility risk as lower wages or a job transfer directly reduces retirement benefits.[15] Indeed, compared to DC schemes, DB schemes suffer from less investment risk but more human capital risk. DB schemes feature less diversification of risk than DC schemes do; not only labour income but also retirement income depends on the individual wage level.

Governments may impose regulations on DB schemes (e.g. shortening vesting periods or requiring indexation of vested rights) to enhance insurance against job mobility by improving portability. In doing so, a trade-off between flexibility and commitment emerges.

External Conditions. Table 7.2 summarizes the economic conditions affecting the trade-off between commitment (under DB schemes) and flexibility (under DC schemes). The first class of conditions involves the value of commitment. Commitment is particularly valuable if investments in firm-specific human capital are widespread. Asset specificity is important if high search, hiring, and training costs imply that employers have to incur substantial sunk costs when hiring new staff. These substantial hiring costs may be due to lack of information about the features of potential workers. Furthermore, human capital and knowledge should be firm-specific. In particular, knowledge should be tacit rather than codified so that it not easily transmitted between firms. A related condition is that most technological advances occurs in established firms rather than in innovative start-up firms (see also Section 2.4.3).

Another class of conditions determines whether external flexibility is important. The value of external flexibility is relatively small if firm-specific shocks are relatively unimportant. In that case, adjustments occur within rather than across firms. Moreover, workers face only small risks in linking their pension benefits to wages and the performance of one specific firm.

A final class of conditions determine whether firms can make credible commitments. As regards commodity markets, firms should have some consistent market power in order to back up the benefit promise and insure agents against macro-economic shocks (see Section 7.1.2).[16] Furthermore, some degree of labour immobility, which may be due to high search costs, enables firms to

---

[14] Tying benefits to *average* rather than *final* pay may weaken this trade off.

[15] This trade-off between dynamic labour market incentives and insurance against human-capital and job-mobility risks reflects the trade-off between incentives and risksharing discussed in Chapter 2.

[16] This market power may originate in tacit (i.e. firm-specific) knowledge.

Table 7.2 Commitment versus flexibility in old-age insurance

	DB schemes	DC schemes
Strengths	Promotes firm-specific investments Discourages workers from shirking	Enhances external labour market flexibility Enhances diversification of risks
Conditions		
Labour market		
Training and hiring costs	high	low
Human capital	firm-specific	general
Information costs		
About features worker	high	low
About behaviour worker	high	low
Technology		
Knowledge	tacit	codified
Technological advances	incremental in established firms	radical in start-up firms
Shocks		
Firm-specific shocks	infrequent	frequent
Macro-economic shocks	frequent	infrequent
Commodity market		
Turnover of firms	low	high
Market power firms	substantial	fleeting

redistribute resources between older and younger workers.[17] Indeed, DB schemes seem particularly attractive if labour and commodity markets are imperfect and exit and entry barriers (and hence asset specificity) are substantial.

7.2 Pensions in Germany and the Netherlands

7.2.1 Introduction

A Three Pillar System. Pension schemes serve various objectives, including poverty-alleviation and insurance against longevity and income risks in old age. Depending on the particular objective, different types of pension scheme may be most appropriate. In particular, alleviating old-age poverty is best accomplished by a nationwide public PAYG system that provides a minimum standard of living in

[17] Labour mobility across industries may be rather limited. Hence, branches of industry tend to be able to make more credible promises than individual firms.

old age. This system should be mandatory, redistributive, and can be financed from current tax revenues.

Another objective is relatively uniform insurance against longevity and income risks in old age. To avoid moral hazard involving means-tested benefits and adverse selection in annuity markets, and to facilitate intergenerational risksharing, this function may require compulsory insurance. This insurance can be provided by funded private schemes of either the DC or DB type. These schemes are not explicitly aimed at poverty alleviation. Accordingly, contributions levied on labour income can be more closely linked to benefits, thereby mitigating labour-market disincentives.

Those workers who want to go beyond the mandatory level of pension insurance can use voluntary supplementary pension plans of the DC type. These schemes can be particularly important for high income-earners who are better able to deal with the investment risks associated with DC schemes.

The World Bank (1994) argues in favour of separating the various functions in three separate pillars. Such a three pillar system does indeed seem an attractive model for old-age insurance.[18] A separation of tasks would optimize the trade-off between incentives and solidarity by avoiding non-transparent and perverse redistribution. Another important reason for adopting a mix of pension systems is to diversify macro-economic risks; workers should not put all their eggs in one basket to avoid excessive exposure to the substantial political, investment, and human-capital risks over a long horizon.

The Dutch pension system is closer to the three pillar model than the German system. Germany, like France and Italy, has integrated the first two functions of pension schemes (i.e. poverty alleviation and old-age insurance) into a single comprehensive public pension system. In the Netherlands, in contrast, the public sector provides only a minimum benefit, leaving the second function of old age insurance to private occupational pension schemes of the DB type. Hence, occupational pensions play a more important role in the Netherlands than in Germany. Both Germany and the Netherlands have a rather small third pillar because the aspirational level for collective pensions is quite high in the two countries. Accordingly, this section focuses on describing the public pensions (in Section 7.2.2) and occupational pensions (in Section 7.2.3) in Germany and the Netherlands. After Section 7.2.4 deals with the level of collective pension benefits, Section 7.2.5 concludes this section by placing the Dutch and German pension systems on the most important trade-offs identified in Section 7.1.3.

---

[18] For other insurances, the combination of minimum public provisions and supplementary private insurance may result in overinsurance associated with excessive moral hazard (see Chapter 6). For old-age insurance, in contrast, eligibility conditions (i.e. age) are easily verified. Hence, moral hazard is not relevant, except when benefits are means-tested.

Table 7.3 Public and occupational pension schemes

	Public scheme (PAYG)		Occupational scheme		
	Coverage	Type of benefit	Coverage (% working pop.)	Type of benefit	Financing
Germany	all workers	linked to average earnings[a]	65%	lump-sum or salary linked	mainly book reserve
Netherlands	all residents	lump-sum[a]	95%	final-pay or average salary	funded
United States	all workers	linked to average earnings[b]	50%	defined benefit (47%) or defined contributions (53%)	funded

[a] During retirement linked to average after-tax wages in the economy.
[b] During retirement linked to price index.

Source: Pestieau (1992) and Quinn (1990).

7.2.2 The Public Pension

The Dutch public sector provides only a minimum benefit. This benefit is flat (i.e. independent of premiums paid during the working life) and depends on personal circumstances. In particular, single persons receive a higher benefit than married persons do.

German public pensions, in contrast, are linked to the earnings history.[19] Hence, by relying strongly on the insurance principle, the German public sector goes beyond providing a minimum benefit (see Tables 7.3 and 7.4). The advantage of the insurance principle is that it alleviates work disincentives. For example, by tying pension benefits to premiums paid, women face a strong incentive to enter

[19] The working life is defined rather broadly. To illustrate, some of the time that married women care for the children is included. Moreover, periods of education and training may increase a person's rights while so-called imputations [Zurechnungen] are allowed for certain groups of immigrants.

Table 7.4 Replacement rate of public pension in various European countries, 1992

	Final gross salary[a] of $ 20,000	$ 50,000
	%	
UK	50	26[b]
Germany	70	59
Netherlands	66	26
Sweden	69	49
Denmark	83	33
Ireland	47	19
France	67	45[c]
Italy	77	73
Spain	90	60
Belgium	63	40
Portugal	69	68

[a] For married men.
[b] Includes state earnings related pension scheme (SERPS). For those contracted out, the ratios are 35% and 14%.
[c] Includes ARRCO.

Source: Davis (1996)

the labour force.[20] Moreover, benefits are individualized. Hence, in contrast to the Dutch system, the German system does not discourage elderly from living in two-person households.

A disadvantage of the insurance principle, which reflects the trade-off between incentives and solidarity, is that the insurance premiums are a heavy burden for vulnerable low skilled workers.[21] Furthermore, groups with a weak attachment to the labour market are not adequately covered by social security, thereby burdening social assistance and creating moral hazard. Finally, by providing high benefits to the middle-incomes, the German system reduces the need for supplementary private schemes, which are funded. This discourages saving and makes the German pension system vulnerable to aging.

[20] However, if the compulsory insurance level exceeds the level that would be selected voluntarily, the tax character of premiums is maintained to some extent.

[21] Low-wage earners, however, do benefit from special provisions.

Table 7.5 Assets of pension funds[a] in various European countries, end-1993

	Stock of assets $ bn	% of GDP	% foreign assets
United Kingdom	717	82	31
Germany	106	6	8
Netherlands	261	85	21
Sweden[b]	39	16	1
Denmark	26	19	4
Ireland	18	44	41
France	41	3	2
Italy	12	1	4
Belgium	7	3	37
Spain	10	2	10
Portugal	5	7	10

[a] Includes only independent funded schemes and thus excludes bookreserves.
[b] 1991.

Source: Davis (1996).

7.2.3 Occupational Pensions

Relative Importance of Occupational Pensions. Supplementary occupational pension benefits are more important in the Netherlands than in Germany, primarily because the Dutch public pension scheme provides only a flat minimum benefit, which is relatively low compared to middle- and higher incomes (see Table 7.4). The Dutch occupational pension provisions are negotiated in the private sector by the social partners. Hence, the private sector plays a more important role in pension provision in the Netherlands than in Germany. Nevertheless, government regulations that make the negotiated supplementary pension provisions and premiums compulsory for all firms in a particular sector play an important role in facilitating intergenerational risksharing in DB schemes.[22] The flat public pension together with compulsory participation in supplementary funded schemes has resulted in the accumulation of considerable pension savings (see Table 7.5). Accordingly, compared to Germany, the Netherlands relies more on capital funding and less on pay-as-you go financing.

[22] Indeed, industry-wide schemes are the most common occupational pension funds. Also single employer schemes are possible, but they have to meet certain criteria before they can be set up. In particular, they must offer benefits that are at least as generous as those provided by the relevant industry-wide scheme.

DB Schemes. In Netherlands and Germany, occupational pension schemes are generally of the DB type rather than the DC type. Hence, the link between individual premiums and accrued benefits is typically rather weak. Private pensions in both countries thus stress intergenerational risksharing on the trade-off of risksharing versus incentives. Moreover, DB schemes can provide little individual choice to workers concerning the level and composition of pension benefits.

Investing Pension Assets. Supplementary occupational pensions are funded in different ways in Germany and the Netherlands. The Dutch law stipulates that the pension assets backing occupational pension obligations must be held outside the sponsoring firm by independent pension funds. In Germany, in contrast, the tax system has encouraged the sponsoring company to hold pension assets within the firm as book reserves rather than in independent pension funds, which invest outside the firm. These book reserves in effect act as a cheap source of financing for the company.[23]

The Dutch arrangements yield some advantages for the allocation of capital. First, the pension funds diversify their investments and hence reduce investment risk. Second, they stimulate the development of capital markets, thereby facilitating the reallocation of capital away from older, mature firms towards younger, growing firms. This may yield a more efficient allocation of capital across the economy.

The advantage of the German system is that most pension savings find their way into the domestic corporate sector. Until recently, Dutch pension funds invested mainly in low-risk government bonds rather than equities (see Table 7.6). In recent years, however, Dutch pension funds have significantly increased their holdings of domestic equities. Indeed, the long horizon of funds with DB obligations should allow these pension funds to invest in high-yielding equities with volatile returns.

Compulsory Participation in Pension Funds. The Dutch system of compulsory participation of firms in sectoral pension funds allows these funds to keep the pension premiums relatively stable without endangering their pension promises. In this way, the funds can engage in intergenerational risksharing. The disadvantage of this system is that wage negotiators may fail to internalize the costs of wage increases in terms of higher pension costs because part of the additional costs of higher pension benefits due to higher wages can be shifted to the future. Moreover, at the sectoral level, social partners and pension funds in sheltered sectors may feel little competitive pressure to keep costs under control. Finally, compulsory participation of firms reduces diversity of pension plans.

In Germany, by investing their pension assets in their own company, employees have a direct stake in the financial health of their firm. This enhances incentives

---

[23] Pension liabilities are reinsured by the Pension-Sicherungs-Verein. 75% of the German occupational schemes are based on book reserves.

Table 7.6 Pension funds' portfolio distributions in various European countries (percentage allocations), 1992

	Equities	Fixed income	Property	Liquidity and deposits
UK	80	11	6	3
Germany	6	80	13	1
Netherlands	24	60	14	2
Sweden	2	91	2	6
Denmark	19	67	12	2
Ireland	66	24	7	3
France	20	67	11	2
Italy	14	72	10	5
Belgium	31	50	8	11
Spain	3	94	2	1
Portugal	18	57	5	19

Source: Davis (1996).

for wage moderation, effort on the job, and long-term investments in firm-specific human capital. The other side of the coin is that workers are more exposed to firm-specific shocks. Hence, a trade-off emerges between intergenerational solidarity and risksharing (under the Dutch system) and incentives to keep pension costs under control and moderate wage claims (under the German system).

Portability of Pension Rights. Vesting periods and provisions for transferring pension rights differ considerably between the Netherlands and Germany. For pension rights to be vested, a German employee must have reached 35 years of age and must have been with the employer for at least 10 years. If a worker moves to another company, transferring contributions to the other employer is typically not possible. In the Netherlands, in contrast, vesting periods are shorter than one year. Moreover, many employees can transfer the value of their accrued pension rights to another employer.

On the one hand, the German system restricts the mobility of labour and exposes the worker to high job-mobility risk. On the other hand, it encourages workers not to shirk by increasing the costs of lay-offs. Hence, whereas the Dutch system allows external flexibility, the German system encourages commitment and firm-specific investments in human capital. Moreover, the German system provides strong incentives for effort on the job. The Dutch system provides more insurance against job mobility and firm-specific shocks.

Table 7.7 After-tax pension benefit as a percent of (indexed) average after-tax wage during complete career

	One-earner family	Single person	Two-earner family
Germany[a]	69-82-89	78-92-99	78-92-99
Netherlands[b]	103	92	80

[a] The three numbers assume 0%, 10%, and 15% gross occupational pensions of average gross wage, respectively.
[b] The numbers assume that the overall pension (including the public and occupational pension) amounts 70% of the before-tax finale wage.

Source: CPB calculations.

7.2.4 Collective Benefit Levels

Collective pensions aim to achieve a pension of 70% of final earnings before taxes. In after-tax terms, the aspiration level is even higher because the elderly do not pay social security premiums for the public retirement scheme and benefit from other tax privileges. Pensions are taxed even more lightly in Germany than in the Netherlands.[24] People over 65 receive broadly the same collective pension in both countries. The Dutch public pension is lower than its German equivalent (see Table 7.4) but this difference is fully offset by additional Dutch occupational pensions.

Table 7.7 contains after-tax replacement rates of collective pensions (i.e. public and occupational pensions) in case of a complete career of 40 years. Two-earner families and single people receive higher collective benefits in Germany while couples with a single earner are better off in the Netherlands. Dutch replacement rates are highest for couples with a single earner because Dutch occupational pensions supplement the public pension to 70 % of the final wage under the assumption that individual retirees receive a public pension for a married couple, which exceeds that of a single person. The relatively high replacement rate for a couple compared with a single earner indicate that the Dutch pension system discourages partners of breadwinners to participate in the labour market.

[24] Taxes and social insurance premiums paid by workers have increased substantially during the past decades. Accordingly, the aspiration level in after-tax terms has risen. In the Netherlands, for example, the aspiration level for wage earners with the modal income rose from 78 % in 1960 to 88 % in 1994.

7.2.5 Conclusions

This section discusses the position of the Dutch and German pension systems on the most important trade-offs.

Scale versus Diversity. Both countries stress scale at the expense of diversity by relying on collective PAYG and DB schemes rather than personal pensions of the DC type.[25] Hence, the after-tax replacement rates provided by collective schemes are quite high (see Table 7.7). On the one hand, the relatively small German occupational pension sector is more diverse than the corresponding Dutch sector because collective labour agreements do not force individual firms to join sector-wide pension funds. On the other hand, the Dutch two-pillar system allows for somewhat more diversity by having a relatively large occupational pension sector, which differentiates pensions across various sectoral pension funds. Indeed, Germany stresses scale by integrating old-age insurance and poverty alleviation in a single public system.

Intergenerational Risksharing versus Incentives. Both countries focus on intergenerational risksharing. Germany accomplishes intergenerational risksharing by relying heavily on a public PAYG system. The Netherlands facilitates intergenerational risksharing not only through a public PAYG system but also by forcing firms to join sectoral pension funds and adhere to pension provisions negotiated in collective labour agreements. Indeed, Dutch occupational pension plans focus more on intergenerational solidarity and risksharing than German occupational schemes, which emphasize labour-market incentives and encourage bonding between the employee and the firm.

Intragenerational Risksharing versus Incentives. The Dutch PAYG system relies less on the insurance principle and is thus more redistributive than the German public system. On the one hand, this produces a higher marginal tax wedge, which reduces the number of hours worked and discourages partners of breadwinners to participate in the labour market. On the other hand, it contains the premium burden on low-skilled workers with low incomes. This helps to maintain the access to work for these vulnerable groups.

Commitment versus Flexibility. By facilitating the portability of pension rights, Dutch occupational pensions allow for external flexibility, thereby providing more insurance against job mobility and firm-specific shocks. In Germany, in contrast, occupational pensions are less portable. German occupational pensions thus

---

[25] This implies also that both countries stress insurance against market rather than insurance against political risk.

Table 7.8 Average benefit levels, 1970 and 1992, in terms of purchasing power parities

	Germany		Netherlands	
	1970	1992	1970	1992
	in euros			
Old age/surviving dependants	1300	10,000	1300	10,700
Unemployment/disablement	1800	10,400	3100	16,000
Family support[a]	200	2400	200	1200
Sickness[b]	200	1500	100	1200

[a] Related to children aged 0-18.
[b] Related to the labour force.

Source: Eurostat (1994).

encourage commitment and firm-specific investments in human capital. Moreover, they provide strong incentives for effort on the job. These institutional differences in occupational pensions between Germany and the Netherlands are consistent with the differences on the labour market more generally. In particular, the German labour market is more oriented towards commitment, whereas the Dutch institutional arrangements involve a mix between commitment and flexibility (see Chapter 8).

7.3 Performance of the Pension Systems

This section discusses the performance of the Dutch and German pension systems. Section 7.3.2 explores the impact of pensions on old-age poverty. After Section 7.3.1 discusses retirement behaviour, Section 7.3.3 examines other aspects of labour-market behaviour. Section 7.3.4 deals with the return on pension premiums and investigates the effects of the pension systems on the capital market.

7.3.1 Old-Age Poverty

On average, people over 65 receive broadly the same pension in both countries (see Table 7.8). The figures include both the basic public pension and supplementary pensions. The Dutch public pension is lower than its German equivalent, but this is fully compensated by the supplementary pensions. It is unclear what effect this situation has on income differentials among pensioners. Around 80% of all Dutch pensioners are entitled to a supplementary pension, while the remainder has to make do with the basic pension. Whereas the relatively low Dutch public pension should lead to wider income differentials among Dutch pensioners than among their German counterparts, it should be remembered that the German basic pension is related to the earnings history of each individual. In Germany, however,

Table 7.9 Annual minimum income of people aged 65 and over[a] in ECU based on purchasing power parities

	Single person		Married couple	
	Germany	Netherlands	Germany	Netherlands
Standard pension		7476		10680
Social assistance standard rate	3511		6436	
Supplements	469		867	
Housing subsidies	2777	664	3732	1119
Fixed health insurance premium		156		312
Total disposable income	6756	7984	11034	11487

[a] Levels refer to second half of 1996.

means-tested social assistance provides a relatively high retirement income to the poor (see Table 7.9). In both countries public pension levels are indexed to general earnings.

7.3.2 The Retirement Age

The effective retirement age has declined to rather low levels in both countries over the past two decades (see Tables 7.10 and 7.11). Various policies encouraged older workers to leave the labour market in order to alleviate the adverse social effects of industrial restructuring and to preserve employment opportunities for younger workers.

In Germany, the qualifying age for the public pension benefit is variable: the earlier a person retires, the lower the yearly pension benefit becomes. However, the decline in pension benefits is far less than would be actuarially fair. Consequently, most of the eligible population retires before the legal retirement age of 65 year. Disabled and unemployed workers receive full retirement benefits already at age 60. Hence, the public old-age pension system includes a substantial amount of hidden unemployment. By supplementing public benefits with extra-statutory benefits, firms are able to dismiss older workers with only small costs to the company. The dismissed workers have little incentive to return back to work.

In the Netherlands, the statutory retirement age for the public scheme is fixed. However, the effective retirement age is much lower. Employers could shift the costs of early retirement unto the public disability scheme.[26] In addition, private

[26] Recent and prospective reforms of the disability scheme have made this more difficult. See Chapter 6.

Table 7.10 Participation rates and effective retirement age in the EC, Japan and the US, 1990

	Participation rates					Retirement age	
	50-54	55-59	60-64	65-69	70-74	Effective	Statutory
Belgium	54.0	34.2	12.1	1.9	0.4	59.5	65/60
Denmark	84.1	72.7	37.5	16.4	2.3	62.6	67
France	74.8	51.6	16.3	4.5	1.4	59.9	60
Germany	73.2	58.7	21.4	4.6	1.7	60.8	65
Greece	61.9	50.8	33.1	14.6	4.1	63.1	65/60
Ireland	57.4	49.3	35.2	15.4	6.8	63.9	66
Italy	59.0	42.0	21.1	7.8	1.6	61.1	65
Luxembourg	57.4	35.4	13.2	0.0	0.0	59.2	65
Netherlands	61.3	46.3	17.1	6.4	2.3	60.8	65
Portugal	66.0	54.8	37.7	23.3	8.1	64.0	65/62
Spain	57.5	48.8	31.0	6.5	1.1	62.5	65
United Kingdom	79.0	67.0	38.0	10.7	3.3	62.4	65/60
Austria	73.1	53.3	15.1	2.6	2.1	59.9	65/60
Finland	77.9	58.3	28.6	3.4	2.8	60.9	65
Sweden	92.6	82.8	56.4	9.8	3.1	63.1	65
EC	69.5	53.8	25.5	7.3	2.3	61.3	65
Japan	82.0	71.5	54.7	24.4	23.9	64.8	60/55
United States	80.0	66.1	44.2	11.5	6.3	62.8	65

Source: Besseling and Zeeuw (1993).

early retirement schemes (VUT), which are financed on a pay-as-you-go basis, facilitate early retirement. Moreover, unemployment insurance can be used as a way to retire workers early as unemployed workers older than 57 1/2 years do not have to apply for work in order for them to be eligible to unemployment benefits, which are related to the final wage[27]. Finally, tax-advantaged individual saving schemes provide for early retirement benefits. Hence, just as in old-age pensions more generally, the social partners play a more important role in determining the effective retirement age in the Netherlands than in Germany. In recent years, various reforms in both countries have aimed to increase the effective retirement age (see Box 7.2).

[27] Unemployment benefits are not reduced if employers provide supplementary benefits. Hence, by providing relatively small supplementary benefits, employers can assure that older laid-off workers can maintain their standard of living during early retirement.

Table 7.11 Participation rate, effective retirement age and life expectancy, 1950-1980

	Participation rate age group 55-64		Effective retirement age		Life expectancy at birth	
	1950	1980	1950	1980	1950	1980
Belgium	46.0	38.3	63.8	61.2	67.5	73.7
Denmark	59.6	58.5	64.2	62.7	71.0	74.5
France	57.7	45.7	64.4	61.0	66.5	74.7
Germany	49.8	43.1	63.7	61.0	67.5	73.9
Greece	48.9	43.3	65.2	63.1	65.9	74.7
Ireland	55.4	50.2	65.8	64.1	66.9	73.1
Italy	45.5	31.7	63.9	60.3	66.0	74.6
Luxembourg	50.0	28.6	64.4	59.9	65.9	73.3
Netherlands	50.9	40.9	64.6	62.2	72.1	76.0
Portugal	47.3	44.7	65.4	63.1	59.3	72.2
Spain	49.2	41.2	65.5	62.9	63.9	75.8
United Kingdom	53.9	61.9	64.4	62.8	69.2	74.0
EC average	51.3	45.1	64.3	61.8	67.0	74.4
Japan	63.0	64.5	64.7	64.0	63.9	76.9
United States	57.2	55.8	64.4	63.0	69.0	74.5

Source: ILO (1986); United Nations (1989); own calculations.

7.3.3 Other Labour-Market Effects

The Dutch pension system harms labour supply of younger workers. In particular, the PAYG system adds to the marginal wedge, thereby discouraging labour supply. The link between individual contributions and benefits is weak also in the final-pay occupation DB schemes. However, the portability of pension rights facilitates the efficient allocation of labour.

Compared to the Dutch system, the German system provides less disincentives to labour supply. However, the lack of portability of pensions harms the efficient allocation of labour. Moreover, the long vesting periods protect insiders at the expense of young workers entering the labour market.

7.3.4 The Return on Pension Saving and the Capital Market

The Netherlands features a better balanced mix of various pension systems than Germany. This latter country relies heavily on PAYG financing, which makes the German economy vulnerable to aging and to low wage and employment growth (see Box 7.1). Indeed, the aging of the population implies a lower return on PAYG contributions, which necessitates a rather rapid rise in German pension contributions (see, e.g., Börsch-Supan, 1993). The returns on German occupational

Box 7.2 Reforms in old-age insurance in Germany

A pension reform was enacted in 1992 in Germany. Pensions were indexed to net rather than gross wages. Moreover, the retirement age is to be increased from 63 for men and 60 for women to 65 for both men and women in several steps between 2001 and 2012. These measures were expected to cut in half the expected increase of the premium rate up to 2030 (BMA, 1997a). In 1996, this latter period for a gradual increase in the retirement age was brought forward to the period between 1997 and 2004. Moreover, pension credits for years spent in training are to be reduced. The 1996 reform measures[a] further reduce the pressure on the insurance scheme, but are not sufficient to halt the increase in the premium rate. Including these measures, the premium rate is expected to increase from a current level of 20.3 % of gross wages to 21.3% in 2010 and 25.5 in 2030 (BMA, 1997b). Without the 1996 reform measures, the premium rate would have been between one and two percentage points higher in 2010 (Sachverständigenrat, 1996: 228). A June 1997 bill proposes further reform measures to be executed from 1999 onwards.[b] Concerning old age benefits, the main elements are a gradual reduction of the aspiration rate, a strengthening of the occupational pension schemes, and a shift towards tax finance. Introduction of a demographic factor in the old age benefit scheme reduces the increase of the benefit through time. It eventually results in an old age benefit of 64% of net wages for an average income earner with 45 year of premium payments, compared with a current level of almost 70%. This measure is expected to reduce the premium rate by 1 %-point in 2010 and 1.5 %-points in 2030 (BMA, 1997b). The second pillar is strengthened by reducing its adverse effects on mobility. The waiting period until a pension right is vested will be reduced in 1999 from 10 years to 8 years and in 2008 to 5 years. The associated age limit will be lowered to 33 years in 1999 and to 30 years in 2008. Finally, as regards financing, a one percent reduction of the premium rate will be financed by a higher contribution out of the general government budget. The reform proposal states that the exact way of financing still has to be decided within the context of current tax reform proposals.

---

[a] *Sachverständigenrat (1996: 123) contains a complete overview of these reform measures.*
[b] *See Box 6.5 in Chapter 6 for the disability component of the 1999 Rentenversicherung reform.*

---

pensions are rather vulnerable to the performance of the German corporate sector. Book reserves do not allow the risk to be diversified across various firms or countries. Moreover, investing pension savings in mature, existing firms runs the risk of an inefficient allocation of capital in the European capital market, which will become increasingly integrated within EMU.

Dutch pension funds are increasingly investing in equity. This facilitates the investment of pension saving in high-yielding projects in the corporate sector, enhances capital mobility within the corporate sector, allows a higher expected return over a long horizon, makes the return less sensitive to unexpected inflation, and may help to improve corporate governance.

Table 7.12 The impact of trends on three major trade-offs in the pension systems

Trade-off: Trend	solidarity ⇔ incentives	scale ⇔ diversity	commitment ⇔ flexibility
German unification	⇐		⇒
Aging	⇔	⇒	⇔
Financial innovation	⇒	⇒	
Internationalization	⇐		⇒
Preferences			
– more heterogeneity	⇐	⇒	⇒
– individualization	⇒	⇒	⇒
Features of individuals			
– more heterogeneity	⇔	⇒	⇒
More elastic labour supply	⇒		
Technology			
– less tacit			⇒
– more complex			⇐
– skill biased	⇐		

7.3.5 Conclusions

Compared to the German pension system, the Dutch system seems better prepared to deal with the aging trend because it relies less heavily on PAYG financing. Moreover, the public system is better targeted at poverty alleviation. However, a weak link between premiums and benefits harms the incentives to supply labour.

7.4 Trends

This section discusses the impact of various trends on three major trade-offs discussed in Section 7.1.3 and 7.1.5, namely the trade-offs between solidarity and incentives, scale and diversity and commitment and flexibility. Table 7.12 summarizes the discussion.

7.4.1 Unification

Need for Solidarity. German unification has increased the demand for solidarity and insurance provided by the government. Indeed, following unification, the West German system of old-age insurance was extended to East Germany. This increased East German pension expenditure substantially, requiring large transfers from Western Germany.

Need for Flexibility. German unification demands substantial flexibility from the German economy. In particular, both capital mobility and labour mobility seem important in helping the German economy adjust to new circumstances. This need for flexibility shifts the optimal position on the commitment-flexibility trade-off towards flexibility.

7.4.2 Aging

PAYG Schemes. PAYG systems, and to a lesser extent DB schemes, are particularly sensitive to the expected decline in the worker/retiree ratio due to the expected aging of the population. Indeed, if the participation rates of the various age cohorts remained constant, aging would cause the average worker/retiree ratio in OECD countries to decline from 3 currently to about 1½ in the course of the next five decades. Table 7.13 shows projections for the old-age dependency ratio in Germany and the Netherlands. The relatively low German birth rate implies a rather high dependency ratio. The dependency rate is expected to almost double in both Germany and the Netherlands between 1992 and 2040.

Aging makes the commitment of firms and younger workers to DB schemes and that of younger generations to PAYG schemes more expensive to maintain. This reduces the credibility of this commitment.

Fortunately, the demographic factors that cause aging provide some offsetting effects on labour supply. In particular, lower fertility tends to raise the participation rate of women. At the same time, increased life expectancy should allow for a rise in the effective retirement age. Also market forces are likely to reduce the negative first-order effects of aging on labour supply as higher wages induced by labour scarcity raise both labour productivity growth and labour supply. For example, as labour becomes scarcer, employers are likely to invest more in older workers.

Funded Schemes. Not only PAYG but also funded schemes may be vulnerable to aging. By reducing labour supply, aging makes capital less scarce compared to labour, thereby depressing the return on capital. However, by investing capital in non-OECD countries with relatively young populations and abundant labour, funded schemes can exploit the phasing differential in aging between, on the one hand, the aging OECD countries and, on the other hand, the non-OECD countries, which are expected to age only later. Accordingly, whereas labour mobility (i.e. inward migration) may sustain PAYG schemes in aging countries, capital mobility (i.e. capital exports) may help funded schemes in these countries to maintain high

Table 7.13 Persons older than 60 years as a ratio of persons between 20 and 60 years, 1992-2040

	1995	2000	2010	2020	2030	2040	2050
Germany	35.8	40.8	44.8	53.1	73.2	76.4	...
The Netherlands	30.6	31.8	39.3	48.6	61.0	62.0	60.8

Source: CPB (1997) and Siebert (1997).

returns and diversify risks.[28]

The Aaron Condition. The well-known Aaron condition shows how demographic shocks, wage growth, and the return on capital impact the attractiveness of PAYG vis-à-vis funding (see Box 7.1). Aging of the population reduces the attractiveness of PAYG by decreasing the growth rate of employment. However, aging is also likely to make labour scarcer relative to physical capital. This may raise wage growth and depress the rate of return on capital. Accordingly, the overall effect of aging on the Aaron condition is ambiguous. Moreover, non-demographic trends may impact the Aaron condition. To illustrate, enhanced international capital mobility may boost the return on capital and increase the scope for diversifying risks in capital markets, thereby making funding more attractive.

7.4.3 Financial Innovation and International Financial Integration

Financial innovation and globalization of financial markets produce more sophisticated financial instruments that allow investors to reap higher returns and hedge better against inflation (e.g., indexed bonds) and other country-specific macro-economic risks. This reduces the need for intergenerational risksharing, thereby shifting the position on the trade-off of risksharing versus incentives in the direction of incentives. Insurance through markets allows also for more diversity.

7.4.4 Internationalization

Globalization of international markets of capital, goods and services increasingly exposes individual firms to competition from abroad. This trend gives rise to more

[28] However, sizable net capital flows may be difficult to achieve in practice. The large trade imbalances that are required to sustain the capital flows may give rise to major movements in real exchange rates, yielding serious trade tensions. Moreover, political risks and inadequate information about local circumstances may inhibit large capital inflows into the non-OECD countries.

firm-specific shocks. More volatility increases the demand for insurance. This trend thus moves the position on the risksharing versus incentives trade-off in the direction of insurance.

At the same time, more firm-specific shocks increase the importance of flexibility. Moreover, fiercer competition implies that firms cannot easily capture monopoly rents while international mobility gives the firm more opportunities to opt out of implicit contracts. This reduces the credibility of the commitment of firms to benefit promises in DB schemes. Accordingly, the position on the commitment-flexibility trade-off shifts towards flexibility.

7.4.5 Social Trends

More Heterogeneity and Solidarity. A heterogeneous population exerts ambiguous effects on the trade-offs that affect the choice between mandatory PAYG and DB schemes and voluntary DC schemes. On the one hand, more heterogeneity among the elderly population makes solidarity more expensive (see Box 7.3). On the other hand, more heterogeneity increases the danger of adverse selection in old-age insurance. Moreover, more disparities in before-tax incomes increases the need for solidarity. These two factors make mandatory schemes more attractive by shifting the position on the trade-off between, on the one hand, risksharing and solidarity, and, on the other hand, incentives, towards risksharing and solidarity.[29]

More Heterogeneity and Other Trade-Offs. More heterogeneity increases the need for pension contracts that are tailor-made to individual circumstances. The position on the scale-diversity trade-off thus moves towards diversity. Moreover, with more heterogeneity, tastes tend to shift faster. This results in more volatile markets and firm-specific shocks as the need for product innovation increases. Accordingly, the importance of flexibility in the commitment-flexibility trade-off increases.

Individualization. Individualization may erode intergenerational altruism, so that the implicit intergenerational contract between generations may weaken. Furthermore, a better educated population is able to make responsible long-term decisions about old-age insurance. These trends move the positions on the risksharing-incentives trade-off towards incentives, on the scale-diversity trade-off towards diversity, and on the commitment-flexibility trade-off towards flexibility.

[29] However, a more heterogeneous population may increase political risk and the transaction costs of the political process determining the level of mandatory insurance.

Box 7.3 Heterogeneity and the costs of solidarity

How much the two objectives of solidarity and incentives conflict in old-age insurance depends on income heterogeneity within generations compared to heterogeneity across generations. Paying public benefits and providing tax privileges to all elderly irrespective of income is appropriate from the point of view of poverty alleviation if the old are a homogeneous group that is poorer than the young. However, if the pensioner income distribution widens, if slow growth of low-skilled wages causes poverty among young workers, and if aging narrows the contribution base, these policies favouring the old would become less effective in alleviating poverty. Indeed, sizable amounts of public spending would accrue to elderly persons collecting high incomes.

If the income distribution within any generation becomes more heterogeneous, the government has to supplement information on age with information on income to determine which people are poor. If it wants to alleviate poverty through the pension system, the government has to transfer resources from rich to poor pensioners. This implies that the link between individual contributions and benefits in pension schemes becomes less tight. Accordingly, pensions contributions are perceived as a tax rather than a price paid for a future pension benefit. As a direct consequence, the pension scheme discourages labour supply. The associated distortions worsen the trade-off between efficiency and equity. Indeed, with a more heterogeneous population, poverty alleviation becomes more expensive.

Flexible Labour Markets. Labour-supply distortions due to high marginal tax rates rise with the wage elasticity of labour supply. This elasticity can be expected to rise as working, career, and retirement patterns become more flexible and diverse. The labour supply elasticity of older workers, who have the option to retire, may become particularly high. At the same time, more two-earner families and a more flexible labour market provide more insurance through, respectively, the family and the market. Finally, heterogeneity increases the costs of solidarity by making it more difficult to find proxies for vulnerable groups that cannot be manipulated (see Box 7.3). All these trends shift the positions on the trade-offs between, on the hand, solidarity and, on the other hand, incentives in the direction of incentives.

7.4.6 Technology

Medical Technology. Life expectancy is increasing due to advances in medical technologies. Moreover, technological advances potentially increase the information about life expectancy. If this information remains private to the individual, it increases the danger of adverse selection in annuity markets.

Less Tacit Knowledge. Information technology makes knowledge less tacit so that it is more easily transmitted across firms, people, and countries. This implies that knowledge becomes less relation specific, thereby reducing the importance of commitment (see Table 7.2 and Section 7.1.4).[30] However, the tacit knowledge that remains becomes increasingly important in determining first-mover advantages on competitive markets. Hence, commitment remains important in encouraging cooperation within firms and the accumulation of firm-specific human capital. This is especially so in incremental and complex technologies (see also Section 2.5 in Chapter 2).

Need for Solidarity. Technological and organization developments increasing the importance of marketable skills make unskilled workers more vulnerable (see also Section 6.4.2 in Chapter 6). This increases the need for solidarity.

7.4.7 Conclusions

Table 7.12 summarizes the impacts of the trends on the trade-offs. The position on the scale versus diversity trade-off moves in the direction of diversity. Most of the trends shift the position on the commitment versus flexibility trade-off towards flexibility. The overall impact on the solidarity versus incentives trade-off is not clear. Whereas some trends move the position on this trade-off towards incentives (financial innovation, individualization, and more elastic labour supply), others shift this position towards solidarity (internationalization and volatility, more heterogeneity, skill-based technological change).

7.5 Policy Options

7.5.1 Policy Options for the Netherlands

Strengthen the Insurance Element. The Dutch pension system implies a high marginal and average tax wedge, thereby distorting labour supply. Moving away from final-pay to average-pay occupational schemes would reduce the marginal and average wedge by tightening the link between premiums and benefits.[31]

Increase Investment in the Corporate Sector. The system of book reserves implies that German pension savings directly increase the supply of capital to the corporate sector. Dutch pension funds, in contrast, have traditionally invested a large share of their capital in government bonds. More recently, however, Dutch pension funds are increasingly investing in corporate equity. This facilitates the

---

[30] As knowledge ages faster, the importance of firm-specific knowledge is reduced further. Moreover, faster technological change requires more flexibility. Both these trends shift the commitment-flexibility trade-off towards flexibility.

[31] This would also enhance labour participation of the elderly by promoting wage flexibility in old age. See Section 7.5.4 below.

Box 7.4 Reconciling intergenerational risksharing and flexibility

The government can reduce the need for intergenerational risksharing through collective pension funds by conducting more of this risksharing itself through the tax system. In particular, it could levy a tax on the investment income of pension funds. The tax rate should rise with the average return on all pension saving. If the average return is low, the government can transfer resources to the pension funds. Since the tax rate depends on the average return of all pension funds rather than the individual return of each pension fund, this tax treatment does not remove the incentive to invest in high-yielding assets.

This tax treatment yields a number of advantages. The government, in fact, insures the pension funds against long-run investment and inflation risks that these funds cannot hedge against on financial markets. Consequently, the risk premium in pension contributions can fall, thereby lowering wage costs and improving international competitiveness. Moreover, DC schemes become more attractive. By reducing the tax wedge on labour, this improves the functioning of the labour market. Furthermore, since pension funds no longer need to transfer resources across generations, workers and firms can be left free to select their own pension plans. This allows more competition among pension funds, which may reduce the overall costs of pension provisions. Moreover, it allows pension provisions to better fit the diverse needs of a heterogeneous population. This system thus amounts to a combination of the coordination mechanisms of competition and control. Whereas all pension funds would be required to participate in this risksharing arrangement, firms and workers would be free to select their own pension fund.

As an alternative to this system, which may suffer from substantial political risk, the government may bear only part of the macro-economic risk, for example, by issuing indexed bonds. In this way, pension funds are protected against inflation risk but still bear real interest-rate risk. By issuing longer maturities, however, the government can absorb part of this risk, as well. The disadvantage of indexed government bonds compared to risksharing through the tax system is that pension saving would not directly flow into the corporate sector. Hence, pension funds would contribute less to enhancing corporate governance.

investment of pension saving in high-yielding projects in the corporate sector, enhances capital mobility within the corporate sector, allows a higher expected return over a long horizon, makes the return less sensitive to unexpected inflation, and may help to improve corporate governance. By investing a larger share in venture capital firms, pension funds could help increase the supply of risk-taking capital for starting entrepreneurs. Alternatively, if the collective part of old-age insurance is reduced (see Section 7.5.3.), starting entrepreneurs can be allowed to invest a larger share of their previously accumulated pension saving in their own firm, thereby increasing the supply of capital to new, growing firms.

More Diversity in the Second Pillar. Increasing the possibilities for firms to opt out of industry-wide pension funds is consistent with the trend towards more heterogeneous preferences, which requires more diversity. Moreover, more opt-out possibilities increase competitive pressures on pension funds to improve their performance. At the same time, financial innovation and a better educated workforce reduce the need to protect individuals against risks through collective pension insurance. To meet these trends, firms could be required to participate in industry-wide pension funds only for pension benefits with lower aspiration levels, especially for middle- and higher incomes. The government could reduce the need for intergenerational risksharing through collective pension funds by issuing indexed bonds, which provide insurance against inflation risk (see also Box 7.4).

Offering not only firms but also workers more options to select their own pension fund would meet the trend towards more heterogeneity, which requires tailor-made solutions. However, these individual options may give rise to adverse selection and high transaction and information costs, thereby raising pension costs. Accordingly, more individual options should be introduced carefully, for example by reducing the aspiration level for collective insurance for middle- and higher incomes.

7.5.2 Policy Options for Germany

Less Public Insurance. Germany may want to focus the public pension scheme more on poverty alleviation by gradually reducing PAYG benefits for those earning higher incomes. This yields a better balanced portfolio between funded and PAYG schemes as workers with middle- and higher incomes would substitute private pensions for public PAYG benefits. The 1999 reform proposals reduce the growth of the benefit level, yet not differentiated according to income level (see Box 7.2).

The first pillar could be financed from general tax revenues rather than payroll taxes.[32] Relying on broad-based taxes paid by the entire population rather than payroll taxes alleviates the tax burden on workers by shifting this burden in part unto those outside the labour force, including the retired. The 1999 reform proposals are a first step in this direction (see Box 7.2).

Reducing net public benefits for and increasing taxes on the richer elderly makes the welfare state less vulnerable to the aging process.[33] Table 7.14 indicates that especially the German welfare state seems vulnerable to aging because at present a large part of public transfers accrues to the elderly.

Reducing PAYG benefits for and increasing the tax payments by the more affluent elderly is also consistent with the trend towards a more heterogeneous older

---

[32] The Dutch public pension system is still financed almost entirely by premiums on the young. In the future, however, an increasing part will be financed from general tax revenues as current premium rates are fixed with the balance financed from taxes.

[33] Reducing tax privileges for the elderly also reduces tax subsidies for pension saving that originate in the gap between the marginal rates at which pension contributions can be deducted and the marginal rates applied to the benefits. These tax subsidies suffer various drawbacks. See Bovenberg and Van der Linden (1997).

Table 7.14 Social expenditures and their age distribution

	Transfers to elderly/transfers to non-elderly	
	1980	1993
Australia	1.3	0.7[a]
Canada	1.2	1.2
New Zealand	1.8	0.8[a]
United Kingdom	1.6	1.0
United States	2.3	2.5
Denmark	0.6	0.6
Finland	1.1	0.8
Norway	0.9	0.7
Sweden	1.0	0.9
Austria	2.5	2.2
Belgium	1.0	1.2[a]
France	1.5	1.6
Germany	*1.9*	*1.7*
Italy	2.7	3.5
Netherlands	*0.7*	*0.7*
Spain	1.3	1.3
Japan	3.4	5.5[a]

[a] 1992 instead of 1993
Source: OECD Social Expenditure Database

population. Since age is no longer a good indicator for poverty, information on age should increasingly be supplemented by other information (in particular on incomes) to identify those in need of income support (see also Box 7.3). The literature on optimal tax and benefit structures suggests that the optimal structure is a flat benefit for all the elderly that is clawed back at higher incomes through the tax system (see, e.g., Dilnot *et al.* 1994). As the number of richer pensioners increases, the case becomes stronger for having the higher marginal withdrawal rates start further down the income distribution in order to prevent large amounts of public money from accruing to affluent pensioners.[34]

[34] Means-tested benefits suffer from various disadvantages. They may be stigmatizing and create disincentive effects. Moreover, they may undercut political support of the middle class for public pensions.

Accordingly, as the older generation becomes more heterogeneous, tax privileges and public benefits that are granted to the richer elderly should be reconsidered. Indeed, since the elderly lead longer, healthy lives, they are in a position to be net contributors to the budget for a longer time.

Another advantage of reducing tax privileges to the elderly is that progressive taxes can play a more effective role in intra- and intergenerational risksharing. Hence, the tax system can pool risks and shift these risks to those who can best bear them. This is especially important now that more risks seem to shift to the beginning of the life cycle.[35]

The Transition. The presently retired generation has not been able to anticipate lower public benefits. Moreover, it cannot adjust easily because it has already depreciated its human capital. The short horizon of the elderly implies that they are risk averse and value stable rules. Accordingly, the case for changing the rules of the game (i.e. reducing PAYG benefits and increasing taxes on the elderly) in a gradual fashion is strong.[36] However, extensive grandfathering provisions protecting those who are currently old are expensive. Indeed, it implies that young generations have to pay not only for their own benefits but also for the benefits of the currently old.[37] Hence, also here, the government faces a trade-off between flexibility and stability. To enhance confidence and trust in a stable social contract while at the same time facilitating timely adjustments, governments should announce early any prospective changes in the social contract. This allows the babyboom generation to anticipate reduced public transfers in retirement.

Independent Pension Funds. The second pillar in Germany stresses commitment at the expense of flexibility. However, various trends, including German unification and European (monetary) integration, call for more flexibility (see Section 7.5). In this context, the case for removing the tax obstacles against setting up independent pension funds is strong. The current system of book reserves discourages the development of modern financial markets, inhibits the efficient allocation of capital across firms, and does not allow pension savings to be diversified. Moreover, it prevents pension saving from benefiting from higher returns and more diversification abroad.

---

35 See Chapter 6 and OECD (1997).

36 One way to reduce relative PAYG benefit levels gradually is to index benefits to prices rather than wages.

37 This high burden on young generations can raise wage costs, thereby harming employment. To spread the costs of such a transition over various generations, the government may want to finance part of its existing PAYG obligations through public debt issue.

Portability of Pension Rights. To enhance flexibility in the German labour market, the vesting period for pension benefits could be shortened. The 1999 reform proposals do indeed entail a reduction of both the vesting period and the vesting age, albeit at a rather moderate pace (see Box 7.2). Furthermore, increased portability of pension rights, e.g. along the lines of the present Dutch system for transferring pension rights, would facilitate labour mobility.

7.5.3 Addressing the Trends

The policy options in the previous two sections provide a good starting point for reforming the pension systems in the two countries. However, these policy options and the reforms currently being implemented (see Box 7.2) are not sufficient to adequately deal with the trends identified in Section 7.5. This section, therefore, contains some additional, more speculative, suggestions about the future of old-age insurance in the two countries in view of various non-demographic trends. The next section discusses how labour-market reforms can address aging.

Less Collective Insurance. In setting the mandatory, collective level of pension insurance, one needs to trade off, on the one hand, providing enough risksharing and, on the other hand, tuning pensions to individual needs. Setting the mandatory level too low harms inter- and intragenerational risksharing, may induce workers to exploit means-tested benefits, and may lead to underinsurance due to adverse selection. Setting the level too high, in contrast, results in overinsurance by forcing some households to save more than they would like. The associated implicit tax distorts saving and harms employment.

In both Germany and the Netherlands, the third, voluntary, pillar, which can cater to individual preferences, is small because the mandatory, collective level of pension insurance is quite high. Indeed, as tastes have become more heterogeneous and the aspiration level has increased in after-tax terms (see Section 7.2.4), many workers are likely to have become overinsured.[38]

Accordingly, the shift in the position on the diversity-scale trade-off towards diversity (see Table 7.12) calls for a reduction in the collective part of old-age insurance for the middle- and higher incomes. The earners of these incomes are typically better able to deal with old-age risks. One way to increase the flexibility and personal responsibility in pension insurance would be to reduce high compulsory levels of collective pensions and provide more tax privileges to individual accounts that would insure individuals against not only old-age risk but also other human-capital risks such as unemployment and obsolescence of human capital (see Box 7.5).

---

[38] The fact that many elderly save substantial parts of their incomes provides evidence for overinsurance.

Box 7.5 More flexibility in pension insurance; tax-favoured accounts

Current Tax Treatment of Pensions. *Pensions are typically taxed on a cash-flow (or consumption-tax basis) basis: pension premiums are deductible for the personal income tax but pension benefits are subject to the income tax. The outflows of tax-favoured pension schemes are tightly regulated. In particular, pensions typically have to be paid out as an annuity that insures against longevity risk. This in order to avoid myopia and combat moral hazard associated with means-tested benefits. However, various trends that demand more flexibility call for less tight restrictions on what type of saving would be eligible for consumption-tax treatment.*

Registered Accounts. *Individuals would be allowed to have a registered account that would be taxed on a cash-flow basis. Hence, inflows (i.e. saving) would be tax deductible while outflows would be taxed. The capital income (i.e. interest, dividends, capital gains) earned in the account would not be subject to the income tax. Tax-deductible inflows would be subject to a ceiling. Moreover, investments would be subject to regulations in order to reduce information and transaction costs and combat moral hazard associated with risky investments. Also the forms and timing of outflows would still be subject to certain restrictions. These restrictions, however, would be less tight than those currently applying to tax-favoured personal pensions. To facilitate a shift from collective to individual insurance, the government could at the same time reduce the tax privileges for collective pension schemes (e.g. reduce the ceiling for tax-deductible premiums in collective plans).*

Human Capital. *Subject to a certain minimum balance, individuals could be allowed to take out some funds from the registered account before the retirement age, for example to invest in their own human capital or to care for their children (i.e. to invest in the human capital of their children). This would help individuals to deal with risks early in life. Moreover, it would allow individuals to save for old-age risks in the form of not only financial but also human capital; by investing early in life in human capital, individuals may be able to work longer (see Sub-section 7.6.4 on the need to increase the effective retirement age). For example, individuals could draw on the account when unemployed in order to invest in training to improve their position on the labour market. One could draw on the account also to retire in a gradual fashion at an early stage. Thus, these accounts would facilitate flexible retirement at an actuarially fair price. In this way, these tax-favoured registered accounts meet the trend towards a less rigid allocation of learning, working, and retiring over the life cycle. More generally, the accounts could be viewed as an insurance device against human-capital risk (due to not only old age but also unemployment and obsolescence of human capital during the working life).*

Entrepreneurship. *To encourage entrepreneurship and home-ownership, individuals could be allowed also to invest part of their registered account in their own firm or their own home. Hence, tax-favoured saving would flow not just through large institutional investors*

Box 7.5 More flexibility in pension insurance:tax-favoured accounts (continued)

Integrate tax privileges. *Various tax privileges applying to capital income (not only tax-favoured personal pensions and annuities but also tax-free dividend and interest income for small savers and for employees investing in their own firm) could be integrated in the tax favoured account. By increasing the scope for individuals to choose the way in which they want to save in a tax-favoured fashion, the government would create a level playing field between various financial institutions offering insurance and investment products. It would create also more neutrality between various types of saving (for example in the form of human capital, the own firm, the own house, annuities). In this way, it would free up resources that are currently tied up in finding out how best to exploit various tax privileges that apply to various types of saving.*

Social insurance. *The registered account could also help to reduce the need for collective unemployment insurance, which becomes increasingly vulnerable to moral hazard.*[1] *If experiments show such accounts to be successful, the government could move a larger part of its social insurance system in this direction.*

In order to protect vulnerable groups, the government could top up the contributions of poor people or compensate those with little human capital (for example because of a handicap) in the form of a higher initial balance. In this way, the accounts would shift more responsibility to the individual without relinquishing redistributive goals.

Social assistance. *When an individual would have exhausted the account due to long-term unemployment (the individual would be 'bankrupt' and experience solvability rather than liquidity problems), the individual could resort to social assistance. In order to avoid moral hazard, social assistance would provide conditional transfers that would balance the carrot of the benefit with the stick of certain obligations (see also Sub-section 6.5.3 in chapter 6).*

[1] *The accounts could be integrated with so-called unemployment support accounts (see Snower, 1996). Under these schemes, employed people would be required to contribute to their own unemployment support accounts. They could draw on these accounts during periods of unemployment.*

7.5.4 Addressing the Aging Trend in the Labour Market

The aging trend provides serious challenges for the systems of social insurance, including old-age insurance. In addressing these challenges, policy makers should act on several fronts in order to diversify risks. Just as in social insurance more generally (see Chapter 6), the use of several instruments is attractive not only from the point of view of risksharing but also for political reasons: costs and benefits are spread over various groups. Moreover, by using both carrots and sticks, policy makers prevent specific groups from being alienated and ensure that various groups become stakeholders in the reform process. For example, the age at which public retirement benefits are paid may be raised. However, without supplementary policies strengthening the labour-market position of the old, such a policy would risk alienating the elderly generations.

A major way to improve the sustainability of present arrangements in the face of aging is to boost labour-force participation. As stressed in Chapter 6, a well-functioning labour market with a high level of employment is a prerequisite for generous social insurance. This section first discusses labour participation of the elderly. Subsequently, it deals with the labour market more generally.

Raising the Effective Retirement Age. Encouraging early retirement is an increasingly costly policy. It not only directly reduces labour supply but also harms employment of the younger generations by raising premium and tax rates. In particular, it raises these rates both by narrowing the contribution base and by raising the required financing for the early retirement benefits.

Indexing the statutory retirement age to life expectancy is the most natural way to insure society against a longer average life of its citizens so that people spend part of their longer life in work and part in retirement. A higher retirement age implies that the human capital embodied in the elderly is used more intensively. This raises the return on effort and schooling, thereby facilitating life-long training. By redistributing human capital more equally over various generations, a higher retirement age attacks the potential fiscal and social problems due to aging at the root. The elderly rely less on the solidarity of the young and more on their own human capital. Indeed, labour income of the elderly could become another major pillar of old-age insurance. By keeping older workers longer employed, governments reap a double dividend. The elderly not only reduce social spending but also broaden the contribution base.

More Reforms Needed. Current reforms (see Box 7.2) do not seem sufficient to significantly raise the effective retirement age. In particular, raising the effective retirement age requires a stronger labour-market position of elderly workers. Employers can be encouraged to employ elderly workers not only by increasing the skills of the elderly but also by tightening rules against age discrimination and by reducing wage costs. To achieve this, age-related pay schemes may have to be reconsidered so that wages can be better adjusted to individual productivity levels. This may also require modification of social security schemes. For example, occupational pension systems and unemployment insurance schemes that link benefits to final pay, discourage gradual retirement through occupational downgrading with lower rates of pay. Furthermore, social security systems that let benefits increase with age reduce the labour-force participation of elder workers.

Efficient Retirement Decisions. Different people may want to leave the labour force at different times and in different ways. To facilitate efficient decision making by workers with diverse needs and preferences, pension systems should confront potential retirees and their employers with the social costs of retirement. In other words, early and delayed retirement benefits should be actuarially fair.

Various routes for withdrawing from the labour force may be substitutes. Accordingly, in confronting workers with the social costs of their labour-supply decisions, governments should pursue a comprehensive approach. Various conditional social security benefits, such as unemployment and disability benefits, are subject to moral hazard. As the work force ages, these moral hazard problems become more serious as older workers are subject to higher disability and unemployment risk. These considerations increase the need to reform social insurance along the lines outlined in Chapter 6.

Labour Supply of the Young. Higher labour supply of the young strengthens the base for financing old-age benefits. One way to accomplish this is to enhance labour supply of vulnerable groups with little marketable skills through a more activating social insurance system (see Chapter 6). Another way is to increase labour supply of women. Following the drop in fertility, many women have moved from the informal into the formal sector. However, in both countries, there is still considerable scope for women to increase their labour supply. Improved child care, which can be provided by elderly workers, may enhance labour-market participation of women with young children. A higher female participation rate strengthens the labour skills and human capital of women. This allows them to rely less on public transfers when old; an added benefit from the point of view of reducing the claim of old-age pensions on the public budget.

8 Labour Market: Institutional Environment

At present, the Dutch labour market receives acclaim for its strong job growth and decreasing unemployment rate. From a Dutch perspective, the high skill level and internal flexibility of German workers stand out. How can these and other differences in current performance be linked to labour market institutions? And, do economic trends require more flexible and diverse labour relationships, or is there a future for long-term commitment and cooperative exchange?

To address these core questions, Chapter 8 and 9 examine the strengths and weaknesses of German and Dutch labour market institutions in view of current and future economic conditions. In this examination, the American labour market is used as a benchmark. Labour market institutions are broadly defined as arrangements that structure the interactions between individual employers, workers and outsiders. They govern labour relations between employers and employees, managers and employees, and affect the position of outsiders (the unemployed) and insiders. Hence, both labour market regulations and cooperative arrangements between (organised) employers and employees are considered.

The structure of the analysis is as follows. Chapter 8 starts with the analytical framework. Next, it compares labour market regulations that provide the institutional environment for cooperative exchange and competition on the German, Dutch and American labour markets. Labour market regulations regarding dismissals, working time, short-time work and atypical contracts are taken into consideration. Chapter 9 deals with cooperative exchange and competition in labour relationships. It compares systems of collective bargaining, vocational employee training and co-determination. Finally, Chapter 9 presents several policy options.

8.1 Analytical Framework

The analytical framework explores how labour market institutions impact labour market performance. The core of the analysis is that international differences in labour market institutions result in different positions of countries on the four main economic trade-offs (Chapter 2). In turn, these differences impact labour market performance: labour market participation, human capital, job quality and living standards. To illustrate this line of reasoning, Section 8.1.1 explains why free labour market competition may fail. Subsequently, Section 8.1.2 presents the way in which two stylized institutional models address these market failures. Next, Section 8.1.3 to 8.1.7 provide a better understanding of the various institutions at work in both models. Finally, Section 8.1.8 gives an overview of the main strengths and weaknesses of the models in view of the economic conditions that are conducive to their performance.

8.1.1 Market Failures in Labour Relationships

The Need for Labour Market Institutions. A pure neoclassical labour market does not need labour market institutions. Perfect product and labour market competition prevents rent-extracting and results in an equilibrium wage level that equals both marginal productivity and the reservation wage, thereby clearing the labour market. Moreover, labour relationships are perceived to be similar to other market transactions: they are a market exchange of effort against wages. Labour contracts are complete and monitoring compliance to contract specifications is not prohibitively costly.

In practice, however, competition is imperfect and labour contracts are incomplete. Indeed, the four types of market failure explained in Chapter 2 pertain also to labour relationships. Market power and externalities exist even in a static world with complete labour contracts. The incompleteness of labour contracts causes two additional market failures related to a dynamic labour market characterized by firm-specific investments and fundamental uncertainty.

Bargaining Power. Bargaining theories relax the heroic assumption of perfect competition. For two reasons, the competition of workers for jobs and the competition of firms for workers does not result in the neoclassical equilibrium wage level equal to the marginal productivity of labour and the reservation wage of workers. First, workers and employers can extract rents. Especially if employers face high search costs to replace workers and if firm-specific skills make insiders difficult to replace, insiders can exploit these entry barriers to obtain insider wage premia at the expense of providers of capital, consumers and job opportunities of outsiders (Nickell, 1995; Layard *et al.*, 1991). Bargaining power of employers may cause labour to be paid less than its marginal product in some markets, especially if workers cannot adequately signal the value of their human capital to other employers or if they face high mobility costs. Second, employers may wish to pay wages above the reservation wage of workers in order to attract high quality workers, stimulate worker effort or prevent quits. Competition for jobs of unemployed outsiders with lower reservation wages does not induce employers to cut wages, because the resulting loss of operational efficiency would outweigh the reduction of wage costs (Akerlof and Yellen, 1986).

Externalities. External effects result from interdependencies between individual preferences that are outside the price system and therefore are not considered in decisions of individual workers, employers or outsiders. They imply that individual employers and employees cannot fully capture the benefits or do not incur all the costs of their decisions. Two well-known examples are the poaching externality related to transferable human capital and the external effect of a decentralized wage agreement on the unemployment level. If wages are below the marginal product of labour, a poaching firm may capture part of the human capital investments of workers and the firm that provided the training (see Booth and Snower, 1996). Since workers and employers cannot fully capture all returns to investments through higher wages and profitability, they will underinvest (Section 8.1.6). Wage bargaining at a decentralized level involves externalities on the unemployment level. Individual employers and workers at the individual firm-level drive up wages, because they fail to consider the adverse effect of the wage bargain on unemployment.

Specificity and Commitment. A labour relationship differs fundamentally from a market transaction of effort against wages (see also Hartog, Polachek and Theeuwes, 1993). In particular, labour contracts do not fully specify the division of rents from shared investments in firm-specific worker quality, such as in firm-specific human capital and internal flexibility of workers. It is not feasible to determine the productivity and pay rises that should result from every type of investment in all future circumstances. Hence, employers and employees are vulnerable to possible exploitation by the other party once they have invested in their mutual labour relation. They fear that the other party "grasps the fruits of the first party's cooperative stance" (Marsden, 1995), since they have little means to enforce commitment.[1] For instance, once employers have invested in the relationship, workers may threaten to quit or shirk on the job unless they receive higher wages. Likewise, employers may threaten to fire workers who have invested in relationship-specific assets in order to lower their wages. As a result of incomplete contracts, a lack of commitment discourages shared investments in firm-specific quality (Chapter 2).

Uncertainty. Because of failures of the private insurance market related to adverse selection, moral hazard and interdependent risks, a private insurance market for human capital is missing (Chapter 2 and Chapter 6). Hence, the market fails to provide insurance against the loss of income related to involuntary unemployment

---

[1] Some specifications in labour contracts may help to enforce commitment. For instance, contract specifications may forbid workers to transfer particular assets, such as client-networks, to other employers. However, due to transaction costs, contract specifications alone cannot prevent opportunistic behaviour (see also Chapter 2).

and inactivity. This lack of insurance erodes solidarity between insiders and outsiders. Moreover, it creates uncertainty regarding the returns to firm-specific investments in human capital, thereby discouraging firm-specific investments by outsiders and insiders alike. Outsiders do not sufficiently invest in skills and job search to improve the quality of a future job match (Blank (ed.), 1994). Insiders do not take the risk to invest substantially in the quality of a labour relationship.

The Role of Institutions. The four types of market failure described above may lower labour market activity and human capital investments, leading to a loss of welfare for the economy as a whole. Labour market institutions address the four market failures by employing the four coordination mechanisms introduced in Chapter 2. Some institutions aim to safeguard free competition. They restrict the bargaining power of powerful interest organisations and impose only limited labour market regulation in order to enhance the freedom to act at a decentralized level. Other institutions replace competition by more visible means of coordination in the form of control and cooperative exchange.

8.1.2 Two Stylized Models of Labour Relationships

Two stylized models of labour market institutions present extreme ways to address labour market failures. The *competitive model* can be associated with the American labour market, while the *cooperative model* corresponds roughly with labour relations in Germany (Figure 8.1).[2] These stylized models occupy extreme positions on the four economic trade-offs explained in Chapter 2. Accordingly, they are useful as a starting point for the more detailed comparison of German and Dutch labour market institutions in the rest of this Chapter and Chapter 9.

The Competitive Model. Institutions of the competitive model reduce market failures by supporting competition through the reduction of entry and exit barriers, thereby more closely approximating the ideal of a pure neo-classical labour market. Hence, this model relies on external labour market flexibility, tailor-made solutions, diversity and financial incentives to promote the *allocative efficiency* of the labour market. As a result of low entry barriers to the labour market, this model promotes also *opportunities for outsiders* to participate on the labour market. The increased access of workers to the labour market reduces the risk of prolonged involuntary inactivity.

---

[2] Their main characteristics regarding labour market institutions correspond to the features of the socio-economic orders of the two models (Chapter 5). The distinction between the cooperative and competitive model defines also the analytical framework on Chapter 10 on Corporate Governance.

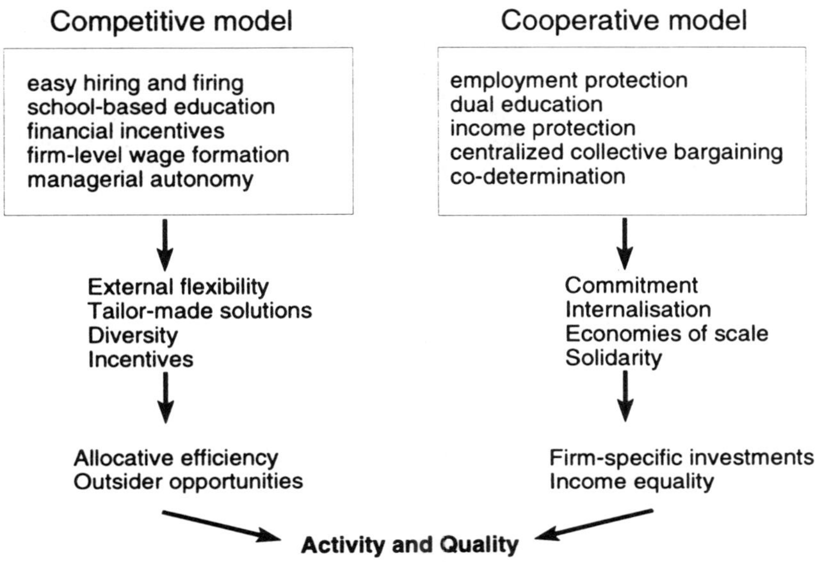

Figure 8.1 Institutional models, behaviour and performance

Competition implies ample freedom to act at the decentralized level. This promotes *external flexibility*: individual employers can easily adjust employment, working hours or wages to output fluctuations. In turn, school-based education promotes external flexibility because it provides workers with a stock of general human capital at the start of their career. To enhance job opportunities in a labour market environment characterized by external flexibility, employees invest in general training to enhance their employability.

The competitive model discourages specific investments and thus suffers from the market failures associated with specificity. However, by reducing exit and entry barriers, it decreases specificity as much as possible and benefits from the allocative advantages and the external flexibility of the market. The competitive model resolves externalities (i.e. missing markets) through market creation. The determination of labour conditions at a decentralized level allows *tailor-made solutions* that correspond with specific economic conditions.

In such a competitive labour market, control measures primarily aim to safeguard competition by reducing exit and entry barriers so as to avoid the market failure of market power. Institutions thus discourage the emergence of centralized interest organisations, which could yield market power. In this way, institutions promote *diversity* of labour conditions. Moreover, they hamper both influential centralized collective bargaining associations and substantial direct influence of worker representatives within firms. This supports autonomy of management in setting individual labour conditions. Workers have little scope to use voice. Instead, they rely on their employability and exit options to discipline management and to combat opportunistic behaviour of management (see also Chapter 10).

Furthermore, regulations provide a minimum degree of employment and income protection to deal with negative social consequences of the competitive labour market environment. Yet, the extent of job and income security in this model is relatively modest. This provides strong *financial incentives* to participate, search, accept and perform on a job (Chapter 6). The competitive model replaces markets of risk pooling by risk reduction through increased flexibility, mobility, employability, and adaptability (see also Subsection 6.4.4 in Chapter 6).

The Cooperative Model. Institutions of the cooperative model, in contrast, support cooperative exchange as a way to address labour market failures. Accordingly, control measures provide the institutional environment in which cooperative exchange takes place by restricting the individual freedom to act. As a result, this model emphasizes commitment, internalisation of external effects, the realisation of economies of scale, and solidarity.

The institutions of this model that restrict the individual freedom to act strengthen the *commitment* of employers and workers to keep to implicit agreements in labour relationships, for instance regarding the distribution of the returns to *firm-specific investments* in the quality of labour relations (Chapter 2). In two ways, institutions limit the scope for opportunistic behaviour once firm-specific investments have been made: they delegate collective bargaining power to a higher level of aggregation and give workers a voice to influence management on matters that are decided at the firm level.

Collective exchange between organized employers, workers and the government at the centralized level encourages interest groups to *internalize* external effects in their bargaining objectives. Encompassing interests groups incorporate the macroeconomic results of their decisions in their bargaining objectives. In particular, centralized bargaining internalizes the external effect of the wage bargain on the unemployment level. Moreover, collective exchange helps to reduce the external effects related to the transferable nature of employee training. Centralized wage bargaining reduces the poaching threat, whereas consensus building regarding the contents and organisation of human capital formation increases the private returns to shared investments.

In addition, interest associations of workers or employers can realize *economies of scale*. Centralized agreements between representatives of relatively homogeneous groups of labour and capital, for instance between sectoral trade unions and employer organisations, or between works councils and management, reduce the transaction costs related to the conclusion of a large number of individual agreements.

For the outsiders of this system, social security benefits guarantee a minimum income level.[3] *Solidarity* not only increases income equality, but also supports the search for a good job match. Moreover, it gives workers an incentive to invest in firm-specific skills, because they are insured against shocks that affect the value of these investments.

8.1.3 Employment Protection

Employment protection enhances the job security of workers, but reduces the freedom to act of individual employers. An employer cannot use particular arrangements without risking legal sanctions (Grubb and Wells, 1993). Firing regulations and legal support of co-determination are the main channels of employment protection. Firing regulations restrict the circumstances that permit dismissals and make firing procedures more costly. A collective voice of workers at the work floor through co-determination strengthens the protection of insiders against dismissals, because an important objective of workers is to enhance job security (Koene and Slomp, 1991).

Employment protection reduces employment flexibility; i.e. the scope for employers to adjust the employment level to fluctuations in activity.[4] Hence, whatever strategy employers choose to deal with employment protection, it makes the allocation of human resources more sluggish: sector or firm-specific shocks do not trigger swift labour flows from firms in unfavourable circumstances to firms in favourable circumstances, and insider protection hampers the job opportunities of outsiders. These effects have been confirmed by empirical research (Jackman *et al.*, 1995; Abraham and Houseman, 199[illegible]). Another disadvantage of unemployment protection is that it makes employers more hesitant to hire new workers. This reduces the access of outsiders to jobs. This, in turn, may harm labour supply.

Exit barriers provide an incentive for high quality human resource strategies and internal flexibility of the workforce, because they strengthen the commitment of employers to the labour relations with their employees. High employment

---

3 This is especially important in the cooperative model because entry and exit barriers tend to increase the risk of prolonged periods of involuntary inactivity.

4 The overall effect of reduced flexibility on unemployment is ambiguous. On the one hand, higher adjustment costs foster strategies of labour hoarding during economic downturns. On the other hand, they augment labour costs and make employers more cautious to hire during economic upswings (Gelauff and Graafland, 1994). Both the inflow to and the outflow from unemployment decline. Yet, employment protection may increase unemployment by reinforcing the scope for insiders to extract rents Empirical research on the employment and unemployment effects of protective regulations is inconclusive. Büchtemann (1989) finds marginal effects. Jackman *et al.* (1995) do not find a significant effect on unemployment, but find that the limited access of outsiders to stable employment discourages labour supply, thereby reducing the employment level.

adjustment costs stimulate workers to take a long-term perspective and invest in relationship-specific assets. Analogously, the semi-fixed character of core employment increases the need for enterprises to invest in worker quality. Empirical research by the OECD (1993: 119-155) shows that tenure and investments in employee training are positively correlated. However, the causality of this relationship is unclear.

A legal obligation on universally guaranteed individual employee rights increases the efficacy of worker protection. If, in the absence of collective dismissal protection, a single firm applies a policy of justifying each dismissal, it might attract a relatively large proportion of shirking-prone workers. The firm can only prevent such a process of adverse selection by a high cost screening policy. Legal employee rights prevent this process of adverse selection.

If employment protection is excessive, a strong commitment of employers may go hand in hand with weak incentives for insiders to invest and put effort in their labour relationship and strong incentives for insiders to extract rents. Both a lack of incentives to perform on the job and insider power to extract rents reduce the returns to high-quality human resource strategies and decrease the incentive for employers to make firm-specific investments. This points to the importance of a balanced division of commitment between both parties.

Employment Protection and Performance of Both Models. Limited employment protection of the competitive model supports an efficient use of human resources because it promotes *external flexibility* (Table 8.1). Outsiders with up to date stocks of human capital can easily get access to the labour market. This contributes to frequent flows in and out of unemployment (see for instance OECD, 1994a: 48). Workers have strong incentives to put effort in their labour relationship in order to reduce the dismissal threat. Yet, easy exit options of employers cause short-termism. Workers do not make substantial firm-specific investments in the long-term quality of their current labour relationship, because the returns to these types of investments are highly uncertain. Rather, they focus on explicitly defined tasks to reduce the dismissal threat. Moreover, they invest in general human capital to enhance their employability as an insurance against possible future job loss.

Because of more extensive employment protection, the cooperative model is better at accumulating firm-specific human resources. Job security supports employer *commitment* (Table 8.1). This promotes a long-term perspective towards labour relationships and encourages firm-specific quality of human capital and internal flexibility of workers. Yet, a strong focus on job security reduces the incentives not to shirk, hampers swift re-allocation of transferable human resources and outsider job opportunities.

Table 8.1 Institutional characteristics and position on the trade-offs

	Competitive model	Cooperative model
Employment protection	*Limited*	*Extensive*
– extent of job security	flexibility	commitment
Income protection	*Limited*	*Extensive*
– fall-back position	incentives	solidarity
Collective bargaining	*Decentralized*	*Centralized*
– bargaining level	flexibility	commitment
– bargaining objectives	tailor-made solutions	internalisation
– level of representation	diversity	economies of scale
Employee training	*Decentralized*	*Consensus-building*
– bargaining level	flexibility	commitment
– training objectives	tailor-made solutions	internalisation
Co-determination	*Absent*	*Substantial*
– extent of job security	flexibility	commitment
– worker objectives	tailor-made solutions	internalisation
– level of representation	diversity	economies of scale

8.1.4 Income Protection

Social security protects individuals against income decline during periods of inactivity. On the one hand, income protection may weaken the financial incentives for activity and effort. Extensive unemployment benefits, characterized by a high instant replacement rate, a long benefit duration, easy eligibility conditions and low monitoring activities, reduce the "terrors of unemployment" (Jackman *et al.*, 1995). Therefore, they may reduce the search intensity of unemployed and the probability that a job offer is accepted (Gelauff and Graafland, 1994). Moreover, they may weaken the effort of workers in their current labour relation, because insurance against job loss reduces the disutility of losing a job.

On the other hand, income protection promotes solidarity. This increases income equality. Moreover, it improves the opportunities for the unemployed to invest in job-search and skills in order to improve the quality of a future job match. Because of changing skill requirements of jobs, unemployed can often not expect to find a job that matches their current skills. In this case, income protection in combination with retraining "helps them make their skills appropriate to changing jobs" (Booth and Snower, 1996; Blank (1994). Moreover, benefits insure workers against a possible future loss of their firm-specific assets, thereby encouraging workers to take the risk to invest in firm-specific worker quality.

Income Protection and Performance of Both Models. The effects of income protection illustrate the trade-off between adequate market *incentives* for activity and worker effort in the competitive model, versus *solidarity* through the insurance of investments in the quality of current and future job matches in the cooperative model (Table 8.1). On the one hand, cutting benefits may increase the incentives for search, acceptance and effort and reduce insider power. On the other hand, it may lead to socially unacceptable living standards, underinvestments in firm-specific assets and inadequate job search (OECD, 1996b: 52).

8.1.5 Collective Bargaining

The extent of centralisation is a key feature of collective bargaining. The extent of centralisation not only depends on the predominant collective bargaining level, but also on coordination between employees and employers and government involvement. The decentralized end of the spectrum consists of collective bargaining at the firm (or plant) level, guided neither by coordination nor by strong government involvement. At the centralized end of the spectrum, cooperative exchange between interest associations and the government is more dominant. Economy-wide units bargain, with strong government influence through regulations, tripartite concertation or direct interventions.

This section first discusses the basic theory about how centralization affects wages and employment. It then explores how the product market environment and efficiency wage considerations may affect this basic relationship. With these refinements, the theoretical relationships appear to be largely in accordance with the empirical evidence. The section then shifts to the impact of centralization on commitment. It closes by reviewing the major trade-offs in collective bargaining.

Centralisation and the Wage Level. Calmfors and Driffill (1988) describe the relationship between the degree of centralisation and the level of wages as an inverse U-curve. They argue that decentralized collective bargaining at the individual firm-level limits the bargaining power of organised workers. At this level, product market competition tends to be fierce. Accordingly, excessive wage demands result in a considerable loss of market share and employment, thereby endangering the position of the insiders (see also OECD, 1994b: 11). As a result, the wage bargain is close to the neoclassical outcome: the wage level reflects marginal productivity.

Centralisation raises the bargaining power of trade unions and affects their bargaining objectives. The price-elasticity of product demand is generally lower for the industry than for the individual firm, because the sectoral bargaining unit comprises firms producing relatively close substitutes (Calmfors and Driffill, 1988). Sectoral trade unions can demand wages that exceed the neoclassical level, knowing that the firm can more easily translate wage premia into higher output prices without losing its market share. Yet, as centralisation rises further, the difference between outsiders and insiders disappears (Teulings, 1996). Trade unions internalize the effects of the wage bargain on job opportunities and have less incentives to drive-up wages. In a cross-country-analysis, Jackman *et al.* (1995) confirm the wage moderating effects of centralisation. They find that a higher collective bargaining coverage drives up wages, but that a higher degree of centralisation moderates this effect.

This suggests that a sufficient degree of either decentralisation or centralisation prevents excessive wage demands. An intermediate degree of centralisation, i.e. sectoral bargaining without strong economy-wide coordination or government involvement, yields the worst employment performance. Trade unions are powerful but their incentives to internalize the position of outsiders are weak. In such a bargaining setting, both decentralization or further centralisation, for instance through coordination by confederations of interest organisations and government involvement, helps to bring the wage level closer to the market clearing neoclassical level (Calmfors and Driffill, 1988; see also Van de Wijngaert, 1994; Teulings, 1996).

Various factors may upset the basic relationship between centralization and wages. On the one hand, even sectoral unions may lack market power if the sector faces international competition. On the other hand, decentralized workers may feature market power if individual firms face imperfect competition or cannot perfectly monitor individual workers. We now turn to these two refinements of the basic relationship.

Impact of Product Market Environment. The impact of centralisation on the wage level depends on the product market environment. If the industry encounters fierce international product market competition, sectoral trade unions in an intermediate bargaining setting have little scope to drive up wages (Layard *et al.*, 1991). Accordingly, sectoral trade unions in industries trading homogeneous products on the international market can hardly extract rents.

If product market competition is imperfect, however, workers and employers are able to drive up wages also in a decentralized bargaining setting. Product market competition between companies within an industry is often imperfect due to a technological lead, differentiated products or sunk costs. In this case, incentives for rent extracting are relatively strong, even in a decentralized bargaining setting.

A firm-level trade union has a strong motivation to extract rents because it is too small to internalize employment opportunities of outsiders (Teulings and Hartog, 1997; Nickell, 1995). Local insider power causes persisting wage differentials between identical workers in firms with high and low product market rents, and makes employment growth in prosperous firms more sluggish (Layard *et al.*, 1991; Teulings, 1995 and 1996). Similarly, fluctuations in product market rents create wage differentials between insiders and new hires within a particular firm. After a period with positive product market rents, the insiders attempt to keep their high wage level and to translate a worsening of firm performance into lower starting wages for new hires (Hartog, Van Opstal and Teulings, 1994).

Decentralisation and Efficiency Wages. In addition to imperfect competition on commodity markets, other factors may drive up wages above the neoclassical equilibrium level in a decentralized bargaining setting. High monitoring costs (Chapter 2) create an incentive for individual employers to raise wages above the market-clearing rate in order to enhance the motivation, loyalty and effort of their work force (Akerlof and Yellen, 1986; Layard *et al.*, 1991: 29). Efficiency wage premia enhance labour productivity by making outside opportunities relatively unattractive compared to inside opportunities. Clearly, this behaviour induces leapfrogging behaviour of other employers with the same motive. The resulting higher wage level raises unemployment. In equilibrium, unemployment rather than high relative wages acts as a "worker discipline device" by providing an incentive to maintain work effort. Hence, efficiency wages correspond with a positive level of equilibrium unemployment.

Efficiency wage considerations differ across companies. Accordingly, efficiency wage premia persistently differ between identical workers in different firms (Akerlof and Yellen, 1986). For firms with a high firm-specific skill intensity of production and high monitoring costs, efficiency wage premia will be relatively high.

Empirical Evidence. Empirical evidence finds that wage dispersion related to firm or industry characteristics is relatively large in countries with a decentralized bargaining system such as the United States, Canada and the United Kingdom (Layard *et al.*, 1991: 188; 212; Teulings and Hartog, 1997; Teulings, 1996; Hartog, Van Opstal and Teulings, 1994).[5] Adjustment processes to local shocks, efficiency wage considerations and insider power of local trade unions contribute to wage dispersion. Unfortunately, these three causes are difficult to separate empirically. In a dynamic environment with continuous firm-specific shocks, the identity of high productivity and low productivity firms continuously changes. Wage differentials between firms in a dynamic environment may be needed to provide an incentive for workers to overcome mobility costs and migrate to profitable locations (Bertola and Ichino, 1995). Moreover, differences in efficiency wage considerations across companies cause wage differentials between workers with identical human capital characteristics.

Yet, empirical evidence suggests that also local insider power yields wage differentials. In particular, the large size of trade union wage markups in the

---

5 Although unobserved skill differences, varying pleasantness of jobs or imperfect mobility of labour may play a role, these factors cannot completely explain the relatively large and persisting wage differentials between firms (Layard *et al.*, 1991).

United States and the United Kingdom, i.e. the difference in wages between identical workers depending on whether they are covered by a collective agreement, suggests that insider power plays a role. In unionized firms with product market power, significant wage markups exist (Stewart, 1990). In contrast, union mark-ups are small for firms that encounter fierce product market competition. In addition, the effect of product prices on the wage level is relatively large in countries with a decentralized bargaining system (Teulings and Hartog, 1997; Teulings, 1996). Moreover, in the United States new hires pay the price for insider wage premia (Waaijers, 1996; Teulings, 1996: 58-59). Also this suggests the existence of insider power, because efficiency wage considerations do not discriminate between new hires and existing workers.

Centralisation and Commitment. Centralisation of collective bargaining supports commitment of employers and employees to keep to a predetermined division of the returns from investments in their labour relationship (Teulings and Hartog, 1997; Teulings, 1996 and 1995). Opportunistically changing the way rents are shared becomes more difficult, because individual workers and employers have delegated their bargaining authority to a higher level of aggregation. Hence, they have a negligible influence on wages during periods of renegotiation. Whereas wages can be adjusted to changes in macroeconomic or sectoral circumstances, they thus cannot be adjusted to changes in the ex-post bargaining position of individual workers and employers.[6] For instance, insiders cannot easily extract the rents from an unexpected increase in firm performance or demand higher wages in response to an improvement of their outside options. This increases the certainty for individual employers and workers that the other party will not opportunistically capture a larger share of the returns to investments in firm-specific assets.

Collective Bargaining and the Performance of Both Models. In the competitive model, labour conditions are determined at a decentralized level, either between individual workers and employers or between firm-level trade unions and individual employers (Teulings and Hartog, 1997). The bargaining process is neither guided by strong government involvement nor by encompassing interest groups of workers and employers at a higher level.

Decentralized wage formation enables *flexible* adjustments of wages in response to local shocks. The absence of centralized interest associations promotes *diversity* and *tailor-made solutions*, in particular concerning efficiency wage differentials between types of firms or types of workers (Table 8.1). For instance, employers that have made considerable firm-specific investments in worker quality pay higher

---

6 Teulings and Hartog (1997) argue that alternative more simple external institutions for renegotiation, such as formulas for wage growth, cannot easily determine how wages need to be adjusted to external shocks.

efficiency wages in order to prevent quits of workers with firm-specific skills. These factors promote allocative efficiency. However, efficiency wage considerations drive up the wage level and increase unemployment. Furthermore, bargaining power of local trade unions causes insider wage premia that hamper employment growth in prosperous firms. Moreover, decentralized wage formation promotes a short-term view towards labour relationships. Some companies strengthen commitment by fixing the wage level for a period of several years, but this hampers the possibility to adjust wages to shocks during the duration of the contract (Teulings and Hartog, 1997; Teulings, 1996).

In the cooperative model, collective bargaining predominantly takes place at sectoral level. The bargaining process is guided by cooperative exchange between social partners and the government at economy-wide level. Centralized collective bargaining curbs local insider power, *internalizes* external effects and supports *commitment* (Table 8.1). Moreover, trade unions and employers organizations may realize *economies of scale* in representing individual workers and employers. This reduces transaction costs related to a large number of individual transactions. Yet, an intermediate degree of centralisation may drive up the wage level, because trade unions gain bargaining power but have insufficient incentives to consider the position of outsiders. Moreover, centralisation reduces flexible wage adjustments to shocks in firm-specific economic conditions and compresses efficiency wage differentials across firms.

8.1.6 Employee Training

Becker (1962) demonstrates the importance of distinguishing between general and firm-specific training. Workers have an incentive to finance general human capital, because the returns to this type of education are valued on the labour market through higher wages. Investments in firm-specific human capital, in contrast, are valuable only to a single employer. These investments require that the employer and worker share the initial costs and the future benefits in order to give both parties an incentive to continue the labour relationship and capture their share of the returns. Hence, if general and firms-specific training can be separated and adequately financed, there can be a market for both types of human capital.

In practice, however, market failures may cause underinvestments in both general and firm-specific human capital. Employees may not be able to capture the returns to general training investments through higher wages, because incomplete information prevents them from adequately signalling the value of their general human capital investments to employers. Hence, general skills are not transferable. Investments in general skills are discouraged also because employees with low incomes tend to have only limited access to capital markets due to moral hazard and adverse selection. Hence, employees are not able to finance investments in human capital. With respect to shared investments in firm-specific human capital, a lack of commitment regarding the future division of rents between the employee and the training firm may discourage investments.

The mixed characteristics of most training investments makes investment decisions even more complex. Most employee training features both general and firm-specific elements, or can be applied in a limited number of companies, for instance within a specific industry. The market for this type of human capital is incomplete: because skills are not purely general, they are imperfectly transferable. Hence, individual employees cannot fully capture the returns of their training investment on the labour market. Because of the firm-specific component, employers need to finance part of the investment in employee training. Yet, also employers tend to underinvest, because the general component of employee training causes positive externalities: a poaching firm can obtain part of the rents from the shared training investments of workers and the training firm (Stevens, 1996).

Cooperative Exchange and Employee Training. Cooperative exchange at a centralized level regarding wages and the organisation of employee training helps to strengthen commitment and reduce poaching externalities. This increases the incentives for employers and workers to invest in employee training with partly firm-specific and partly general characteristics (Booth and Snower, 1996; Soskice, 1994).

Centralized wage formation strengthens commitment to keep to a predetermined division of returns from the training investment (see also Section 8.1.5). In addition, it reduces externalities, because employers have less scope to poach skilled workers of other companies by offering higher wages (Soskice, 1994). Analogously, individual workers face less incentives to quit and opportunistically capture part of the returns to transferable quality investments made by the current employer.

Consensus-building on the finance and contents of employee training between interest groups of employers, workers and the government helps to increase the private returns to shared investments by employees and the training firms. For instance, relatively low wages during the training period increase the returns to the training firm, and make the investment worthwhile even if part of the employees quits after a relatively short tenure (Soskice, 1994). Moreover, consensus-building on the contents of training at centralized level helps to increase the general labour market value (or transferability) of the training certificate to workers (Van Lieshout, 1996) and to make the employee training match employer requirements (Den Broeder, 1995).

Employee Training and Performance of Both Models. The competitive model promotes investments by workers in purely general, transferable human capital. The school-based initial educational system supports this focus on general skills, by providing workers with a stock of general human capital. This human capital is easily transferable across firms because clearly defined characteristics limit information asymmetries. The limited job and income security of this model encourages these investments as a way to strengthen the *flexibility* and *employability* of workers (Section 8.1.3 and 8.1.4).

Yet, this model does not support investments in imperfectly transferable employee training with partly firm-specific and partly general characteristics. Decentralized wage formation aggravates the poaching externality related to the general component of employee training. Decentralized wage formation and limited job and income security discourage investments, because they result in a lack of commitment and insurance of firm-specific assets. Both factors provide a disincentive for investments in this type of employee training (Table 8.1).

The cooperative model, in contrast, supports investments in imperfectly transferable employee training. Centralized collective bargaining reduces the *poaching threat* caused by the general component and strengthens *commitment* needed to encourage investments in the firm-specific component. In addition, relatively extensive employment protection strengthens commitment, whereas social security provides insurance against a loss of firm-specific assets. Moreover, consensus-building helps to *internalize the external effects* from shared investments, for instance through a higher general value of the training certificate and a shorter pay-back period (Table 8.1). However, this model suffers also from disadvantages. Cooperative exchange at centralized level diminishes the scope for tailor-made training solutions at the firm level. Moreover, consensus-building at centralized level is time-consuming and causes slow adaptations of the contents of training to changing economic conditions (Van Lieshout, 1996).

8.1.7 Co-determination

Co-determination rights, i.e. the institutionalized participation of workers in decision-making by management, support the commitment of labour relationships and influence the quality of managerial decision-making.

In two ways, co-determination strengthens commitment. First, it is a form of employment protection (Section 8.1.3). This gives workers an incentive to consider their labour relation from a long-term perspective and invest in firm-specific human capital, efficient information flows and internal flexibility. Worker representatives often support the demand of employers for recurrent investments in quality or internal flexibility, because they see this as a way to preserve the employment level (Jacobi *et al.*, 1992). Evidence on the effects of co-determination generally confirms that co-determination stabilizes employment. For instance, Frick (1996) finds that the presence of a works council significantly lowers both quit and dismissal rates in German companies.[7] Second, co-determination gives workers a tool to monitor the way management handles their investments in firm-specific quality. This precludes unilateral decisions of management to renege on implicit agreements in labour contracts.

The direct influence of workers on management impacts the quality of management, because managers cannot opportunistically pursue their own goals without considering the interests of workers. For instance, worker influence may curb managerial empire building. Besides, work-floor suggestions may improve production processes or product quality. However, co-determination rights also hamper the short-term flexibility of management decisions, because consensus-building at the work-place is time-consuming. If worker-representatives become too influential, they may behave opportunistically, instead of participating in effective cooperation. In extreme cases co-determination may even result in a deadlock, which lowers labour quality within the firm instead of improving it.

Some empirical studies address the impact of German co-determination on firm performance, but their findings are mixed (Addison *et al.*, 1996; Gurdon and Rai, 1990; Fitzroy and Kraft, 1993).[8] Making use of a relatively large data set, Addison *et al.* (1996) find that the presence of a works council lowers profitability, but does not discourage innovative activity. Hence, rent seeking of works councils does not appear to spill over to other performance dimensions and their findings neither support nor contradict a positive effect of works councils on firm performance.

Co-determination and Performance of Both Models. The competitive model lacks substantial co-determination rights, i.e. the institutionalized participation of workers in decision-making by management (Hepple, 1993; Biagi, 1993). The lack of co-determination arrangements enhances *flexible* employment adjustments and managerial decision-making, but provides a disincentive for workers to make firm-specific investments, because they bear the risk of losing the returns to these investments (Table 8.1).

Extensive co-determination rights of the cooperative model, in contrast, promote the *commitment* of labour relationships. Moreover, interest representation of individual workers *overcomes externalities* related to monitoring by individual workers and accomplishes *economies of scale* in interest representation (Table 8.1).

---

[7] Frick (1996) suggest that the voice instrument may replace the exit option of workers and that a higher training incidence further lowers the incidence of separations.

[8] This is not surprising, since it is difficult to disentangle the effects of co-determination from other factors, such as the quality of the schooling system or of other business strategies. Moreover, empirical studies suffer from methodological problems, for instance regarding the way to measure long-run firm performance, and from data problems (Nickell, 1995; Owen Smith, 1994: 307).

However, co-determination also causes sluggish decision-making. Moreover, as the primary objective of worker representatives is to protect the position of workers, it delays the adaptation of employment to economic conditions (Abraham and Houseman, 1993; Owen Smith, 1994). This hampers the re-allocation of employment and the labour market opportunities for outsiders.

8.1.8 Assessment

Strengths and Weaknesses of Both Models. Table 8.2 summarizes the main strengths and weaknesses of both models. The competitive model is better in using human resources efficiently: to adjust flexibly to changing economic circumstances, to determine labour conditions according to diverse economic conditions and to create employment opportunities for outsiders. The lack of employment protection, limited income support and the absence of centralized interest organisations with bargaining power *reduces the scope for rent-extracting* by insiders and helps to prevent dualism between insiders and outsiders.

Yet, the emphasis on competition as the main coordination mechanism results in a short-term focus towards labour relationships. A *lack of commitment and of certainty* curbs firm-specific investments in the quality of labour relationships: for instance in firm-specific human capital, in internal flexibility of workers or in improvements of managerial decision-making through direct worker influence. This makes the competitive economy strongly dependent on general, marketable skills and less attractive as an investment site for firm-specific knowledge intensive activities. The lack of encompassing interest groups reinforces this focus on purely general skills, because institutions do not solve the *poaching externality* related to shared investments of employers and employees in human capital with partly general and partly firm-specific characteristics. Moreover, decentralized interest representatives within prosperous firms have the scope and incentives to *extract rents*. Finally, *uncertainty* caused by limited employment and income protection may cause social fragmentation, i.e. an unacceptable degree of income dispersion and job and income insecurity.

The cooperative model, in contrast, performs better in accumulating firm-specific assets and in providing income equality and job and income security. The focus on long-term labour relationships supports *commitment* and leads to internal rather than external flexibility: working-time adjustments and quality adjustments through training or internal re-allocation of labour. Insurance against a possible loss of income reduces fundamental *uncertainty* and reinforces the focus on firm-specific investments. In addition, centralized interest associations *internalize external effects* and thus consider the realization of general welfare. At the same time they curb local insider power and allow adjustments of wages to macro-economic or sectoral shocks without reducing the commitment of labour relationships.

However, the larger emphasis on control and cooperative exchange as coordination mechanism prevents labour conditions to reflect local conditions,

Table 8.2 Strengths of the two models

Competitive model	Cooperative model
(External) flexibility efficient re-allocation of labour, diffusion of general knowledge, outsider job opportunities, swift management decisions	*Commitment* internal flexibility, firm-specific quality, job security
Tailor-made solutions individual preferences, adjustments to local shocks	*Internalisation* general welfare, adjustments to macro-economic shocks
Diversity less powerful interest associations, heterogeneous conditions	*Economies of scale* less scope for local insider power, efficient interest representation
Incentives search and effort, investments in general knowledge	*Solidarity* income equality, investments in firm-specific quality

makes labour markets inflexible and weakens financial incentives for search, job acceptance and effort. Moreover, if the degree of centralisation is insufficient, economies of scale in interest representation may create *bargaining power* of trade unions without providing adequate incentives to incorporate external effects. These weaknesses may yield an inefficient allocation of human resources and also hamper equity: outsiders receive income support but have limited job opportunities.

Balancing Strengths and Weaknesses. The distinct strengths and weaknesses of both stylized models imply that a single optimal institutional model does not exist. There is no unique set of institutions that succeeds in solving the four types of labour market failures. Hence, the design of labour market institutions involves balancing their relative strengths and weaknesses in view of the position on the trade-offs and current and future economic conditions. Some economic conditions require a competitive labour market, whereas other conditions benefit from cooperative exchange. More specifically, the relevancy of the competitive versus the cooperative model depends on preferences, technological change, skill requirements, type of companies and product market conditions (Table 8.3).

The competitive model is conducive to performance in a risk-taking, diffusion-oriented, heterogeneous economic environment with fierce product market competition and frequent firm-specific economic shocks. Risk-taking preferences and few equity considerations do not require more extensive income and employment protection. Flexible labour flows promote the diffusion of general knowledge embodied in workers and the re-allocation of labour in response to

Table 8.3 Economic conditions conductive to performance of the two models

	Competitive model	Cooperative model
Preferences	heterogeneous	homogeneous
	risk taking	risk averse
	few equity considerations	strong equity considerations
Technological change	short life cycle, radical	incremental
	diffusion-oriented	R&D in established firms
Skill requirements	general knowledge	firm-specific knowledge
Type of company	start-up companies	established companies
Product market	volatile	stable
	heterogeneous	homogeneous
	firm-specific shocks	macro-economic shocks
	competitive	imperfect competition

changes in volatile and diverse firm-specific economic conditions. Start-up firms benefit from flexible conditions to promote entrepreneurial risk-taking. Fierce product market competition ensures that economic agents at the decentralized level cannot easily capture monopoly rents.

The advantages of the cooperative model, in contrast, are more important in an environment with high risk aversion, strong equity considerations, firm-specific knowledge intensity, stable and homogeneous preferences and macro-economic shocks. Job and income security correspond with risk averse preferences and strong equity considerations. Homogeneous preferences and economic conditions increase the scope for consensus-building at centralized level. The long-term orientation of labour relationships is conducive to incremental technological change within established companies that is based on the exploitation of firm-specific assets. Established R&D intensive firms with firm-specific assets benefit from institutional support of commitment.

8.2 Employment Protection in Germany and the Netherlands

What is the impact of the German "internal labour market" versus the Dutch system of "flexicurity"? This section addresses the employment protection regulations that provide a framework for competition and cooperative exchange on the German and Dutch labour markets. First, it takes a closer look at German employment protection to explain the German focus on commitment between employers and workers within long-term labour relationships. Second, it examines the Dutch regulations, to illustrate that Dutch labour market regulations result in a mix between labour market flexibility and commitment. In this analysis, the American regulations are often used as a benchmark.

To these aims, employment protection is broadly defined as constraints on flexibility in employment, working-hours and types of contracts. This definition emphasizes that not only firing rules impact flexibility. If firms can easily adjust working hours or hire temporary workers, firing rules do not have to hamper overall labour market flexibility (Blank (ed.), 1994). For instance, employers may rely on hours adjustments through lenient working-time regulations, part-time work or short-time working arrangements to introduce some flexibility within a system of long-term labour relationships. As an alternative, they may choose a dual hiring strategy. According to this strategy, "flexible" and "rigid" workers coexist. The former category of workers provide flexibility, whereas the latter category develops firm-specific quality. Hence, Section 8.2.1 to 8.2.4 focus on four types of labour market regulations: firing rules, working-time regulations, short-time work arrangements and regulations regarding flexible contracts. Subsequently, Section 8.2.5 presents the main findings from the institutional comparison.

8.2.1 Firing Rules

From a broad economic perspective, firing regulations in Germany and the Netherlands are broadly similar. Viewed from an American perspective, they are relatively strict. Firing procedures in the United States are limited, since periods of notice or severance payments are not obligatory (OECD, 1994b: 73). Experience rating in the unemployment benefit system and lawsuits in case of firings that may contradict other laws (for instance regarding discrimination) are the American forms of employment protection (Bovenberg and De Mooij, 1996). Viewed from a European perspective, however, the difficulty of laying off workers can be considered as "intermediate": procedures are not as strict as in Italy, Greece, Portugal, or Spain, but more severe than in the United Kingdom, Denmark or Ireland (Grubb and Wells, 1993).

At a closer look, firing rules in Germany and the Netherlands differ.[9] This section compares the most important aspects, concentrating on individual and collective dismissals for economic reasons (Table 8.4). The distinction between individual and collective dismissals depends on the number of workers that become redundant within a specific period of time: in the Netherlands, a dismissal is considered collective if at least 20 workers become redundant within a period of three months (SER, 1994: 67 or IDS, 1995a: 39). In Germany, collective dismissals

[9] This section describes only legal minimum conditions. Collective agreements often specify improvements for workers on those conditions. Especially in case of dismissals at the executive level, considerable severance payments and outplacement services can be offered (IDS). Moreover, regulations regarding firing procedures are different for members of the management board, since firing a member of the board of directors is decided by the general meeting of shareholders or the supervisory board (Chapter 10).

Table 8.4 Overview of firing rules

	Germany	Netherlands
	Individual dismissal	
procedures	consultation works council	prior authorization
delay before notice	7 to 10 days	4 to 6 weeks
notice period	2 to 26 weeks[a]	1 to 26 weeks[b]
compensation	1 to 18 months pay[a]	1 to 26 weeks pay[b]
probationary period	6 months at most[c]	2 months at most
	Collective dismissal	
procedures	notice employment office, works council	notice employment office, worker representatives
delay before notice	1 month	1 month extra
severance pay	15 to 25 weeks pay[d]	1 to 2 months pay[d]

[a] Depending on age, tenure and type of job (blue-collar or white-collar or civil servant).
[b] Depending on tenure and age.
[c] This is no legal maximum (EC, 1994).
[d] Estimate. Amounts strongly vary.

Sources: Grubb and Wells (1993); Hunt (1994); Abraham and Houseman (1993); IDS (1995a); Jacobs (1993).

only apply to firms with at least 20 workers. It depends on the number of dismissed workers and the size of the firm whether a dismissal is collective.[10]

Individual Dismissals. German firing procedures are to a large extent concentrated within the firm. Employers do not need to ask permission from the employment office, but have to consult the works council (at least if a works council is present in the company). Consequently, worker protection depends on the strength of employee representation at firm level (Bosch, 1988). This procedure generally takes a shorter time compared to the Dutch procedure of obtaining prior authorization. However, if the works council disagrees, the particular worker has the right to remain employed until appeal to labour court (Büchtemann, 1989; Hunt, 1994; Jacobs, 1993). This happens in only a minority (8%) of dismissal

[10] In Germany, dismissals are collective if more than 6 workers or 20% of workers in companies with 20-59 employees, more than 37 or 20% in companies with 60-249 employees, more than 60 or 15% in companies with 250-499 employees and more than 60 or 10% in companies with 500 or more employees become redundant within a period of 30 days (Hunt, 1994: 5).

cases (Jacobs, 1993). Even if the works council agrees with a dismissal, however, workers can appeal in court. If a dismissal is considered unfair, compensation instead of reinstatement is common (Jacobs, 1993: 115).

German employment protection is limited for small companies. The possibility to appeal in court does not apply to workers in small firms. Moreover, small firms usually do not have a works council.[11] Recently, a policy proposal has been accepted that raises the lower limit for dismissal protection from five to ten workers.

In the Netherlands, the administrative procedure of obtaining prior admission from the regional employment office for each dismissal is unique in Europe. The procedure generally lasts up to six weeks. Only a minority of the actual[12] requests (6%) is rejected (Van den Boom, 1993). A recent policy proposal aims to shorten the length of dismissal procedures by allowing the authorization and notice period to partly overlap, and by reducing the maximum period of notice to four months (Box 8.2). Workers can appeal in court afterwards if they think that the dismissal is unfair, but this is not a common procedure (SER, 1994: 36). However, if a dismissal is judged unfair through a court procedure, the worker receives compensation payments for being unjustly dismissed, since reinstatement is rare. Employers also have the possibility to appeal in court if authorization is refused (IDS, 1995a). Finally, the probationary period for new hires is relatively short in the Netherlands, which gives employers little time to screen new hires.[13]

Collective Dismissals. In case of collective redundancies, additional - more complex - firing procedures need to be followed. In Germany, the criteria for a collective redundancy were altered in 1985 with the policy-objective of facilitating firing procedures by reducing the number of collective dismissals (AFG 1985).[14] In addition to the consultation of the works council, the state employment office must be informed. This procedure includes an obligatory waiting period of approximately one month, although the period of notice can already start during this period (Hunt, 1994; Jacobs, 1993: 129). The involvement of the works council becomes more extensive: the works council influences which persons will be

---

[11] The only restrictions are that the dismissal is not contrary to provisions in general laws, for instance regarding discrimination.

[12] Of course, the administrative procedure may discourage employers from requesting dismissal.

[13] During this period the employer can dismiss a worker without having to obtain prior authorization (IDS, 1995a: 31).

[14] Before 1985, a dismissal in Germany was considered to be collective if more than 5 workers in firms with 21-59 employees, more than 25 or 10% of workers in firms with 60-499 employees or more than 30 workers in firms with at least 500 employees become redundant within a period of 30 days (Hunt, 1994: 3).

dismissed and negotiates a social plan with the employer, including severance payments and retraining measures.

In the Netherlands, an additional waiting period of one month - before the beginning of the procedure to obtain prior authorization by the regional employment office - is obligatory in order to discuss alternative solutions and compensation schemes with union representatives. Moreover, the works council has to be consulted on the intended dismissal. If the dismissal goes through, severance payments are specified in a social plan which the employer determines together with worker representatives (SER, 1994: 78). In practice, large firms frequently pay compensation to redundant workers, but in return demand that workers help to minimize procedural inconveniences (NRC Handelsblad, 1995). Moreover, the fairness of the choice which workers will be dismissed is determined by the regional employment office (SER, 1994). Employers need to justify their choice of workers who are to be fired, which is usually based on the last in, first out criterion (see also Grubb and Wells, 1993).

Summary. The procedures involving dismissals feature many similarities. In both countries, preventive regulations, involvement of worker representatives and court procedures exist. Major differences concern the involvement of the works council versus the prior authorization procedure in the Netherlands, the difference between employment protection in small and large companies in Germany and the maximum length of the probationary period. The Dutch procedure of obtaining prior admission by an external third party is lengthy but prevents costly court procedures (see also IDS, 1995a). In addition, the German dismissal protection is limited for workers in small companies: a works councils is usually absent and the possibility to appeal in court is weak. For large companies, in contrast, both the involvement of the works council and the possibility to appeal in court protect workers against dismissals. The maximum probationary period for new workers is relatively short in the Netherlands, which allows employers less time to screen new workers in order to reduce subsequent "firing-risks".

8.2.2 Working-time Regulations

Working-time regulations protect the safety, health and well-being of workers in relation to their labour market participation. Rules relate to the number of hours that can be worked on an average working day, minimum resting periods, work at irregular hours and variation in the daily working time of individual workers. They constrain the scope for employers to vary working-hours according to variations in production.

German and Dutch Regulations. In Germany, working-time rules were deregulated in 1994. Nowadays, fluctuations in daily working time can be compensated within a period of six months. Moreover, there is more scope to

Box 8.1 Working-time: the trade-off between reductions and flexibility

During the 1980s, the resistance of many employers against a shorter work week diminished because of enhanced working-time flexibility.

Between 1975 and 1985, the major German trade union IG-Metall aimed at a reduction of the 40 hour work week, but failed to achieve this. In 1985, trade unions achieved a breakthrough after a harsh labour dispute: a shorter work week was agreed upon in return for an increased flexibility in working hours. Weekly and daily working hours of individual workers could fluctuate over a period of two months around the average of 38.5 hours per week. Since that time, working time gradually decreased further to a 35-hour work week in 1995, with variable individual working time over a six months period (Bosch et al., 1993).

Other sectors followed these agreements. In 1995, 4,5 million workers, among which workers in the engineering and paper and printing industry, on average worked 35 hours per week (SZW, 1994). A wide variety in working patterns emerged. The incidence of shift work in the metal industry has risen (OECD, 1995a). Some firms in the car industry have agreed upon work at Saturday so as to increase operating hours. In the chemical industry, variable working time (between 35 and 40 hours per week) has been introduced in 1994 (SZW, 1994). Variable working time now applies to 26% of employees (SPU, 1996).

In the Netherlands, developments were similar. The need for shorter working time was stated in a central agreement of the Foundation of Labour in 1982, and was followed by decreases in working time in sectoral agreements (Van der Heijden et al., 1995). Working-time reductions were combined with increased flexibility in working hours, facilitating work at irregular hours and variable working time. Currently, more than 1.1 million Dutch workers, an equivalent of 17% of all workers, are covered by a collective agreement that specifies a 36 hour-work week, with varying forms and degrees of working time flexibility (data from FNV). Variable working hours are not yet common practice, but are becoming more popular. In the private sector, large companies such as Akzo-Nobel, KPN, V&D and KBB have agreed upon or are experimenting with variable working hours.

change working-time conditions through collective bargaining agreements, even if this implies less worker protection. For instance, collective bargaining can result in longer working days.

In the Netherlands, former legal regulations stem from 1919. Rules used to be very detailed, but allowed many exceptions through a licence system. New regulations were gradually implemented in 1996. They specify general minimum conditions. However, these minimum conditions are less strict for firms that negotiate upon working time through collective bargaining agreements or through co-determination at firm level. For a majority of firms, the latter set of rules is relevant, which implies that the new regulations can actually lead to more flexibility. Only if bargaining is unsuccessful, the standard restrictions apply (see also De Lange, 1995).

Table 8.5 compares the main aspects of current working-time regulations. In both countries, the working day cannot be longer than 8 or 9 hours on average, whereas working time on a particular day is possible up to 9 or 10 hours. Extra

Table 8.5 Working-time regulations

	Germany	The Netherlands	
		standard	with agreement
maximum number of average hours per day (per week)	8	8 (40)	9 (45)
maximum number of working hours per day (per week)	10	9 (45)[a]	10[b]
maximum compensation period	6 months	13 weeks	13 weeks
minimal number of resting hours after work day (week)	11 (35)	11 (36)	11 (36)
minimal number of holiday days (of a full-time worker)	24	20	20
work at irregular hours: Sundays	restricted[c]	restricted[d]	restricted[e]
work at irregular hours: nights	restricted[f]	restricted[f]	restricted[f]

[a] Up to 11 hours in case of incidental overtime (a maximum of 45 hours per week over a period of 13 weeks including incidental overtime applies).
[b] Up to 12 hours in case of incidental overtime (a maximum of 48 hours per week including incidental overtime over period of 13 weeks applies).
[c] Allowed for special reasons only, with a minimum of 15 free Sundays per year.
[d] Allowed for special reasons only, with a minimum of 4 free Sundays per 13 weeks.
[e] Allowed for special reasons only, with a minimum of 13 free Sundays per year.
[f] Restrictions relate to a minimum rest period, a maximum duration and number of night-shifts.

Sources: Second Chamber of the States General, 1993-1994; SZW (1995); Anzinger (1994).

working time needs to be compensated within a maximum period of 13 weeks in the Netherlands and six months in Germany. This is a significant difference, since it allows more scope for fluctuations in daily working time in Germany. Moreover, in Germany it remains possible to lengthen this period even further through collective bargaining (Anzinger, 1994).

In both countries, the Sunday is still principally considered as a day off, but in practice many exceptions are possible. For example, after much debate it was decided that international competition can be a reason for work on Sundays in Germany (Anzinger, 1994). Analogously, the new Dutch regulations specify that work on Sundays is allowed if the type of work or economic reasons require this. Still, certain conditions apply, such as a minimum number of free Sundays per year. Work at night is possible in both countries, but is restricted in terms of duration and rest periods.

The effects of deregulation measures strongly depend on collective bargaining agreements. The scope of legal arrangements is usually not fully applied. With respect to the length of the work week and the number of holidays, collective agreements are usually more favourable to workers than the legal minima (Anzinger, 1994; SZW, 1994; De Jong, 1995). Yet, irregular and flexible working-time patterns are becoming more common. Table 8.6 shows that the incidence of irregular working-time patterns in both countries is currently relatively low from an EC perspective. Besides work at irregular working hours, collective agreements increasingly include flexible working-time provisions (Box 8.1).

Summary. In both countries, recent deregulatory measures have increased flexibility in working-hours.[15] They facilitate working at irregular hours (weekends, nights). In addition, the length of the working-week of individual workers can vary in order to deal with variations in activity. The trend towards more flexibility in working hours induced bargaining at the firm level over working time provisions. Usually, sectoral collective agreements provide the framework, but exact specifications can be concluded at the firm level. In this case, the works council is the bargaining partner of management. As to differences between both countries, it can be concluded that regulations concerning variable working time are slightly more flexible in Germany.

8.2.3 Short-time Work

Short-time work enables employers to temporarily reduce both the quantity of hours worked and the corresponding wage costs. Employees are partly compensated for the loss of wage income that results from the temporary reduction in working hours, because they receive unemployment benefits. On top of that, collective agreements often specify that the remaining wage gap for workers is reduced through additional wage payments of employers (Table 8.7).

Short-time work can be considered as a form of employment protection. It aims to stabilize labour relations and to prevent unemployment in case of a temporary slowdown of business activities. Hence, it an be considered as a subsidy on internal rather than external labour market adjustments to shocks (Büchtemann, 1989). Empirical research indicates that short-time work is one of the factors that explains why the German employment level is relatively unresponsive to output fluctuations, but the number of working hours is responsive (Abraham and Houseman, 1993). This promotes a long-term perspective towards labour relationships: employers have less hiring and firing costs and both workers and employers are encouraged to invest in firm-specific human capital.

---

[15] The introduction of new regulations is related to an EU-directive concerning working time (Second Chamber of the States General, 1993-1994: 21-25).

Table 8.6 Work at irregular hours, 1995

	Germany	Netherlands	EU
	% of employment		
Working at night	13.9	12.0	15.0
Sunday working	21.6	23.2	27.2
Shift working	10.6	7.5	12.1
Evening working	30.0	27.7	32.7

% of employees who usually or sometimes works at irregular hours.

Source: EC Labour Force Survey (1996)

German Regulations. Short-time work (or Kurzarbeit) is a prominent feature of German labour markets. The Employment Promotion Act (Arbeitsförderungsgesetz or AFG) allows employers to use short-time working arrangements to deal with a wide range of difficulties. These include general economic difficulties (such as the business cycle situation), structural changes (such as the introduction of new technologies or reorganisations) and other unavoidable circumstances (such as a fire).[16] In all three cases, the reduction in business activity must be temporary, unavoidable and impossible to solve in any other way (see also SZW, 1994).

Employers, worker representatives and the government jointly decide whether the use of short-time work is appropriate. The regional employment office[17] needs to approve the employer's request for short-time work. The works council has to give its opinion in advance on the intention of management to use 'Kurzarbeit' and will generally only agree if other solutions have failed. Then, the works council usually agrees with 'Kurzarbeit' as a strategy to maintain the current level of employment. It is even possible that works councils directly request short-time work. Finally, trade unions play a role in ensuring that the regulations laid down in the Employment Promotion Act are followed (Linke, 1993).

The period for which short-time work can be used is usually 6 months, but this period can be lengthened up to a period of 12 months in case of structural sector-specific or regional problems, or even up to 24 months in case of more general structural problems.[18] For some branches in the metal industry, spells of 36 months have been applied during the 1980s (SZW, 1994). However, the majority of short-time spells lasts up to 6 months. The reduction of working time has to

[16] Organisation-specific or seasonal circumstances are excluded.

[17] Or the 'Bundesministerium für Arbeit und Sozialordnung' in case of a request for structural reasons.

[18] Source: BMA (1994a) and (1994b).

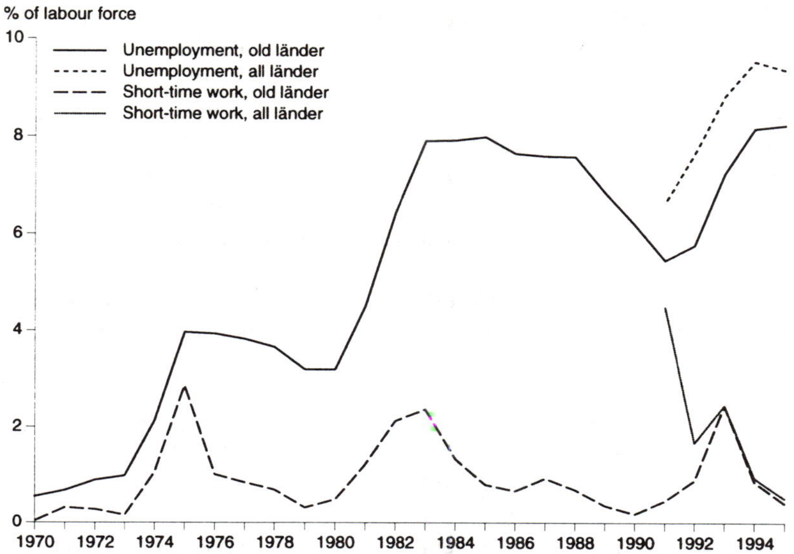

Source: Bundesministerium für Arbeit und Sozialordnung, Statistisches Bundesamt

Figure 8.2 Short-time work and unemployment in Germany

amount to 10 percent or more of the normal working time for at least one third of the number of workers for a period of four weeks or more. For most workers, the number of hours worked decreases by 10 up to 50% (Bundesanstalt für Arbeit, 1994).

The Incidence of Short-time Work in Germany. The use of short-time working arrangements in Germany is strongly and inversely correlated with the business cycle situation: the use of short-time work is correlated with the unemployment level (Figure 8.2). Yet, short-time work is also used for restructuring purposes (Linke, 1993). During the 1980s, short-time work for structural purposes has been applied in the old Länder. The efficacy of short-time work to support restructuring is debatable. In the car industry, short-time work has indeed encouraged successful restructuring, but in shrinking branches of the metal industry short-time work with a duration of up to three years could only delay but not prevent mass dismissals during the 1980s (Linke, 1993). In the new Länder, short-time work became widely used for restructuring purposes in the new Länder after unification (Figure 8.2). This resulted in a booming participation amounting to nearly 20% of the East German labour force in 1991 and "allowed in extreme (but common) cases a large part of wages to be paid by the state for workers who were producing nothing" (OECD, 1992: 82). The wide use of short-time work could postpone, but not prevent a rise in open unemployment. Consequently, the use of short-time work for structural reasons is debatable. In recent years, the use of short-time work in the new Länder as well as in the old Länder has been reduced.

The Dutch Situation. Dutch regulations concerning short-time work are relatively strict. Only in case of a reduction of business activity that is substantial (amounting to at least 20% of the usual activity level), temporary and not related to structural factors or normal business risks, short-time working arrangements can be used, usually for a period of six weeks. However, this period can be lengthened up to six months.

A significant difference to the German situation is that structural problems, such as reorganisations, cannot be a reason to make use of short-time work. The Dutch regulation is based on the conviction that short-time benefits for structural reasons subsidize loss-makers and hamper necessary restructuring. Moreover, the business cycle situation is considered as a "normal risk" and is consequently not regarded as a sufficient condition to make use of the arrangement (SZW, 1994). Procedures to apply for short-time work are also different in the Netherlands, since there is no formal influence of trade unions or works councils.

The common reduction in the number of hours worked in the Netherlands amounts to 50% or less (Table 8.7). As in Germany, workers are compensated for their loss of income through unemployment benefits. On top of that, many Dutch employers supplement the entire remaining income gap. In that case, net income does not decrease at all while the wage bill of employers temporarily diminishes. Table 8.7 also provides rough estimates of the corresponding effects on wage costs and wage levels in comparison to those in Germany. As a consequence of the more restrictive Dutch regulations, the use of short-time work is comparatively low in the Netherlands.

Summary. Dutch regulations regarding short-time work are more strict than their German counterparts. The purposes for which short-time work can be used are restricted to such an extent that short-time work is not a significant tool to enhance labour hoarding and promote flexibility of working-hours and wage costs. In contrast, the German regulations do not only allow short-time work to overcome temporary difficulties, but also to prevent or postpone dismissals in case of structural difficulties. This difference in regulations corresponds with the German focus on commitment within long-term labour relationships. The Dutch system to a larger extent relies on flexible employment adjustments, as the following section illustrates.

8.2.4 Part-time and Flexible Contracts

Part-time and flexible contracts provide labour market flexibility. Part-time work is characterized by a less than full-time length of the working week, and is usually

Table 8.7 German and Dutch short-time working arrangements compared

	Germany	Netherlands
Reasons for use	business cycle/structural	'exceptional' problems
Maximum duration	6-24 months	6 weeks-6 months
Net income of workers (% of former wage)[a]	up to 90%	up to 100%
Reduction in wage costs (% of former wage)[b]	43.5%	35%
Participation (% of labour force)	1.0	0.2
Short-time payments (% of unemployment benefits)	12	<1
Duration of short-time spell (months)	5	2.5

[a] Including additional wage payments based on collective agreements.
[b] Assuming a 50% reduction in working time and maximum additional payments.

Sources: Abraham and Houseman (1993), table 2; Grubb and Wells (1993); SZW (1994); Bundesanstalt für Arbeit.

of unlimited duration.[19] It may correspond with worker preferences or with capacity and flexibility considerations: employees wish to work part-time, certain jobs do not need a full-time cover, and part-timers may cover busy periods and provide working-time flexibility related to regular weekly fluctuations in business activity (Delsen, 1995: 22,72; OSA, 1995; OECD, 1994b). A flexible contract, in contrast, is characterized by a limited duration or a variable number of contractual working hours.[20] This type of contract provides employment or working-hour flexibility.

The Incidence of Part-time Work. "Part-time work has become a key feature of the Dutch labour market" (OECD, 1995b: 61). Since the 1970s, the share of part-time work in the Netherlands has risen much more strongly than in Germany. Nowadays, the Netherlands stands out in an international perspective because of its high share of part-time workers, whereas the corresponding German share is relatively low (Table 8.8). The higher share of part-time work is the most

[19] Although the incidence of part-time work among workers with a flexible contract is relatively high, see for example Bierings and Imbens, 1992: 59.

[20] A standard contract specifies a fixed number of working hours and is of unlimited duration.

Table 8.8 Types of employment

type of contract	US	UK	Ger[a]	Neth	Swe
part-time (% employment)[b]	19	24	16	34[c]	24
full-time (% employment)[b]	81	76	84	66	76
flexible (% employees)[d]	2	7	10	12	14
standard (% employees)[d]	98	93	90	88	86

[a] Total Germany.
[b] 1996, CBS, data by fax, for Neth; 1995, OECD (1996b: 192-194) for the other countries. Note that the definition of part-time varies across countries. Ger, UK: based on classification of respondent. Neth: working less than usual hours of full-time job, US, Swe: working less than 35 hours.
[c] The Dutch figure assumes that the incidence of part-time work among flexible workers equals that among workers with a contract of unlimited duration. This slightly underestimates the Dutch part-time share.
[d] 1996, CBS for Neth; OECD (1996b: 8) for the other countries of reference. US: 1995, UK, Ger, Swe: 1994. Note: Figure for the US in % of total employment. Note that the definition of flexible employment differs across countries. Neth: Limited duration (< 1 year) or variable working hours. Ger: Limited duration, including apprenticeships.

important explanation for the difference in average working hours between a Dutch and German employee (Chapter 3, Table 3.8). Especially Dutch women work part-time, but the incidence of part-time work among Dutch men is also high from an international perspective: 26% of part-time jobs is held by men, compared to 13% in Germany.

Worker preferences turn out to be the dominant reason for part-time employment in Germany and the Netherlands (Delsen, 1995: 83; OECD, 1996a: 122). In both countries, the majority of part-time workers works part-time voluntarily (Delsen, 1995: 36, see also Chapter 3). Survey-information reveals that German workers (on average) prefer to work less hours (Hof, 1995; OECD, 1996a). A considerable share of Dutch male workers also prefers to work less hours per week (OSA, 1995). Dutch women, in contrast, more often want to work more hours. This is related to the large number of Dutch women with small part-time jobs.[21]

[21] In 1994, 15% of male workers would like to work less hours, but 8% would like to work more hours. Among female workers, 17,5% would like to work more hours, but 14,5% would like to work less hours. (OSA, 1995).

The Impact of Institutions. To what extent can the difference in part-time the incidence of part-time employment in Germany and the Netherlands be explained by institutions? The less extensive use of part-time employment in Germany could be related to differences between both countries in the employment protection and social security entitlements and contributions of part-time workers.

In both countries, the employment protection of part-time workers is carefully regulated. In Germany, the legal position of part-time workers is equal to that of full-time workers since 1985. This implies an equal (or proportionally equal) treatment of part-time workers as regards labour conditions (SZW, 1994; Passchier, 1995: 84). In the Netherlands, the equal legal position of part-time workers has been arranged since november 1996, but in many collective agreements, part-time workers were already treated (proportionally) equal to full-time workers.

Moreover, both countries try to promote part-time employment through additional regulations. German policy makers consider the high percentage of part-time workers in the Netherlands as an example ('Niederländisches Modell'). Since 1994, the German Employment Promotion Act provides an incentive for part-time work through the unemployment benefit system: if a worker reduces his or her weekly working time and eventually becomes unemployed, the unemployment benefit level will be based upon the former (longer) working time (SZW, 1994).[22] This regulation also applies to unemployed who accept a part-time job which they lose again within a period of three years. In the Netherlands, this type of financial incentive does not exist. Yet, a new regulation has been proposed that gives Dutch workers the right to work part-time (80% of a full-time work week).

Differences exist regarding social security benefits and contributions. In Germany, social security entitlements of part-time workers are often less well arranged due to minimum thresholds ('Geringfügigkeitsgrenzen'). These thresholds imply that workers with a small part-time job[23] have no access to unemployment, illness and disability insurance schemes (Passchier, 1995: 84 and BMA, 1994b: 51; Delsen, 1995: 118-119). Social security entitlements of Dutch part-time workers are more extensive, since many thresholds in social security coverage have been abolished (Second Chamber of the States General, 1994-1995). Part-time as well as full-time workers have access to unemployment benefits, as long as they lose

---

[22] Provided that the working time has been reduced by 20% or more and that he or she has worked longer hours for a period of at least 6 months, not longer than 3 years ago (AFG).

[23] With a weekly labour time of less than 15 hours *and* a wage level below 1/7 of the average full-time wage level, *or* with less than 50 working days per year.

more than 50% or more than 5 hours of their usual weekly working time (Elsevier, 1995: 83).[24]

Consequently, it is difficult to relate the relatively low share of part-time employment in Germany to these institutional differences. Employment protection of part-time workers is well arranged in Germany. Until recently, minimum thresholds in social security also existed in the Netherlands. Apart from differences in the regulatory framework, other factors may explain the different share of part-time work, for instance the supportive attitude of Dutch trade unions. In contrast, differences in the sectoral production structure - i.e. the large German industrial sector - hardly constitute a satisfactory explanatory factor, since the Dutch share of part-time workers is higher in the industrial as well as in the service sector (Hof, 1995: 243, data from Eurostat). Finally, also different preferences of workers between the Dutch and German labour force seem an inadequate explanation, as German workers often prefer to work less hours. However, the recent increase in the traditionally very low participation rate of Dutch women may help to explain the high share of part-time employment in the Netherland. In particular, part-time work facilitated the access of women to the labour market.

Flexible Contracts. The total share of flexible contracts differs considerably between the countries of reference (Table 8.8). As could be expected, the American share of flexible contracts is relatively low. This points at the limited importance of a dual labour market as a way to increase employment flexibility in the United States. In the Netherlands the overall share of flexible contracts is rising. Between 1987 and 1996, the Dutch share of flexible employment rose from 8 to 12 percent, whereas the German share has remained approximately stable at a level of approximately 10% (CBS, and OECD 1996b: 8). Demand-factors predominantly determine the incidence of flexible work, since most workers - ceteris paribus - prefer the higher degree of income security and legal protection related to a part-time or full-time contract of unlimited duration (OECD, 1994b; Golden and Appelbaum, 1992; Delsen, 1995).

Not only the overall share of flexible contracts differs between Germany and the Netherlands, but also the type of flexible contract that is most frequently used, i.e. a fixed-term contract, a temporary contract through a temporary-work agency (TWA) or a variable-hour contract (Figure 8.3).

In Germany, the extensive dual education system corresponds with a considerable number of fixed-term contracts (Section 9.2). The duration of these fixed-term

---

24 Two other necessary conditions are that an employee has worked on 26 of the past 39 weeks, and has received wage for at least 52 days - regardless of the number of hours worked on those days - in four of the past 5 years (Voorlichtingscentrum Sociale Verzekering, 1995: 53-55). However, these two conditions are not disadvantageous to most part-time workers.

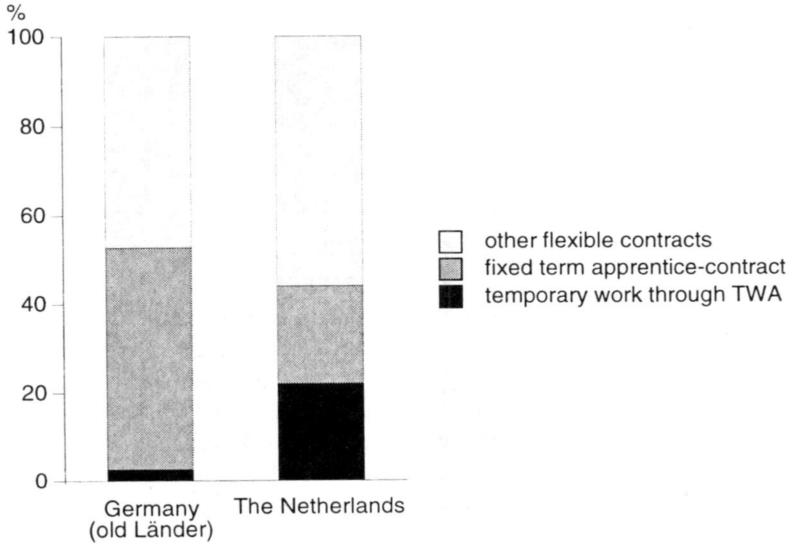

Source: CBS, Eurostat

Figure 8.3 Rough estimate of flexible employment per type of contract

contracts equals the training period of two to three and a half years. In 1994, the number of apprentices amounts to 1.6 million, or 4.5% of total employment (Statistisches Bundesamt, 1996, all Länder). The reason for employers to hire apprentices temporarily is a combination of screening and external flexibility: employers exploit the training period to gather information on the quality of a trainee, but the decision to hire him or her after graduation will also depend on the (expected) activity level at that moment. Approximately half of all fixed-term jobs are converted into a "standard" contract (OECD, 1996a).

Dutch employers hire workers for a fixed term as a screening device, a way to deal with seasonal fluctuations or with temporary assignments. Screening appears to be the most significant reason, because two thirds of temporary contracts is changed into a standard contract after expiration (Van Bolhuis, 1996). The number of fixed-term contracts for apprentices is lower than in Germany: the employment share of Dutch apprentices amounts to nearly 2% of total employment in 1994, but not all Dutch apprentices have a fixed-term labour contract (CBS, 1997; Den Broeder, 1995).

In the Netherlands, temporary work through temporary work agencies (TWAs) is relatively popular, also from a broader international perspective. The share of temporary workers is high and has risen during the 1980s and 1990s: in the beginning of the 1980s the share of temporary work in total employment fluctuated from 0.5 up to 1%, but from 1985 onwards this share fluctuates around 2% in the Netherlands and the 1990s showed a further increase towards approximately 3%

Table 8.9 Jobs with a tenure of less than 1 year

	US	UK	Ger	Neth	Swe
	% of jobs				
1985	29	15	9	12	na
1991	29	19	13	24	na

Source: OECD (1996b).

in 1995 (SCP, 1994: 143 and CPB, 1997). The predominant motivation to hire this type of flexible workers is to deal with fluctuations, temporary assignments or to replace absent workers. Screening appears to be less important, because only 15% of employers predominantly use this type of flexible contracts as a screening device (Van Bolhuis, 1996). In contrast, temporary work through TWAs is much less popular in Germany, where it fluctuates around 0.3% of employment (see Grubb and Wells (1993) for an overview of different data sources)[25].

Information on the total share of flexible contracts and on the incidence of types of flexible contracts in both countries suggests that flexible contracts in the Netherlands are to a larger extent used to enhance short-term employment flexibility. Information on the share of jobs with a short tenure confirms this picture (Table 8.9).

Regulations Regarding Flexible Contracts. The use of flexible contracts is related to the regulatory framework. Regulations that restrict the use of flexible contracts are generally more liberal in the Netherlands (Table 8.10). The use of fixed-term contracts is not restricted to certain circumstances and regulations do not specify a maximum duration. Consequently, employers not only use fixed-term contracts for extra projects or to replace absent workers, but can also easily use fixed-term contracts as a screening device or to deal with fluctuations in business activity. In the near future, Dutch regulations will probably become even more liberal in the near future (Box 8.2). In contrast, German employers can use fixed-term contracts for only special reasons such as the replacement of temporarily absent workers, seasonal work, an occasional task, the start of a new business, etcetera. Moreover, fixed-term contracts have a maximum duration of 18 months (or 24 months for exceptional reasons) and cannot be renewed beyond that period.

[25] The remaining category of Figure 8.3 consists of fixed-term contracts and variable-hour contracts. For the Netherlands, approximately half of this category consist of variable-hour contracts, whereas the other half consists of fixed-term contracts and a tiny share consists of work at home (in 1991, Bierings and Imbens, 1992).

Table 8.10 Regulations related to use of flexible contracts

	maximal duration	contract renewals	other restrictive regulations
Fixed-term contracts			
Germany	18 months[a]	only allowed within period of 18 months	not allowed for all types of work
The Netherlands	no maximum	allowed, but restricted	allowed for all types of work
Temporary contracts through temporary work agencies			
Germany	6 months	allowed, but restricted	not allowed for all types of work
The Netherlands	6 months or 1000 hours	allowed, but restricted[b]	allowed for all types of work[c]

[a] Except for apprentice contracts.
[b] A period of 31 days or more before the renewal is required (STAR Foundation of Labour (1996).
[c] Except in the building sector, where temporary work is not allowed, although this restriction will be abandoned in the near future.

Sources: Grubb and Wells (1993); Abraham and Houseman (1993); SZW (1994); Schömann *et al.* (1995).

In 1985 and in 1996, German regulations were liberalized. Since 1985, employers do not have to specify a reason for using fixed-term contracts in case of a transition period after termination of an apprentice contract or in case of first hirings of unemployed (Schömann *et al.*, 1995 or Grubb and Wells, 1993). Recent policy changes will lengthen the maximum duration of fixed-term contracts from 18 months to two years.

Regulations related to temporary work through TWAs are similar in both countries as regards their maximum duration and the possibilities for contract renewals. A difference concerns the type of labour contract. In Germany, workers usually have a fixed-term labour contract with the TWA (Jacobs, 1993: 57-58). For Dutch workers through TWAs, regulations regarding their labour contract are currently changing (Box 8.2). In contrast to the German practice, Dutch employers do not need to have a special reason to make use of temporary workers. In addition, rules regarding the maximum duration are not always adhered to in practice, since an informal agreement allows longer durations without sanctions, anticipating future deregulatory policy proposals (Box 8.2).

In addition, the use of flexible labour, and of different types of flexible contracts can be related to differences in the institutional framework regarding the firing

Box 8.2 Flexicurity advice of Dutch foundation of labour

Before taking policy measures aimed at enhanced labour market flexibility, Dutch policy makers have consulted the Foundation of Labour about the policy options they have in mind. The advice of the employer and worker representatives in this foundation touches upon the trade-off between employment security and flexibility. Their advice comprises the following main elements:

More security

With respect to temporary work through TWAs

- *flexible workers through TWAs can get a fixed-term labour relation with the TWA for the duration of their assignment, but after three assignments and a minimum total tenure with the TWA, they finally get a contract for unlimited duration.*

More flexibility

With respect to firing rules

- *the maximum period of notice can be reduced to 4 months*
- *the period of authorization and the period of notice can partly overlap*

With respect to temporary work through TWAs

- *abolish the legal maximum on the duration of the temporary assignments*
- *TWAs do not need a licence*

With respect to fixed-term contracts

- *the introduction of a (short) probationary period for fixed-term contracts*
- *more scope to renew a fixed-term contract (without the required period of 31 days in between)*

Source: STAR Foundation of Labour (1996)

protection of core workers (Section 8.2.1). Protection of workers with a standard labour contract may induce employers to hire a core of workers with a standard contract and a periphery of flexible workers. This argument appears to be relevant for Germany as well as for the Netherlands. Yet, empirical research on this relationship is inconclusive. For instance, loosening of dismissal protection in Germany in 1985 did not significantly lower the use of fixed-term contracts (Hunt, 1994), but this evidence is not overwhelming since firing protection was altered only slightly. Survey information reveals that many employers indeed regard employment protection related to hiring and firing as an important obstacle to hire more staff (Grubb and Wells, 1993).

Summary. Part-time and flexible contracts are more common in the Netherlands than in Germany. This makes the Dutch labour market flexible compared to its German counterpart. Part-time employment is relatively popular in the Netherlands. This increases working time flexibility with respect to regular fluctuations in work loads. In Germany, the share of part-time employment is much lower. This cannot be satisfactorily explained by different worker preferences, the sectoral distribution in employment or differences in regulations.

The incidence of flexible work is also higher in the Netherlands and the purpose of flexible contracts differs. German employers to a larger extent use fixed-term contracts as a screening device for apprentices. In the Netherlands, fixed-term contracts are predominantly used as a screening device and for flexibility purposes. In addition, the demand for employment flexibility is to a larger extent fulfilled by flexible contracts of temporary workers through TWAs. This situation corresponds with relatively permissive regulations.

8.2.5 Assessment

The comparative examination of regulations shows that Dutch and German workers have a more secure labour market position than their American counterparts. Firing regulations are roughly comparable in both countries and stricter than in the United States. Working-time regulations are comparable as well. Both countries have recently deregulated working time regulations. In collective agreements, provisions for work at irregular times and variability in working hours of individual workers have become more common. This enhances labour market flexibility without hampering the commitment of employees. At a closer look, some significant differences between the German and Dutch regulations emerge. Remarkable differences concern the more extensive use of short-time work in Germany, versus the greater popularity of part-time work and flexible contracts through TWAs in the Netherlands.

These differences make the German labour market oriented towards commitment within long-term labour relationships, whereas the Dutch labour market results in an intermediate position on the trade-off between flexibility and commitment. The German way of providing flexibility through working-hour adjustments stimulates labour hoarding. This enhances commitment but makes labour markets more rigid and reduces the access of outsiders to work. Moreover, the efficacy of short-time work for structural purposes is doubtful. In contrast, the Dutch way of providing working-hour flexibility through part-time employment allows workers to deal with systematic fluctuations in activity and corresponds with worker preferences. In addition, the more extensive use of temporary employment through TWAs in the Netherlands enhances employment flexibility. However, this type of contract may reduce commitment.

9 Labour Market: Institutional Arrangements

This chapter deals with cooperative exchange on the German and Dutch labour market. The structure is as follows. First, Section 9.1 addresses the collective bargaining systems in both countries. Next, Section 9.2 compares the German apprenticeship system to the Dutch system of vocational education at upper secondary level. Subsequently, Section 9.3 turns to the co-determination arrangements in both countries. Finally, Section 9.4 presents the main policy options from the labour market analysis in Chapter 8 and 9.

9.1 Collective Bargaining in Germany and the Netherlands

What are the strengths and weaknesses of the German 'Tarifautonomie' versus the Dutch system of consensus building? In order to examine the performance of both collective bargaining systems, this section addresses their main similarities and differences. To put the comparison in a broader international perspective, the United States is chosen as a country of reference. In addition, collective bargaining is looked at from a European perspective, with The United Kingdom and Sweden as reference countries.

To start with, Section 9.1.1 describes the main characteristics of collective bargaining, focusing on types of collective agreements, the predominant bargaining level, the degree of organisation and the coverage of collective contracts. Next, Section 9.1.2 compares how regulations impact the objectives and relative bargaining power of trade unions in Germany and the Netherlands. Subsequently, Section 9.1.3 takes a closer look at the extent of centralisation of collective bargaining, concentrating on the extent of coordination and government involvement and on decentralisation tendencies. Finally, Section 9.1.4 presents the main conclusions from the international comparison.

9.1.1 Collective Bargaining Characteristics

Types of Collective Agreements. Collective agreements can be defined as "agreements entered into by one or more employers or employer associations with full legal rights to bargain and one or more worker organisations with these rights; in which terms and conditions of employment are regulated; and which must be adhered to in employment contracts between individual employers and individual workers" (IDS, 1995b). They do not only arrange the growth and structure of wages, but encompass other labour conditions such as working time, holiday entitlements, training provisions and supplementary payments in case of sickness and disability.

Sectoral bargaining is common in many OECD-countries, including Germany and the Netherlands. This differs from the American and English bargaining systems, where single employer bargaining at firm-level is predominant (Table 9.1). Sectoral collective agreements apply to an entire industry or an industry within a certain region of the country. In spite of a similar bargaining level, the German bargaining system results in a relatively large number of collective agreements because of regional collective agreements, Paralelltarifverträge and separate parts of agreements.

Due to the federal structure, German sectoral collective agreements (Flächentarifverträge) are in most cases concluded per region (Land or part of a Land). However, the regional variation in the contents of sectoral agreements is usually small. In addition, separate but identical agreements are concluded if more than one trade union represents the workers of a particular industry (Paralleltarifverträge). Furthermore, different agreements are concluded for different aspects of collective bargaining. These collective agreements have variable durations, ranging from one to several years. General labour conditions (for instance regarding working time or sickness benefits) and conditions regarding the wage structure are usually fixed for a period of several years, whereas negotiations on wage growth in most cases take place on a yearly basis (Verdonk and Wiggers, 1994, Paqué, 1993).

Dutch agreements do not have a regional dimension, and one agreement usually covers all aspects. As in Germany, more than one trade union can participate in sectoral negotiations. In this case, coordination in advance is the common practice, but it is also possible that the employer concludes an agreement with one of the trade unions (Korver, 1993). Most collective contracts have a duration of one, or sometimes two, years (De Kam *et al.*, 1995).

Trade-Union Density. From a broad international perspective, German and Dutch trade-union density rates are roughly similar (Table 9.1). Nevertheless, the difference in trade-union membership between both countries is noteworthy. Dutch workers are less inclined to join a trade union than their German counterparts. This picture results from diverging trends in trade-union density over the period 1960-1995.

Until quite recently, overall German density rates remained remarkably steady. This masks differing tendencies within industries: membership within the manufacturing sector rose until 1985, but the public sector already experienced a declining membership during this period (OECD, 1991). Between 1990 and 1991 total membership took a jump, because the organizing territory of West German

Table 9.1 Overview of collective bargaining characteristics, 1990

	US	UK	Ger[a]	Neth	Swe
	% of employees				
union density[b]	16	39	33	26	83
employers' organisation density[c]	–	–	90	90	na
collective bargaining coverage[d]	18	47	90	71	83
effect of collective extension[e]	–	–	3	14	–
predominant bargaining level	firm	firm	sector	sector	sector

[a] Figures refer to western Germany.
[b] Employed union members as a percentage of wage- and salary earners.
[c] Van de Wijngaert (1994). In the new German Länder, the organisation rate of employers amounts to approximately two thirds of the work force (OECD, 1996a).
[d] Number of employees covered by a collective agreement divided by total number of wage- and salary earners (corrected for employees excluded from bargaining rights), including coverage through extension of agreements, 1990, 1992 for Germany (OECD, 1994b).
[e] Effect on collective bargaining coverage.

Sources: Schilstra and Smit (1996), OECD (1996a and 1994b), Van de Wijngaert (1994), Layard *et al.* (1991), SZW (1996).

trade unions spread to the East (Baethge and Wolf, 1995: 254). Membership of the largest trade-union confederation (the DGB) increased from almost 8 to almost 12 million, which equals a rise of 5 percent points in terms of trade-union density. From 1991 onwards, however, membership started to fall (The Economist, 1996). Nowadays, the total trade-union density level of the DGB approximately equals the 1990 level of the former western Länder (Figure 9.1).

Dutch trade-union density, in contrast, started to decline much earlier. During the 1960s and 1970s it gradually fell, but during the 1980s it plunged. Membership declined within nearly all industries, including the traditionally highly organised manufacturing industry and public sector. Quite recently, however, Dutch trade unions have succeeded to reverse this strong downward trend into a modest rise (Figure 9.1).[1]

The earlier decline of Dutch trade-union density, as opposed to stable density in Germany, can be to some extent attributed to differences in the presence of trade unions within firms (Hancké, 1993). In Germany, trade-union representation has strong linkages with local employee representation at the firm level. This enhances

[1] Sectoral shifts cannot satisfactorily explain why trends in trade-union membership diverged between both countries (OECD, 1991: 114-115).

union influence at the firm level and promotes the recruitment of new union members. In contrast, Dutch sectoral trade unions hardly have a voice at the firm level. They are weakly present in the firm and do not have a strong influence through the works council (Koene and Slomp, 1991; Visser, 1995). Quite recently, however, Dutch trade unions have become more active in promoting worker interests through works councils, for instance through support of the possibility of works councillors to propose members for the supervisory board (Berkhout and Tamminga, 1997; see also Section 9.3.2).

Collective Bargaining Coverage. Two types of extension mechanisms explain why German and Dutch collective bargaining coverage, i.e. the share of employees that is covered by a collective agreement, exceeds trade-union membership by far (Table 9.1). First, "firm-level" extension, which is common practice in OECD countries, makes the collective agreement binding for non-unionized workers within a firm.[2] Second, collective extension makes a collective agreement legally binding for the entire industry (or the industry within the region), including for employers who are not affiliated to the employer organisation.[3] The indirect effects of collective extension may be considerable. In industries where collective extension is in force, employers have an incentive to join the employers' association in order to have some influence on labour conditions (OECD, 1994a). Even in industries where agreements are not legally binding, the threat of collective extension may prevent non-organized employers from paying lower wages than their organized competitors (Paqué, 1993).

The significance of collective extension differs between Germany and the Netherlands. From a broad international perspective, both countries have "interm-ediate" collective extension practices (OECD, 1994b). The importance of collective extension is smaller than in countries such as Australia, Austria, Belgium, France or Portugal, but nevertheless considerable. In contrast, collective extension mechanisms do not exist in the United States, the United Kingdom and Sweden (Table 9.1).[4] At a closer look, it turns out that collective extension is more widely used in the Netherlands than in Germany: 60% of Dutch employees is covered by an agreement to which collectively extension applies, whereas this share amounts

---

[2] A Dutch employer is obliged to apply the contents of collective agreements to the non-unionized workers (Schuit, 1995). In Germany this is not a legal requirement, but it almost always holds in practice through a voluntary clause in the collective agreement or individual labour contract (Verdonk and Wiggers, 1994; Jacobs, 1993).

[3] Both extension mechanisms allow free rider behaviour of workers, which may partly explain moderate trade-union density rates.

[4] In the former two countries, this follows from the predominance of firm-level bargaining. In Sweden, in contrast, sectoral bargaining is predominant, but non-organised employers are not bound to keep to a sectoral agreement.

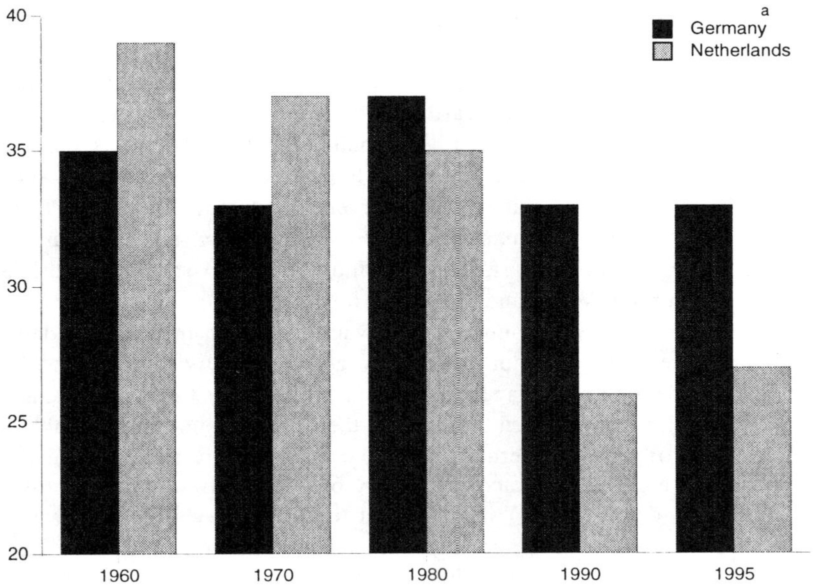

Source: Hancké, 1993, OECD, 1994b and 1991, Visser (1995), CBS, 1995:65.

Figure 9.1 Development of trade-union density
[a] Until 1990 old Länder, 1995 total Germany

to 25% in Germany. Yet, in both countries the direct effect of collective extension on coverage is much lower, because most employers are affiliated with the employer association. It amounts to 14% of all employees in the Netherlands, and only 3% in Germany (Table 9.1).[5] Moreover, collective extension in Germany mainly relates to "general working conditions" and not to wages (OECD, 1996a).

9.1.2 Regulations and Trade-Union Behaviour

Regulations impact trade-union behaviour. They provide the boundaries for collective bargaining outcomes, because the issues dealt with in collective bargaining and through regulations to a large extent overlap (Paqué, 1993). Moreover, they impact the process of bargaining, as they provide a framework for the way of bargaining, influence bargaining objectives as well as the reach of

---

[5] In Germany, collective extension mainly applies to small firms in the construction, textile and retail trade sectors.

bargaining outcomes. This section addresses legal minimum wages, collective extension rules, strike rules and income support (Table 9.2).

Minimum Wages. Legal minimum wages put a lower limit on collective bargaining outcomes. German 'Tarifautonomie' prohibits direct government involvement in collective bargaining. Formally, the government is entitled to impose minimum conditions if it considers the bargaining outcomes as socially unacceptable, but in practice this type of intervention has never been used (Jacobs, 1993: 156).[6] Therefore, German bargaining partners are not constrained by restrictions on wages. In contrast, legal minimum wages exist in the Netherlands (through the Minimum Wage and Holiday Allowance Act).

Yet, the absence of lower boundaries on wage formation in Germany does not result in a relatively low minimum level of wages in collective agreements. In the metal industry, the minimum wages for German white collar workers are relatively low, but blue collar workers earn the same as their Dutch counterparts (Table 9.2). The lowest level of wages in German collective agreements varies between sectors and regions, but a crude estimate by Ministry of Social Affairs and Employment (1996) based on Vogels (1994) suggests that the lowest level of gross wages of German employees is on average higher for blue collar workers but lower for white collar workers, compared to the Dutch legal minimum wage level.[7]

Collective Extension. Regulations regarding collective extension strengthen the bargaining power of sectoral trade-unions, because they eliminate wage competition within the industry. The regulatory framework regarding collective extension slightly differs between Germany and the Netherlands. In Germany, collective extension (Allgemeinverbindlichkeit) is only allowed if more than 50% of the employees in the extension domain have participated in the bargaining process. In this case, an agreement is legally binding if a request of the signatory employers' or employees' representatives has been approved. The federal Minister of Labour and Social Affairs (Bundesminister für Arbeit und Sozialordnung) and subsequently a bargaining commission consisting of representatives of employers and workers ('Tarifausschuss) needs to favour the request (Paqué, 1993). A necessary condition for approval is that it serves the public interest (Verdonk and Wiggers, 1994).

---

[6] An agreement is considered socially unacceptable if workers or employers in a particular sector are hardly organized; if agreements are not collectively extended; and if the existing labour conditions are below accepted minimum standards.

[7] These figures do not include wages for apprentices. In Germany, apprentices earn roughly one third up to half of the lowest collective wage (Paqué, 1993; see also Section 9.2). In the Netherlands, legal minimum wages of young people (up to 23) are lower than the values shown in Table 9.2. For instance, the legal minimum wage of workers of 20 years old amounts to 61% of the legal minimum wage for adults.

According to Paqué (1993) this procedure is not a strong obstacle, as the public interest is in practice defined as a "defense against undermining collectively agreed terms by outsider competition". Hence, the outsider perspective is hardly considered in the procedure.

The Dutch procedure is similar, but the criterion for the approval of collective extension by the Minister of Social Affairs and Employment is more loosely defined: a request is approved as long as it is not contrary to general interests and if the agreement already covers an "important majority" of the industry (Schuit, 1995).[8] In practice, collective extension is almost always permitted in the Netherlands (Lever and Marquering, 1995).

Strikes. In both countries, strikes are considered as a last resort option and strike activity is low from an international perspective.[9] In Germany, strikes are not allowed if the current collective agreement is still in force. Moreover, a strike needs to be approved by the trade union, must address a topic that is included in the bargaining outcome and can only be started if negotiations have resulted in a deadlock (Paqué, 1993, Verdonk and Wiggers, 1994). Workers on strike do not receive wages or unemployment benefits, but are paid by the unions. The employer may respond to a strike with a lock-out. In this case, even the workers who are not on strike are not able to work. They do neither receive wages or payments by the union, nor unemployment benefits (Jacobs, 1993).[10] In the Netherlands, strike activity is limited to periods of collective negotiations as well (Koene and Slomp, 1991). Workers on strike are paid through trade-union funds, as they are not entitled to wages or unemployment benefits (De Gier *et al.*, 1994). Lock-outs are no attractive option for employers, since they have to continue paying wages (OECD, 1994c).

Social Security. The social security system affects the objectives of trade unions, in particular the value they attach to wages versus job opportunities. Generous benefits encourage trade unions to concentrate on the level of wages because they provide a relatively high fall-back income for workers that become unemployed. Furthermore, generous benefits and few measures of active labour market policy may reduce the search intensity of unemployed and diminish the sensitivity of wages to the unemployment level (Section 8.1.4 and 8.1.5). Only if trade unions are completely centralized, they internalize the budgetary constraint of the

---

8 Before the government decides, it consults the Foundation of labour (Korver, 1993).

9 In 1994, strikes caused 8 lost working days per 1000 Dutch employees, and 7 per 1000 German employees. For the US, this figure amounted to 34 in 1993 (Eurostat and ILO).

10 A change in the Employment Promotion Act (Arbeitsförderungsgesetz) removed the entitlement of these workers to unemployment benefits (Baethge and Wolf, 1995: 241). Yet, lockout-activity is low (BMA, 1996).

Table 9.2 Characteristics of the institutional environment, 1993

	US	UK	Ger	Neth	Swe
gross legal minimum wage level (EC= 100)	93[a]	86[b]	–	157	–
gross collectively agreed minimum wage level for the metal industry (EC=100)	–	74[c]	148/105[d]	148	na
average replacement rate (%)	41	63	68	78	na
active labour market policy (1995, spending as % GDP)	0.20	0.53	1.33	1.06	3.00
average wedge for apw[e]	32 to 37[a]	29	41	44	na
average wedge for min wage[f]	17 to 19	-16	20	32	na
marginal wedge for apw[e]	30 to 39[a]	40	53	54	na
marginal wedge for min wage[f]	37 to 42	74	50	59	na

[a] Figures vary across states. Texas, New York and California are considered in CPB (1995).
[b] Only in the agricultural sector.
[c] In the textile industry.
[d] Minimum wage in collective agreement for blue and white collar workers respectively.
[e] Average Production Worker.
[f] At the minimum wage level.
Source: CPB (1995: 21,26,29), Vogels (1994), OECD (1996b: 210-212).
Note that Dutch figures include holiday payments, whereas German figures do not.

government or social security funds into their objective function. They realize that higher wage claims will drive up social security costs, thereby lowering net wages or employment. In this case, generous social security will not drive up wages. Yet, empirical evidence for the Netherlands suggests that real wage resistance plays a role, whereas evidence for Germany is mixed (see also Box 9.1).

The broad indicators in Table 9.2 suggest that the Dutch social security system does not strongly encourage trade unions to consider employment opportunities: the average replacement rate is high compared to the American value, whereas spending on active labour market policy lags behind compared to the Swedish system. In Germany, both indicators are slightly more favourable to outsider considerations.[11] Table 9.2 moreover shows that the value of the wedge is the highest in the Netherlands, especially at the low end of the earnings distribution. Assuming that real wage resistance plays a role, the high wedge will drive up wage costs.

---

[11] At the lower end of the earnings distribution, however, replacement rates for couples are equally high in both countries and amount to almost 100% (CPB, 1995: 14).

Box 9.1 Real wage resistance

Two conflicting models describe the effect of the wedge (i.e. the gap between wage costs and net wages) on wage formation. Layard et al. (1991: 108) argue that the burden of the wedge will be totally absorbed by workers and does not increase wage costs. The reason is that a (proportional) increase of the average wedge equally affects the net benefit and the net wage. Since trade unions are interested in the difference between both values, their gross wage claims will not change, unless the marginal wedge is affected. In contrast, Graafland and Huizinga (1996) and Gelauff and Graafland (1994) argue that a rise of the wedge induces compensating wage demands, referred to as real wage resistance. The reason is that workers demand a certain level of net earnings, not only to make working more attractive than receiving benefits, but also to make the official labour market more attractive than the household sector or the underground economy. In this view, the burden of the wedge increases the gross wage level.

Empirical evidence on the effects of the wedge on wage costs is inconclusive. Generally, evidence from macroeconomic time series analysis is mixed. Tyrväinen (1994) suggests that real wage resistance is extremely high in Germany, indicating that the burden of taxes are not shifted onto labour but result in higher wage costs. In contrast, Carruth and Schnabel (1993) find no effect of the wedge on German wage costs. For the Netherlands, Graafland and Huizinga (1996) find that a rise in the average wedge (and a corresponding rise in the marginal wedge) increases wage costs in the long run by approximately 40%. In a cross-section analysis of OECD countries Jackman et al. (1995) find that the wedge does not significantly affect wage costs.

9.1.3 The Extent of Centralisation

Although sectoral bargaining prevails in Germany and the Netherlands, the extent of centralisation differs. Dutch collective bargaining results in a *mixed system* with centralized and decentralized elements. On the one hand, consensus building, i.e. coordination and government involvement at centralized level, enhances the extent of centralisation. On the other hand, the broad nature of consensus-building, the higher incidence of firm-level bargaining and the existence of firm-level variations within sectoral agreements allow tailor-made solutions. German collective bargaining, in contrast, is less strongly guided by coordination in advance at economy-wide level. In addition, 'Tarifautonomie' constrains government involvement, whereas firm-specific variations turn out to be smaller. Hence, the extent of centralization can be considered as *intermediate* (Section 8.1.5). To explain these differences, this section compares coordination, government involvement and decentralisation tendencies of collective bargaining.

Coordination. Coordination enhances the degree of centralisation of the collective bargaining process. The OECD (1994b: 171) defines coordination as the degree of integration between the different bargaining levels. It is overt, if bargaining units coordinate wage claims in advance and subsequently try to realise coordinated bargaining objectives. For instance, trade unions take the viewpoints of their confederation as a starting point for their wage claims, or peak level representatives of workers and employers jointly decide upon common bargaining objectives. It is covert, if key agreements set the stage for collective bargaining in other industries or firms. In this case, a system of pattern-bargaining evolves.

The degree and type of coordination strongly differs across the countries of reference. In the United States and the United Kingdom, employers and trade unions predominantly bargain at the firm-level, with little coordination from a higher level of aggregation. In Sweden, Germany and the Netherlands, in contrast, national confederations of trade unions and employer organisations perform a supportive and coordinative role in the bargaining process, but do not participate directly. In the Netherlands and in Sweden, coordination is predominantly overt, but in Germany it is mainly covert.

In Germany, regional divisions of sectoral bargaining units coordinate their demands in advance, but overt coordination between sectoral bargaining units in their peak level organisations weaker than in the Netherlands (OECD, 1996a; Slomp, 1995). Moreover, the peak level organisations of employers' and workers do not interact on a regular basis. They have no formal system of joint discussions at the national level between social partners (Soskice, 1990; Koene and Slomp, 1991). In contrast, covert coordination is relatively strong: collective bargaining in key sectors sets the stage for other sectors (OECD, 1996a; Katz, 1993). The largest trade union of the metal industry (IG Metall) plays the most prominent role in this process (Baethge and Wolf, 1995: 236).

In the Netherlands, overt coordination is more extensive. Dutch trade unions usually use the recommendations of their confederation as a starting point for negotiations, although these guidelines allow some freedom for variations in bargaining positions across sectoral trade unions to take account of sector-specific conditions (De Kam *et al.*, 1995). As a counterbalance, employer confederations decide upon a common position vis-à-vis trade unions as well, although this common position is not binding (IDS, 1995b). Based on the general positions of confederations, consultation and discussion at an economy-wide level between employers' and unions' confederations takes place in the bipartite Foundation of Labour (Stichting van de Arbeid).[12] The government is also involved in this process. The discussions at the Foundation of Labour incidentally lead to economy-wide recommendations that serve as guidelines for negotiations the sectoral

[12] The Foundation of Labour was founded in 1945. It is the exclusive representative employer-employee institution where sectoral or company negotiations can be coordinated. The foundation can make recommendations to sectoral trade unions and employers associations, but can also make recommendations to the government (Korver, 1993).

level.[13] Besides overt coordination within and between peak level organisations, covert coordination through trend setting collective agreements also exists in the Netherlands (De Kam *et al.*, 1995; Graafland and Verbruggen, 1993). However, this type of coordination is of less significance than in Germany, because of stronger overt coordination in advance.

Government Involvement. Government involvement, through direct interventions or persuasion, steers collective bargaining outcomes towards national policy objectives. The extent of government involvement significantly differs between Germany and the Netherlands.

In Germany, the system of 'Tarifautonomie' prohibits direct government interventions in wage bargaining (Paqué, 1993). The government tries to influence wage bargaining through persuasion or exerting political pressure (Baethge and Wolf, 1995).[14] Yet, formalized tripartite wage debates at economy-wide level do not take place at a regular basis. Concerted Action meetings existed between 1967 and 1977, but were generally not very effective in changing actual bargaining outcomes (Soskice, 1990). Recently, rising unemployment rates have stimulated the re-introduction of a tripartite debate on the need to moderate wage costs in order to reduce unemployment (the Bündnis für Arbeit).

The Dutch government is more strongly involved in wage formation. Government influence evolved from direct wage determination by the government until 1963 to collective bargaining between trade unions and employers associations, influenced by the government through wage interventions and consensus-building. Between 1963 and 1982, direct wage interventions regularly took place. The 1982 agreement of the Foundation of Labour made social partners more independent and coincided with the end of direct wage interventions (Chapter 5). Nowadays, the government may still directly intervene in the bargaining process, but only in exceptional circumstances.[15] Quite recently, in 1993, the threat of a possible wage intervention had the impact of restricting the scope for wage growth. Tripartite wage debates between the government and confederations in order to reach consensus on "sensible wage growth" are common practice. Persuasion is

---

[13] The 1982 recommendation was especially significant because it stated the primary responsibility of employers and employee organisations for wage bargaining and coincided with the end of direct government intervention in wage bargaining (De Kam *et al.*, 1995: 37, see also Chapter 5).

[14] Additionally, the opinion of independent institutions, notably the Deutsche Bundesbank and the Council of Economic Experts (Sachverständigenrat zur Begutachtung der gesamtwirtschaftlichen Entwicklung) influences collective bargaining.

[15] The criteria for wage interventions are that "the interests of the national economy require intervention because of sudden external shocks to the economy" (Van der Heijden *et al.*, 1995).

usually directed at the Foundation of Labour, the meeting place of employer and worker representatives at the economy-wide level (Korver, 1993). The government has tried to moderate wages also by reducing the burden of taxes and social security premiums.

Decentralisation Tendencies. Although the sectoral level is predominant, the firm level is gaining importance. Collective bargaining becomes more decentralized because of an increasing number of firm-level agreements, and because of an increasing scope for firm-level variations within sectoral agreements.

The first trend is more profound in the Netherlands. The number of firm-level agreements has increased from approximately 600 to 900 between 1982 and 1994, and they now cover 13% of employment. The increased presence of firm-level bargaining coincided with an increase in coverage, because the number of sectoral collective agreements remained stable at a level of approximately 200 (Schilstra and Smit, 1996).[16] Yet, firm-level bargaining is usually influenced by sectoral trade unions and the recommendations of their national confederations (Slomp, 1995). In Germany, firm-level agreements are less significant than in the Netherlands. Only one third of the number of agreements in total Germany are now concluded at the firm level (OECD, 1996a), compared to 80% in the Netherlands. A prominent example of a large German firm that bargains at the firm level is Volkswagen AG, but generally firm-level agreements mainly concern small firms that closely follow sectoral agreements (Slomp, 1995).

Quite recently, however, the firm-level appears to be gaining importance in Germany. Especially in the new Länder, employers increasingly withdraw their membership from employer associations, or succeed in paying wages below the agreed wage bargain (OECD, 1996a). This is related to the convergence of eastern to western wage levels after unification, causing wages rises by far exceeding labour productivity growth and providing a strong incentive for employers to depart from the established bargaining arrangements (Section 3.1.3). A recent agreement between government, employers and trade unions aims to increase the number of firm-level agreements for the new Länder (Het Financieele Dagblad, 1997). This agreement may imply a future tendency towards decentralisation of collective bargaining.

The rising importance of the firm level does not only concern the new Länder. An increasing number of firms in the old Länder is leaving or wants to leave the employer organisation and bargain at the firm (OECD, 1996a). Yet, the persistence of this trend is uncertain. Although individual employers complain about the lack of wage flexibility related to sectoral bargaining, they benefit from their membership in a number of ways, for instance because the employer organisation

---

[16] The number of employees covered by a firm-level agreement as a percentage of total coverage slightly increased from 15% in 1982 to 18% in 1990 (Schilstra and Smit, 1996).

provides legal advice and cooperation, for instance with respect to employee training (Soskice, 1990).

Apart from firm-specific agreements, less specific elements of sectoral agreements leave scope for enterprise-level bargaining with local worker representatives, for instance regarding working time. In Germany, the (trade-union-dominated) works council is the main firm-level bargaining partner. In the Netherlands, this depends on the presence of trade unions or works councils, on provisions in collective agreements and the issue at stake.

However, in both countries the scope for firm-level variation of wages within sectoral agreements is, until now, limited. In Germany, collective agreements specify minimum conditions regarding wages (Verdonk and Wiggers, 1994). Formally, works councils have no influence over supplementary wage increases, and these are unilaterally decided by management.[17] In practice, however, the works council may be involved informally or has a say about wage-related issues such as performance premia (Soskice, 1990; OECD, 1994b). Lower wages than the sectoral agreement are not allowed, unless opening clauses in the sectoral agreement explicitly state this possibility. The recent textile and clothing industry agreement allows lower wages to be payed by firms facing financial difficulties. In the chemical industry, the agreement allows lower wages for previously long-term unemployed (OECD, 1996a). In the Netherlands, the majority of sectoral collective agreements also specify minimum conditions with respect to wages. Therefore, the employer can only deviate from the agreement in favour of the employee.[18] Firm-level bargaining with worker representatives about wages above this minimum is possible, as long as local agreements do not contradict provisions in the collective agreement. In practice, however, employers are not inclined to give workers at the firm level a voice in determining wages, since this would undermine their position in collective wage-bargaining and may cause conflicts within the company (see also Teulings, 1996).

---

[17] Local employee-representatives do not have collective bargaining rights on wages at the firm level, irrespective of the fact that the contents of the sectoral agreement (i.e. the specification of a minimum) theoretically leaves room for such negotiations. Management can autonomously decide to pay more than the agreed collective wage increase to all workers, but not to some workers, because this affects the wage structure, an area on which the works council has a say (Jacobs, 1993: 175;176).

[18] Minimum wage agreements apply to 65% of covered employees. Additional types are standard agreements that leave no scope for firm-level deviations (17%) and min-max agreements with two-way restrictions on deviations at the firm level (18%). Source: Second Chamber of the States General, 1993-1994.

9.1.4 Assessment

What does this overview of bargaining institutions tell about the relative position of Germany and the Netherlands? From a broad international perspective, both bargaining systems are similar. In contrast, the American and also the British system have a decentralized collective bargaining setting with a relatively low coverage of collective agreements. This makes wage formation closer to the features of the competitive model (Section 8.1.5). Institutions do not support the existence of powerful interest associations, but make bargaining over labour conditions a firm-level issue. The predominance of firm-level bargaining promotes wage flexibility and diversity, but reduces the commitment of labour relationships.[19] Moreover, local insider power may result in large insider wage premia between firms and between insiders and new hires. Yet, insiders cannot easily prevent downward wage adjustments in case of severe negative shocks, since limited employment protection and a low fall back position diminishes their bargaining power.

In contrast, collective bargaining in Germany and in the Netherlands is closer to the cooperative model: cooperative exchange between organized interest associations plays a dominant role in wage formation (Section 8.1.5). Institutions support the bargaining power of trade unions, in particular through "firm-level" and collective extension mechanisms and through aspects of the social security system. Institutions also support the commitment of labour relationships. Sectoral bargaining reduces the scope for rent-extracting at firm-level, whereas regulations regarding strike activity govern conflicts of interests between trade unions and employers associations. Because of the sectoral bargaining level, wages can be adjusted to changes in supply and demand affecting the industry or economy. Yet, firms bear the adjustment costs related to fluctuations in local business conditions. If a worsening of firm-specific business conditions is temporary, it will sooner lead to a period of labour hoarding and lower profit rates than to downward wage adjustments, whereas a more persistent firm-specific shock will eventually lead to a downward adjustment of employment.

At a closer look, however, it turns out that a different degree of centralisation in Germany and the Netherlands impacts the performance of collective bargaining. The Dutch system performs better, because it mixes centralized and decentralized elements. Collective bargaining is more centralized because of the greater role of a priori consensus building on "sensible wage growth" through interaction between the peak level organisations of employers and workers and the government.

---

[19] By consequence, some collective agreements in the United States have a relative long duration of three years as a way to enhance stability (Layard *et al.* 1991: 90). However, this type of stability does not reduce the appearance of the hold-up problem during periods of renegotiations, whereas the long duration makes wage formation rigid.

Government involvement in consensus-building is supported by the, although strongly constrained, possibility to intervene in wage formation. The greater reliance on tripartite overt coordination is a strong element of Dutch wage formation, because it moderates wage growth, as trade unions tend to internalize external effects of the wage bargain on unemployment. Meanwhile, the Dutch system also leaves more scope for tailor-made solutions within the framework of consensus-building, because of the larger number of firm-level agreements, sectoral deviations from broad economy-wide guidelines regarding wage growth and the (limited) scope for firm-specific variations within sectoral agreements. Yet, even firm-level bargaining is influenced by consensus-building at the economy-wide level.

The German system, in contrast, is characterized by an intermediate degree of centralisation. By consequence, it neither fully captures the advantages of decentralized bargaining nor those of centralisation. The sectoral level has greater autonomy in determining bargaining outcomes, because direct government involvement is not allowed and institutions do not support persuasion and overt coordination. Instead, covert coordination influences collective bargaining outcomes, but this is less effective from the perspective of internalizing external effects and sooner promotes leapfrogging than wage moderation.

9.2 Vocational Education in Germany and the Netherlands

The most outstanding feature of education in Germany is its extensive apprenticeship (or dual) system: approximately two thirds of young people combine learning in schools with in-company training. The system of dual education is considered a main determinant of Germany's high quality labour force and relatively low youth unemployment (Figure 4.7 and Table 3.6). In the Netherlands, dual education also exists, but full-time education in schools is more popular.

This section compares the German apprenticeship system to the mix of full-time and dual education of Dutch vocational education at upper secondary level. It focuses on institutions that determine differences in the popularity of dual education between both countries. The structure of this section is as follows. First, Section 9.2.1 provides a brief overview of the main characteristics of vocational education at upper secondary level in both countries, focusing on the educational structure and enrolment per type of education. Next, Section 9.2.2 and Section 9.2.3 examine the organisation and finance of German and Dutch apprenticeships respectively. Subsequently, Section 9.2.4 explains the main reasons why German employees and employers have greater incentives to participate in this system than their Dutch counterparts. Finally, Section 9.2.5 provides the main conclusions.

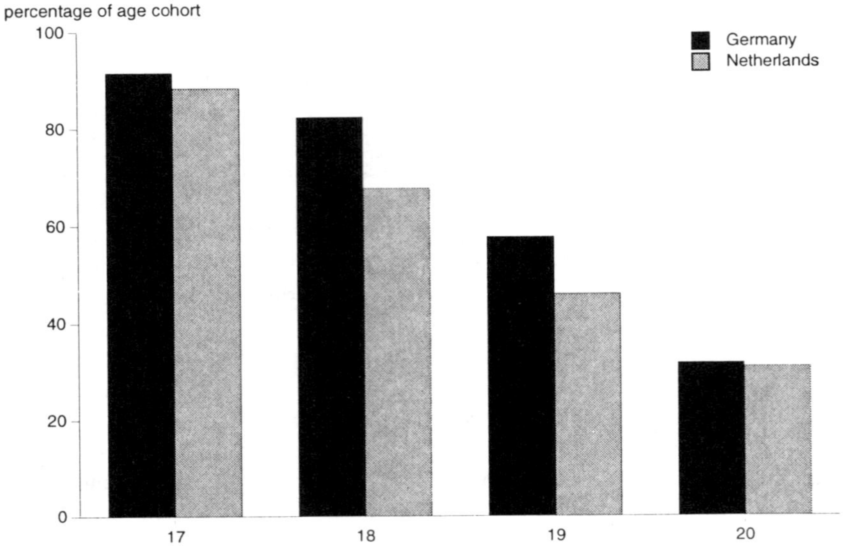

Source: OECD (1996), Education at a glance

Figure 9.2 Participation in secondary education, 1994

9.2.1 A Comparison of Vocational Education

Enrolment and Educational Attainment. Currently, the educational attainment level of the German population by far outperforms that of its Dutch counterpart (Figure 4.7). This is mainly caused by a larger share of people with a qualification at the upper secondary level in Germany.

Current enrolment rates reveal that the Dutch educational attainment level is engaged in a process of catching up (see also De Jager, 1996). In 1994, total net enrolment rates in secondary education are only slightly lower than in Germany (Figure 9.2). In both countries, a large majority of youngsters continues to follow upper secondary education when they are out of the compulsory age range, either in general or in vocational education (see Box 9.2 for an overview of the main learning routes in both countries).

Yet, enrolment per type of education substantially differs (Table 9.3). In Germany, apprenticeships are the most important type of upper secondary education. There is a high demand for training places by young persons and a high demand for trainees by industrial and commercial firms of all sizes in almost all sectors (Steedman, 1993). In contrast, a majority of Dutch pupils chooses full-time instead of dual vocational education. Enrolment in full-time vocational education has strongly risen between 1970 and 1994. Relative participation in general education diminished, but is still higher than in Germany.

Box 9.2 Learning-routes in upper secondary and tertiary education compared

The structure of upper secondary education is broadly similar in both countries. Pupils can follow general or vocational education, the latter via a full-time or a dual route. Dual education combines school-based and enterprise-based training.

In Germany, general education at the upper secondary level is provided by the 'Gymnasium' (and its counterpart at the integrated school type 'Gesamtschule'). This type of education gives access to university and non-university tertiary education. Dutch general upper secondary education comprises two types of schools ('havo' and 'vwo') that give access to higher vocational and university education respectively.

Regarding vocational education, the relative position of the full-time and the dual route differs. In Germany, dual education leads to a full qualification (as Facharbeiter). Full-time vocational education is not equivalent to the dual system. It usually does not lead to a full qualification in vocational education: the greater part of the full-time schools prepare students for the dual system[a] *or provide the possibility to improve the level of general upper secondary education combined with some education in the vocational field.*[b] *In the Netherlands, in contrast, both dual education ('llw') and full-time education ('mbo') lead to a full qualification in vocational education. However, full-time upper secondary vocational training gives access to higher vocational education but, as in Germany, apprenticeship certificates don't.*

In Germany, tertiary education encompasses university and non-university tertiary education, as well as post-secondary vocational education. The former types cannot be entered with an apprenticeship certificate only. The latter type consists of 'Schulen des Gesundheitswesens', 'Berufsakademien' and 'Fachschulen'. The entry qualification is a completed education in the dual system.[c] *Approximately, 'Fachschulen', which train for middle-class executive jobs and specialized Fachkräfte, form the equivalent of (3-4 years) full-time vocational education in the Netherlands. On the other hand, 'Fachschulen' also consist of 'Meisterschulen', a particular German school type at a higher level than Dutch full-time qualifications. In the Netherlands, higher education consists of higher vocational and university education.*

Source: Van Lieshout (1996)

[a] *Viz. the 'Berufsgrundbildungsjahr', the 'Berufsvorbereitungsjahr', 'Berufsvorbereitende Bildungsmaßnahmen' and some 'Berufsfachschulen'.*

[b] *Viz. 'Berufsaufbauschulen', 'Fachoberschulen' and some 'Berufsfachschulen'.*

[c] *Additional entry preconditions are a qualification of the 'Berufsschule' and a period of work experience in the same field of vocational specialization.*

Although apprenticeships are the most significant type of education in Germany, policy makers worry about its diminishing popularity. Table 9.3 reveals that full-time education at the upper secondary level has gained importance compared to dual education. However, the implication that the dual system is loosing its attractiveness turns out to be exaggerated: as a share of the young population, the number of apprenticeships rose between 1970 and 1986. Since then, it slightly diminished (Van Lieshout, 1996). German pupils more often follow a full-time course before they enter dual education, for instance because they want to enter higher education after having completed an apprenticeship. Hence, the apprenticeship system has lost attractiveness compared to higher education as a final qualification, but many students follow an apprenticeship before they enrol in higher education (Van Lieshout, 1996: 70-73).

The Position of Dual Education. For three reasons, the German apprenticeship system has a different position within the upper secondary education system compared to its Dutch counterpart. First of all, German apprenticeships practically form the only adequate way to obtain a full vocational qualification at upper secondary level (Box 9.2). They offer possibilities for a wide ability range, including for students with a 'Gymnasium' qualification ('Hochschulreife').[20] Apprentices with the lowest qualifications, such as drop-outs or 'Hauptschule' graduates, are concentrated in the 'Handwerk sector' (craft sector), whereas apprentices with higher pre-entry qualifications are concentrated in the manufacturing and service sectors (Gordon, Jallade and Parkes, 1994; Münch and Henzelmann, 1993; Steedman, 1993). This differs from the Dutch mixed system, which does not attract many pupils who have already obtained a full-time upper secondary qualification (Den Broeder, 1995). As the German system is more strongly embedded in the initial education system, it mainly attracts youngsters. The Dutch system, in contrast, also provides further education to adults (Van Lieshout, 1996).[21]

Second, there are no formal pre-entry conditions to enter an apprenticeship in Germany. In practice, however, pre-entry qualifications influence the type of training place that can be found. In the Netherlands, a lower secondary vocational certificate ('vbo') or general lower secondary certificate ('mavo') is usually required to enter apprenticeships, although these entry requirements are not always applied in practice.

Third, the German qualification for graduates of the dual system is always that of a skilled worker or 'Facharbeiter'. In the Netherlands this depends on the level at which the apprenticeship has been followed. A semi-skilled, skilled or specialized skilled qualification can be obtained (Dercksen, Van Lieshout *et al*, 1993).

---

[20] In 1990, 14.6% of the apprentices obtained this qualification before entering the dual system (Tessaring, 1993)

[21] In 1992-1993, 16% of entrants in the Dutch dual system was older than 27, compared to less than 1% in Germany.

Table 9.3 Participation in upper secondary education per type of school

	Germany[a]			Netherlands		
	1970	1990	1994	1970	1991	1994
	in %					
general	16	21	23	44	32	30
full-time vocational	16	23	23	30	46	45
apprenticeships	68	57	55	26	21	25
total	100	100	100	100	100	100

[a] 1970 and 1990, Old Länder, 1994 total Germany

Source: 1994: OECD (1996c: 123); Earlier years: Behringer and Jeschek (1993), Ganga (1992) and CBS Statistics Netherlands

9.2.2 Organisation and Finance of German Apprenticeships

Organisation. In dual education, theoretical education is combined with working experience and practical learning. The duration of apprenticeships in Germany is two to three and a half years, depending on the occupation. During this period, most apprentices follow enterprise-based training on the work floor for four (or three) days a week and attend classes ('Berufsschule') one (or two) days a week.

German employers are not obliged to hire apprentices, but if they do so they are obliged to let them go to school during work time and to provide the enterprise-based part of their training according to national standards. These standards are determined per occupation, through cooperative exchange between the government and employers representatives. Worker representatives also play a role, but their influence is more limited (Van Lieshout, 1996).

The development of these standards differs between the school-based and the enterprise-based component. The contents of the school-based component of dual education are determined at the 'Länder' level, through cooperation between the regional governments, chambers of industry and commerce, and trade unions (Soskice, 1994). This does not mean that the school-based part of the system strongly differs per Land, because the sixteen Länder cooperate on a voluntary basis (OECD, 1994c). The contents of enterprise-based training, in contrast, are determined at the federal level (Green and Steedman, 1993). This involves a complex and time-consuming process in which the federal government, the governments of the 'Länder', chambers of industry and commerce, and trade unions participate. This process ensures that the minimum quality of enterprise-based training is the same in all Länder. At the operating level, competent bodies (mostly Chambers of industry and commerce) monitor the quality of training, whereas works councils also monitor the adherence of employers to training regulations (Soskice, 1994). For instance, only a certified teacher[22] is allowed to give enterprise-based training.

Individual employers have to train according to national standards, but have some freedom to choose their own training methods and improve upon the required minimum training quality (OECD, 1994c). Over time, the ways to provide enterprise-based and school-based training have become more diverse. Nowadays, parts of enterprise training can be provided through extra-plant training centres in order to improve the quality of training and to facilitate the provision of some parts of the training for small or medium sized firms. Public funds were used to build and equip these centres (OECD, 1994c). However, some (larger) firms also provide the school-based part of the training within the firm.

Qualifications are awarded on the basis of written and practical examinations, set and marked by external examiners (Münch and Henzelmann, 1993). So called competent bodies (mostly chambers of industry and commerce) issue certificates, which are recognised throughout Germany. The examinations result in the skilled worker ('Facharbeiter') status and indicate that the pupil has obtained the necessary practical and theoretical knowledge according to the standards of the Vocational Training Act. After graduation, skilled workers also have the possibility to participate in adult education, for example to study for the 'Meister' certificate.[23] 'Meister' in the 'Handwerk' sector can set up a business and all 'Meister' are allowed to train apprentices.

Finance. Training costs are shared between the government, employers and workers. The governments of the Länder pay for the school-based component. Employers finance enterprise-based training, such as remunerations for apprentices, instructor salaries, equipment and examination costs. Evidently, apprentices bear a part of the costs as well, since apprenticeship wages are relatively low compared to the wage of young unskilled workers: unskilled earnings can be three to four times as high as the apprentice wage (Soskice, 1994). Apprentices with very low wages receive an allowance from the government, but this concerns a small group (Behringer and Jeschek, 1993).

---

[22] Who has completed apprenticeship training and has obtained the Trainer Aptitude or the 'Meister' certificate.

[23] A minimum period of work experience, lower secondary qualifications and an apprenticeship certificate are the entry conditions for the 'Meister' study. This study takes approximately two years and the study level is the same as that of a higher vocational study, but the 'Meister' certificate does not give access to higher education. Apart from the 'Meister study' skilled workers have the possibility to participate in a further technical study (Münch and Henzelmann, 1993) or to study for the Trainer Aptitude exams, which enables them to provide enterprise-based training (OECD, 1994c).

After graduation, Facharbeiter can apply for a skilled worker's job with their current employer or look for a job with another employer. A job with the current employer is not guaranteed, because apprentices have a labour contract of limited duration. There are clear links between the skilled worker certificate and the status of a skilled worker job. Collective bargaining agreements specify (minimum) wages for Facharbeiter, who are included in collective bargaining agreements as a separate category. Earnings and career perspectives strongly vary per occupation.

9.2.3 The Dutch System of Dual Education

Organisation. The Dutch dual system is organized on the basis of occupations and is divided into study levels. In principle, people of 16 years old or older can enter the dual system. In practice, young people with a low pre-entry qualification have more difficulties in finding a training place. Three study levels are distinguished: primary, secondary and tertiary apprenticeships. Participation in primary apprenticeships is highest. A primary apprenticeship lasts two to three years, in which pupils usually go to school for one (or two) days a week and are trained on the job for the rest of the week. Graduates from the dual system receive a nationally acknowledged leaving certificate. The three levels correspond to three certificates which are all classified at the upper secondary level.[24]

Employers who hire apprentices have to train according to the standards set by national apprenticeship organisations. The contents of the school-based as well as the enterprise-based component are determined by the national organisations of the apprenticeship system, in which representatives of the government, employers, trade unions and the training system participate (Hövels and Meijer, 1994). In addition, these organisations supervise the implementation of apprenticeship contracts and the examination process (Römkens and Visser, 1994).

Finance. The government and employers share the costs of training. The government pays for the school-based part of apprenticeships, finances the national apprenticeship organisations and also subsidizes enterprise-based training. Firms pay the costs of the enterprise-based training, and often share a part of these costs through payments to schooling funds (see also De Vries and Heere, 1993). Some (smaller) firms choose to provide enterprise-based training together.

In most cases, wage costs for the apprentice are the largest cost component for employers (according to estimates of De Vries and Heere, 1993). Wage costs vary considerably and depend on the form of the apprenticeship contract. In some cases

[24] Approximately, the level of primary apprenticeships corresponds to that of 2 year full-time vocational education at upper secondary level ('kmbo'), whereas the level of secondary and tertiary apprenticeships is comparable to that of 3 or 4 year full-time vocational education ('mbo').

the apprentice does not get a labour contract and hence does not receive a regular wage but only an allowance (see also De Vries and Heere, 1993).[25] However, most apprentices (94% of all primary apprenticeships according to Frietman and Hövels, 1994) have a labour contract of limited or unlimited duration, and receive a regular wage. The minimum wage of apprentices with a labour contract equals the legal minimum wage on a part-time basis (4 days a week), but 88% of primary apprentices earns more than that (Frietman and Hövels, 1994; Hövels and Meijer, 1994). This implies that trainees often do not incur large opportunity costs, because trainee wages are not substantially lower than the unskilled wage level.

Graduates from the dual system are not explicitly considered as a separate group of workers in collective labour agreements, which implies that their salary after graduation will depend on their function and age group and not directly on their skilled worker status.

9.2.4 Attractiveness of German versus Dutch Apprenticeships

The organisation and finance of German apprenticeships, as well as the institutional environment, provide incentives for many young workers and companies to participate (Finegold, 1991; Soskice, 1994; Van Lieshout, 1996). This section focuses on these aspects and explains why these incentives do not exist to the same extent in the Netherlands.

Employee Incentives. From the perspective of young workers, there are three main reasons that make the German system more attractive than the Dutch system.

First, German youngsters have hardly access to an alternative labour market besides the dual system.[26] In addition, the absence of pre-entry requirements makes the dual system relatively easily accessible in Germany.This differs from the Dutch situation, where wage differentials between unskilled workers and apprentices are much smaller and most apprenticeships have pre-entry requirements.

Second, the dual system in Germany is attractive for a wide ability range. The system has succeeded in attracting a growing number of pupils with upper secondary qualifications, whereas low achievers can still find a training place in the 'Handwerk' sector. In contrast, the Dutch system turns out to be less attractive for a wide ability range. Low achievers are constrained by pre-entry requirements,

---

[25] A minority of apprentices does not even have an apprenticeship contract, since it is also possible to follow the school-based part of an apprenticeship only.

[26] This is mainly caused by the relatively low apprenticeship wages compared to unskilled wages, which creates an incentive for employers to offer training places instead of unskilled jobs.

whereas high achievers more often opt for school-based vocational education, which provides better opportunities for further education.

Third, the skilled worker certificate has a high labour market value in Germany. This value is not so much determined by a high relative wage, but rather by a high chance for skilled workers compared to unskilled workers to find a job. The skilled worker certificate can be seen as a general entry certificate for the labour market: it is even relevant for occupations which strongly differ from a worker's field of apprenticeship training. The function of the skilled worker certificate as an entry certificate to the labour market is related to the status of the dual system in Germany and to transferable elements of the training. Moreover, the explicit link between the skilled worker certificate and labour market conditions enhance its general value to workers. 'Facharbeiter' who find a job in their training occupation receive the skilled worker wage. On top of that they receive additional benefits, for instance related to social security entitlements (Van Lieshout, 1996).

In the Netherlands, the labour market value of a completed apprenticeship training is less evident. Collective bargaining agreements do specify skill requirements related to certain functions, but generally do not make a distinction between dual or full-time education. Moreover, the differentiation within the dual system makes the value of a certificate even less clear: there are three levels within the system and pupils can also partially participate in the training.

Employer Incentives. From the perspective of employers, the central question is whether it is worthwhile to invest in human capital through apprenticeships. Uncertainty about the future benefits of training investments results from the transferable nature of the training investment. In Germany, labour mobility after completion of an apprenticeship is substantial.[27] Apparently, training firms are able to extract enough rents from these investments despite labour turnover.

There are several reasons why investments in dual education are worthwhile in spite of labour mobility. First, the relatively low trainee wages make training attractive compared to hiring unskilled workers. In small firms in the Handwerk sector, the returns to some apprenticeships are often already positive during the period of the apprenticeship contract (Oulton and Steedman; 1992).[28] Hence, the poaching problem is of less importance, even though labour mobility in this sector is relatively high. In larger firms in the 'Industrie und Handel' returns are often

[27] Six months after graduation, 41% of the graduation cohort 1984/85 still worked for the same employer with a contract of unlimited duration (Winkelmann, 1994). Approximately 70% of 'Facharbeiter' leave their training firm within a period of 5 years (Harhoff and Kane, 1993).

[28] Apprentices can be trained during slack periods, when 'Meister' are less engaged in production work. Because of relatively low apprentice wages and training costs, returns can be positive.

negative during the training period, because full-time trainers and more expensive training equipment are needed (Steedman, 1993). In this case, poaching can be a problem. Yet, this does not mean that apprenticeship training is an unprofitable investment. If labour mobility is not too high, apprenticeships are still worthwhile, because a part of all 'Facharbeiter' will stay with the firm long enough to make the investment worthwhile on average (Harhoff and Kane, 1993). According to Soskice (1994), labour turnover is lower in these types of companies than in the Handwerk sector, which helps to increase the private returns to the training firm.

Second, German employers have difficulty in recruiting skilled workers on the external labour market. Poaching skilled workers from other firms as an alternative to training is hampered by the collective bargaining system. The sectoral bargaining level and the involvement of works councils at firm level makes it more difficult for companies to use wages for new hires as a means to poach (Soskice, 1994). In addition, the recruitment of skilled workers from the full-time educational system is hampered by a lack of full-time vocational learning routes at upper secondary level.

Third, a reason for German firms to hire apprentices is that they can benefit from the highly regulated training infrastructure. Their involvement in the development of training standards can improve the match between training and occupation-specific human capital requirements, whereas the in company element strengthens the match with firm-specific requirements.

Finally, apprenticeship training entails a number of indirect benefits. The status related to being an 'acknowledged training firm', which is monitored by the chambers of industry and commerce, functions as a quality signal to customers (Den Broeder, 1995). In addition, employers can use the training period also as a screening device that helps them to select workers (Van Lieshout, 1996).

In the Netherlands, these incentives are weaker. The private costs of employee training for employers are not substantially higher than in Germany (see Van Lieshout, 1996 for an overview of empirical studies). Yet, wage costs of apprentices are hardly lower than those of young unskilled workers. This makes hiring trainees a less attractive alternative compared to hiring unskilled workers. Moreover, hiring graduates from full-time vocational schools provides a cheap alternative to apprenticeship training. Indirect benefits may also be smaller in the Netherlands. For instance, the quality signal of being a training firm is weaker, because of the lower significance of apprenticeship training.

9.2.5 Assessment

Because of the more extensive apprenticeship system, the German educational system corresponds with the features of the cooperative model (Section 8.1.6). The Dutch system, in contrast, results in a mix between the school-based full-time education of the competitive model and the extensive dual educational system of the cooperative model. This implies that the German economy is to a larger extent specialized on the formation of human capital with partly general and partly firm-specific characteristics. The Dutch system, in contrast, is more specialized on the provision of general skills through full-time education.

The greater attractiveness of dual education in Germany can be partly explained by institutions that strengthen the commitment between employers and employees and that help to internalize external effects of the training investment. In particular, the lack of equivalent full-time educational routes, the easy access and clear labour market value of the system enhance the general value of apprenticeship training to workers. For employers, the system is attractive because of relatively low trainee wages, moderate mobility rates, a limited scope to attract skilled workers on the external labour market, as well as cooperative exchange on the contents of dual education and a number of indirect benefits. Hence, both the organisation of the system and related labour market institutions codetermine the high training equilibrium in Germany.

9.3 Co-determination in Germany and the Netherlands

German workers have a strong voice in managerial decision-making.[29] Workers' representatives have access to firm-specific information, advise employers on business policy and co-decide on personnel matters. German co-determination or 'Mittbestimmung', which is defined here as the institutionalized influence of worker representatives on management, takes place through two different channels. At the enterprise level, worker representatives are present on the supervisory board of most public or private limited liability companies. In addition, workers in many firms are represented at the work-floor level through works councils.

In comparison to the lack of co-determination arrangements in the United States, the Dutch system of co-determination is broadly similar to that in Germany. The interests of American workers at the firm level are, if at all, protected by trade unions. Works councils are not compulsory and direct employee representation on the board of directors does not exist (Hepple, 1993; Biagi, 1993). From a European perspective, Dutch co-determination is relatively close to the German system as well, since co-determination is extensive in both countries (Turner, 1993). However, a closer look reveals that both systems differ. In the Netherlands, workers are not represented on the supervisory board and works councils are not compulsory in small firms (see Table 9.4 for a summary). However, Dutch works councils have more influence on managerial financial-economic decisions regarding reorganisations, mergers, etcetera.

The organisation of this section is as follows. First, Section 9.3.1 focuses on German co-determination institutions. Subsequently, Section 9.3.2 compares Dutch co-determination institutions to those in Germany. Based on this comparison of

[29] This chapter has also been published in Gelauff and Den Broeder (1997).

Table 9.4 Indicators of co-determination

	United States	Germany[a]	Netherlands[b]
	in % of workers		
Workers represented on supervisory board	_	26.5	_
Presence of works council is employee right	_	85.2	68

[a] 1980. Streeck (1984: 404), Niedenhoff (1990: 14).
[b] 1995. CBS Statistics Netherlands, rough estimate, private sector workers in firms with 35 workers or more.

worker influence on management, Section 9.3.3 presents the main conclusions regarding the extent of worker influence in Germany and the Netherlands.

9.3.1 The German System of Co-determination

This section describes the two types of German co-determination institutions: worker representation on the supervisory board and co-determination at the work-floor level. Subsequently, it addresses the integrated character of German co-determination.

Co-determination at the Enterprise Level. Co-determination at the enterprise level is closely related to corporate governance, since it takes place through worker representatives on the supervisory board (Aufsichtsrat) who supervise management together with shareholder representatives. The size, sector and legal form of enterprises determines which part of the supervisory board consists of workers' representatives (Table 9.5). Worker representatives on the supervisory board have two main tasks: they control management together with shareholders, but also promote the interests of the workers they represent (Section 10.2.1).

Co-determination through workers' representation on supervisory boards was first introduced in 1951 (Co-determination Act of 1951) for the coal, iron and steel industries, where arrangements are still most strict: parity representation is required, which means that half of all board members consist of workers' representatives and the other half of shareholders' representatives. One additional member, the chairman, is co-opted by the entire supervisory board in order to prevent a deadlock of votes (Streeck, 1984: 393). Moreover, the management board needs to contain a worker representative, i.e. the labour director or 'Arbeitsdirektor', whose appointment is approved by the worker representatives on the supervisory board (Streeck, 1984; Owen Smith, 1994). However, this particular Co-determination Act is now of limited importance because employment in this industry has declined (Jacobi *et al.*, 1992).

Table 9.5 Worker representation on the German supervisory board

Legal form	Firm size (number of workers)			
	1-500	501-1000	1001-2000	2001-
Public limited liability company	_[a]	1/3	1/3 (1/2)[b]	1/2
Private limited liability company	_	1/3	1/3 (1/2)[b]	1/2
Unlimited liability company	_	_	_	_

[a] Founded after August 10, 1994.
[b] In brackets: parity applying to coal, iron and steel industry.

Sources: Gurdon and Rai (1990); Streeck (1984); Koene and Slomp (1991); Niedenhoff (1990)

Soon after the introduction of co-determination in the coal, iron and steel industries, participatory management was extended to other industries: The Works Constitution Act (WCA of 1952) required worker influence on the supervisory boards. However, requirements were less strict compared to those in the coal, iron and steel industries, as only one third of seats was allocated to worker representatives. The main principles of this Act are still valid today (WCA of 1972).

Co-determination rights were further expanded during the 1970s. In particular, near-parity representation on the supervisory board and the presence of a labour director became obligatory for very large firms in all sectors (Co-determination Act of 1976). Small differences to the parity model according to the Co-determination Act of 1951 (which still applies to the coal, iron and steel industries) remained: the casting vote of the chairman is held by a shareholder representative, which implies near-parity instead of parity. Moreover, the labour director is appointed in the same way as other managers, namely through voting of the entire supervisory board (Streeck, 1984). Quite recently, however, policy changes reduced co-determination rights at enterprise level. Since 1994, newly founded small public companies are no longer required to have worker representatives on the supervisory board (Section 10.2.1).

Co-determination at the Work-floor Level. Co-determination at the work-floor involves daily management issues and is therefore often considered to be more influential than enterprise-level co-determination (Turner, 1993). Moreover, in contrast to enterprise-level co-determination, the advancement of worker interests is the only objective of worker representatives at the work-floor level. Institutionalized participation at the work floor takes place through works councils. These councils are particularly influential regarding social or personnel policies (with the exception of wage formation), but weaker in relation to business strategies (Jacobi *et al.*, 1992: 243).

Workers in private-sector plants that usually employ six or more workers have the legal right to start a works council. The employer is required to support the establishment of a works council (Jacobs, 1993: 167). This right applies to approximately 85% of the total number of employees (Table 9.4).[30] The works council is elected by all employees of minimal 18 years old. Only workers who have worked within the firm for a period of at least six months can be elected (Jacobs, 1993: 168).

Regulations regarding works councils stem from the 1950s (Works Constitution Act of 1952).[31] During the 1970s, the influence of works councils slightly expanded, for instance through enlargement of the works councils (Works Constitution Act of 1972). Nowadays, works councillors have information, consultation and co-decision rights, but these rights are related to the obligation to work with managers in a way which benefits both the workers and the company. For instance, works councillors are not allowed to organize a strike (Niedenhoff, 1990).

Compared to information or consultation rights, co-decision rights give workers most influence, because management cannot implement particular changes without approval of the works council. Co-decision rights apply to personnel policies related to hiring and firing, transfers, employee training, work environment, working hours, holiday arrangements, performance monitoring and remuneration policies, *e.g.* bonuses, piecework rates (Turner, 1993; Jacobs, 1993). If an agreement cannot be reached, an internal settlement board ('Einigungsstelle') provides binding arbitration. These rights are combined with access of councillors to the relevant firm-specific information.

As regards financial and economic matters (such as re-organisations or the introduction of new technologies) the influence of the works council is confined to information and consultation rights. These rights apply to works councils in firms with 20 or more workers (Koene and Slomp, 1991). Influence of the works council is limited, because the worker representatives on the supervisory board are viewed as the main institution for worker influence on financial and economic decisions. Consequently, consultation rights of works councils are restricted to the social consequences of managerial decisions (Jacobs, 1993: 173). Management should inform the works council in advance and has to listen to comments and suggestions of works councillors. For instance, in the case of mass lay-offs the works council has to be informed in advance and has the right to give advice about alternative solutions. Once this procedure has been followed, the works council is

---

30 This figure includes the public sector, where parallel legislation exists regarding "staff councils" that have somewhat less influence: co-determination over social issues is similar but there is no right to information on business policy (Jacobi *et al.*, 1992).

31 The first German co-determination laws already existed at the end of the 19th century. In 1933 every form of co-determination was abolished. After the war, arrangements were re-established and further developed (Niedenhoff, 1990).

entitled to negotiate a social plan for redundant workers. These negotiations can be very detailed and often include compensation schemes and retraining measures (Niedenhoff, 1990).

Integration and Interaction with Trade Unions. The two channels of co-determination can be seen as an integrated system of worker representation. Communication between works councillors and worker representatives on the supervisory board is common practice (Streeck, 1984; Koene and Slomp, 1991). Moreover, worker representatives on the supervisory boards are often also members of works councils. The relationships between the supervisory board and the works council improve the access of works councillors to information regarding investment strategies and of the supervisory board to work-floor information.

Co-determination is also linked to worker influence through trade unions. Trade-union power has facilitated the development of co-determination institutions, since trade unions generally favoured worker influence at firm and plant levels. According to Turner (1993), legal co-determination rights cannot easily be developed in countries with little trade-union power. In addition, the various channels of worker influence are intertwined. Formally, works councils are independent of trade unions, but in practice they are dominated by trade-union members. Consequently, trade unions have an indirect say at the work-floor level. In large firms, one or more worker representatives work full-time for the works council, and these councillors are often trade-union members (Jacobs, 1993: 170). In contrast, the direct representation of trade unions at the work floor is only weak. Trade unions attempted to set up a distinct system of work place representation through local trade-union representatives, but in many cases this was not successful (Owen Smith, 1994: 301). Therefore, a major work-floor task of trade unions is to support the functioning of works councils (Biagi, 1993).

The degree of integration of trade unions and co-determination arrangements poses the question which objectives predominate: general trade-union objectives or the interests of workers in a particular firm. As works councils are dominated by trade-union members, they are often "vehicles for the expression of union interests" (Turner, 1992: 96). However, councillors tend to "identify with their company" and to protect the position of insiders. Therefore, in case of discrepancies between general trade-union objectives and the firm's direct interests, the latter tend to prevail (Owen Smith, 1994: 302; Streeck, 1984: 398).[32]

---

[32] For instance, some works councils in the car industry have recently agreed to work on Saturdays, although this contradicted trade-union policy.

9.3.2 The Dutch System of Co-determination

This section compares the Dutch institutions regarding co-determination at enterprise and work-floor level to those in Germany.

Co-determination at the Enterprise Level. Dutch co-determination at the enterprise level is virtually absent. Members of the supervisory board are elected by the general meeting of shareholders (common model) or appointed through cooption (structural model), but are not elected by workers directly (Section 10.2.1). Members of the supervisory board can be shareholders but, in contrast to the German situation, employees of a firm are prohibited to occupy a seat on the firm's supervisory board (Van het Kaar, 1995).

Only in large firms to which the structural model applies, employees have an indirect say in the composition of supervisory boards.[33] In particular, works councillors are allowed to advise on the appointment of new members. If the works council in these large firms disagrees with the appointment of a particular supervisory board member, the appointment is cancelled, unless the opinion of the works council is overruled in court at the Chamber of Company Law (Ondernemingskamer), the Dutch court specialized in corporate law. Moreover, it is common practice but no legal right, that at least one member of the supervisory board has somewhat closer connections to the works council. This member is concerned with social aspects or is recommended by the works council (Koene and Slomp, 1991; Van het Kaar, 1995).

Co-determination at the Work-floor Level. Regulations concerning co-determination at the work floor stem from 1950 (Works Council Act or WOR). At that time, works councils became compulsory for firms with 25 workers or more (Vanwersch *et al.*, 1993). They had an advisory task and were directed at the interests of the entire enterprise. In 1979, their influence was strengthened. Works councils became an instrument directed at the protection of workers' interests (WOR 1979). As in Germany, they obtained co-decision rights on social and personnel policies (Albers, 1995; SER, 1991), for instance regarding hiring and firing[34], transfers, employee training, work environment, working hours, holiday arrangements, performance monitoring and remuneration policies (e.g. profit sharing, pension plans). As in Germany, co-decision rights do not apply to wage formation.

The employer has to consult the works council in advance on matters of business policy, such as important organisational changes and investments (SER, 1991: 104), as well as on the appointment and dismissal of directors and higher

[33] Section 10.2.1 describes the specific conditions that pertain to the structural and the common model in the Netherlands.

[34] Co-decision does apply to firing policies in general but not to individual dismissals.

staff (SER, 1991: 108; Teulings, 1987). The advisory rights of work councils are more extensive than those in Germany. A Dutch employer must consult the works council on any 'important' economic decision (Jacobs, 1993; Teulings, 1987: 2; Biagi, 1993; Vanwersch *et al.*, 1993). In contrast to the situation in Germany, the advisory rights not only pertain to the social consequences of a decision but also to the decision itself.

From an international perspective, legal advisory rights are strong. The works council can appeal at the Chamber of Company Law if it is not rightly consulted, presumes that the interests of all stakeholders in the firm are not carefully taken into account, or is convinced that managers should not have disregarded its advice (SER, 1991). If management has neglected advisory rights or if managers did not sufficiently consider the interests of all stakeholders, the Chamber of Company Law often prohibits implementation of a particular management decision. In contrast, if the works council has been consulted but its advice has not been followed, appeals by the works council are hardly ever successful. Accordingly, advisory rights rarely stop an investment plan, although the works council sometimes succeeds in changing business policies, especially in case of reorganisations (Teulings, 1987; Koene and Slomp, 1991).

The reach of works councils has changed over time. Nowadays, all firms in the private sector that usually employ 35 workers or more[35] are obliged to have a works council (SER, 1991). Members of the works council must have been employed by the firm for at least one year, whereas workers with a minimum tenure of half a year are allowed to vote (SER, 1991). The influence of works councils is larger in firms with 100 workers or more. For instance, in firms with 35 to 100 workers consultation rights apply only to matters that affect the labour market position of at least 25% of all employees, whereas this restriction does not apply to large firms (Koene and Slomp, 1991).

The right to start a works council does not apply to very small companies. Workers in small firms, with 10 to 35 workers, merely have limited advisory power via obligatory biannual personnel meetings. According to a rough estimate, approximately 68% of Dutch workers have the right to start a works council, whereas this right applies to approximately 85% of German workers (Table 9.4). However, a considerable number of workers, especially those in small firms, do not use their co-determination rights because they do not start a works council. Table 9.6 shows that currently German workers are relatively more active in medium-sized firms, while activity is similar in large firms. This implies that works councils are still more common in Germany. However, these activity rates may converge in the future, since activity in medium-sized Dutch firms is increasing (Van der Burgh and Kriek, 1992).

---

[35] 35 workers or more who work (on average) more than 1/3 of a full-time work week, or a minimum of 100 workers. The 1/3 criterion will be abolished in the near future.

Table 9.6 Presence of a works council in Germany and the Netherlands

	Germany	The Netherlands
	% of firms	
Small firms, 6-10 workers	10	–
Medium-sized firms 50 to 100 (Ger), 35 to 100 workers (Neth)	60	41
Large firms, 100 workers or more	80	83

Source: Koene and Slomp (1991: 234)

Dutch co-determination is still gaining ground (Second Chamber of the States General, 1996a and b). Five institutional changes imply a stronger influence of workers. Firstly, the law regarding works councils (WOR) is extended to the public sector, which will strengthen co-determination in this sector after the implementation of the new regulations in May 1997 (Vanwersch *et al.*, 1993). Evidently, government policy is excluded from co-determination rights.

Secondly, the influence of works councils will strengthen in some areas. Co-decision rights will also apply to instruments of performance monitoring and to the registration of personal information of employees. Advisory rights will be extended to technological changes (instead of being limited to new technologies that correspond with important investments), to systems of environmental care as well as to important granting of credit.

Thirdly, firm-level agreements between management and employees will get a more formal status. This change is related to the increasing importance of the works council as a bargaining partner at the firm level, for instance regarding working-time conditions. Within the boundaries of the contents of a collective agreement, the works council in many firms negotiates with management over firm level issues, and lays down the outcome in a firm-level agreement. Such an agreement involves not only co-decision rights but often also other issues, since the influence of the works council can be extended through provisions in a collective agreement or by management. The more formal status of these agreements implies that management cannot easily change the contents of this type of firm-level agreements without involving the works council. However, in contrast to the German situation, firm-level agreements do not have the same status as collective agreements.

Fourthly, a EU-directive obliges member countries (except the United Kingdom) to implement co-determination requirements for multinationals in their national legislation (Berentsen, 1995). Hence, international co-determination by a European works council or similar committee will become obligatory for multinationals.[36] The influence of this institution will be confined to information and consultation rights related to management decisions at the international level (Sanders, 1995). Of course, this directive will also alter the German legislation.

Fifthly, the scope of co-determination will be enhanced in the near future, because part-time workers as well as temporary workers through employment agencies will obtain the same status as full-time workers with respect to co-determination regulations. Nevertheless, the requirement of a minimal tenure before voting and membership rights become effective remains intact.

9.3.3 Assessment

The comparison of German and Dutch co-determination institutions shows that, from a broad international perspective, workers have a relatively strong voice in both countries. The significance of cooperative exchange between worker representatives and management corresponds with the features of the cooperative model (Section 8.1.7). Many aspects of co-determination are similar. For instance, co-decision rights are alike, since they apply to many matters of personnel policy except to wage bargaining. Moreover, in both countries the works council mainly has a passive role; initiatives are exceptional.

Yet, for three reasons worker influence is somewhat stronger in Germany. Firstly, the potential influence of works councils is relatively small in the Netherlands, since small firms (with less than 35 employees) are not required to have a works council, whereas Germany small firms are legally required to support the establishment of a works council.

Secondly, many aspects of German worker influence are more concentrated within the firm. Hence, works councillors do not need to share influence with external institutions. Firing procedures provide an example: a German employer informs the works council in advance in case of an individual dismissal, since works councillors have advisory rights. Moreover, in case of mass lay-offs, the works council negotiates about the contents of a social plan. In contrast, in the Netherlands the regional employment office determines whether individual dismissals are appropriate. In case of mass lay-offs, trade unions usually negotiate with the employer about a social plan. As another example, internal settlement boards arbitrate if the German works council and management disagree. In contrast, Dutch works councillors can make use of non-binding arbitration by committees in matters related to co-decision rights (Bedrijfscommissies). However,

[36] The new regulations will apply to multinationals (private or public sector companies) with 1000 employees or more, and at least 150 workers in two or more membership countries.

if arbitration is not successful they need to appeal in court. If disagreement is related to advisory rights, the Chamber of Company Law decides.

Thirdly, the legal basis of worker influence is stronger in Germany because some instruments of works councils are formalized in Germany but not in the Netherlands (Jacobi *et al.*, 1992). For instance, works councillors in Germany can conclude formal agreements that have a similar status as collective agreements. As another example, the internal settlement boards that solve disputes between managers and works councillors are required by law (Koene and Slomp, 1991). Yet, legislation is not a sufficient condition for worker influence at the work floor, because the government cannot control work-floor activities. The absence of works councils in smaller firms clearly illustrates this. However, legislation does provide workers with a powerful means to ensure that co-determination is effective in case of disagreements with management.

There is one aspect of Dutch co-determination institutions that gives workers a comparatively strong influence, namely the advisory rights of works councils. Works councillors can advise management to cancel a major investment project. Their advice can be enforced through the Chamber of Company Law, although this rarely happens in practice. Only if management has made procedural mistakes or has not carefully considered the position of all stakeholders, investment plans or re-organisations sometimes have to be cancelled, postponed or amended. Therefore, advisory rights do mainly imply that managers need to operate carefully in case of major investment plans or reorganisations.

The integrated character of German co-determination presents a mixed picture. Worker representation on the supervisory board facilitates access of employee representatives to information on the companies' financial and strategic planning (Turner, 1993). Moreover, compared to the Netherlands, communication between supervisory board members and works councillors is more common in Germany. In the Netherlands, works councillors, management and supervisory board members are required to organise meetings on a regular basis, but informal contacts between the works council and the supervisory board are much less common (Van het Kaar, 1995; Koene and Slomp, 1991).

However, the German situation shows that enterprise-level co-determination does not constitute the main channel for the advancement of worker interests. The objectives of worker representatives on the supervisory board are potentially conflicting. In particular, business policies that are in accordance with the long-run strategy of the firm may not agree with the protection of worker interests. Moreover, many companies have reduced the significance of the supervisory board meetings in order to limit the influence of worker representatives. Hence, joint representation diminishes the efficacy of the board.

In summary, German institutions to somewhat a larger extent promote the commitment within labour relationships through cooperative exchange between management and organized workers. However, future extensions of legal co-determination rights in the Netherlands will strengthen the influence of Dutch workers.

9.4 Policy Options

9.4.1 Policy Options for the Netherlands

Apprenticeships. The organization of German apprenticeships as a combination of learning in schools and in-company training seems particularly attractive. First, it is consistent with the trend towards more integration of work and learning. Second, the involvement of companies ensures that training enhances those skills that are in demand in the private sector. Third, screening of young workers by employers and job shopping by younger workers occur simultaneously with training. Hence, flexible contracts that allow screening and searching do not hurt the accumulation of skills, thereby reconciling flexibility and investment in human capital. Fourth, the screening of potential apprentices provides incentives for youngsters to perform well at school.

To encourage Dutch firms to invest more in portable training[37], two main elements seem important. First, cofinancing of workers should be increased, thereby boosting the returns of the firm on apprenticeship contracts. Collective labour agreements may have to provide more flexibility to adjust apprenticeship wages to training costs and the situation in the labour market. Cofinancing of workers is especially important if certificated skills make these skills more easily portable across firms and industries, thereby facilitating job mobility.[38]

However, the use of the competitive coordination mechanism in the form of cofinancing of workers is subject to limitations. In particular, given their limited collateral, young workers have only limited access to capital markets and hence cannot resort to borrowing to finance investment in their human capital. Accordingly, further developing institutions based on cooperative exchange that protect firms from poaching is called for. This would allow firms to reap a larger part of the return on their investments in workers. Dutch employers organizations can play an important role in discouraging poaching and in providing advice about and monitoring a company's training performance. Also compulsory extension of training provisions in collective labour agreements can prevent free-rider behaviour

---

[37] This portable component of training (e.g., the ability to learn) is likely to become increasingly important in the future as firm-specific skills age faster due to rapid technological change and a more volatile economic environment.

[38] More certification of skills should increase the value of the investment from the worker's point of view. However, increasing the transparency of the labour market through more certification may reduce the value of training to the employer because it increases the risk that trained workers leave the company.

of individual firms.[39] More generally, the industrial relationships between social partners in the Dutch consultation economy can facilitate the strengthening of institutions addressing market failures. Indeed, the consultation economy could be a fertile soil for developing new mixes of the coordination mechanisms of control, cooperative exchange, and competition.

German experience also shows that the apprenticeship system should be diverse enough to be attractive for a wide ability range. In particular, in Germany low achievers still have relatively easy access to the system. Moreover, the German system appeals also to high achievers.

Collective Extension. In Germany, separate collective labour agreements for wages and general labour conditions allow collective extension to be confined to general labour conditions. In the Netherlands, in contrast, collective extension usually relates to an integrated collective agreement, covering both wages and other labour conditions. This allows less scope to deal with firm-specific conditions and preferences. Moreover, the compulsory extension is not limited to provisions involving positive externalities across firms, but also restrains competition in wage formation.

Co-determination. Theoretical arguments and case-studies support the view that co-determination can improve firm performance in the long run. Hence, the recent extensions of co-determination in the Netherlands are not expected to hamper the performance of established firms, although co-determination may reduce external flexibility somewhat by protecting the position of the insiders within the firm.

9.4.2 Policy Options for Germany

Short-time Work. The German labour market relies more heavily on internal rather than external flexibility. Extensive short-time work provisions provide working-hour flexibility. In principle, short-time work can combine the advantages of flexibility and commitment. In practice, however, the efficiency of short-time work is often doubtful, because it can result in a subsidy on loss-making activities, thereby hampering employment flows towards more profitable activities.

More Flexibility. The Dutch system results in a mix between flexibility and commitment, whereas the German system remains more oriented towards commitment. The social and international trends towards individualisation, more

---

[39] Another way to internalize the external effects of imparting general skills is to provide tax incentives. However, the government may find it difficult to check whether companies do indeed provide training. In this way, asymmetric information may give rise to rentseeking.

volatility, and more heterogeneity suggest that a mix of commitment and flexibility will tend to be better able to deal with the new economic environment than a strong reliance on commitment alone. With respect to labour market regulations, the main differences between Germany and the Netherlands are the more extensive use of short-time work in Germany, versus the greater popularity of part-time work and flexibility through flexible contracts (especially through a temporary work agencies or TWAs) in the Netherlands. More liberal regulations with respect to the use of flexible contracts in Germany could increase the access of unskilled workers to the labour market. Moreover, more flexible contracts may meet the more heterogeneous needs of employers and workers. Not only a more flexible labour market but also deregulation of sheltered sectors may enhance the access of vulnerable groups to work.

Collective Bargaining. With respect to wage formation, the Dutch system involves a "pragmatic" mixture between commitment and flexibility and between centralization and decentralization. Consensus-building (or overt coordination) at the centralized level makes labour relations at the firm level less confrontational, improves the internalization of external effects and strengthens commitment. A number of firm-level agreements can account for firm-specific conditions and preferences, although these agreements are still influenced by the central level. In addition, some scope for firm-specific variations in sectoral agreements renders the system of collective bargaining more flexible.

In Germany, sectoral collective bargaining is less strongly influenced by overt coordination at a centralized level. This hampers the internalization of external effects and may reduce the sensitivity of wage formation to the unemployment level. Rather, it may induce leapfrogging, by giving leading sectors a large autonomy in collective bargaining. Since Germany is much larger than the Netherlands and hence features more diversity, part of the centralized coordination could occur at the regional rather than the national level. This would allow for more experimentation and diversity as regional actors could adjust to regional circumstances (see also Chapter 5). Moreover, the building of consensus tends to be easier at a lower level. In order to ensure that regional agents internalize the effects of their bargain on the unemployment level, the regional level may have to assume a larger budget responsibility for unemployment insurance.

Firm-level agreements are currently less popular in Germany than in the Netherlands. Only the trend towards firm-level variation within sectoral agreements, for instance concerning working-time provisions, is similar. The German system thus captures neither the advantages of centralization nor those of decentralized wage bargaining. Hence, more scope for firm-specific and regional-specific variations in sectoral agreements is desirable in order to arrive at a better mix of the coordination mechanisms of competition and corporative exchange. Various trends and the need for regional differentiation after German unification demand more flexibility, diversity, and experimentation in collective bargaining.

Table 9.7 Performance, main findings

	US	Ger	Neth
	relative performance (−−, −, + or ++)		
Quantity			
net participation	+	−	−
working hours per head	+	−	−−
low long-term unemployment	+	−	−
Quality			
current educational attainment level	++	+	−
vocational skills	−	++	+
match between education and work	−	++	+
employee training courses	-	+	++
avoiding poverty	−	+	+

9.4.3 The Unfinished Agenda

Table 9.7 summarizes the main findings regarding labour market activity and quality in the context of a comparison with the performance of the US labour market. The American labour market performs well in stimulating activity. In Germany and the Netherlands, labour-force participation is still quite low as vulnerable groups have only limited access to work. This is reflected in the high share of the long-term unemployed in overall unemployment. If expressed in working hours per head, activity is at a low level in Germany but especially in the Netherlands, reflecting a larger share of part-time work.

Labour-force participation in Germany and the Netherlands can be increased through three channels: First, activating people drawing on social security (see Chapter 6); second, increasing the effective retirement age (Chapter 7); and third, increasing average working hours per worker.

The popularity of part-time work in the Netherlands provides working-hour flexibility and, according to survey information, often corresponds with worker preferences. However, many small jobs depress the Dutch overall activity level. Moreover, the current preferences for (small) part-time jobs may be influenced by the current regulations that hamper a combination of work and care and by a high wedge on additional labour income. To encourage labour supply and boost the tax base of the government, a further reduction of the overall tax burden would be welcome. A lower aggregate tax burden would reconcile the need to, on the one hand, increase the access to work of low-skilled labour by reducing tax rates in lower incomes and, on the other hand, encourage workers to increase their working hours by reducing marginal tax rates. In this connection, lower marginal tax rates could help to boost labour supply of women and to increase the effective retirement age.

10 Corporate Governance

Why does this study focus on corporate governance: the institutions that govern stakeholder relationships between management, shareholders and creditors? Two reasons motivate the analysis. First, corporate governance institutions are important for company performance. Because of conflicting objectives of various agents and the incompleteness of contracts, corporate governance institutions are needed to strengthen company performance. Second, these institutions differ across countries, in particular between the United States and Germany. So a comparative study may provide scope to learn about the impact of such institutions.

Being hired to run the company, managers constitute the primary decision-making unit of a limited liability company. They operate far from autonomously, however, but depend on shareholders and creditors for the survival of the company.[1] These stakeholders all strive for the continuity and prosperity of the firm, because they have invested in the company. Nevertheless, they have partly conflicting interests. For instance, in case of financial difficulties, shareholders may opt for a risky strategy. Creditors, however, may prefer quick liquidation, whereas managers may aim to safeguard their position. Stakeholders can opportunistically pursue private goals, because bounded rationality makes the contracts between the stakeholders of a company incomplete (see Section 2.1.2). Hence, institutions are needed to ensure stakeholders that their interests are taken into account. This makes company performance dependent on the design of corporate governance institutions.

International differences between the Anglo-American, German and Dutch corporate governance institutions provide scope to learn. In Anglo-American countries, shareholders and creditors govern management mainly through external control. In Germany, in contrast, internal control through long-term relationships between management, shareholders and banks stands out. The Dutch system holds a position in between these extremes.

---

[1] This chapter focuses on stakeholder relationships with financiers. Additional stakeholders of a company are employees, suppliers, procuring firms, competing firms and consumers; see Chapter 9 for the relationships with employees.

The structure of this chapter is as follows. To start with, Section 10.1 addresses the analytical framework. Subsequently, Section 10.2 compares corporate governance institutions. Finally, Section 10.3 presents the policy options from the analytical framework and international comparison.

10.1 Analytical Framework

The analytical framework provides the theoretical background for this chapter. It starts in Section 10.1.1 with an explanation of stakeholder objectives. Next, Section 10.1.2 describes two stylized institutional models. They represent extreme positions on the trade-off between flexibility and commitment. Finally, Section 10.1.3 gives an overview of the main strengths and weaknesses of both models.

10.1.1 Stakeholder Objectives

Shareholders and Creditors. What are the objectives of investors? The interests of the two categories of providers of external financial capital, shareholders and creditors, diverge to some extent (Prowse, 1994). Shareholders, the owners of the company, exert a residual claim on the profits of the firm (Box 10.1). In an efficient stock market, they receive the highest return on their investment if the value of the firm's equity is maximized. They benefit most from successful high-risk strategies, while the costs of bankruptcy in case of total failure of high-risk strategies are divided between shareholders and creditors. Therefore, influential shareholders may try to persuade the firm to engage in risky strategies. Moreover, when shareholders lack sufficient information about possible long-term gains of investment projects, they may attach a greater value to projects with short-term returns than to strategies with a long-term horizon. This type of myopic shareholder behaviour indicates stock market inefficiency, because shareholders with full information would invest in profitable long-term projects (Nickell, 1995; Gelauff and Den Broeder, 1996: 35-37).

Creditors, in contrast, never make a higher return than repayment including interest, and thus aim at maximizing the probability to be repaid in full. They are best off if the firm minimizes the possibility of a bankruptcy, are less inclined to invest in risky projects, but encourage management strategies with a high probability of return.

Management. What are the objectives of management and how do they relate to the objectives of investors? The general objective of management follows from the separation between equity ownership and management control (Box 10.1). Being hired by shareholders to exercise residual control, managers should maximize the residual returns of shareholders, which equals the value of equity or the discounted sum of future profits (Monks and Minow, 1995: 41).

Box 10.1 Aspects of ownership

From an economic point of view, two crucial aspects of ownership are the right on residual returns and the right of residual control (Milgrom and Roberts, 1992: 289-293). Both these aspects follow from the incompleteness of contracts: in a world of comprehensive contracts the complete allocation of revenues and the full division of control rights would be specified contractually.

The ***right on residual returns*** *specifies that owners exert a residual claim on the operating revenues of a firm. From its operating revenues, the firm has to pay rents to other stakeholders, i.e. wages for its workers, interest on loans and payments to suppliers. The remaining profits can be used to pay dividends to owners or to finance investments. Investments raise future revenues and in that way indirectly benefit owners as well. However, if revenues fall short of wages, interest payments and costs of supplies, the company will not pay any dividends and losses will reduce the owners' wealth.*

The ***right of residual control*** *entails the right to make any decisions concerning the asset's use after all legal and contractual obligations have been fulfilled. Hence, residual control of a firm's assets is permitted only in so far as control is not restricted by law or other contracts.*

On the one hand, to properly take advantage of opportunities, managers need sufficient freedom to act (Blair, 1995: 32). Too much influence of shareholders with a short time horizon may lower the equity value of the company. Managers may focus on strategies with visible short-term returns, instead of exploiting their information advantage to engage in strategies that increase the equity value of the company in the longer run (Nickell, 1995). Likewise, too much creditor influence may induce a risk-averse strategy and also reduce the equity value of the company.

On the other hand, too high a degree of managerial discretion provides opportunities for managers to depart from value-maximization in order to pursue their own private goals. These goals involve the spending of free cash flow[2] within the company and the protection of their own position within the firm. Managers may indulge in empire-building, which includes investments in large offices, in staff departments or in R&D activities, launching of over-extensive advertising campaigns or acquisitions (Prowse, 1994; Yafeh and Yosha, 1995). To safeguard their position, managers can entrench themselves in the company by writing contracts or making investments, which raise the costs of replacing them (Shleifer and Vishny, 1989; OECD, 1996). Examples are golden parachute contracts, binding of valuable employees to managers instead of to the company, or excessive expansion of current lines-of-business and aversion to new activities if current operations correspond best to the management abilities of the incumbent management.

[2] Free cash flow constitutes earnings of the company in excess of the funds needed for investments in projects with a positive net present value.

Opportunistic management behaviour primarily harms shareholders' interests, because creditors are protected by a fixed interest rate. The existence of debt finance may even discipline management, because obligatory interest repayments constrain the residual control span of managers and reduce their scope to pursue private gains (Hart, 1995; Scholtens, 1996). Yet, also a lending relationship is not free from possible exploitation (Van Damme, 1994). Management may not use a loan for the purpose it indicated by application, but instead finance projects that yield high private gains. This may harm creditors because the chance of a default or a bankruptcy increases and because the agreed interest rate does not reflect the actual risk associated with the loan.

10.1.2 Two Stylized Models of Corporate Governance

Corporate governance institutions align the partly conflicting goals of managers, shareholders and creditors. Putting too much emphasis on the objectives of one of these groups of stakeholders may hamper company performance. The purpose of corporate governance institutions is to ensure stakeholders that their interests will be adequately considered. The competitive model and the cooperative model represent two extreme ways to deal with partly conflicting stakeholder objectives (Figure 10.1). In many respects, the competitive model can be considered as a stylized version of Anglo-American institutions. The cooperative model, in contrast, can be associated with the German system of corporate governance.[3]

The Competitive Model. The competitive model solves potential conflicts between stakeholders by delegation of responsibility and by coordination through competition. Managerial discretion and external control characterize this model. Financial investors delegate a large degree of autonomy to the management team for a certain period of time. Management can flexibly re-allocate resources to maximize the value of the company's equity, without direct involvement of investors. In turn, financial investors can also flexibly re-allocate their resources. If management performance is disappointing, investors switch their resources to better performing companies. In addition, if investors do not agree with corporate strategies they may even replace management through a hostile takeover. Thus, management teams from different companies permanently compete for financial resources. By consequence, competition and flexibility of both management and financial investors characterize the competitive model.

Three types of institutions strengthen the degree of external shareholder control. First, the stock market is easily accessible and transparent. Institutions ensure the transparency of trading through extensive accounting rules, large fines on the use

[3] See De Jong (1991), Bishop (1994), Moerland (1995), Nickell (1995) for features of both systems.

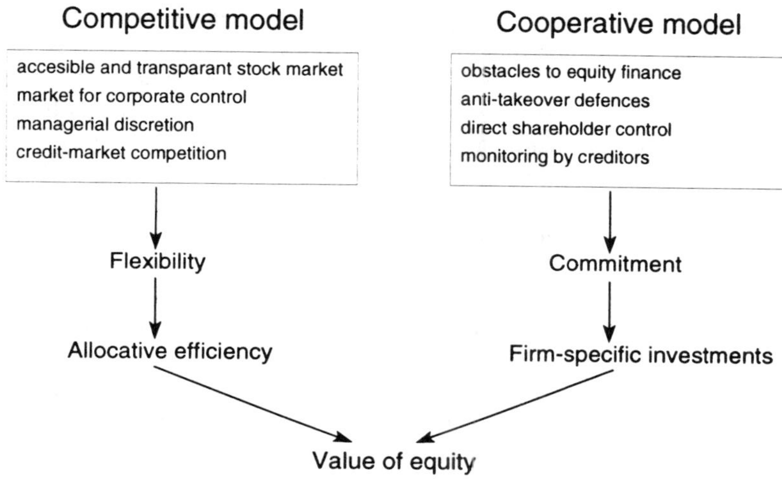

Figure 10.1 Institutional models, behaviour and performance

of insider information and strict disclosure requirements (OECD, 1996: 128). This facilitates screening and monitoring by (potential) investors. Second, extensive managerial shareholdings aim to persuade managers to act in the interest of shareholders. Third, on the market for corporate control, shareholders, frequently the management of another company, can replace management through a hostile takeover. Regulations constrain protective measures of management against hostile bids.

Although shareholders can exert a strong influence through the stock market and the market for corporate control, direct shareholder influence on management decisions is only limited. The Chief Executive Officer (CEO) runs the company as highest manager in charge and has substantial freedom to act. Opportunities to influence management by voice are costly for individual investors with a relatively small stock of shares (Blair, 1995: 76). External effects related to individual monitoring induce free-rider behaviour. As this model discourages concentrated shareholdings,[4] the scope for direct shareholder monitoring is limited. In addition, strict insider trading rules hamper informal communication between shareholders and management (Fukao, 1995). Still, shareholders may exert some influence

[4] To prevent monopoly power of large investors, regulations constrain the holdings of large blocks of shares. In particular, antitrust law and dividend tax rules discourage cross holdings of shares between large companies. Moreover, securities laws restrict investors with concentrated share holdings from active involvement in corporate policies.

through the board of directors, because they have the formal right to elect this board. The main functions of the board of directors are to select, evaluate and dismiss the CEO and senior executives, to review financial objectives and strategies of the company, and to counsel top management (Monks and Minow, 1995: 183). However, the task of the board of directors as a monitor on behalf of shareholders is limited. The board of directors and management are strongly linked. The CEO is often also the chairman of the board, and a considerable number of board members are company managers (Gelauff and Den Broeder, 1996: 28-29; OECD, 1996).

External control characterizes also the corporate governance role of creditors. Accounting rules facilitate screening and enhance monitoring possibilities of creditors. If screening or monitoring results are disappointing, creditors may raise risk premia, demand collateral or ration debt finance. Yet, they have little direct influence on corporate strategies. Especially American banks face strong restrictions. Regulations do not allow banks to provide more than 15% of their capital to a single borrower (OECD, 1996: 136)[5] and banks are prohibited to hold any shares on their own account (the Glass-Steagall Act of 1933, OECD, 1995b: 75). This prevents them from being active investors. Even in case of severe financial difficulties, the direct influence of creditors is limited, because regulations shield the current management team from creditor claims (OECD, 1996: 141; Fukao, 1995: 40). This encourages high risk strategies that reduce the chance of creditors to be repaid in full.

The Cooperative Model. The cooperative model aims to align conflicting interests through direct consultation and involvement of a limited number of stakeholders. Internal control and long-term relationships characterize this model. Cooperative exchange coordinates decisions between management and financial investors with a long-term attachment to the company.

Internal control by shareholders is substantial. Concentrated shareholdings give an incentive to monitor firms, through voting rights on the general meeting and through representation on the supervisory board. Limited liability companies are usually[6] organized according to a two-tier principle: a supervisory board exerts control over the management board. The two-tier structure helps shareholders to use voice and increases their access to firm-specific information. In addition, shareholders also get firm-specific information from other companies or research institutes with close relationships to the firm (Carlin and Soskice, 1997).

In this model, creditors exert direct influence as well. Bank intermediation is extensive and regulations enable banks to act as active investors. Bank intermediat-

---

[5] In Germany, this upper limit amounts to 50 percent (OECD, 1996: 136).

[6] In Germany, it depends on the legal form and size of the company whether a two tier structure is obligatory (see Section 10.2.1).

ion in debt finance facilitates risk diversification and reduces the external effects of monitoring of firms by a large number of small lenders. Close and long-term bank-firm relationships may develop, in which banks have more intensive contacts with a firm, gain access to tacit firm-specific information and more directly influence management.

Regulations strengthen the role of banks as active investors. First, in case of severe financial difficulties, bankruptcy laws give creditors priority over most other stakeholders (Fukao, 1995). Moreover, banks can both grant loans to a firm and own part of its equity. Hence, they can apply their influence as shareholders also to benefit their creditor position. In particular German universal banks play a prominent role in corporate governance, as they combine concentrated debt claims with shareholdings. On the one hand, this may enhance bank influence, because it creates economies of scale in screening and monitoring and solves conflicts of interests between creditors and providers of equity (Stiglitz, 1985; Prowse, 1994).[7] On the other hand, it may weaken the disciplining effect of the lending position of the bank (Boot, 1994): the threat of withdrawal of a loan becomes less credible, since a withdrawal would harm the value of the bank's shareholdings.

In contrast, the stock market plays a relatively unimportant role. This can be related to past and current legal obstacles restricting access to non-bank sources of finance and to lack of market transparency. For instance, accounting information in Germany is more relevant to tax policy than to the purpose of obtaining a proper insight in the equity value of a company. Until their removal at the end of 1991 authorization requirements on issuance of shares and taxation of securities raised the costs of equity compared to debt financing (Prowse, 1994: 27). Disclosure requirements were relatively permissive and legislation prohibiting insider trading has only recently been established. External control weakens further because the market for corporate control is virtually non-existent. Concentrated holdings of shares in the hands of founding families or enterprises, and bank control of voting rights at general meetings through proxy votes reduce the chance of a hostile bidder to acquire a majority of votes. In addition, regulations with respect to the number of votes required to replace management shield companies from hostile takeovers.

10.1.3 Strengths and Weaknesses of Both Models

The Competitive model. Extensive equity finance encourages risk-taking in the competitive model. The liquidity of the stock market allows shareholders to diversify risks and promotes the swift re-allocation of financial capital. Hence, the model performs well in moving capital out of declining sectors into promising new sectors and start-up firms. Also debt finance is characterized by strong competition

---

[7] In Chapter 2 this is referred to as the ownership solution.

Table 10.1 Strengths of the two models

	Competitive model	Cooperative model
Dominant type of finance	equity finance promotes risk taking	debt finance disciplines management
Equity finance	enhances flexible re-allocation promotes start-up activity	supports long-term finance promotes firm-specific investments
Debt finance	promotes flexible re-allocation	close relationships may reduce risk aversion and benefit existing SMEs

and flexible re-allocation. These characteristics explain that risk-taking and external flexibility are the strong features of the competitive model (Table 10.1).

The flexible re-allocation of the competitive model promotes the finance of new activities in start-up companies. The accessible and liquid stock market makes risk-taking finance easily available for innovating start-up companies and gives investors an incentive to finance these companies by facilitating risk diversification. For technostarters with an exceptional risk that the regular stock market tends to refuse, specialized financial instruments provide start-up finance by screening companies and diversifying risks over this market segment. In the United States, venture capital provides finance to these types of companies (OECD, 1995b: 76). American venture capital companies benefit from the well-developed stock market, to reap the benefits of their investments by converting venture capital into equity after a number of years.

However, a lack of stakeholder commitment constitutes the crucial drawback of this model (Nickell, 1995). Little institutional support of informal agreements creates a hold-up problem, which hampers direct involvement of shareholders in the company's financial conditions. Limited direct involvement reduces the possibility for shareholders to acquire firm-specific information. This discourages investments in projects with less visible, long-term results. Moreover, because shareholders cannot easily use voice they will sooner use their exit option: instead of supporting managers who encounter problems and may need more time, they abandon the firm by selling their shares (Porter, 1992; Blair, 1995: 136; OECD, 1995b: 83). Selling does not entail a substantial loss of relationship-specific assets, because shareholders have made little firm-specific investments in screening and monitoring. The threat of a hostile takeover further hampers shareholder commitment to the current management team and stimulates managers to focus on short-term results.

Analogously, the credit market is characterized by a lack of long-term relationships. Arm's length financing benefits companies that can signal their creditworthiness or are able to put up collateral, but the lack of close relationships puts SMEs without a strong reputation or sufficient fixed assets to put up as collateral at a disadvantage.

The lack of long-term implicit contracts between shareholders, creditors and management hampers also a credible commitment of management to other stakeholders. In particular, management in this system has difficulty in offering a commitment to employees and suppliers, because their own relationships with shareholders and creditors are unstable (Blair, 1995; Fukao, 1995: 42-43). For instance, the threat of a hostile takeover undermines investments of employees in firm-specific skills (Carlin and Soskice, 1997). This adds to the lack of commitment to workers created by the work governance structures of the competitive model (compare Chapter 9).[8]

The Cooperative Model. The cooperative model, in contrast, provides long-term finance and encourages firm-specific investments (Table 10.1). The institutional support of direct involvement of shareholders in corporate strategies diminishes the hold-up problem and thus lowers information asymmetries between shareholders and management. This reduces shareholders' short-term orientation by giving insight into the potential gains of long-term investments. Moreover, this model enables shareholders to use voice instead of exit options. Incentives and possibilities to monitor make shareholders less willing to leave the firm and lose the returns to their firm-specific screening and monitoring investments. They want to continue their relationship with the firm so as to capture the benefits, because the costs of their firm-specific investments are irrecoverable once made (sunk costs). This strengthens shareholder commitment and enables management to focus on longer-term projects and make firm specific investments, for instance in their relationships with shareholders. Hence, support of commitment is the strong feature of this model.

The greater importance of debt finance in this model also strengthens commitment. Close bank-firm relationships discipline management and reduce the information asymmetry between creditors and management. By consequence, the risk-aversion of banks may fall and their willingness to finance longer-term projects increases, unless a bank becomes so influential that it can opportunistically pursue its own goals (Gelauff and Den Broeder, 1996: 64). This points to the importance of a sufficient degree of competition among banks in this model. SMEs particularly benefit from close bank-firm relationships, because they have less opportunities to attract equity finance or to signal their creditworthiness through credit ratings, or to put up collateral (Van Damme, 1994: 21).[9] For large established companies, empirical evidence for Germany concludes that banks improve firm performance because they partake in the network of cross-share-

---

[8] See Gelauff and Den Broeder (1996) for an overview of inter-firm relationships.

[9] Admittance criteria, for instance a minimum enterprise age and a minimum size of the equity capital, hamper stock market access of smaller firms. In addition, young small firms have had less scope to raise equity through retained profits (OECD, 1995b).

holdings, but empirical studies do not find an additional influence of the combination of equity and debt finance by banks (Gorton and Schmid, 1996).

Yet, this model suffers from inflexibility and risk-aversion. The focus on long-term relationships tends to make the re-allocation of financial capital too rigid. Therefore, unprofitable investment projects may not be terminated quickly enough and start-up companies may have difficulty to establish themselves in the system of long-term relationships with investors (Fukao, 1995: 70). In this way, rigidities also hamper employment opportunities in new enterprises. Moreover, long-term relationships with block shareholders hinder investments in uncertain risky projects, because uncertainty makes it inherently impossible to assess the expected returns to these kinds of investments. Therefore, long-term shareholders do not benefit from a reduction of information asymmetries with managers, because managers are also very uncertain. On the contrary, risks incorporated in these projects frequently discourage block shareholders to put their reputations at stake by providing equity finance (Jenkinson and Mayer, 1992). In addition, the more dominant position of debt finance may cause risk-aversion, because creditors, even if they have a long-term relationship with the company, are more interested in certain fixed returns than in higher residual returns.

Balancing Strengths and Weaknesses. Because of their distinct strengths and weaknesses, superiority of one of the two stylized models cannot be established (see also Jenkinson and Mayer 1992; Fukao, 1995). Corporate governance institutions of the cooperative model strengthen the commitment of stakeholders not to exploit each other. Yet, these institutions limit flexible market transactions by making stakeholders more dependent on the continuity of their relationship with the company. This signifies the existence of a trade-off between the flexibility and commitment of stakeholder relationships (compare Chapter 2).[10]

Conditions. Institutions should strike an adequate institutional balance between flexibility and commitment. This balance is not constant over time and across industries, but depends on the economic environment. Some technologies benefit from long-term relationships, whereas others benefit from flexibility (Franks and Mayer, 1995). More specifically, the relevance of the competitive versus the cooperative model depends on preferences, the type of technological change, type of company and the product market environment (Table 10.2).

In contrast to the cooperative model, the competitive model thrives in a heterogeneous and risk-loving environment. Diverse preferences and a heterogeneous population ask for efficient allocation. A risk-loving environment concurs with the competitive model being more conducive to risk compared with the cooperative model. If people easily start-up entrepreneurial activities or if firms

[10] Gilson (1995) derives a similar trade-off between commitment and adaptability.

Table 10.2 Economic conditions supporting the two models

	Competitive model	Cooperative model
Preferences	risk taking, heterogeneous	risk averse, homogeneous
Technological change	radical, marketable knowledge	incremental, firm-specific knowledge
Types of companies	start-up firms	established firms
Product market environment	volatile, competitive	stable, economies of scale, sunk costs

easily switch between activities, merge or outsource activities, they demand a flexible financial system. In addition, heterogeneity makes it difficult to support commitment, because more possibilities exist to renege on informal agreements and diversity complicates monitoring of informal agreements. In contrast, relatively homogeneous preferences in a risk-averse and stable environment more easily support commitment in the cooperative model.

Technological development through radical innovations supports the competitive model (Carlin and Soskice, 1997). Radical innovations make use of marketable assets, such as general human capital or external know-how, rather than firm-specific assets and knowledge that needs to be developed internally (OECD, 1995b: 61, 87). Because of their use of marketable assets and relatively high risks, radical innovations demand flexible financial institutions and a high amount of risk finance. Moreover, the availability of equity finance for new activities promotes the spread of new technologies through the economy. Flexibility is a strong asset in a quickly changing, competitive and diffusion-oriented environment of enterprises (Hellwig, 1995).

In contrast, incremental technological change within established companies and the need to meet idiosyncratic customer requirements, shifts the balance towards the long-term finance opportunities and long-term customer-relationships of the cooperative model (Jenkinson and Mayer, 1992; Carlin and Soskice, 1997). Active block shareholders are better able to assess the risk and expected returns from incremental rather than radical innovations and therefore are more willing to provide equity finance. Analogously, long-term relationships with banks may strengthen the focus on incremental innovations. Close relationships increase the willingness of banks to finance long-term projects, but debt finance reduces the scope to finance more risky radical innovations. Long-term customer relationships enable companies to design products tailored to the needs of a procuring company, because the associated investment in firm-specific knowledge requires corporate governance institutions that enhance commitment.

The exploitation and development of firm-specific knowledge within established companies makes the cooperative model more suitable to a stable product market environment with economies of scale. These features add to the impact of other institutions. A well-developed system of vocational training, technology policy, employment protection regulations and co-determination arrangements, also support the specialisation on innovations that rest on the internal development and use of firm-specific assets (Carlin and Soskice, 1997; see also Chapter 9).

10.2 Corporate Governance in Germany and the Netherlands

The objective of this section is twofold. First, it provides a more detailed picture of the actual German institutions. Most characteristics of the German institutional system are consistent with the stylized characteristics of the cooperative model. Yet, some recent institutional changes imply a moderate shift towards the competitive model. Second, it analyzes the position of Dutch corporate governance institutions on the trade-off between flexibility and commitment. To address both issues, Sections 10.2.1 and 10.2.2 compare the extent of internal and external shareholder control. Subsequently, Sections 10.2.3 and 10.2.4 turn to the corporate governance role of banks and pension funds, respectively.

10.2.1 Internal Shareholder Control

Internal control of shareholders takes place through voting at the general meeting of shareholders, using voice through the supervisory board, or informally approaching management. Hence, both the ownership structure of shares and the extent of supervisory board influence determine the incentives and scope to monitor.

Ownership Structure. Concentrated shareholdings provide stronger direct monitoring incentives for German shareholders compared to the Netherlands. Small shareholders have little incentives to invest in acquiring information and direct monitoring. In contrast, shareholders with concentrated shareholdings and commercial ties to the company have greater opportunities to influence management by voice. This puts German shareholders at an advantage. In Germany, non-financial enterprises and banks own relatively large percentage of shares. Moreover, their shareholdings are far more concentrated than in the other countries of reference (see Table 10.3). Information on the cross shareholdings among the largest 100 enterprises in Germany further illustrates this (Figure 10.2). For 46 of these companies, at least some shares are in the hands of other companies of this group. For a substantial number (24) the percentage of shares held by large companies lies in the range of 20% to 50%, and four companies are almost completely owned by other companies from the largest 100. In the Netherlands, the direct monitoring role of non-financial companies and banks is relatively modest and shareholdings are widely dispersed. The share ownership of pension funds is increasing, however, as well as their monitoring activities (Section 10.2.4). In the

Table 10.3 Distribution of share ownership, 1993

	Germany	Netherlands	United Kingdom	United States
Ownership of shares (%)[a]				
–households	16.6	20.0	17.7	50.2
–non-financial enterprises	38.8	9.6	3.1	14.1
–banks	14.2	0.7	0.6	0.0
–investment funds	7.6	1.5	9.7	5.7
–pension funds	1.9	7.9	34.2	20.1
–insurance companies	5.2	5.5	17.2	4.6
–government	3.4	0.0	1.3	0.0
–foreign	12.2	54.8	16.3	5.4
Share of largest shareholder[b]				
> 25%	85.	–	13.	–
> 50%	57.	22.	6.	–
> 75%	22.	–	1.	–

[a] Source: Germany, 1993, Deutsche Bundesbank (1994: 68, 69) and CEPS (1995: 31, 32); the Netherlands, 1993, CPB extension of Swank *et al.* (1989); United Kingdom, 1993, CEPS (1995: 13) and OECD (1995b: 88); United States, 1990, Prowse (1994: 21).

[b] % of large firms in which the share of the largest shareholder exceeds 25, 50, 75%. Source: Germany and the United Kingdom, Franks and Mayer (1993); the Netherlands Cantrijn *et al* (1993: 47).

United States, households still hold the largest proportion of all equity, and cross-shareholdings are limited (OECD, 1996). However, institutional shareholdings have also become more important over time, and especially pension funds have become more active (OECD, 1996).

The German Supervisory Board. The German two-tier system is obligatory for all public limited liability companies (AGs) and for private limited liability companies (GmbHs) with more than 500 employees. Expressed as a share of employees, this model applies to approximately half of all limited liability companies.[11] The remaining half generally have a managing director, who is directly responsible to shareholders. Yet, they are free to install an advisory board (Beirat), which provides advisory services to management, or to install a supervisory board voluntarily.

---

[11] Approximately 54% of all employees works in a limited liability company, and approximately 27% of employees works for a company where the two-tier system is obligatory. Sources: Statistisches Bundesamt, 1994, Streeck, 1984, see Gelauff and Den Broeder, 1996: 51.

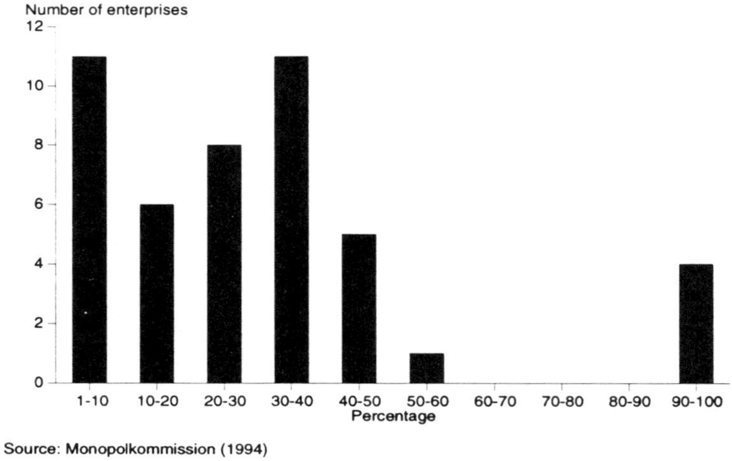

Figure 10.2 German largest 100 enterprises distributed by the percentage of shares owned by other enterprises among the largest 100.

The supervisory board (Aufsichtsrat) combines shareholder control with employee co-determination (compare Section 9.3). In companies with 500 to 2000 employees, two thirds of the seats of the supervisory board are assigned to shareholders' representatives.[12] In companies employing over 2000 workers,[13] seats are divided evenly over shareholders' and workers' representatives. Shareholders' representatives elect the chairman of the supervisory board, who has a casting vote in case of a voting deadlock.[14]

The main task of the supervisory board is to exert control over the management board (Vorstand). Supervisory board members monitor financial conditions, ratify important investment decisions or acquisitions and approve the annual profit-and-

---

[12] Small public companies (with less than 500 employees) founded before 10 August 1994 are also required to have employee representatives on their supervisory board. The 1994 Law on Small Public Companies and Deregulation of Equity Legislation has abolished this requirement for newly founded small public enterprises in order to make it more attractive for small and medium sized enterprises (SMEs) to become a public company.

[13] By law the total number of seats on the supervisory board equals 12 for companies with 2000 – 10,000 employees, 16 for companies with 10,000 – 20,000 employees and 20 for companies with over 20,000 employees (Edwards and Fischer, 1994: 78).

[14] This right is laid down in the 1976 Codetermination Act. The only exception to this rule are companies in the coal and steel sector (Streeck, 1984: 401). The earlier 1951 Codetermination Act obliges supervisory boards of these companies to coopt an additional member to prevent a deadlock of votes.

loss statement, balance sheet and the amount of dividend pay-outs (Table 10.4). To this aim, the chairman of the supervisory board is usually informed and consulted by management at least once a month (Edwards and Fischer, 1994: 210).

Only in public companies, supervisory board members also control the composition of the management board. They appoint managers and can dismiss them for a major cause, like neglect of duty or loss of confidence (Charkham, 1994: 22, Edwards and Fischer, 1994: 191). In private limited liability companies, in contrast, the general meeting of shareholders rather than the supervisory board has the right to appoint and dismiss managers (Edwards and Fischer, 1994: 79).

Management generally does not feel unduly constrained by the supervisory board (Lane, 1992: 78). The board does not have a right of initiative: it can not impose alternative strategies on the management board. Moreover, a number of important management decisions are often not presented to the supervisory board. According to Gerum *et al.* (1988), only in less than 20% of large public companies the supervisory boards must approve the general product or market strategy or investment finance plans. Finally, in 86% of the companies the supervisory board meets only the legal minimum of twice a year.

The Dutch Supervisory Board. The presence and tasks of the Dutch supervisory board depend on the size and ownership structure of the limited liability company. Accordingly, three types of supervisory board systems can be distinguished: the structural model, the "mitigated" structural model and the common model (Table 10.4).

The structural model makes the presence of a supervisory board obligatory and gives this board most influence. This model applies to limited liability companies that fulfil three criteria: a subscribed capital of at least 25 million guilders, at least 100 employees employed in the Netherlands, and the presence of a works council.[15] Companies that fulfil the three criteria but are a subsidiary of a structural holding company are exempted from the structural model. According to a rough estimate, approximately 37% of employment in private or public limited liability companies fulfils these criteria (Statistics Netherlands, see Gelauff and Den Broeder, 1996: 51). As a share of the number of Dutch listed public companies, almost two thirds belongs to the structural model (Corporate Governance Committee, 1996: 36).

Four features characterize the supervisory board (Raad van Commissarissen) of the structural model. Firstly, its members are appointed by cooption, i.e. members of the seated supervisory board elect new members. Yet, shareholders, workers and management have some influence on the process of cooption. The general meeting

[15] Honée, 1986; Voogd, 1989; Rietkerk, 1992, Van het Kaar, 1995.

Table 10.4 Presence, composition and tasks of the supervisory board

	Germany			Netherlands		
type of limited liability company	public	private large[a]	small	structural	structural mitigated	common
Presence obligatory	yes	yes	no	yes	yes	no
Composition	elected	elected	elected	coopted	coopted	elected
Tasks						
– monitor and ratify	yes	yes	limited	yes	yes	yes
– determine statement of account	yes	yes	no	yes	no	no
– appoint management	yes	no	no	yes	no	no

[a] More than 500 employees.

of shareholders and the works council can propose or reject new board members.[16] The management board (Raad van Bestuur) merely has a right to propose new members, but in practice substantially influences the composition of the supervisory board (Van der Knoop, 1991: 150; Van het Kaar, 1995: 16). Secondly, the supervisory board ratifies important managerial decisions, like share issues, major investment projects, mergers and acquisitions or significant restructuring processes. Thirdly, it determines the annual statement of accounts, which however requires approval by the general meeting of shareholders (Voogd, 1989: 247). Fourthly, supervisory board members appoint and (for major causes) dismiss members of the management board, although the influence of current management in this process is substantial (Van der Knoop, 1991: 83).

A mitigated form of the structural model applies to companies that fulfil the three criteria but are majority owned by foreign enterprises.[17] This model also prescribes the presence of the supervisory board, but reduces its influence in order to ensure a sufficient degree of control of foreign companies over their Dutch subsidiaries. In particular, the general meeting of shareholders rather than the supervisory board determines the annual statement of accounts and appoints and dismisses members of the management board.

Companies that do not fulfil the criteria of the structural model belong to the common model. This model applies to approximately 63% of employment in limited liability companies (Gelauff and Den Broeder, 1996: 51). These companies

---

[16] Only a legal procedure can overrule objections by the general meeting or the works council against proposed members of the supervisory board (Koene and Slomp, 1991: 48-50; Honée, 1986: 9).

[17] At least 50% of the shares of these companies is owned by a company with a majority of its employees working abroad (Voogd, 1989: 245; Slagter, 1994: 332).

may voluntarily install a supervisory board, but – unless they explicitly adopt the structural model – its influence is more limited. The general meeting of shareholders appoints supervisory board members, determines the annual statement of accounts and appoints the management board. Hence, its competencies are confined to ratifying important management decisions.

Discussions on Supervisory Board Performance. With respect to their task to monitor and ratify management decisions, the German and Dutch supervisory boards have much in common. Yet, the performance of the supervisory board in both countries suffers from distinct weaknesses. In Germany, the discussion on possible improvements centres on co-determination through the supervisory board. In the Netherlands, it focuses on the system of cooption.

In Germany, the presence of worker representatives on the German supervisory board appears to reduce the efficacy of internal shareholder control. Both shareholder representatives and management try to limit the importance of the supervisory board in order to constrain worker influence. A number of companies have reduced the responsibilities of the supervisory board to the legal minimum (Schröder, 1995). Because shareholder representatives do not like to criticize management in front of employee representatives, they organize informal meetings with managers to discuss controversial or confidential issues. This may explain why meetings of the German supervisory board are often characterized by the absence of debate and by consensus.

In the Netherlands, the system of cooption limits the direct influence of shareholders (Rietkerk, 1992). Hence, the quality of internal control above all depends on the supervisory board members themselves. In well-managed companies, members of the supervisory board and directors recognize the need for a competent supervisory board. However, in companies with an incompetent supervisory board, members will select congenial candidates.[18] Hence, the Dutch supervisory board is expected to be of less uniform quality compared to its German counterpart. Furthermore, cooption may increase risk-averse behaviour of companies (Boot, 1995). As shareholders have little direct influence on management, the Dutch model puts much weight on disciplining management by creditors. The latter have an incentive to promote risk-averse strategies (Section 10.1.1).

In both countries, discussions on these and related supervisory board weaknesses intensified, but have up to now not led to policy proposals to substantially reform the supervisory board. Rather, they have caused proposals for gradual improve-

---

[18] Slagter (1993: 196) states: '...The current system has a contrary effect: a member of the supervisory board who wants to intervene is looked upon as a rebel and forced to resign. The failing members hold their positions whereas they should be dismissed instead of the innovating member.'

ments.[19] In Germany, the near collapse of Metallgesellschaft in 1994 (Fisher, 1995) and large financial problems with several other companies have reduced confidence in the ability of the supervisory board to monitor firm performance. Yet, after the difficult and lengthy political struggle in the 1970s to introduce the co-determined supervisory board, most participants in the debate consider abolishing it politically infeasible. A recent policy proposal, which will probably be implemented in the beginning of 1998, aims to improve the German system of corporate governance. Among other things, it proposes to reduce the maximum size of the supervisory board to twelve members and to increase the required minimum number of yearly supervisory board meetings (de Waard, 1996; Seibert, 1997). Meanwhile, members of supervisory boards are becoming more alert at properly executing their task as a result of the large financial problems in some German companies (Goudzwaard, 1994).

In the Netherlands, an independent Corporate Governance Committee (1996) has considered ways to strengthen shareholder control and to improve supervisory board performance. Yet, this committee does not recommend to leave the system of cooption. Rather, it proposes to improve the efficacy of internal shareholder control within the current institutional system through a greater independency of supervisory board members from the management board, more careful (re-)appointment procedures for board members and a more active role of shareholders at the general meeting. The Committee tries to persuade companies to effectuate these changes through self-regulation.

In addition, jurisdiction has increased the consequences of failing supervisory board control for individual board members. They increasingly run the risk that they personally will be held liable if a company fails because of mismanagement (Tamminga, 1995). In some recent bankruptcy cases, the Dutch court has convicted former members of the management board and of the supervisory board for mismanagement. The conviction creates opportunities for aggrieved shareholders to submit claims for compensation or to demand a financial settlement.[20]

---

[19] For instance, in both countries experts recommend to reduce the number of supervisory board seats per person, to make the composition of the supervisory board more independent from that of the management board and to install supervisory board committees, such as an audit committee, a nominating committee or an investment committee (Corporate Governance Committee, 1996; Schneider-Lenné, 1995; see also Gelauff and Den Broeder, 1996: 60-63).

[20] Boot (1995) warns against proposals to further increase personal liability of members of the supervisory board, because it encourages risk-averse behaviour of board members.

10.2.2 External Shareholder Control

The Role of the Stock Market. The importance of the Dutch stock market holds a position in between the small German and the extensive Anglo-American stock market (Table 10.5). The difference in size between the German and Dutch stock market is not caused by a different share of limited liability companies. The employment share of these companies amounts to 54 and 57% in Germany and the Netherlands respectively (Gelauff and Den Broeder, 1996: 51). Rather, fewer German limited liability companies obtain a listing at the Stock Exchange.

The small size of the German stock market can be related to institutions that discourage stock market access and transparency. Until recently, little attention has been paid to insider dealing. Hardly any formal sanctions existed and self-corrective actions only occurred after a transaction had been exposed to publicity in the press. Moreover, accounting practices do not primarily aim to present a 'true and fair view' of the financial position and profits of the company, but aim to comply with fiscal regulations (Nobes, 1992; Offeren, 1992; Charkham, 1994: 31).[21] Finally, before 1994 the required employee representation on the supervisory board of small public companies put up a barrier to stock market financing in Germany (Borio, 1990; Prowse, 1994; Chapter 9).

Yet, recent and future regulatory reforms imply a shift of German institutions towards the market transparency and stock market accessibility of the Anglo-American system. Firstly, authorization requirements on issuance of shares and taxation of securities, which raised the costs of equity compared to debt finance, were removed at the end of 1991 (Prowse, 1994: 27). Secondly, the German Law on Small Public Companies and Deregulation of Equity Finance aims to make the legal form of a public company more attractive to SMEs. The number of people needed to found a public company has been reduced from five to one. In addition, newly founded small public companies are no longer required to have employee representatives on their supervisory board (see also Section 10.2.1). Thirdly, since August 1994 heavy fines, up to five years of imprisonment, have been put on insider dealing.[22] A related change concerns the obligatory disclosure of shareholdings above 5%. Before, a secret build-up of a large stock of shares was possible up to 25%. Fourthly, the new draft policy proposal to enhance German corporate governance (see Section 10.2.1) also suggests ways to improve the transparency of accounting practices, for instance through stricter requirements regarding the independence of accountants (Seibert, 1997).

---

[21] Conservative measurement often results in an undervaluation of the company (see also OECD, 1995a: 106).

[22] A Federal Supervisory Office for Securities Trading (Bundesaufsichtsamt für den Wertpapierhandel) now monitors share transactions and publication of relevant information by companies. Activities of this office resulted is some convictions for insider dealing.

Table 10.5 The role of the stock market, 1993

	Germany	Netherlands	United Kingdom	United States
capitalization[a]	25.1	61.5	132.4	83.5

[a] Value of equity as a % of GDP. Source: CEPS (1995: 7).

Meanwhile, companies face pressure to disclose their performance on a more comparable basis (Fukao, 1995). In 1993, Daimler Benz became the first German company that obtained a listing on the New York Stock Exchange, and reported accounts under GAAP and German rules (OECD, 1996). Until now, only a few German companies have followed this example.

Dutch institutions hold a position in between the extreme market transparency of the Anglo-American system and the current German regulations. Especially Dutch accounting rules more closely resemble those in Anglo-American countries (Nobes, 1992). Accounting is micro-based and commercially driven. Yet, rules are not as strict as the American "generally accepted accounting principles" (US-GAAP) of the Security and Exchange Commission (SEC) and allow substantial variations in accounting methods across companies (Beckman, 1993). Since the changes of German regulations, insider trading and disclosure rules have become similar in Germany and the Netherlands. A 1989 legal provision in the Dutch criminal code prohibits insider dealing (Amsterdam Stock Exchange, 1994).[23] Currently, the Dutch government considers measures to increase the effectiveness of regulations, because prosecution was not very successful in some recent cases. As in Germany, investors must disclose shareholdings of 5% or more. In both countries, disclosure regulations are less strict than in Anglo-American countries. Managers in the US and UK have to disclose their transactions in company-shares, whereas such openness is not required in Germany and the Netherlands. Because of an increasing use of stock option plans, this difference gains in importance.

The Market for Corporate Control. Hostile takeovers, *i.e.* stock market bids on the shares of an enterprise without the consent of its management, are rare in Germany and in the Netherlands. Although both countries have different defense mechanisms to discourage hostile takeovers, this makes the German and Dutch corporate governance systems different from the Anglo-American system. Note

[23] Since 1992, this provision is part of the more general Act on Supervision of Securities Trading. An independent Office on Supervision of Securities Trading monitors transactions on the stock exchange and can commission the Bureau of Control of the stock exchange to investigate specific cases.

Box 10.2 The efficacy of the market for corporate control

The debate on the efficacy of the market for corporate control as a disciplining device ranges between its positive indirect 'contestability' effect and arguments that raise doubt on its efficacy. The threat of a hostile takeover may urge management to perform efficiently and to give shareholder value highest priority. This 'contestability' effect may preclude the necessity for a hostile takeover to actually take place, only the threat suffices. Of course, its indirect impact makes it difficult to obtain empirical evidence in favour of a strong market for corporate control.

In contrast, several arguments have been raised why hostile takeovers turn out to be a blunt and rather ineffective device to discipline management. Firstly, available evidence on actual takeovers shows that in practice disciplining companies does not constitute the primary motivation for a hostile takeover. The "typical hostile target is not a very badly performing company" (Nickell, 1995: 59). According to Franks and Mayer (1996), three out of four empirical measures indicate that the pre-bid performance of target companies does not differ significantly from that of companies engaged in friendly acquisitions or from companies not engaged in mergers. Empirical evidence further suggests that in particular the former shareholders of target firms appear to gain from hostile takeovers, whereas the gains to bidding managers are less certain (Nickell, 1995).

Secondly, even if the market for corporate control might be effective in curbing outright abuses, it does not assure more effective decision-making afterwards. Pound (1995) emphasises that corporate failure frequently is not caused by managerial incompetence or abuse of power but by failures of judgement, stemming from general characteristics of human decision making and the way organisations operate.

Thirdly, the takeover mechanism is less useful during a period of economic downturn, when funds to finance the takeover are difficult to obtain and the threat of a hostile takeover may be less credible (Prowse, 1994: 65).

Fourthly, hostile takeovers are a costly instrument, both in terms of direct costs to launch the takeover and in terms of indirect costs inflicted upon the target company. Indirect cost arise because a takeover bid distracts management from normal management tasks and causes turmoil among employees (Jenkinson and Mayer, 1992).

that, while aiming to curb management opportunism, also in the Anglo-American system the efficacy of the market for corporate control as a disciplinary device turns out to be debatable in practice (Box 10.2).

In Germany, one obvious reason for a less-developed market for corporate control is the limited importance of the stock market. Yet, also for listed companies hostile takeovers are difficult to effectuate. Block shareholders (Table 10.3) have a long-term attachment to the company and often refuse to sell to a hostile bidder. The proxy-voting rights of banks (Section 10.2.3), which imply that banks control a substantial number of votes on the general meeting, functions as an additional defence against a raider.

Moreover, regulations thwart hostile take-overs. The most important of those is that 75% of the votes at a shareholders' meeting is required to replace shareholders' representatives on the supervisory board before their term of appointment ends (Edwards and Fischer, 1994: 191).[24] Once a raider owns 75% of the shares and has replaced shareholders' representatives on the supervisory board (or has persuaded current members to accept the take-over), replacement of the management board can easily be effectuated by a majority decision of shareholder representatives at the supervisory board.

Hostile takeovers are uncommon in the Netherlands as well. The Dutch structural model of corporate governance acts as one of the defensive devices. The supervisory board is elected through cooption, and in turn appoints members of the management board. This shields managers from shareholders (Rietkerk, 1992). However, under two conditions the structural model can be overruled: if a raider is itself a structural company and if a raider is a foreign takeover company.[25] Moreover, the raider can exert pressure on the supervisory board to give in to the raider, for instance by objecting to the appointment of new members of the supervisory board or by refusing to approve the annual statement of accounts. (Voogd, 1989: 249-269; Van der Grinten, 1990; Gelauff and Den Broeder, 1996: 80). Furthermore, for a number of Dutch companies the common model is relevant, which offers no defence at all.

Because the structural model offers no absolute defence and the protection through block shareholdings is much lower than in Germany (Table 10.3), Dutch companies utilize a wide range of additional anti-takeover defences (Box 10.3). Approximately 90% of companies listed at the stock exchange use at least one means of defence (Cantrijn *et al.*, 1993: 28-29; Van Fredelikslust and van Veldhuizen, 1996). Apart from voting caps, these devices are not used in Germany.

In the near future, new regulations will – somewhat – lower these types of defense walls around Dutch companies. After lengthy discussions, a proposal for new regulations to facilitate hostile takeovers has been agreed upon: a majority of shareholders, owning 70% of the shares for a period of at least one year, can start a legal procedure to pull down anti-takeover defences. The shareholders appeal to the Chamber of Company Law, who approves the takeover if criteria related to the continuity of the company and the position of employees are found satisfactory

---

[24] As an additional barrier to hostile take-overs, some public companies have a cap on voting rights at a shareholders' meeting, which means that the number of votes cast by a single share owner is restricted. However, voting caps offer no absolute protection because they can be circumvented by share owners acting in concert.

[25] If a Dutch structural takeover company owns at least 50% of the target's equity capital, the structural model of the target company can be abolished. If a foreign takeover company acquires a majority of the equity capital of a Dutch target company, the mitigated structural model instead of the structural model applies to the target. By consequence, the supervisory board neither appoints nor dismisses management and cannot prevent the foreign takeover company to replace the management team through voting at the general meeting of shareholders (see also Section 10.2.1).

Box 10.3 Dutch juridical anti-takeover defences

This box summarizes the main juridical anti-takeover defences applied by Dutch companies.

Preference shares *are most widely applied as defence mechanisms. They carry the same voting rights as ordinary shares, but give a right to a fixed dividend percentage before ordinary shareholders become entitled to dividend. Preference shares discourage hostile takeovers because specific foundations, aimed at protection of the company, often own the stock of preference shares. This reduces the influence of ordinary shares through votes at the general meeting.*

Priority shares *are the second important anti-takeover device in the Netherlands. A company can assign special rights to holders of priority shares, like proposing or preventing the appointment of particular new members on the management and supervisory boards, approving the issue of ordinary shares, liquidation of the company or changing the articles of association. Hence, they also curb the voting power of ordinary shares.*

The issue of ***tradable depositary receipts*** *is also widespread. The company deposits its share capital at an administrative office, which instead trades depositary receipts on the stock market. Even if a raider obtains the majority of these depositary receipts, voting power at the general meeting still rests with the administrative office. Since the administrative office usually is a business connection of the company, a substantial anti-takeover defence has been raised.*

As another option, ***voting caps*** *are also, within certain bounds, allowed in the Netherlands. Voting caps restrict the number of votes cast by a single shareholder regardless of the size of the stock of that shareholder. However, they have proven to provide insufficient defence against a hostile takeover: straw-men at the general meeting can circumvent voting caps. Bloemsma (1973) mentions the example of a large Dutch company, which founded 860 small limited liability companies to undermine the voting caps of a company it intended to take over. Hence, voting caps are scarcely used.*

Finally, anti-takeover devices like ***poison pills, crown jewels and greenmail,*** *became prevalent in the United States during the 1980s, but are not very common in the Netherlands. Poison pills give shareholders certain conditional rights, which may raise the costs of a takeover. For instance, the company can sell additional shares to current shareholders at a low price (Jacobs, 1991: 93). The protection of crown jewels, i.e. valuable business units, aims to cut the chain between the firm and its crown jewel. For instance, a crown jewel of a possible target company can be sold to a 'white knight' or is protected by preference shares. Greenmail, i.e. sending the raider an envelope filled with dollars, entails the repurchase of the stock of shares already in possession of the raider at a higher price. It is not very effective in the Netherlands because repurchase of shares is only allowed to a maximum of 10% of the share capital.*

Besides utilizing the above defences, Dutch legislation furthermore permits public limited liability companies (under the common model) to considerably diminish the influence of the general meeting on the composition of the management board through binding nominations. The general meeting elects the management board, but chooses from a binding nomination of at least two persons for every seat. Only a two-third majority at the general meeting can overrule this nomination. Because current members of the boards draft the nomination, their control over the composition of the board increases.

(Gelauff and Den Broeder, 1996: 84).

The implementation of this policy proposal will sooner lead to a shift towards the German system than towards Anglo-American takeover practices. In anticipation of the policy change, Dutch companies are already turning to institutional investors or multinational companies to place large blocks of shares (Gelauff and Den Broeder, 1996: 84-85). This may signify a future shift towards long-term relationships between managers and block shareholders. In this case, direct shareholder influence will increase in the Netherlands, but hostile takeover activity will not.

10.2.3 The Corporate Governance Role of Banks

This section focuses on the corporate governance role of banks in large established companies. In Germany, the specific corporate governance role of banks in these companies follows from their shareholdings, which add to the concentrated shareholdings among non-financial enterprises. The shareholder position is strengthened by the system of proxy voting, which permits a bank to vote at the general meeting of shareholders for shares it holds in custody.

Share Ownership of Banks. Shareholdings of German banks are relatively large compared to those in other countries. In 1993, German banks owned over 14% of the stock of shares (Table 10.3). Comparable figures are negligible in the United Kingdom and the Netherlands and zero in the United States, where the law prohibits universal banking.

Yet, for a number of reasons the direct bank influence on non-financial companies in German may be smaller than this figure suggests. Firstly, a substantial part consists of participations in other financial companies such as insurance companies, mortgage banks or other subsidiaries. From the total stock of shares owned by banks, only 40% are shareholdings in German non-financial enterprises (Schröder, 1995). Secondly, public companies constitute only a small part of the German enterprise sector.[26] If all limited liability companies are considered, the ten largest private German banks own only 0.4% of their total nominal capital (in 1994, Bundesverband Deutscher Banken, 1995). These figures illustrate that the direct shareholder position of banks is not extremely important.[27] Thirdly, the supervisory board representation of banks is more limited than

[26] Employment in public companies, as a percentage of employment in all limited liability companies, amounts to 26%. The corresponding turnover share is 45% (Statistisches Bundesamt, 1994; Edwards and Fischer, 1994).

[27] The relevance of the shareholder position increases for listed public limited liability companies: the ten largest private banks own 4.1% of the equity capital of the 30 largest German listed non-financial companies.

could be expected on the basis of their voting power. The number of bank representatives on the supervisory boards of the largest 100 companies amounted to 7.2% in 1992 and 6.3% in 1993 (Monopolkommission, 1994: 232; Bundesverband Deutscher Banken, 1995). Moreover, it is by no means self-evident that bank representatives act in concert.

Over the last decades, German banks reduced the size of their block shareholdings (Bundesverband Deutscher Banken, 1995). Large participations (over 25%) in non-financial companies fell, while participations of 10% to 25% rose. Banks reduced large shareholdings in individual companies in order to diversify their investments more adequately over branches of industry and countries (Schröder, 1995: 12). Moreover, the reduction of large holdings became interesting after the threshold, above which double taxation on corporate income from municipal taxes and wealth tax can be avoided (Schachtelsteuerprivileg), diminished from 25% to 10% in 1977. Current bank shareholdings are still substantial, but to a larger extent require coalitions with other block shareholders in order to influence firm policy or offer protection against hostile takeovers.[28]

Proxy Voting. Proxy voting strengthens the shareholder position of German banks: owners of shares deposit their shareholdings with a bank and authorize the bank to vote on their behalf at the general meeting. This system aims to increase the representation of shareholders at the general meeting (Kümpel, 1995; Schneider-Lenné, 1992; Schröder, 1995). Since many share owners do not instruct banks on their voting preferences, this voting system substantially strengthens the influence of banks.

The scope of these proxy votes can be quite substantial. In 1988, banks owned 8.1% of the total shareholdings, while another 53.5% of the total stock of shares had been deposited with the banks (Edwards and Fischer, 1994: 112). Moreover, 45% of the shares deposited with the banks were held by the three German large banks (Deutsche bank, Dresdner Bank and Commerzbank). Hence, proxy votes may provide banks a voting majority at the general meeting, especially in large firms without other majority owners (Baums and Fraune, 1995; see also OECD, 1995a: 96).

Yet, three qualifications restrict the voting power of banks. First of all, some depositors, i.e. companies and the government, will probably instruct the bank how to vote.[29] Secondly, concentrated shareholdings of non-financial enterprises

---

[28] See Zwiebel (1995) for a theoretical analysis of the impact of the size of blocks of equity of a firm and control benefits to shareholders on the resulting shareholder structure within and across firms.

[29] From the 53.5% of shares deposited in 1988, the shares owned by non-financial enterprises amounted to 17.5 %-points and the shares owned by the government to 4.3 %-points. Hence, the maximum percentage of proxy votes directly under the banks discretion

reduce the dominance of bank influence through proxy voting, because block shareholders dominate the general meeting.[30] Thirdly, banks have to follow a formal voting procedure. For instance, they must inform each depositor on their intended voting behaviour and ask for instructions. A current policy proposal, aiming to improve the German system of corporate governance, intends to reduce the dominant influence of large banks at the general meeting: banks with a participation of more than 5% will have to choose between exercising proxy votes or voting on their own behalf (de Waard, 1996; Seibert, 1997). This policy proposal will probably be implemented in the beginning of 1998.

Despite these qualifications, the viability and extent of proxy voting in Germany is remarkable. The system not only provides a channel to monitor companies more strongly, but also provides the management of banks with a substantial voting power on their own general meeting of shareholders. Since most of the banks are public companies with widely dispersed equity capital, they can strongly influence voting behaviour through proxy votes. For example, voting shares controlled by a bank on its own general meeting were 32% for Deutsche Bank, 44% for Dresdner bank, 18% for Commerzbank, 32% for Bayerische Vereinsbank and 24% for Bayerische Hypothekbank (Baums, 1996: 14). Hence, proxy voting gives these five banks a combined majority vote at each of their individual general meetings.

In the Netherlands, proxy voting is allowed but hardly exists. This may be related to the relatively small power of the Dutch general meeting of shareholders (De Vijver, 1980). Anti-takeover defences and the system of cooption lower the opportunities for the general meeting to exercise control (Section 10.2.1 and 10.2.2) and thus reduce the need for and benefits of proxy voting. Recent developments, however, make the introduction of proxy voting in the Netherlands more likely. The current policy proposal to lower anti-takeover defences will make a system of proxy voting more effective. In addition, institutional investors, large internationally-oriented Dutch companies and foreign investors advocate proxy voting and the Corporate Governance Committee (1996) favours proxy voting as a way to enhance the activity of the general meeting.

The Degree of Bank Influence. Share ownership, supervisory board influence and proxy voting suggest that German banks play an important role but do not totally control the German enterprise sector. Edwards and Fischer (1994) state that the position of banks in corporate governance fits into the general view of extensive cross holdings between enterprises in Germany. Gorton and Schmid (1996) empirically corroborate that conclusion. Firm performance is related to block

---

diminishes to 31.7%. In 1993, households owned 16.6% of the stock of shares, which indicates the relevance of proxy voting (Table 10.3).

[30] The evidence by Baums and Fraune (1995) on large voting majorities of banks refers to only 24 of the largest companies.

holdings of majority shareholders in general, including banks, but no additional influence exists of share holdings by banks or through proxy voting (see also Section 10.1.3).

The analysis shows that the role and ambitions of Dutch banks in corporate governance differ considerably from that of German counterparts. Recent developments indicate that Dutch banks become more engaged in equity finance, but do not aim at active shareholder monitoring of companies (see for instance, Tamminga, 1996). They primarily monitor companies from a creditor perspective and in this sense closely resemble Anglo-American banks. Hence, they do not substantially contribute to internal shareholder control, but also do not weaken their creditor position due to their shareholdings, as may be the case with German banks (see Section 10.1.2).

10.2.4 The Corporate Governance Role of Pension Funds

Share ownership of Dutch pension funds (7.9%) considerably exceeds the percentage of shares (1.9%) owned by their German counterparts (Table 10.3). Therefore, the role of Dutch pension funds in corporate governance needs further clarification. To what extent do Dutch pension funds influence decision making in large companies and how does their role compare to that of German banks?

Pension Funds' Share Ownership. Shareholdings of German pension funds are small because of the extensive pay-as-you-go public pension system and the retainment of most private pension fund contributions within companies (compare Chapter 7). Assets of German pension funds and life insurance companies amount to only 5% of GDP. Moreover, pension funds are risk averse to such an extent that they invest less than 10% of their cover stock in shares, although the legal room for investment in shares equals 30% of their cover stock (Schneider-Lenné, 1992: 13).

In the Netherlands, the private pension system is far more elaborate than in Germany. Total assets invested by Dutch pension funds amount to 73% of GDP in 1992 (CS First Boston, 1993).[31] The large Dutch civil servant pension fund (ABP) is worth nearly half of this sum. Due to risk-aversion, however, the share of equity capital owned by pension funds is much smaller compared to that in the United Kingdom and the United States (Table 10.3).[32] Related to the total cover stock, shareholdings by pension funds in the Netherlands merely comprise 14% of total assets, while the comparable figures for the United Kingdom and the United States are in the order of 65% and 45% respectively (CEPS, 1995).

---

[31] The comparable figure for the United Kingdom is 59% of GDP.

[32] The former legal restriction for the civil servant pension fund that no more than 20% of the cover stock of the fund can be invested in shares has not been binding.

Box 10.4 Investment policies of the Dutch civil servant pension fund (ABP)

The civil servant pension fund, which has been privatized in 1996, aims to raise the average return on its investments through an increase of its total equity investment from 13% of the cover stock in 1995 to 30% in 2000 (Barentsen, 1995). Holdings in Dutch companies will increase from 7% to 10% of the cover stock. This implies a higher concentration of shareholdings: the size of current participations in some Dutch companies will rise from just below 5% to some 8 to 10% (Bakker and Schlaghecke, 1995). Another aim of the fund is to participate in smaller securities, venture capital and foreign equity. The latter type of investment is intended to increase most: from 6% to 20% of the cover stock. The target of 30% equity investment is still relatively modest compared to some other Dutch pension funds, which already have larger shareholdings and are also expanding their shareholdings (Gelauff and Den Broeder, 1996: 76).

Accordingly, the civil servant pension fund has thoroughly reconsidered its role as shareholder (Barentsen, 1995). Exit options, i.e. the selling of shares if the performance of the company is disappointing, become less attractive as the size of participations increases, because the stake of the fund in a specific company is so large that exit would drive down the share price. Therefore, the fund aims at using voice as a governance instrument to promote their interests. It will not confine itself to financial data to develop an opinion on the performance of the company, but also want to become knowledgeable on corporate strategies and the quality of management. Its aim is to have a relatively small group of specialists monitor the companies in which the fund participates. These specialists will gather information on the performance and strategies. Yet, the civil servant pension fund does not aim at direct representation of fund managers in supervisory boards of companies (see Bakker and Schlaghecke, 1995).

Pension Fund Activism. Currently, the investment policy of Dutch pension funds is changing. An example concerns the change in investment policies of the civil servant pension fund (Box 10.4). Increasing and more concentrated shareholdings of pension funds suggest that Dutch institutional investors may become the vehicles for stronger internal shareholder control in the Netherlands. The pension funds' equity stakes in a company may become large enough to solve the free-rider problem that confronts small shareholders (Section 10.1.2). Some developments indicate increasing involvement of pension funds. Dutch pension funds oppose the cumulation of anti-takeover defences applied by Dutch companies, pay more attention to shareholder value of enterprises, and show an increasing interest in corporate policy and nomination of members of supervisory boards (Frijns *et al.*, 1995).

Developments in several other countries also indicate increasing pension fund activism. In the United Kingdom and the United States, institutional investors become stronger involved in monitoring management performance (Bishop, 1994; Blair, 1995; Crist, 1995). Moreover, active pension funds in the United States have improved management of some poorly performing companies (Blair, 1995: 173). However, the focus of American pension funds differs from that of their Dutch counterparts. Because of the defined contribution pension system in the United States, American pension funds have a shorter time horizon. The Dutch defined benefit system, in contrast, promotes a long-term orientation (compare Chapter 7).

The Influence of Pension Funds. Despite their increasing activism, the corporate governance role of Dutch pension funds differs markedly from that of German block shareholders. The link between shareholdings and supervisory board representation is much weaker in the Netherlands, due to the system of cooption. By consequence, pension funds have less direct means available to convince management of their views and have to seek informal contacts with management. This may reduce their monitoring opportunities. Furthermore, pension funds mainly monitor from an investment perspective. German block shareholders, in contrast, also have commercial, technological or lending relationships with the company. On the one hand, a purely shareholder perspective makes monitoring more effective by making the investor less dependent on the continuation of the relationship with the company (Section 10.1.2). On the other hand, it may also reduce the monitoring scope of pension-funds because fund managers have less entrepreneurial experience. The involvement of the pension fund with corporate strategies invokes high monitoring costs. For each individual company the fund has to amass detailed knowledge of strategic variables such as product development, production processes, internal organization, technology, market opportunities, worker motivation, etc. (Blair, 1995: 183). Because these variables differ substantially between companies, returns to scale may be moderate. Hence, Dutch pension funds will probably strengthen internal shareholder control in the Netherlands, but the extent of their influence may be weaker than that of German block shareholders.

10.3 Trends and Policy Options

What can be learned from the analytical framework and the comparison of corporate governance systems in the United States, Germany and the Netherlands?

The analysis of conditions in Section 10.1.3 points out that the choice of an optimal system of corporate governance also depends on the social, technological and economic environment. Moreover, corporate governance institutions are linked to other institutions concerning work governance, technology policy, product market regulations and so forth. This complicates single policy changes in the field of corporate governance, as changes may affect the coherence of the entire institutional system.

Does this imply that learning from abroad is impossible because each country already has the corporate governance system that optimally fits its economic and institutional environment? The analysis rejects this conclusion. For two reasons, it is still possible to learn from institutions abroad. First, some institutional changes would imply a better performance of the corporate governance system of a country. Second, trends in the economic environment create challenges for strategic

Table 10.6 Corporate governance: opportunities for shareholder influence

	Germany	Netherlands	United States
External control			
role stock market	small	intermediate	large
market transparency	weak, improving	intermediate	transparent
hostile takeovers	rare	rare	more frequent, efficacy doubtful
Internal control			
share ownership	concentrated	intermediate	dispersed
board	two-tier, co-determined	two-tier, cooption	one-tier, autonomous CEO
role of banks	active monitoring, block shareholders, proxy voting	creditor perspective, small shareholdings	creditor perspective, no shareholdings
role of pension funds	negligible	increasingly active, long-term investor perspective	increasingly active, investor perspective

institutional changes. They may require a shift towards more flexibility or more commitment in the field of corporate governance and related institutions.

Therefore, to provide a background for the derivation of policy options, Section 10.3.1 starts with a survey of relevant trends. Section 10.3.2 reviews the performance of the systems of corporate governance in the United States, Germany and the Netherlands in the light of the trends and formulates the policy options. As a point of reference, Table 10.6 summarizes the main features of the system of corporate governance in Germany, the Netherlands and the United States.

10.3.1 Trends and Institutional Change

Structural changes in society, demography, technological orientation and international product and financial markets may require a change in corporate governance institutions. Table 10.7 summarizes the most important economic trends and points out whether they enhance the relevance of the competitive or the cooperative model.

Social Trends. An increasingly heterogeneous population, individualisation, quickly shifting tastes and risk taking induce a shift towards the competitive model and create challenges for the German system of corporate governance. Increasing heterogeneity makes it more difficult to monitor informal agreements and to support commitment. More diverse tastes that quickly adapt to various fashions create swings of creative destruction, which require flexible financial reallocation.

Table 10.7 Impact of economic trends on the strengths of both models

	Competitive model	Cooperative model
Social		
– heterogeneity, individualization, risk taking	+	–
Demography		
– ageing: role of stock market	+	–
– ageing: scope to monitor	–	+
Technological change		
– codified and market oriented	+	–
– learning and customization	–	+
Product and Financial markets		
– internationalisation	+	–

+ positive impact – negative impact

Reviewing the conditions supporting the competitive model, Section 10.1.3 concluded that flexibility is a strong asset in a quickly changing and diverse environment. To some extent social trends also point at increased risk taking. People are more inclined to hold part of their savings in equity or in mutual funds that invest in equity. Higher prosperity also raises the amounts invested in more risky assets. Increasing supply of higher-risk assets more easily finds its way to companies in a model with a well-developed stock market.

Demography. The ageing of the population leads to an increasing activity of pension funds. One the one hand, the American and Dutch system are better able to deal with this trend, because of a larger size of the stock market and of increasing shareholdings by pension funds. The inflexible German bookreserve system, in contrast, prevents a flexible re-allocation of pension fund capital. Moreover, the passing of generations requires a better access to stock market finance, because individuals or families who founded and own a company need to find external sources of finance once they retire. Therefore, ageing requires a shift of German institutions towards the better stock market access of the competitive model.

On the other hand, both the American and the Dutch system lack strong direct monitoring possibilities for institutional investors. Because pension funds have considerable shareholdings, they do not want to rely only on their exit options, but want to influence corporate strategies by voice. For instance, American pension funds increasingly propose to vote on important company issues at the general meeting (proxy proposals). Yet, they usually have a minority of votes and strong proxy regulation limits possibilities to contact other shareholders before the general meeting (Karpoff et al., 1996; Ligtenberg, 1997). In the Netherlands, the system of cooption together with the far-reaching responsibilities of the supervisory board restrict direct shareholder control by pension funds.

Technological Change. Technological trends do not clearly indicate a structural change in the relative importance of both models of corporate governance. On the one hand, information technologies have made knowledge more codified. As a result, innovations can more easily spread through the economy and innovating companies can to a larger extent make use of codified knowledge from the external knowledge base as input for their own innovations. The competitive model is better able to deal with these trends, because its flexibility is conducive to radical innovations based on general, marketable knowledge and the diffusion of new knowledge through the economy.

On the other hand, trends towards firms that function as learning organisations and the need to meet idiosyncratic customer requirements, enhance the performance of the cooperative model. A learning organisation rests on cooperation between dedicated employees and consultation with financiers and suppliers. Innovations that meet idiosyncratic requirements of procuring companies are based on knowledge from firm-specific investments in customer relationships (Carlin and Soskice, 1997). Moreover, besides flexible diffusion of radical innovations, continuous incremental innovations within companies constitutes an alternative approach to deal with a quickly changing technological environment (compare Section 2.5). The cooperative model deals better with these types of innovations, because long-term relationships between customers, workers and financial investors promote technologies based on the internal development of firm-specific knowledge.

International Markets. Internationalisation and liberalisation shift product market competition towards the world market and increase access of companies to foreign sources of finance. This requires a convergence of stock market rules, accounting practices and disclosure regulations towards international standards. Currently, Anglo-American institutions are better able to deal with this trend, because of the larger stock market access and transparency of their financial markets. Hence, internationalisation requires a shift of German and Dutch institutions towards these features of the competitive model.

This institutional shift is already taking place. Recent policy changes in Germany aim to increase the stock market access of companies through more strict disclosure rules, insider dealing legislation and an easier stock market access of small companies. Moreover, a draft policy proposal aims to make accounting rules more micro-based and commercially driven. Meanwhile, companies with a multinational investor base face pressure to disclose their performance on a more comparable basis (Fukao, 1995). In the Netherlands, market transparency was already larger than in Germany, mainly because of more transparent accounting practices. Yet, in both countries financial markets are still less transparent than in the United States. Disclosure rule and accounting practices still diverge considerably from American practices and insider regulation is less strict.

The institutional shift towards a greater market transparency increases access to international sources of finance. Together with the increasing orientation on international product markets this development may imply a further shift towards the features of the competitive model, because it poses a threat to the long-term relationships between management and financial investors of the cooperative model. The more easy access to foreign sources of finance makes management less committed to long-term relationships with investors. Once these investors try to exert direct control and constrain managerial freedom to act, management may try to attract less directly involved investors on the international market in order to reduce the constraints on their autonomy. Hence, the outside option of management may reduce their commitment and curb investments of financiers in screening and monitoring activities. Moreover, foreign investors may have less close commercial ties to the company and may own smaller blocks of shares. In addition, the greater distance to the management team as well as more restrictions on the informal information exchange imposed by stricter insider trading regulations may reduce their capability to monitor.

10.3.2 Policy Options

Table 10.7 shows that trends towards the competitive model dominate trends towards the cooperative model. Although full convergence of corporate governance institutions is unlikely because different technological specializations create niches for different institutional arrangements among countries, social and international trends generate a greater demand for flexibility in the cooperative model. Against the background of these trends, which policy options can be derived from the review of corporate governance institutions in this chapter?

The United States. Trends towards flexibility give the American model of corporate governance an advantage. Yet, in some respects flexibility and market orientation are fairly strong in the American system and may harm relationship-specific investments. Some steps towards commitment are justified to redress the balance between shareholders and other stakeholders and promote a long-term view. OECD (1996) emphasizes that the market oriented American model promotes flexibility and radical innovations, but also states: 'Many observers believe that the US system is in need of greater monitoring'. Increasingly arguments are raised that too much attention on 'shareholder value' entails high costs in terms of human capital forgone, due to extreme 'downsizing'. Moreover, 'incentive-compatible' share options schemes bring about overly excessive revenues for top management (Ligtenberg, 1997). Ill representation of employees in American corporate governance curbs commitment to employees (see Chapter 9). The direct influence of creditors is also rather limited. To enhance the involvement of creditors, proposals have been raised to overhaul the Glass-Steagal act so as to ease restrictions on banks' securities operations (OECD, 1996: 152).

In addition, the more prominent role of pension funds in corporate governance demands more room for direct monitoring in the United States. American pension funds are becoming more active, but face difficulties in reaching and convincing other shareholders with dispersed shareholdings due to strong proxy rules. Recently, some minor institutional changes have increased the scope for direct monitoring. Since 1992, regulations permit easier communication between shareholders, for instance regarding their voting intentions at the general meeting. Moreover, shareholders have more opportunities to propose issues for voting at the general meeting (OECD, 1996: 139; Blair, 1995: 72-75). However, OECD (1996: 150) presents a substantial list of reform proposals that could further strengthen direct shareholder involvement and thus enhance commitment. Examples are: easing shareholder communications, facilitating access to the proxy process or tax exempts for investment companies with large shareholdings for the purpose of monitoring.

A policy option for the United States from the Netherlands and Germany, is to create more independent boards of directors. The CEO chairing the board and the presence of a substantial number of executive directors thwart board performance. To some extent the process towards more independent boards is already taking place. Internationalisation, fast technological change and shareholder activism increase pressure on American companies to improve their performance. In some instances companies perceive the advantage of an independent board that not only supervises management but also acts as a discussion partner. By consequence, the number of outside directors increases and boards become smaller and more assertive (OECD, 1996: 135).

Germany. The trends toward flexibility pose challenges to the German model of corporate governance. In Germany internal control is strong. Representatives of block shareholders monitor management. Supervisory board representation by banks and firms is related to considerable cross-holdings of equity among companies. German institutions perform weakly on risk-taking and the flexible reallocation of financial capital. Increasing heterogeneity and internationalisation of product markets and financial markets may also considerably weaken the commitment of long-term stakeholder relationships.

Analogously to the German interlocking politics (Politikverflechtung) in intergovernmental relationships (compare Section 5.2.2), interlocking checks and balances in corporate governance restrict flexibility and hamper exchange of information. The supervisory board forms the nexus of all the checks and balances between stakeholders. The supervisory board has to represent the interest of independent shareholders, who primarily focus on the equity value of their shareholdings. Its worker representatives supervise management on how it handles labour issues. Representatives of banks have to take care of the interests of the bank as a shareholder, of the private shareholders that the bank represents as proxy holder, and frequently also take into account that the bank has a lending relationship with the company. Representatives from non-financial companies, may combine their interests as a block shareholder with supervision of a supplier relationship or of cooperation in R&D. Members of the supervisory board who primarily have been appointed on the basis of their personal qualities (such as professors, lawyers or civil servants), may take a more independent view. However, they always are representatives of either capital or labour, which a priori restricts their position. This combination of the interests of many stakeholders in one institutional body complicates decision making, may narrow down the discussion to rather general observations and hampers exchange of information, because of a fear of loss of confidentiality.

A stronger division of responsibilities among different actors and different institutional bodies may still provide checks and balances to sustain commitment, while at the same time enhancing their performance and increasing flexibility. Besides the current initiatives to enhance the performance of the supervisory board, for instance by reducing its size and increasing the number of meetings, two institutional adjustments come to the fore: replacing the co-determined supervisory board and more intense use of supervisory board subcommittees. In addition, current policy proposals to restrict the voting power of banks also contribute to disentwining interlocking checks and balances.

Replacing the co-determined supervisory board does not necessarily imply a reduction of worker influence within the company. Currently co-determination reduces the efficacy of the supervisory board, because it restricts information flows to the board and hampers open discussions. As such, it not only limits supervision by shareholders, but it also restricts the influence of employees and may endanger employment or workers' wages if the supervisory board performs poorly. Confining supervision of the relationship between labour and management to a strong works council and negotiating labour conditions by encompassing peak organisations of employees and employers (see Chapter 9), more clearly defines responsibilities while preserving the possibility to build up mutual trust and commitment that support long-term relationships. This may enable employees and management to openly discuss issues relevant to labour and may even revitalize their relationship. Some steps in this direction already have been taken: since 1994 newly founded small public companies are no longer required to install a supervisory board with worker representatives.

Supervisory board committees, such as an audit committee, a nominating committee or an investment committee, may improve the exchange of information between management and specific stakeholders, because participants share information on a more confidential basis. Committees facilitate contacts between management and specific stakeholders on topics relevant to their relationship, which lowers the risk of disclosure of information to other stakeholders or to competitors. For instance, the audit committee allows specialized members of the supervisory board to intensify their contacts with the company's accountants. In a nominating committee, members of the supervisory board can discuss the quality of the management board on a confidential basis. Subject of discussion in investment committees are the mission and strategies of the company and major investment plans. Introduction of specialized committees requires legal action. A verdict of the German court currently prohibits the installation of committees without joint representation (Schilling, 1994).

Current policy proposals to prevent conflicting interests of banks also serve to delineate responsibilities more clearly. A bank that holds five percent or more of a company's equity capital must choose whether it votes at the general meeting on behalf of its own participation or as a proxy representative of private investors. Together with the current tendency towards falling share ownership of banks, this may improve monitoring from a creditor's perspective.

The Netherlands. The Dutch system of corporate governance holds a remarkable position between the competitive and the cooperative model. Cooption of members of the supervisory board and juridical takeover barriers almost completely shield management from shareholders. Where members of the German supervisory board represent the interests of a substantial number of stakeholders, the Dutch supervisory board does not entail any direct representation at all. The supervisory board elects its own members and has to promote the interest of the company as a whole. However, the independent position of the supervisory board can be called into question, because in practice management substantially influences its composition.

The influence of management on the composition of the supervisory board and the latter's autonomy, makes Dutch corporate governance highly dependent on the quality of management. If a competent management board governs a company, the Dutch system of corporate governance strikes a favourable balance between commitment and flexibility. Shielded from short-term stock-market pressure and the risk of hostile takeovers, management can develop a long-term view. Separate institutions like the works council enable management to enhance commitment in its relationships with stakeholders, which promotes investment in relationship-specific assets such as specific human capital. Because of its relative autonomy, management can retain sufficient flexibility to adjust investments to emerging opportunities. Moreover, if management recognizes the gains from a high-quality independent supervisory board, the supervisory board may act as a discussion partner that supports management in enhancing the performance of the company.

In contrast, hardly any institutions exist to correct a poorly performing management that dominates the supervisory board. Neither shareholders nor other stakeholders have any direct means to change the composition or the actions of the supervisory board. The position of the supervisory board and juridical takeover barriers also shield weak management from the market for corporate control.

Hence, the only alternative available to shareholders is their exit option. Paraphrasing Stiglitz (1991: 32): 'if the management board is competent the company may perform well, but if it is incompetent it will perform badly'.

Institutional adjustments are required, because Dutch corporate governance institutions offer too little guarantee for high-quality management and supervision. In a sense the causality runs in the wrong direction: high-quality management guarantees high-quality governance. Trends towards ageing and internationalization reinforce the need for adjustment. Pension funds are becoming more active as direct monitors with considerable long-term shareholdings. Large foreign investors demand a say in the composition of the management board and in company strategy.

Some modest steps have recently been taken to adjust Dutch corporate governance. New regulations will somewhat reduce juridical defenses against hostile takeovers. This will probably increase internal rather than external shareholder control, because companies try to attract block shareholders as a way to protect against hostile takeovers. Hence, in this respect Dutch institutions will shift towards the cooperative model in the near future. In addition, the Dutch Corporate Governance Committee recommends to strengthen the opportunities for shareholders to use voice through the introduction of proxy voting, enabling shareholders to share screening and monitoring costs. In addition, some suggestions for the improvement of supervisory board performance within the current institutional setting have been made, for instance restricting the number of former managers in the supervisory board. However, the Committee tries to persuade companies to effectuate these changes through self-regulation. This does not solve the dilemma that a high-quality management board will recognize the usefulness of these recommendations, but that no instruments are available to persuade ill-performing management to adopt these measures.

To raise the efficacy of Dutch corporate governance in safeguarding the quality of both management board and supervisory board, the influence of shareholders on the supervisory board has to increase. A policy option from the German model is to leave cooption and to require a substantial majority of votes in the general meeting to replace the supervisory board. To some extent these adjustments will restrict the autonomy of high-quality management boards. Yet, this constitutes a relatively low price for enhancing effective governance, because shareholders have less incentives to interfere with the strategies of a well-performing company. These changes may give the Dutch corporate governance institutions a relatively strong centre position on the trade-off between commitment and flexibility, because this system would neither suffer from the inefficacy of a co-determined board nor from a short-term orientation or frequent hostile takeover practices.

11 Science and Technology Policy

Over the last years, German and Dutch policy makers have brought forward a series of initiatives in science and technology policy. In Germany, this is partly the result of the 'Standort' debate, in which the diminishing attractiveness of the German economy as a location for private research activities has been a popular topic of discussion. Furthermore, there is an on-going debate among German economists about the innovative performance of traditional sectors like machinery and chemistry. One of the main initiatives has been the merger of two ministries with separate responsibilities for science policy and for technology policy, into the new Bundesministerium fur Bildung, Wissenschaft, Forschung und Technologie. An other initiative concerns recent measures to support specific new technologies like biotechnology. In the Netherlands, the decreasing private R&D intensity in recent years has raised much concern among policy-makers. This has lead to an influential report 'Kennis in Beweging' (EZ/OCW/LNV, 1995) with a 'plan de campagne' for strengthening the knowledge base of the Dutch economy. One of the measures has been the funding of four technological top institutes that were jointly proposed and initiated by firms, universities and research institutions.

The aim of this chapter is to is to put these policy measures into perspective by comparing science and technology policy in Germany and the Netherlands from an institutional point of view.[1] Such a comparison between countries constitutes a pragmatic way to learn about the possible advantages and disadvantages of different institutional setups. Note in advance that current insights only partially cover the many, highly complicated aspects of the interaction between science, technology and the economy (Dasgupta, 1987: 21; Mowery, 1995: 544). 'More so than many other areas of policy, the technology policy maker is limited by bounded rationality. (...) The outcome of policy action is always uncertain and

[1] This approach takes into account the fact that actual technology policy is often not deliberately designed. Nelson (1993: 349-350) remarks in this context that 'there is no presumption that the system was, in some sense, consciously designed, or even that the set of institutions involved works together smoothly and coherently. Rather, the systems concept is that of a set of institutional actors that, together, play the major role in influencing innovative performance.' (cited in Audretsch, 1995: 17).

there is much sense in the view that the policy maker should use many instruments and none to excess' (Metcalfe, 1995: 410). Consequentially, at times the analysis remains somewhat sketchy.

Section 11.1 presents some theoretical backgrounds, stressing the different roles of science and technology for the production of innovations. Next, Section 11.2 and 11.3 analyze science and technology policies in Germany and the Netherlands, respectively. Section 11.4 reviews relevant trends and derives policy options.

11.1 Analytical Framework

In retrospect, one can distinguish three major stages in the economic thinking about technological change. The first stage is the work of Schumpeter who set forth a broad view of the relationship between technological change and the economic process. The second stage is the formal empirical confirmation of Schumpeter's view that economic growth indeed to a large extent can be attributed to technological progress (Solow, 1957). The third stage is the translation of Schumpeter's ideas in formal theoretical models. Examples are the industrial organization literature on the relation between market structure and innovation, and the new growth theory.[2] The notion that innovations are endogenous, that is, firms invest in research and development with the purpose of generating innovations, is central to this stage.

Currently, a new, fourth stage seems to emerge: a growing literature stresses the role of institutions for technological change. At the firm level, one could interpret the endogenization of innovation as taking the institutions of R&D labs properly into account. But also at the country level, a consensus is growing that the institutional setup matters. Looking at national R&D expenditures alone provides too narrow a view. A broad perspective as expressed in the concept of a *national System of Innovation* presents a more complete picture: a national system of innovation consists of those 'elements and relationships which interact in the production, diffusion and use of new, and economically useful knowledge ... and are either located within or rooted inside the borders of a nation state' (Lundvall, 1992; see also Metcalfe, 1995).

This section addresses the German and Dutch national systems of innovation from an institutional angle. The comparison distinguishes between science and technology policy, because both science and technology are important for the generation of innovations, but each in a different way. In terms of other well-known classifications, science loosely corresponds to invention and basic research, *i.e.* the generation of ideas. Technology corresponds to innovation and diffusion and to applied research and development, *i.e.* the development of those ideas into marketable products and the spread of these products. For both science and

---

[2] See Kamien and Schwartz (1982) for an overview of the industrial organization literature. See Grossman and Helpman (1991) for the new growth literature.

technology, this section describes the main market failures that may arise, reviews alternative coordination mechanisms and presents relevant trade-offs. Moreover, it pays attention to the link between science and technology and the diffusion of technological knowledge through the economy.

Analogously to the other chapters, the analytical framework presents a stylized model. It differentiates between science and technology to clearly identify relevant market failures and trade-offs. Of course in practice, both concerning research activity itself and concerning the relevant institutions, the two fields are not completely distinct. Science can bring forward ideas that turn out to be commercially successful, yet innovation is not a linear process that runs only from scientific research to technology and development. In contrast, interaction- and feedback mechanisms exist between science and technology (Kline 1985, Cobbenhagen 1990). Science can also solve problems that appear in technological research or address practical problems. Technological problems and objectives influence basic research in universities, in particular in fields like engineering, health, agriculture, or defence (Rosenberg and Nelson, 1994). In these fields, universities specialize on fundamental understanding, motivated by practical goals like fighting cancer or AIDS, whereas companies focus more on short-term problem-solving R&D.

The broad spectrum from pure basic research to commercial R&D with many feedback mechanisms is also manifest in the institutions of science and technology policy. University research ranges from largely basic research in theoretical physics or astronomy to much more applied research in engineering. In new fields such as biotechnology, basic research and technological R&D are even quite closely linked. Research institutes exist on the basic and on the applied side of the spectrum. Yet, even the applied institutes have to perform some basic research to maintain an adequate knowledge base and to keep informed on new developments in science. Therefore, after the stylized theoretical framework, the analysis of institutions in subsequent sections is organized according to the main characteristics of these institutions, without applying a strong distinction between science and technology. In the analysis of institutions the theoretical aspects of science and technology, further elaborated in this section, act as an organizing principle.

11.1.1 Market Failures and the Role of Policy in Science and Technology

The interaction between science, technology and the economy concerns four main fields: the generation of scientific knowledge, the incorporation of scientific knowledge in technological research, the creation of technological knowledge, and the diffusion of technological knowledge throughout the economy.[3] Each of these fields entails several market failures that may require institutions to support performance. This section starts with a review of the main characteristics and market failures in scientific research and in technological research. Subsequently, from the characteristics of science and technology, the linkage between the two fields is seen to present some serious challenges for policy. The final part of this section analyses which market failures exist in the diffusion phase.

Generation of Scientific Knowledge. Scientific research entails some serious market failures. Non-rivalry, non-excludability and uncertainty are present in every type of research and in every stage of the innovative process (see Arrow, 1962). In scientific research, however, they exist in their most extreme form. Because scientific output is not oriented on specific applications, the wide potential use of science in technological research implies a high degree of non-rivalry. Use of scientific results in one technological application does not restrict the use in many other applications. On the contrary, repeated usage of knowledge frequently leads to a continuous process of improvements, which ameliorates knowledge instead of depreciating it. Furthermore, scientific knowledge without direct applications is hard to appropriate in an economically meaningful way, which makes scientific research also largely non-excludable. Uncertainty in scientific research is proverbial, a well-considered research strategy does not guarantee success. In contrast, at times serendipity guides scientific progress: breakthroughs sometimes arise by chance as a byproduct of the search for something completely different.

Non-rivalry and non-excludability turn scientific knowledge into a public good, which requires institutions to encourage production. Enhancing excludability by granting property rights (patents, copyrights) is difficult, because non-competitive market structures may easily arise and because the value of scientific research is difficult to quantify (Dasgupta and David, 1994: 496). Hence, science requires public provision either in public scientific research institutes or in subsidized private institutes that in general must disclose the results of their research to anyone interested.

Public provision, uncertainty and information asymmetries create information problems and incentive problems in scientific research. Information problems pertain to the definition of the total research budget and the allocation of the budget over different scientific research areas. Moral hazard arises in reward structures, because it is difficult to distinguish low effort of researchers or the pursuit of personal goals from poor research performance. Problems of ex-post verification are present because it is hard to observe the ability of researchers,

[3] Note that various relations and feedbacks exist between these fields. The discussion below shows that innovation is not a linear process that only runs from science to technology and diffusion.

again, because failure of a project may be due to intrinsic technical problems or to low ability of researchers. Thus research institutes may use subsidies for other purposes than the project agreed upon and claim that the project failed because of inherent uncertainty.

Competition for priority of discovery forms the basic incentive structure in scientific research that motivates researchers to exert effort and to disclose their results (Dasgupta and David, 1987, 1994; Stephan, 1996). Most scientists aim to be first to communicate a certain advance in knowledge. By establishing priority of discovery and completely disclosing their findings, scientists can intellectually 'appropriate' knowledge. It strengthens their reputation in the scientific community, enhances their ability to obtain research grants and provides a basis for a career in science.

Priority of discovery in scientific research intensifies the public character of scientific knowledge. Public disclosure of new findings forms the basic prerequisite to obtain an intellectual property right. Disclosure lowers information asymmetries and enables peer groups to screen scientific results for accuracy. Moreover, disclosure broadens the diffusion of scientific results, which raises the value of science to society (Dasgupta and David, 1994: 500).

Technology. Science and technology differ in generating public versus private knowledge. Science adds to the stock of public knowledge, whereas technology adds to the stream of rents that may be derived from possession of private knowledge (Dasgupta and David, 1994: 498; Stoneman, 1995: 4). For private firms R&D must be profitable, *i.e.* R&D revenues must exceed R&D costs.

All four main market failures distinguished in Chapter 2 exist in technological research: market power, externalities, specificity and uncertainty (compare Geroski, 1995). Some are similar to those in scientific research, be it less extreme, others are specific to technological research.

Market power may arise because R&D often involves large fixed costs. Economies of scale make the market for information non-competitive (Dasgupta, 1987). One of the questions that has occupied industrial economists for decades is the optimal market structure for innovation. The so-called Schumpeterian hypothesis states that market power is conducive for innovation. Schumpeter argued that large scale is necessary because of large fixed R&D costs (cost spreading argument) and that monopoly profits are necessary to finance R&D because of imperfections on the capital market. Recent literature emphasizes that the Schumpeterian hypothesis may not be correct, because a competitive threat is needed to encourage innovation (Nickell, 1996). Hence, a trade-off exists between moral hazard and scale.

Two opposite *externalities* determine whether there is too much or too little R&D competition on the market (compare Chapter 12). The business-stealing effect means that firms do not take the impact of their effort on the value of their competitors' research effort into account. This leads to wasteful duplication of fixed R&D costs, and therefore induces too much competition. The product-diversity effect means that the consumer surplus of a new variety is not appropriated by the innovator. This causes too little competition. The two opposite effects create a trade-off between diversity and scale. Which effect dominates depends on product market characteristics. In markets characterized by technological competition for one specific innovation, the business-stealing effect often dominates (Reinganum 1989). In markets where firms compete through product differentiation (quality, design), the product-diversity effect often dominates.

Externalities in the form of knowledge spillovers are less present in technology than in science. The first reason is that technology is more application-oriented and therefore there is less 'spillover potential': the part of scientific research at the basic end of the spectrum is not application-oriented at all. The second reason is that firms have private means to appropriate knowledge and associated returns, such as secrecy, exploitation of first-mover-advantages and marketing efforts to build brand loyalty (Levin *et al.*, 1987). Nevertheless, the risk of imitation may result in a socially suboptimal level of innovation, which calls for institutions like patent protection.

Often, technological research and development entails *specificity* and sunk costs. Specificity follows from investments in knowledge tailored to the technological problem at hand that may be difficult to apply in other situations. Another type of specificity concerns a technical product standard in an industry. If contracts were complete and verifiable, the market could handle specificity. However, generally, it is hardly possible to write a complete contract on R&D activities: because the innovation is not exactly known beforehand, the contract is incomplete and thus will not be verifiable in court. These features may give rise to hold-up problems in technological research, for instance concerning investments in firm-specific knowledge by workers (see Chapter 9), in the relationship between a private R&D laboratory and a customer firm, in joint R&D projects by several firms, or in relationships between a supplier and a procuring firm (compare Chapter 2).

Generally, information asymmetries preclude reducing *uncertainty* in technology through risk sharing in insurance markets. Two types of uncertainty characterize technological research. Analogously to scientific research, technical uncertainty exists. Investing in technology does not guarantee an innovation since there is always a chance of technical failure. In addition, innovation-generating activities are subject to market uncertainty as it is unclear beforehand whether the innovation will succeed on the market. These strong uncertainties may lead to underinvestment in technology, unless the risks can be insured against, for example by spreading them among several external capital suppliers. Then, however, the problems of asymmetric information and incentives, mentioned above, arise. The limited possibility to insure innovations on the capital market means that innovation is frequently funded out of the internally generated profits of established firms, which creates path-dependency in the innovation process and limits financing available to small firms (Metcalfe, 1995: 486). To a certain degree specific institutions, such as venture capital, reduce this market failure.

The Linkage between Science and Technology. Science and technology are linked in several ways, yet at the same time some fundamental differences exist between the two fields, as shown by the discussion above. This turns the linkage between science and technology into a delicate subject for public policy. To see why, this section addresses three questions. How does science contribute to technology? Which feedbacks exist between technology and science? What is the risk of strengthening the impact of technology on science by making science more market oriented?

Three main contributions of science to technology stand out (compare Brooks, 1994; Dasgupta and David, 1994; Mowery, 1995). The first is the provision of *higher education*, which not only takes care of training of researchers but also of other high-quality human capital. Technological research in firms benefits from the inflow of trained scientists who are acquainted with new scientific insights, master new techniques, and strengthen the networks between firms and universities. In particular the combination of a basic university education and several years of experience in scientific research at a university forms a valuable asset for a company, because it enables the company to screen potential employees on their research abilities (Dasgupta, 1987). Incentive structures in science encourage researchers to disclose their results and thus provide a public screening service to technological companies. Besides training future technologists, high-quality human capital also enhances the exploitation of the fruits from R&D. Employees need proper skills and training to be able to use innovations. Finally, positive externalities exist because high-skilled human capital raises productivity and thus stimulates economic growth from which others benefit as well.

The second contribution of science concerns the provision of a *broad general knowledge base* from which a wide set of firms can tap and which facilitates absorption and diffusion of knowledge. This broad knowledge base is built up through research on a broad front, mainly in universities and in large public research centres. Knowledge bases not only consist of new scientific knowledge, but also comprise research methods, techniques and instruments.

The third contribution of science to technology consists of *specific knowledge bases*, meant to support industry. If the market failures in technology mentioned above, prevent crucial industries to create their own dedicated scientific research base, the government may provide public research institutes that perform this task. Research carried out at these institutes must be application-oriented to some extent ('oriented basic research' according to the Frascati Manual), since it is eventually meant to support industry. Specialized large research institutes carry out in-depth basic research to support specific sectors. More broadly oriented are the applied scientific research institutes that aim to commercialize technology by transforming public knowledge and basic technologies into specific applications, in particular for small and medium-sized firms. This concerns the Fraunhofer Gesellschaft in Germany and the Netherlands Organization for Applied Scientific Research (TNO).

Strengthening the Linkage between Science and Technology. Arguments exist for strengthening the impact of technology on science. The fundamental differences between science and technology described above imply that 'scientists will not obviously provide what technologists require nor that technologists will pick up what the scientists are doing' (Stoneman, 1995: 4). Then, a stronger feedback from technology to science may direct university research more closely to the needs of industry, which may enhance a country's technological research base and raise productivity. For this reason, American legislation in the 1980s encouraged universities to licence R&D results to business, to establish centres for industrial technology and to form technology transfer alliances with business (Lee, 1996: 844).

However, increasing the impact of technology on science through the market mechanism entails a number of risks that may generate a *dynamic market failure*, which in the long run slows down rather than increases the rate of innovation. The fundamental differences between the objectives and incentive structures in science and technology lie at the heart of these risks. Scientific research (partly) financed by companies runs the risk that short-term issues crowd out long-term research subjects. Moreover, companies may exert pressure on researchers to withhold or delay publication (Lee, 1996). Also, in a number of cases the scientific insights and methods used to design marketable technologies are relatively old and thus offer few or no prospects for publications or academic careers (Rosenberg and Nelson, 1994: 340). These effects reduce the motivation of scientific researchers. In addition, a stronger orientation of science on technology makes the two fields closer substitutes, which lowers the income differential required to pull talented young researchers out of science into technology (Dasgupta and David, 1994: 514). The signalling value of academic experience may even reverse when most of the talented researchers opt for a career in technology. Hence, companies will face increasing difficulties to attract researchers with a number of years experience in science and spillovers from science to technology diminish. Companies benefit less from science and increasingly have to perform basic research themselves. However, because private research is secret compared to open scientific research, duplication of basic research intensifies, which slows down the rate of technological progress.[4]

---

[4] Note that to some extent positive evolutionary effects from duplication of R&D, as described by Geroski (1991), counteract this dynamic market failure (see also Van de Klundert, 1997: 83). Duplication increases the probability of positive mutations, *i.e.* the emergence of entirely new products that may create new markets and boost economic growth. These positive effects of duplication occur at the start-up phase of the product life cycle. Therefore, duplication of scientific research by companies in particular will create a

Because of this dynamic market failure, a stronger orientation of scientific research on economic objectives should not replace government support for basic research by funding from private industry and by the establishment of property rights on scientific research (Dasgupta and David, 1994; Rosenberg and Nelson, 1994; Lee, 1996; Nelson and Romer, 1996). Instead, a reorientation should be found in a reallocation of funds in science policy budgets towards topics that are relevant to the needs of industry. 'This would require advisory committees knowledgeable about industry needs, and decision criteria and proposal evaluation systems that are sensitive to those needs' (Rosenberg and Nelson, 1994: 346). In addition, university evaluation standards have to include user relevance criteria, which encourage scientists to perform user-oriented research through prospects for tenure and promotion (Lee, 1996: 861).

Diffusion of Technological Knowledge. Diffusion of technological knowledge is crucial for economic welfare. The spread and use of innovations and knowledge throughout firms and industries strongly enhances a country's productive potential.

Three main sources of market failure relate to the diffusion process: imperfect information, market power and externalities (Stoneman and Diederen, 1994). *Imperfect information* may concern the lack of information not only on the very existence of an innovation, but also on its current and future technical and economic characteristics. These two aspects complicate the link between uncertainty and diffusion. Uncertainty about available technologies may retard adoption, but certainty about future developments may slow down adoption as well. The reason is that providing information about potential future improvements in technology may induce companies to wait for new or cheaper technologies to arrive on the market. Also, when it is not clear which will be the dominant standard in the market, a firm may wait before adopting.

Market power in the industry that supplies an innovation generates intertemporal price discrimination. However, if buyers are aware of price discrimination and anticipate future prices to decrease, they delay adoption of a new technology. In these circumstances market power of the supplier industry produces a diffusion path that is too slow from a welfare point of view (Stoneman and Diederen, 1994: 923). Hence, a system of property rights, such as a patent system, slows down diffusion, although at the same time it may form a prerequisite for markets for innovations to exist, because without patent protection suppliers would not produce innovations at all.

The third source of market failure concerns various *adoption externalities*, both negative and positive. The advantages of adopting an innovation may provide too

---

dynamic market failure in the expanding and mature phases of the product life cycle. Since established companies in these phases have substantial financial means to attract researchers from science, the adverse effect is likely to dominate the evolutionary counter effect.

strong incentives, resembling the business-stealing effects explained above. In this case diffusion will be too high. There are also positive externalities. A firm that adopts early provides indirectly useful information about the innovation to firms that wait and see. Market and technical uncertainty thus tends to decrease along the diffusion path. Network externalities may also be present: the larger the group of adopters, the larger the benefits per adopter. This implies that an early adopter receives less benefits. By consequence, information externalities and network externalities may slow down the diffusion process.

Diffusion of technology is a highly complex process. From a social welfare point of view, delay in the adoption of new technologies may be economically desirable. The various market failures impact the diffusion process in contrasting ways and may make diffusion either too slow or too fast, compared to the optimal path. In addition, diffusion may depend also on the user firm's capacity to perform R&D, when research experience is required to evaluate and adopt new technologies (Levin *et al.*, 1987; Cohen and Levinthal, 1989). Together with the observation that in general technologies develop further along the diffusion path, this links technology diffusion to technology development (Metcalfe, 1995: 482). Development is needed for diffusion, but diffusion also shapes development: the two processes are mutually interacting. Moreover, the interaction with development makes diffusion a path-dependent process. In still more general terms, diffusion will depend on firms' capability to learn, *i.e.* its human capital, its current technological knowledge base and its organisational structure. The latter features link diffusion to a broad set of institutions in a country's system of innovation, covering education, the labour market, financial markets and product markets and to the social acceptance and public attitude towards new technologies. This explains both why diffusion is crucial for economic development and why the process is only partly understood. Indeed, innovation is much more than merely R&D (see Minne, 1992; Jacobs, 1996).

11.1.2 Institutions of Science Policy

Frequently, different institutions deal with market failures in science and technology. These institutions affect economic performance in different ways and thus give rise to trade-offs. This section reviews trade-offs in science policy, the next section addresses technology policy. Here, the description of science policy includes institutions that affect the linkage between science and technology. Technology policy includes institutions that affect the diffusion of technological knowledge throughout the economy.

The discussion below first turns to the three main contributions of science to technology, *viz.* higher education, broad knowledge base and specific knowledge base. Subsequently, the institutions that affect the feedback from technology to science are discussed.

Higher education. Education is a special good in two respects. First, to a certain extent it is a non-rival good: the marginal cost of one extra student in a lecture-room is relatively low.[5] Hence, increasing returns exist in providing education. Second, from an economic and technical point of view, education is an excludable good: it is possible to exclude students who do not pay from receiving education. However, in many countries, social and political reasons make education largely non-excludable. For social reasons, also persons who cannot pay for education should be able to have education.

To the extent that social reasons restrict excludability, education increasingly becomes a public good that calls for public intervention (compare Box 2.3). This forms a major difference between the American system of higher education and the European system.[6] Excludability is relatively high in the American system, which is based more on the coordination mechanism of competition. Private American universities in general have to compete to attract students. Reputation, price, quality of education and differentiation are their means of competition. Competition has its price: large tuition fees must be paid to enter a top university. Compared to the expensive top private universities, state universities are cheaper but often of lower quality. In contrast, coordination through control and more homogeneous quality characterize the European system. European universities to a large extent receive basic funding from the government. Therefore, competition with other universities, through reputation and differentiation, is less present than in the United States. In addition, hardly any private universities exist in Europe (some business schools form the exception).

This stylized representation positions the American and the European systems of higher education on two sides of the trade-off between diversity and scale, the trade-off between experimentation and certainty and the trade-off between incentives and solidarity (see Table 11.1). The American system promotes diversity and experimentation among different methods and qualities of education and enables flexible adjustment of curricula. The more homogeneous European system more strongly exploits economies of scale and stresses the certainty of a uniform quality of education above experimentation. Finally, the less competitive European system provides insurance both to students and to the providers of education compared to the American system that entails more incentives.

---

[5] The marginal costs of increasing the number of students of course differ among the various science fields. For instance, marginal costs in technology and medicine exceed those in the social sciences, because of a larger cost share of equipment and practical training. Also switches from classroom lectures towards more individually oriented teaching methods increase the marginal costs.

[6] Here 'European' system refers to main characteristics in comparison to the United States. Of course within Europe systems of higher education differ on many aspects.

Table 11.1 Trade-offs in science policy

Higher education	*Competition (US)*	*Broad admission (Europe)*
– knowledge base	diversity	scale
– quality	experimentation	certainty
– uncertainty	incentives	solidarity
Broad knowledge base: financing institutions	*Peer-review grants (US)*	*Institute approach (Europe)*
– science base	diversity	scale and scope
– research orientation	flexibility	commitment
– uncertainty	incentives	solidarity
Specific knowledge base: financing institutions	*Contract funding*	*Basic funding*
– knowledge base	diversity	scale and scope
– tailored to industry	flexibility	commitment
Feedback from technology to science	*Contract funding, licensing, etc.*	*Networks*
– research orientation	flexibility	commitment

Broad Knowledge Base. Besides the priority of discovery rule, financing institutions address the incentive and principal-agent problems in scientific research. Two different systems exist in practice: the peer-review grants system frequently used in the United States and the institute approach commonly applied in European countries (Stephan, 1996). The American system consists of competition among scientists for individual grants, allocated on the basis of reviews by peers. In addition to competition, also common values and norms within the relevant peer group structure this system. The European system, in contrast, finances specific institutes and leaves the choice of research topics and research methods to the institutes. By delegating responsibility to the institutes, the European system more strongly applies cooperative exchange as a coordination mechanism.

The American and European financing systems occupy opposite positions on three trade-offs (Table 11.1). The American system generates a diversity of research projects, flexibility to adjust the knowledge base to new developments, and an incentive for scientists to remain productive. Diversity and flexibility create an environment conducive to the emergence of radical innovations. Disadvantages are the transaction costs involved in writing and judging proposals and the fact that short-term, well-defined projects are more successful in obtaining finance than projects with a longer term horizon. The European system of financing institutes instead of individuals has the advantage of exploiting economies of scale and scope and facilitating commitment of scientists to research projects that are more uncertain on the longer term. Moreover, the institute approach enhances solidarity because it pools risks among a group of researchers. These features of the European system encourage incremental innovations.

Specific Knowledge Base. Trade-offs arise from two financing methods of specific research institutes: contract funding versus basic funding (Table 11.1). Contract funding strengthens competition and has the potential to create a more diverse knowledge base. Moreover, it enhances flexibility to respond to new sources of innovations or to short-term shifts in interests of industry. Basic funding more strongly enables research institutes to benefit from economies of scale. In addition, it promotes commitment to invest in research topics and methods tailored to the long-term needs of the industry the institute is meant to support. Basic funding creates a knowledge base that supports industry by enhancing its long-term potential to innovate. However, these trade-offs only exist to a limited extent, because the research technology requires a minimum efficient scale and a certain degree of specificity to match the industry needs.

The Feedback from Technology to Science. The main trade-off regarding the feedback from technology to science results from institutions that support competition versus institutions that support cooperative exchange. As mentioned above, various institutions may enhance competition, like making scientific research more dependent on funding by companies and granting universities the right to benefit from the fruits of their research through licensing agreements, etc. These institutions link scientific research more closely to the needs of enterprises and enable flexible adjustment, but may weaken commitment of researchers to engage in science, which hampers long-term investments.

In contrast, cooperative exchange supports basic research with a long-term relevance for technology. Its commitment and internal flexibility promote incremental research activities, but reduce external flexibility. Cooperative exchange can be found in networks that link scientific research institutes to enterprises (Metcalfe, 1995: 466). Networks promote exchange of information, identification of important topics for research and common agreements on the definition of standards. Moreover, networks facilitate the flow of researchers not only from science to technology, but also vice versa for instance through professorships for top technological researchers. Industry associations may play a role in enforcing the implicit contracts that underlie network relationships (Carlin and Soskice, 1997).

Table 11.2 Trade-offs in technology policy

Scope of patents	*Narrow*	*Broad*
– R&D	diffusion	experimentation
– product market	diversity	scale
Subsidies	*Generic*	*Specific*
– technologies	experimentation	certainty
	incentives	solidarity
– type of firm	diversity	scale
– R&D cooperation	flexibility	commitment
Promoting diffusion	*Information, subsidies*	*Common views / standards*
– design	experimentation	certainty
– specific technologies	flexibility	commitment

11.1.3 Institutions of Technology Policy

This section briefly reviews the trade-offs present in various institutions of technology policy.[7] It starts with institutions that affect technology development and also affect technology diffusion: patents and subsidies. Thereafter it addresses institutions oriented at the diffusion process: provision of information and reduction of uncertainty.

Patents. Patents define property rights, which support markets for innovations. As mentioned above, the scope of patent protection generates a trade-off between diffusion and experimentation (see Table 11.2). A limited scope promotes diffusion, whereas a broad scope encourages experimentation in technological research (Klemperer, 1990; Matutes *et al.*, 1993). A very broad patent system may even create too strong incentives for R&D from a social welfare point of view, because of a patent's 'winner-take-all' feature. This induces wasteful duplication of fixed R&D costs that are necessary to enter a patent race. On the product market broad patents provide much market power to large individual firms, whereas patents with a limited scope leave room for competition and therefore diversity.

Subsidies. Subsidies are conceivable, when the market provides too low a level of R&D. Table 11.2 shows that, depending on the type of subsidy, all four main trade-offs from Chapter 2 are relevant. Generic R&D subsidies that leave the

---

[7] For more extensive surveys of institutions for technology policy see Stoneman and Vickers (1988), Geroski (1995), Metcalfe (1995), and Mowery (1995).

choice of technology to the market, such as the exemption of R&D activities from taxation, promote experimentation and create incentives to engage in R&D. Subsidies that support specific technologies or specific firms promote certainty and contain elements of solidarity with companies active in the relevant technological fields.

Subsidies that differentiate according to firm size produce a trade-off between diversity and scale. Subsidies that support start-ups and small firms promote diversity, whereas specific procurement contracts often go to large firms. For example, a limited number of large defense firms in the United States perform most defense-related R&D for the government.

Subsidies may also soften the hold-up problem between firms that cooperate in R&D. Subsidies for R&D cooperation increase the benefits from cooperation for the firms involved, which may reduce incentives for opportunistic behaviour by partners in a research joint venture. Hence these subsidies strengthen commitment.

Promoting Diffusion. The theoretical arguments above provide no general policy advice to either increase or slow down the rate of diffusion. Yet, practical measures in the field of diffusion policy all attempt to increase the speed of diffusion (Stoneman and Diederen, 1994: 927). In particular, they aim at small and medium sized enterprises, which seem most vulnerable to the market failures associated with too slow a rate of diffusion. Examples are regional innovation centres, business parks or network facilities.

Governments can promote diffusion by increasing the flow of information, by subsidizing early adopters or by aiming at common perceptions and standards among the participants in specific research areas. The previous examples all increase information flows, just as demonstration projects or advertising campaigns do. On the one hand, reducing uncertainty through the provision of information and providing subsidies for early adapters enhance competition for new technologies and thus promote experimentation and flexibility (compare Table 11.2). On the other hand, together with companies, business associations and research institutes, policy makers may try to develop a common view on important technologies and relevant interface standards to disseminate these technologies among companies (Carlin and Soskice, 1997). In that case, cooperative exchange favours the certainty of a dominant design and the commitment to invest in the relevant technologies and standards. Once these investments have been made diffusion proceeds relatively fast.

In addition, as mentioned above, many other institutions affect the rate of technology diffusion, because diffusion strongly depends on conditions that affect investments and on society's learning capabilities. As emphasized by David (1986: 387), innovation adoption decisions are investment decisions, which relate to a broad range of institutions, such as macroeconomic policies that affect interest rates, financing institutions or competition policy. Learning capabilities strongly depend on a nation's 'human infrastructure', i.e. its educational system, institutions that promote lifelong learning etc. These features link technology diffusion to most of the other chapters in this study.

11.1.4 The Impact of Country Size and Openness

More than for many of the institutions addressed in previous chapters, country size and openness matter for science and technology policy. Hence, the difference in size between Germany and the Netherlands warrants some specific attention to the impact of this condition. This section first presents the main arguments for a closed and an open economy. Next, it reviews the consequences for science and technology policy.

Country Size and Technological Specialization. Due to the impact of two market failures, firms in a small closed economy tend to be smaller than firms in a large closed economy. Firstly, the size of the market limits economies of scale. Firms in small countries will be of smaller scale, since large scale cannot be achieved in the domestic market. Secondly, the incentive for firms to invest in R&D is larger in large countries. While R&D costs are largely fixed, revenues depend on market size. Therefore a larger market provides more opportunities to fully capture the revenues from R&D activity.

Openness adds another market failure: international knowledge spillovers. On balance, these may benefit a small country because inward spillovers may well exceed outward spillovers. The small country is able to free ride on knowledge production of larger countries.

In contrast, openness reduces the market failures related to market size, because it to some extent enlarges the size of the market. For several reasons, foreign markets and the domestic market are no perfect substitutes: firms have better knowledge of the home market, exports involve transport costs and uncertainties, *etc.* To the extent that the domestic and foreign markets are imperfect substitutes, the impact of country size remains present. In that case, firms in larger countries benefit relatively more from a large home market. Hence, the degree of substitution co-determines firm size and investment in R&D in the small country.

If openness enhances incentives for R&D in a small country, the national resource base, and the knowledge base in particular, becomes a limiting factor. Because fixed costs of R&D require sufficient scale and because the resource base is limited, domestic firms will grow large and more R&D intensive, and domestic markets will become more concentrated and specialized. As a result: 'Only large countries can afford to distribute their innovations more uniformly across technologies. Small countries, on the contrary, are to some extent forced to specialize in selected niches, suggesting that they are more dependent on international technology flows and cooperation than large ones.' (Archibugi and Pianta, 1992: 117).

Box 11.1 International R&D spillovers and productivity

Total Factor Productivity (TFP) indicates how much an economy grows more than can be expected on the basis of increases in labour and capital inputs. It is an indirect measure of the effects of R&D on productivity. In the period 1973-1979, both Germany and the Netherlands are above the OECD average TFP growth. In the next period of 1979-1992, however, TFP growth decreased to the OECD average.

A study by Coe and Helpman (1995) gives a more detailed picture of the structure of TFP growth of 21 OECD countries during the period 1971-1990. Their study focuses on international spill-overs: what is the impact of domestic versus foreign R&D expenditures on domestic growth? International trade constitutes the vehicle for R&D spill-overs. For the Netherlands Coe and Helpman find that an increase of the domestic R&D stock of 10% leads to a 0.7% increase in productivity. An identical increase of foreign R&D leads to a larger productivity increase of 1.5%. Especially American and German R&D have a positive impact on Dutch productivity. Germany turns out to be much less sensitive to foreign R&D and much more to domestic R&D. A 10% increase of German R&D leads to a 2.3% increase in German productivity, while the same increase of foreign R&D has a much lower impact of 0.7%. American R&D in particular is important for Germany, Dutch R&D not at all.

A similar study by Eaton and Kortum (1996) takes foreign patents in a country, rather than international trade, as the channel through which R&D spreads. It finds similar results: the Netherlands benefit largely from foreign spill-overs, in particular from the US but also from Germany and Japan, while Germany has to rely more on domestic R&D, although it benefits largely from US spill-overs as well.

These studies concur with the analysis in Section 11.1.4. The small open Dutch economy should focus relatively more on absorption of knowledge, whereas the larger, more closed German economy should focus more intensively on generating innovation itself.

Specialization implies that the small country is less insured against external shocks that hit its sectors of specialization. Large countries with many large firms and many specializations are better diversified and therefore less vulnerable to shocks. This problem is even more severe, because external shocks may hit small countries relatively hard so that these countries are in need of better insurance.

The Position of Science. Since market failures and incentive structures differ between science and technology, the impact of country size and openness on science differs from that on technology. The above arguments primarily apply to technology where knowledge to a larger extent is secret and can be appropriated. Hence, returns to scale, barriers to entry and concentration are most relevant for technology.

In science, international spillovers are large and developments in information technology further increase the speed of information dissemination. In addition, fixed costs and therefore economies of scale are less than in technology. Internationalization of science facilitates diffusion, access to scientific knowledge and international cooperation. As a consequence, to a certain degree diversification replaces specialisation in scientific knowledge, also in small countries (for empirical evidence see Archibugi and Pianta, 1992). In contrast, internationalization increases locational competition between national knowledge bases (see Section 11.4.1). Hence, increasingly competition on the international scientific 'market' requires high-quality research and sufficient scale.

Policy Implications. How can a small country's science and technology policy deal with inherent technological specialization? Resources of a small country are too limited to create many new large scale specializations. Policy makers also lack the information to pick the winning specialisations for the future. Therefore, policy may attempt to make the country's knowledge base on a broad front more adoptive to foreign knowledge spillovers and more flexible to pick up developments in science and technology (see also Box 11.1). Compared to innovation, absorption of new technologies provides insurance, first, because much uncertainty is resolved once innovations are on the market and, second, because the country is not dependent on the success of the few technologies of domestic firms. The fact that international knowledge spillovers are relatively large for small, open countries fits very well in this absorption strategy.

How can the absorption strategy be implemented? In order to be able to absorb foreign spillovers, a country also has to carry out scientific research herself. Therefore, a diversified and flexible scientific knowledge base appears most suitable for small countries. In addition, firms need high-quality human capital to be able to absorb spillovers. This also implies that a small open country should focus its science policy more at higher education and at developing a broad scientific knowledge base, which can be relatively large compared to large countries. Only in a few specific fields a small country might develop a high-quality scientific research potential that competes on a world-wide scale. A reasonably large research potential may also be needed in some key technologies that permeate many business sectors, so as to provide a sufficiently large knowledge base to support these sectors. All together, these features put the small country more on the diversity and flexibility side of the trade-offs in Table 11.1.

In its technology policy, a small country should focus on creating a relatively broad industrial research potential, in particular aimed at facilitating the diffusion of foreign knowledge spillovers to domestic firms. A large country, on the contrary, should focus on enhancing current industrial research, which is both well-diversified and of sufficient scale, by supporting firms and industries with specific basic research in their technologies. Hence, a small country is closer to the experimentation and flexibility side of the trade-offs in Table 11.2.

11.2 The Institutions of German and Dutch Science Policy

Section 11.1.1 states that the main contributions of science to technology consist of higher education, the provision of a broad knowledge base and the provision of a specific knowledge base. With respect to higher education, this section focuses on universities as the main source of education for scientific researchers. The broad knowledge base in the Netherlands comprises universities and basic research institutes, such as the institutes of the Royal Dutch Academy of Arts and Sciences (KNAW) and those of the Dutch Organisation for Scientific Research (NWO). Also in Germany the major part of basic research takes place at universities. In addition, characteristic for Germany is the Max Planck Gesellschaft (MPG), worldwide renowned for its high-quality basic research. Public research institutes engaged in oriented basic research create the specific research base in both countries.

Section 11.2.1 focuses on the institutions and funding of higher education and the broad knowledge base in Germany and the Netherlands. Section 11.2.2 turns to the specific knowledge base. Section 11.2.3 addresses current issues in science policy and in that context also touches upon the feedback from technology to science. Note that the scope of a subject like higher education and scientific research is too large and complex to analyze in full detail in the limited space available here. Therefore, the emphasis lies on the integration of readily available information, leaving many topics for further elaboration.

11.2.1 Higher Education and the Broad Knowledge Base

Both Germany and the Netherlands have organized their scientific knowledge base according to the European institute approach of mainly basic funding of research institutes (compare Section 11.1.2). Yet, differences in the system of funding and the orientation of activities of institutes exist. This section reviews some of these differences. Relevant topics are the sources of funding, the system of distribution of financial resources, and the evaluation of research performance.

An Empirical Overview. With 0.6% of GDP, Dutch R&D in higher education is among the highest in the OECD (see Table 11.3). Germany is at the higher end of a large group of countries with higher-education R&D intensities of about 0.4% of GDP. In terms of total R&D expenditures, the relative importance of higher-education R&D differs even more between Germany and the Netherlands, because private R&D in Germany exceeds that in the Netherlands.

A further distinction concerns the scientific fields in which R&D is carried out. According to Table 11.4, the German share of research in natural sciences substantially exceeds that of the Netherlands. In contrast, Dutch higher-education research more strongly focuses at agricultural sciences, social sciences and humanities. Recently, Dutch research in higher education to some extent is shifting away from social sciences and humanities towards engineering and technology (see Table 11.4). Between 1990 and 1994 nominal expenditure on social sciences and humanities increased by 3.5%, whereas nominal expenditure for the other categories combined increased by 19% and nominal expenditure for engineering

Table 11.3 International comparison of main fields of R&D expenditure, 1994

	Higher education		Government[a]		Business enterprises		Total
	% R&D	%GDP	% R&D	%GDP	% R&D	%GDP	%GDP
Denmark[b]	22.8	0.41	18.8	0.34	58.3	1.04	1.79
France	16.2	0.39	21.9	0.52	61.8	1.47	2.38
Germany	18.7	0.44	15.2	0.35	66.0	1.54	2.33
Japan	20.2	0.57	13.7	0.39	66.1	1.88	2.84
Netherlands	28.8	0.59	19.6	0.40	51.5	1.06	2.05
Norway[b]	27.3	0.48	19.2	0.33	53.5	0.93	1.74
Sweden[b]	24.5	0.80	5.1	0.17	70.5	2.31	3.28
United Kingdom	17.5	0.38	17.3	0.38	65.2	1.43	2.19
United States	15.6	0.39	13.4	0.34	71.0	1.80	2.53
EU	20.6	0.39	17.6	0.33	61.9	1.18	1.90
OECD	17.8	0.38	15.3	0.33	66.8	1.43	2.14

[a] Including private non-profit institutions. [b] 1993.
Source: OECD Basic Science and Technology Statistics database.

and technology rose by 30% (CBS, 1996: 117). The shares in Germany are relatively stable.

Funding Higher Education. Three major sources of funding R&D at institutes of higher education exist: basic funding, contract research and peer review grant funding. Basic funding, consists of a block grant from central or local government. The extent of basic funding underscores the institute approach in Germany and the Netherlands. It covers 65% (10600/16228) of total higher education funding in Germany and 72% (2839/3920) in the Netherlands (see Table 11.5). Measured as a percentage of GDP, basic funding appears to account for the difference in higher education R&D intensity between Germany and the Netherlands. Both contract funding and peer review grant funding constitute a similar percentage of GDP in the two countries.

In the Netherlands contract funding considerably increased since the early 1980s, partly as a response to falling basic funding by the government (VSNU, 1997). Private non-profit organisations commission a substantial part of the contract research in Dutch universities. These organisations predominantly finance medical research: they collect money from the public to stimulate medical research, for instance regarding cure and prevention of heart diseases. Moreover, compared to Germany, Dutch universities appear more easily to find their way to international sources of finance, mainly from participation in EU research projects. In contrast, the financial link between firms and higher education research is stronger in Ger-

Table 11.4 Distribution of R&D expenditure in higher education among fields of science

	Germany		Netherlands	
	1989	1993	1990	1994
Agricultural sciences	4.6	4.7	6.6	7.2
Natural sciences	29.5	28.8	18.6	18.1
Engineering and technology	20.6	19.7	20.4	22.8
Medical sciences	25.5	27.0	28.0	28.4
Social sciences and humanities	19.7	19.7	26.3	23.5

Source: Germany, BMBF (1996), Table VII/20;
Netherlands, CBS (1996), Table A.2.2.1 and Table A.2.2.2.

many than in the Netherlands.[8]

As a percentage of GDP, German peer review grant finance of university research equals that in the Netherlands. These funds are allocated through research councils like the Deutsche Forschungsgemeinschaft (DFG) in Germany and the Dutch Organisation for Scientific Research (NWO). The relatively large share of enterprise R&D in Germany makes peer review grant finance as a percentage of total R&D (2.2%) to fall below the Dutch figure (2.5%), In contrast, the large share of basic funding of Dutch higher education research makes the German 10% (1698/16228) share of peer review grant finance in total higher education R&D to exceed the Dutch figure of 8% (318/3920). From an international perspective these shares are relatively low: comparable figures for Belgium, Denmark, France and the United Kingdom lie in the order of 20% (OCW, 1996b: 54).

This empirical overview gives a first indication on the position of Germany and the Netherlands on the relevant trade-offs in Table 11.1. The similar size of contract funding and peer review grant funding in terms of GDP seem to place the two countries in the same position on the trade-offs. The larger share of basic funding in higher education makes the institute approach appear even more predominant in the Netherlands. However, a more precise positioning requires a more closer look at the institutions that surround financing institutions, in particular

---

[8] Co-authorship of scientific articles puts this observation in a somewhat different perspective. NOWT (1994) found that business firms in the Netherlands in the field of basic research cooperate more with universities and other business firms, but less with research institutes than business firms in Germany. However, these observations have to be interpreted with care, because co-authorship between firms and universities is relatively limited, since firms perform little basic research. In the Netherlands, cooperation between firms and universities concerns 2.7% of the total number of co-authored publications on average (NOWT, 1994; 97). For the technical and natural sciences this percentage equals 6.3 and 3.6, respectively.

Table 11.5 Composition and funding of the German and Dutch broad knowledge base

	Germany			Netherlands		
	mill DM	% R&D	% GDP	mill *f*	% R&D	% GDP
Higher education total[a]	16228	20.9	0.49	3920	31.3	0.64
Higher education (OECD)[b]	14530	18.7	0.44	3602	28.8	0.59
Basic funding, of which:	10600	13.7	0.32	2839	22.7	0.46
– Bund[c]	1991	2.6	0.06	–	–	–
– Länder	8609	11.1	0.26	–	–	–
Contract research, of which:	3930	5.1	0.12	763	6.1	0.12
– international org. (EU)	150	0.2	0.00	123	1.0	0.02
– government[c]	2580	3.3	0.08	292	2.3	0.05
– non-profit org.	–	–	–	204	1.6	0.03
– firms	1200	1.5	0.04	144	1.1	0.02
Peer review grant funding	1698	2.2	0.05	318	2.5	0.05
Basic research institutes	1496	1.9	0.05	274	2.2	0.05
Basic funding, of which:	1303	1.7	0.04	274	2.2	0.05
– Bund	648	0.8	0.02	–	–	–
– Länder	655	0.8	0.02	–	–	–
Own funds + contracts	193	0.2	0.01	–	–	–
Total	17724	22.8	0.53	4194	33.6	0.69

[a] Higher education including peer review grant finance (own definition).
[b] OECD Basic Science and Technology Statistics definition: sum of basic funding and contract research, but excluding peer review grant finance of university research.
[c] German investment in construction of university buildings (545 mill. DM) transferred from Drittmittel to basic funding.

Source: Germany BMBF (1996), Tables VII/3, VII/8, VII/10, VII/20, Figure II/9, tables on page 399 and 409; the Netherlands CBS (1996) Tables 4.1.1a, 4.3.1, OCW (1993), OCW (1996a); own computations.

basic funding because of its importance. Therefore this section continues with a review of basic funding institutions in German and Dutch higher eduction. Section 11.2.3 pays more attention to contract funding and peer review grant finance in the context of the links that these types of funding may provide between technology and science.

Basic Finance Institutions in German Higher Education. Within the German federal system, the Länder have the main responsibility for higher education

(Frackmann and de Weert, 1994: 141). They provide most of the basic funding for research at institutions of higher education (Table 11.5). An advantage of financing at the more decentral level is that regional governments are closer to private firms and have better knowledge of the regional environment. At the national level primarily the Bundesministerium fur Bildung, Wissenschaft, Forschung und Technologie finances scientific research. Federal funding largely covers investments in higher education and special programs.

The main centres of power in German higher education are the Länder governments and the chair holders, the individual professors. The Minister has to approve the 'organizational structure of the institutions, including the establishment, modifications, or closing down of departments, institutes or central units' (Frackmann and de Weert, 1994: 145). Within the framework of the national legislation, Land's laws determine the management and decision making structure in universities. The Minister also appoints a professor from a three-person list of recommendation, made up by a selection committee. In addition, higher education must be equal and equivalent throughout Germany (Frackmann and de Weert, 1994: 151). Therefore, elaborate coordination mechanisms exist to guarantee equality and equivalence, for instance with respect to examination regulations, and individual institutes have little freedom to differentiate curricula (Frederiks and Westerheijden, 1996: 22). The state has no decision power on research priorities: the German constitution guarantees academic freedom. Researchers are free to choose research projects and individual professors have many rights and leeway to attract and allocate research.

The influence of the Land government on basic funding of higher education institutes is also substantial. Funding is largely incremental, *i.e.* based on previous year's budget with no dependency on student enrolment or the number of graduates (Frackmann and de Weert, 1994: 152). Accordingly, the budget mechanism does not provide incentives for reducing the length of studies, which on average is seven years and thus rather high in Germany. The institutes' budgets define several specific expenditure categories (Frackmann and de Weert, 1994: 146). Funds allocated to one expenditure category may not be spent for other purposes. Institutes' personnel budgets are specified according to 'positions', *i.e.* according to the number of seats for professors, assistant professors, researchers etc. During the fiscal year no transfers of financial funds between positions can take place. Also, transfer of funds over the years is not allowed. Hence, basic funding of German higher education features little autonomy for institutes, few incentives and much regulation. Therefore, academic freedom primarily concerns individual research autonomy within the limitations set by a rigid financial environment.

Recently, in some Länder a shift is taking place towards more autonomy for universities. In particular Niedersachsen and Baden-Württemberg increased the institutes' autonomy by allowing more flexibility to reallocate non-personnel budgets among expenditure categories and to carry over funds to the next fiscal year. This shift corresponds with experiments starting in 1995 to introduce quality control through peer reviews, which are largely comparable to the Dutch system (see below), although without full publication of the assessment report (Frederiks and Westerheijden, 1996: 23). Outside these experiments, and therefore still relevant for a large part of German higher education, quality control depends on voluntary efforts of individual researchers and teachers. Government regulations provide some quality assurance, but mainly on the input side of the educational process (entry qualifications, curricula) so as to guarantee equality and equivalence throughout the country (Frackmann and de Weert, 1994: 157).

Basic Finance Institutions in Dutch Higher Education. Recent reforms in the Dutch legislative framework result in a greater autonomy of universities in the Netherlands compared to Germany. Since the mid 1980s, in the Netherlands coordination between the government and universities shifted from control to cooperative exchange. Several motives caused this shift: control appeared too detailed and ineffective, responsibilities of the institutes were undervalued, and quality control was underdeveloped (Goedegebuure *et al.*, 1993: 196).

The reduction of control measures in the Netherlands becomes apparent in the regulatory burden on universities, in the system of basic funding, and in the system of quality control. The number of regulations fell from about 2000 to somewhat above 300. Where previously total basic funding for teaching and research depended on discipline-related weighted figures on student enrolment, the current method of calculation more strongly differentiates between teaching and research. The share of the budget related to education depends on the number of students that have studied less than four years and the number of degrees awarded (VSNU, 1997). Hence, this method provides an incentive for universities to devise efficient methods of education. The share of basic funding related to research for 80 % depends on the budget in the previous year. The number of students and final degrees determines a further 15% of the budget. The remaining 5% consists of bonuses for doctoral theses and recognized research schools (Goedegebuure *et al.*, 1993: 206). Universities receive the total amount of basic funding as a lump sum amount and are free to allocate it in accordance with their specific objectives (Goedegebuure *et al.*, 1993: 203).

Quality control in the Netherlands shifted towards a system of self-assessment and peer review, which strongly increased the influence of the academic community on quality control and enhanced the responsibility of universities to respond to quality assessments. The government enlarged universities' autonomy on the condition that they would guarantee an adequate degree of quality. Each faculty evaluates the education and research of all its research groups. In addition, the Association of Universities in the Netherlands (VSNU) organizes a revolving system of peer-review quality assessments through visiting committees, separately for education and research performance (Frederiks and Westerheijden, 1996;

VSNU, 1997).[9] The procedure for education and research evaluation is largely the same. VSNU installs a committee of independent (foreign) experts that visits and reviews all faculties in a specific science field. Prior to the review each faculty writes a self-assessment report, which also contains its objectives for the future. After consultation and review, the committee publishes its final assessment report. In their annual reports, faculties are obliged to give account of the measures they took in response to the assessment. Publication and citation evidence demonstrates a relatively good quality of Dutch science compared to Germany and in a broader international comparison (Box 11.2).

The peer-review has no direct budgetary consequences. Yet as an ultimate sanction, the Minister of Education, Culture and Science has the authority to stop financing a poorly performing course. Until now, in practice this instrument has not been used, but its presence may form an incentive to take quality evaluation seriously. Yet, because the university receives a lump-sum amount, in principle it has the freedom not to execute the desired measures. But then, of course it has to solve the budget cut in some other way. No comparable ultimate sanctions are available in case of a negative research evaluation report.

In conclusion, the institutions of basic funding of university education and research show a difference between control in Germany and cooperative exchange in the Netherlands. A substantial degree of autonomy in the Netherlands coincides with an elaborate system of quality control (Frederiks and Westerheijden, 1996: 44). In Germany, detailed regulation corresponds with largely absent quality control, except for some experiments with lump sum finance and quality control in Niedersachsen. This positions the Dutch system closer to diversity and experimentation, whereas Germany is more on the scale and certainty side of the trade-offs in Table 11.1. Because they have more authority and responsibility, Dutch universities are also closer to incentives, whereas more risk sharing in Germany promotes solidarity. Moreover, incentives in the basic funding of institutions to restrict the length of studies are stronger in the Netherlands.

Basic Research Institutes. In Germany, the Max Planck Gesellschaft constitutes the umbrella organisation of a large group of basic research institutes. The Max Planck Gesellschaft consists of about 70 institutes, 30 labour groups and some other institutions, covering the entire range of scientific fields, although clearly specialized in natural sciences and engineering. Max Planck institutes perform basic research, supplement university research by stimulating research in new areas, cooperate with universities and provide access to large-scale research

---

[9] Visiting committee quality assessment for education started in 1988. The first series of visits ended in 1994. Currently, education in about half of the disciplines has been assessed in the second series of visits. Quality assessment of research started in 1993 and currently covers the first series of visits (VSNU, 1997).

Box 11.2 Scientific performance indicators

Public disclosure is the main method for scientists to obtain intellectual property rights on their findings. Disclosure usually takes place through publication in scientific journals. Because, on average, better scientists publish more, publications can be used as an output indicator for scientific research. Recently, a study on scientific publication patterns (Science, 7 February 1997) found that the Netherlands perform relatively well on the publication front. The share in the total publications of the world top countries in science over the years 1981 to 1994 has been 2.0% for the Netherlands and 7.0% for Germany. In terms of publications relative to public R&D personnel, this comes down to 109 publications per person for the Netherlands and 67 for Germany. Over the full range of countries, the Netherlands ranks six and Germany 17th on this indicator.

Opponents argue that publications are just a quantity measure and do not indicate quality of research. A way to assess quality is counting the number of times a publication is cited in publications by colleague scientists. This gives an idea of the reputation, peer group esteem and impact of the scientist. The same report finds that Germany has a share of 6.0% of total citations and the Netherlands 2.2%. Once corrected for R&D employees, this means 96 citations per person in the Netherlands and 49 in Germany. The positions of the two countries in the ranking order for this indicator are six and sixteen respectively.

The intrinsic value of a publication is measured by the Relative Citation Index (RCI), which is the number of citations per publication. The Dutch RCI was 1.10 thereby ranking the Netherlands sixth. Germany ranked fifteenth with an RCI of 0.86.

The overall conclusion must be that the Netherlands performs relatively better than Germany concerning scientific research. Once corrected for country size, both the quantity and impact of Dutch scientific publications is higher. In addition to the emphasis on quality evaluation, other causes may underlie these findings. Firstly, German researchers may publish a relatively large part of their results in German. However, internationalization of science would make that a less appropriate strategy. Secondly, the share of higher education in the Dutch scientific knowledge base exceeds that in Germany and scientists at universities face the strongest incentives to publish their results. Thirdly, the high teaching load at German universities crowds out research.

equipment for scientists at universities (BMBF, 1996: 409). In the Netherlands, the institutes of the Royal Dutch Academy of Arts and Sciences (KNAW) and those of the Dutch Organisation for Scientific Research (NWO) perform basic research and manage large-scale research facilities.

At the German Max Planck Gesellschaft, project funding, contract funding and own funds (like revenues from licensing agreements) are relatively more important than at the Dutch institutes. These make up 13% of MPG funding (see Table 11.5), and put MPG more at the side of diversity and flexibility on the trade-offs of Table 11.1 compared to the Dutch institutes. Experience with contract funding and patenting at MPG illustrate the tension between the objectives and incentives of science and those of technology. Scientists state that companies are inflexible, want results too quickly, lack qualified discussion partners, refuse to give access to the company's expertise and knowledge base, and are not interested in long-term relationships (Reinhard and Schmalholz, 1996: 86). Scientists show little interest in patenting their innovations, despite the facilities available at the special Max Planck institute for technology transfer: Garching Innovation. Some scientists also believe that applying for a patent is not worth the trouble because yields for the applicant are too small. They appear to be unaware of the financial incentive structures available at MPG to encourage patenting (MPG forwards 30% of patenting revenues to the innovator). A possible reason might be that they are more interested in scientific esteem than in financial revenues (compare Reinhard and Schmalholz, 1996: 92).

11.2.2 Specific Knowledge Base

The composition of the specific knowledge base differs markedly between Germany and the Netherlands. Related to the size of the countries, the German knowledge base incorporated in specialized research institutes (large research centres plus Blue List institutes) considerably exceeds the Dutch one (see the bottom lines in Table 11.6). Relative to GDP, the German large research centres (0.12%) are twice as large as those in the Netherlands (0.06%). Adding another 0.04% for the Blue List Institutes, the size of the German specialized institutes relatively to GDP is more than 2.5 times that of the Netherlands. In contrast, the Netherlands stands out on the applied scientific research institutes. On a relative basis, the size difference of these institutes is remarkable. It implies that relative to GDP the size of the specific knowledge base in the Netherlands exceeds that in Germany.

Large Research Institutes. These institutes have a relatively large scale to carry out oriented basic research to support specific economic sectors. In-depth covering of scientific and technological areas requires large investments in knowledge and equipment. In the Netherlands, five such large research centres exist (Grote Technologische Instituten, GTIs). The two largest are ECN (Energy Research Foundation Netherlands) and NLR (National Aerospace Laboratory), specialized in energy and aviation and aerospace research, respectively. The remaining three specialize in maritime research (MARIN), geotechnics (GD) and hydraulics research (WL). Germany has 16 large research centres (Grossforschungs-einrichtungen, GFEs). Like in the Netherlands, the German GFEs are exclusively active in the natural sciences and engineering fields, but due to their larger number cover a broader range of fields.

In addition to the large centres, Germany has smaller research centres, the so-called Blue List Institutes, with on average 120 researchers each. These smaller institutes operate in the complete range of scientific fields. About one-third is specialized in fields from the social sciences and humanities, the remaining two-third in the natural sciences and engineering. Expressed in terms of expenditures the difference is larger: 23 versus 77% (BMBF, 1996: 570). The more costly

Table 11.6 Financing structure of German and Dutch applied scientific research institutes

	Germany			Netherlands		
	mill DM	% total	% contr.	mill *f*	% total	% contr.
Large research institutes	3942	100		359	100	
Basic funding	2884	73		153	43	
Contract research[a]	1058	27		206	57	
Blue List institutes	1370	100				
Basic funding	1120	82				
Contract research	250	18				
Fraunhofer / TNO[b]	1142	100		745	100	
Basic funding	536	47		297	40	
Contract research, of which:	606	53	100	448	60	100
– international organizations	32	3	5	110	15	25
– government	289	25	48	110	15	25
– non-profit org.	28	2	5	–		
– firms	216	19	36	228	31	50
– other	41	4	7	–		
DLO				355	100	
Basic funding				235	66	
Contract research, of which:				120	34	100
– international organizations				30	8	25
– government				30	8	25
– firms				60	17	50
Key totals		% R&D	% GDP		% R&D	% GDP
Large institutes + Blue List	5312	6.9	0.16	359	2.9	0.06
Applied scientific institutes	1142	1.5	0.03	1100	8.8	0.18
Total	6454	8.4	0.19	1459	11.7	0.24

[a] Germany: Excluding financing of closing down of old nuclear reactors at Forschungszentrum Karlsruhe (369 mill DM, see BMBF, 1996: 454).
Netherlands: of which international 63, government 42, firms 81 and own funds 20.

[b] FhG (1995: 92-95); TNO: 1995; DLO, 1994

Source: Germany BMBF (1996), Table VII/8, tables on page 427, 441-456, FhG (1995: 92-95); Netherlands CBS (1996) Table 4.1.1a, OCW (1995), OCW (1996a), TNO jaarverslag 1995, DLO: NOWT (1996, 216); own computations.

research facilities in natural sciences and engineering may well explain this difference. Hence, the German specific knowledge base not only covers a broader range of scientific fields with its large research centres, but at the same time covers a wide research area with the many small Blue List Institutes.

The difference in size of Germany and the Netherlands explains not only the broader scope of the German GFEs, but also their larger size. With more than 800 employees each, the two largest Dutch institutes are among the medium-sized German institutes. The other three Dutch institutes are smaller than the small German institutes, which employ about 500 people each. In addition, Germany hosts three very large institutes with a staff of 3500 to 4000 people.

The financing structure of the German and Dutch specialized research institutes shows that the German institutes rely more on basic funding (Table 11.6). The share of basic funding equals 73% for the large research centres and 82% for the Blue List Institutes, compared to 43% for the Dutch GTIs. Partly this may follow from the fact that the German GFEs are located more towards the pure basic research side on the R&D spectrum (NOWT, 1996). Maintaining a specialised knowledge base requires a considerable part of basic finance to invest in long-term and uncertain research projects. Project and contract research constitute an incentive for the research centres to prevent inflexibility and lock-in effects. Indeed, the GTIs and GFEs all represent scientific areas that support economic sectors that were strong some decades ago (see also Klodt, 1996). Critics of the Blue List Institutes add that their research has never been subject to systematic quality control (Abbott and Schiermeier, 1996). The smaller share of basic funding suggests that the Dutch institutes are closer to flexibility on the flexibility-commitment trade-off and may more easily adapt to the demands of economic agents that benefit from their knowledge.

Applied Scientific Research Institutes. Both German and Dutch science policy supports institutes where research is carried out at direct request of firms or with the goal of translating scientific research into potentially useful knowledge for private firms. The Netherlands Organization for Applied Scientific Research (TNO) is the most important actor in Dutch applied R&D with 13 research institutes and other related centres and laboratories in various technical fields. Although TNO is mainly directed towards applied research, part of the research, roughly that part financed by basic funding, has an oriented-basic character. This type of research enables TNO to maintain its knowledge base. Besides TNO, another, more specialized institute in applied research is the Agricultural Research Service (Dienst Landbouwkundig Onderzoek, DLO). It comprises 11 research institutes, mainly concentrated around the Agricultural University of Wageningen.

In relation to the size difference of the two countries, TNO is relatively large compared to its German counterpart, the Fraunhofer-Gesellschaft (FhG). Although the number of institutes of the FhG exceeds that of TNO by a factor three (47 against 13), employment of the two institutes only differs by a factor 2 and operating income by 50% (compare Table 11.6). Adding the revenues of DLO, total income of the combination of TNO and DLO is close to that of Fraunhofer, whereas German GDP is about six times as large as Dutch GDP. The relatively large size of TNO is partly explained by its broader range of research subjects. The remaining size difference fits the observation in Section 11.1.4 that a small country needs a relatively large research potential aimed at enhancing the absorption capacity of firms. TNO primarily focuses on small and medium sized enterprises without own R&D activities. This type of company is relatively important in the Netherlands compared to Germany, where larger medium-sized companies with own R&D facilities are more numerous. In that respect the Netherlands resembles other small countries, like Denmark, Finland and Norway, which also host large applied scientific research institutes. Hence, the relatively large size of TNO/DLO compared to Fraunhofer corresponds with the size difference and different sectoral structure between the Netherlands and Germany.

Contract funding comprises 53% of the revenues of Fraunhofer, 60% for TNO and 34% for DLO (see Table 11.6). For TNO and DLO combined, the share of contract funding equals that of Fraunhofer. Both for TNO and DLO, the share of contract funding commissioned by enterprises (50%) exceeds that of Fraunhofer (36%). In addition, the larger share of funding commissioned by international organisations shows that the international orientation of TNO exceeds that of Fraunhofer. Hence, compared to Fraunhofer, TNO and DLO are closer to flexibility on the relevant trade-off in Table 11.2.

To some extent, the funding system of the Fraunhofer institutes contains an incentive to increase contract funding. Financing of contract research at the FhG for 70% consists of direct revenues from contracts entered and for 30% consists of government basic finance related to these direct revenues (BMBF, 1996: 426). By consequence, an increase of contract research directly raises the revenues from basic government financing, which is an additional incentive to increase contract research activities. Analogously to TNO, basic government financing is used by the FhG to investigate self-selected research topics and to develop new technologies so as to secure its scientific proficiency. This system of funding forms an incentive to increase flexibility at Fraunhofer.

11.2.3 Policy Developments: Quality, Cooperation and Relevance

Both in Germany and the Netherlands science policy is concerned with the strength and quality of the scientific knowledge base, with cooperation between research institutes and with the social and economic relevance of scientific research (BMBF, 1996; OCW, 1996b). The increasing role of knowledge in society, challenges posed by internationalization, the importance of scientific research as a basis for technology, and companies that withdraw from long-term basic research motivate policies to strengthen the scientific knowledge base and to enhance the link between science and technology. Policy aims at promoting interdisciplinary research, because it perceives a potential for innovations on the border lines between scientific disciplines, and because addressing social questions requires a combination of insights from different disciplines. In addition, aspects from several other disciplines, such as design, marketing, or management, complement engineering and technological R&D in fostering successful innovations. Cooperation between research institutes may also improve the quality of their research.

The search for quality, cooperation and relevance manifests itself in the various components of the scientific knowledge base. Quality, flexibility, and selectivity feature prominently in higher education research policy. Strengthening peer review grant finance constitutes a way to improve flexibility. Shifts in funding to contract research, stimulates research organisations to enhance the quality of their research and their orientation to societal needs. Studies attempt to identify promising research areas from a social and economic perspective. This section reviews these developments.

Developments in Higher Education. Crowding out of research by teaching poses a significant threat to the German knowledge base in higher education. Since 1977, the number of students increased by 75%, whereas the scientific staff increased by only 11% (BMBF, 1996: 35).[10] During the same period the average length of studies rose to 7 years. Many students already have completed vocational education when entering university, which further raises the length of learning routes and the average age of university students. Reduction of the time students spent in higher education and discussions on limiting access to higher education feature in the German political debate.

Competition and differentiation are other important topics in German science and education policy discussions[11]. Autonomy of universities should increase, differences between institutes of higher education should become more visible and financing institutions should become more flexible and should promote competition among institutes (Frackmann and de Weert, 1993: 151; BMBF, 1997a). However, legislation that imposes equality and equivalence throughout Germany largely prevents differentiation. Extensive coordination mechanisms within the federal system and with the relevant actors also make change proceed slowly. Differentiation at the level of the institutes of higher education necessitates shifts of power from the Länder level and the level of individual scientists to the institutes. Also,

---

[10] Expecting a decline of the student population in the mid 1980s, the Prime Ministers of the Länder decided to generally 'open' higher education to anyone with the required qualifications in their 1977 'Öffnungsbeschluss' (Frackmann and de Weert, 1993: 135, 149). Universities temporarily had to carry a 15% teaching overload. However, increasing participation in upper secondary education raised the number of potential students and a larger share of these school leavers decided to enter university. These two factors more than offset the demographically expected decline in student population. In addition, the Länder did not keep pace with the financial need of the institutes of higher education. Together these factors contributed to the current high teaching load in German universities.

[11] BMBF (1997a) also mentions other problems such as a lack of international compatibility of German degrees, the absence of a credit transfer system and too much regulation.

institutes are more likely to constitute a transaction cost efficient intermediate level of governance, because they are close enough to research and education to obtain the necessary information and at the same time distinct enough from individual researchers to assess their performance and execute quality control. Yet a shift towards the institutes requires a strengthening of their management and may be blocked by the many interest groups affected (Frackmann and de Weert, 1993: 159). For these reasons, the road from policy discussions to the actual implementation of differentiation and competition measures may be a long one.

In recent years, the Netherlands has established a network of research schools to bundle the expertise among research groups in higher education. Research schools bundle research activities by scientists from one or several universities with the aim to raise quality and to design a coherent research program. Hence, research schools may promote interdisciplinary or interuniversity research activities. In addition, research schools aim to improve the education of future researchers. Research schools have to be accredited by a committee from the Royal Dutch Academy of Arts and Sciences. Currently 106 research schools exists, which cover all scientific fields.

The size of the Dutch science budget necessitates selectivity (compare Section 11.1.4). Science policy therefore aims to select the 10 most promising research schools, which will receive additional funding to develop into internationally acknowledged centres of excellence for a period of 10 years (OCW, 1996b: 56). The Dutch research council (NWO) will perform the selection process (see below). In addition, recently four technological top institutes have been established in which universities and enterprises cooperate (EZ/OCW/LNV, 1995: 32; OCW, 1996b: 58). The aim of these institutes is to perform internationally excellent basic research, in the fields of metals, nutrition, polymers and telematica that serves the needs of the companies involved. Participating companies made a financial commitment to the technological top institutes by supplying part of their funding.

Peer Review Grant Finance. The trade-offs in Table 11.1 show that peer review grant finance promotes diversity and flexibility, and strengthens incentives. Hence, it constitutes an instrument to reallocate research and to enhance flexible adjustment of research priorities to social and economic priorities. Moreover, it surpasses the boundaries between institutes and thus in principle may also easily shift funds to qualitatively promising institutes.

An important disadvantage of peer review grant finance in Germany and the Netherlands concerns the lack of financial resources to accept valuable research proposals (Reinhard and Schmalholz, 1996: 72; OCW 1996a: 13). In the Netherlands acceptance rates differ considerably among science fields. In technical sciences acceptance rates lie in the order of 40%, in some fields of the social sciences and humanities they come down to about 10%. In Germany proposals also fail because universities lack funds to finance basic facilities (housing *etc.*) that DFG is not allowed to finance. Because the low probability of acceptance does not warrant the considerable effort to draft research proposals, scientists lose interest to apply for funds. As a result, the research councils (DFG and NWO) lose their impact on scientific fields.

To strengthen peer review grant finance, the German government increased the DFG budget by 5% a year over the period 1990-1996 (Abbott and Schiermeier, 1996). In addition to the basic support activities that cover about 40% of its budget, DFG has two special programs at its disposal that require participation of several institutes. The core activity program ('Schwerpunktprogamme') comprises cooperative research projects that involve participation of scientists from different regions. These projects generally cover a period of 6 years and in 1994 took up 13% of the DFG budget (DFG, 1997; BMBF, 1996: 196). Special research areas ('Sonderforschungsbereiche') particularly pertain to long-term interdisciplinary research activities. They exist between 12 to 15 years and cover 25% of the DFG budget in 1994. Frequently also non-university research institutes participate. Since July 1996 DFG aims at enhancing technology transfer by supporting transfer activities within the special research areas. Together with other research institutes and companies, universities that participate in a special research area may apply for funding of projects to convert scientific findings into practical prototypes.

In 1996 an international committee evaluated the Dutch research council NWO (OCW, 1996a). Amongst others, the committee identifies the following possibilities for improvement. To alleviate the shortage of funds, it recommends an increase of the NWO budget. In addition, it observes inflexibility in fund allocation, which is largely based on historical grounds. Of course, inflexible fund allocation would jeopardize many advantages of a peer review grant system. To more strongly tailor funding to scientific challenges, the committee recommends a system for project applications that resembles the procedure at DFG. Furthermore, the committee suggests the Minister of Education, Culture and Science to take a more active role in defining research priorities and to make NWO the main instrument for the administration of long-term research projects initiated by the government. It also proposes to simplify the NWO organisation to increase its flexibility. Such a reorganisation is currently taking place.

Several recent policy proposals strengthen the position of NWO in stimulating high-quality research. OCW (1996b) announces a program that involves NWO in promoting excellent research schools. About 7% of universities' basic funding (*f*200 million) is earmarked for that purpose. Half of this budget will be used to finance a small group of excellent research schools to be selected by NWO. The other half of the budget will be used by universities to support specific research schools. Before putting these support measures into practice, universities have to ask NWO's judgement.

Strengthening Basic Research Institutes. The German government aims to strengthen the scientific knowledge base by increasing the budget for basic funding of the Max Planck Gesellschaft. The amount of basic funding rose from 1.3 billion

DM in 1994 (see Table 11.5) to 1.4 billion in 1995 and 1.5 billion in 1996 (BMBF, 1996: 87). Accordingly, the share of the Max Planck Gesellschaft in the government's science budget increased from 16.9% in 1994 to 17.7% in 1996. In 1996 MPG started the organisation of a quality evaluation of its institutes assisted by international experts. According to the Ministry of Education, Science, Research and Technology, the MPG has already reached a high degree of flexibility and autonomy (BMBF, 1997b).

In the Netherlands, policy focuses more on reinforcing the quality and effectivity of basic research institutes than on increasing their funding. The Ministry of Education, Culture and Science, the Royal Dutch Academy of Arts and Sciences (KNAW) and Dutch Organisation for Scientific Research (NWO), prepare a new organisational model for the basic research institutes (OCW, 1996b: 64). The aim is to combine the institutes in one organisation, based at KNAW. This would facilitate an integrated policy towards the institutes and would separate the management of the institutes from the project funding activities of the research council NWO, so as to prevent conflicts of interests. In particular, separation is important because another purpose of the reorganisation is to raise the current low level of project funding at the institutes, which will increase their dependence on NWO grants. In addition, quality control at the institutes will be enhanced and adjusted to the methods used in higher education research. To increase the quality of their research activities and to create more dynamism in the research fields covered by the institutes, quality evaluation may have rather drastic consequences, such as a redefinition of the mission of an institute or even closing it down completely.

The Large Research Institutes. Recent policy initiatives in Germany aim at shifting the research activities of the large research centres (GFEs) towards priorities identified by the Minister of Education, Science, Research and Technology (BMBF, 1996: 437). A second objective is to increase the extent of contract finance to strengthen the link with enterprises. Some evidence illustrates that the link with customers indeed needs to be enhanced. Although their position is more towards the applied side of the research spectrum, the share of revenues from patents in total GFE finance is less than that of the Max Planck institutes (Reinhard and Schmalholz, 1996: 124). Reinhard and Schmalholz (1996: 92) argue that, analogously to the Max Planck institutes (see Section 11.2.1 above), incentives for individual scientists to apply for a patent are weak: scientific publications are more rewarding. In addition, financial incentives at some GFEs appear weaker than at the Max plank institutes.

Also funding of the large research centres is under pressure. The growth in basic finance for large research centres has been very modest in recent years, so that their share in total government funding of R&D has fallen by 2.3 percentage points over 1994-1996. The Ministry of Education, Science, Research and Technology has proposed to shift funds from individual research centres towards their umbrella organisation: the Helmholtz Society (Abbot and Schiermeier, 1996). Accordingly, the senate of the Helmholtz Society could more easily reallocate funds towards priority areas. The independent senate consists of external members, among which representatives of the enterprise sector. In 1998 this process will start with a strategy fund of DM 150 million, financed out of the basic funding of the research centres (FAZ, 1997). The position of the institutes is strengthened by a more flexible organisation and the freedom to create a financial buffer out of revenues from contract research or licensing agreements. Instead of size, interdisciplinarity becomes a more important characteristic of these institutes. In a more distant future, part of the funding of the research centres may be transferred towards peer review grant funding from the Deutsche Forschungsgemeinschaft (DFG).

Comparable plans for the Blue List Institutes are in a further stage. Currently, the Scientific Council ('Wissenschaftsrat') is evaluating all Blue List institutes. If the Council concludes that a certain institute no longer satisfies the conditions to be included in the Blue List, the Ministry will terminate its basic funding (BMBF, 1997b). Moreover, recently the Ministry has proposed the Länder governments to transfer 5% of Blue List Institutes' basic funding to DFG. These plans increase competition between the Blue List Institutes and the universities for peer reviewed funding, which may improve the quality of research at the Blue List Institutes.

In the Netherlands, the government also aims at focusing the mission of the large research centres (GTIs) and enhancing their market orientation. A closely defined mission prevents inefficient competition between institutes and ineffective use of public funds, which is important to maintain a knowledge base in a small country like the Netherlands (EZ/OCW/LNV, 1995: 31). Adjustments in the basic funding of the Energy Research Foundation Netherlands (ECN) illustrate the shift towards a stronger orientation on the market. In its basic-funded research programs, ECN has to cooperate more closely with companies and the energy sector. A new system of quality evaluation will also contain criteria like the extent of commitment of enterprises and the energy sector, or the incorporation of research projects in strategic research cooperatives (EZ/OCW/LNV, 1995: 38).

A Stronger Market Orientation of the Applied Scientific Research Institutes. Compared to the 1980s, in the early 1990s the circumstances for the applied scientific research institutes turned harsher. For the Fraunhofer-Gesellschaft the 1980s was a period of substantial growth. Driven by German economic growth and a rising demand for R&D, from 1981 until 1991 total expenditure of the FhG increased fourfold. This picture changed in the early 1990s. Restructuring and concentration on core activities by enterprises reduced the growth rate of demand for R&D research by companies. Moreover, government budgets for R&D in the old Länder fell. By consequence growth of the FhG in the old Länder came to a standstill and employment declined slightly. Yet, the establishment of nine new institutes in the new Länder, which became operational in 1992, has countered the development in the old Länder. In the Netherlands, TNO has also been confronted with falling contract research commissioned by governments and enterprises, leading to a decrease of employment in full-time equivalents by more than 10% over the four year period 1991–1994.

In recent years several developments pose considerable challenges. Due to budgetary constraints, government project finance stagnates (FhG, 1996). In addition, increasing competition by basic and specialized research institutes put FhG and TNO under pressure. The larger share of basic funding of the basic and specialized research institutes raises doubts on the fairness of their competition. A problem specific for FhG is the recent decision by the Federal Fiscal Court that contract research is not a public utility but tax-liable business. In the field of personnel policy a challenge is to shift the capacities of the staff from long-standing technologies towards future oriented fields of research. Both institutes tackle these challenges by a closer orientating to the market, by quality improvement, by higher efficiency, by closer collaboration between the different research divisions, and by shifting their orientation towards the international market for applied research and to the service sector.

In contrast to the financial linkage between basic finance and contract finance at FhG, the Dutch government aims at monitoring more closely the contents of TNO's research activities. To obtain basic finance, from 1997 onwards TNO has to present the Ministry of Education, Culture and Science a research plan every four years. The plan has to report on research priorities, expansion of the knowledge base, and has to contain a market analysis. The Ministry evaluates the research plan against developments in the market, in society and in policy (EZ/OCW/LNV, 1995: 36). Compared to the stronger financial incentives incorporated in the FhG system of basic funding, which enhance flexibility, the Dutch system is closer to commitment. In addition, specific basic funding ('doelfinanciering', about 50 million guilders in 1996) from the Ministry of Economic Affairs will be based on research programs drafted by TNO and interested companies. Companies have to make a clear commitment to these programs, for instance through participation in funding. Specific basic funding from other ministries (140 million) does not require such co-financing.

Identification of Research Priorities. If governments want to guide the scientific knowledge infrastructure closer to social and economic issues, an important question is how to identify these issues and how to translate them towards research areas and into specific research programs.

During 1992-1996, in the Netherlands a Foresight Steering Committee (Overlegcommisie Verkenningen) performed an in-depth survey of seventeen scientific fields, including the social sciences and the humanities. The objectives of the committee were to 'strengthen the foundations and boost the vitality of the Dutch knowledge system' and to 'increase that system's sensitivity to any changes in its social environment' (OCV, 1996: xi). The committee identified four main trends in the scientific environment (information and communication, sustainability, internationalisation and regionalisation, improving the quality of life) and from that recommended a focus on ten themes for future research (OCV, 1996: Ch. 2). In addition, it provided four recommendations to improve the strategy and organisation of scientific research. Subsequently, for each of these recommendations the Ministry of Education, Culture and Science has designed some more or less concrete policy proposals (OCW, 1996b: Ch. 2).

Germany uses Delphi studies to identify important future technological developments. In 1992/1993, the first of these was held both in Germany and Japan, in cooperation with a Japanese institute. It inquired about 1000 scientific experts about expected developments in their field of science over the next 30 years (BMBF, 1996: 34). The study strengthened understanding in the scientific community about conditions and priorities in 16 scientific fields. After a small scale German Delphi study in 1995, currently another broad-based study is in progress, which asks over 2450 experts to review scientific developments in twelve main themes (ISI, 1997).

11.2.4 The Scientific Knowledge Base and Science Policy in Comparison

Which conclusions come forward from the comparison of the German and Dutch scientific knowledge base and the developments in science policy? A general conclusion is that the structure of the scientific knowledge base in the two countries reflects their difference in size and industrial specialization (see Section 11.1.4). Relative to GDP, higher education constitutes a larger share of the Dutch knowledge base. Also on a relative basis, in the specific knowledge base the large research centres and the Blue List institutes dominate in Germany, whereas the applied scientific research institutes (TNO) strongly dominate in the Netherlands.

The larger size of Dutch *higher education* primarily results from a larger amount of basic funding. On a relative basis contract funding and peer reviewed funding are identical in the two countries. A substantial degree of autonomy in Dutch higher education together with an elaborate system of quality control, positions the Dutch system closer to diversity and experimentation compared to Germany. Germany is more on the scale and certainty side of the trade-offs, because of detailed regulation and largely absent quality control. A high teaching load hampers research in German higher education. Differentiation and competition feature prominently in the German debate on higher eduction, but do not appear to translate into concrete policy measures. In the Netherlands the search for quality and relevance resulted in proposals to establish centres of excellence and technological top institutes, co-funded by the government and enterprises respectively. In both countries a shift from basic funding to peer reviewed funding is taking place. The German system of peer review finance forms an example to reorganise the Dutch system, which currently is considered to be too inflexible.

The financing structure of the German *basic research institutes* reflects more diversity and flexibility. The quality of the Max Planck institutes and their agenda setting research activities result in a increasing flow of funds from the government over the last six years. In a future organisational model, the Dutch basic research institutes obtain a more independent position from the research council.

The size of the German *large research centres* and their large share of basic finance, reflects an emphasis on scale and commitment. In the Netherlands flexibility and the absorption potential are higher, because of the relatively large share of applied scientific research institutes in the specific knowledge base. In both countries policy aims at lowering basic funding and at tying research activities closer to the demand of customers.

Finally, in both countries projects to identify promising new research areas and societal demand for scientific research are underway.

11.3 Institutions of German and Dutch Technology Policy

Technology policy aims at stimulating, supporting and facilitating the R&D of firms. This subsection describes some of the instruments of technology policy that were defined in the theoretical part. It focuses on direct instruments like patents and subsidies in Section 11.3.1 and on applied scientific research institutes in Section 11.2.2.

11.3.1 Direct Instruments

Patents. Since the institution in 1978 and widespread use thereafter of the European Patent System, patent protection does not constitute a difference between Germany and the Netherlands. Both German and Dutch firms in practice make use of the same European Patent System. In theory, firms could still use the national patent systems, but the lower costs of one single procedure to obtain patent protection in more countries make them often choose the European route. Whereas the old national systems of Germany and the Netherlands provided strong patent protection, the European system can be said to provide intermediate protection (see Van Dijk, 1994).

Subsidies in Germany. Unification considerably influences German subsidies in the field of technology policy. In 1994 the German government spent DM 4600 million on R&D subsidies. Almost half of this amount, DM 2100 million, consists of defence projects, about which little additional information is available.[12] The Ministry of Education, Science, Research and Technology supplies about two thirds

---

[12] Note that these defence subsidies concern subsidies to private companies. In addition the government finances defence research in public research institutes. For instance, in the Netherlands basic funding of TNO includes nearly *f*100 million finance of defence related research from the Ministry of Defence (OCW, 1996b: 92).

of the non-defence subsidies and the Ministry of Economic Affairs the remaining part. Table 11.7 presents the division of subsidies among major spending categories, subdivided into amounts allocated to the old and the new Länder. In addition, it contains the part of the subsidies directed at small and medium-sized enterprises (SMEs), defined as firms with less than 500 employees. The main distinction in the table is between subsidies for specific technologies and generic subsidies aimed at stimulating innovation or knowledge diffusion. In particular, a large part of the generic subsidies pour into the new Länder.

Specific subsidies, mainly stemming from the Ministry of Education, Science, Research and Technology, aim at stimulating particular technologies through project funding. According to Table 11.7, companies in the old Länder receive the major part of these subsidies. Moreover, the table shows that these subsidies primarily benefit large companies. Over 1992–1995, the amount of specific subsidies decreased by nearly 25%, while their composition is changing from older to new key technologies (BMBF, 1996: 96). Subsidies fell for R&D in space exploration, fossil fuels, renewable energy, nuclear energy, and environmental technology. Subsidies increased for information technology, micro systems, manufacturing technology, biotechnology and aviation.

Almost all of the generic subsidies benefit SMEs and about three quarters of these subsidies apply to the new Länder. The categories start-up finance and other subsidies completely aim to improve innovativeness of companies in the new Länder. Start-up finance entails a subsidy to establish a R&D-intensive company in the new Länder[13]. The category of other subsidies pertains to two programs. The first program subsidizes 35% of the development costs of new products for SMEs in the new Länder. The second one subsidizes projects commissioned by companies to enterprise-related research institutes in the new Länder.

Subsidies to encourage R&D cooperation between companies and subsidies aimed at diffusion apply both to the new and the old Länder, yet with a relatively large share of funds directed at the new Länder. Subsidies for R&D cooperation between companies already exist since 1954 (BMBF, 1996: 252). The 'Arbeitsgemeinschaft Industrieller Forschungseinrichtungen' (AiF) administers this program. The AiF is a private mother organization of about 100 small industrial research associations. These institutes carry out branch-specific research at the service of about 50,000 SMEs (BMBF, 1996: 407). In addition, a program that subsidizes R&D cooperation between companies in the old and the new Länder, in particular aims at strengthening innovation in the new Länder. Subsidies to stimulate technology diffusion, for a substantial part finance the establishment of technology transfer centres and comparable facilities in the new Länder.

---

[13] These data do not include programs to co-finance investments of young or small technology oriented companies, administered by the Kredietanstalt für Wiederaufbau (see BMBF, 1996: 251).

Table 11.7 German and Dutch non-defence R&D subsidies and tax exemptions in 1994

	Germany 1994 (millions of DM)				Netherlands
	Old Länder	New Länder	Total	SMEs	1996 (mln *f*)
Specific technologies	1401.2	211.0	1612.2	370.9	294.1
Generic subsidies	212.1	465.4	677.5	651.3	278.8
– start-up financing	27.3	42.1	69.4	69.4	85.1
– R&D cooperation	166.8	136.7	303.5	279.0	125.6
– diffusion	18.0	57.1	75.1	73.4	56.3
– other		229.5	229.5	229.5	11.8
Tax exemption					
– personnel		85.3	85.3	85.3	450.0
Total	1613.3	761.7	2375.0	1107.5	1022.9

Source: Germany, BMBF (1996) Tables II/17, II/20, II/22a, II/22b; the Netherlands, OCW (1996b: 94), own computations.
Note: because of different definitions of the private sector in different source tables of BMBF (1996) the above totals do not correspond completely with the source tables.

Finally, in Table 11.7 personnel contributions have been distinguished as a separate category because in the Netherlands this concerns a tax exemption, which generally is not included in R&D subsidy statistics. In Germany, personnel contributions comprise a 40% subsidy on wage costs of researchers employed at a company with less than 1000 employees, seated in one of the new Länder (BMBF, 1996: 249). Hence, this also concerns a generic instrument to enhance the technological position of the new Länder.

In conclusion, three main subject areas exist in Germany in the field of R&D subsidies: subsidies for specific key technologies developed at large companies, subsidies that enhance R&D cooperation between SMEs, and a broad range of subsidies designed to build up innovative capacity for companies in the new Länder.[14] The high degree of specificity, augmented by the DM 2100 million 100% specific amount of defence projects, put Germany on the certainty side of the relevant trade-off in Table 11.2. Ministries identify which technologies require financial support. In contrast, subsidies that encourage R&D cooperation between SMEs promote diversity and flexibility. The group of subsidies aimed at the new Länder are also more on the flexibility, experimentation and diversity side of the trade-offs.

[14] Some programs in the latter group of subsidies (start-up finance, product development) have ended in december 1995.

Subsidies in the Netherlands. On a relative basis Dutch R&D subsidies exceed those in Germany.[15] Specific information on Dutch R&D subsidies is available only for 1996 in OCW (1996). Table 11.7 contains the main data. Amounting to 0.16% of GDP, on a relative basis Dutch subsidies exceed those in Germany. Including the large German defence subsidies the German total equals 0.14 % of GDP, excluding defence it equals 0.07% of GDP. During the end of the eighties Dutch R&D subsidies have been decreasing. Since the early nineties the subsidies and exemptions are steadily increasing.

The composition of Dutch R&D subsidies shows some striking differences with Germany. Even excluding the German defence subsidies, Dutch specific subsidies are relatively small, whereas relative to GDP the amount of generic subsidies exceeds that in Germany. Hence, on a relative basis, the Netherlands is closer to experimentation compared to Germany.

For the Netherlands the tax exemption for R&D personnel (under the WVA[16]) stands out. Per company, the exemption covers 40% of the taxes and premiums for employees engaged in R&D up to a wage sum of *f*150000 and 12.5% above that sum. In addition, the annual amount per company has been limited to 15 million guilders. Hence, companies with relatively small R&D activity benefit most from this instrument. The forerunner of this subsidy, WBSO, was mainly (75%) used by SMEs (EZ/OCW/LNV, 1995: 30). Tax exemptions for R&D personnel constitute the most important Dutch R&D instrument. This corresponds with the structure of the Dutch entreprise sector, which consists of a relatively large number of small companies that frequently lack sufficient finance to perform R&D. In Germany this type of subsidy only exists as a temporary tool to improve innovation in the new Länder.

Subsidies for R&D cooperation are the second important Dutch instrument. The aim of this instrument is to strengthen cooperation between companies and research institutions and among companies (EZ/OCW/LNV, 1995: 39; EZ, 1996: 82). On a relative basis, subsidies for R&D cooperation in the Netherlands exceed those in Germany, but not to a considerable degree. Another difference is that in Germany a branch research organisation administers the program, whereas in the Netherlands administration is in the hands of a subsidiary organisation of the Ministry of Economic Affairs (Senter). To a certain extent a branch research organisation may be more knowledgeable about the R&D issues that concern companies, which may increase the effectivity of the instrument. In addition, the German program mainly aims at SMEs, whereas in the Netherlands both large and small companies may apply for these funds.

---

[15] Unless otherwise indicated, here total amounts include tax exemptions

[16] WVA stands for Wet Vermindering Afdracht Loonbelasting en Premie Volksverzekeringen Speur en Ontwikkelingswerk. Previously, it was known as WBSO, Wet Bevordering Speur en Ontwikkelingswerk.

On a relative scale, subsidies to enhance diffusion are also high in the Netherlands, which is in line with the difference in size of the countries and the relevance of foreign R&D spillovers (compare Box 11.1). A part of these funds finance Innovation Centres, which aim to enhance technology diffusion.

11.3.2 Consensus on Key Technologies

Specific for Germany are institutions that create consensus among companies, business associations, research institutes, universities and the government about key technologies relevant for the future competitiveness of German industry (Carlin and Soskice, 1997: 67). Standing committees that link these different actors discuss and identify emerging technologies and the necessary standards to disseminate these technologies among the various participants. Diffusion programs contribute to the building up of competencies in these technological fields at research institutes and companies. These programs are subsidized by the government and administered by the branch organisations, in particular the 'Arbeitsgemeinschaft Industrieller Forschungseinrichtungen' (see the subsection on German subsidies above).

Common competencies facilitate long-term implicit relationships between companies both horizontally and vertically in supplier-procurer relationships. Quality competition and mediation by branch organisations support these relationships. Quality competition through concentration on market niches, lowers direct price competition and reduces incentives to renege on implicit contracts. Branch organisations act as an informal arbiter in case of conflicts between companies. These organisations are close enough to the individual companies to understand their position, yet at the same time they hold enough distance to form an independent opinion. Therefore, they have a relatively strong position to effectively deal with the dispute in a way that is acceptable for both parties. Hence, this also supports the long-term technological relationships.

Compared to the Netherlands, where such an elaborate system of technology transfer does not exist, German cooperative exchange favours the certainty of a dominant design and the commitment to invest in the relevant technologies and standards. These institutions in particular fit the German specialization in incremental product and process innovation with medium-tech technologies (compare Table 3.13 in Section 3.4). Competition prevails more strongly in the Netherlands, which positions the Netherlands closer to diversity and flexibility. Hence, direct adjustment of research activity to new technologies may take place relatively fast in the Netherlands. Yet, once investments in standards and technological competencies have been made, diffusion on an broad scale proceeds relatively fast in Germany.

Table 11.8 Impact of trends on science and technology

Trend	Impact on science and technology
Social	
– heterogeneity	diversity
– quickly changing tastes	flexibility
– societal questions and challenges	multidisciplinary research
International economy	
– spillovers increase	absorption capacity, flexibility
– demand for learning and cooperation	commitment
– locational competition between knowledge bases	high quality

11.4 Trends and Policy Options

11.4.1 Trends Affecting Science and Technology

What is the impact of social and economic trends on the trade-offs in science and technology policy? On the one hand, social trends towards heterogeneity and quickly changing consumer tastes require flexible adaptation of the technological knowledge base, which, although to a less extent, also creates an increasing demand for flexible scientific foundations (see Table 11.8). On the other hand, society demands cooperation and multidisciplinary research. More complex technologies, the speed of scientific developments and the increasing role of knowledge in society demands a scientific knowledge base aimed at societal needs. Society faces important questions and challenges, which require a bundling of knowledge from different disciplines. Examples not only concern the development of technologies to enhance economic performance and the shift in the sectoral structure from manufacturing towards services, but also problems related to multicultural societies, sustainable development, acceptance of new technologies in society, the capability of citizens to deal with information technologies, the ability for life-long learning, *etc.* These examples not only require cooperation between disciplines in the natural sciences, engineering and technology, but increasingly also inputs from social sciences and humanities. More and more scientists from currently remote disciplines have to cooperate to address important issues in society.

Internationalization results in several, partly contrasting effects[17]. Spillovers between countries increase. In particular for 'open' science, national boundaries largely disappear. By consequence, domestic science more and more has to compete on the international 'market' and international scientific standards increasingly impose constraints on the selection of research topics and on methodology and increasingly determine quality norms. For large companies the link between domestic science and technology weakens, because more and more these companies draw upon the international scientific knowledge base (OECD, 1992: 225). To keep an overview on international scientific developments, large companies cooperate with universities and research institutes in several countries and exchange and coordinate scientific information among divisions in different countries. Also in the technological field spillovers increase. Spillovers call for flexibility and a strong absorption potential of the scientific and technological knowledge base, so as to be able to quickly take up international developments.

In contrast to competition and flexibility, internationalization demands also learning and cooperation. Technological knowledge to a considerable degree remains tacit and incorporated in researchers, who benefit from personal contacts with scientists in universities and research institutes. Tacit elements even gain importance, because internationalization increases the significance of knowledge as a decisive factor in international competition between enterprises. Many firms lack sufficient human and financial capital to perform all necessary R&D on their own. Therefore, they increasingly rely on cooperation with other companies and with research institutes to enhance their knowledge potential (Acs and Preston, 1997). The greater emphasis on learning and cooperation calls for commitment in the interaction between companies and a country's knowledge base.

In addition, internationalization intensifies locational competition between national knowledge bases. Large multinational companies allocate their research activities to countries with the most appropriate high-quality scientific knowledge base. Domestic SMEs increasingly have to raise the knowledge intensity of their products and production processes to deal with intensified competition. Indirectly, this also increases competition between national policies that strengthen the knowledge base supporting SMEs. Locational competition and a more important role of knowledge, require a high-quality national knowledge base.

In conclusion, internationalization intensifies the trade-offs between diversity and flexibility on the one hand and scale and commitment on the other hand. Countries need to enhance their absorption capacity, through sufficient diversity and flexibility of their system of higher education and of their research infrastructure.

---

[17] Of course internationalization and technological developments are interrelated. Developments in information technology to a considerable extent drive the process of internationalization. Since this chapter focuses on conditions and trends affecting science and technology, technological trends are not addressed separately.

At the same time they have to provide high-quality research capacity to attract foreign R&D and research-intensive companies that produce high value added. This makes great demands on science and technology policy.

11.4.2 Policy Options for Germany and the Netherlands

Developments in the field of science and technology policy emphasize quality, cooperation and relevance. How do these stand out in the light of the analytical framework of Section 11.1 and the above trends?

The Trade-offs Revisited. The most important lesson from the analytical framework is to recognize the existence of trade-offs. To some extent increasing relevance may enhance quality, if a larger share of contract finance urges researchers to leave well-trodden paths and improve quality. Cooperation in multidisciplinary teams may create economies of scale and thus also enhance quality. Yet, trade-offs put boundaries to these synergy effects and require science and technology policy to administer a sometimes delicate balance.

Relevance and quality touch upon the trade-off between flexibility and commitment (see Table 11.1). Building a high-quality scientific knowledge base requires a long-term focus, and compliance with the incentive structures in scientific research, i.e. priority of discovery. Experiences at the Max Planck Institutes and the German large research centres show that these incentive structures may conflict with priorities set by economic agents that operate in a competitive environment. Hence, science policy should not lose sight of the long-term foundations of the scientific knowledge base by emphasizing relevance too much (see also OCV, 1996: 9). This trade-off also manifests itself in attempts to strengthen the quality of science through peer review. Peer review emphasizes scientific evaluation criteria, *i.e.* compliance with international research priorities and with views on innovativeness, the extent to which scientific results observe the existing research methodology, the quality and number of publications, *etc.* To some extent, a stronger emphasis on these criteria pushes scientists away from projects and research interests with high (short-term) value for society, because in a number of disciplines the latter type of research operates less at the forefront of scientific evolution.

Multidisciplinary research relates to the trade-offs between flexibility and commitment and between diversity and scale. Cooperative exchange underlies multidisciplinary research. Hence, the motivation of scientists from different disciplines to make their own preferences and methods subservient to the common goal, is crucial to the success of this type of cooperation. However, to some extent that demand is at odds with incentives and quality evaluation within each single discipline. Even if universities and institutes could lower the dividing lines between disciplines, scientific journals do not easily deal with interdisciplinary publications, peer review quality committees primarily apply standards from their own specific scientific field, while funding organisations are also organised by discipline. In addition, a competitive scientific environment that emphasizes the quality of individual researchers, may hamper the formation of multidisciplinary research teams. For these reasons, economies of scale in multidisciplinary research are not obvious and a trade-off arises between cooperation and quality. OCW (1996a: 15) warns against promoting multidisciplinary research for its own sake: '..., there is no intrinsic merit in multidisciplinary research. Most research can be carried out perfectly within one discipline. Too much top-down pressure for multidisciplinary research results in collaborations that do not naturally arise from scientific needs'. Hence, science policy has to find an adequate position on the trade-off between problems in society that demand a multidisciplinary approach and incentive structures within science.

The lesson not to neglect trade-offs, can be operationalized into a policy option to systematically examine the impact of specific measures on the main policy objectives. This would lower the risk of disappointment when policies meant to improve one objective, worsen another. In particular, synergy elements may be small and trading off objectives becomes important, if the budget constraint is tight as has been the case in the Netherlands and increasingly becomes the case in Germany. Then, intensifying policy on one subject entails a price on other subjects. In these circumstances, a statement like 'The alleged contradiction between fundamental research and social embedment of research is illusory' (OCW, 1996b: 7), only is valid to the extent that it may be useful to apply criteria of societal relevance in research. Yet, different incentive structures in science and technology create trade-offs and necessitate policy makers to choose between objectives. Against this general background, some more specific policy options come to the fore.

Higher Education. In the field of higher education the Dutch experience may be of interest to German policy makers. Dutch higher education policy constitutes an interesting experiment to find an adequate balance on the trade-off between diversity and scale and on the trade-off between flexibility and commitment. Autonomy and quality control enhance flexibility, research schools provide a framework to bundle competencies and recent initiatives to establish centres of excellence and top research schools strengthen the position in locational competition between national knowledge bases.

Analogously to the policy options mentioned in Chapter 5, strengthening subsidiarity may promote differentiation and flexibility in German higher education. Diminishing national coordination and a peer review system of quality control may increase experimentation to reduce the length of studies and to curtail the high teaching load. Locational competition between Länder and financial incentives may support this process. An example of a financial incentive is the Dutch system that relates basic funding to the number of students with an enrolment of four years or less.

A smaller teaching load provides room to enhance flexibility and quality of research in higher education. In addition, it may be worthwhile to consider financial incentives that promote the international orientation of science. Shifting some part of basic funding to internationally cooperative research or to visiting scientists may increase exposure to international scientific developments and may give an impetus to quality.

The trade-off in university research between quality and multidisciplinary research needs attention from Dutch policy makers. A tension exists between scientific quality norms in the committees that recognize and evaluate research schools and the objectives of policy makers. If policy makers emphasize relevance and multidisciplinary research, whereas recognition and evaluation committees implicitly or explicitly apply monodisciplinary criteria and emphasize coherency in research programs, individual research groups may face incompatible requirements. The process of trying to comply with these requirements may become time and resource consuming and frustrating.

Peer Review Finance. The organisation of the German system of peer review finance provides an example for the Netherlands. Both countries aim at increasing flexibility and quality by strengthening peer review finance in higher education. Cooperation, technology transfer and relevance increasingly become criteria to assess project proposals. For peer review finance to achieve the objective of flexible adjustment of scientific research to new developments, a flexible financing organisation is essential. Therefore, a successful reorganisation of the Dutch research council is essential to achieve flexibility.

Research Institutes. The German Max Planck Gesellschaft provides an example, both for the Dutch basic research institutes and for the large research centres in the two countries. It not only performs high-quality basic research but also explores new scientific areas and as such is agenda setting for German higher education R&D. Hence, it combines quality and flexibility. Despite its stronger orientation on basic research and the conflict of interests between scientific incentives and market incentives, patenting activity with the Max Planck Gesellschaft exceeds that of the German large research centres. A flexible set of institutes under a common umbrella organization, supported by special facilities such as Garching Innovation, appears to be a strong asset in the German research infrastructure. On this issue Germany provides an interesting case for the Dutch policy initiatives to concentrate the basic research institutes in a separate and flexible organisation. Of course, the Dutch basic research institutes will never reach the scope and size of their German counterparts, due to the difference in size of the countries.

Their size makes the large research institutes vulnerable to the risk of becoming locked in technologies of the past. This risk is relevant to Germany in particular, because the large research centres constitute a significant share of the specific knowledge base. Germany applies financial incentives to increase flexibility of the large research institutes and the Blue List institutes. Incentives for the Blue List institutes are strongest because part of their funding has been transferred to the German research council (DFG), where they have to compete with universities. That may be a suitable policy option for the large research centres as well. By involving companies and sectoral organizations in the drafting of basic funded programs, the Netherlands more strongly relies on cooperative exchange.[18] If the aim is to promote flexibility, the German policy appears more effective and the Netherlands may further consider increasing the share of peer review finance or contract finance for the large research centres.

A point of attention for policy makers, related to strengthening incentive structures and a stronger orientation towards societal needs, concerns the transaction costs associated with increasing competition within the scientific research base. Transaction costs not only concern the often substantial costs to draft proposals to apply for funding, but also the costs of lower investments in a specific institute's knowledge base. On the long run this may reduce quality. Hence to some extent policy makers should lean against the winds of internationalization and flexibility to protect sufficient commitment among the scientific research base to maintain a high-quality knowledge base. In addition, policy should guard a level playing field among the research institutes to prevent unfair competition from institutes with a relatively large degree of basic funding.

Direct Instruments. The relatively large size of subsidies for specific technologies and the elaborate system of creation of consensus on key technologies among all actors in the technological field, strengthen commitment and long-term relationships in German science and technology. Competition put the Netherlands closer to flexibility and diversity. The recent shift in focus towards and the building up of a strong position in biotechnology clearly show the strength of the German system. The integrated character of this set of institutions and the difference in size of the countries make it difficult to derive any policy options on this subject.

[18] A comparable difference between competition and cooperative exchange exists with the applied scientific research institutes FhG and TNO.

12 Regulation and Competition Policies

The central theme of this study is the effect of institutions on the economic performance of countries. This chapter discusses regulation and competition policies in the market for goods and services in Germany and the Netherlands. Current discussions on privatization and market liberalization illustrate the practical and policy relevance of this theme. Germany and the Netherlands have not been leaders in this field, but are catching up, affected by developments in the Anglo-Saxon countries, the creation of an internal European market, technological developments and modern market and regulation theory. Dutch examples are the large scale competition encouragement and deregulation operation and privatization of public enterprises, such as telecoms. In Germany the discussion on these themes is part of the so-called *Standort*-debate, which started in the early eighties.

This chapter aims to assess the current situation of Germany and the Netherlands. The aim is not to cover the complete field; that would be too extensive. We focus on the sheltered sectors where Dutch and German governments are sovereign to create institutions, and where there are thus potential policy options to be learned both for Germany and the Netherlands. The exposed sectors are less interesting, since they are largely subject to European rules and policies. Furthermore no attention will be paid to the gigantic privatization operation after unification.

The organization of the chapter is as follows. First, the deeper theoretical motives behind regulation and competition policy are explained. To this end, we use arguments from the modern industrial organization and regulation literature by distinguishing four market prototypes. Second, recent developments in actual (de)regulation and competition policy in Germany and the Netherlands are sketched. We combine the theory and recent developments to assess the impact of specific (de)regulation and competition policy measures. Finally, we draw policy options that can be learned from the experiences in Germany and the Netherlands

12.1 Theoretical Backgrounds

The common starting point of analysis in this study is the presence of market failures. The logic of competition and regulation policy is to alleviate market failures in the markets of goods and services. The question then is, first of all, what failures do occur in these markets? Secondly, what is the impact of these failures? Next, what are the principal coordination mechanisms used by competition and regulation policies to alleviate these failures and what are the major trade-offs they imply? These are the questions this section addresses. Section 12.1.1 discusses the market failures that are relevant for the markets of goods and services, as well as their impact. Whereas other chapters apply the benchmark of social efficiency, for regulation and competition policy one needs to state more precisely which notion of social efficiency is used. At a higher level of detail, the benchmark of social efficiency incorporates three concepts: allocative efficiency, technical efficiency and dynamic efficiency. Of these, allocative efficiency is traditionally the most-often used benchmark for social efficiency. A market outcome is allocatively efficient if the combined surplus of firms and consumers together is at its highest possible level, given the current state of technology. It is technically efficient if firms have costs that are not higher than those in agreement with the most efficient technology of that moment (for example, the potential of economies of scale must be well exploited, but also X-inefficiency must be absent). It is dynamically efficient if firms take 'sufficiently' care of innovation and new technology. The incidence and impact of failures differ strongly from one market to the other. Section 12.1.2 therefore presents a simple framework of four categories of markets to discuss the prevailing market failures as well as the trade-offs that occur.

12.1.1 The Rationale for Regulation and Competition Policy

Market Power. The most important source of market failure in the context of regulation and competition policy is market power. From an allocative efficiency point of view, a monopolist charges a price that is too high and causes deadweight losses. If the price were lower (equal to the marginal cost), the sum of consumer and producer surplus would be higher. From a technical efficiency point of view, one could say that the necessity to produce efficiently is less present for a monopolist than for a competitive firm. An inefficient competitive firm is unlikely to be profitable, a inefficient monopolist can be. A recent empirical study (Nickell, 1996) found evidence that competition indeed may be conducive for technical efficiency. From a dynamic efficiency point of view, conclusions are harder to draw. The debate whether monopoly or competition leads to more innovation has been going on since Schumpeter (1943). Recently, consensus among economists seems to grow that competition is typically more conducive for innovation, but arguments for either case can be given.

Specificity. A second source of market failure in the markets for goods and services is specificity. As explained in Chapter 2, the hold-up problem can frustrate specific investments. Without a commitment not to behave in an opportunistic way, investments may not be carried out at all, although they are mutually beneficial.

Obviously, this is not conducive for allocative efficiency, since an improvement in resource allocation is possible. Moreover, since these investments can concern R&D investments of suppliers in industrial supplier-customer relationships, dynamic efficiency may get worse as well. A second channel through which specificity cause market failure is by creating market power, with all the detrimental effects explained above. Specific investments (or sunk costs, see Box 12.1) can be used by firms to raise entry barriers in a market. More generally, specificity implies dependency which can easily lead to (abuse of) market power.

Externalities. Another source of market failure that can give rise to competition and regulation policy are externalities. Most important to competition and regulation policy are entry externalities. These occur if firms do not take into account the full effects of their strategies on other firms or consumers. One is the product diversity effect: a firm cannot completely appropriate the consumer surplus of a new product and has thus not enough incentive to introduce new products. The other is the business-stealing effect: when entering, a firm does not take into account the loss caused to other firms at the market. Besides these entry externalities, the R&D externalities that were explained in the chapter on science and technology policy, are relevant as well.

Asymmetric Information. Finally, asymmetric information between market parties may cause market failure. This problem can take the form of adverse selection (hidden information) and moral hazard (hidden action). An example of a market with adverse selection problems is the insurance market, where uncertainty about the risk profile of consumers can lead to the situation that high-risk consumers are served while low-risk consumers are not. Adverse selection problems are present at markets with uncertainty about the product quality (for example, second-hand cars, professional and financial services). Moral hazard problems can also be illustrated with the insurance market: a consumer who is insured has less incentives to be prudent. This can lead to too much consumption or too little provision of some insurances, from an allocative efficiency point of view.

Regulation and Competition Policies. Both regulation and competition policy aim at correcting these market failures, but each in a different way. Notice beforehand that definitions are not clear-cut and that the exact distinction between both policies is hard to make. The following, necessarily sketchy definitions are applied here. Competition policy 'lays down a set of rules by which firms should behave in markets' while regulation 'prescribes a set of contracts which determine the basis on which firms supply goods and services' (Jenkinson and Mayer, 1996: 2). In other words, competition policy defines the rules of competitive behaviour on the market, while regulation policy more directly affects the structure of the market. Market power (in some cases the consequence of specificity) is the source of market failure competition policy primarily deals with. One of the main problems of competition policy is to distinguish between the competition reducing effects of collusion and concentration and the efficiency enhancing effects of cooperation. Competition authorities have to perform an act of striking a balance between the goal of allocative efficiency on the one hand and the need to enhance the technical and dynamic efficiency on the other. In some cases, depending on market conditions, allocative efficiency is decisive and stimulated by encouraging rivalry among firms. Situations can also arise in which higher concentration ratios or massive investments might be tolerated, for instance when there are pronounced gains from economies of scale or cooperation which may enhance technical and dynamic efficiency.

The other sources of market failure are primarily controlled for by regulation policy. Externalities, for example, may be dealt with by entry regulation, uncertainty by quality standards regulation. If technical efficiency requires a natural monopoly, market power is dealt with by price and quality regulation.

Competition and regulation policies are to some extent complementary policies. Regulatory reform may make changes in competition policy necessary. Deregulation aims at more competition at markets, but at the same time creates the need for new regulation and more stringent competition policy in order to control for undesirable effects of more competition.

12.1.2 Four Market Prototypes

A Simple Framework. Of course, the market failures do not occur in each market. In some markets a certain market failure is more likely to occur than in other markets. To analyze this in a more systematic way this section presents a simple framework in which four market-prototypes are distinguished. For our purposes two dimensions are crucial (after Sutton, 1992):

- The degree to which the production technology involves *fixed costs*. Loosely speaking, the size of the fixed costs in relation to the size of the market determines the number of firms that can be active on a market. Given the long-term character of production technology decisions (machinery and capacity, once chosen, indeed are fixed in the short term), their main effect is in shaping the structure of a market.

- The degree in which product *differentiation* is present. The degree of product differentiation affects the toughness of competition in a market. Competition is more relaxed if products are differentiated; firms then have some local market power. Homogeneous products generally lead to more intense competition as products become closer substitutes. As opposed to fixed costs, product differentiation (or 'demand technology') affects more short-term strategies of firms, like pricing strategies.

Table 12.1 Four market prototypes

Fixed cost Product differentiation	Low	High
Low	Atomistic Competition	Natural Monopoly
High	Monopolistic Competition	Natural Oligopoly

The two dimensions give rise to four prototypes of market structures (see Table 12.1): atomistic competition, monopolistic competition, natural monopoly and natural oligopoly.

Market Failures and Market Prototypes. The presence of market failure and the trade-offs that occur depend on the market dimensions and thus differ for different market prototypes. The dimension of fixed cost is related to three sources of market failure: market power, specificity and externalities. The dimension of differentiation is related to the market failures of externalities and asymmetric information.

First, market power exists when there are few suppliers on a market who face non-horizontal demand curves. If the fixed costs are large relative to the market size, a market equilibrium with a few firms in the market is the only one sustainable. For relatively small fixed cost, many firms can be present on the market and more diversity is obtained. Market power is thus more of an issue in the right-hand side of the Table, where natural monopoly and natural oligopoly are located.

Specificity as a potential source of market failure is closely related to the extent that fixed cost are sunk. In the prototypes atomistic competition and monopolistic competition, fixed costs, and thus sunk costs as well, are low. One could say that this is beneficial for flexibility, for example, in the supplier-customers relationship. Since many parties are on the market, customers always have alternatives (which makes, as is characteristic of these prototypes, demand relatively elastic). In the natural monopoly case, the large fixed cost is typically sunk to a large extent. This requires a commitment from the side of the regulator in the relationship between the regulator and the regulated natural monopoly. Without a commitment of the regulator to keep the contract and to reward the regulated firm, this firm is not prepared to incur sunk costs in the first place. In the natural oligopoly case, sunk costs can be used strategically to raise entry barriers and to create market power. Further, to the extent that costs are sunk, the hold-up problem may arise in relationships between firms. Again, commitment is more needed in this case.

Third, entry externalities can occur. Whether, from an allocative efficiency point of view (or dynamic efficiency because new products are often concerned), too

Box 12.1 Fixed and sunk costs

A fixed cost is defined as a cost that is independent of the production volume (at least in the short term). Production plants are an example. Characteristic of a sunk cost is that it is irrecoverable once made. Examples are firm-specific plants, research and development expenditures and advertising outlays. These definitions already signify a relationship between fixed and sunk costs. Sunk costs are always fixed. Fixed costs can but need not to be sunk. In practice all fixed costs are sunk to some extent (Tirole, 1989: 307).

The point of this distinction is that it has important implications for market structures. Pure fixed costs (i.e., without a sunk part) are deterministic for the number of firms on a market. There are just so many firms on the market that one extra firm would make losses. Incumbent firms just cover their fixed costs and do not make profits (more precisely: they make normal profits). This configuration is due to the possibility of free entry. Contrary to old beliefs in industrial organisation (for example, Bain, 1956), pure fixed costs do not establish entry barriers and supranormal profits. Contestability theory (Baumol, Panzar and Willig, 1982) has made this clear. The very threat of entry can discipline the market to zero profits.

Sunk costs, however, can act as genuine entry barriers. These costs can be used in a strategic way. 'Strategic' here means 'with the purpose of influencing the behaviour of other' (in the spirit of Schelling, 1960). For instance, an incumbent firm can invest in extra capacity with the purpose of looking aggressive and thus deterring entry by other firms. Strategic behaviour of this kind requires irreversible commitment; if capacity could be sold once entry has taken place, the investment would not have strategic value. Sunk costs, as opposed to pure fixed costs, have this property. The consequence is that positive profits can be present at a market without attracting new entrants.

In his book on the relationship between sunk costs and market concentration, Sutton (1992) distinguishes two types of sunk costs: exogenous and endogenous. The acquisition of a plant of minimum efficient scale that all firms must incur in order to enter the market is an example of an exogenous cost, for it is determined by the nature of the underlying production technology. In markets where sunk costs are mainly exogenous, concentration is determined very much like in the case of fixed costs. That number of firms for which the sunk cost is just covered, is present in the market. The result is different for endogenous sunk costs. R&D investments or advertising outlays are choice variables to firms and are thus examples of endogenous sunk costs. In this case, Sutton argues, the strategic use in general leads to a competitive escalation of outlays, which in turn can lead to higher concentration for a given market size than in the case of exogenous costs. Think of one firm advertising more where others react aggressively by spending even more, in order not to lose market share.

---

much or too little entry (or diversity) occurs in a market, depends on two opposing externalities that are at work (Mankiw and Whinston, 1986). If the product diversity effect dominates, then too little entry is more likely because consumer surplus is not completely appropriated. The product diversity effect is strongest in markets where consumers appreciate product differentiation (monopolistic competition and natural oligopoly). If the business-stealing effect dominates, too much diversity (or entry) is more likely to occur because entrants do not take all effects on incumbent firms properly into account. In general, the business-stealing effect causes larger efficiency losses if the fixed costs to enter are higher. It is intuitively clear that the economies of scale originating from the fixed costs are best exploited by few firms. Entry of more firms not only means too little production per firm but also wasteful duplication of fixed setup costs. In short, too much entry (diversity) is more likely to occur if fixed costs are large. Too little entry (diversity) is more likely if products are differentiated. Besides entry externalities, R&D externalities can occur as well. They are more likely to occur when fixed costs are large, since most R&D costs are fixed. They are related to product diversity as well, as most R&D is aimed at product innovation.

The final source of market failure is asymmetric information. This is more of a problem in differentiated markets than in homogeneous markets. Adverse selection can be present at markets with uncertainty about the product quality (for example, second-hand cars, professional and financial services). Low quality providers may exploit the fact that consumers cannot distinguish between low- and high quality goods. Using the reputation of high-quality providers, low-quality providers may pretend to sell high-quality goods and charge too high prices. The result may be that not enough high-quality goods are offered at the market. The consequence for the trade-off in fighting this market failure is that commitment and enforcement are necessary in differentiated markets (in order to deal with the adverse selection problem). In homogeneous markets these problems do not occur; therefore these markets can be more flexible and open.

The presence and likelihood of market failures is now checked for the specific market prototypes. Implications for the trade-offs, efficiency benchmarks and competition and regulation policy are presented as well.

Atomistic Competition. Low fixed costs establish that many firms can enter the market. As a consequence, concentration is low. Moreover, because products are homogeneous, the market is typically characterized by fierce price competition. Market power is usually not an issue. Firms in this prototype typically make zero (or normal) profits. Collusive behaviour between firms may be possible but is unlikely to occur because there are many suppliers. Furthermore, sunk costs are low so that investment problems due to specificity do not play a role. Atomistic competition indeed is characterized by high flexibility in supplier-customer relationships. As products are homogeneous and the market is transparent, asymmetric information problems do not occur. Since both the business stealing and product diversity effects are absent, entry externalities as a source of market failure are also absent.

R&D externalities, however, can cause problems in these markets, as scale rather than diversity may be conducive for R&D. Several arguments exist as to why small and competitive firms may not overcome R&D externalities and have too little incentive to invest in R&D (Kamien and Schwartz, 1982: 47). Small firms have lower sales volumes to recover the (relatively low) fixed R&D cost; the so-called cost-spreading argument. Small firms are less able to appropriate the returns to their R&D because unforeseen innovations that come out of their R&D cannot be exploited and economies of scale in R&D neither. Moreover, the imperfection of capital markets feeds the need to finance R&D with past profits, which are typically absent in atomistic competition. This is also a problem of asymmetric information in financing.

The result of these features is that with respect to the benchmarks of allocative and technical efficiency, atomistic competition performs very well. With respect to the benchmark of dynamic efficiency, performance may be worse.

Monopolistic Competition. Like in the case of atomistic competition, low fixed (and thus low sunk) costs give rise to easy entry and low market concentration. Price competition, however, is typically more relaxed because products are differentiated. Market power is not likely to occur as a source of market failure. Monopolistic competition is truly characterized by diversity (in the sense of both many and diverse firms). There are neither problems as a result of specificity because sunk costs are typically low. Flexibility in the supplier-buyer relationship is thus obtained. Entry externalities can cause too little entry. As fixed costs are low, the business stealing effect is typically weak. Because products are differentiated, the product diversity effect is strong. Since this last effect is likely to dominate, too little entry may occur. The other potential source of market failure is asymmetric information. As products are differentiated, uncertainty about their quality indeed may exist and give rise to adverse selection problems.

Concerning the performance benchmarks, entry externalities not only cause allocative efficiency losses, because there are not enough firms at the market, but dynamic efficiency losses as well, if one considers entry to be introduction of product innovations. Entry and product subsidies are instruments of regulation policy to correct this market failure. The problem of asymmetric information causes allocative efficiency losses. Minimum-quality standards (for example, hygiene regulation for restaurants, standards for construction materials, minimum education requirements for personnel) and entry licences are possible regulation measures to deal with these problems. These measures improve allocative efficiency but since they establish legal entry barriers, the risk is that they may induce technical inefficiency because of lack of competitive threat.

Natural Monopoly. Large fixed costs make that the market is concentrated. In fact, in most cases, such as utilities, these costs are so large that only one firm is active on the market. The production of the goods in this market type often exhibits economies of scale everywhere. Scale is thus not only a feature of this market type; it is also a virtue. As there is only one firm at the market, market power is an obvious problem. The presence of the specificity problem is closely related to the extent that fixed cost are sunk. In the natural monopoly case, the fixed cost is usually sunk to a large extent. This requires commitment in the

Box 12.2 Natural monopoly regulation: The trade-off between incentives and rent extraction

Asymmetric information gives rise to a basic trade-off for the regulator, namely one between providing incentives to reduce costs (to promote technically efficiency) and extracting the rents of the monopolist (to be sure society does not pay too much for the good the monopolist supplies, that is, to promote allocative efficiency). To illustrate the trade-off, suppose the regulator imposes a price cap (maximum price permitted to charge) to the monopolist. This makes the monopolist eager to keep costs low because the difference between the price permitted and the actual costs remains with the monopolist (the monopolist is said to be the 'residual claimant', a feature of so-called high-power incentive schemes). However, with respect to rent extraction this measure scores worse. On the other hand, suppose that the regulator transfers the costs plus some mark-up to the monopolist. In that case the monopolist does not gain by keeping costs low, but society gains because no rents remain with the monopolist (cost-plus contracts are low-power incentive schemes).

Source: Laffont and Tirole (1993)

relationship between the regulator and the regulated natural monopoly. Without commitment of the regulator to reward (or provide the cash and profit) to gain back investments, the regulated natural monopolist will not invest in the first place. This is the familiar hold-up problem in the context of regulation. For the government it implies a trade-off between commitment and flexibility.

How does this market type score with respect to the efficiency concepts? Market power leads to allocative inefficiency. From a technical efficiency point of view, however, it is best to have one firm, that is, a natural monopolist, in order to optimally exploit economies of scale. Price regulation of this natural monopolist is then needed from an allocative efficiency point of view. Indeed, traditionally natural monopolies have been subject to strong price regulation.[1] A fundamental problem regulators face in this matter is information asymmetry with the natural monopolies. For example, to impose the price a monopolist should charge (to prevent deadweight losses caused by unregulated pricing), a regulator must know the cost structure. The best source of this information is the monopolist himself, but he has every reason to overstate his costs so as to be permitted to set higher prices (see Box 12.2). The regulator must take this problem into account when formulating contracts with the natural monopolist.

Another problem of market power that may also occur in a natural monopoly concerns dynamic efficiency. The following arguments have been put forward (Kamien and Schwartz 1982). In favour of innovativeness of monopolists are the

[1] The focus of the extensive regulation literature has almost exclusively been on natural monopolies (see Laffont and Tirole, 1993). Competition policy is less relevant here, although recent deregulation gives rise to it.

presence of profits which makes self-financing of R&D possible and avoids external financing problems. Moreover, the (often) large scale of monopolies makes it easier to appropriate returns to R&D. Finally, large scale establishes that the fixed R&D costs are spread over a higher production volume and are thus sooner recovered. Argument against monopolies are their low incentive to innovate. The monopolist's incentive to innovate is the difference between his profits before and after innovation. Since current profits are high (that is, to the extent that the regulator does not take them), this incentive is generally low; monopolists tend to 'rest on their laurels'.

Natural Oligopoly. Large fixed costs - usually sunk to a large extent - lead to concentrated market structures. However, as opposed to the case above, economies of scale are less important because competition takes place in quality (or innovation, service, advertising) rather than in price. This prototype is the natural territory for competition policy, as market power is the main source of market failure. Other possible market failures are asymmetric information concerning quality and entry externalities.

The market power argument is the main motive behind government intervention in this prototype. Of course, as markets are concentrated, firms naturally have some market power. The point is that this power should not be abused, and competition policy must check just that. Since the fixed costs are usually sunk to a large extent, they can be used to raise entry barriers. A practice that is not allowed is monopolization of the market. Possible ways to push competitors out (or, similarly, deter entry) and monopolise the market are predatory pricing (first setting low prices and later increase them once competitors are out) or imposing standards. Other practices that are suspicious from the point of view of competition policy are mergers and acquisitions. The motive behind these may be exploitation of economies of scale or scope, but there is the risk that a firm obtains excessive market power. In other words, there lies a trade-off between scale and diversity. Vertical restraints are yet another practice of possible abuse of market power. Vertical foreclosure, for example, may prevent a competitor to obtain an essential input. Other examples of vertical constraints are exclusive dealerships, vertical price binding, tying and price discrimination.

Despite the fact that competition policy particularly applies to this type of market, regulation policy still plays some role. In the insurance and banking sector, for example, market failures that are due to asymmetric information give rise to entry or quality regulation. Minimum quality standards, entry licences or certificate requirements are examples of regulation policy of this kind. As these measures often impose legal entry barriers, the lack of competitive threat may be at the cost of technical and allocative efficiency.

Finally, two types of externalities may be a source of market failure in this prototype. First, the by now familiar entry externalities. Notice that both the product diversity and the business-stealing externalities are present. Beforehand,

Table 12.2 Market prototypes and trade-offs

	Fixed cost		Low	High
Product differen-tiation	*Market failure* ⇒ ⇓ trade-off ⇒ ⇓	*market power* *specificity*	diversity ⇔ flexibility ⇔	scale commitment
	information asymmetry (quality)	*Externalities* ⇒ ⇓	efficient entry ⇔ little R&D ⇔	business stealing: too much entry R&D (over)supply
Low	flexibility	efficient entry	**atomistic competition**	**natural monopoly**
	⇔	⇔		
High	commitment / enforcement	product diversity: too little entry	**monopolistic competition**	**natural oligopoly**

How to read this table?

This table combines the general analytical framework and the classification of markets used in this chapter. The dimensions that underlie the market classification, fixed costs and product differentiation on the axes of the table, each have specific impact on the presence of market failure and the trade-offs that occur in correcting these. The horizontal axis of fixed cost can be linked to the market failures of market power, specificity and externalities. For low fixed cost these market failures are hardly present and, naturally, the trade-offs point more towards diversity, flexibility and efficient entry. For high fixed cost, typically sunk to a large extent, the mentioned market failures can be particularly strong. Naturally, the trade-offs are biased towards the scale, commitment, too much entry and R&D extremes.

The vertical axis of product differentiation can be linked to the market failures of information asymmetry and entry externalities. The information asymmetry market failure is particularly strong if products are differentiated and for example quality is uncertain. Being able to provide commitment to deliver quality is then an issue. The problem of entry externalities is also mainly present if products are differentiated because of the product diversity effect described in the main text.

it is not clear which effect dominates and thus whether there is too much or too little entry. There is some theoretical evidence that technological competition, where few firms race against each other for some innovation, leads in general to excessive R&D investments from an allocative efficiency point of view. More generally, Sutton (1992) finds that in oligopoly structure where sunk costs are endogenous for example, R&D, quality, advertising, firms tend to get involved in an upward spiral of expenditures. This is unlikely to be beneficial for allocative efficiency. As these sunk costs constitute entry barriers, too little entry takes place and too much scale is established.

The second type of externalities are R&D spill-overs between firms. Spill-overs reduce the incentive to innovative are therefore not conducive for dynamic efficiency. Competition policy can take the form of allowing cooperation in R&D,

Box 12.3 New technology in telecommunications, regulation and market structure

In the telecommunications sector, technological development has undermined the natural monopoly argument for regulation. In a natural monopoly situation, exclusive rights can be defended on the argument that competitive entry would lead to wasteful competition (technical efficiency requires one firm). Networks of fixed-wires telecoms have been a natural monopoly traditionally. In combination with a rapidly growing demand for a variety of services new technology (in the form of optical fibre) has strengthened the economic case for open network provision in the form of non-discriminatory access for service-providers. Moreover, it has weakened the economic argument for having a single long distance network, for the costs of setting up such networks (for a given capacity) have declined enormously. New technology in mobile telephones has further impaired the natural monopoly character.

By contrast, in the absence of cable-TV networks, the so-called local loop (connections to homes and businesses) remains a natural monopoly, at least for the time being. The opening up of the infrastructure part of the telecommunications industry for competition in 1998 will presumably have the effect of national telecom companies making alliances with companies of other countries and with firms in the data and TV industries to protect their own markets and to penetrate foreign markets. Possible alliance partners will also be utilities with access to a network infrastructure (like railway and electricity companies). Newcomers will probably try to secure a position in niche markets.

Source: CEPS (1996).

whereas usually other cases of cooperation, for example, in prices, are at least suspect according to most competition policies. Here a trade-off may occur between dynamic efficiency and allocative efficiency. Dynamic efficiency asks for the internalization of spill-overs and the sharing of fixed costs through R&D cooperation. The risk that two firms that cooperate in R&D are more likely to cooperate in the product market, is undesirable from an allocative efficiency point of view. Table 12.2 summarizes the presence of trade-offs in the four market prototypes.

12.2 Sea Changes: The Impact of Trends

A number of developments has contributed to the increasing concern for improving the functioning of markets in general, and the shift towards regulatory reform policies in sheltered sectors in particular (Høj *et al.*, 1995; Geelhoed, 1993).

For a long time market failures have been considered as *sufficient* conditions for government intervention. The trend in recent years has become to consider them just as *necessary* conditions. The presence of market failure does not automatically lead to public action. The general opinion is that government can fail too. Indeed, the trade-off is one between market failure versus regulation failure. In many countries, including Germany and the Netherlands, the political outcome of this trade-off seems to have changed over time.

Table 12.3 The impact of trends on trade-offs

Trends	Impact on trade-offs
Higher visibility of government failure Political feeling of lack of dynamism Technological change (lower fixed costs) European integration Increasing international competition More heterogeneity	diversity ← scale flexibility ← commitment much entry ← little entry

There is wide recognition nowadays that traditional regulatory instruments can result in serious allocative, technical and dynamic efficiency losses. Partly as a result of new economic theory from countries like the United States and United Kingdom (see Kahn, 1988; Vickers and Yarrow, 1988), regulation failure has become more visible and regulation programs have been scrutinised. For example, regulation measures to deal with the adverse selection problem in monopolistic competition and natural oligopoly, restrict entry and thus leads to allocative efficiency losses. Under regulation failure one can classify several costs: the administrative costs associated with regulation measures (compliance costs), the distortive effects of tax raising and the cost of technical inefficiency of regulated firms. The vulnerability of the political decision process to the influence of pressure groups, the so-called regulatory capture, is another potential source of regulation failure.

Secondly, a feeling of lack of dynamism has lead to another vision on the driving forces behind economic growth, with competition as the main thrust. This has led to a wave of regulatory reforms. Deregulation has made more competition possible at previously protected markets. This trend to market liberalization has required more focus on other forms of regulation as well as on competition policy.

Thirdly, rapidly changing technologies are increasingly creating opportunities for competition in areas where it did not exist to any substantial extent before. In telecommunications, for instance, technology is increasingly allowing entrants to challenge monopolies by a twofold development (see Box 12.3). New technologies, by lowering entry costs, not only challenge the technical network monopoly of incumbent national companies, but also contribute to creating a demand for and supply of new information services. Existing regulation can therefore become obsolete very quickly.

Fourthly, the creation of the Single Market as well as the internationalisation of economic relations in general are forcing economies to rapidly adapt and adjust to changing circumstances, especially to a growing intensity of competition in sectors that were formerly sheltered from international competition. To a great extent, this is due to the opening-up of capital markets and hence the erosion of many of the

Box 12.4 Regulatory reform in the United Kingdom

The regulatory reform programme in the United Kingdom started in 1979 under the Thatcher government. Privatization and the promotion of shareholder ownership by private citizens was a major drive behind it. Originally, privatization concentrated on state owned companies that already operated in a market environment, like the oil and car industry. Firms like British Aerospace, Cable and Wireless, British Petroleum, Jaguar and British Airways were sold. Later, firms in semi-public sectors like the energy sector, the transport sector and other utilities were privatised. British Telecom for instance was privatised in 1984 and the gas companies in 1986. The firms concerned all enjoyed a dominant position on their respective markets. Therefore, these privatizations often underlined the need for stimulating competition by for instance splitting up companies and by regulatory reform measures. In sectors like gas, water and telecommunications, restrictive rules were abolished, networks were uncoupled and independent regulatory agencies (like Ofgas, Ofwat and Oftel) were installed. The agencies had the task of monitoring market behaviour of the privatised companies and correcting them if necessary. One of their instruments is price cap and access price regulation. In addition to the combined privatization and deregulation operations, regulatory reform measures were especially directed at the financial and services sectors.

An example of an industry that has been privatised is the railway industry. It has been separated into an infrastructure part, which runs the networks and the stations (Railtrack), and a potentially competitive part. Train operations are organised by three rolling stock leasing companies and 25 (potential) operators to run the train services. The Office of Passenger Rail Franchising determines service requirements and arranges competitive bidding for different services. Franchises are given for a period of 5-10 years. The Office of the Rail Regulator has been assigned the task of facilitating and controlling the efficient running of the system. One of the complex issues arising is the interoperability of tickets and the maintenance of reduced-price travel cards.

After a relative standstill at the end of the eighties due to the economic recession, in recent years a new impulse has been given to the process of deregulation. Regulations in a.o. telecommunications, transport, construction and the wholesale distribution are being reviewed by task forces. Their recommendations are discussed and implemented by special deregulation units at the ministries, with a supervisory role for the Prime Minister. To date, the plans of the new Labour government in these issues are uncertain but likely to be of little consequence for the regulatory reform.

Sources: Armstrong, Cowan and Vickers (1994); Bishop, Kay and Mayer (1995); CEPS (1996); Koedijk and Kremers (1996).

barriers to foreign direct investment. This has not only increased the degree of international competition, but also the sense of urgency for streamlining regulations that do not contribute positively to national competitive positions.

Finally, the notion is gaining importance that society is becoming more and more heterogeneous and complex. Legislators and administrators therefore can not identify objects and aims of regulations as easily as before. They may lead to a tendency of regulations becoming more and more complex and costs for compliance increasing (Geelhoed, 1993). One way of escaping from this risk is to look for other, more effective and efficient coordination mechanisms for meeting pluralistic demands.

These trends have impact on the trade-offs that were distinguished in Section 12.1. As Table 12.3 shows, all trends point at an increasing role for competition as coordination mechanism. The trends shift the trade-offs towards diversity, flexibility and more entry.

Instruments of regulation and competition policy should be designed accordingly to become in line with these trends. In the seventies and the eighties, policy experiments in the United States and the United Kingdom have taken place to achieve this (see Box 12.4). Continental Europe is now catching up with new policies of regulatory reform. In general, two main elements/instruments of deregulation programmes can be distinguished. Firstly, liberalization, that is, the removal of restrictions on competition (Armstrong *et.al.*, 1994: 99). Examples are the abolishment of quality regulation that restricts entry, but also unbundling potentially competitive parts from natural monopolies. Secondly, privatization, that is, the transfer from public ownership into private ownership. In particular privatization with the aim of introducing more competition, rather than raising income for the government, is relevant here.

Deregulation in the form of liberalization can be applied in most of the market types we have distinguished. It can take the form of entry and quality standards deregulation, but also of restructuring firms and industries. The instrument of privatization in itself does not establish more competition. Privatization of public firms is often complementary to liberalization; it is often needed to create a level playing field after liberalization and entry of private firms. Another consequence of privatization is that the technical efficiency may improve. In general private shareholders are expected to be more strict in monitoring managers than the government. Firms under government control often face a soft budget constraint, which implies that managers do not have strong incentives to improve technical efficiency. A final instrument to achieve more competition is a tougher competition policy.

12.3 Regulation in Germany and the Netherlands: The Current State of Flux

This section reviews per market type most of the regulatory reform measures that are planned or have taken place in Germany and the Netherlands. Atomistic competition is not dealt with because there is not much regulation in the first place. The process of regulatory reform in *Germany* started in 1988 with an independent commission of experts that evaluated a large number of regulations in terms of their costs and benefits. In 1991 it published a report on the institutional impediments to a more flexible functioning of markets in Germany. A novelty was the fact that the commission evaluated existing regulations in terms of costs and benefits and thus in economic terms. The report evaluates regulations on the basis of three guiding principles. Firstly, a regulation is adjusted or abolished if it is not needed to correct a market imperfection or to serve a non-economic objective. Secondly, the same holds if the envisaged benefits of a regulation do not outweigh its costs. Thirdly, if possible, a regulation that is desirable in itself, is replaced by an alternative regulation that carries lower costs or is less detrimental for competition.

A parliamentary steering group chaired by the Minister of Economic Affairs discussed the measures and presented an implementation report, adopting most proposals. In 1992 the federal government decided to implement 58 out of 97 measures proposed by the Deregulation Commission (Van Bergeijk and Haffner, 1996). Part of the regulatory reform measures was recommended and implemented because European Union internal market guidelines prescribed such policy changes. The other part primarily had the objective of deregulating predominantly sheltered sectors as an instrument for stimulating intra-border adaptability and competition. Concrete measures relate to liberalization in the fields of insurance, energy, technical inspection, legal advice and to a certain extent also the labour market.[2] Privatization measures concerned state participation in, for example, the national air line company, railways. and postal services.

Traditionally, in the *Netherlands* an impressive number of regulations have hampered the functioning of the markets for goods and services, especially in the sheltered sectors. Examples are public transport, telecommunications, energy and gas, and health care. These prominently came to the fore in several studies, e.g. in the 1993 OECD-country survey on the Netherlands. Interventions are motivated either by the natural monopoly character of activities or by social considerations. Discontent with the performance of the markets for goods and services inspired a government policy resting on three pillars. Firstly, legal steps were taken to intensify competition policy. This is the subject of the next section. Secondly, a cross-ministry project was started in 1994 investigating the effects of several regulations on the functioning of markets and suggesting measures for improvement. The so-called Market performance, deregulation and quality of legislation-project (MDW) was started to give an impetus to deregulation. It is part and parcel of the coalition agreement and aims to increase economic dynamism by creating a healthy and competitive business environment. Among others, the 'Market and government' project is part of it. This project aims at stimulating the functioning of markets in (semi-)public sectors. In particular this second pillar is dealt with here. The third pillar is an action programme aiming at curtailing the administrative

---

[2] In particular proposals concerning public notaries, transport, taxi-regulations and most labour market proposals were turned down by the steering group.

burden of existing and proposed legislations for firms by doing away with or simplifying rules and regulations wherever possible.

Monopolistic Competition. Since 1994 liberalization of establishment regulations in *Germany* has facilitated the exercise of an independent craft and, in addition, enabled craftsmen to supply a broader spectrum of services, while retaining the master craftsman's certificate. Also shop opening hours were partially liberalized recently to take effect in November 1996. This measure has given an impetus to economic activity in a substantial part of the service sector.

In the transport sector European Union initiatives have contributed to liberalization measures. Road transport can be considered to be a market of monopolistic competition, with relatively low fixed costs and differentiation through service. Free entry usually prevails but transport in Germany was traditionally heavily regulated. By consequence, strong barriers to entry on the German market existed and the degree of internationalisation of national transporters was relatively low. The deregulation operation has led to an extension of the capacity for long distance road goods transport within the existing system of quotas on licences. Binding tariffs for goods transport have been abolished as of 1994 for all means of transport. By consequence, in road haulage, prices fell by some 30 per cent following deregulation of prices in 1994 (OECD, 1996). A substantial reduction in the number of empty rides (visualizing a technical efficiency gain) has contributed significantly to this price fall.

In the *Netherlands*, in the first year of the deregulation operation, working groups of experts and civil servants, chaired by an independent person, evaluated the Shop Opening Act, taxi regulations, driving time regulations, and the process monopoly of lawyers.[3] These measures in particular affect monopolistic competition markets. Based on the specific proposals put forward by each of these working groups, government has drawn conclusions that are worked out and prepared for sending them to parliament. Parliamentary decision making is expected to lead to among others deregulation of the taxi market, a considerable reduction of the number of licences required for environment related activities, the removing of several legal obstacles to introducing more flexibility in the planning of driving times and resting hours of drivers and workplace safety standards replacing detailed specifications.

As a first result of the activities of the MDW-commission, as from June 1996 shop opening hours have been substantially liberalised. Furthermore, the process monopoly of lawyers has been abolished in order to allow other legal experts (from e.g. consumer organisations, trade unions and insurance companies) to represent their members or firms in legal procedures. Among the subjects that are part of the second round of the deregulation operation are the legislation on food, regulatory

---

[3] In addition the working group reviewed environmental and working place regulations.

obstacles in the market for health care provision, and obstacles to a market-oriented operation of educational institutions. Working groups have already presented their reports on these subjects and their proposals are being discussed in the Cabinet, after which decisions will be sent to Parliament. The subjects of the third round pertain to legislations that concern the construction sector (see Box 12.5), accountants, product related regulations and competition and pricing in the health care sector. In addition, a sharply liberalised Establishment Law[4] was introduced under the former government, which reduces entry barriers and is therefore presumed to considerably increase mobility in the retail sector.

Natural Oligopoly. Another group of liberalization measures concerns natural oligopolies like the banking and insurance sectors. The *German* banking law has been amended in conformity with various European Union banking directives. In insurance, mandatory implementation of European Union directives also aimed at intensifying competition on the European market. Before 1990, German competition law exempted banking and insurance from the general ban of horizontal and vertical price agreements and subjected these to abuse control. With the fifth amendment of the Cartel Law, exceptions for banks and insurance companies have been appreciably pruned back.

Furthermore, in Germany a privatization programme has substantially reduced the state holding of companies.[5] As in other European countries, these concentrated first on state ownership of companies that provided goods and services for (near-) competitive markets. The government holding of Lufthansa shares, for instance, has been substantially reduced and completion of the privatization proceeds. Other candidates for privatization are the federal participations in airports and harbours, as well as the holdings of banks and telecoms.

In the *Netherlands* an example of a deregulated natural oligopoly is public transport, where the extent of government involvement is steadily decreasing. Subsidies to public transport are being reduced through a combination of fare increases and improved efficiency. Regional transport companies have been made more independent to allow them to become more flexible and responsive to market signals. These companies next merged into one big company, holding a near monopoly in regional bus transport, Verenigde Streekvervoerbedrijven Nederland (VSN). Although this merger was not in line with the political aim of more competition, no instruments were available to prevent it. In the mean time, plans have been developed to introduce more competition in this sector. By way of experiment, one concession was given to a small private company. For the time

---

[4] This law came into force on 1 January 1996 and decreased the number of types of establishment licences from 88 to 8.

[5] Privatization efforts have reduced the holding of companies from 956 in 1982 to about 400 at the end of 1994; see OECD, 1995.

Box 12.5 The construction market

The construction market is a market of monopolistic competition. Regulation affects the construction market in various forms. First, there is technical regulation with respect to the product. Minimum quality standards of products and materials, and quality control fall in this category. German regulation on this point is more stringent than Dutch regulation. Second, there is entry regulation. In order to enter one needs certificates. Also on this point, Germany has a more stringent policy. Entry barriers stemming from this source are thus higher in Germany. In Germany, policies with respect to the construction sector have hardly changed in the last five years. In the Netherlands, in 1996 more liberal regulation has been introduced with respect to entry. Starting a business is easier and does not require as many certificates as it did before 1996.

Another way the government affects the construction market is through housing policy. In the Netherlands, housing policy has been less liberal and the government has constituted a large demand. Partly as a result of this, the construction sector in the Netherlands is more industrialized, whereas Germany is more characterized by old-fashioned craftsmanship. The trend in construction is to put more weight at stages before the actual building. More and higher-quality prefab materials make building more efficient. The large scale and uniformity of social housing projects in the Netherlands has encouraged experimentation with new building techniques. This has lead to a cost advantage in materials, which is an important advantage in this increasingly open market. The housing policy in the Netherlands has become more liberal now.

As opposed to this positive effect, there is the potential negative effect of collusion among construction firms when bidding for public projects. In the Netherlands until 1994 the rules concerning bidding in public tendering were set by the construction sector itself (the rules of the so-called Uniform Prijsregelend Reglement (the Uniform Price-regulating Rules) of the association of constructors, the Vereniging van Samenwerkende Prijsregelende Organisaties (the Association of Cooperating and Price-regulating Organizations)). Construction firms had to make bids on the basis of independent calculations. After that, bids were compared and the project was attributed by a meeting of construction firms to the bidder with the lowest price. The bidders that were not elected got compensation for the costs of making the bid. An extra margin was set on the winning bid to pay for this compensation. The principal had no information about this process and only saw the final bid. This practice of market allocation was allowed for by the lax competition policy in the Netherlands. From January 1994 measures are in force to deal with the most severe forms of anti-competitive behaviour.

Competition policy in Germany has been more stringent from the start. In addition to the overall competition law, special rules are designed for public tendering by the German government (the Verdingungsordnung für Bauleistungen). Despite the rules, however, some anti-competitive behaviour may be present. The practice of underhand (selective) tendering, for example, that is common practice in Germany. Instead of a public tender where every firm can bid, two or more construction firms are selected and asked for bids. In practice, projects often go to local construction firms, which can be an indication of non-transparent markets. Up to now no measures have been taken against these practices.

Source: Stoffers (1995).

being, VSN and local transport companies in bigger cities still own monopoly positions.

Other Dutch measures have concentrated on liberalization of markets with public as well as private firms (so-called mixed markets). These markets often have a natural oligopolistic nature. As noticed above, the 'Market and government' project makes up the third pillar of government policy aiming at improving the functioning of markets. A working group has recently made an inventory of situations in which public companies are (potentially) in competition with private firms. More precisely, it has indicated the factors that build up a competitive advantage of public firms and has given solutions that contribute to levelling the playing field of both private and public firms. Definitive measures have not been taken yet.

Natural Monopolies. Most measures have been taken in what used to be considered as natural monopolies. Potentially competitive parts of former natural monopolies have been opened for competition. Only the truly natural monopolistic parts, such as networks, remain regulated. Indeed, in terms of the market classification, a shift from natural monopoly towards natural oligopoly is taking place in some markets.

With respect to the utilities, a number of initiatives in *Germany* have been stimulated by the Single Market, for example, concerning the gas and electricity sectors.[6] Regarding rail transport, a reform in 1994 implied the corporatisation of the Federal Railway system. This reform followed the line of a Single Market directive. Four separate units have been established under a publicly-owned stock company, for short distance and long distance passenger traffic, freight traffic and the rail network respectively. The federal government is responsible for investment in the rail network and charges the rail network for depreciation. The divested train operating company is deprived of any privileges. Train services can be offered by this company but also by other operators. Therefore access rules have been specified and the infrastructure operator has set access prices for utilisation of the network by railway operators. Originally a price system was set up that gives rebates to big operators. This rebate scheme was adjusted after it had been criticised for strongly favouring in-house operators.[7]

From 1996 onwards, the Länder are responsible for the operation of short distance passenger traffic. Although it is too early to judge the overall effects of the reform on competition, it can be noted that just making the market open has had the effect of improving service to customers (OECD, 1996).

In the *Netherlands*, former state monopolies with a presumed natural monopoly character are being restructured. The old state-owned railway company has been

---

[6] The energy sector is the subject of Chapter 13.

[7] Nevertheless, under the original rebate, there were about thirty third-party operators, who had only very little traffic.

divided into three publicly-owned stock companies, *viz.* for passenger transport, freight transport, and the rail network respectively. As in Germany the federal government is responsible for investing in the rail network. With respect to railway transport services, for a long time the Dutch Railways has been the only supplier. This near monopoly has recently been contested and a private company has obtained concessions from the Transport Ministry on some minor lines. Dutch Railways are heavily opposing and recently further concessions on main-lines were refused. Moreover, Dutch Railways, the regional bus services (VSN), and local transport companies in big cities have announced the setting up of a close cooperation programme to prevent potential competitors from attacking their positions (De Volkskrant, 18-9-1996).

European directives also set the pace in *Germany* for liberalization of the communications sector and for privatization of state-monopolies. The Postreform I-operation has divided the federal post office into three public enterprises (postal service, post-bank and telecommunications) and opened up parts of the communications market competition for third parties (equipment, teletext, mobile functions). The Postreform II-operation entailed the organisation of the main units as joint-stock companies, although originally the shares continued to be owned by an agency of the Ministry of Post and Telecommunications. A first part of the Telekom shares was floated in 1996. The sector will be fully liberalized in 1998, meanwhile opening up some other parts of the market to third parties. Licences to operate voice telephony, for instance, will be available to all firms satisfying certain safeguard criteria. Despite the progress that has been made in this field, entry in basic telecommunications still is of a limited character. This is worsened by the fact that Telekom is one of the few (formerly) monopolistic operators in Europe that controls the cable net. Giving up its dual ownership of both the telephone- and cable TV-network is a necessary condition to arrive at genuine liberalization and competition in the telecommunications industry (Monopolkommission, 1996: 32).

Guided by European Union-proposals for liberalising parts of this sector, some progress in opening up markets has also been made in the postal sector. Because the differences between the future telecommunications regime and the European Union-proposals for reforming the postal sector are considerable, privatization in postal services is not expected to proceed as far as in the telecommunications sector.

In the *Netherlands*, the state-owned communication firm KPN has been privatized. With respect to liberalization, the admittance of a second supplier on the market for mobile communication, in addition to KPN, has created a duopoly. This entrant has built its own network. Two more firms will be admitted before long. Network competition will be introduced also in basic telecommunications. The voice telephony monopoly of the former state-owned telephone company in supplying telephone services will be abolished. The sector has been opened up through the granting of more licences, to other private network suppliers. Unlike the German situation, the Dutch telecommunications company does not own the TV-cable network. So in principle opportunities exist for admitting more suppliers to the market.

Competition in the postal services sector so far is limited. The KPN has maintained an exclusive statutory concession for postal deliveries, while, among others, the markets for express and direct mail, have been opened up to other companies. In the near future, an independent regulator will be installed, the OPTA, in order to watch over the postal and telecommunication sector. In addition, the new competition authority (see section below) will control competition matters in this sector.

12.4 Competition Policy

This section compares the Dutch and German competition policy systems and their implementation. It first distinguishes two basic philosophies in competition policies, then describes the main characteristics of both regimes and signals relevant similarities and differences and finally compares competition policies in the light of recent developments and discussions. In particular the market type of natural oligopoly is relevant for competition policy.

12.4.1 Two Basic Philosophies: Abuse and Prohibition Principles

Competition policy is primarily concerned with three kinds of problems: restrictive business agreements, the abuse of dominant market positions, and the creation or strengthening of a dominant position through mergers and acquisitions. Two basic philosophies underlying competition legislation can be discerned. These are usually characterised by the way they handle restrictive business agreements. In this respect a distinction can be made between systems based on the prohibition principle (like most of the European Union member states) and systems based on the abuse principle. Under the prohibition principle restrictive business agreements are prohibited and violations are sanctioned. By contrast, the abuse principle basically allows restrictive agreements but comprises the right of government to interfere if agreements are considered as contrary to the public interest. This principle characterised Dutch competition policy until recently (see Box 12.6). Driven by concerns about the dynamism of the Dutch economy and by the need to confirm to European Union laws, an entirely new Economic Competition Act has been prepared that is based on the prohibition principle. This new act comes into force January 1998. Anticipating this bill, a number of major adjustments to the old competition law have already been administered, which already shift the focus for the most harmful competitive restraints from the abuse principle towards a prohibition based policy.

The German competition policy regime is for the most part laid down in the Act against Restraints of Competition of 1958 (ARC). This law contains a system of

Box 12.6 The old Dutch Act on Economic Competition

The Dutch Act on Economic Competition of 1956, which still applies but will be replaced by a new one shortly, is founded on the abuse principle. According to the Dutch competition rules, agreements between producers on for instance pricing or market sharing are not prohibited, except if they are contrary to the public interest. It is up to the authorities to prove in each individual case that the public interest has been impaired, after which the Minister of Economic Affairs has the authority to nullify the agreement. Only collective vertical price agreements and individual vertical price agreements for a list of specified goods have been prohibited since 1964. Agreements have to be reported to the government and are filed in the Cartel Register.

The old Dutch Act does not prohibit dominant positions or abuses of dominant positions, but only allows for corrective action if dominant positions are against public interest. Until the latter fact has been ascertained, no legal basis exists for the administration to interfere. Moreover, prior to a formal decision, dominant behaviour is perfectly legal and cannot be sanctioned.

The old Dutch competition regime does not have a merger control mechanism similar to that in Germany or in the European Union. Mergers and acquisitions are regulated to some extent by the Merger Code, but the aim of this code is only to protect the interests of shareholders and workers, not to regulate competition. It is enforced by the Social and Economic Council, that can only issue a public admonition.

Although an abuse control based competition regime does not necessarily prevent the authorities from pursuing a stringent competition policy, the enforcement of the provisions left much to be desired (Uitermark, 1990, chapter V). Enforcement has even been qualified as 'without doubt hardly impressive' by the member of government in charge of competition policy (Van Rooy, 1992). Not surprisingly, CPB concluded in 1992 that in the Netherlands competition on the markets for goods and services was avoided rather than looked for (CPB, 1992, 100).

Two reasons can be given for the weak enforcement of the law. First, it can be attributed to the presumption in the law that restraints of competition are not harmful by definition. As a result in every individual case the burden of the proof that the public interest was impaired lies with the competition authorities. Because this public-interest criterion was not defined or specified in law, it hardly functioned as a useful reference frame in concrete situations. Secondly, the testing of the competitive effects of collusive behaviour requires a lot of effort from the competition authorities because advantages and disadvantages of restraints have to be weighed continuously. This time-consuming character of enforcing the legal provisions is more or less inherent in an abuse system. It was at the expense of the detection of non-filed cartels and the testing of newly filed ones. Consequently, formal policy was of little relevance. Enforcement was based mainly on informal action by the competition department of the Ministry of Economic Affairs, triggered by complaints by competitors. It rested on consulting the firms involved in an agreement on possible adaptations of its provisions to confirm to law (Uitermark, 1990). Another result was that the Cartel Register was far from complete by tradition, despite the fact that arrangements had to be reported within one month.

Source: Peeperkorn (1987), Uitermark (1990).

bans, sanctions and approval possibilities that serves to ensure "freedom of competition and remove economic power where this can inhibit the effectiveness of competition and its inherent tendencies to improve performance and jeopardise the best possible supply to consumers. The German competition policy regime can be regarded as a mixture of the two basic philosophies. Horizontal agreements between enterprises are subject to a prohibition based policy, while most vertical restraints of competition are governed by an abuse system. The ARC originally did not apply to sectors such as transport, banking and insurance, agriculture, gas, electricity and water. Since 1 January 1990 however, the exceptions for transport, banking and insurance and utilities have been appreciably pruned back by the legislator. The ARC is enforced by the Federal Cartel Office (FCO), a highly independent authority with wide ranging powers.

12.4.2 The German and Dutch Competition Regimes

The legal foundations of European competition policy have served as the principal reference framework for designing the new Dutch Act on Economic Competition. Moreover, most European provisions have more or less been duplicated in the draft act. Accordingly, a comparison of Dutch and German competition policy comes close to comparing European and German competition policy provisions and their enforcement. It should be noticed beforehand, that European competition authorities have an exclusive competence in affairs that are likely to exert an appreciable effect on trade between member states.[8] Thus, national competition authorities in both countries exclusively deal with all intra-border affairs.

Restraints of Competition. A central rule of the *German law* is the prohibition of restrictions of competition, either by contract, decision or coordinated behaviour, under Section 1. This provision is very similar to Section 1 of the United States Sherman Act (see Box 12.7 below). Contrary to American antitrust law, there are some exceptions to the general ban on cartels to be found in German law. According to Section 2 to 8 two groups of cartel agreements can be authorised by the Federal Cartel Office:

- agreements that are supposed to improve the competitive process;
- agreements that are supposed to improve the efficiency of the firms concerned.

The first group comprises of agreements on uniform business, delivery and payment conditions, agreements on technical standards and on rebate-schemes. These agreements can be permitted under certain conditions. The second group of cartel agreements that may be authorised comprises specialisation and

---

[8] In principle, an agreement does not have an appreciable effect where the undertakings concerned do not have a market share of more than 5% in the relevant market and the combined turnover does not exceed 200 million ECU.

rationalisation cartels (Sections 5 and 5a) and crises cartels which are 'necessary to bring about a planned adjustment of productive capacity to demand' (Section 4). The anti-competitive effects of agreements that are forbidden under Sections 1 of the ARC cannot be balanced against competing economic or social goals. Only one exemption to this principle exists: in specific circumstances cartels that are forbidden under the other provisions of the law, can be exempted because of reasons of public interest. However, the decision to grant these exceptional permissions is a political one and the power to decide is given to the Minister of Economic Affairs and not to the Federal Cartel Office (FCO) (Kantzenbach, 1990).

In contrast to the general prohibition of horizontal restraints in German law, vertical restraints are subject to an abuse regulation. In distinguishing vertical from horizontal restraints, according to Section 1 of the ARC, the decisive criterion is the aim of an agreement. Restraints are considered to be horizontal if the parties in the agreement in question have a common goal. This does not have to be an identical goal, nor the only one. A parallelism in interests suffices to mark an agreement as horizontal. Vertical price-restraints are exempted from the abuse principle and are prohibited. So are price recommendations. Non-binding uniform retail prices, however, can be recommended to partners in SME cooperations.

The prohibition of restrictive practices in *the Netherlands* is in conformity with article 85(1) of the European Union-Treaty. Article 85(1) prohibits agreements and concerted practices affecting trade between member states and motivated by the prevention, restriction or distortion of competition within the common market. Exemptions of this prohibition are dealt with in Article 85(3). The exemptions mainly concern types of vertical agreements. Some horizontal agreements, for example cooperation in R&D under certain conditions, are exempted as well. In addition to these types of agreements, certain sectors (for example, agriculture, airlines) enjoy (limited) exemptions. Article 6 of the new Dutch competition act is similar to Article 85(1) of the European Union-treaty. The Dutch act has taken over all the European exemptions with reference to Article 85(3). So far as common trade is not affected, the Dutch act has some specific exemptions, such as a threshold exemption for mergers and acquisitions, an exemption for individual vertical price restraints in the market for daily papers and exemptions concerning temporary maximum prices and sales obligations for the retail sector.

Abuse of Market Power. The second pillar of competition policy in *Germany* is the supervision of firms to prevent them from abusing a dominant market position. Dominance is to be presumed when the market share of one firm reaches one third. In the case of oligopoly, market dominance is presumed when the largest three suppliers have a market share of one-half, or in the case that the five largest suppliers have a total market share of two-thirds and no substantial competition exists among the firms in the oligopoly in their internal relations. The FCO will take action only if a case of abuse has been established. First the FCO will ask the enterprise to desist from the practice, next it can forbid the practice or declare a

Box 12.7 Main characteristics of American antitrust policy

Two major provisions of the Sherman Act of 1890 still form the pillars of current United States antitrust law. Section 1 declares unlawful contracts and combinations in restraint of trade. Section 2 declares it illegal to 'monopolize, or attempt to monopolize'. The third pillar is found in Section 7 of the Clayton Act of 1914. It laid the foundation for United States merger control policy as it prohibited acquisitions that 'substantially ... lessen competition, or ... tend to create a monopoly'.

Just like German law, the American law traditionally is based on the general assumption that free competition is in the public interest. Likewise, there is no room for balancing the goal of free competition against possibly competing goals such as export promotion or employment. The prohibition of restraints of competition is a basic component of United States antitrust policy. The most flagrant forms of collusive behaviour, such as price-fixing agreements, certain market-sharing arrangements and vertical restraints like for instance resale price maintenance and tying arrangements were found illegal perse. Other types of arrangements were examined under the 'rule of reason'. Under this rule it had to be not only demonstrated that a particular behaviour had anti-competitive effects, but also that these dominated any alleged justifications of this behaviour. The rather straightforward enforcement of competition policy was visible also in the vigorous and successful prosecution of not only horizontal, but also vertical and conglomerate mergers. The highwater marks undoubtedly were the antitrust cases in which companies with market shares as low as 5% of the national market and 7.5% of a local market were prevented from merging (Mueller, 1996).

Source: Comanor (1990), Mueller (1996).

contract null and void. Neglect of FCO decisions by an enterprise can be punished by imposing a fine.

In *the Netherlands*, under the proposed new Competition Act, abuse of dominant market positions will be explicitly prohibited. Contrary to the old law, abuse of dominant market positions will be illegal from the moment abuse behaviour starts and not from the moment a formal decision has been reached by the competition authorities. Hence, sanctions can apply also to the period before the authorities conclude their inquiries. Nevertheless, inquiries have to be substantial to actually prove that abuse occurred. No presumptive criteria will exist in the Netherlands. Instead, the definition of dominance that is used by the European Court of Justice is followed.[9] It states that dominance is a position of economic strength enjoyed by one or more undertakings which enable them to hinder the maintenance of effective competition by allowing it to behave to an appreciable extent independently of its competitors, suppliers, buyers and consumers. Furthermore, the Court has indicated that a market share for one or more economically related firms of

[9] This is given in Case 27/76 (United Brands versus Commission).

one half in itself is a prove of dominance; with a lower market share, additional factors are taken into consideration.

Merger Control. Since 1973 also merger control in *Germany* is regulated by the Act against Restraints on Competition and enforced by the FCO. Mergers may be prohibited only if they would give rise to market dominance or strengthen an already dominant position. This may be the case with the combination of market shares in a horizontal merger, but also in vertical or conglomerate mergers. Exemptions exists for mergers in which small or medium-sized enterprises are involved.[10] Another exemption, comparable to the anti-cartel legislation, is the ministerial consent clause in the ARC. The Federal Minister of Economics can approve a merger already prohibited by the FCO if this is justified by compelling reasons of public interest or by broader economic advantages. Increased competitiveness on export markets, employment consequences or national defence may be relevant considerations in this sphere.

The application of control provisions to horizontal mergers has been substantially facilitated by presumptive criteria. The criteria for assessing dominance are the same as those used in the supervision of abuse of dominant behaviour (see above). A merger resulting in such a dominating position must be prohibited by the FCO, unless the enterprises concerned prove that the merger will improve competitive conditions that will outweigh the disadvantages of market dominance. Although the presumptive criteria do not relieve the Cartel Office of its duty to thoroughly examine and evaluate all the circumstances of a merger, they have greatly influenced the decision-making practices of the Office and of the courts (Kantzenbach, 1990).

With regard to vertical and conglomerate mergers, the law also expressly provides for their control. The ARC requires that in determining market dominance, in addition to market shares, the financial strength of the companies involved, their access to procurement markets, interlocking relationships with other companies, and entry barriers to other companies be taken into consideration. The application of merger control to vertical and conglomerate mergers has proved much more difficult. This has to do with the fact that the effects of vertical and conglomerate mergers on competition are not undisputed in competition theory (Kantzenbach, 1990).

At the moment, *the Netherlands* do not have a merger control mechanism similar to that in Germany or in the European Union. Mergers and acquisitions are regulated to some extent by the Merger Code, but the aim of this code is only to

---

[10] Only mergers where the enterprises involved together have annual sales of over 500 million DM can be vetoed. Prohibition does not apply to the takeover of a small company with sales less than DM 50 million or to mergers in small markets with total market sales of less than DM 10 million.

protect the interests of shareholders and workers, not to regulate competition.[11] No judicial punitive measures can be taken against firms not respecting the code. In the near future, however, a merger control procedure will come into force. It is based on the European Regulation on the Control of Concentrations between Undertakings of 1989. Mergers will be prohibited if they create or strengthen a dominant position as a result of which effective competition in the Dutch market will be significantly impeded. The merger control procedure will extend also to vertical and conglomerate mergers. Mergers involving small and medium-sized companies are exempted from merger control.[12] In case a merger is prohibited by the competition authorities, the Minister of Economic Affairs will have the power to overrule the decision because of public interest reasons.

Institutional Framework. As noticed above, in *Germany* implementing the ARC is assigned to an autonomous competition authority. The Federal Ministry of Economic Affairs exercises the appropriate administrative supervision. Competencies of the two institutions are strictly separated. With regard to restraints of competition for instance, the FCO decides on applications for permission to form cartels. It therefore checks if notified cartels satisfy the formal criteria for granting exemptions and assesses their competitive effects. The FCO also has an exclusive responsibility for merger control. The ministry can not interfere directly with the decision making processes. It nevertheless has two possibilities for influencing the outcome of FCO-activities. First, it has the right to overrule disapprovals of cartels and mergers by the FCO for compelling reasons of public interest. Secondly, with respect to restraints of competition, it can give general instructions to the FCO which apply to the issue or non-issue of orders. These have to be officially published. So far, this facility has only been used once, in 1972.

In *the Netherlands* a civil office, the Dutch Competition Authority is intended to enforce the new competition law from 1 january 1998 onwards. Eventually, after a three year transition period, the autonomy of this office will be comparable to that of the Bundeskartellamt. Initially, however, this authority will be semi-autonomous and seems a midway between the German and the European solutions for administering competition laws. During these first years, the Director General of the Dutch Competition Authority is subordinate to the Dutch Minister of Economic Affairs, who can give general instructions like in Germany. The minister may issue directives as to individual cases but such directives will be published.

---

[11] It is enforced by the Social and Economic Council, that can only issue a public admonition.

[12] The competitive intervention threshold is fixed at a total annual sales volume of the companies involved to the amount of 250 million guilder. An additional condition for being subjected to the merger control procedure is a sale volume of 30 million guilder for at least two of the companies involved.

12.4.3 A Comparison

Restrictive Business Agreements. A comparison of European and new Dutch provisions with German regulations relating to restrictive business agreements learns that, despite of the existence of differences in formal provisions, there are many parallels in day-to-day policies towards horizontal as well as vertical restraints. First of all, the most harmful cartels like those relating to price-fixing and market sharing are prohibited perse in both countries. Moreover, also the most severe vertical restraints, i.e., resale price maintenance, will be forbidden in both countries. Secondly, the possibilities for exempting groups of cartels that may promote efficiency show some similarities. Thirdly, although at first sight the German regulations seem to be more generous towards some horizontal cartel forms because they have more possibilities for group exemptions, it must be noted that the European and future Dutch systems are more flexible in principle: the more abstract wording of conditions for granting exemptions, spelt out in article 85(3), can allow cartels that qualify not easily for a group exemption in the codified German regime.

Abuse of Dominant Positions. With respect to the abuse of dominant positions, the presumptive criteria for dominance that are used in Germany, allow conducting a more strict policy in principle, but in practice German policy tradition towards enterprises being accused of abusing a dominant position is not regarded as very successful, especially with regard to vertical cases of abuse. One of the major difficulties in enforcing this provision of the law is that the enterprises concerned stop objectionable conduct ahead of formal prohibitions (OECD, 1992). Another one is related to conceptual problems. In the supervision of price abuses for example, the fact that often hypothetical reference values have to be relied upon, and the high evidentiary requirements made by German courts in market domination and abuse cases have all contributed to the FCO's poor record in this area (OECD, 1995). By contrast, in the Netherlands this element of competition policy can be considered as relatively strong, even under the old competition act. However, this is probably partly explained by its functioning as a substitute for less effective anti-cartel instruments (NERA, 1992). The new Dutch act will enhance possibilities for competition authorities for handling abuse, because this will be prohibited from the moment the behaviours starts and not just after a formal decision has been reached.

Mergers and Acquisitions. Mergers and acquisitions may even be more effective in restraining competition than cartels because no complicated mechanisms to coordinate decisions and to enforce agreements are required any more. The respective policies towards mergers and acquisitions that create or strengthen a dominant position also show important similarities. In both countries competition authorities have no possibilities for judging mergers on other than competition

Table 12.4 Comparison of main characteristics of European and Dutch competition policies with German policy

	The Netherlands	Germany
Horizontal restraints	prohibition based; group exemptions covering e.g. specialisation and R&D-agreements with special attention given to SME's.	prohibition based; group exemptions covering e.g. general terms of business, crises and specialisation cartels, rationalisation agreements for SME's.
Vertical restraints	prohibition based; resale price maintenance forbidden; non-binding price recommendations permitted; group exemptions covering for e.g. exclusive purchasing, selective distribution, franchising agreements.	abuse based; resale price maintenance forbidden; on-binding price recommendations permitted.
Abuse of dominant position	dominance is defined as a position of economic strength enjoyed by one or more undertakings which enable them to hinder the maintenance of effective competition by allowing it to behave to an appreciable extent independently of its competitors, suppliers, buyers and consumers; a market share for one or more economically related firms of one half in itself is a prove of dominance, with a lower market share additional factors are taken into consideration; abuse behaviour is illegal from the start.	presumptive market share criteria: one firm holds at least one third, two firms hold one half and three firms hold two-thirds; abuse behaviour *can* be forbidden.

effects. Efficiency or other arguments formally have to be set aside by competition authorities if competition is substantially hindered. Only the Ministers of Economic Affairs in the respective countries can overrule decisions by competition authorities on compelling reasons of public interest. They can approve mergers that have already been prohibited.[13]

[13] Note that a similar provision is absent in European competition policy.

Table 12.4 Comparison of main characteristics of European and Dutch competition policies with German policy (continued)

	The Netherlands	Germany
Mergers and acquisitions	preventive control; concentrations can be forbidden which create or strengthen a dominant position as a result of which effective competition in (a substantial part of) the common market would be significantly impeded; with a market share of less than a quarter generally no dominance is presumed; competition-effects criterion, no formal efficiency defence.	preventive control; presumptive market share
Institutional framework	autonomous administrative office (after three years); minister can give general instructions; minister can overrule decisions on mergers on public interest grounds.	independent competition authority (FCO); minister can give general instructions; minister can overrule decisions on cartels and mergers on public interest grounds.

It must also be noted, however, that the German policy on the control of horizontal mergers generally is more strict and straightforward than the Dutch policies will probably be since in Germany there are legal criteria for assessing dominance whereas the draft Dutch law does not provide for them, but only gives some factors (like e.g. the market shares of competitors, the technological and financial position of the firms concerned, the alternatives available to suppliers and consumers) that must be taken into account in assessing dominance. By consequence, there will most likely be more room for administrative discretion in judging on mergers and acquisitions in the Netherlands. This unmistakably creates opportunities for giving factors like efficiency in production and distribution or innovative capacity a higher weight in deciding on individual cases and therefore contributes to flexibility. However, there is a risk of commitment to a straightforward competition policy being adversely affected.

Institutional Framework. With regard to the institutional framework, it can be concluded that at least for the first three years from 1998 the position of 'semi-autonomy' of the competition authority in the Netherlands is a midway between the European and the German solutions for administering the competition laws. Because a clear-cut separation of competencies between the Ministry of Economic Affairs and the competition authority is necessary for transparency of decisions and avoids problems of potential conflict of interests, after three years, following the German example, the Dutch competition authority will be more autonomous and the problems sketched are likely to disappear. As described above, in Germany the Minister of Economic Affairs has no competencies in competition matters and can only explicitly overrule decisions on public interest considerations.

12.5 Assessment and Policy Options

Most deregulation measures that have been taken in Germany and the Netherlands are in line with the trends that stress encouraging competition as a coordination mechanism (see Table 12.5). Liberalization and privatization are proceeding steadily and seem to be supported in both countries by a broad political momentum. Much, however, remains to be done. Countries like the United States and United Kingdom, that are further in the deregulation process, have carried out interesting regulatory experiments from which Germany and the Netherlands can learn. Next, albeit modestly, Germany and the Netherlands can learn from each other's experiences. Finally, many plans are still waiting to be approved and executed.

What Can We Learn from Other Countries. Despite the impetus that has been given to regulatory reform in Germany and in the Netherlands, both countries are still considerably lagging behind countries like the United States and the United Kingdom. An assessment of the German and Dutch regulatory reforms can be based on a comparison of the United States and the United Kingdom experience. In general, one could argue that in the Netherlands in some cases debatable institutional arrangements have developed. One example is the emergence of a monopoly in regional bus transport. Only to the extent that the gains through prevention of coordination problems between bus lines outweigh the monopoly costs, this monopoly seems justified. It must be said that at the moment the monopoly was created, the government had no instruments available to prevent it. In the mean time, plans have been made to introduce more competition. Another example is the organisation of the electricity market, which seems to be out of line with the goal of encouraging competition (see Chapter 13). Furthermore, the networks of the utilities like Dutch the telecom, rail, gas and electricity are not really separated from the competitive parts. This leaves room for these firms to raise entry barriers and obstruct competition. Separation in combination with independent regulators, like in the United States and the United Kingdom, seems to be best practice to deal with the problems that occur after deregulation.

With respect to competition policy, an interesting development takes place. Whereas the United States antitrust provisions once were the most rigorous and most vigorously enforced antitrust statutes in the world, in recent years the merits of this policy have been questioned (Mueller, 1996). Several industrial organisation economists, particularly from the Chicago University, claimed that high concentra-

Table 12.5 The impact of instruments per market prototype

Market type	Instrument	Impact
Monopolistic competition	Liberalization	
	- entry deregulation	too little entry → more entry
	- quality deregulation	flexibility ← commitment
	Tougher competition policy	diversity ← scale
Natural oligopoly	Liberalization	too little entry → more entry
	Privatization	flexibility ← commitment
	Tougher competition policy	diversity ← scale
Natural monopoly	Liberalization	too little entry → more entry
	- uncoupling networks	diversity ← scale
	Privatization	flexibility ← commitment

tion was the consequence of some firms being more (technical) efficient than others, and thus having grown to be larger, rather than of large firms colluding to raise prices. Similarly, authors like Oliver Williamson (1975) emphasized the forces of competition in selecting organisational forms and (interfirm) relationships and advocated a welfare trade-off approach to mergers in which anti-competitive effects were weighed against their efficiency gains.

This new thinking about antitrust issues is very influential in policy enforcement. In the Vertical Restraints Guidelines, that were issued in 1985 under the Reagan Administration, the Department of Justice indicated that it would employ a rule of reason approach to vertical restraints, even if the courts would continue to view certain practices like tying arrangements and resale price maintenance as perse illegal. These guidelines were repudiated under the Clinton administration.

Likewise, in the area of merger control, under the Reagan administration a more permissive antitrust policy became visible. The 1984 Merger Guidelines introduced an efficiency defense in governmental practise. They stated that a merger would go unchallenged if it was expected to result in economic efficiencies that would outweigh its anti-competitive effects. The least visible shift in antitrust policy and standards is in regard to price-fixing and market sharing arrangements. But even here, more opportunity is given for following a rule of reason approach (Mueller, 1996: 427). The issue of efficiency permeated the antitrust enforcement agencies from the start of the Reagan Administration in 1981 and finally resulted in a major decline in enforcement by the Department of Justice and the Federal Trade Commission. Nowadays antitrust enforcement policies have become a partisan issue and can be expected 'to become dependent more directly on which political party is in power' (Comanor, 1990). European competition policy seems to be of a less partisan nature.

This development towards less stringent competition policy in the United States does not take place in Europe. On the contrary, European competition policies are becoming tougher. An illustrative example in case is the presumed merger between aerospace firms Boeing and McDonnell Douglas, which has been allowed for by the American competition authorities, but which may be objected by the European competition commissioner Van Miert (Financial Times, 19/22-5-97). Of course, strategic trade and industrial policies may also partially be behind this European position.

Mutual Policy Options. With respect to competition policy, two preliminary remarks must be made, before drawing conclusions. First, the draft Act on Economic Competition has passed through parliament, but is not really operative yet. Secondly, in Germany there is considerable disagreement about several proposals that the government has launched for harmonising competition law to European regulations through the next amendment to the ARC. Both the Federal Cartel Office and the Monopolies Commission oppose them (Die Welt, 1996; Monopolkommission, 1996, Norman, 1997). The outcome of these debates is not completely clear yet.

Nevertheless, two observations emerge. Firstly, for the future of German and Dutch competition policies a general picture arises of convergence to the European competition regime. The similarities between European, Dutch and German competition policy regimes clearly dominate the mutual differences between the systems. Cartel regulations in the Netherlands, which were originally based on the abuse principle, will shortly be completely based on a prohibition system under the new Competition Act, that can be seen as a close copy of the European competition policy provisions. As far as Germany is concerned, it has to be awaited to what extent the adjustment to the European competition provisions that the government has announced, will completely materialize. However, some additional harmonisation of provisions that already are rather comparable in their practical effects on competition, is to be foreseen.

Secondly and closely related to the first conclusion, one of the most marked differences between the European competition policy regime on the one hand and the German scheme on the other, is in their institutional design. According to the Monopolies Commission the main disparity between German and European competition regimes is in the diverging objectives of German and European competition policies and, closely linked to these, in their respective institutional structures. Whereas the main objective of German policy is to safeguard competition and to protect the freedom of competitors, in European policy practice an intermingling of competition goals with other social or economic objectives, like for instance industrial policy goals, cannot be excluded. The reason is the absence of a clear and indisputable separation of responsibilities in European competition policy practice (Monopolkommission, 1996).

In the Netherlands a similar issue played a role during the preparations of the New Competition Act. In the initial plans, the new competition authority was semi-autonomous, creating a possibility for active involvement of the Minister of Economic Affairs in individual cases. A lesson from Germany, which is implemented in the mean time, is to make the competition authority more autonomous. Indeed, after three years the new Dutch competition authority will be (almost) completely independent, following the Bundeskartellamt.

Independency is also desirable for the (future) regulators in Germany and the Netherlands. Neither Germany nor the Netherlands are yet so far in the deregulation process that a complete network of regulators exists, for example like in the United Kingdom and the United States. Following their examples, it seems best not only to make the (future) regulators independent from the now responsible Ministries, but also to place them under the competition authorities. This way knowledge and expertise can be shared and the risk of regulatory capture is smaller. This principle seems to be easier to implement in Germany, where the Bundeskartellamt is already organized mainly along industry-specific departments.

An additional lesson for the Netherlands could be found in the useful task performed by the German Monopolies Commission. This is an independent commission of experts with the task of reporting regularly on the state of development of concentration among enterprises. Every two years it produces a report for publication by the government. It can also at its discretion produce special reports on sectors.

Unfinished Agenda. With respect to regulation policy, many other measures still have to be worked out into details. Both Germany and the Netherlands are in the process of implementing European Union directives, mainly aimed at liberalising sectors with a natural monopoly nature. In telecommunications, competition will be intensified by more network competition and a less restrictive concessions policy. Germany is somewhat behind in this respect as German Telecom is one of the few monopolistic operators in Europe that controls the cable TV network. Giving up its dual ownership of both the telephone- and cable-network is a necessary condition for creating competition in the communications industry. With respect to the liberalization of postal services Germany is ahead of the Netherlands. In public transport, competition is practically non-existent in both countries and will be hard to establish without additional government actions. It must be concluded that stimulating competition in these industries is an important challenge in both Germany and the Netherlands. Furthermore, exploring privatization opportunities at the more decentralized government levels should be encouraged. Possible examples are waste management and public housing.

Special attention should be given to initiatives aimed at levelling the playing field of private and public companies in sectors where these are in competition directly or potentially. In the Netherlands the Commission Cohen has recently published a report with a list of proposals to deal with mixed markets of public and private firms. With respect to Germany, for this purpose the OECD recommends to review the overall regulatory structure (OECD, 1996). It is obvious that a levelling of playing fields of (semi-)public and private firms, where these are in direct competition, is crucial in removing distortions in resource allocation.

In this respect also lower levels of government, have a substantial potential for privatization, especially in the fields of housing, utilities and transport. Whereas privatization is proceeding rather steadily at the federal level, action at the Länder and local levels was much more subdued. There are several indications that lower government objects to initiatives aimed at further privatization (OECD, 1995 and 1996). First, local governments do not seem to be very eager to place private and public providers of services to municipalities on a more equal basis. Furthermore, Länder governments prove to be slow in introducing European Union directives, aimed at contributing to the internal market, in particular those regarding public procurement.

13 Electricity and Gas Markets

The previous chapter offers a broad overview of the development of public institutions through the introduction of market forces in general. This chapter analyses in depth this theme in one field, namely the electricity and gas markets. This sector provides an excellent illustration of the topicality and relevance of the introduction of market forces. For decades it was taken for granted that electricity and gas provision were natural monopolies requiring heavy government intervention. This view is now subject to criticism. With competition the key word, the institutions in these markets are now being reformed in many countries, including Germany and the Netherlands, with the overriding aim of increasing efficiency.

Several factors provide the backdrop to this revolution. The most fundamental was doubtless the growing dissatisfaction with the performance of the utilities, especially in the United States and the United Kingdom (Joskow, 1989: 149-163; Newbery and Green, 1996: 58). Following on from this, new theoretical insights were developed on policies towards natural monopolies. Two insights were particularly influential: firstly, the view that competition, wherever possible, is important for efficiency; and secondly, that competition is possible at several junctures in the energy market. According to this perception only the networks which take care of transmission and distribution in the electricity and gas markets are natural monopolies. The generation and sale of electricity can in principle take place in competitive markets. Technological trends, such as decentral combined heat-power plants and information technology, support this development. And specifically for Europe, the preparation of the European energy market has also cast its shadow before it in recent years.

This shift in thinking makes a balanced evaluation of the strengths and weaknesses of the energy market institutions in Germany and the Netherlands more difficult. In policy terms there is little point in comparing the *existing* institutions, since they do not yet reflect the new thinking. At the same time the implementation of the proposals will take some time, so that it is not yet possible to pass judgement on the new institutions on the basis of their actual performance. That is why the approach in this chapter is different from that in most other chapters of this study. Section 13.1 first outlines the shift in thinking on the role of government in natural monopolies. This is an elaboration of Section 12.2 in the chapter on market forces. Section 13.2 examines the existing institutions in the German and Dutch electricity and gas markets, and evaluates the performance of this sector on the basis of several factors. Section 13.3 analyses and evaluates the current proposals to liberalize the two markets. To provide a benchmark, this section also looks at the situation in the United Kingdom, which now has five years of experience with the operation of a highly liberalized electricity market. Moreover, it also looks at the state of affairs surrounding the European energy market. Section 13.4 formulates conclusions and policy options, focusing on the future situation. Reference to the British situation provides these options with an empirical underpinning.

13.1 The Shift in Thinking on Natural Monopolies[1]

The Traditional View. Because of their network characteristics the electricity and gas markets have traditionally been regarded as natural monopolies. Furthermore the provision of electricity and gas services is characterized by economies of scope. Economies of scope can be defined as the (negative) difference between the cost of producing a number of products all in a single firm and the total cost of producing these products in specialized firms (see Berg and Tschirhart, 1988: 35-36). An example are day and night services in the electricity sector. Economies of scope tend to promote cooperation between those responsible for production, transmission and distribution. That is why vertical integration is common in the electricity and gas markets. The traditional view of these natural monopolies is that the government must regulate them tightly to ensure they do not abuse their favoured market positions. In a number of countries, the United Kingdom for instance, they were even nationalized. The aim of regulation is almost invariably to imitate the results of a competitive market. In practice this has often been given shape through the cost-plus-rate-of-return method. Under this system the regulated companies are allowed to pass on their costs in full, together with a fixed profit mark-up.[2] To promote a stable investment climate, there is no free entry to the market and there is no contract freedom on the supply side.

In the course of the interaction between theory and practice dissatisfaction with this regulatory regime gradually spread, first and most strongly in the United States, but later also in other countries such as the United Kingdom. In the 1960s economists gained the impression that the monopolies were abusing their favoured

---

[1] Much of the information in this section is derived from Armstrong, Cowan and Vickers (1994), and Joskow (1989). Box 13.1 provides an overview of the concepts used in this chapter.

[2] In addition to the cost-plus-rate-of-return method there is also price-cap regulation, which is applied less often, however. For a discussion of the various methods of regulating prices in a monopoly situation, see Chapter 12, Box 12.4, as well as Chapter 6, Section 6.1.5.

Box 13.1 Definitions of the concepts used

Captives: *consumers of energy that are not allowed to choose between suppliers and therefore have no freedom to contract*
Central generation: *production of electricity by producers in charge of public supply of electricity to final customers or distribution firms*
Dispatch *(technical): tuning of energy demand and supply*
Distribution: *transport of electricity on the medium-voltage and low-voltage grid (also referred to as distribution grid), sometimes including sale*
Economic dispatch: *dispatch that secures the least-cost generation of electricity by using powerstations in order of (variable) costs ('merit order')*
Economies of scope: *reduction of production costs achieved through horizontal or vertical integration*
Eligibles: *consumers with freedom to contract*
Generation: *production of electricity*
Horizontal integration: *a company performs at least one of the activities of generation sale, transmission, distribution or sale of electricity and gas*
Interconnector: *equipment used to link electricity systems*
Operator: *authority in charge of dispatch and transport also responsible for maintenance and safety of the grid and the reliability of energy supply*
Regulator *(in the United Kingdom): authority in charge to investigate complaints, monitor and encourage competition in the market, reset price caps, issue new licenses, revise licenses and influence capacity decisions*
Sale: *merchandising of electricity services to the end user*
Single-buyer: *any legal person who is responsible for centralized electricity purchasing and selling*
Supervisory authority: *tasks are comparable to those of regulatory authority, except that the supervisory authority has no regulatory power.*
Supply: *process of transmission/distribution and sale to customers*
Third-party access (TPA): *access to the high- and low-voltage grid and the pipeline network for everyone at equal, reasonable and transparent charges*
Transmission: *transport of electricity on the high-voltage, or central grid with the aim of delivery to final customers or distribution firms*
Unbundling: *operational and in some cases also administrative and juridical separation of production, transmission and distribution involving the same energy carrier; strict unbundling implies divestment of these activities*
Vertical integration: *a company performs two or more of the activities of generation, sale, transmission and distribution*

positions despite the regulatory constraints. The problem which the regulator encountered was the information asymmetry between the regulator and the regulated companies. In terms of chapter 2 there were problems of hidden features (adverse selection) and hidden action (moral hazard). The critics suspected that as a result insufficient information is generated about efficient cost-levels. Prices in the regulated sector were consequently higher than would be reasonable on the basis of actual costs. Moreover, costs were often higher than necessary because with cost-plus the monopoly had no incentive to cut costs (Joskow and Schmalensee, 1983: 5; McKinsey, 1996: 10). It is also true that the cost-plus mechanism gave rise to an asymmetry between the severe social implications of a blackout and the moderate costs of overcapacity. This has resulted in a tendency towards overcapacity (Gilbert *et al.*, 1996: 11). Another disadvantage of strong regulation is the effect, signalled by a number of researchers, that over time the regulator increasingly identifies with the industry's vested interests. This has been dubbed *regulatory capture.*

During the 1970s the opposite situation developed. After the first oil shock the US regulators took a very cautious line in allowing the utilities to pass on the steep cost hikes in their rates or they allowed them to do so only after considerable delays. The utilities responded by scaling down their investment plans. This chain of events revealed another weakness of regulation, namely uncertainty about the regulator's stance. The regulator's inability to precommit itself on regulated prices in particular can, in combination with the utilities' strong sunk-cost character, lead to a structurally low investment level, which can give rise to capacity problems over the long run. This so-called regulatory risk creates the familiar hold-up problem.

The Shift in Thinking. Because of these developments the realization dawned that regulation was not always the most efficient instrument to control the utilities' natural monopoly. More than that, it became evident that regulation could create its own failures (see also Chapter 12)! This regulatory failure sparked renewed interest in and appreciation of the benefits of the market mechanism. This laid the foundation for the process of regulatory reform. A subsequent key insight was that not all the utilities' activities could be regarded as strong natural monopolies. In the electricity and gas markets it is above all the transport networks that are the natural monopolies. Electricity generation and sale, as well as gas production and sale, can in principle take place in competitive markets, i.e. markets characterized by free price setting, freedom to contract, free entry, and freedom to import and export.

But to bring about such a situation, the natural monopoly, i.e. the network, has to become accessible at a reasonable charge to every market player who wishes to enter it. This is called third-party access (TPA). The most transparent manner of doing so is to strictly deintegrate the natural monopolies from the competitive activities in the market to exclude the misuse of market power. Such a radical separation has a price, however, namely the potential loss of the economies of scale and scope achieved by the integrated generation-transmission and transmission-supply activities. Concretely, what is at stake are operational reliability and efficient dispatch.[3] This also highlights the fundamental trade-off which policy

---

[3] See Joskow (1989: 187); this is less true for gas.

Box 13.2 Overview of conditions affecting the trade off between traditional regulation and competition in the energy markets

	Traditional regulation	*Competition*
Strengths	*exploiting economies of scale and scope*	*allowing diversity* *reducing informational rents* *reducing regulatory failure*
Conditions		
Technology		
– *economies of scale and scope*	*important*	*less important or of decreasing importance*
– *progress*	*incremental*	*radical*
Information	*symmetric*	*asymmetric*
Products, production processes	*homogeneous*	*heterogeneous*
Political process	*efficient*	*inefficient*
Preferences		
– *risk aversion*	*high*	*low*
Uncertainty		
– *environment*	*stable*	*unstable*

makers face in the formulation of a liberalization policy for utilities: a wider role for market forces promotes the elimination of the monopoly's informational rents, thus improving its allocative efficiency, but at the same time economies of scale and scope will be lost (Armstrong *et al.*, 1994). Other factors which have to be weighed in the balance are the opportunities for effective regulation of the natural monopoly and the opportunities for maintaining operational coordination between, say, generation and transmission in a different way (Joskow, 1989: 192). This balancing process is strongly influenced by a number of conditions, which are summarized in Box 13.2.

The stronger the importance of economies of scale and scope the more important is coordination through regulation. Regulation is also supported by conditions such as a stable economic environment, technical progress with a strong incremental character as well as an efficient political process. The reverse is true when economies of scale are rather unimportant and technical progress has a radical character. Inefficiencies in the political process and instabilities in the economy also point in the direction of competition.

Network Operator. It also emerges that, besides strict deintegration, a liberalized market still requires regulation; in fact, with regard to the network, regulation becomes even more important. For regulation has to guarantee that everyone who wants to use the network has access to it in a non-discriminatory way and at a reasonable and transparent charge. Independence of the network operator offers the best guarantee of this. Independence in this context means concretely that the network operator has no interest in the generation, distribution or sale of electricity or gas. If it did, it could be in a position to abuse the market power which the natural monopoly creates (see Huygen and Theeuwes, 1996; see also Box 13.3).

Regulator. A regulator independent of the government monitors whether the network operator carries out the tasks entrusted to it properly. The reason why the regulating authority should be independent of government and industry and have a clear mandate is that all hints of political interference or confluence of interests should be eliminated as much as possible. Experience in the sphere of monetary policy shows that stability, transparency and independence strongly promotes the credibility and effectiveness of policy. In addition to supervising network access and the conditions and charges applied in this area, the regulator also ensures that the network operator meets its statutory obligations in terms of safety, distribution, reliability of supply and use of sustainable energy sources. During a transition to a free market the regulator may also have the task of preventing abuse of captive customers.

Customers and suppliers in the market will usually work with long-term contracts to enhance supply reliability and smooth price fluctuations. Because electricity cannot be stored and demand can vary wildly over the short run, a short-term market is created, which constantly balances supply and demand. Crucial to the effective performance of this pool is that there are sufficient numbers of customers and suppliers. Otherwise the large producers have an opportunity to use their peak-load supplies (when the number of competitors often falls sharply) to subsidize their base-load supplies. In the United Kingdom this strategic behaviour has proved effective in denying smaller producers access to the market. An effective transmission grid also supports competition, because it lowers the transport costs of electricity.

Privatization. A final point concerns the role of privatization. In practice it has become clear that of itself regulated privatization is not enough to achieve the efficiency improvements which the introduction of market forces promises. Empirical studies show that, once the market has been liberalized, private ownership does produce better results than public ownership (Gilbert *et al.*, 1996: 9). An important reason for this is the disciplining effect which the financial markets exert on management. This leads to better cost control and more innovation. Liberalisation is thus more important than privatisation and is an important condition for successful privatization.

13.2 German and Dutch Energy Market Institutions: The Present Situation

13.2.1 Actors and Markets in Germany

Electricity Market. Table 13.1 provides an overview of the players in the market and their share in production. Whereas the electricity market comprises more than 800 utilities, almost 85% of public demand is produced by nine producers. By means of agreements known as horizontal demarcation contracts these producers have divided up the country into nine areas in which each producer operates an independent high-voltage electricity network. Hence there is no national grid network, although the grids are connected and if necessary exchange of electricity takes place. In its own region each producer is responsible for the production and transport of electricity, and in some cases also distribution. The companies, which cooperate in the German Association of Interconnected Transmission Systems (Deutsche Verbundgesellschaft, DVG), differ substantially with respect to size and scope, with the Rheinisch-Westfälische Elektrizitätswerke (RWE) by far the largest. Producers are obliged to maintain sufficient capacity for peak hours. Likewise, each producer must guarantee, and thus properly plan, the production capacity in its own production region. Six of the producers are publicly owned, while three are in private hands.

There are two types of distribution companies: regional and local. These enterprises are mainly owned by the regional public authorities. In 1992 this applied to 69% of the companies, while another 15% were mixed property (with government shares between 25-95%). There are 70 regional distribution companies, mainly established in the western federal states. These utilities supply both directly to end users and to local distribution companies. Of their electricity demand they obtain around 80% from one of the DVG companies and produce the rest themselves. They are represented by the Board of Regional Energy Distribution Companies (Arbeitsgemeinschaft Regionaler Energieversorgungsunternehmen, ARE).

Distribution on a local level is taken care of by around 800 companies, represented by the Association of Local Enterprises (Verband Kommunaler Unternehmen, VKU). These companies obtain their energy from the DVG and ARE companies and produce only a small amount of electricity themselves. They also distribute natural gas, water and heat.

German law allows for several kinds of generators, and there are no restrictions on autoproduction, which currently amounts to around 14% of total production. By law, utilities are required to pay 63-90% of retail prices for power from autoproducers (up to 5 MW) that use renewable energy sources or cogeneration.

The federal government defines the policies and policy goals, for example with respect to competition, environment and energy (e.g. the mandatory use of coal in

Table 13.1 Players on the German electricity market and their share in production, 1992

Players electricity market	Ownership	Share in production	Peak-level organization
9 large producers	6 government 3 private	72%	DVG
70 regional distribution firms	mainly public	14%	ARE
800 local distribution firms	mainly public	-	VKU
Decentral producers	mainly private	14%	-

electricity production). The federal states implement these policies, grant permits for the building of production facilities on their territory, and determine end-user tariffs. At the municipal level concession rights for energy distribution companies are granted. Representatives of municipalities and states are on the board of virtually every utility (McKinsey, 1996: 10). At the firm level the government has a profound influence: since private shares are often exempt from voting rights, public authorities command a majority vote in more than 83% of all enterprises, accounting for 93% of demand.

Gas Market. Of total natural gas production 80% is supplied by the three largest companies. A total of 15 companies, including some of the production companies, are involved in the transport of natural gas. Distribution of natural gas is taken care of by around 500 companies, most of which operate on a local level. Horizontal integration with electricity companies is a common phenomenon. Production, transport and distribution companies are mainly privately owned.

13.2.2 Competition in the German Electricity and Gas Markets[4]

As discussed in Section 13.1, the main prerequisites for competition in a market are the freedom to set prices, the freedom to conclude contracts and the freedom to enter the market. In a market with network characteristics, such as the energy market, this requires third-party access. This section examines how the German energy market institutions perform on these points.

[4] Because German regulation treats the electricity and gas markets very much the same, the discussion in this section covers both markets.

Currently strong and decentralized government intervention characterizes the German energy sector. The main regulating institution is the federal Energy Act (Energie Wirtschaftsgesetz, EnWG), which dates from 1935. It provides a legal basis for the exclusive territory concept which resulted in the so-called demarcation contracts. In these contracts, which divide up the supply areas of distribution and transport, utilities horizontally agree to restrict themselves to specific delivery areas, while vertically producers commit themselves to refrain from directly supplying the distribution companies' customers (except for very large consumers).

The energy sector is also explicitly exempted from the most important regulations of the federal Anti-Trust Act (Gesetz gegen Wettbewerbsbeschränkungen, GWB). This exemption made possible the practice of exclusive concession rights, according to which an enterprise obtains the exclusive right to supply a region with energy. In exchange for this right, granted by the municipal authorities, the energy firm has the obligation to supply the whole region with energy, at equal prices. In addition, the energy firm must pay concession rights and a tax on the profits made.[5] Since the 1990 revision of the GWB the maximum period of an exclusive concession contract is limited to 20 years; in practice this new provision has not changed much.

Energy companies are furthermore subject to price controls with respect to retail prices. The general price structure is specified at the federal level by the Federal Rate Regulations for Electricity (Bundestarifordnung, BTO). Execution rests with the Energy Supervisory Authority (Energieaufsichtsbehörde) of the federal state where the utility is located. The guidelines allow for a cost-oriented price, and so price regulation by the states is based on the cost-plus-rate-of-return principle. There are significant differences in implementation between the states, however, for example with respect to the allowed rate of return on capital. For industrial users prices are determined through contracts negotiated with the electricity suppliers and controlled by the Federal Anti-Trust Office. Natural gas prices are based on the price of oil.

In practice there is no freedom to contract. While in theory large users are allowed to conclude contracts with suppliers of their own choice, this is strongly hampered by the existing market structure in which there is no free entry. Firstly, the entry to the market for public energy supply is prevented by exclusive concession rights and the lack of a third-party access obligation in case of transport for commercial purposes. Furthermore, existing utilities cannot enter other regions than agreed upon in the voluntarily concluded demarcation contracts. Competition by regional producers is limited by the 5 MW capacity restriction and many other legal barriers, among which the required permits for construction and operation,

[5] At the moment total concession payments are estimated to run at around DM 6 billion per year (FAZ, 1996).

limitations on the use of certain primary energy sources, and a requirement for franchise agreements (OECD/IEA, 1994b: 211). The only other way entry can be established is when a direct connection is built between the new producer and its customers. Due to high costs this has prevented entry in the past.

In short, then, despite the large number of energy companies the German energy market institutions do not allow for competition but have resulted in numerous monopoly areas instead. In terms of the trade-off between scale and scope versus diversity, Germany thus comes down squarely on the side of scale and scope.

13.2.3 The German Coal Market

The coal market is strongly connected to the electricity market, since most lignite companies are owned by electricity companies or have power plants associated with their mines. Lignite is produced in the former East Germany and the Ruhr area. The coal market is among the most densely regulated, subsidized and protected sectors of the German economy. This stems from the low competitiveness of this sector in comparison with other producer countries, due to high wages, unfavourable geological conditions in coal mining, and the growing supply of superior energy products such as oil and natural gas.

The lack of competitiveness of German coal is clearly demonstrated by the coal prices faced by utilities: in 1994 these amounted to DM 97 per tonne for imported steam coal against DM 311 per tonne for German coal (OECD/IEA, 1996a: 123). To protect the domestic coal industry from cheaper imports, a complicated system of laws and private contracts has been established. It aims to secure sales in the two most important markets, namely electricity, which used around 60% of total coal production in 1991, and steel, with a share of around 35%. In the western federal states the Electricity from Coal Act (Jahrhundertvertrag), the Steel Mills Contract (Hüttenvertrag) and four smaller programmes have supported the hard coal industry until now.[6]

Until 1996, under the so-called Jahrhundertvertrag the power generators, industry and the German *Bundesbahn* committed themselves to buying a total of 40 million tonnes of domestic hard coal each year. These amounts equalled around 87% of the electricity generators' needs for domestic coal at prices covering the coal producers' break-even costs. To compensate the electricity producers for the higher costs incurred through using domestic coal, a special fee was levied on the bills of electricity consumers, the coal penny (Kohlepfennig). In 1994 the Federal Constitutional Court in Karlsruhe ruled that the Kohlepfennig violated the constitution, however, and it has not been levied on electricity bills since 1996. Since that year utilities can buy German coal via individual contracts and at world

---

[6] In the new federal states the lignite industry is not subsidized and imports of coal are free from any restrictions.

prices.[7] The difference between the world market price and the domestic coal price is subsidized by the German government.

In the coming years the amount of subsidies will be drastically reduced, however. In recent years resistance to the support for uncompetitive sectors has been growing. This has partly been induced by the budgetary consequences of German reunification, which are even more problematic as the transition to EMU imposes strict budgetary constraints. Furthermore, the directives of the European Commission permit government support only if a modernization plan to improve the economic viability of a sector is submitted in advance. Under current plans, more than a third of the coal mines will be shut down between now and 2005 and subsidies will be reduced from DM 8.9 billion in 1997 to DM 5.5 billion in 2005 (Bundesregierung, 1997).[8]

13.2.4 Actors and Markets in the Netherlands

Electricity Market. Since the Electricity Act of 1989 production and distribution of electricity are operationally unbundled in the Netherlands. In 1996 around 74% of Dutch electricity production is generated by four regional electricity companies; two of them are owned by distribution companies and two by regional and local authorities. Several small-scale producers with private and mixed ownership generate the remaining 26%.

The four regional electricity companies cooperate within the Association of Electricity Producing Companies (Samenwerkende Elektriciteits Produktiebedrijven, SEP), of which they are the shareholders. The SEP owns the high-voltage grid and is responsible for planning the central production and transmission capacity. Functioning as central dispatcher, the SEP optimizes the deployment of power stations; that is, it ensures that those plants with the lowest costs are used first. A final responsibility of the SEP is the construction and maintenance of the high-voltage grid system, as well as the transport of electricity through the system.

Around 24 distribution companies take care of distribution, all of them directly owned by regional or local authorities. Most companies are horizontally integrated and manage the distribution (including retail) of electricity as well as other energy products such as natural gas and heat. In some cases they also supply non-energy products such as cable television. All distribution companies cooperate in EnergieNed, which represents the companies in the central tariff negotiations with the SEP and the government.

---

[7] In 1996, after the ending of the Jahrhundertvertrag, the power generators remained the largest customers of the German coal industry: they concluded contracts for around 30 million tonnes of coal.

[8] In 1997 the coal subsidies amount to around DM 100,000 per worker.

With respect to decentral production, the 1989 Electricity Act allows private firms and joint ventures between private firms and distribution companies to produce electricity without restrictions. Distribution firms are obliged to buy the surplus of electricity produced by decentral production at prices based on the avoided costs principle.[9]

The central government regulates the generation, transmission and retail of electricity under the terms of the Electricity Act. It grants production licences and distribution concessions, controls maximum tariffs, and approves the production and transmission capacity plan made by the SEP. This helps the government to realize its general goals in the energy field of a reliable, affordable and clean energy provision.

Gas Market. The importance of the Dutch gas market is illustrated by the fact that Dutch natural gas production accounts for around 25% of all marketed natural gas in IEA Europe. Whereas natural gas accounts for around 50% of the Dutch total primary energy supply, in Germany this is only 17%. With a yearly added value of NLG 25-30 billion the gas sector contributes around 4.5% to Dutch GDP.

The central pivot in the natural gas market is Gasunie, half of which is owned by the government and a quarter each by Shell and Exxon. Although the supply of gas is not a legal monopoly, in practice only Gasunie has transport pipelines at its disposal. Until recently, Gasunie had the 'right of first refusal', which meant that all domestically produced natural gas had first to be offered for sale to Gasunie. Although Gasunie had no formal TPA-obligation negotiated access has been provided by Gasunie ever since 1972. There is no formal restriction to the import of gas. Until now, however, only the SEP has been able to import gas for its electricity production. Consequently Gasunie has always been the single supplier for the distribution companies and large natural gas users. Around half of Dutch natural gas production is exported by Gasunie, of which 62% to Germany. Gasunie prepares an annual plan for the sale of gas for the next 25 years, which has to be approved by the Minister of Economic Affairs.

The fact that Gasunie lost its right of first refusal two years ago, and has had to offer third-party access since, has had no practical consequences. At the moment Gasunie still buys almost all natural gas produced, and no additional gas imports have taken place. Three factors are probably responsible for this: long-term contracts, a price structure that favours selling to Gasunie instead of end users, and the lack of a really competitive gas supply from abroad. Recently, there are a number of signs that this will change in the near future, i.e. next year cheap British gas will become available on the Dutch market through the interconnector between the United Kingdom and Belgium.

[9] Avoided costs are costs that would have been incurred by the distribution companies if they were to purchase electricity from one of the central power plants.

Concessions of the Nederlandse Aardolie Maatschappij (NAM), a subsidiary of Shell and Exxon, take care of 80-90% of total natural gas production. Eight other producers are active in smaller fields. Energie Beheer Nederland (EBN), a trustee firm of the Dutch government, takes care of the participation of the Dutch State in all concessions. Some 70% of the revenue from natural gas production flows to the government.

Gasunie distributes natural gas directly to the electricity sector and to around 400 large consumers and distribution companies. In addition to 24 horizontally integrated distribution companies, there are 11 companies that solely distribute natural gas. Like the integrated distribution companies, these companies are owned by local authorities and participate in EnergieNed.

Except for gas production, there is no act governing the gas market. Policy is based on the Nota De Pous (named after the then Minister of Economic Affairs) of 1961, which established the gas supply as a government task. Under this policy Gasunie was established as a public-private partnership. The government regulates the maximum amount of natural gas to be exploited by means of concessions, while prices are based on the market-value principle. This principle implies that the price of natural gas is based on the costs of alternative energy sources, such as oil. Furthermore, the government has stimulated the exploitation of the smaller, economically less profitable, gas fields via profitable contracts offered by Gasunie.

13.2.5 Competition in the Dutch Energy Market

Electricity Market. Price setting is not free; purchase tariffs are determined according to administrative procedures. The electricity price is made up of several parts. Firstly, the national base tariff is derived from the pooled costs of all producers. Distribution companies must pay the regional base tariff, which is the national tariff plus a mark-up for additional production costs incurred by the specific production firm.[10] A maximum is set for the regional tariff, agreed between the SEP, EnergieNed and the Ministry of Economic Affairs. The same is true for the tariffs for end users, which equal the regional tariff plus a mark-up for distribution costs.

The 1989 Electricity Act slightly improved the *freedom to conclude contracts*. Distribution companies are now allowed to export and to choose between the different electricity producers, so-called horizontal shopping. Large energy users (+20 GW) are allowed to engage in horizontal shopping among different distribution companies. In addition, these users are allowed to import and export

[10] The mark-up offers the opportunity for each producer to create a price difference with the other three firms. In this way the mark-up should create an efficiency incentive for producers to reduce their costs. In practice, due to price agreements, tariffs differ only slightly among the four producers.

Box 13.3 The unforeseen impact of the 1989 Electricity Law: stimulus for further liberalization

The 1989 Electricity Act marked an important step towards liberalization. Before 1989, the energy market consisted of regional monopolies of horizontally and vertically integrated government-owned firms. During the 1980s high energy prices and the resulting call for energy saving increased the attractiveness of highly efficient cogeneration of heat and power (CHP)[1]. However, until the end of the decade the market structure remained unfavourable to a significant increase in CHP capacity.

In 1989 the desire to increase efficiency and save energy finally resulted in a new Electricity Act. Important features of the new law that were included to stimulate the development of (decentral) CHP were the separation of production and distribution and the obligation for distribution companies to buy every supply of decentrally generated electricity at avoided costs. Furthermore, through participation in joint ventures with private firms distribution firms were allowed to build new CHP capacity without the involvement of the SEP. Combined with subsidies and special gas prices for CHP these measures were designed to pave the way for the development of decentral CHP. This policy proved highly successful, but in the end it became the victim of its own success.

In fact, this set of measures assured investors in CHP of a profitable investment, regardless of whether their investments created excess capacity. Through a vicious circle these effects were enhanced: the increase in CHP meant that the fixed costs of the central capacity had to be spread over less demand, which increased the national base tariff. This in turn automatically pushed up the price that distributors were obliged to pay for centrally produced electricity, further stimulating new decentral capacity building, and so on. Hence consumers in the regulated market have partially subsidized producers as well as consumers in the free market. At present, decentral production accounts for around 20% of total production and CHP production for around 30%.

To correct this unforeseen development, CHP subsidies have been cut and government and electricity industry have agreed that new commercially exploited decentral capacity must be matched by supply contracts concluded in advance. More fundamentally, it has become apparent that central planning is no longer appropriate when a significant number of the investment decisions are taken decentrally. Given the general trend to increase competition, liberalization of the energy market seems a logical answer. In this way the unforeseen development of CHP capacity stimulated the wide-ranging reforms that are now being prepared.

[1] Cogeneration of heat and power has a total generating efficiency of about 80%, compared to 40% in the case of separate generation of electricity.

as well as function as intermediate suppliers. The freedom to contract has hardly been used, however, due to high or unknown transaction costs, intransparency of transport rates and only small price differences. This is also true for the freedom to import, especially due to the fact that Dutch electricity prices have been low compared to international prices.

The small price differences between domestic suppliers point to the lack of competition caused by the *barriers to enter* the production and distribution market.

Entry on the distribution market is impossible because of the exclusive supply rights granted to distribution companies in a specific region. With respect to the production market, the Electricity Act states that electricity production for the central grid (with capacity exceeding 5 MW) is only permitted for producers with minimal 2,500 MW capacity and a licence from the national government.[11] In reality, however, foreign producers will not easily be granted a licence to build a power plant. The entry by decentral producers has not generated price competition, since distribution firms are obliged to buy the surplus of electricity at prices based on the avoided costs principle. In practice the strong growth of decentral generation, mainly combined heat and power, has led to overcapacity and a price increase following the forced reduction of central electricity production. This is elaborated in Box 13.3.

To enable the contracting freedom offered, owners of transportation and distribution networks are obliged to offer *third-party access* to eligible users at a reasonable compensation charge.

Gas Market. Like the electricity market, the gas market is dominated by the administrative coordination mechanism. This implies that the *price for natural gas* is not determined by the market. For large consumers the tariff is fixed by Gasunie, while smaller end users pay the price negotiated between EnergieNed and Gasunie plus the distribution costs of the respective distribution company. Startingpoint in the price negotiations is the market-value principle. End-user tariffs are bounded by a nationally determined maximum advised by EnergieNed.

Although there has never been a formal restriction on the *freedom to contract*, in practice it was impossible for small users to freely conclude contracts since the distribution companies had exclusive rights to supply in certain areas (with Gasunie as their sole supplier). Since the beginning of this year these exclusive rights have been declared null and void, however. The implication of this recent development is not yet clear. For large users Gasunie's obligation to offer *third-party access* to the transport network has thus far not led to any competition from abroad or between domestic producers. The long-term contracts have also prevented competition among the domestic gas producers on the export market. Although there is no formal restriction on exports at prices approved by the Minister of Economic Affairs, Gasunie still holds a near-monopoly in the export market.

Conclusion. Based on the criteria of free price setting, contract freedom, freedom to entry, and third-party access, the following conclusions can be drawn for the Dutch electricity and gas markets (see also Table 13.2). On the electricity market a certain amount of contracting freedom exists, but lack of entry and of free price setting have prevented the emergence of real competition. The gas market shows

---

[11] The 2,500 MW minimum is set by the government to enlarge the scale of production.

Table 13.2 Determinants of competition in the German and Dutch energy markets, under present institutions

	Netherlands	Germany
Price setting	administrative	administrative
Firm ownership		
– electricity	local government	government/private/mixed
– gas	mixed	government/private/mixed
Grid ownership		
– central	production	production
– low voltage	distribution	distribution
– gas	sale	production/distribution
Access to grid		
– electricity	producers, distributors and large users	no formal restrictions, in practice very limited due to lack of TPA obligation
– gas	no formal restrictions	no formal restrictions, in practice very limited due to lack of TPA obligation
Freedom to contract		
– electricity	producers, distributors, large users	not in practice
– gas	distributors, large users	yes, for transmission
Free foreign trade		
– electricity	producers, large users	yes, but in practice only DVG firms
– gas	yes	production, distribution, large users
Investment control	central government	regional government
Other features	electricity production owned by distribution	in practice exempted from competition law
Conclusion	competition very limited	no competition

a similar picture. Although the large users and distribution firms have freedom to contract, supported by provision of third-party access, competition is still largely absent. Thus, as in the case of Germany, in the Dutch energy sector the scale factor strongly dominates in the trade-off between scale and diversity.

13.2.6 Performance and Evaluation of the German and Dutch Energy Sectors

As the previous two subsections and Table 13.2 illustrated, in both the German and Dutch energy markets competition is virtually absent under the present institutions. A next question is how both countries perform with respect to affordability, reliability and sustainability. This section will judge these criteria and compare them to the results in the United Kingdom and the United States to assess the influence of the institutional structure.

Affordability. To compare the affordability of energy, Table 13.3 shows the prices of electricity and gas for households and businesses, excluding VAT and other end-user taxes. It appears that Dutch electricity and gas prices are competitive from an international perspective. Dutch natural gas prices are only to a limited extent distorted by subsidies, only the Dutch horticultural sector profits from substantial implicit subsidies. German energy prices are relatively high, however.

A first factor that contributes to this is the high price of German coal input. As can be seen from Table 13.3, a second important factor that explains the high electricity price is low labour and total factor productivity in Germany.[12] Unfortunately, for the Netherlands no comparable data on total factor productivity are available. McKinsey (1996: 5) attributes the productivity gap between the United States and Germany to a less than optimal utilization of assets due to a lack of market incentives in combination with the absence of a narrow price cap. As can be seen from Table 13.3, both Germany and the Netherlands have created a reserve margin that is higher than the efficient margin of 15-20% (Gilbert *et al.*, 1996: 11). Another factor which can be held responsible for the low capital productivity in Germany are the higher capital expenditures required to create an equivalent level of capacity (McKinsey, 1996: 7). This stems from stricter environmental standards. This also plays a role in the Netherlands.

Reliability. In 1987 a comparison of European data on electricity outages by an international committee showed large differences between the European countries. The Netherlands scored remarkably high, its average duration of electricity outages of about 20-30 minutes per customer being twice to seven times as low as the other countries. Compared to the Netherlands, both Germany and the United Kingdom underperformed with an average duration of 60 and 80 minutes, respectively. Unfortunately, since 1987 no further comparisons have been made. In the mean time the 1987 figures can have changed much. France, for example, has greatly improved its electricity supply system and recent figures point at a halving of the average duration of electricity break-downs from 220 minutes to about 100. In contrast, German unification will have worsened the German figure because of the obsolete electricity supply system in the New Länder. With respect

[12] Comparison of productivity data has two pitfalls, however. Firstly, since the data include the number of employees in the distribution sector, productivity data reflect the productivity and volume of the distribution sector as well. Secondly, differences in labour productivity might be caused by differences in the capital coefficient and compensated by a higher capital productivity. Comparing total factor productivity is therefore more appropriate.

Table 13.3 Measures of performance of Electricity and Gas markets in Germany, the Netherlands, United States and United Kingdom, 1994/1995

	Germany	Netherlands	United States	United Kingdom
Electricity				
Electricity price households, excl.tax ($/KWh,1995)[a]	0.164	0.112	0.084	0.115
Electricity price industry, excl tax ($/KWh,1995)[a]	0.093	0.070	0.047	0.068
Labour productivity (GWh/employee,1993)[b]	2.20	3.08	8.18	2.51[c]
Total factor productivity[d]	66	n.a.	100	n.a.
Capacity utilization index (public supply; OECD=100,1994)[e]	102.8	100.7	101.3	106.8
Reserve margin (%, 1995)[f]	32.9	32.6	21.6	17.3
Estimated mark-up ratio, 1980-92[g]	1.39	1.25	1.34	1.34
Gas				
Gas price for households, excl. tax ($/$10^7$kcal, 1994)[h]	353.5	259.3	246.7	291.7
Gas price for industry, excl. tax ($/$10^7$kcal,1994)[h]	159.0	109.6	113.3	141.6

[a] Converted with exchange rates; for Germany excluding the Kohlepfennig. Source: OECD/IEA (1996b)

[b] This measure of labour productivity takes all employees in the electricity sector into account, including distribution. Source: OECD (1997).

[c] Due to recent productivity gains, a 1995 preliminary estimate of U.K. productivity would put its level at about 3.2 GWh per employee. Source: OECD (1997).

[d] Source: McKinsey & Company (1996).

[e] Ratio of gross electricity production to generating capacity. Source: OECD (1997).

[f] Difference between total generating capacity and peak demand, as percentage of peak demand. Source: Künneke (1996).

[g] Estimated mark-ups in electricity, gas and water, using the Roeger method. Source: OECD (1997).

[h] Source: OECD/IEA (1996b).

to the United Kingdom it is of major interest how privatisation and liberalisation have influenced reliability. In 1992-1993 the number of supply interruptions per 100 customers showed a better-than-average result compared to the performance over the last ten years (Littlechild, 1994: 143). However, as the average duration of interruption might have increased, no firm conclusion can be drawn.

Sustainability. The environmental effects of electricity generation are influenced by the fuel mix used. As shown in Table 13.4, in all countries except the Netherlands coal constitutes around 50% of fuel input in electricity generation. Although in the other countries the share of nuclear power is large relative to the Netherlands, emissions of SO_2 are more than 11 times higher. In addition, in the United States and United Kingdom emissions of NO_x are more than twice as high as in Germany and the Netherlands.

Conclusion. Combining Table 13.2 with Table 13.3 and Table 13.4, justifies the conclusion that the Netherlands, in contrast with Germany, combines a low level of competition with a rather good performance. In terms of price level and productivity, the Dutch electricity market even equals the liberalized and privatized British market. It must be noted, however, that efficiency in the United Kingdom has been greatly enhanced since 1990. If this trend continues the Netherlands will fall behind in the future. The German performance is relatively weak, especially with respect to productivity and price. Judging from the situation in United States, there still exists a huge potential to enhance performance in both countries.

13.3 Regulatory Reform

The immediate cause for the reform of the national energy institutions in the Netherlands was dissatisfaction with the functioning of the new Electricity Law of 1989. In addition, in both Germany and the Netherlands there was a major shift in the importance policy-makers attached to competition for the performance of market economies. The British electricity and gas markets are particularly important in this regard because the British are already well down the road of liberalization. The experiences in the United Kingdom can therefore offer a yardstick in the evaluation of the German and Dutch reform proposals. Hence this section starts with an outline of the reforms in the United Kingdom and the state of affairs surrounding the European energy market. It then examines the German and Dutch reform proposals against this background.

13.3.1 The Example of the United Kingdom

Previous History. Before 1990, when the reforms were launched, the electricity sector in England and Wales consisted of two vertically integrated segments, both owned by the central government. Electricity generation and transmission, via the

Table 13.4 Electricity generation by source and environmental effects, 1994

	Coal	Gas	Oil[a]	Nuclear	Other[b]	$CO2^c$	SOx^d	NOx^d
	in %					kg/kwh	g/kwh	
Germany	56.7	7.6	1.7	28.8	5.1	0.71	5.46	0.99
Netherlands	34.4	54.5	3.8	5.0	2.3	0.72	0.35	0.83
United States	52.5	14.3	3.5	20.1	10.1	0.63	4.06	2.08
United Kingdom	50.5	14.4	5.4	27.3	2.4	0.63	6.49	1.77

[a] Petroleum products.
[b] Comb.renew. & waste, solar, tide, wind, hydro.
[c] 1993.
[d] 1993; data for Germany refer to 1992.

Source: OECD/IEA (1994a, 1995); OECD (1995).

high-voltage grid, were in the hands of the Central Electricity Generating Board (CEGB), which sold the electricity on the basis of a regulated bulk charge to 12 area boards. These boards held a monopoly on the distribution and delivery to end users, also at a regulated charge. Both segments thus enjoyed a monopoly in their respective spheres of operation. The British electricity sector was characterized by major inefficiencies, especially in terms of investment. According to Newbery and Green (1996: 67), power stations in England and Wales cost 50-100% more to build than in other industrialized countries, for instance. After an earlier attempt at reform (providing among other things for decentral generation) had yielded only modest results, the government decided on more radical reform measures in 1988.

The Reforms of 1990-91. The starting point for the reform is the reduction of inefficiencies by means of privatization and the introduction of competition for those parts of the electricity sector which do not form natural monopolies. On the generating side in particular this idea has been applied fairly rigorously, through the opening of the market to entrants and the so-called vertical break-up of the CEGB into a generation and a transmission segment. The generation segment was divided horizontally into three companies: National Power, PowerGen and Nuclear Electric. The transmission segment was organized in the National Grid Company (NGC). The NGC operates the national grid and provides non-discriminatory access to the network on the basis of regulated transmission charges.

The 12 public area boards became private regional electricity companies (RECs). The RECs can buy electricity from the electricity generators in two ways: through the day-ahead market, the so-called pool, or through longer-term contracts to avoid fluctuations in pool prices. At the moment around 95% of electricity is supplied on a contract basis. Via the interconnectors Electricité de France and the Scottish electricity producer can also buy and sell electricity in England and Wales.

The natural monopoly of the distribution grids was not split up. Distribution is restricted to the RECs. In the first instance the RECs also became owners of the NGC, but they were only allowed to control it at arm's length. The retail of electricity, however, is open to competition. The RECs are obliged to provide access to licensed retail companies on the same conditions as the RECs themselves. At the moment around 30 companies sell electricity. Users who consume more than 1 MWh have had contract freedom since 1994. This freedom will be extended to all users in 1998. Until then these so-called captive markets will be monitored by the Office of Electricity Regulation (OFFER).

OFFER, headed by the Director-General Electricity Supply (DGES), is the independent regulator of the British electricity market. It is regulated in turn by the Mergers and Monopolies Commission, an independent supervisory body.

Gas Market. The genuine liberalization of the British gas market started later than the liberalization of the electricity market. But British Gas, which owns the national grid and a large section of the distribution network and also has major interests in the sale of gas, was privatized much earlier than the CEGB and the area boards. At the time of privatization there was a formal liberalization of the gas market. But because of the lack of regulation British Gas was able to exploit the market power of its natural monopoly to the full. Several years ago a regulatory reform was implemented to reduce British Gas's market dominance (compare Spottiswoode, 1995: 53-60). This reform has three elements. The first is a stronger regulation mandate for the regulator, the Office of Gas Supply (OFGAS), which operates independently of government. The second is operational and juridical separation of the natural monopolies from competitive activities, intended to guarantee non-discriminatory access. To this end British Gas has established a separate transport company, TransCo, a subsidiary which is to be separated from the rest of British Gas by Chinese walls, and a separate trading company, Centrica. Here the government ignored the recommendation of the Monopolies and Mergers Commission, which had called for a complete break-up of British Gas. The third element is free competition on the domestic gas market from April 1998.

13.3.2 The European Context

The Internal Electricity Market. In 1992 the European Commission made a first proposal for a directive on the opening of the electricity market. Due to wide differences in the organization of national energy markets, it was not until June 1996 that the Energy Council was able to reach an agreement. This agreement seemed a very watered-down version of the 1992 proposal, which had called for unrestricted third-party access. The present directive allows for the coexistence of

Box 13.4 The single-buyer system versus third-party access

When liberalizing their electricity markets, the member states of the European Union can choose between two systems: single-buyer or third-party access.

If they adopt the third-party access system, member states can choose between negotiated access to the network or regulated access. In case of negotiated access to the network the member state must take the necessary measures to enable electricity producers and eligible customers to negotiate access to the network with the relevant transmission/distribution network operator, so as to conclude supply contracts with each other on the basis of voluntary commercial agreements. The system operators must publish an indicative range of prices for use of the network. If a country opts for a regulated system of access procedure, eligible customers do not have to negotiate with the relevant network operator. They have a right of access on the basis of published tariffs for using the transmission and distribution network. This reduces the opportunities for barring access, which in turn raises the chances of a successful liberalization. It is always possible, however, for the system operators to refuse access to a potential operator on the grounds that it lacks the necessary capacity.

If a member state chooses the single-buyer system, it designates a vertically integrated electricity company to be the single buyer within the territory covered by the system operator. It can choose whether the single buyer acts as a broker or a dealer. In the first option, the single buyer is obliged to purchase the electricity contracted by an eligible customer, while in the second option the single buyer allows regulated or negotiated third-party access on its transmission system. The Electricity Directive has ordered that the single buyer should operate separately from the generation or distribution activities of the vertically integrated company. It is clear that the single buyer system is less sure to create a competitive market compared to the third-party access system with strict unbundling of the grid network from production and distribution. Although formally forbidden, the so-called chinese walls between the single buyer and production or distribution may leave room for information flows between them. This might provide the company with strategic information about the contracts of competitors and so lead to a competitive advantage. Note that this argument also applies to the third-party-access system in which the grid network is not strictly unbundled from production and distribution.

the single-buyer system and the third-party access system. Box 13.4 explains the characteristics of these systems.

According to the Electricity Directive, which came into effect in February 1997, EU-countries must progressively increase the share of consumers eligible for freedom to contract over a period of six years. In the first three years member states must open 22% of their market for final consumption. This percentage is based on the EU share of electricity consumed by final consumers consuming more than 40 GW. Subsequently, the threshold is increased to 28%, corresponding to consumption of 20 GW at the EU level. Finally, by 2003 member states must have opened up 33% of the electricity market, corresponding to 9 GW at the EU level. Each member state is free to determine which consumers will represent the shares. On the basis of a European Commission report on the functioning of the internal electricity market the European Parliament and the Council of Ministers will then consider the possibility of a further opening of the market after 2006.

The directive does not require an unbundling of the generation, transmission and distribution activities. Integrated enterprises are only obliged to keep separate accounts for these activities. Nor does the directive provide for the creation of an independent national supervisory authority.[13] The directive thus provides only a rough framework for liberalization. That is why the degree of freedom to contract will vary from country to country, and the outcome of the liberalization process is difficult to predict. It is further complicated by the fact that the directive foresees a reciprocity clause to protect countries that experience a faster national liberalization against unbalanced energy trade with those countries in which the liberalization process lags behind. It must be noted, however, that the reciprocity clause can only be invoked in those cases where a customer is eligible in one of the two countries.

An additional difficulty for the liberalization process is created by the capacity constraints of the already heavily utilized European grid network. It is thus unclear how the increase in energy streams following the liberalization can be realized in practice. Expansion of the grid increasingly creates spatial problems.

The Internal Gas Market. The proposed organization of the internal gas market relies heavily on the ideas developed for the internal electricity market. One important difference between gas and electricity, however, is that the single-buyer principle will not be applied to the gas market. This means that third-party access will be possible everywhere in the EU. As with electricity, EU member states can choose between negotiated access and regulated access. Negotiations on the phasing of the liberalization are still in progress. Nor is it clear at this stage how far the liberalization will go. A particular issue is whether small users will be allowed to operate in the EU gas market. A technical complication is created by the take-or-pay contacts, see Box 13.5. The Dutch presidency aimed to conclude the negotiations in the first half of 1997; the Gas Directive could then take effect on 1 January 1999. This attempt failed, however.

Impact of the Internal Energy Market. On behalf of the European Commission, the gains and costs of completing the single European energy market have been estimated by London Economics, a British consultancy. Their survey shows that whereas the transaction and administrative costs may be extensive, estimated at tens of millions of ECU per year, gains are forecasted to be of the order of billions of ECU per year. These gains stem from the competition that arises between

[13] The directive does oblige member states to designate a competent authority, which must be independent of the parties, to settle disputes relating to the contracts and negotiations in question. This authority does not have to be independent from the government, however.

Box 13.5 The problems with take-or-pay in the preparation of the European internal market

Take-or-pay contracts, which are really take-and-pay contracts, are contracts which oblige the customer to buy gas at an agreed price or price formula. These contracts help to solve a hold-up problem for the gas producers. Gas production carries a large sunk cost. Without take-or-pay contracts the gas producers run a major risk of not being able to cover their fixed costs. Until recently these contracts did not pose a problem because the buyers delivered the gas on to others under long-term contracts. For the buyers these contracts provided long-term reliability in gas supply. Liberalization of the gas market will change this. Clients will be able to walk out creating a substantial financial risk for the intermediary, especially if gas prices start to fall in the wake of liberalization. The total value of these contracts is estimated at about 45 billion guilders. Recently British Gas became the first company to solve the take-or-pay problem successfully by renegotiating terms with the gas producer British Petroleum. To alleviate the problems of take-or-pay in the internal market it is suggested at the EU level to maintain the right of distribution companies to refuse access of third parties to their grid. This, however, would restrict access to the internal gas market to the distribution companies and large users with a direct connection to gas pipelines of producers.

countries after completion of the internal energy market, and are larger when more countries choose for regulated TPA instead of negotiated TPA. This is reflected by the difference between the upper and lower figure in Table 13.5 showing the benefits of competition in the gas and electricity markets.[14] In addition Table 13.5 shows the benefits from deregulation of the UK electricity market. Also in the other European countries additional gains may be attained when the European measures are supplemented by the introduction of competition within countries (London Economics, 1996: 51).

13.3.3 Reform Proposals in Germany

The Federal Minister of Economic Affairs recently presented a bill for the replacement of the Energy Act (EnWG) which dates from 1935, and a revision of the Anti-Trust Act (GWB). The proposed changes apply equally to the natural gas and electricity markets, so that both markets become subject to identical regulation. The objective of the new EnWG and revised GWB is to create more competition on the markets for electricity and natural gas, and thus to achieve a lowering of Germany's high energy prices.

---

[14] These figures are based upon the assumption that under regulated TPA there is access to the network, both within a country and between countries, and all distribution companies and large consumers have the right to buy electricity from any source. Under negotiated TPA this market opening is restricted to direct imports by large consumers.

Table 13.5 Benefits of liberalisation of the UK energy market (1990-1996) and expected benefits from the internal European energy market (1995-2020)

	Electricity			Gas
	United Kingdom	Germany	European Union	European Union
	% changes			
Energy consumption growth		8	2 - 3	0.7 - 1.1[a]
Price decrease	10	15		
industrial use			8	3[b]
residential use			2 - 4	0
Capacity utilisation increase	10[c]		16	0
Labour productivity increase	100 - 120	100		
Capital productivity increase	15[c]	25		
Cross border trade increase (% of total consumption)			6 - 15	0
	bln ECU per year			
Savings in capacity investments[e]			0.48 - 1.08[e]	
Total cost savings[f]			3.9 - 6	0.9 - 1.4

[a] Calculated as expected consumption growth (2-3 bcm p.a.) divided by yearly consumption (280 bcm).
[b] Prices to the power sector are expected to fall 5 to 8%.
[c] Source: OECD (1997).
[d] Savings due to a reduction in investment costs and more efficient capacity utilisation.
[e] Total estimated savings until 2020 (12-27 bln) divided by 25.
[f] According to NTPA scenario. Electricity figure excludes reduction of construction costs due to competition, estimated at maximal 4.6 bln ECU p.a.

Source: London Economics (1996:25,39,52,53,113) for United Kingdom and European Union; OECD (1997) for Germany.

Towards a New EnWG and GWB. The main element of the reform, which is supposed to increase competition, is that the exemption of the anti-trust law is lifted. This implies the abolition of the demarcation contracts and exclusive concession rights. Furthermore possibilities will be created for the building of new networks. The practice of granting exclusive concession rights will also be banned. Termination of the energy companies' exceptional legal position means that regional authorities will no longer be allowed to grant energy companies exclusive rights for the construction and operation of network facilities on their territory. Instead, local authorities are to open their domain without discrimination for the building and use of additional network facilities. This measure will not automatically reduce their income from concession rights, because municipalities will still be permitted to demand payment of concession rights by every utility firm that uses their territory. The federal government will be entitled to set a maximum to the amount of the concession payment per kWh, which may vary according to the number of inhabitants or the type of customers supplied. The control of new investments in generation capacity and networks will be abolished.

Exclusive rights will still apply to the public supply to captives, however. Under the new EnWG households, small and medium sized firms, and agricultural firms will remain captive. For their supply the local authorities are allowed to conclude contracts with electricity suppliers for a maximum period of 20 years. In the first instance these exclusive supply rights will be given to suppliers which at the moment hold the exclusive concession rights in a region. These concessions have all been renewed recently (see Section 13.2.2) and will apply to the end of the contract period (20 years). Each regional firm has a supply obligation to captives and is subject to tariff control by the federal government.

In the bill the abolition of territorial monopolies and the possibility to build new network lines are not supplemented with specific regulations for third-party access. Neither will there be an independent network operator. Under German competition law third-party access can be negotiated. If negotiated access is refused, however, the third party can complain to the Bundeskartellamt. In contrast to the United Kingdom, German policy-makers trust that the threat of new network facilities as well as of strict enforcement of German competition policies will be sufficient to create more efficiency in the electricity and gas markets.

13.3.4 Reform Proposals in the Netherlands

More Competition and Better Exploitation of Scale Economies. Regulatory reform in the Netherlands is inspired by a number of factors. In addition to those already mentioned in the introduction, the evaluation of the 1989 Electricity Act plays an important role. The proposals for regulatory reform have been laid down in the Third White Paper on Energy Policy (1995). A general characteristic of the reforms is that they try to combine more competition with better exploitation of economies of scale and scope. In fact, in terms of the trade-off, it tries to square the circle by aiming to improve both sides of the trade-off at the same time!

Electricity Market. To achieve more competition, the policy proposals intend to create freedom to contract, to set prices and to enter the market, as well as third-party access to all the networks. This will not apply to all consumers from the start; rather, the Ministry of Economic Affairs foresees a transition period of some length. While the new electricity law is due to come into effect in January 1998, it will take until 2007 before all customers have contract freedom. The step-by-step procedure, described in Box 13.6, is deemed necessary because of the existence of technical difficulties and excess capacity.

Box 13.6 The step-by-step transition to a liberalized electricity market

To secure a smooth transition towards a liberalized Dutch electricity market, the Ministry of Economic Affairs proposes a step-by-step procedure. Firstly, large users (i.e. those with a connection of more than 2 MW), will be allowed freedom of choice as soon as possible. With respect to the electricity market this will probably start in January 1998, the moment the new electricity law becomes operative. Implementation of this phase will lead to a situation in which 28% of electricity consumption can be freely contracted; this involves about 400 customers.

*After a period of at most five years another 33% of the electricity market is due to be liberalized by allowing contract freedom to medium-sized users (i.e. those with a connection of more than 3*80 Ampère). After ten years all consumers are to be given contract freedom.*

In 2007 production will also be completely free. When a customer both produces and consumes energy, its position on the demand market must equal its position on the supply market. Thus captive and protected in demand the customer does not have free access to the network for its supply but is assured of sale at a fixed price.

In order to enhance economies of scale and scope, the policy proposals foresee a complete merger of the four public production companies and their joint subsidiary the SEP in a single *large-scale production company* (LPC). Arguments in favour of this merger run in terms of efficiency gains.[15] In the Ministry's view, a merger is also needed to enable the Dutch industry to compete in the European energy market. The present generators are considered too small and financially too weak to survive full-fledged competition on the European market. This point is elaborated in Box 13.7.

The creation of one central production company might seem to conflict with the aim of increasing competition. After all, the LPC will have a market share of around 76% in 1996. However, the regulatory reform will facilitate entry, because the minimum condition for installed capacity (currently 2,500 MW) will be abolished. The Ministry expects, moreover, that entry barriers will be lowered in the next decade as a result of the EU internal energy market and technological developments, such as CHP. It is still uncertain, however, whether the merger will take place. The Ministry of Economic Affairs has no formal means to impose its plans on the local authorities.

In order to accomplish non-discriminatory access, the national and distribution grids will be administratively, legally and financially separated from the production and distribution companies. To achieve this they will be placed in separate legal entities owned by the production and distribution companies. These separate network operators will be banned from involvement, directly or indirectly via

[15] Estimates of the economies arising from joining the four production companies amount to around 200 mln guilders per year, which is about 3% of total costs (NRC Handelsblad, 1997). These efficiency gains result from lower overhead costs and less employees.

Box 13.7 Scale of production and financial position of the Dutch electricity industry

Estimates suggest that the minimum efficient scale of production is around 400 MW for fossil-fuel capacity and 800 MW for multiple-unit operation. These numbers double for nuclear generation. As Figure 13.1 shows, in Germany and the Netherlands even the capacity of the smallest multiple-unit firm meets this standard, so that the Dutch operators attain productive efficiency. By enlarging their scale they can still achieve some additional efficiency gains, for example by reducing overhead costs. Figure 13.1 also shows, however, that Dutch electricity producers are among the smallest in Europe: even their joint capacity is smaller than many single companies. In an internal market this could lead to takeover threats. Takeovers are more of a threat to small companies for the simple reason that they are more affordable than larger companies. In addition, a small scale firm will be more sensitive to firm-specific shocks in demand and investments in new plants comprise a relatively large share of total production capacity.

Concerns about competitiveness and takeover threat are increased by the fact that Dutch utilities have a poor liquidity position and are highly indebted. This unhealthy financial position partly results from the unbundling of production and distribution after the adoption of the 1989 Electricity Act. During this reorganization, distribution firms acquired a disproportional share of total capital.

subsidiaries, in potentially competitive activities.[16] After the establishment of the LPC there will thus be one operator for the central grid and several operators for the distribution grid.

The network operators will be responsible for ensuring such matters as fair access, grid maintenance and investments, safety and reliability of supply. In order to obtain a reliable energy provision, the operators must mutually cooperate and conclude contracts with producers that make them hold sufficient (spinning) reserve capacity. The transport prices they charge must be efficient (i.e. cost-covering) and transparent. They will be allowed to make a profit commensurate with a reasonable return on their capital.

The present proposals do not address the issue of economic dispatch. It is expected that a varied and dynamic pattern of dealers, contracts and spot markets will evolve. The usual anti-trust legislation will apply in the electricity market. Coordination between the network operators must provide for technical dispatch.

Supervision of network operation and supply to captives will be carried out by a newly created service that, like the competition authority, functions directly under the Ministry of Economic Affairs. This service determines the network tariffs based upon a proposal by the operators. Anti-trust supervision will be carried out by the national competition authority. Both services must agree on their individual tasks and possibilities for cooperation.

[16] They are, however, allowed to operate other monopolistic networks, for example natural gas or water.

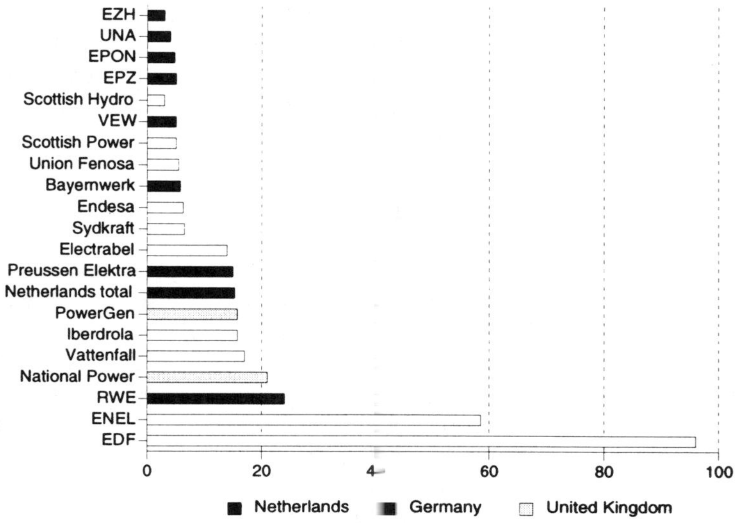

Source: EZ (1996)

Figure 13.1 European electricity firms: production capacity in GW, 1993

Another important aspect is the ownership structure of the utility companies, now dominated by local government property. The proposed regulatory reform implies no major change. The plan is that the LPC will be owned by the distribution companies. The central and distribution grids will, although in a separate entity including an independent supervisory board, remain in the hands of production and distribution companies, respectively. In the short term there are no plans for privatization.

Gas Market. Once the new electricity bill has concluded its passage through parliament at the end of 1997, the government intends to table a Gas Act in the States General. This should benefit greatly from both the new Electricity Act and the European Gas Directive, which it is hoped will have been adopted by the Energy Council by then. With respect to contract freedom, the Gas Act will be modelled on the Electricity Act. This implies that eventually – in the year 2007 – *all* users will be granted contract freedom. This is also the main aspect in which the Netherlands, together with the United Kingdom and several other countries, is ahead of the European field.

In other respects there will be major differences between the Electricity and Gas Acts. In the gas market there will be negotiated instead of regulated third-party access. Furthermore the national grid will remain in the hands of Gasunie. This also applies for the distribution networks. The activities related to the natural monopoly will have to be separated from the other activities only in accounting

Settlement Authority, however, will ensure non-discriminatory access on the basis of transparent and objective criteria. One probable consequence of the creation of a free gas market will be that the coupling of the gas price to the oil price will become much looser. The gas price might for longer periods follow its own price path on the basis of supply and demand conditions on the gas market.

13.4 Conclusions and Policy Options

Section 13.2 concluded that currently there is not much competition in the German and Dutch energy markets. In both countries it is generally recognized that this situation implies scope for increasing welfare, and in both countries proposals have been put forward to strengthen the role of market forces in this sector. These proposals were discussed in Section 13.3. This section evaluates these reforms for the purpose of formulating policy options for Germany and the Netherlands. The first question in this evaluation is what effects the reforms are likely to have. One problem in this context is that as yet the reforms exist only on paper: they still have to be adopted by the German and Dutch parliaments, and only when they are law implementation can begin. The real impact of the reforms will thus only become apparent in several years' time at the earliest. But it is possible to make an initial evaluation of the German and Dutch proposals indirectly, namely by drawing on the experiences in the United Kingdom. That is why this section starts with an evaluation of British policies. It will then return to the German and Dutch situations and try to use the conclusions from the British experiences to formulate policy options for the German and Dutch reform proposals.

13.4.1 Evaluation of and Policy Options for the Electricity Market

Evaluation of the British Reforms. Although it is still early in the day to come to a considered verdict on the British reforms, interim balances are made up at regular intervals. The provisional judgement is usually cautiously positive. The most striking effect since the changes has been the doubling of labour productivity. The British electricity sector was apparently heavily overstaffed in the past. Capital productivity has also improved, albeit less spectacularly, by 15% (OECD, 1997: Table 2.2). These productivity gains were achieved through the closure of a number of coal-fired power stations and their replacement with modern combined-cycle gas-turbine power stations. One beneficial side effect of this has been that the British electricity industry is now considerably greener. Another important factor is that these positive developments have not compromised the system's short-term operational capabilities (see Littlechild, 1994:125-149). A first conclusion which can be drawn is that it seems possible to introduce more competition in the electricity market without greatly impairing economies of scale and scope.

A frequently cited disappointment is the modesty of the price cuts achieved thus far. Real prices for consumers started to fall only in 1995, and have now come down by around 10%. Combined with the productivity gains and lower fuel prices this has led to a surge in profits. Electricity company shares have outperformed the stock market by over 100% (Green and Newbery, 1997:44). In the meantime the high returns have also tempted independent generators to enter the market. As a result of this, the market share of National Power and PowerGen has fallen from around 78% to around 45%. Yet there is a consensus that competition has been slow to develop and that National Power and PowerGen are still too dominant with regard to the non-base load. In this situation the DGES has sought to exert strong counterpressure over the last few years to rein in the two companies' market power. For this reason Yarrow (1994: 86) even argues that the establishment of the independent regulator has been the key factor in securing the modest success of the reforms.

A second conclusion which has been drawn is that the positive effects of liberalization could have been greater if the British government had made an even more radical break with the past (see also Ruff, 1994: 26; Vickers and Yarrow, 1994: 65-66; Armstrong *et al.*, 1994: 319-322; Green and Newbery, 1997: 45). Especially the creation of the duopoly among the generators is considered a major flaw. This gave National Power and PowerGen too strong a position in the market place. Entry based on high monopoly rents has lead to concern about inefficient excess capacity (Armstrong, Cowan and Vickers, 1994: 279-322). In addition the RECs were dominant in their captive markets, in part also through their ownership of the NGC. This judgement has already led to a number of modifications to the regulatory structure in the last few years

Firstly, the DGES instructed the generators to shut down or sell part of their capacity in order to limit the scope for strategic behaviour in the pool. In July 1996 the eight most advanced nuclear power plants were jointly privatized as British Energy. And after reviewing the position of the NGC with a view to increasing its independence, the DGES instructed the RECs to sell the company. The NGC has now been floated on the stock market as an independent company. The DGES is also considering splitting off the distribution grids from the RECs, because there are signs that the RECs are abusing their natural monopolies to strengthen their position in the retail supply (Beesley, 1995: 114; see also Helm and Jenkinson, 1997: 1-14). Despite all these measures a recent report of London Economics concludes that proper competition is still lacking in electricity generation (Financial Times, 1997).

Evaluation of the German Proposals. The liberalization law, coupled with the introduction of the European electricity market (in which Germany has opted for negotiated third-party access) and the abolition of the mandatory use of coal, will trigger major changes in the German electricity market. German electricity prices are likely to fall appreciably, by about 15% according to provisional estimates.

Table 13.6 Key characteristics of the German and Dutch reform proposals for electricity in comparison with the situation in the United Kingdom

	Germany	Netherlands after 1998	United Kingdom
Price setting free	only eligibles	yes, in 2007	yes
Ownership			
- generators	mixed	distributors	private
- distributors	mixed	local government	private
- central grid	mixed	generators	private
- distribution grid	mixed	distributors	distributors
Grid operator independent			
- from production	no	no strict unbundling	yes
- from sale	no	no strict unbundling	no
Access to grid	negotiated TPA	regulated TPA	regulated TPA
Freedom to contract	only for eligibles	yes; until 2007 only for eligibles	yes
Foreign trade free	yes	yes	yes
Independent supervision	yes	in 2003	yes
Merger policy	general competition regulation	merger of all public generators	dismantling of monopolies

Moreover, electricity generation will also become far less polluting, because much of the hard coal and lignite will be replaced by gas. But a number of significant differences will remain compared to the British and Dutch situation, especially with respect to third-party access, independence of the grid, as well as price and contract freedom. In fact, the threshold for effective competition will remain much higher than in these countries. Ultimately, more competition in Germany will depend on the enforcement of the competition law. As a result, it remains to be seen whether the German reforms can fulfil the high expectations that exist with respect to more efficiency and lower prices. Therefore it cannot be excluded that in a few years' time additional reforms have to be undertaken.

Evaluation of the Dutch Liberalization. As Table 13.6 shows, in many respects the Netherlands is going further down the road of liberalization than Germany (or the EU). This is most prominent with respect to third-party access to the natural monopolies, contract freedom and free price setting. But also with respect to grid access and independence of the grid operator the Dutch are clearly in the lead. On these points the Dutch are much closer to the British position than the Germans. Two main differences remain:

- the formation of a single large-scale production facility (LPC) comprising the current four regional generators;
- ownership relations within the new electricity sector: the distribution companies will own the LPC which in turn will remain the owner of the national grid; the distribution companies are owned by the municipalities and provinces, which thus directly and indirectly own the whole electricity sector.

The choice for an LPC stresses economies of scale and scope, adding some further efficiency gains to the current cooperation and coordination of the four producers in SEP. It would create a player with some weight on the future European market (see Figure 13.1). Unlike the UK grid, the Dutch electricity grid is well-connected with the grids of neighbour-countries. As a result, technically about 40% of Dutch electricity consumption can be imported from other countries, as opposed to only 2% for the United Kingdom. Hence the Dutch market is much more open to foreign competition than the UK market, and through regulated TPA foreign producers will gain real access to an increasing share of the Dutch market. The current four producers might be too small and too weak to remain independent on the European market, while the efficient Dutch producers deserve a fair start on a level playing field. And although a foreign take-over would not impair competition, it would create a political-strategic risk in maintaining a reliable national electricity network.

In contrast, the shift in thinking on natural monopolies emphasizes a strong role for market forces, independent ownership relations, in particular for the network operator, and a strong independent regulator (see Section 1.3). This reduces the risk of abuse of market power, exploitation of informational rents, and cross subsidization to prevent market entry by competitors. The British experience constitutes a case in point. While in the UK the DGES has taken measures in recent years to protect and accelerate vertical and horizontal deintegration, the Dutch proposals move in the opposite direction. The efficiency of the current four Dutch producers does not suggest that they run below optimal scale, but it should be remembered that they do cooperate closely, e.g. in investment decisions. If the size of investments in new plants creates substantial risks for a single producer, the scale of the four production companies may be too small. Technological developments towards less scale-intensive technologies may reduce this problem, environmental regulations demanding substantial investments intensify it. In addition, creating truly independent ownership runs into substantial, though transitory, transaction costs. Just like central government cannot impose the proposed merger, neither can it push through a different ownership structure in any simple way. However, the proposed structure makes the task of the supervisor in preventing collusion more difficult.

Reviewing these arguments, it remains an open question whether the current proposals can achieve the dual aim of introducing more market forces and better exploitation of economies of scale and scope. In particular the combination of a single large-scale production facility and the proposed ownership relationships creates risks that too few checks and balances will be built into the Dutch structure to prevent abuse of market power. Also in wider perspective, for example in comparison with other small economies such as Norway and Sweden, the Dutch proposals seem to take an exceptional position. Both Scandinavian countries deregulated their electricity supply industries in the past years. Just like in Britain the central grids were separated (including ownership) from the state- owned generation companies. The main difference with the British situation is that the networks are not privatised, but transferred to state-owned enterprises.

Policy Options. The conclusion is that from the point of view of the functioning of markets, doubts remain about the effectiveness of the reform proposals. How can the government improve the chances for effective liberalization? For Germany obvious policy options are to introduce regulated third-party access, separation of the grids and more contract freedom. With these measures the prospects for competition would be greatly strengthened.

What are policy options for the Netherlands in this respect? The most effective way to strengthen the forces of competition on the domestic market would be the conversion of the four existing regional generators into independent production companies. This would open the way for genuine competition between the major domestic generators provided they get a fair start on a level playing field. The separation of the central grid would also follow naturally from this line of argument. Indeed, putting the grid in the hands of one of the generators could easily lead to complaints of unfair competition from the others.

Economies of scale and the competitive position on the European market may constitute arguments to combine the generators into an LPC. To secure competition this option would more strongly demand effective separation of the grid and independent ownership relations. Moreover, it requires a powerful Supervisory Authority. The Swedish example shows that independent ownership not necessarily requires complete privatisation of the entire energy sector. Therefore, from the perspective of strengthening market forces, separation and full independence constitute policy options that are worthwhile considering.

13.4.2 Policy Options for the Gas Market

Although there are important differences between electricity and gas, for example with respect to storage, there is also one crucial similarity from the perspective of market regulation: the existence of network-characteristics. This would seem to imply two policy conclusions for Germany and the Netherlands, which came to the fore also with electricity: the need to separate the natural monopoly from competition activities and the need for independent supervision. For the same reasons as in the case of electricity, it raises doubts – as part of an exercise to introduce more market forces – to leave the grid in the hands of parties that also have interests in the sale of gas.

Difference in Markets. On further consideration, however, there is one important difference between electricity and gas. First of all, *already now* competition in the European gas market is much more advanced than in the electricity market, because only a few countries in Europe dispose of natural gas resources. At the same time, the share of gas in total energy use has continuously risen during the past decades and for the future a further strong increase is expected. This gives the many European countries without major natural gas resources, such as Germany, a strong interest in strengthening free trade and competition in the gas market to secure reliable gas supply at low prices. For these reasons, confidence seems justified that the European gas market will be opened up further. From this perspective, the steps Germany has taken up to now to liberalize the gas market seem to be modest. Additional policy options to stimulate competition would be the introduction of regulated instead of negotiated TPA and strict unbundling of the networks. A first step would be a no-regret policy option to promote regulated TPA on a European scale to maintain a level-playing field. However, the size of the German market also creates room for more unilateral steps. These initiatives could induce other countries to take the same steps.

Difference Between the Dutch and the German Case. The position of the Netherlands differs from that of Germany and of other European countries, because it is one of the few European countries with large natural gas reserves. In fact, the Dutch government itself is the *de facto* owner of both these reserves and, through Gasunie, part of the grid. As a result, the Dutch government faces an important trade-off between competition and the rents of natural gas, which largely flow to the central government. What counts, in particular, for the Dutch economy as a whole is the loss of rents from abroad. Strict adherence to the British example by separating the grids will only add to those losses, because it will eliminate also domestic monopoly rents Gasunie gains through the grid. The Dutch government has chosen to accept the reduction of rents from abroad as a result of the internal gas market, but is not prepared to walk in front and lose even more (domestic) revenues for the sake of (international) competition. Given this position, there is only limited room for further liberalization. One option would be to introduce regulated TPA instead of negotiated TPA, but to prevent predatory pricing by foreign suppliers and to create a level playing field, this policy would require similar steps in other countries.

Final Remark. There is one other trade-off European governments have to consider, with respect to the creation of internal electricity and gas markets: the trade-off between more competition and the environment. More competition will lead to lower prices, which in turn will increase the use of electricity and natural gas and concomitantly of emissions. These side-effects can be mitigated by the introduction of energy taxes and levies, or through direct regulation (see CPB, 1997: Ch. 5).

14 Health Care

In recent years, the health care systems in most industrialized countries have undergone considerable diagnostics and treatment by analysts and policy makers. The symptoms that prompted the attention were the large increases in health care expenditures as a percentage of GDP, the increase in real per capita health care expenditures and the rapid rise in the cost per unit of health care relative to increases for other goods, especially in the United States. The Netherlands and Germany, as well as the United Kingdom exhibited the above symptoms to a lesser extent than the United States (see Figure 14.1) but they required considerable political effort to maintain control over health care budgets. Furthermore, there is the prospect of potential future increases in expenditures as a result of aging and more heterogeneous populations, increased affluence, and new technologies.

At the same time, Figure 14.1 also suggests that possibilities exist to learn from comparing the experiences in different countries. Expenditure ratios differ widely, while life expectancy differences - a crude indicator of quality - are much smaller. Cross-country comparisons may point the way towards the design of a better system. In principle, a rising share of GDP being allocated to health care may not be undesirable. The real problem lies in trusting the working of the institutions of health care enough to be sure that the level of spending reflects social desires, that the health care services provided are the most efficient in meeting patients' needs, and that the services are produced in the most efficient manner. These properties can be summarized by the goals *quality, accessibility, and affordability*, (see White, 1995). Quality refers to the best possible care, given the needs of the patient. Accessibility reflects the commitment of resources to provide services when and where necessary, while affordability points to the most efficient delivery of the required services.

In order to design institutions that improve upon the functioning of the health care sector, the driving forces of the health care system must first be understood. The analytical framework, developed in Chapter 2, is customized for the health care sector in Section 14.1. The framework tries to clarify the special character of health care as well as the market failures that would emerge in a free health care market. The framework also identifies the principle trade-offs governments face when they try to alleviate the failures, as well as the external conditions that influence the trade-offs.

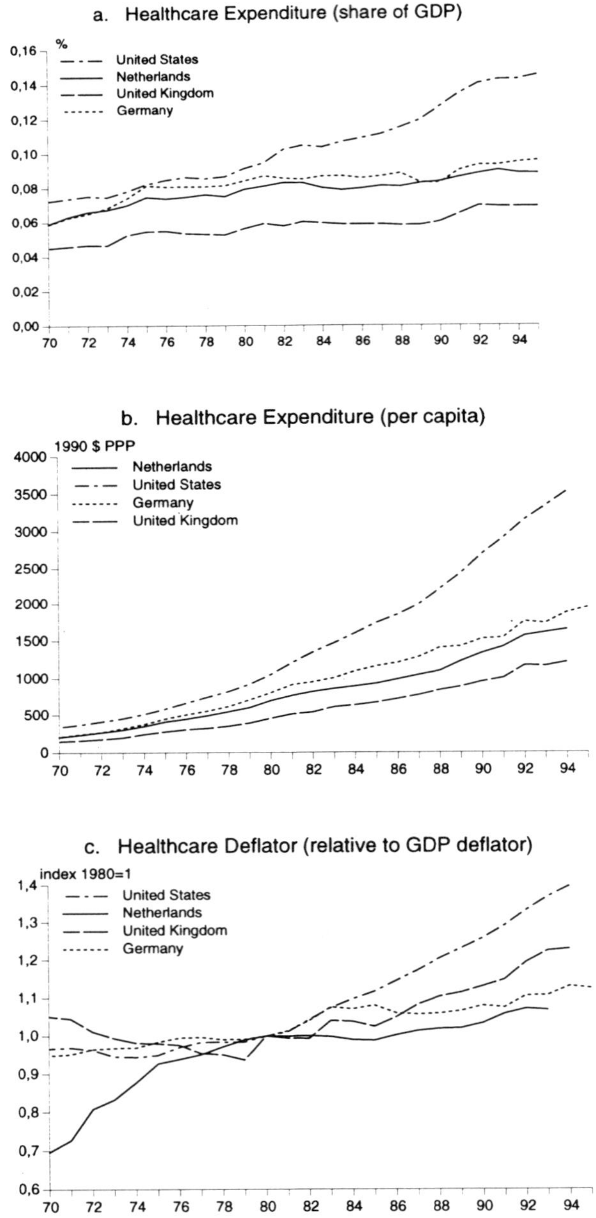

Source: OECD Healthdata 1996

Figure 14.1 Health care expenditure

Following the discussion of the analytical framework, Section 14.2 describes the institutional choices that have been made in Germany and the Netherlands with respect to health care financing, delivery systems, and the interactions between payers and providers. Next, Section 14.3 evaluates the actual performance of the German and Dutch health care system in the context of the analytical framework. The effects of emerging trends on the institutional trade-offs are the subject of Section 14.4. The final section concludes the comparative analysis with policy options for Germany and the Netherlands and provides thoughts on the unfinished agenda.

14.1 Theoretical Framework: Market Failures and Trade-offs

This section gives a summary of problems which would occur in a free market for health care and describes mechanisms which are used to alleviate the problems in two stylized models, Managed Competition (MC) and National Health (NH). The strengths and weakness of the two approaches under changing external circumstances are then assessed.

14.1.1 Market Failures in a Free Health Care Market

Infrequent, Unpredictable, Costly. Consumer preferences for health care are unlike those for traditional goods. The need for health care is subject to a special form of risk, with infrequent but unpredictable and very costly events. Consumers are unable to use savings to cover the risk because of the uncertain timing of the event, while they are unable to borrow because their state of health makes them bad credit-risks. In general, these conditions give rise to a market for pooled savings, or insurance, to ensure accessibility. Insurance markets, however, will not function efficiently when confronted with adverse selection, or moral hazard. Precisely these problems crop up because of informational asymmetries in the market for health care, as described below.[1]

Moral Hazard. Consumers lack information about the need for health care services and thus defer to the judgment of those with medical training to determine required provisions. Essentially, suppliers have the market power to create their own demand, and thus have incentives to provide excessive (or inefficient) care. Moral hazard also exists on the demand side of the market, because insured consumers no longer face a budget constraint when making health care purchasing decisions.

---

[1] For an early discussion on the role of uncertainty in health economics, see Arrow (1963).

Finally, the complexity of insurance contracts allows insurers to exercise market power in the provision of insurance because individuals have high transaction costs in making informed choices.

Dynamic Inefficiency. As a result of moral hazard on the part of consumer and supplier, the system has a predisposition towards creating and adopting cost-increasing technologies. As long as customers benefit without bearing the financial burden they will demand use of the best technology.

Adverse Selection. Another characteristic of health care demand is its skewness across consumers: In one study, 1 percent of patients accounted for 28 percent of total costs (see Newhouse, 1986). Although only a small portion of the probability of health care need can be predicted using readily available indicators such as age and gender, screening high-risk individuals could be very profitable for competing insurers. If actuarially fair rates are charged to different groups, asymmetric information of health situation will result in high risk individuals in each group choosing insurance, while low-risk individuals will not. Rates will thus rise to reflect the higher risk of the insurees, which causes further selection. Adverse selection thus can cause a death-spiral of worsening risk-pools until insurance no longer is offered (see Schut, 1995).

Externalities. Finally, consumers may be affected by the health situation of others. The presence of contagious diseases and the danger of epidemics are clear cases of externalities. The interdependence of risks from contagious diseases makes insurance coverage problematic; mandatory immunization programs are a more reliable means of stemming the danger.

The Impact of Market Failures. Due to adverse selection a free market leads to gaps in coverage and exclusion from insurance for segments of the population. Moral hazard results in over-provision of high-cost and low-efficiency health care to insured persons. The asymmetric information as well as the lack of oversight and review of care render it difficult for consumers to assess the quality of care. Another drawback of a free market is high transaction costs owing to the complexity of insurance contracts. Unfettered competition in the market for health care thus will fail to ensure quality, accessibility, and affordability.

14.1.2 Coordination Mechanisms in Health Care

Two Models of Health Care Systems. The free market system as described above is not characteristic of the health care sector in any particular country. A portion of the United States health care market, however, could be considered to fit the description, as could parts of the German and Dutch systems in the 1970s and 1980s. The resulting escalation of costs and diminution of accessibility, especially

Box 14.1 Definitions of terms used in Chapter 14

cap	*Maximum reimbursement allowed for covered items in a given period*
capitation	*Method of giving provider a fixed payment for each patient in a given period, regardless of services provided*
co-insurance	*Means of reducing moral hazard by shifting some insurance risk to customers*
co-payment	*A method of co-insurance, where customer pays a small fixed amount or percentage for each provided service*
community rating	*Insurance premiums based on the risk-profile of all customers*
coverage	*List of services which are reimburseable under an insurance policy or health plan*
deductible	*A method of co-insurance, where customer is at risk for fixed amount per period before insurance coverage commences*
delivery	*Provisions utilized in care or treatment*
fee-for-service	*Method of paying provider for each provision supplied*
health plan	*Entity which offers integrated financing and delivery of health care service, under system of Managed Competition*
HMO	*Health maintenance organisation. Common form of health plan found in the United States*
OOP maximum	*Out-of pocket maximum. Maximum amount of co-insurance risk placed on insuree per calender year*
prepayment	*Coverage purchased directly from providers for a charge which is fixed in advance*
provider	*An entity supplying health care services, including general practitioner, specialist, hospital, group practice, etc.*
risk-adjustment	*Transfer of fees among insurance providers based on ex-ante risk characteristics of insurance pool*
sponsor	*Entity which acts as agent for demand side under system of Managed Competition*

in the United States, lead to heightened interest in health care policy. The purpose of health care policy is to search for coordination mechanisms which reduce the market failures. Instead of relying on the strawman of perfect competition as one archetype coordination mechanism, two models will be distinguished which try to cope with the market failures: the managed competition model (MC), and the national health model (NH). MC was developed during the last two decades, among others by Enthoven (see Enthoven, 1988). At the other end of the coordination spectrum, stands the system of control as practised, until recently, in the United Kingdom by the National Health Service (NHS).[2] Both systems compre-

[2] Since 1991, fairly radical restructuring of the NHS has been taking place, with the introduction of 'quasi-markets' for the delivery of health care services (see Galjaard-Middel, 1996).

hend the market failures endemic in a free health care market and provide interventions to solve the problems. Managed competition places great weight on inefficiencies brought on by government intervention and on the benefits of the incentives from competition. The NHS circumvents the problems associated with insurance by creating an entitlement to health care for the entire population and by providing, and controlling, the supply outright. The health care systems in most countries contain elements of both stylized models. Under pressure from rising health expenditures, most Western European countries have cautiously introduced some elements of MC. In the United States, where pressures were even greater, managed competition is being approached from the free market side.

After providing a brief overview of the characteristics of the two models, this section sketches their strengths and weaknesses and provides an interpretation of the choices made in terms of the trade-offs. Box 14.1 provides definitions of some terminology used throughout the chapter.

Managed Competition. Managed competition refers to a system where agents have incentives to behave as they would have in a market satisfying all necessary conditions for perfect competition (see Table 14.1). Price signals and competitive pressures are designed to bring cost-conscious consumers and capable profit-seeking providers together in an efficient manner. Informational asymmetries, adverse selection, and moral hazard are dealt with by imposing some ground rules and creating certain institutions. The first step is to enable integration of the financing and delivery of health care. The second rule is to allow several of such integrated providers (henceforth called health plans or plans) to compete for customers. As a result of these, the moral hazard of providers to over-provision is mitigated. The third rule is to create a sponsor.

Sponsor. A sponsor is an entity which acts as a purchasing agent for a pool of consumers in a community (say, everyone in a region) and lays the ground rules for competition among health plans. Examples of sponsors may be large employers, regional-, or national governments. A crucial feature is that a minimum level of insurance is mandatory for all persons, mitigating adverse selection. Health plans offer potential customers an insurance contract with coverage at or above the sponsor-set minimum, at a price based on the level of coverage and on the risk characteristics of the entire risk pool (community rating). However, because competing plans are required to accept any customer at the offered price, they have an incentive to compete for customers whose risk is better than the community average. The sponsor therefore makes an adjustment to plans based on the ex-ante risk characteristics of their customers. Collecting information on ex-ante risk is costly for the sponsor, but requires much fewer resources than competing firms each expending effort on risk selection. With ex-ante risk adjustment, plans can focus their efforts on providing better care in order to gain a competitive advantage, rather than on risk selection.

Table 14.1 Key characteristics of managed competition

- The managed elements
  - health plan: integrated financing and delivery systems
  - sponsor: organization to provide competence on the demand side
  - customer: minimum coverage mandatory
  - plan receives risk-adjusted per capita pre-payment
  - effective competition policy
  - quality monitoring and control by sponsor

- The competitive elements
  - Customers:
    * freedom to choose plans
    * limited freedom to choose providers within plan
  - Plans:
    * freedom to set price
    * freedom to select/exclude providers
    * freedom to invest

The sponsor collects information on the quality of care and on the level of offered service in order to provide the customer with information to make an informed choice among plans, thereby lowering transaction costs. To promote competition among plans, customers are allowed to choose freely among plans at regular, predetermined, intervals. Although the MC model does not specify explicitly any features for solidarity, the model does not preclude it either. Without explicit redistribution across customers, solidarity would occur between high-risk and low-risk customers in the community. Income solidarity could be built in, for example, by providing progressively financed vouchers for the lowest priced plan. For competition among plans to succeed, customers must be free to choose more expensive plans, but must be liable for any difference price. Finally, sponsors mitigate moral hazard on the part of the consumer by introducing some form of co-insurance. (see Box 14.2).

Health Plans. Health plans have an incentive to work efficiently because they are pre-paid according to the ex-ante risk profile of their customers. As such, they get rewarded for cost-reductions below the level expected given their customers' risk characteristics but suffer losses with higher costs. Under managed competition, plans can experiment with any variety of organizational forms, with market forces weeding out the unsuccessful ones. Plans can pay their physicians, or other providers, on a capitation basis, have them on salary, make them share-holder/partner of the organization, or even pay a fee-for-service. Plans are free to contract and exclude providers, giving them a strong bargaining position. In any case, the plan has incentives to monitor, control, and optimize the physicians' care

Box 14.2 The RAND Health Insurance Experiment

The RAND Health Insurance Experiment was designed to study the effects of co-insurance on health care service use and on health outcomes.[1] *Two thousand families were randomly assigned to various fee-for-service insurance plans, with varying rates of co-payments and varying OOP maxima, for three-to-five year periods in the late 1970s.*

The principle findings are that higher co-payments significantly reduce health care service utilization. A co-payment of 95 percent, up to the OOP maximum, was seen to reduce utilization of services by about 25 to 30 percent compared with full coverage. The results did not depend on level of the OOP maximum, which ranged from 5 to 15 percent of family income. For all but the poorest families, health outcomes did not vary with co-payments or OOP levels. However, the health of the poorest 6 percent of families was adversely affected by co-insurance. In the United States, insurers have generally responded to the findings of the RAND experiment by lowering OOP maxima and increasing co-payments.

Besides testing the effect of co-insurance on reducing moral hazard on the part of customers, the RAND group conducted a limited experiment on provider moral hazard in different institutional provider settings. Delivery trajectories were compared between one HMO and traditional fee-for-service providers. To control for selectivity bias, families were randomly assigned to the two provider types. Overall, RAND found that HMOs were able to care for patients with 39 percent fewer hospital admissions and 28 percent lower expenditures, with similar health outcomes. The use of preventive services was higher at the HMO.

[1] *Newhouse (1993).*

delivery choices, because the market will penalize inefficient providers.

Health plans, likewise, are punished or rewarded by the market for making good intertemporal choices regarding investments and health care delivery trajectories. Plans can reduce costs or improve quality of output by investing in capacity, new equipment, and new technology. Given the uncertainty regarding future technology and consumer demand, investments to which plans have committed themselves may or may not work out, ex-post. Further, plans have an incentive to improve the intertemporal path of health care delivery, for example, by promoting preventative medicine, or by initiating early treatment. Likewise, plans find it in their interest to conduct research into more cost-effective treatments, at least if the research results are (partly) appropriable.

Several such integrated providers, called "managed care," currently exist in the United States and the United Kingdom. Besides the popular health maintenance organizations (HMOs) in the United States, where a full range of providers are usually on staff, managed care is practised through utilization review and at-risk gatekeepers. With utilization review, insurers require selected physicians to obtain permission to make certain provisions before reimbursement is allowed, while patients pay lower co-insurance if they visit these selected physicians. The at-risk gatekeeper, in the United Kingdom called a GP-fundholder, is a primary care physician, or group of physicians, who is given a fixed budget by the plan for total

Table 14.2 Key characteristics of National Health Care

- Control Elements
  - total budget
  - administered allocation
  - quality control
  - mandatory participation
- Freedoms
  - choice of physician
  - no freedom in pricing
  - no freedom of enrolment
  - no freedom to invest

expected health care costs for each insured patient, and thus has an incentive to review and optimize provisions by secondary care givers.

On a more negative note, competing plans continue to have an incentive for sneaky selection of low-risk customers within the categories for which risk-adjustment takes place. Also, plans may have moral hazard towards under-provision because they receive a pre-payment per customer. The sponsor attempts to mitigate these problems by trying to monitor and prevent cream-skimming behaviour of the competing plans, and by mediating on behalf of the customers who feel that they have been denied provisions which they thought were covered. Nonetheless, the tasks of the sponsor are difficult, and market failures still may persist.

National Health Care. In a national health care system, such as the National Health Service (NHS) in the United Kingdom prior to reforms of 1991, a central budget for health care services is financed through taxes (see Table 14.2). The budget is allocated across regions and across several sectors of health care, such as salaries, materials, medicine, and investments. All providers are on salary, and hospital capacity, such as number of beds and operating facilities, is planned.

Yet, national health does provide solutions to some of the market failures mentioned earlier. Access to service is an entitlement, so that no adverse selection can take place. Because providers do not get a fee-for-service, the moral hazard of over-provision is avoided. Externalities are internalized, and optimal decisions can be made, in principle. Moral hazard from the side of the consumers can still occur, although waiting lists which often arise may induce the same behavioral effect as co-insurance.

14.1.3 Managed Competition and National Health: Strengths and Weaknesses

Both the managed competition model and the national health model have mechanisms which alleviate the market failures inherent in free health care

Table 14.3 Strengths and weaknesses of managed competition

- Strengths
  - promotes diversity, experimentation, drive for best practice
  - adoption of efficient technology
  - reflects consumer preferences
  - reduces political risks
- Weaknesses
  - solidarity; divergence in levels of service
  - under-provision as a result of pre-payment
  - conflicts concerning coverage
  - sneaking adverse selection
  - high administration costs

markets. However, the models do so to a different extent, and both models introduce new problems along the way. An overview of the strengths and weaknesses implied by the two models is given in Tables 14.3 and 14.4.

Strengths of Managed Competition. MC chooses for incentives, diversity, and experimentation. In principle, these choices are the same as for free competition, but much less extreme. The strength of competitive markets lies in the incentives for experimentation, resulting in the creation and adoption of new ideas together with the market selection and diffusion of the best ideas. Further, free choice of consumers concerning the level of care they wish to purchase above the floor given by the least expensive plan, leads to a macro level of expenditures which reflects consumer wishes at the margin. For politicians, the system does not require frequent intervention, nor can problems be blamed directly on politicians.

Weaknesses of Managed Competition. The principle weaknesses of MC are less solidarity and scale, which express themselves in divergences in service-levels, sneaking adverse selection and high administration costs. The extent of the weaknesses are difficult to quantify in advance. This is all the more true because MC has not yet fully been tested. Debates on pros and cons, as a result, are mainly based on theoretical arguments. The lack of solidarity, for example, depends on the implementation. In order for competition between plans to work, consumers must face the incremental costs of choosing more expensive plans. However, the sponsor could effectuate a redistribution across consumers by compressing (or expanding) the cost differences between plans progressively with income. A proper rate of progressivity could result in a neutral effect on the aggregate amount of insurance purchased. Furthermore, the under-provision which may arise because of the pre-payment capitation may be countered by long-run profit incentives of the plan. Under-provision this year, may result in higher expenditures for the patient in the

Table 14.4 Strengths and weaknesses of national health

- Strengths
  - equity/solidarity
  - transparency of market
  - low administration costs

- Weaknesses
  - micro-efficiency
  - rationing when supply is tight
  - rationing undermines quality and equity
  - political risks
  - little experimentation
  - dynamic inefficiency

future, while consumer complaints may lead to loss of market share. The same market discipline may mitigate conflicts arising between customers and plan over covered benefits. Sneaking risk selection and under-provision can also be countered by altering slightly the method with which the sponsor pays plans, as suggested by Newhouse (1996): By providing a mix of fee-for-service and capitation payments to the plan, the incentive for risk selection and the incentive towards under-provision would be reduced.

Strengths and Weaknesses of National Health. In general the strengths of the National Health model are the weaknesses of Managed Competition, and vice-versa. By circumventing the need for insurance, the market under national health becomes simple and transaction costs for consumers are reduced. The system guarantees access, through mandatory enrolment and tax generated revenue. Administration costs are low, and the overall budget becomes very predictable and easier to control. Providers have the 'simple' task of triage, or allocating the fixed capacity among consumers. However, moral hazard of providers may result in low effort and under-provision. The system relies strongly on the values of medical professionals to provide the best care possible, given the budget. Waiting lists are often used as the method of allocating scarce capacity; they also tend to reduce moral hazard on the part of the consumer. Tight funding is more readily reflected in reduced capital budgets than in current operating expenses, leading to slow adoption of new technology and underinvestment in future capacity. Complaints about the system, especially about excessive waiting periods, can lead to political problems. During the 1980s the problems became severe enough to lead to radical change in the form in the direction of managed competition.

14.1.4 Fundamental Trade-offs

The strengths and weaknesses of both models can be translated in the trade-offs of Chapter 2; the trade-offs of the health care sector are quite similar to those of social protection; compare Section 6.1.3. Therefore explanation of these trade-offs will be brief.

First of all there is the trade-off between incentives versus solidarity. Managed competition stresses incentives. The beneficial effects of incentives are that they promote efficiency. Therefore they provide the best instrument to cut back moral hazard on the side of providers and customers. Incentives also induce risk-selection behaviour among providers, however, which makes risk-sharing much more difficult. Furthermore, incentives allow for greater differences in service levels of health care. In conclusion, the stronger incentives are applied the greater the lack of solidarity and inequality of health care provision will be.

In the NH-model the reverse is true. National health eliminates incentives for risk selection. National health therefore facilitates risk-sharing as well as solidarity and equal treatment. The other side of the coin is that incentives to fight moral hazard although not absent, are less strong than in the MC-model and concern under-provision rather than over-provision. The NH-model will therefore be characterized by more micro-inefficiencies.

The second trade-off relates to scale versus diversity. The NH-model with a centralized budget and administration can profit from economies of scale while the MC-model offers the advantages of diversity and experimentation. It stimulates trying out of new ideas and provides better incentives for dynamic efficiency.

Finally there is the trade-off between the political risk in the NH-model versus the market risk in the MC-model.

14.1.5 The Impact of External Conditions

External conditions influence the merits of different systems as a means of coping with market failures. Table 14.5 shows the conditions under which the two stylized coordinating systems have an advantage in alleviating the economic problems in health markets. Because many relevant conditions also play a role in various other chapters, such as Chapter 6 and 7, discussion here will be brief. Three groups of conditions can be distinguished: First of all, conditions which determines whether society attaches a high value to insurance and solidarity; Secondly, conditions which determine the magnitude of the market failures, and finally other conditions.

In general, if conditions are such that insurance markets fail, then the case for NH is strengthened. Specifically, the stronger the incentives towards selection, the better national health compares with managed competition. The case for MC, on the other hand, becomes stronger when conditions are such that moral hazard is an important problem. Other conditions which support MC are a changing technologi-

Table 14.5 Conditions favouring the stylized systems

	National Health	Managed Competition
Strengths	exploiting economies of scale	allowing diversity
	reducing information costs	reducing political risk
	facilitating solidarity	reducing moral hazard
	facilitating risk sharing	enhancing incentives
Conditions		
Conditions Group 1:		
Preferences		
- risk aversion	high and homogeneous	low and heterogeneous
- preference for equity	high	low
Conditions Group 2:		
Information		
- information about ex-ante risk features	asymmetric	symmetric
- information costs about insurance contract	high	low
Uncertainty		
- uncertainty	fundamental	not fundamental
- predictability of event	poor	good
- predictability of care outcome	good	poor
- (technological) environment	stable	changing
Conditions Group 3:		
Information		
- information about provider effort	symmetric	asymmetric
- information about consumer behaviour	symmetric	asymmetric
- information about best practice	good	poor
Preferences		
- norms constraining moral hazard	strong	weak
- preference for free choice	low	high
- responsiveness of supplier effort to incentives	low	high
- responsiveness of customer demand to incentives	low	high
Political process	efficient	inefficient

cal environment with fundamental uncertainty regarding best treatment paths. The reason is that MC provides flexibility and incentives for learning.

14.2 Health Care Institutions in Germany and the Netherlands

This section analyzes the exact nature of the existing institutions in Germany and the Netherlands against the background of the analytical framework. First it describes the relationships between customers and financing schemes, followed by an overview of the interactions between financing schemes and the health care delivery system and between patient and provider. It evaluates the institutions with regard to how their characteristics compare with the NH or MC model. It closes with an evaluation of how we, theoretically, expect the institutions to perform in terms of accessibility, affordability, and quality.

14.2.1 Customers and Insurers

Mixed Insurance System. In the Netherlands, the insurance system is of a mixed type, with both private and social ('sickness funds') insurance providers. In 1992, sickness funds provided mandatory coverage for 62 percent of the population and private insurers covered most of the remainder on a voluntary basis. These insurance schemes do not cover all health care provisions: A special fund called 'AWBZ', mandatory for all residents, pays for long-term care and exceptional health care costs. In Germany, the arrangements are similar, with compulsory sickness fund insurance covering two-thirds of the population. The private insurance companies, however, have to compete with the sickness funds for the remaining residents; the majority choose the sickness funds.[3] In Germany, a new insurance form covering the whole population, the 'Pflegeversicherung', has been introduced to cover daily care caused by illness or handicap. This scheme is comparable to the Dutch AWBZ, but very much narrower in coverage. The special insurance scheme reduces the pressure on the normal insurance funds to screen out potential high risk applicants. Table 14.6 provides some key information on health insurance premiums in both countries.

Customers and Sickness Funds. Table 14.7 summarizes the main characteristics of the market for sickness fund insurance in Germany and the Netherlands, using concepts described in the analytical framework. For reference, the key characteristics of MC also are included. First of all, sickness funds in both countries have a strong solidarity element. Payments for sickness fund insurance are made as a percentage of income, up to a maximum, with a certain share of the total premium

---

[3] Private insurance companies have rates that appeal to single persons earning incomes above the income ceiling for the sickness fund, and disfavour families with children.

Table 14.6 Health insurance premiums in Germany and the Netherlands, 1997

	Germany		Netherlands
Sickness funds		% of gross wages	
employer rate	6.66		5.55
employee rate	6.66		1.35
		USA $ PPP	
fixed per adult			104
insurance ceiling	36000		29348
contribution ceiling	36000		25091
average premium	1603		815
maximum premium	4795		1836
		%	
share of expenditures	80		38
Special insurance	Pflegeversicherung		AWBZ
	% of gross wages		% of taxable income
employer rate	0.85		
employee rate	0.85		8.85
		USA $ PPP	
fixed per adult			69
contribution ceiling	36000		22203
average premium	205		742
maximum premium[a]	612		1965
		%	
share of expenditures	10		45
Private insurance		USA $ PPP	
average premium[b]	2718		849
		%	
range high-low	65-140		75-130
share of expenditures	10		17

Source: CPB, VWS (1996), BMG (1995).
[a] Assuming family of four.
[b] Single person, 40 years old.

nominally paid for by the employer. The premium does not vary with household composition of the employee, although in the Netherlands, a small fixed-fee is charged per adult-equivalent member of the household. The premium thus mixes insurance with income re-distribution, as it entails solidarity with large families, the elderly, and the poor.[4] In both countries insurance is compulsory below an income ceiling. Together with solidarity, this ensures that the rather comprehensive coverage is accessible to all, without regard to financial position, age, or health history.

Accessibility and affordability are slightly reduced with the co-insurance that has been introduced in both countries to reduce moral hazard on the part of the consumer. In Germany, sickness funds require co-payments for most items. Solidarity is maintained somewhat by excluding co-payments for children and low-income households, and by having a progressive OOP maximum ranging from 2 percent to 4 precent of income per year. In the Netherlands, sickness funds experimented with co-payments between 1988 and 1990, and in 1997 re-instated co-insurance of up to 20 percent with a relatively low OOP maximum of fl 200 per annum.

The next elements relate to competition. Although some conditions required for the MC model are increasingly fulfilled in both countries, other important conditions remain to be met. Table 14.7 shows that the sickness funds in Germany and the Netherlands meet three or four out of six conditions.

In Germany, workers traditionally were not allowed to change from their local, trade based, or company specific fund. Beginning in 1997, customers will be able to switch freely between funds. In the Netherlands, compulsory insured persons have been able to switch between sickness funds at regular intervals, starting in 1992.

Restrictions on entry into the sickness fund market remain prohibitively strong in Germany, with only limited leeway for new trade based or company funds. Industry concentration has increased, especially in local funds, following loosening of restrictions in 1993 on changes in fund structure. In the Netherlands, entrance of new companies and joint operations between private insurers and sickness funds are now allowed. Mergers between funds and between funds and private insurers have caused the number of funds to drop from 48 in 1986 to 26 in 1994. The increased concentration, however, has not called forth action from the competition policy authorities.

Another requirement for competitive interactions in the insurance market is the ability of funds to attract customers with lower rates or better service. Since coverage is uniformly set, and quality is difficult for a consumer to observe, especially when no sponsor is present, price competition is the name of the game. At present, sickness fund contribution rates are set nation-wide in the Netherlands, and funds can vary contributions only minimally through changes in the small fixed-fee part of the premium. In Germany, differences can, and do, exist in the contribution rates, which ranged from 8 percent to 15 percent of gross wages for

---

[4] The income redistribution scheme may cause the same marginal wedge problems which occur with other income based taxes.

Table 14.7 Key characteristics of sickness funds

	Germany	Netherlands	MC
Access/affordability			
- enrolment under ceiling	mandatory	mandatory	
- enrolment above ceiling	allowed	not allowed	
- solidarity	income/family/age	income/family/age	community
- coverage	complete	complete	at least basic
- co-insurance	yes	yes	yes
Competition/control			
- free choice of insurer	yes	yes	yes
- free entry insurers	no^{+}	yes	yes
- sponsor	no	no	yes
- freedom to set prices	yes	no^{+}	yes
- ex-ante risk adjustment	yes^{-}	yes^{-}	yes
- select/exclude providers	no	yes^{-}	yes

company funds and from 11 percent to 17 percent for regional funds in 1993. The effect of allowing free choice between funds is likely to narrow these ranges substantially in Germany in the years to come.

In order to reduce risk selection problems, the managed competition model prescribes ex-ante risk adjustment. In Germany there is the newly instated risk structure settlement (Risikostrukturausgleich). This scheme transfers contributions from funds with a lower risk pool to funds with higher risk members, where risk is measured by nation-wide expected expenditures broken down by region (East, West), age, and gender. The German risk-adjustment scheme remains somewhat simplistic, as it does not take into account other relevant parameters for evaluating the risk structure, such as occupation or income. Although it is better than no risk-adjustment, it still leaves the door open for some risk selection behaviour of insurers.

In the Netherlands the mechanism to compensate funds for variation in ex-ante risk profiles also is based on age, gender, and region. A further adjustment is made for the number of subscribers under worker disability. Although still simplistic, this is an improvement, from the point of view of the MC model, over the previous situation. Until recently, redistribution of fund contributions in the Netherlands was not based on ex-ante risk, but nearly fully on ex-post expenditures. Each fund received, or paid, 90 percent of the difference between actual and budgeted expenditures, while the government made up 75 percent of any remaining shortfall (the so-called after-calculation). As a result, even though there was no danger if risk selection, there was no incentive for the insurers to try to reduce the moral hazard on the side of the providers. Starting in 1996, fixed hospital outlays still

Table 14.8 Key characteristics of special insurance

	Germany	Netherlands	NH
Access/affordability			
- enrolment	mandatory	mandatory	mandatory
- solidarity	income/age	income/age	income/age
- coverage	narrow	broad	broad
- co-insurance	yes	yes	yes
Competition/control			
- free choice of insurer	no	no	no
- free entry insurers	no	no	no
- sponsor	no	no	no
- freedom to set prices	no	no	no
- ex-ante risk adjustment	no	no	no
- select/exclude providers	no	yes$^-$	no
Provider payments	FFS[a]	FFS[a]	salary

[a] Fee-for-service

will be subject to 95 percent after-calculation, but redistribution and after-calculation are scheduled to be phased out in three years for variable hospital costs and all other provisions.

Finally funds barely have the tools to influence the major source of their expenses, namely payments for health care provisions. At present, the sickness funds in Germany and the Netherlands are not allowed to integrate with providers. Funds still cannot participate in the delivery of health care services, or invest in capacity. Since 1992, funds in the Netherlands do have limited ability to vary the conditions of contracts with independant providers.

Customers and Special Insurance. In both countries, a separate compulsory insurance scheme has been created which covers the whole population for long-term health expenses. Fund contributions are a fixed percentage of income up to a ceiling. In the Netherlands, the fund (AWBZ) is rather comprehensive, and in 1992 covered nearly half of all health care expenses. The scheme was originally meant to provide universal coverage for difficult to insure health risks and for long-term nursing care, but since 1992, mental health care, family care, pharmaceuticals, medical devices, and rehabilitation were also covered. In 1996, the latter three items were excluded, shifting 12.5 percentage points of health expenses back to sickness funds and private insurance. In Germany, ''Pflegeversicherung,'' or nursing care insurance is being introduced to cover the risk of daily care caused by illness or handicap, and will absorb about 3 percent of total direct health care

Table 14.9 Key characteristics of private insurance

	Germany	Netherlands	MC
Access/affordability			
- ensured access	no	yes	yes
- co-insurance	yes	yes	yes
- solidarity	no	no	community
- coverage	varies	varies	transparent
Competition/control			
- free choice of insurer	yes$^-$	yes$^-$	yes
- free entry insurers	yes	yes	yes
- freedom to set prices	yes	yes	yes
- ex-ante risk adjustment	no[a]	no[a]	yes
- select/exclude providers	no	yes$^-$	yes

[a] premiums are risk-rated.

costs.

The special insurance appears to resemble the National Health model, to a large degree, as shown in Table 14.8. There is mandatory participation and a centralized budget for current expenses and investments. However, the providers are not directly under contract but deliver services on a negotiated fee-for-service basis. This makes controlling the variable portion of the budget rather difficult, owing to supplier-induced demand problems.

Recently, co-insurance has been instated in the AWBZ for most provisions. However, given that the nature of provision covered, it seems aimed more to help finance the system, rather than to alter consumer incentives.

The special insurance provides an important relief valve for the pressures of health plans in managed competition to engage in risk selection. Because the use of health care is very skewed among insurees, as mentioned before, the incentives for risk selection are very high, even with ex-ante risk adjustment. If these low probability, high cost events are covered by special insurance, it would let plans dis-enroll such patients after the fact, thus reducing the incentive for selection. Further, special insurance compensates for a tendency towards under-insurance owing to myopic behaviour towards catastrophic events on the part of consumers.

Customers and Private Insurance. Both Germany and the Netherlands have private insurance available for individuals whose income is above the compulsory insurance limit. Table 14.9 shows some key characteristics of the interactions between private insurers and customers. In the Netherlands, 31 percent of the population is privately insured, compared with 9 percent in Germany.[5] In the Netherlands, individuals can freely choose among insurers; even high-risk customers are ensured of some form of coverage.[6] In Germany insurers can exclude risky individuals or offer prohibitively expensive contracts.[7] Coverage, co-insurance, and premiums can vary per insurance contract. The risk-rated premiums generally vary according to age, and in the Netherlands sometimes gender of the insured.

Adverse selection problems, which arise with risk-rated insurance, are dealt with in the MC model through ex-ante risk adjustment. This feature, however, is lacking in both Germany and the Netherlands.[8] Other deviations from the MC model which hamper competition relate to the inability of insurers to selectively contract with providers; insurers therefore can not gain competitive advantage by offering access to care with a better price/quality ratio. Lastly, coverage and premiums vary so widely across contracts that customers may have difficulty in making economically sound choices in an environment without a sponsor.

A subtle but important obstacle to competition exists in the premium structure of German private insurance. Although risk clearly varies by age, individuals pay a constant premium based on their expected remaining lifetime risk. This scheme mixes insurance with forced savings. Unfortunately, the accumulated savings are not transportable and therefore lock customers into a particular insurance contract. Insurance companies in Germany thus focus their marketing attention on those earning above the compulsory insurance ceiling who are not yet privately insured. Possibly, insurers give low quotes of the lifetime premium in order to attract new customers, and then later adjust the rates when faced with higher costs, or a steeper age-cost profile. Increases in premiums for existing older customers, for the above and other reasons, have become prevalent in recent years.

14.2.2 Insurers and Delivery Systems

This section looks at delivery systems in Germany and the Netherlands. From a medical point of view, remarkable variations in delivery exist between and within countries; see also Table 14.14. From an economic perspective, however, both

---

[5] In Germany, customers whith income above the mandatory ceiling may voluntarily enroll in a sickness fund, instead of purchasing private insurance. Many choose to do so, because the private insurance premiums disfavour families with children.

[6] The Law on access to health insurance (WTZ) sets a maximum price and minimum coverage for contracts which insurers must offer to any customer.

[7] Insurers may not dis-enroll existing customers. Further, high-income individuals with pre-existing conditions may still enroll with a Sickness Fund, in most cases.

[8] In the Netherlands, a transfer takes place from private to sickness fund insurance, based on the relatively low enrolment of elderly in private insurance.

Table 14.10 Payment methods for care

	GP[a]	Specialist	Pharmacy	Hospital
Netherlands				
Sickness fund	Cap	FFS*	FFS	FFS*
AWBZ		FFS*	FFS*	FFS*
Private insurance	FFS*	FFS*	FFS	FFS*
Germany				
Sickness fund	RVS	Sal+	Bdgt	FFS*
Private insurance	FFS	FFS	FFS	FFS
NH	Sal	Sal	Bdgt	Bdgt
MC	free to contract, usually Cap or Sal			

[a] For Germany, ambulatory specialist have been included in GP column.
FFS: Fee-for-service; RVS: relative value scale & conversion
Cap: Capitation payment; Sal: Salary; Bdgt: Planned
* negotiated budget or tariffs.

countries show great similarities with respect to delivery. In essence in both countries policy makers try to keep delivery per health sector within predetermined budgets. The delivery systems are therefore quite close to the NH model. In both countries governments try enforce these budgets almost completely; often budget control remains an elusive goal. This section describes delivery institutions per sector of health care in more detail.

Payments to Providers. Table 14.10 displays the method with which various insurance schemes reimburse providers for delivered services in the comparison countries. The fee-for-service (FFS) method allows a provider to bill for every service. Sometimes, the fee schedule is the result of negotiations between interested parties, rather than unilaterally set by the providers; this is denoted by a '*' in the table. Very similar to negotiated fee-for-service is the relative value scale (RVS). This payment method assigns weights or points to each provision, usually determined by the providers, while the conversion factor between the points and a monetary value is determined through some form of negotiation. Capitation (Cap) is a fixed fee paid for each potential customer in a given time period. In some instances, providers are paid on a straight salary basis, or salary plus some other form of compensation (denoted with a '+'). As shown in the table, fee-for-service is the norm, even though total budgets are negotiated as a means of controlling prices.

General Practitioners. General practitioners in the Netherlands receive a capitation fee from the sickness funds, but can charge a fee-for-service for privately insured individuals. The capitation fee and the tariffs for the fee-for-service are set at a national level by the COTG, the Central Agency for Health Care Tariffs (see COTG, 1994).

GPs are the gatekeeper to the system and will prevent sickness fund patients from visiting a specialist if they deem it unnecessary. On the other hand, the capitation payment GPs receive for sickness fund patients provides an incentive to pass them on to secondary care givers, instead of providing primary care.

In Germany, GPs and ambulatory specialists are paid using a relative value scale (RVS). The relative fee schedule is negotiated among the physicians, while the conversion factor depends on the total federal budget, negotiated by fund representatives, doctors and the so-called committee "Konzertierte Aktion," in which are represented sickness funds, insurers, physicians and local government. The precise conversion factor is negotiated in a decentralized manner within each Land, by each fund or each private insurer, with the doctors union. Physicians submit the treatment points for each patient to the union, which collects from the sickness funds and insurers and pays the physicians. Although this method is administratively simple for the physicians, and provides a transparent way of fixing an aggregate budget for physicians services, it may induce higher utilization of other health care items.

Under FFS* or RVS, each physician has an incentive to increase the number of treatments, as this will increase her salary for any given tariff or conversion factor. It is a typical collective action problem that the increased treatment performed by all physicians results in a lower conversion rate, given a global budget, and thereby leaves average income unchanged. The burden on the overall health care budget, however, increases owing to increases in the volume of complementary treatments, such as hospital admissions, diagnostics, or pharmaceutical prescriptions. The problem becomes especially severe when physicians have a stake in diagnostic equipment, as they can over-utilize these to supplement stagnating income; indeed, doctors who have their own X-ray equipment prescribe far more images per patient than doctors who do not (see Sachverständigenrat, 1988).

Hospital-based Specialists. Hospital based physicians in Germany are generally on staff, and receive a salary. However, the "Chefarzt," the leading physician, can often quadruple his hospital salary, of around DM 120,000, by accepting patients with private insurance into the ward and billing them on a fee-for-service basis. Often the care of these patients is provided by staff physicians at a lower position in the hierarchy, such as the "Oberarzte" or even residents and interns.

In the Netherlands, hospital based specialists are paid a fee-for-service, with the fees negotiated at a national level by the COTG. In 1989, under threat of government interference, specialists and insurers agreed on a method to control expenditures. The so-called Five-Party-Agreement set out to fix the number of provisions at the 1989 level for three years. In case of an excess, the tariffs were to be reduced in the subsequent year, to maintain spending levels. Further, the tariff structure of the sickness fund and private insurers was to converge following a transition period.

The Agreement failed to work as planned - as witnessed by increased expenditures from 1989 through 1992 - for a variety of reasons. Demography and technological change put upward pressure on the number of provisions, but mostly specialists, faced with the collective action problem, increased provisions, or shifted to more profitable provisions. The increases in provisions led to a substantial reduction in tariffs in 1993. Since then, rather than allowing physicians to determine the relative values per treatment category on their own, the government determines the appropriate average income level for each medical specialty. From this normative income level, a price per unit provision is backed out, given the current pattern and number of provisions. If the number of provisions rises in a subsequent year, the tariffs are reduced accordingly. In 1996, the tariffs were reduced by 18 percent. Besides control of the physicians incomes, the number of physicians is directly controlled by limits on available positions at hospitals.

Hospitals. Hospitals in Germany receive funds by charging a bed-day rate or by receiving a prospective payment for patients admitted for one of 26 diagnosis related illness groups. The latter scheme puts hospitals at-risk if they use more resources than budgeted for a typical patient in one of the groups. The bed-day rate for patients falling outside the 26 groups is determined by evaluating actual costs in the previous year and dividing by the planned number of bed-days. If the hospital exceeds the number of budgeted bed-days, every additional bed-day is paid for at 10% of the rate, while planned bed-days not used receive 50% of the bed-day rate. Although this seemingly provides an incentive to limit the number of bed-days, the use of actual costs to determine future budgets outweighs this effect and results in over-utilization. Some form of cost-control has been built into the payment system, however, as sickness fund insurance only reimburses the rate of the two most efficiently operated suitable hospitals in the region. Hospital capacity in Germany is planned to achieve an 85% occupancy rate, and the investment is provided by the Lands.

In the Netherlands, the COTG sets national rates for secondary services provided in the hospital. The bed-day rate is then determined by subtracting the payments of the secondary provisions from planned acceptable costs and dividing the remainder by planned bed-days. Acceptable costs vary according to the catchment population, hospital capacity, expected production (e.g. bed-days, daily care, policlinic visits), depreciation, maintenance, and other costs. Shortfalls or surpluses in a hospital's budget are compensated by an adjustment to the bed-day rate in the following year. Hospital capacity, in beds and specialists positions, have traditionally been planned by the central government. Following reductions in capacity between 1991 and 1995, hospitals will have more liberty to determine their own capacity in the future. However, their plans, usually financed by banks, will remain subject to government approval.

Pharmaceuticals. Delivery of pharmaceuticals is subject to the same problems of asymmetric information between patient and physician, and of disconnection between consumption and payment, as the provisions discussed above. The problems are further exasperated by the fact that pharmaceutical manufacturers often have monopoly power, through patents. Of course, patent protection is a well accepted means of getting close to a dynamically efficient economic environment, where firms can charge more than the low marginal cost of production in order to recoup the R&D investment needed for creation of the knowledge-intensive good. Nonetheless, attempts have been made in Germany and Netherlands to control expenditures in various ways.

A first method of achieving lower prices is the substitution of generic drugs for high priced name brands, once a patent has expired. This seemingly straightforward option is hampered by anti-competitive behaviour in the distribution chain, inertia or lack of information among physicians, and indifference among consumers. Some combination of these problems must be tackled in order for the substitution to take place.

In Germany, pharmacists are obliged to substitute the cheaper alternative if a physician prescribes a drug by its substance name, or states that substitution is allowed. In the Netherlands, a pharmacist *may* substitute in this case, but not in case of a brand-name prescription. Unfamiliarity with substance names, as well as the ease of writing down the short well-known name brand, has been shown to influence physicians' perscription-writing habits (see Hellerstein, 1994). Further, even if a physician states the substance name, the Dutch rule won't stimulate substitution unless the incentives for the pharmacist are in favour of providing the generic drug, or if the consumer faces a co-payment which is higher for the name brand. Given volume discounts, reductions in purchase price, and bonuses from brand-name manufacturers, pharmacists can realise very high mark-ups on brand names and find substitution financially unattractive.

Reductions in prices also can occur through lowering of the margins of wholesalers and pharmacists, either through increased competition or by direct regulation. Technological advances in inventory control, just-in-time ordering and logistics have greatly reduced costs of technically similar distribution operations, and should allow for reduced margins, while maintaining reasonable income levels for the well-trained pharmacists. Deregulation measures in the Netherlands in 1996 allow for competition, such as mail-order pharmacies and insurer-run dispensaries, and should speed adoption of these technologies.

More effective towards price reductions are methods of reducing consumer indifference towards pharmaceutical prices by means of co-insurance. In both countries, new compensation schemes have been set up which limit insurance reimbursement for each category of drugs, and make the consumer responsible for any excess charge. In the Netherlands, the average price of the alternative drugs in a category is the maximum allowed for reimbursement, while in Germany the lowest available price is the maximum allowable charge. The scheme relies on a list of available drugs for each therapeutic effect, or with similar active components, in order to allow cost-effective choices. The effect of these schemes has been an increase in market share of generics, and reductions in prices of the name brands. However, pharmaceutical firms attempt to circumvent the system by marketing slightly altered versions of drugs for which no alternative exists.

Direct price controls in the Netherlands, based on the Law on Pharmaceuticals, take the form of a maximum price within each drug category equal to the average price of the same drugs in neighbouring countries. This measure is a response to clear price discrimination by pharmaceutical companies which resulted in high drug prices in the Netherlands. The effects of this price setting, which is being phased in starting in mid-1996, are expected to be significant.

The other approach towards reducing pharmaceutical expenditures is through constraining number of prescriptions. In the Law on Health Reform (Gesundheitsreformgesetz 1988) Germany instated a fixed maximum prescription volume for every physician, with an investigation in case of excesses. Further, a 'Negativliste' was compiled with drugs which became ineligible for compensation; mostly the list covered drugs which are considered over-the-counter in other countries. Overall, the success of these measure in reducing volume (growth) has not become apparent in the data. Germany continues to have much higher per capita pharmaceutical usage than the Netherlands, where drug use is among the lowest in Europe.

14.2.3 Assessment of Institutions

Given the similarities in the economic institutions of the health care systems in Germany and the Netherlands, especially when compared with the stylized MC and NH models, what has been learned from comparing the details? Both countries have a system which contain competitive and control mechanisms. The political attempts to manage costs relies on a three-pronged attack: First, limiting the cost of premiums, mostly by cautiously introducing competitive elements, such as free choice of insurer. Next, keeping costs of provisions at or below available premiums, lastly through limiting the supply of provisions. The method to achieve the latter two goals still relies heavily on control mechanisms.

Insurance. The insurance schemes available in Germany and the Netherlands resemble each other, but also have some subtle differences. The sickness funds and private insurance markets have been moving in the direction of managed competition, but major impediments remain. The lack of a sponsor who collects information about coverage, premiums and quality of care impairs the ability of customers to make rational choices. Further, free choice by customers has increased the incentives for risk-selection by insurers. Most importantly, insurers still lack the tools necessary to influence the payments to health care providers, either by affecting price or quantity. The competitive elements introduced thus may increase efficiency in the administrative tasks of the insurers, but cannot affect the largest component of expenditures. Consequently, if the system fails to perform as envisioned by proponents of more competition, this can not be considered as evidence for failure of the MC model.

The special insurance schemes in both countries resemble the NH model. An important deviation exists, namely that provisions are reimbursed under fee-for-service. The control of allocated budgets may be difficult to implement.

In conclusion, the insurance systems have moved toward MC, but competitive forces are held in check through remaining impediments, and the scope for improvement is limited without an integrated link to the delivery system.

Delivery. The delivery systems in Germany and the Netherlands are subject to many forms of control, especially with regard to budgets, and therefore resemble to a certain degree the NH model. Hospital capacity is planned, hospital budgets and occupancy rates are targeted, pharmaceutical prices are capped, among other forms of control. However, the key market failure of moral hazard on the provider side continues to put upward pressure on the amount of treatment. This is the key difference from the NH model where salaried providers, if anything, have an incentive to under-provide. The German and Dutch system of paying physicians based on tariffs that get reduced if over-treatment takes place at the macro level is rather indirect and continues to place incentives at the micro-level for over-provision.

In conclusion, the delivery systems have thus moved toward the NH system, but the benefits of NH cannot be reaped because a key market failure is not addressed.

14.3 Performance of Health Care Institutions

How do the institutions affect the performance of the health care systems in Germany and the Netherlands? To measure performance, it seems logical to measure the extent to which the systems achieve the principle goals, namely accessibility, affordability and quality. How does one measure these achievements? For access, this is relatively straightforward: simple criteria are the share of uninsured population and the width of coverage. Suitable criteria for quality are much harder to define, because the 'output' of the health care sector, namely good health, depends on many other factors. Appropriate affordability indicators also require well defined health care output measures. Consequently, for quality and affordability, one must rely on partially informative data on system inputs and throughputs.

Table 14.11 Access-indicators

	D	NL	GB	USA
	in %			
Insured population	99	99	100	85
Coverage	broad	broad	varying	broad

14.3.1 Performance Indicators

Accessibility. In Table 14.11, access indicators are presented for Germany and the Netherlands, as well as for the benchmark countries, the United States and the United Kingdom. Only in the United States is a high percentage of the population uninsured. In the other countries, all low-income families enjoy compulsory insurance, with broad coverage of primary and secondary care, and at least adequate coverage of pharmaceuticals and long-term care.

Quality. Most studies use life-expectancy and mortality rates at various ages to measure health care quality. These data are shown in Table 14.12. The data provide some information on quality. The relatively high life expectancy of the elderly in the United States may be explained by the high level of care given to them. On the whole, however, these indicators do not show much variation and might therefore suggest that quality differences are minor. This conclusion is premature. The link between life-expectancy and health care is rather weak, and has been shown to depend on many other factors (see Box 14.3).

Affordability. The task of comparing the performance of the health care systems in Germany and the Netherlands would have been rather straightforward if data on inputs and outputs were directly available. A methodology used for comparisons of performance in manufacturing could then be used to construct total factor productivity measures and to compare the efficacy with which technologies, capital, and labour inputs were utilized in the respective countries. Observed differences in these measures, over time and across countries, could then be ascribed to differences in financing, regulation, and other institutional arrangements. Unfortunately, such detailed information does not exist. Only recently, a pilot-project has been started to collect this information; see Box 14.4. Alternatively, useful insights on affordability can also be obtained by studies that try to unravel increases in health care expenditures, such as undertaken by Cutler (1996); see Box 14.5.

Health Care Expenditures. Owing to the lack of reliable output measures for the health care sector, we have to fall back on traditional indicators of affordability

Box 14.3 The relationship between health and health care

The data on life expectancy and infant mortality are crude indicators of health status. Health care services may be aimed at improving quality of life, rather than at prolonging life. Health also is affected by factors other than health care services, such as income, crime and violence, smoking, eating patterns, environment, socio-economic background, and genetics. Thus, '...infant mortality rates and average life expectancies [...] do not by themselves imply anything about the allocation of health care resources.' (Aaron, 1996: 92).

Advances in medical science and increases in the quantity of health care services, over time, significantly contribute to reductions in morbidity and mortality. Nonetheless, '...differences in health levels within or between developed countries are not primarily related to difference in the quantity or quality of medical care.' (Fuchs, 1996: 3).

Indeed, a prognosis of the future of public health in the Netherlands by RIVM (1993), does not limit itself to studying the role of the health care sector (care and cure). It also places particular emphasis on the salutary effects on longevity and health status of prevention policy (preventative medicine, education on effects of life style choices) and intersectoral policy (environmental and occupational hazards, transportation safety, agricultural policy).

such as expenditures per capita or as a percentage of GDP. Table 14.13 shows health care expenditures for the comparison countries as a percentage of GDP and in 1990 purchasing power parity dollars per capita, respectively. Although precise comparisons may be clouded by statistical problems remaining in the OECD health care data, the broad picture is clear. As mentioned, the United States spends nearly 15 percent of gross domestic product on health care goods and services. Lowest is the United Kingdom share, at close to 7 percent of GDP, while the German rate is slightly higher than in the Netherlands. The United States started diverging significantly from the European countries in the early 1980s, as shown in Figure 14.1. The high expenditures in the United States occur in most categories, with an exception for pharmaceuticals, where Germany spends a larger fraction of income.

By category, the Netherlands spends more per capita than Germany on in-patient and ambulatory care, while Germany spends more on pharmaceuticals. Overall, however, Germany and the Netherlands do not vary all that much in their macro-level health care expenditures. Differences in the age structure and income may have resulted in the slightly higher levels of spending in Germany, but point towards faster increases in the coming years in the Netherlands.[9]

Health Care Inputs. Affordability also is affected by efficient utilization of health care services. Some striking differences in patterns of use may reflect provider incentives rather than medical efficacy. Some comparative data on inputs into

[9] In recent years, Germany has had nearly 3 percentage points more population over 65 years of age than in the Netherlands, boosting German expenditure share on health care by roughly 1 percentage point.

Table 14.12 Life-expectancy and mortality rates for 1991

	D	NL	GB	USA
Life expectancy				
At birth				
male	73.8	74.6	74.2	72.3
female	79.3	80.3	79.5	79.0
At age 45				
male	34.9	35.7	35.9	35.5
female	40.6	41.0	40.6	40.7
At age 60				
male	18.0	18.1	18.3	18.9
female	22.4	22.8	22.4	22.8
At age 80				
male	6.3	6.2	6.7	7.2
female	7.8	8.1	8.6	9.0
Other indicators (rates)				
Infant mortality	.6	.5	.6	.8
Perinatal mortality	.6	.8	.9	.8
Medical complications	3.5	1.4	4.4	10.5

Source: OECD (1996)

health care are shown in Table 14.14.

The number of general practitioners (GPs) per capita reported in the OECD database is more than twice as high in Germany as in the Netherlands. Partly, this reflects a definitional difference: all non-hospital based physicians are labelled GPs in Germany. Even so, the rate of increase of GPs per capita in Germany outpaced that in the Netherlands during the 1980s. In the Netherlands, the GP plays a gatekeeper function in the health care system. All patients insured by the Sickness Funds must first see a GP before being referred to a specialist for further care, if deemed necessary. Because GPs receive a capitation for sickness fund patients, they may be more be more inclined to pass patients on to specialists than to treat them themselves. In Germany, patients can go directly to a specialist, and many specialists, especially in internal medicine, paediatrics, or gynaecology, provide primary care. Despite the incentives to pass sickness fund patients on to specialists, the gatekeeper function of the GP provides a filter for overall health care usage, and may be partly responsible for the relatively low number of specialists in the Netherlands, and the lower number of physician visits by patients.

Significant differences also appear in the number of pharmacists per capita, which is far lower in the Netherlands than in other countries. Partly, this reflects

Box 14.4 McKinsey comparison of health care productivity

McKinsey (1996) attempts to answer the question of why health care expenditures across countries vary so much while life expectancy outcomes show only small differences, by analyzing the productivity with which health care services are performed. Productivity can be measured because the study chose to analyze treatments of a few specific diseases where outcomes and inputs are relatively easily defined. McKinsey studies productivity for treatment of diabetes, cholelithiasis (gallstones), breast cancer, and lung cancer for the United States, the United Kingdom, and Germany. The study analyzes the data in an institutional framework which varies by degree of competition and degree of health care product integration.

The study finds that no country is most productive in treatment of all diseases, but that differences in spending and productivity across countries and diseases can be explained by the institutional setting of the healthcare sector. The United States has the highest expenditures not because of poor productivity, but because of high input costs and administrative costs.[1] *The United States is more productive than Germany in all diseases, but is less productive than the United Kingdom in treatment of diabetes. The United Kingdom out-performs Germany in treatment of gallstones and lung cancer, but loses out in the treatment of breast cancer. Input usage for treatment of the diseases varied more consistently across countries and follows the pattern off aggregate input data. Germany used most resources for treatment of all the diseases, followed by the United States, while the United Kingdom struggled to get by with the lowest available resources.*

McKinsey's recommendations for improving performance in health care are based on their finding that market incentives create powerful forces towards changing behaviour. As such, they suggest that policy makers should allow markets to define health care products and remove regulatory barriers for the provision of integrated care services. Further, they suggest that rapidly evolving technology is best harnessed in a system which allows experimentation and flexibility.

[1] *Remarkably, McKinsey does not count administrative inputs as a relevant factor for productivity measurement, even though they represent nearly 25 percent of total health care costs.*

the low number of prescriptions dispensed per person which is about half the German rate, and partly it reflects the high population density. Pharmacies provide a buffer stock of medicine that is rapidly accessible in time of need, and the high population density allows fewer pharmacies per person while still covering a reasonably sized geographic (travel distance) area.

14.3.2 Overall Performance Assessment

Table 14.15 shows a subjective assessment of the performance of the health care systems in Germany and the Netherlands, as well as in the United Kingdom and the United States for comparison purposes. On balance the relative performance of the German and Dutch systems is good.

Table 14.13 Health care expenditures, 1993[a]

	D	NL	GB	USA
	% of GDP			
Total healthcare	9.56	8.82	6.88	14.50
Public	7.02	6.83	5.80	7.02
In-patient	2.91	4.62	2.95	6.17
Ambulatory	2.49	2.54	...	4.62
Pharmaceuticals	1.76	.94	1.10	1.24
	1990 $ PPP per capita			
Total healthcare	1941	1641	1211	3516
Public	1427	1274	1019	1559
Pharmaceuticals	327	175	186	291
In-patient	540	858	499	1521
Ambulatory	463	472	...	1138
Hospital expenditures	1990 $ PPP			
In patient				
Per bed day	265	426	647	1383
Per admission	4185	14071	5908	11703
Acute				
Per bed day	...	929	953	1385
Per admission	...	8930	4516	7762

[a] Latest available year after 1991, unless noted

Source: OECD (1996).

Accessibility. Accessibility no longer is an issue in most industrialized countries, the United States being a notable exception. The United Kingdom was the first of the comparison countries to provide universal coverage in 1948, with Germany and the Netherlands expanding access during the 1960s. The United Kingdom has provided health care through the NHS, with services available to the whole population. Germany and the Netherlands have a mandatory income-related insurance scheme for the majority of the population (sickness funds), with an escape hatch for wealthiest segment of the population to purchase private insurance. In the United State, less than two-thirds of the population is covered under private or employer group insurance, while an escape hatch exists for the poor and elderly to obtain government funded coverage. However, more than 15 percent of the population is without any form of health coverage.

Box 14.5 Technology and health care expenditure growth

Recently, Cutler (1996) attempted a back-of-the-envelope decomposition of the long run increases in real per capita health care expenditures. He first identified and roughly quantified the contributions of seven potential factors. The factors all were assumed to be independent of each other, so that results could be summed. The residual increase was attributed to changes in technology, and its contribution amounted to roughly half the increase in time. The table below shows the potential causes and their contributions.

Table *Factors contributing to health care expenditure growth in the USA, 1940-1990*

Factor	*Increase due to*	*Contribution*
	percent	
Total increase	*790*	-
Static factors	*399*	*51*
Demographics	*14*	*2*
Income	*37*	*5*
Spread of insurance	*100*	*13*
Relative price changes	*147*	*19*
Administrative expense	*101*	*13*
Factor rents	*0*	*0*
Residual	*391*	*49*

Source: Cutler (1996), Table 3.

Quality. Comparisons are by far the hardest to make. Meaningful output measures are hard to come by, and subjective questions about a population's approval of the health care system may reflect concerns other than quality. Nonetheless, it is probably fair to say that in the United States the latest in medical procedures and technology is at the disposal of those fortunate enough to have insurance, while the uninsured may receive second-rate care. In the United Kingdom fairly rigid capacity often leads to waiting lists for non-vital treatment, causing prolonged discomfort for many patients. Further, adoption of new technology is rather slow. In Germany and the Netherlands, introduction of the very latest in technology also is slightly delayed, and its utilization kept under control. In the Netherlands, supply of care for the elderly, especially in the final stages of their lives, is conservative. On balance, however, it is unlikely that the quality of care in Germany or the Netherlands is below that in the United States on average.

Affordability. Affordability cuts straight to the heart(burn) of policy problems. As shown, the United Kingdom has the most affordable system, either per capita or

Table 14.14 Health care inputs, 1993[a]

	D	NL	GB	USA
	per 100 000 population			
Health care employment	2851.3	2366.4	2006.3	3139.5
Physicians	328.4	250.5[b]	154.2	250.1
GP	110.4	43.4	58.6	22.1
Specialists	181.1	83.4[b]	...	114.5[c]
Pharmacists	53.8	16.1	59.1	74.6
	number per year			
Visits per person	12.8	5.7	5.8	5.9
Prescriptions per person	13.9c	8.0	9.0	6.5d

[a] Latest available year after 1991, unless noted. [b] 1990 [c] 1989 [d] 1984

Source: OECD (1996).

as a percent of income. It is also affordable for all individuals, because the system is funded through general tax revenue and therefore takes its bite out of income. In the United States, aggregate expenditures for health care have ballooned. Moreover, because insurance is generally provided through risk-rating, or community rating in the case of HMOs, low income workers find an increasingly large share of their income going to health care, and many are squeezed out of the system. In the Netherlands and Germany much effort goes into controlling the premiums and expenditures of the sickness funds as well as the quantity of health care provisions, resulting in per capita costs somewhere between the United Kingdom and the United States. However, the current direction of technological change may continue to increase the burden, regardless of the institutional changes made.

14.4 Trends

As described in Chapter 2, exogenous trends may invoke institutional adjustment because the conditions favouring certain institutional arrangements shift under influence of trends. In this section, a description will be given of relevant trends which alter the position on the trade-offs made by existing institutional arrangements. Because most of the trends are also relevant for social protection, topic of Chapter 6, discussion here will be brief. A summary of the impact of trends is given in Table 14.16.

Table 14.15 Performance Assessment

	D	NL	GB	USA
Accessibility	+	+	+	-/+
Affordability	+	+	++	-/-
Quality	+	+	_	-/++

Economic Trends. The clearest economic trend is the continuing increase in per capita income in the Netherlands and Germany. Historically, and across countries, per capita income has been a good predictor of health care expenditures, with expenditures rising more rapidly than income. The latter feature will exacerbate political risks in a system where overall expenditures do not naturally follow customer desires. This strengthens the case for managed competition. Greater opportunities for international mobility point in the same direction. On the other hand the trend towards greater income dispersion, as a result of e.g. biased technological change, strengthens the case for national health to secure accessibility for vulnerable groups.

Demographic Trends. The demographic trend of an aging population puts pressure on the system through a number of channels. First, and foremost, expected expenditures are much higher for the elderly. Second, if health care financing takes place through payroll taxes, the reduction in the active/inactive ratio will reduce available funds. Political pressures resulting from the increased demand on funds will be larger under the national health system than under managed competition. On the other hand elderly people may exhibit a preference for experimentation and flexibility in health care, if it increases the pace of technological advances and their adoption. These characteristics are best provided under managed competition.

Social Trends and Trends in Preferences. The trends of increasing heterogeneity in society as well as less common norms and a greater preference for freedom to choose generally shift the trade-off towards managed competition.

Technological Trends. Information technology provides better opportunities to screen the customers, stimulating risk selection. This trend points in the direction of national health. On the other hand, faster evolution of medical technology would increase the desire for experimentation and flexibility, thus favouring managed care.

Table 14.16 The impact of trends on strengths of NH vs. MC

Trends	National health	Managed competition
Demographic		
Aging: smaller contribution base		+
Aging: desire for commitment and certainty	+	
Aging: desire for new technology		+
Economic environment		
Income level		+
More income dispersion	+	
More institutional mobility		+
Technology		
IT improved screening	+	
Medical: high cost		+
Social		
More heterogeneous risk features		+
Less common norms		+
Preferences		
More heterogeneous		+
More preference for choice		+

14.5 Policy Options

14.5.1 Policy Options for the Netherlands

Although both systems are quite similar and also have moved in the same direction during the last years, some characteristics of the German health care system stand out that provide relevant policy options for the Dutch. Germany does not allow insurer/provider integration as a means of using competitive incentives to curb provider moral hazard. However, the German method of negotiating the relative value scale (RVS) of provisions among physicians, as well as peer review of budget excessive treatment is a cooperative mechanism that may mitigate the problem somewhat. Nonetheless, the Netherlands cannot look to Germany for policy options from an operative MC system.

14.5.2 Policy Options for Germany

Germany utilizes more specialist and hospital care than the Netherlands. The GP as gatekeeper in the Netherlands has often been credited with screening for over-use (see De Melker, 1997). GPs in the Netherlands feature among the lowest pharmaceutical prescription rates in OECD countries, and provide treatments for many simple ills rather than referring patients to more expensive secondary care. It may be worthwhile to assess how such a gatekeeper function could be introduced into the German system.

14.5.3 The Unfinished Agenda

Both health systems performed reasonably well up to now, but not without unremitting policy effort. The systems will come under increased pressure in the years to come because the observed trends are expected to boost demand. This guarantees a continuing public debate on how to strike a balance between affordability, accessibility and quality; as well as on which coordination mechanisms should be used to manage the health care system.

From the perspective of the analytical framework of Section 14.1 the main market failure that both countries have not tackled so far is moral hazard from the side of the provider. Both models of health care, MC as well as NH, address this market failure. Section 14.1.4 concluded, however, that the MC model scores better in aligning the private incentives of providers with desired behaviour than the NH-model does. Because moral hazard toward over-provision is the key market failure that goes unchecked in Germany and the Netherlands, it is a logical step to first explore the scope for more managed competition in the system. More competition also yields more diversity and experimentation, which would fit nicely with a number of trends, such as a more heterogenous population and the radical character of technological change.

More managed competition would come at a price, however. First, the diversity brought about by more managed competition implies more differences in service levels, in other words more inequality. Whereas vulnerable groups may benefit from enhanced efficiency, they may gain less than other groups. Second, although managed competition alleviates risk selection through ex-ante risk adjustment, it is difficult to avoid a tendency for sneaking risk selection which is wasteful of resources. Proper ex-ante risk adjustment is a tricky business, which is likely to involve substantial transaction costs. Third, greater diversity in the health system reduces economies of scale, especially with respect to administration costs. Also this increases the transaction costs of the system.

Counter-arguments to these drawbacks of MC are that high income families can already opt-out of the present system by buying expensive treatments in private clinics. Indeed, this is a well-known phenomenon under the NHS in the United Kingdom. Secondly, sneaking risk selection can be mitigated in the German and Dutch health systems through the special insurance scheme for catastrophic risks.

On balance the price of more managed competition does not seem high enough to obstruct more experimentation with managed competition. In view of the strong preferences for equal treatment in Germany and the Netherlands, we suggest to start with a *limited* experiment, also because managed competition entails sailing into untested waters. This is a major difference with the ill-fated Dekker-Simonsplan, which a few years ago tried to introduce managed competition in the Dutch health system. Whereas that plan was a blueprint for the entire health sector, we suggest a more limited scope initially. In fact, the proposal broadens the range of coordination-mechanisms the government uses to influence the health care sector. The diversification of the policy mix will produce more information on what *does* work and what *does not* work. Moreover, because of its experimental and small-scale character, policy-makers maintain flexibility to adjust the plan or, if results are disappointing, to reverse it.

What could this experiment with managed competition involve? Various experiments would be possible. The transition of sickness fund insurance to a full MC system could be completed. Mostly, this requires allowing unlimited contracting of providers, and fleshing out the tasks of the sponsor. The risk is that expenditures may rise under MC, jeopardizing the political support for solidarity inherent in sickness fund insurance. Instead, we suggest to complete the introduction of managed competition in the private insurance sector and leave the sickness funds and special insurance schemes unchanged, at least initially. Our suggestions contain the following features:

- Mandatory insurance with guaranteed acceptance for all customers not eligible for sickness fund insurance. This resolves adverse selection.
- Insurers vie for customers annually with an offer of coverage at or above a minimum level for a community rated premium. This introduces competition and risk solidarity.
- Insurers receive ex-ante risk adjustment based on actual customer-mix. This features mitigates risk selection problems.
- Tax-deductibility of premiums or reimbursement by employers should be limited to the lowest cost insurance contract. Consumers will bear the cost of extra coverage.
- Insurers may select or exclude providers: accordingly the freedom to contract, to set prices and to invest is introduced in the market for private delivery of medical services. This institutional change empowers insurers to combat the moral hazard of the providers.
- National or regional institutes act as sponsors for customers: in both countries, the sponsor could be the government, in the Netherlands the national government and in Germany regional government. The sponsor specifies minimum coverage level and collects insurers' contract offers. Moreover, sponsor provides unbiased information about the price, quality and coverage of various insurance policies in order to make the market more transparent and empower consumers to combat moral hazard of insurance companies. Sponsor further takes care of the ex-ante risk adjustment.

- An independent office that regulates the market of private health care in order to enhance competition among insurers and providers: This office would fall under the supervision of the national competition authorities.
- The sickness funds should be required to submit a contract offer for their standard coverage. This introduces some certainty about availability of coverage. As an added attraction, sickness funds will benefit from a market-based signal on their ability to compete.

What would be the benefits of this proposal? It could remove the most important market failures in private health care. Hence, consumer preferences and costs would be reflected in delivery. We cannot be sure that the rise in health care expenditures will be contained under managed competition. However, this will no longer be perceived as a social problem because it would truly reflect consumer preferences.

Furthermore, managed competition could change the incentive structures for technological change in medicine. Instead of a focus on high cost - low benefit solutions, it could turn medical research towards more cost-effective treatments. For Germany and the Netherlands, however, this effect is probably quite small, because medical R&D in these countries accounts for only a small part of global R&D in this field.

Finally, managed competition for private insurance could create opportunities for experiments and new ideas about insurance and medical care more generally. If successful, these ideas could be transferred to the sickness funds.

One trajectory is to transform the health care system in a three-pillar system comparable to the pension system. The first pillar would be insured catastrophic risks (AWBZ and Pflegeversicherung); just like at present, this insurance would be modelled on the NH-model. Also the second pillar would be mandatory for the entire population. In this pillar, managed competition would apply, with all necessary features. Although insurers offer contracts with community rated premiums, the sponsor can ensure income and family solidarity by making transfers among customers. The third pillar would provide supplementary insurance with full freedom for insurance companies.

15 Concluding Remarks

15.1 Challenging Neighbours?

To what extent, then, do Germany and the Netherlands provide mutual challenges for institutional change, i.e. for social innovation as it was called in CPB (1992)? And what challenges are put to both neighbours by the apparent trends in the external environment?

The preceding chapters have shown that the choice of coordination mechanisms does differ between the two countries. Of course, both rely heavily on competition as the major coordination mechanism in a market economy. But where the market fails, the German soziale Marktwirtschaft tends to supplement the market with control, while the Dutch consultation economy more readily goes for cooperative exchange. Common values and norms are rarely used as a direct coordination mechanism in the economic fields we have studied, but indirectly broadly shared values and norms are required to support the non-market solutions. Indeed, control relies on codified common values and norms, and cannot remain effective long after those values and norms have eroded. Similarly, cooperative exchange requires a common view of the world and of the goals of economic policy to be an effective coordination mechanism.

As was pointed out in Section 2.3.3, the choice of a non-market coordination mechanism may itself be viewed as a problem of investment in relationship-specific assets, involving a trade-off between commitment and flexibility. Control enforces stated commitments, and provides stability in a changing world. Cooperative exchange is more flexible in redefining commitments, but also more easily made ineffective by external changes that affect the choices of the bargaining partners. This may explain why the Dutch economy was so badly hurt in the seventies, when it took a long time for the main social-economic players to regain a common view of the world. Still today, several arrangements in the Dutch institutional system lack in effectiveness, because the underlying values and norms have eroded. The German economy proved more robust in the turmoil of the seventies, but currently it has a difficult time adapting to major changes in internal and external conditions. Indeed, the German rules and legislation codify strong commitments and therefore tend to be rather rigid.

The mutual challenge is to find new combinations in institutional design, learning from the successes and failures of solutions attempted by the neighbours. While neighbours provide particularly relevant experiences because they share many values and norms, inspiration for solving common problems should rather be found elsewhere. That is one reason why the United States and the United Kingdom have often been used as a benchmark. The policy options derived from the comparative analysis should offer food for thought, and thus contribute to the process of social innovation in both countries.

The trends in the external environment are challenging both neighbours. We identified social trends in individual preferences, demographic trends, trends in technology and internationalization. These trends do not unequivocally point towards this or that side of the four trade-offs that society faces in institutional design. But in many cases it does appear that the Anglo-Saxon countries are better prepared to cope with the likely changes in external conditions. This is another reason why the United Kingdom and the United States have often been included in the analysis of alternative coordination mechanisms in different fields. They provide a relevant extension of the scope of ideas that will be required for future institutional success. The challenge to both Germany and the Netherlands is to find those new combinations in institutional design that can build on domestic common values and norms, and yet offer adequate solutions for newly emerging coordination problems. The present exercise in institutional economics intends to contribute to a better understanding of the relevant policy options and perhaps, where necessary, to reshaping the values and norms that underlie the socio-economic mechanisms in both countries.

After the deep crisis in the early eighties, the Netherlands did in fact start a program of institutional change. Slowly but steadily, several weaknesses that had been exposed in the seventies have led and still lead to new arrangements. In particular in the fields of competition policy and the governance of social protection, the German system has served as an example. This study has identified further relevant policy options for corporate governance, the labour market, and electricity and gas markets. In particular for energy, ideas have come from experiences in the United Kingdom.

Germany has also introduced some reforms in the last fifteen years, but the major challenges have come to the fore only after the unification boom. Indeed, Germany now faces the biggest challenge since post-war reconstruction. Will it be able to bring about a second Wirtschaftswunder? Its Dutch neighbour seems to offer some relevant examples in labour market policies, social insurance and higher education policy. Further relevant policy options relate to energy markets and, the most difficult one, governance of the socio-economic order.

Current performance and trends in external conditions define further items on the agenda for reform for both countries, in addition to the policy options derived from the comparative analysis. The most important topics here are a more active pre-emptive labour market strategy and reform in pensions and health care.

Institutions tend to be strongly interrelated and deeply rooted. Hence institutional changes are difficult and gradual, unless a major disruption forces fast adjustment. A policy of gradual change allows more time for careful design and reduces adjustment costs. It is unwise to wait for a crisis to trigger institutional change, because by then adjustment will have become very costly if not impossible to achieve. But some type of problem or conflict may be required to create the sense of urgency needed for change. There must be a shared assessment that the institutions of the past are no longer acceptable and people must trust that they can be replaced by new arrangements that are fair and effective.

15.2 Strengths and Weaknesses of This Study

The research for this book started as an exercise in applied institutional economics. An exciting exercise, which proved to be more difficult and much more extensive than we anticipated.

Institutions are required to solve highly complex interdependent coordination problems under changing conditions. In our view, the main strength of this study is that it provides an adequate theoretical framework to understand the trade-offs that society faces in institutional design. This framework provided the organizing principle for the book. It is used as a tool to scrutinize the rationale and performance of economic institutions, based on analyses of market and government failure. The framework also helps to study the impact of future trends on the positions of the trade-offs and on the relative merits of the competing properties for economic performance.

The theoretical framework is firmly rooted in micro-economics. Moreover, we found it to be an effective instrument in interpreting most real-world institutional arrangements. Indeed, the theory proved to be so powerful that we could identify some weak spots in institutions; prominent examples are found in corporate governance, health care and the governance of social protection.

The main weakness of the present study is the lack of empirical evidence on the relation between institutional design and economic performance. It proved to be very difficult to link a specific institutional setup to a particular set of economic results. For example, it would have been interesting to measure the effect of alternative systems of corporate governance on indicators of company performance, like profitability or the price of capital. Or to assess the quantitative impact of pension reform on early retirement; the size of the effect of technology policies on economic growth; or indeed the quantitative importance of an alternative socio-economic order.

The problem here is not that we did not do our homework in econometrics. Rather, more often than not such empirical evidence can be derived only from new and unconventional data. Well designed experiments, like the Rand Health Experiment, may provide the type of data needed to answer the relevant empirical questions. Multi-country surveys with sufficient information on institutional detail could help to estimate the performance effects of institutional design.

Other weaknesses of the study are readily listed. Though the preceding chapters do cover a wide range of issues, some relevant areas are hardly touched. Some fields, like infrastructure and environment issues, have recently been covered in other studies for the Netherlands. Others are planned to be studied in the near future.

Not much attention has been given to the question how the current institutional design in Germany and the Netherlands has come about. Which factors in history, economics and culture have shaped the existing system? Such an analysis could contribute further insights into the forces of social innovation and perhaps help find appropriate institutions for either country in the next decades.

Finally, the choice of countries studied in this book clearly is very selective. It had to be, to keep the project manageable. Now that this pilot project has been finished, we or others can apply the instruments that were developed to other countries, perhaps focusing on one or two fields of interest.

Indeed, there is plenty of scope for further research. We do intend to make further contributions at CPB, and welcome all initiatives from colleagues to enhance our knowledge on the relationships between institutional design and economic performance.

References

To present an overview of the literature used for different subjects in the study, the list of references is organized by chapter.

Chapter 1 Comparing German and Dutch Institutions

Albert, M. (1992), *Kapitalisme Contra Kapitalisme*, (Capitalism Contre Capitalism, 1991), Contact, Amsterdam.

Ark, B. van, J. de Haan and H.J. de Jong (1996), 'Characteristics of Economic Growth in the Netherlands During the Postwar Period', in N. Crafts and G. Toniolo (eds.), *Economic Growth in Europe Since 1945*, Cambridge University Press, Cambridge.

Bruno, M. and J. Sachs (1985), *Economics of Worldwide Stagflation*, Basil Blackwell, Oxford.

CPB (1992), *Scanning the Future: a Long Term Scenario Study of the World Economy 1990-2015*, CPB Netherlands Bureau of Economic Policy Analysis, Sdu Publishers, The Hague.

Drazen, A. and E. Helpman (1988), 'The Effects of Policy Anticipations on Stabilisation Programs', *European Economic Review*, 680-686.

EZ (1995), *Competitiveness Indicators*, Dutch Ministry of Economic Affairs, The Hague.

Giersch, H., K.-H. Paqué and H. Schmieding (1992), *The Fading Miracle: Four Decades of Market Economy in Germany*, Cambridge University Press, Cambridge.

Krugman, P. (1994), 'Competitiveness: a Dangerous Obsession', *Foreign Affairs*, 73, 28-44.

——— (1996), 'Making Sense of the Competitiveness Debate', *Oxford Review of Economic Policy*, 12, 17-25.

Lal, D. and H. Myint (1996), *The Political Economy of Poverty, Equity and Growth*, Clarendon Press, Oxford.

Lawrence, R.Z., A. Bressand and T. Ito (1996), *A Vision for the World Economy: Openness, Diversity, and Cohesion*, The Brookings Institution, Washington.

Lindbeck A. (1976), 'Stabilization Policy in Open Economies with Endogenous Politicians', *American Economic Review*, Papers and Proceedings, May, 1-19.

Maddison, A. (1983), 'Economic Stagnation Since 1973, Its Nature and Causes: a Six Country Survey', *De Economist*, 131, 585-608.

North, D.C. (1994), 'Economic Performance Through Time', *American Economic Review*, 84, 359-368.

Olson, M., jr. (1996), 'Big Bills Left on the Sidewalk: Why Some Nations are Rich and Others Poor', *Journal of Economic Perspectives*, 10, 3-24.
Siebert, H. (ed.) (1995), *Locational Competition in the World Economy*, J.C.B. Mohr, Tübingen.
Sinn, G., and H.-W. Sinn (1992), *Jumpstart: the Economic Unification of Germany*, MIT Press, Cambridge, Mass.

Chapter 2 The Interplay of Institutions, Trade-offs, Performance and Trends

Akerlof, G.A. (1970), 'The Market for Lemons: Qualitative Uncertainty and the Market Mechanism', *Quarterly Journal of Economics*, 84, 488-500.
Armstrong, M., S. Cowan and J. Vickers (1994), *Regulatory Reform: Economic Analysis and British Experience*, MIT Press, Cambridge Mass.
Best, M.H. (1990), *The New Competition: Institutions of Industrial Restructuring*, Polity Press, Cambridge.
Blair, M.M. (1995), *Ownership and Control: Rethinking Corporate Governance for the Twenty-First Century*, The Brookings Institution, Washington.
Bovenberg, A.L. and A.S.M. van der Linden (1996), 'Can We Afford to Grow Old?', CPB Netherlands Bureau for Economic Policy Analysis, Research Memorandum no. 134.
Caballero, R.J. and M.L. Hammour (1996a), 'The "Fundamental Transformation" in Macroeconomics', *American Economic Review*, Papers and Proceedings, 181-186.
——— (1996b), 'On the Timing and Efficiency of Creative Destruction', *The Quarterly Journal of Economics*, 805-852.
——— (1996c), 'The Macroeconomics of Specificity', National Bureau of Economic Research, NBER Working Paper no. 5757, Cambridge, Mass.
Carlin, W., and D. Soskice (1997), 'Shocks to the System: the German Political Economy under Stress', *National Institute Economic Review*, 1, 57-76.
Chang, H.-J. (1994), *The Political Economy of Industrial Policy*, St. Martin's Press, New York.
Coase, R.H. (1937), 'The Nature of the Firm', *Economica*, 4, 386-405.
Conlisk, J. (1996), 'Why Bounded Rationality?', *Journal of Economic Literature*, 34, 669-700.
CPB (1992), *Scanning the Future*, CPB Netherlands Bureau for Economic Policy Analysis, Sdu Publishers, The Hague.
Crouch, C. (1993), *Industrial Relations and European State Traditions*, Clarendon Press, Oxford.
Damme, E. van (1994), 'Banking: a Survey of Recent Microeconomic Theory', *Oxford Review of Economic Policy*, 10, 14-33.
Dasgupta, P. (1991), 'The Environment as a Commodity', in D. Vines and A.A. Stevenson (eds.), *Information, Strategy and Public Policy*, Basil Blackwell, Oxford, 71-103.
Dixit, A.K. (1996), *The Making of Economic Policy: a Transaction-cost Politics Perspective*, MIT Press, Cambridge Mass.
Don, F.J.H. and P.J. Besseling, 'Social Security Reforms: Why and How?', *CPB Report*, 96/4, 13-17.
Eggertsson, T. (1990), *Economic Behavior and Instititions*, Cambridge University Press.

EZ (1995), *Toets op het Concurrentievermogen*, Dutch Ministry of Economic Affairs, The Hague.

Gelauff, G.M.M. and C. den Broeder (1996), 'Governance of Stakeholder Relationships; the German and Dutch Experience', CPB Netherlands Bureau for Economic Policy Analysis, Research Memorandum no. 127.

Jong, A.H.M. de, and F.J.H. Don (1995), 'Internationale Trends en de Nederlandse Economie', in L. van der Geest and J. van Sinderen (eds.), *Kracht en Zwakte van de Nederlandse Economie: Naar een Betere Benutting van het Economisch Potentieel*, Barjesteh, Meeuwes & Co, Rotterdam, Syntax Publishers, Tilburg.

Jong, H.W. de (1989), *Dynamische Markttheorie*, Stenfert Kroese, Leiden.

Hart, O. (1995), *Firms, Contracts, and Financial Structure*, Clarendon Press, Oxford.

Hartog, J. and C.N. Teulings (1996), *Corporatism or Competition*, forthcoming.

Katzenstein, P.J. (1989), 'Stability and Change in the Emerging Third Republic', in P.J. Katzenstein (ed.), *Industry and Politics in West Germany*, Cornell University Press, Ithaca, 307-353.

Kay, J. (1993), *Foundations of Corporate Success: How Business Strategies Add Value*, Oxford University Press, Oxford.

Kennedy, P. (1993), *Preparing for the Twenty-First Century*, HarperCollins, London.

Kester, W.C. (1992), 'Industrial Groups as Systems of Contractual Governance', *Oxford Review of Economic Policy*, 8, 24-43.

Laffont, J.J. and J. Tirole (1993), *A Theory of Incentives in Procurement and Regulation*, MIT Press, Cambridge.

Lazonick, W. (1991), *Business Organization and the Myth of the Market Economy*, Cambridge University Press.

MacLeod, W.B. (1995), 'Incentives in Organizations: an Overview of Some of the Evidence and Theory', in H. Siebert (ed.), *Trends in Business Organization: Do Participation and Cooperation Increase Competitiveness?*, J.C.B. Mohr, Tübingen, 3-42.

Magill, M. and M. Quinzii (1996), *Theory of Incomplete Markets*, Vol. 1, MIT Press, Cambridge, Mass.

Matthews, R.C.O. (1986), 'The Economics of Institutions and the Sources of Growth', *The Economic Journal*, 96, 903-918.

Mayes, D. and P. Hart (1994), *The Single Market Programme as a Stimulus to Change, Comparisons Between Britain and Germany*, Cambridge University Press.

McMillan, J. (1995), 'Reorganizing Vertical Supply Relationships', in H. Siebert (ed.), *Trends in Business Organization: Do Participation and Cooperation Increase Competitiveness?*, J.C.B. Mohr, Tübingen, 203-222.

Milgrom, P. and J. Roberts (1992), *Economics, Organization and Management*, Prentice Hall, New Jersey.

Myles, G.D. (1995), *Public Economics*, Cambridge University Press, Cambridge.

North, D.C. (1994), 'Economic Performance Through Time', *American Economic Review*, 84, 359-368.

Olson, M. (1982), *The Rise and Decline of Nations: Economic Growth, Stagflation and Social Rigidities*, Yale Universiity Press, New Haven.

Poire, M. and C.F. Sabel, *The Second Industrial Divide*, Basic Books, New York.

Porter, M.E. (1990), *Competitiveness of Nations*, MacMillan, London.

Romer, P.M. (1990), 'Endogenous Technological Change', *Journal of Political Economy*, 98, 71-102.

Schmalensee, R. (1989), 'Inter-industry Studies of Structure and Performance', in R. Schmalensee and R.P. Willig (eds.), *Handbook of Industrial Organization*, North-Holland, Amsterdam.

Simon, H.A. (1947), *Administrative Behaviour*, MacMillan, London.

——— (1957), *Models of Man*, Wiley, New york.

Sinn, H.W. (1995), 'Social Insurance, Incentives and Risk Taking', National Bureau of Economic Research, NBER Working Paper no. 5335, Cambridge, Mass.

Stiglitz, J.E. (1991), 'The Invisible Hand and Modern Welfare Economics', in D. Vines and A.A. Stevenson (eds.), *Information, Strategy and Public Policy*, Basil Blackwell, Oxford, 12-50.

——— (1993), *Economics*, W.W. Norton & Co, New York.

Streeck, W. (1995), 'German Capitalism: Does it exist? Can it Survive?', Max Planck Institut für Gesellschaftsforschung, Discussion Paper 95/5, forthcoming in C. Crouch and W. Streeck (eds.), *Modern Capitalism or Modern Capitalisms?* Frances Pinter, London.

Streeck, W. and P.C. Schmitter (1991), 'Community, Market, State – and Associations? The Prospective Contribution of Interest Governance to Social Order', in G. Thompson, J. Frances, R. Levacić and J. Mitchell (eds.), *Markets, Hierarchies and Networks*, Sage Publications, London, 227-241.

Tirole, J. (1994), 'Internal Organization of Government', *Oxford Economic Papers* 46, 1-29.

Waarden, F. van (1997), 'Institutions of Socio-Economic Coordination: a European Style?' *Social Policy and Economic Performance*, Dutch Ministry of Social Affairs and Employment, The Hague.

Williamson, O.E. (1975), *Markets and Hierarchies: Analysis and Anti-Trust Implications*, Free Press, New York.

——— (1985), *The Economic Institutions of Capitalism*, The Free Press, New York.

Wolf, C. (1993), *Markets or Governments: Choosing Between Imperfect Alternatives*, 2nd edition, MIT Press, Cambridge, Mass.

World Bank (1994), *World Development Report 1994: Infrastructure for Development*, Oxford University Press, New York.

Wright, D. and A. Jacquemin (1993), *The European Challenges Post 1992*, Edward Elgar Publishing Limited, Aldershot.

Chapter 3 Economic Development in Comparison

Abraham, K.G. and S.N. Houseman (1993), 'Earnings Inequality in Germany', National Bureau of Economic Research, NBER Working Paper no. 4541, Cambridge, Mass.

BMBF (1997), *Zur Technologischen Leistungsfähigkeit Deutschlands. Aktualisierung und Erweiterung 1996*, German Ministry of Education, Science Research and Technology, Bonn.

BMWi (1997), *Reformen für Beschäftigung; Jahreswirtschaftsbericht 1997*, German Ministry of Economic Affairs, Bonn.

CBS (1997), *Statistisch Jaarboek 1997*, CBS Statistics Netherlands, Sdu Publishers, The Hague.

CPB (1994), *Centraal Economisch Plan 1994*, CPB Netherlands Bureau for Economic Policy Analysis, Sdu Publishers, The Hague.
——— (1996), *Centraal Economisch Plan 1996*, CPB Netherlands Bureau for Economic Policy Analysis, Sdu Publishers, The Hague.
——— (1997), *Centraal Economisch Plan 1997*, CPB Netherlands Bureau for Economic Policy Analysis, Sdu Publishers, The Hague.
Deutsche Bundesbank (1996), 'Zahlungsbilanzstatistik Juni 1996', Statistisches Beiheft zum Monatsbericht 3, Frankfurt am Main.
European Commission (1995), 'Annual Economic Report for 1995', *European Economy*, 59, Statistical Annex.
Eurostat (1995), *Ausgaben und Einnahmen des Sozialschutzes 1980-1993*, Eurostat European Communities, Luxembourg.
——— (1996), *Labour Force Survey, Results 1994*, Luxembourg.
Folmer, C. (1995), 'Agricultural Relationships Between Germany and the Netherlands', CPB Netherlands Bureau for Economic Policy Analysis, Research Memorandum no. 122.
Gelauff, G.M.M. (1992), *Taxation, Social Security and the Labour Market: an Applied General Equilibrium Model (AGE) for the Netherlands*, Katholic University Brabant, Thesis, Tilburg.
Graaf, A.C.J.M. de, and H.G.A. Noordman (1995), 'Specialisatie en Prijsconcurrentie van Nederland en Duitsland bij de Handel in Industriële Producten', CPB Netherlands Bureau for Economic Policy Analysis, Research Memorandum no. 123, The Hague.
Hoef, J.D. van de, and H.J.M. ter Rele (1996), 'Een Vergelijking van de Nederlandse en Duitse Overheidsfinanciën', CPB Netherlands Bureau for Economic Policy Analysis, Internal Note no. 96/II/1.
Jager, N.E.M. de (1994), 'German Unification: the Political Miracle, the Economic Cataclysm', CPB Netherlands Bureau for Economic Policy Analysis, Internal Note no. 94/IV/14.
Kam, C.A. de, and M.A. Allers (1993), 'Inkomensherverdeling', in J.J.M. Kremers (ed.), *Inspelen op Europa; Uitdagingen voor het Financieel-Economisch Beleid van Nederland*, Academic Service, Schoonhoven.
Kleinknecht, A. (1994), 'Heeft Nederland een Loongolf Nodig? Een Neo-Schumpeteriaans Verhaal over Bedrijswinsten, Werkgelegenheid en Export, *Tijdschrift voor Politieke Economie*, 17(2), 5-24.
Köddermann, R. (1996), 'Sind Löhne und Steuern Zu Hoch? Bemerkungen zur Standortdiskussion in Deutschland', *Ifo Schnelldienst*, 20, 6-15.
Leibfritz, W., J. Thornton and A. Bibbee (1997), 'Taxation and Economic Performance', OECD Working Papers no. 176.
Maddison, A. (1995), *Monitoring the World Economy, 1820-1992*, OECD, Paris
OECD (1993), *OECD Economic Surveys Germany*, Paris.
——— (1995a), *Labour Force Statistics 1995*, Paris.
——— (1995b), *Employment Outlook 1995*, Paris.
——— (1995c), 'Income Distribution in OECD Countries', Social Policy Studies no. 18, Paris.
——— (1996a), *Employment Outlook 1996*, Paris.
——— (1996b), *OECD Economic Outlook*, 60, Paris.
——— (1996c), *OECD Economic Outlook*, 61, Paris.
——— (1997a), *National Accounts: main aggregates*, Vol. 1, Paris.

——— (1997b), 'OECD in Figures: Statistics on the Member Countries, 1997 edition', supplement to *The OECD Observer*, 206, June/July 1997.

Paridon, C.W.A.M. van (1993), 'Profijtelijke Relatie of Knellende Band: over Economische Ontwikkelingen in Duitsland en de Invloed op Nederland', inaugural lecture, Free University Amsterdam.

——— (1995), *Wer Andern eine Mauer Baut .... Wie die DDR-Wirtschaft Sich Selbst Zugrunde Richtete*, Walter-Raymond-Stiftung, Kleine Reihe Heft 59, Bachem, Köln.

Pilat, D. (1996), 'Labour Productivity Levels in OECD Countries: Estimates for Manufacturing and Selected Service Sectors', OECD economics department, Working Paper no. 169.

Sachverständigenrat (1996), *Reformen Voranbringen*, Jahresgutachten 1996/97, Sachverständigenrat zur Begutachtung der Gesamtwirtschaftlichen Entwicklung, Metzler-Poeschel, Stuttgart.

SCP (1996), *Sociaal en Cultureel Rapport 1996*, Dutch Social en Cultural Planning Office, Rijswijk.

Sinn, G., and H.-W. Sinn (1992), *Jumpstart: the Economic Unification of Germany*, MIT Press, Cambridge, Mass.

Statistisches Bundesamt (1996), *Statistisches Jahrbuch für die Bundesrepublik Deutschland 1996*, Metzler-Poeschel, Stuttgart.

Verdonk, O. and G. Wiggers (1994), 'Loonvorming in Duitsland', CPB Netherlands Bureau for Economic Policy Analysis, Internal Note no. 94/II/17.

WRR (1996), 'Tweedeling in Perspectief', Scientific Council for the Government, Rapport no. 50, Sdu Publishers, The Hague.

Chapter 4 A Structural Comparison

BIB (1994), Bundesinstitut für Bevolkerungsforschung, *Zeitschrift für Bevolkerungswissenschaft*, 19(4), 141.

BMWi (1995), 'Neuere Entwicklungen und Perspektiven für Direktinvestionen', German Ministry of Economic Affairs, Internal Report, Bonn.

Bottani, N. (1995), 'Comparing Educational Output', *OECD Observer*, 193, 6-11.

BP (1994), *Statistical Review of World Energy*, British Petroleum, London.

Brus, D. (1996), *Transport-Infrastructuur en Bereikbaarheid in Nederland en Duitsland*, CPB Netherlands Bureau for Economic Policy Analysis, Internal Note, August.

CBS (1993), *Arbeidsrekeningen 1989-1992*, CBS Statistics Netherlands, Sdu Publishers, The Hague.

——— (1994c), *Vijfennegentig Jaren Statistiek in Tijdreeksen*, CBS Statistics Netherlands, Voorburg/Heerlen.

——— (1997), *Statistisch Jaarboek 1997*, CBS Statistics Netherlands, Voorburg/Heerlen.

CPB (1994), *Centraal Economisch Plan*, CPB Netherlands Bureau for Economic Policy Analysis, Sdu Publishers, The Hague.

——— (1996), 'Immateriële Investeringen in Nederland: een Internationale Positiebepaling', CPB Netherlands Bureau for Economic Policy Analysis in cooperation with CBS Statistics Netherlands, Working Paper no. 86.

Dicken, P. (1986), *Global Shift, Industrial Change in a Turbulent World*, Harper & Row, London.

Economist, the (1997), 'World Education League: Who's Top?', March 29th, 21-22.
European Network for SME Research (1994), *The European Observatory for SMEs*, Zoetermeer.
Eurostat (1993), *Transports 1970-1990*, Brussels/Luxembourg.
——— (1994a), *Demographic Statistics 1994*, Brussels/Luxembourg.
EZ (1991), 'CIM in de Duitse Industrie', Dutch Ministry of Economic Affairs, *Technieuws Bonn*, B.91-02.
——— (1993), *Energy in Figures*, Dutch Ministry of Economic Affairs, The Hague.
——— (1995), *Competitiveness Indicators*, Dutch Ministry of Economic Affairs, The Hague.
Fischer, G., R. Hensel, A. Reinberg, H.D. Reuschel and M. Tessaring (1993), 'Bestand und Bewegung im Bildungs- und Beschäftigungssystem der Bundesrepublik Deutschland: Ergebnisse der Bildungsgesamtrechnung für die Alten und Neuen Bundesländer', Institut für Arbeitsmarkt und Berufsforschung der Bundesanstalt für Arbeit (IAB), BeitrAB 170, Nürnberg.
Hanushek, E.A. and D. Kim (1995), 'Schooling, Labor Force Quality, and Economic Growth', National Bureau of Economic Research, NBER Working Paper no. 5399, Cambridge, Mass.
Jager, N.E.M. de (1996), 'A Comparative Analysis of Current and Future Human Capital in Germany and the Netherlands', in CBS Statistics Netherlands (1996), *De Nederlandse Arbeidsmarktdag 1995; Flexibilisering: het Nederlandse Antwoord op Internationalisering? Arbeidsmarktstrategie in een Mondiale Economie*, Voorburg/Heerlen.
Minne, B. (1992), 'Technologie en Economie: de Nederlandse Positie', CPB Netherlands Bureau for Economic Policy Analysis, Research Memorandum no. 94.
——— (1995), 'Onderzoek, Ontwikkeling en Andere Immateriële Investeringen in Nederland', CPB Netherlands Bureau for Economic Policy Analysis, Research Memorandum no. 116.
OECD (1992), *International Direct Investment, Policies and Trends in the 1980s*, Paris.
——— (1993), *Environmental Performance Reviews Germany*, Paris.
——— (1994a), *Basic Science and Technology statistics*, Paris.
——— (1994b), *International Direct Investment Statistics Yearbook 1994*, Paris.
——— (1994c), *Information Technology Outlook*, Paris.
——— (1995), *OECD Environmental Data, Compendium 1995*, Paris.
——— (1996a), *OECD in Figures, 1996 edition*, supplement to The OECD Observer no. 200 June/July 1996, Paris.
——— (1996b), *International Direct Investment Statistics Yearbook 1996*, Paris.
——— (1996c), *Labour Force Statistics 1973-1993*, Paris.
——— (1996d), *Historical Statistics 1960-1994*, Paris.
OECD/IEA (1996), *Energy Balances of OECD Countries, 1993-1994*, Paris.
Slabbers, M. and B. Verspagen (1994), 'Stemming 1, een Beoordeling van de Nederlandse Technologische Positie op Basis van Kwantitatieve Indicatoren', *mimeo,* MERIT, University of Limburg, the Netherlands.
Statistisches Bundesamt (1995), *Statistisches Jahrbuch für die Bundesrepublik Deutschland 1995*, Metzler-Poeschel, Stuttgart.
——— (1996), *Statistisches Jahrbuch für die Bundesrepublik Deutschland 1996*, Metzler-Poeschel, Stuttgart.

UN (1995), *World Population Prospects 1994*, United Nations, New York.
WEF (1994), *World Competitiveness Report*, World Economic Forum, Geneva.
Witte, J.C., and G.G. Wagner (1995), 'Declining Fertility in East Germany after Unification: a Demographic Response to Socioeconomic Change', *Population and Development Review*, 21, 387-397.

Chapter 5 Governance of the Socio-economic Order: An Economic Perspective

Adams, W.P. (1977), *Die Vereinigten Staaten von Amerika*, Fischer Weltgeschichte 30, Fischer Taschenbuch Verlag, Frankfurt am Main.
Albeda, W., (1993), 'De Toekomst van de Overlegeconomie', in N.A. Hofstra and P.W.M. Nobelen (eds.), *De Toekomst van de Overlegeconomie*, Van Gorcum, Assen/Maastricht.
Alesina A. and H. Rosenthal (1995), *Partisan Politics, Divided Government, and the Economy*, Cambridge Universty Press, Cambridge.
Ark, B. van, J. de Haan and H.J. de Jong (1996), 'Characteristics of Economic Growth in the Netherlands During the Postwar Period', in N. Crafts and G. Toniolo (eds.), *Economic Growth in Europe Since 1945*, Cambridge University Press, Cambridge.
Brady, D., S. Lohmann and D. Rivers (1992), 'Party Identification, Retrospective Voting and Moderating Elections in a Federal System: West Germany 1961-1989, *mimeo*, Stanford University.
Carlin, W. (1996), 'West German Growth and Institutions, 1945-90', in N. Crafts and G. Toniolo (eds.), *Economic Growth in Europe Since 1945*, Cambridge University Press.
Carlin, W. and D. Soskice (1997), 'Shocks to the System: the German Political Economy under Stress', *National Institute Economic Review*, 1, 57-76.
Casson, M. (1991), *The Economics of Business Culture: Game Theory, Transaction Costs, and Economic Performance*, Clarendon Press, Oxford.
CEPR (1993), *Making Sense of Subsidiarity: How Much Centralisation for Europe?*, Centre for Economic Policy Research, Annual Report 1993, London.
Chang, H.-J. (1994), *The Political Economy of Industrial Policy*, St. Martin's Press, New York.
Chang, H.-J., and R. Rowthorn (1995), 'The Role of the State in Economic Change: Entrepreneurship and Conflict Management', in H.-J. Chang and R. Rowthorn (eds.), *The Role of the State in Economic Change*, Clarendon Press, Oxford.
CPB (1992a), *Scanning the Future: a Long Term Scenario Study of the World Economy 1990-2015*, CPB Netherlands Bureau of Economic Policy Analysis, Sdu Publishers, The Hague.
——— (1992b), *Nederland in Drievoud: een Scenario Studie van de Nederlandse Economie 1990-2015*, CPB Netherlands Bureau for Economic Policy Analysis, Sdu Publishers, The Hague.
——— (1996), *Centraal Economisch Plan 1996*, CPB Netherlands Bureau for Economic Policy Analysis, Sdu Publishers, The Hague.
Crouch, C. (1993), *Industrial Relations and European State Traditions*, Clarendon Press, Oxford.
Dertouzos, M.L., R.K. Lester, R.M. Solow and the MIT Commission on Industrial Productivity (1989), *Made in America: Regaining the Productive Edge*, MIT Press, Cambridge, Mass.

Dixit A.K. (1996), *The Making of Economic Policy: a Transaction-Cost Politics Perspective*, MIT Press, Cambridge, Mass.

Gabriel, O.W. and F. Brettschneider (1992), *Die EU-Staaten im Vergleich: Strukturen, Prozesse, Politikinhalte*, Westdeutscher Verlag.

Geelhoed, L.A. (1996a), '1996: Geloofwaardigheid en Vertrouwen', *Economisch Statistische Berichten* 81, 4-9.

——— (1996b), 'Markt, Ordening en Sturing: Schuivende Posities', in A. Nentjes (ed.), *Marktwerking versus Coordinatie*, Preadviezen van de Koninklijke Vereniging voor de Staathuishoudkunde, Lemma, Utrect, 11-35.

Giersch, H., K.-H. Paqué and H. Schmieding (1992), *The Fading Miracle: Four Decades of Market Economy in Germany*, Cambridge University Press, Cambridge.

Hamel, H. (1994), 'Soziale Marktwirtschaft: Anspruch und Realität eines ordnungspolitischen Konzepts' in W. Klein, S. Paraskewopoulos, H. Winter (eds.), *Soziale Marktwirtschaft: Ein Modell für Europa*, Duncker & Humbolt, Berlin.

Hemerijck, A.C. (1992), *The Historical Contingencies of Dutch Corporatism*, Balliol College, University of Oxford.

Katzenstein, P.J. (1987), *Policy and Politics in West Germany: the Growth of a Semi-sovereign State*, Temple University Press, Philadelphia.

——— (1989), 'Stability and Change in the Emerging Third Republic', in P.J. Katzenstein (ed.), *Industry and Politics in West Germany*, Cornell University Press, Ithaca, 307-353.

Kenworthy, L. (1996) 'Balancing Competition and Cooperation', *Challenge*, July/August, 51-58.

Klau, T., (1997) 'Germany Edges Towards Deregulation', *European Voice*, 30/4-6/5.

Lampert, H. (1992), *Die Wirtschafts- und Sozialordnung der Bundesrepublik Deutschland*, 11th ed., Olzog Verlag, München.

Lehmbruch G. (1995), 'From State of Authority to Network State: the German State in Developmental Perspective', manuscript forthcoming in F. Naschold and M. Maramatsu (eds.), *State and Administration in Japan and Germany*, Walter de Gruyter, Berlin.

——— (1996), 'Crisis and Institutional Resilience in German Corporatism', paper presented at the 8th International Conference on Socio-economics, Genève.

Mansbridge J. (1994), 'Public Spirit in Political Systems', in H.J. Aaron, T.E. Mann and T. Taylor (eds.), *Values and Public Policy*, Brookings Institution, Washington, 146-172.

Nye, J.S. (1990), *Bound to Lead: the Changing Nature of American Power*, Basic Books, New York.

Owen Smith, E. (1994), *The German Economy*, Routledge, London.

Paqué, K.-H. (1996), 'Why the 1950s and Not the 1920s? Olsonian and Non-Olsonian Interpretations of Two Decades of German Economic History', in N. Crafts and G. Toniolo (eds.), *Economic Growth in Europe Since 1945*, Centre for Economic Policy Research, Cambridge University Press, Cambridge.

Pekkarinen, J., M. Pohjola and B. Rowthorn (1992), 'Social Corporatism and Economic Performance: Introduction and Conclusions', in J. Pekkarinen, M. Pohjola and R. Rowthorn (eds.), *Social Corporatism: a Superior Economic System?*, Clarendon Press, Oxford.

Rinnooy Kan, A.H.G. (1993), 'De Nederlandse Overlegeconomie in de Jaren Negentig: een Kritische Balans', in N.A. Hofstra and P.W.M. Nobelen (eds.), *De Toekomst van de Overlegeconomie*, Van Gorcum, Assen/Maastricht.

Schlecht, O. (1990), *Grundlagen und Perspectiven der Sozialen Marktwirtschaft*, J.C.B. Mohr, Tübingen

Schlesinger, A.M., jr. (1986), *The Cycles of American History*, Houghton Mifflin, Boston.

SER (1992), *Convergentie en Overlegeconomie*, Social and Economic Council, Adv.ies 92/15, The Hague.

Sinn, H.-W. (1996), 'The Subsidiarity Principle and Market Failure in Systems Competition', National Bureau of Economic Research, NBER Working Paper no. 5411, Cambridge, Mass.

Sinn, G. and H.-W. Sinn (1992), *Jumpstart: the Economic Unification of Germany*, MIT Press, Cambridge, Mass.

Skidelsky, R. (1995), *The World After Communism: a Polemic for Our Times*, MacMillan, London.

Slomp, J.F.W. (1990), *Labor Relations in Europe: a History of Issues and Developments*, Greenwood Press, New York.

Smyser, W.R. (1993), *The German Economy: Colossus at the Crossroads*, 2nd ed., Longman, Harlow.

Streeck, W. (1995), 'German Capitalism: Does It Exist? Can It Survive?', Max Planck Institut für Gesellschaftsforschung, Discussion Paper 95/5, forthcoming in C. Crouch and W. Streeck (eds.), *Modern Capitalism or Modern Capitalisms?*, Frances Pinter, London.

Streeck, W. and P.C. Schmitter (1991), 'Community, Market, State – and Associations? The Prospective Contribution of Interest Governance to Social Order', in G. Thompson, J. Frances, R. Levacić and J. Mitchell (eds.), *Markets, Hierarchies and Networks*, Sage Publications, London, 227-241.

Therborn, G. (1992), 'Lessons from Corporatist Theorizations', in J. Pekkarinen, M. Pohjola and R. Rowthorn (eds.), *Social Corporatism: a Superior Economic System?*, Clarendon Press, Oxford.

Waarden, F. van (1997), 'Institutions of Socio-economic Coordination: a European Style?', *Social Policy and Economic Performance*, Dutch Ministry of Social Affairs and Employment, The Hague.

Watrin, C. (1994), 'Ordnungs- und Wirtschaftspolitische Grundlagen Sozialer Marktwirtschaft' in W. Klein, S. Paraskewopoulos, H. Winter (eds.), *Soziale Marktwirtschaft: Ein Modell für Europa*, Duncker & Humbolt, Berlin.

Weder, R. and H. G. Grubel (1993), 'The New Growth Theory and Coasean Economics: Institutions to Capture Externalities', *Weltwirtschaftliches Archiv*, 129, 489-513.

Wee, H. van der (1983), *De Gebroken Welvaartscirkel: de Wereldeconomie, 1945-1980*, Martinus Nijhoff, Leiden.

Wolf, P. de, and W. Driehuis (1980), 'A Description of Post War Economic Developments and Economic Policy in the Netherlands', in R.T. Griffiths (ed.), *The Economy and Politics of the Netherlands Since 1945*, Martinus Nijhoff, The Hague.

Chapter 6 Social Protection

AAF/AoF: Algemeen Arbeidsongeschiktheidsfonds/Arbeidsongeschiktheidsfonds (1985), *Jaarverslag 1983*, Zoetermeer.

Atkinson, A.B. (1995), *Incomes and the Welfare State: Essays on Britain and Europe*, Cambridge University Press, Cambridge.

BFG (1995), *Daten des Gesundheitswesens, Ausgabe 1995*, German Ministry of Health, schriftenreihe Band 51, Nomos Verlagsgesellschaft, Baden-Baden.

Blomquist, S. and V. Christiansen (1995), *Topping Up or Opting Out? The Optimal Design of Public Provision Schemes*, Uppsala University, Department of Economics, Working paper 1995:13.

BMA (1984), *Die Gesetzliche Rentenversicherung in der Bundesrepublik Deutschland im Jahre 1983*, German Ministry of Labour and Social Order, Bonn.

——— (1995), *Übersicht über das Sozialrecht*, German Ministry of Labour and Social Order, Bonn.

Buist, D. and G. Homburg (1994), *Handhaving Over de Grens*, Ministry of Social Affairs and Employment, The Hague.

Caballero, R.J. and M.L. Hammour (1996), *The Macroeconomics of Specificity*, National Bureau of Economic Research, NBER Working paper no. 5757, Cambridge, Mass.

Carlin, W. and D. Soskice (1997), 'Shocks to the System: the German Political Economy under Stress', *National Institute Economic Review*, 1, 57-76.

CBS (1997), *Statistisch Jaarboek 1997*, CBS Statistics Netherlands, Sdu Publishers, The Hague

Coe, D.T. and D.J. Snower (1997), 'Policy Complementarities: The Case for Fundamental Labour Market Reform', Centre for Economic Policy Research, CEPR Discussion Paper no. 1585.

CPB (1995), 'Replacement Rates: A Transatlantic View', CPB Netherlands Bureau for Economic Policy Analysis, Working Paper, no. 80.

——— (1996), *Macro economische Verkenning 1997*, CPB Netherlands Bureau for Economic Policy Analysis, The Hague.

——— (1997), *Centraal Economisch Plan 1997*, CPB Netherlands Bureau for Economic Policy Analysis, Sdu Publishers, The Hague.

Ctsv (1995), *Kroniek van de Sociale Verzekeringen 1995*, Social Security Supervisory Board, Zoetermeer.

——— (1996), *Kroniek van de Sociale Verzekeringen 1996*, Social Security Supervisory Board, Zoetermeer.

Eurostat (1994), *Ausgaben und Einnahmen des Sozialschutzes 1980-1993*, Eurostat European Communities, Luxembourg.

Frick, B. and D. Sadowski (1996), 'A German Perspective on Disability Policy', in L.J.M. Aarts, R.V. Burkhauser and P.R. de Jong (eds.), *Curing the Dutch Disease: an International Perspective on Disability Policy Reform*, Vol. 1, Avebury, Aldershot.

Hopenhayn, H.A. and J.P. Nicolini (1997), 'Optimal Unemployment Insurance', *Journal of Political Economy*, 105(2), 412-438.

Knight, F.H. (1921), *Risk, Uncertainty and Profit*, Houghton, Boston (etc.).

Lindbeck, A. (1994), 'Uncertainty under the Welfare State, Policy-induced risk', OCFEB Research Centre for Economic Policy, Research Memorandum no. 9403, Erasmus University Rotterdam.

——— (1995), 'Hazardous Welfare-State Dynamics', *American Economic Review*, 85(2), 9-15.

Newhouse, Joseph P. (1996), 'Reimbursing Health Plans and Health Providers: Efficiency in Production Versus Selection', *Journal of Economic Literature*, Vol. 34, 1236-1263.

OECD (1996), *Education at a Glance, OECD Indicators*, Paris.

Prins, R., (1990), *Sickness Absence in Belgium, Germany, France and The Netherlands, A comparative study*, Amsterdam.
Prins, R., T.J. Veerman and M.K. Koster (1993), 'De Uitvoering van Arbeidsongeschiktheidsregelingen in België, Duitsland en Zweden', Social Security Council (SVR), report 9310, Zoetermeer.
Riphahn, R. (1997), 'Disability Retirement and Unemployment: Substitute Pathways for Labour Force Exit?', *Applied Economics*, 29, 551-561.
SB (1985), *Statistisches Jahrbuch für die Bundesrepublik Deutschland 1985*, Statistisches Bundesamt, Metzler Poeschel, Stuttgart.
——— (1996), *Statistisches Jahrbuch für die Bundesrepublik Deutschland 1996*, Metzler Poeschel, Stuttgart.
Sinn, H.-W. (1995), 'Social insurance, Incentives and Risk Taking', National Bureau of Economic Research, NBER Working Paper no. 5335, Cambridge, Mass.
Sinn, G. and Sinn, H.-W. (1992), *Jumpstart: the Economic Unification of Germany*, The MIT Press, Cambridge
Snower, D.J. (1996), *The Modern Welfare State: Problems and Suggested Reforms*, Empirica, Vol. 23, 207-226.
Teulings, C.N., and F. van der Ploeg (1993), 'De Vermoedelijke Ineffectiviteit van de WAO-Maatregelen', *Economisch Statistische Berichten*, Vol. 78, 576-579.
Varian, H.R. (1980), *Redistributive Taxation as Social Insurance*, Journal of Public Economics 14, 49-68.
WRR (1994), 'Belang en Beleid; Naar een Verantwoorde Uitvoering van Werknemersverzekeringen', Scientific Council for the Government, Report no. 45, Sdu Publishers, The Hague.

Chapter 7 Pensions

Aaron, H.J. (1966), 'The Social Insurance Paradox', *Canadian Journal of Economic and Political Science*, Vol. 32, 371-77.
Besseling, P.J. and R.F. Zeeuw (1993), 'The Financing of Pensions in Europe: Challenges and Opportunities', CPB Netherlands Bureau for Economic Policy Analysis, Research Memorandum no. 111.
BMA (1997a), 'Kabinett beschliesst Entwurf für Rentenreformgesetz 1999', German Ministry of Labour and Social Order, Press Announcement 18-6-1997.
——— (1997b), 'Rentenreform wird in Angriff genommen', *Sozialpolitische Umschau*, 23-6-97.
——— (1997c), 'Sozial Sicherung im Überblick', Website of the Bundesministerium für Arbeit und Sozialordnung, www.bma.de., June 1997.
Bovenberg, A.L. and A.S.M. van der Linden (1997), 'Can we Afford to Grow Old?', CPB Netherlands Bureau for Economic Policy Analysis, Research Memorandum no. 134.
Börsch-Supan, A. (1993), 'Macroeconomic Implications of Population Aging', paper presented at a NAKE workshop of the Netherlands Graduate School of Economics, Rotterdam, December 13-17.
CPB (1995), *Replacement Rates: A Transatlantic View*, CPB Netherlands Bureau for Economic Policy Analysis, Working Paper, no. 80, The Hague.

——— (1997), *Bevolking en Arbeidsaanbod: Drie Scenario's tot 2020*, CPB Netherlands Bureau for Economic Policy Analysis, SDU Publishers, The Hague.

Davis, P.E. (1996), 'Pension Fund Investments', in B. Steil et al. (eds.), *The European Equity Markets, the State of the Union and an Agenda for the Millennium*, The Royal Institute of International Affairs, London.

Dilnot, A., R. Disney, P. Johnson and E. Whitehouse (1994), *Pensions Policy in the UK, an Economic Analysis*, Institute for Fiscal Studies, London.

Einerhand et al. (1995), *Sociale Zekerheid: Stelsels en Regelingen in Enkele Europese landen*, SZW

Eurostat (1994), *Ausgaben und Einnahmen des Sozialschutzes 1980-1993*, Eurostat European Communities, Luxembourg.

Gordon, R.H., and H.R. Varian (1988), 'Intergenerational Risk Sharing', *Journal of Public Economics*, Vol. 37, 185-202.

ILO (1986), *Economically Active Population*, Volumes I and II, International Labour Office, Geneva.

Lazear, E.P. (1986), 'Retirement from the Labor Force', in O. Ashenfelter and R. Layard (eds.), *Handbook of Labor Economics*, Vol. 1, North Holland, Amsterdam.

OECD (1997), *Beyond 2000: The New Social Policy Agenda*, Paris.

Pestieau, P. (1992), 'The Distribution of Private Pension Benefits: How Fair Is It?' in OECD, *Private Pensions and Public Policy* Paris.

Quinn J. (1990), *Passing the Torch, the Influence of Economic Incentives on Work and Retirement*

Razin, A., and E. Sadka (1995), *Population Economics*, MIT Press: Cambridge.

Sachverständigenrat (1996), *Reformen Voranbringen*, Jahresgutachten 1996/1997, Sachverständigenrat zur Begutachtung der Gesamtwirtschaftlichen Entwicklung, Metzler-Poeschel, Stuttgart.

Siebert, H. (1997), 'Pay-As-You-Go versus Capital Funded Pension Systems. The Issues', paper presented at the Kiel Week Conference 'Redesigning Social Security', Kiel Institute of World Economics, June.

Sinn, H.W. (1995), 'Social Insurance, Incentives and Risk Taking', National Bureau of Economic Research, NBER Working Paper no. 5335, Cambridge, Mass.

Snower, D.J. (1996), *The Modern Welfare State: Problems and Suggested Reforms*, Empirica, Vol. 23, 207-226.

United Nations (1989), *Long Range World Population Projections*, New York.

World Bank (1994), *Averting the Old Age Crisis; Policies to Protect the Old and Promote Growth*, Oxford University Press.

Chapter 8 Labour Market: Institutional Environment

Abraham, K.G. and S.S. Houseman (1993), 'Does Employment Protection Inhibit Labour Market Flexibility? Lessons from Germany, France, Belgium', National Bureau of Economic Research, NBER Working Paper no. 4390, Cambridge, Mass.

Addison, J.T., C. Schnabel and J. Wagner (1996), 'German Works Councils, Profits and Innovation', *Kyklos* 49, 555-582.

Akerlof, G.A. and J.L. Yellen (eds.) (1986), *Efficiency Wage Models of the Labor Market*, Cambridge University Press, Cambridge.

Anzinger, R. (1994), Arbeitszeitgesetz, Erfolgreich zum Abschluss Gebracht, *Bundesarbeitsblatt*, 6, Bonn.

Becker, G. (1962), 'Investment in Human Capital: A Theoretical Analysis', *Journal of Political Economy*, 70 (5), 9-49.

Bertola, G. and A. Ichino (1995), 'Crossing the River: a Comparative Perspective on Italian Employment Dynamics', *Economic Policy*, October, 361-420.

Biagi, M. (1993), 'Forms of Employee Representational Participation', in R. Blanpain and C. Engels (eds.), *Comparative Labour Law and Industrial Relations in Industrialized Market Economies*, Kluwer Law and Taxation Publishers, Deventer-Boston.

Bierings, H.B.A. and J.C.M. Imbens (1992), 'Werknemers met een Flexibele Arbeidsrelatie, Uitkomsten van de Enquête Beroepsbevolking', *Supplement Sociaal Economische Maandstatistiek*, 5, 57-62.

Blank, R.M. (ed.) (1994), *Social Protection Versus Economic Flexibility, Is There a Trade-off?*, The University of Chicago Press, Comparative labor market series, Chicago.

BMA (1994a), *Arbeitsförderungsgesetz*, German Ministry of Labour and Social Order, Textausgabe, Bonn.

——— (1994b), *Wegweiser durch das Arbeitsförderungsgesetz*, German Ministry of Labour and Social Order, Bonn.

Bolhuis, M. van (1996), *Externe Flexibilisering, een Onderzoek bij Bedrijven*, Dutch Ministry of Social Affairs and Employment, Inspectiedienst SZW, The Hague.

Boom, C.E.M, van den (1993), 'De Preventieve Toets en de Arbeidsmarkt', *Sociaal Maandblad Arbeid*, 48(9), 537-549.

Booth, A.L. and D.J. Snower (eds.) (1996), *Acquiring Skills, Market failures, their symptoms and policy responses*, Cambridge University Press, Cambridge.

Bosch, G. (1988), 'Der Bundesdeutsche Arbeitsmarkt im Internationaler Vergleich: Eurosklerose oder Modell Deutschland?' *WSI Mitteilungen 3/1988*, 176-185.

Bosch, G., P. Dawkins and F. Michon (eds.) (1993), *Times are Changing: Working Time in 14 Industrialised Countries*, International Institute for Labour Studies, Geneva.

Bovenberg, A.L. and R.A. de Mooij (1996), 'Hervormingen in de WW: Zegen of Vloek?', *Economische Statistische Berichten*, October 23, 868-872.

Broeder, C. den (1995), 'The Match Between Education and Work: What Can We Learn from the German Apprenticeship System?', CPB Netherlands Bureau for Economic Policy Analysis, Research Memorandum no. 118.

Bundesanstalt für Arbeit (1994), *Amtliche Nachrichten der Bundesanstalt für Arbeit, Arbeitsstatistik 1993 - Jahreszahlen*, 42 Jahrgang, Sondernummer, Nürnberg.

Büchtemann, C.F. (1989), 'More Jobs Through Less Employment Protection? Evidence for West Germany', *Labour,* 3 (3), 23-56.

Calmfors, L. and J. Driffill (1988), 'Centralisation of Wage Bargaining and Economic Performance, *Economic Policy*, April, 13-61.

CBS (1995), 'Leden van de Vakbeweging', *Sociaal-Economische Maandstatistiek*, no. 95/11.

——— (1997), *Statistisch Jaarboek 1997*, CBS Statistics Netherlands, Voorburg/Heerlen.

CPB (1997), *Centraal Economisch Plan 1997*, CPB Netherlands Bureau for Economic Policy Analysis, Sdu Publishers, The Hague.

Delsen, L. (1995), *Atypical Employment: an International Perspective, Causes, Consequences and Policy*, Wolters-Noordhoff, Groningen.

Elsevier (1995), 'Sociale Zekerheid van Geboorte tot Overlijden', *Almanak voor de Sociale Verzekeringen*, Amsterdam.

European Commission (1994), *Waarnemingspost voor het Werkgelegenheidsbeleid, Situatieoverzicht*, no. 2, Luxembourg/Brussels.

Eurostat (1996), *Labour Force Survey 1996*, Eurostat European Communities, Luxembourg.

Fitzroy, F.R. and K. Kraft (1993), 'Economic Effects of Co-determination', *Scandinavian Journal of Economics* 95, 365-375.

Frick, B. (1996), 'Co-determination and Personnel Turnover: the German Experience', *Labour*, 10, 407-430.

Gelauff, G.M.M. and J.J. Graafland (1994), *Modelling Welfare State Reform*, North-Holland Publishers, Amsterdam.

Golden, L. and E. Appelbaum (1992), 'What Was Driving the 1982-88 Boom in Temporary Employment? Preference of Workers or Decisions and Power of Employers', *American Journal of Economics and Sociology*, 51(4), 473-494.

Grubb, D. and W. Wells (1993), 'Employment Regulation and Patterns of Work in EC Countries', *OECD Economic Studies*, 21.

Gurdon, M.A. and A. Rai (1990), 'Co-determination and Enterprise Performance: Empirical Evidence from West Germany', *Journal of Economics and Business*, 42, 289-302.

Hartog, J., S. Polachek and J. Theeuwes (1993), 'Evaluating Labour Market Performance', in Hartog, J. and J. Theeuwes (eds.) (1993), *Labour Market Contracts and Institutions, a Cross-national Comparison*, Elseviers Science Publishers B.V., Amsterdam, 9-29.

Hartog, J., R. van Opstal and C.N. Teulings (1994), 'Loonvorming in Nederland en de Verenigde Staten', *Economisch Statistische Berichten*, June 8, 528-533.

Heijden, P.F. van der, R.H. van het Kaar, R. Knegt, J. Roebroek, E. Sol and A.C.J.M. Wilthagen (1995), 'Instituties van de Arbeidsmarkt: een Retrospectieve Studie', OSA Organisation for Labour Market Research, preparatory study no. V43.

Hepple, B. (1993), 'European Labour Law: the European Community', in R. Blanpain and C. Engels (eds.), *Comparative Labour Law and Industrial Relations in Industrialized Market Economies*, Kluwer Law and Taxation Publishers, Deventer-Boston.

Hof, B. (1995), 'Teilzeit in Europa, Von der Beschäftigungspolitischen Strategie zum Tragfähigen Personalkonzept', *Sociaal Maandblad Arbeid*, 50, 4, 234-244.

Hunt, J. (1994), 'Firing costs, Employment Fluctuations and Average Employment; an Examination of Germany', National Bureau of Economic Research, NBER Working paper no. 4825, Cambridge, Mass.

IDS (1995a), *Recruitment and Dismissal in the Netherlands 1994/95*, IDS International Documents, Incomes Data services Ltd.

Jackman, R., R. Layard and S. Nickell (1995), *Structural Aspects of OECD Unemployment*, OECD-paper.

Jacobi, O., B. Keller and W. Müller-Jentsch (1992), 'Germany: Co-determining the Future?' in A. Ferner and R. Hyman (eds.), *Industrial Relations in the New Europe*, Basic Blackwell, Oxford.

Jacobs, A.T.J.M. (1993), *Inleiding tot het Duitse Arbeidsrecht*, Gouda Quint B.V., Arnhem.

Jong, F. de (1996), *Flexibilisering van de Arbeid, een Onderzoek naar Flexibilisering in Cao's*, Dutch Ministry of Social Affairs and Employment, Inspectiedienst SZW, The Hague.

Koene, A.M. and H. Slomp (1991), *Medezeggenschap van Werknemers op Onderne-mingsniveau: Een Onderzoek naar de Regels en hun Toepassing in zes Europese Landen*, Dutch Ministry of Social Affairs and Employment, VUGA uitgeverij B.V., The Hague.

Lange, W.A.M. de (1995), 'De Nieuwe Arbeidstijdenwet', *Sociaal Maandblad Arbeid (SMA)*, 50(3), 171-184.

Layard, R., S. Nickell and R. Jackman (1991), *Unemployment, Macroeconomic Performance and the Labour Market*, Oxford University Press, Oxford.

Lieshout, H. van (1996), *Beroepsonderwijs in Duitsland: een Analyse van het Duits Duale Stelsel van Beroepsonderwijs Vanuit Nederlands Perspectief*, Max Goote Knowledge Centre for Vocational Training and Adult Education, Amsterdam.

Linke, (1993), *Kurzarbeit im Strukturwandel, Eine Analyse in der Bundesrepublik Während der Achtziger Jahren unter Einbeziehungen Erster Erfahrungen in den Neuen Bundesländern*, Wissenschaftszentrum Berlin für Sozialforsching (WZB), Berlin.

Marsden, D. (1995), 'Deregulation or Cooperation? The Future of Europe's Labour Markets', *Labour*, Special Issue 1995, 67-91.

Nickell, S. (1995), *The Performance of Companies: The Relationship Between the External Environment, Management Strategies and Corporate Performance*, Blackwell Publishers, Oxford/Cambridge.

NRC Handelsblad (1995), *Shell Betaalt Zelf Ontslaguitkeringen*, October 24.

OECD (1992), *OECD Economic Surveys, Germany*, Paris.

——— (1993), *Employment Outlook 1993*, Paris.

——— (1994a), *The OECD Jobs Study, Evidence and Explanations, part I, Labour Market Trends and Underlying Forces of Change*, Paris.

——— (1994b), *The OECD Jobs Study, Evidence and Explanations, Part II, The Adjustment Potential of the Labour Market*, Paris.

——— (1995a), *OECD Economic Surveys, Germany*, Paris.

——— (1995b), *OECD Economic Surveys, the Netherlands*, Paris.

——— (1996a), *OECD Economic Surveys, Germany 1996*, Paris.

——— (1996b), *Employment Outlook 1996*, Paris.

OSA (1995), *Trendrapport Aanbod van Arbeid 1995*, 21, OSA Organization for Labour Market Research, The Hague.

Owen Smith, E. (1994), *The German Economy*, Routledge, London and New York.

Passchier, C.E. (1995), 'Deeltijdarbeid: het Europees Tekort', *Sociaal Maandblad Arbeid*, 50(2), 82-86.

Schömann, K., R. Rogowski and T. Kruppe (1995), *Fixed Term Contracts in the European Union*, draft paper, European Association of Labour Economists (EALE), conference October 7, Lyon.

SCP (1994), *Sociaal en Cultureel Rapport 1994*, Social en Cultural Planning Office, Rijswijk.

Second Chamber of the States General, 1993-1994, *Bepalingen Inzake Arbeids- en Rusttijden*, no. 23646, Sdu Publishers, The Hague.

——— (1994-1995), *Gelijke Behandeling Deeltijd-Voltijd*, no. 24 020, Sdu Publishers, The Hague.

SER (1994), *Civielrechtelijke Ontslagbescherming*, 94/05, Social and Economic Council, The Hague.

Soskice, D. (1994), 'Reconciling Markets and Institutions: the German Apprenticeship System', in L.M. Lynch (ed.), 'Training and the Private Sector, International Comparisons', National Bureau of Economic Research, NBER Comparative labor market series, The University of Chicago Press, Chicago, 25-60.

SPU (1996), *Presse und Informationsamt der Bundesregierung*, Sozialpolitische Umschau, 26-2-1996.

STAR (1996), *Nota Flexibiliteit en Zekerheid*, no. 2/96, STAR Foundation of Labour, The Hague.

Statistisches Bundesamt (1996), *Statistisches Jahrbuch für die Bundesrepublik Deutschland 1996*, Metzler Poeschel, Stuttgart.

Stevens, M. (1996), 'Transferable Training and Poaching Externalities', in A.L. Booth and D.J. Snower (eds.), *Acquiring Skills, Market Failures, their Symptoms and Policy Responses*, Cambridge University Press, Cambridge, 19-40.

Stewart, M. (1990), 'Union Wage Differentials, Product Market Influences and Division Rents', *Economic Journal*, 100, 1122-1137.

SZW (1994), *Notitie over Arbeidsduurverkorting*, Dutch Ministry of Social Affairs and Employment, The Hague.

——— (1995), *Arbeidstijdenwet, één Nieuwe Regeling voor Bedrijven en Overheid, Info*, The Hague.

Teulings, C.N. (1995), 'Efficiënte Loonvorming door Sociale Partners', *Economisch Statistische Berichten*, May 17, 460-464.

——— (1996), *De Plaats van de Vakbeweging in de Toekomst*, Welboom, Scientific Publications Series, The Hague.

Teulings, C.N. and J. Hartog (1997), *Corporatism or Competition: an International Comparison of Labour Market Structures and their Impact on Wage Formation*, Cambridge University Press, Cambridge.

Voorlichtingscentrum Sociale Verzekering (1995), *De Kleine Gids voor de Nederlandse Sociale Zekerheid*, Social Insurance Information Service, Kluwer, Deventer.

Waaijers, R.J. (1996), *Loonprofielen naar Leeftijd en Anciënniteit: een Internationale Vergelijking*, CPB Netherlands Bureau for Economic Policy Analysis, Internal Report, no. 96/II/13, The Hague.

Wijngaert, R. van de (1994), *Trade Unions and Collective Bargaining in the Netherlands*, Thesis, Tinbergen Institute, Amsterdam.

Chapter 9 Labour Market: Institutional Arrangements

Albers, O. (1995), *WOR: Wet op de Ondernemingsraden, Tekst en Commentaar '95*, Samson Bedrijfsinformatie B.V., Alphen aan den Rijn.

Baethge, M. and H. Wolf (1995), 'Continuity and Change in the "German Model" of Industrial Relations', in Locke, R., T. Kochan and M. Piore (eds.) (1995), *Employment Relations in a Changing World Economy*, MIT Press, Cambridge, 231-261.

Behringer, F. and W. Jeschek (1993), *Zugang zu Bildung, Bildungsbeteiligung und Ausgaben für Bildung, Entwicklungen im Bildungssystem der Bundesrepublik Deutschland*, Deutsches Institut für Wirtschaftsforschung, Beiträge zur Strukturforschung, heft 139, Berlin.

Berentsen, B. (1995), 'De Richtlijn Euro-OR Toegelicht', FNV, *Kort en Bondig*, 7.

Berkhout, K. and M. Tamminga (1997), 'De Rol van Werknemersvertegenwoordigers in de Bedrijfstop, Bang voor Macht, *NRC Handelsblad*, may 17.
Biagi, M. (1993), 'Forms of Employee Representational Participation', in R. Blanpain and C. Engels (eds.), *Comparative Labour Law and Industrial Relations in Industrialized Market Economies*, Kluwer Law and Taxation Publishers, Deventer-Boston.
BMA (1996), *Statistisches Taschenbuch 1996, Arbeits- und Sozialstatistik*, German Ministry of Labour and Social Order, Bonn.
Broeder, C. den (1995), 'The Match Between Education and Work: What Can We Learn from the German Apprenticeship System?', CPB Netherlands Bureau for Economic Policy Analysis, Research Memorandum no. 118.
Burgh, Y. van der and F. Kriek (1992), *Naleving van de Wet op de Ondernemingsraden, Stand van Zaken Medio 1992*, Dutch Ministry of Social affairs and Employment, The Hague.
Carruth, A. and C. Schnabel (1993), 'The Determination of Contract Wages in West-Germany', *Scandinavian Journal of Economics*, 95, 3, 297-310.
CBS (1995), 'Leden van de Vakbeweging', *Sociaal-Economische Maandstatistiek*, no. 95/11, CBS Statistics Netherlands, Voorburg/Heerlen.
CPB (1995), 'Replacement Rates, a Transatlantic View', CPB Netherlands Bureau for Economic Policy Analysis, Working Paper no. 80, The Hague.
Dercksen, W.J., H. van Lieshout, H. Kamps and Y. Wijnands (1993), *Beroepswijs Onderwijs, Ontwikkelingen en Dilemma's in de Aansluiting van Onderwijs en Arbeid*, Sdu Publishers, The Hague.
Economist, the (1996), *Restoring Germany's Shine*, may 4, 11-26.
Finegold, D. (1991), 'Institutional Incentives and Skill Creation, in P. Ryan (ed.), *International Comparisons of Vocational Education and Training for Intermediate Skills*, Falmer Press, London.
Frietman, J. and B. Hövels (1994), *Varianten van Praktijkplaatsen in het Primair Leerlingwezen: Aard en Voorkomen, Eindverslag*, Institute for Applied Social Sciences (ITS), Nijmegen, July.
Ganga, V. (1992), *Deelname, Uitval en Rendement van het Leerlingwezen*, Dutch Ministry of Education, Culture and Science, Zoetermeer.
Gelauff, G.M.M. and J.J. Graafland (1994), *Modelling Welfare State Reform*, North-Holland Publishers, Amsterdam.
Gelauff, G.M.M. and C. den Broeder (1997), 'Governance of Stakeholder Relationships: the German and Dutch experience', CPB Netherlands Bureau for Economic Policy Analysis, Research Memorandum no. 127.
Gier, H.G. de, P.F. Van der Heijden, M. Rojer and M. Vegter (1994), 'Lexicon van Arbeidsrecht en Arbeidsverhoudingen', *Mededelingen van het Hugo Sinzheimer Instituut*, 7, Hugo Sinzheimer Instituut, Amsterdam.
Gordon, J., J.P. Jallade and D. Parkes (1994), *Op Weg Naar een Beroep in Nederland, Duitsland en Frankrijk, Structuren Binnen het Beroepsonderwijs en de Afstemming van het Onderwijs op de Arbeidsmarkt: een Internationale Vergelijking*, European Institute of Education and Social Policy, Paris.
Graafland, J.J. and J.P. Verbruggen (1993), 'Macro Against Sectoral Wage Equations for the Netherlands', CPB Netherlands Bureau for Economic Policy Analysis, Research Memorandum no. 103.

Graafland, J.J. and F.H. Huizinga (1996), 'Taxes and Benefits in a Non-linear Wage Equation', CPB Netherlands Bureau for Economic Policy Analysis, Research Memorandum no. 125.

Green, A. and H. Steedman (1993), 'Educational Provision, Educational Attainment and the Needs of Industry: a Review of Research for Germany, Japan, the USA and Britain', National Institute of Economic and Social Research, NIESR Report Series no. 5.

Gurdon, M.A. and A. Rai (1990), 'Co-determination and Enterprise Performance: Empirical Evidence from West Germany', *Journal of Economics and Business*, 42, 289-302.

Hancké, B. (1993), 'Trade Union Membership in Europe, 1960-1990: Rediscovering Local Unions', *British Journal of Industrial Relations*, December, 593-613.

Harhoff, D. and T.J. Kane (1993), *Financing Apprenticeship Training: Evidence from Germany*, National Bureau of Economic Research, NBER Working paper no. 4557, Cambridge, Mass.

Heijden, P.F. van der, R.H. van het Kaar, R. Knegt, J. Roebroek, E. Sol and A.C.J.M. Wilthagen (1995), 'Instituties van de Arbeidsmarkt: een Retrospectieve Studie', OSA Organisation for Labour Market Research, preparatory study no. V43.

Hepple, B. (1993), 'European Labour Law: the European Community', in R. Blanpain and C. Engels (eds.), *Comparative Labour Law and Industrial Relations in Industrialized Market Economies*, Kluwer Law and Taxation Publishers, Deventer-Boston.

Het Financieele Dagblad (1997), *Duitse Sociale Partners Sluiten Banenverbond*, 21-5-1997.

Hövels, B. and K. Meijer (1994), 'Structures of Vocational Education and Training and the Match Between Education and Work: an International Comparison. Netherlands: National Report', OSA Organisation for Labour Market Research, July.

IDS (1995b), *Pay and Conditions in the Netherlands 1995*, IDS International Documents.

Jackman, R., R. Layard and S. Nickell (1995), *Structural Aspects of OECD Unemployment*, OECD-paper.

Jacobi, O., B. Keller and W. Müller-Jentsch (1992), 'Germany: Co-determining the Future?' in A. Ferner and R. Hyman (eds.), *Industrial Relations in the New Europe*, Basic Blackwell, Oxford.

Jacobs, A.T.J.M. (1993), *Inleiding tot het Duitse Arbeidsrecht*, Gouda Quint B.V., Arnhem.

Jager, N.E.M. de (1996), 'A Comparative Analysis of Current and Future Human Capital in Germany and the Netherlands', in CBS Statistics Netherlands (1996), *De Nederlandse Arbeidsmarktdag 1995; Flexibilisering: Het Nederlandse Antwoord op Internationalisering? Arbeidsmarktstrategie in een Mondiale Economie*, Voorburg/Heerlen.

Kaar, R.H. van het (1995), 'Ondernemingsraad en Vertrouwenscommissaris, Structuurregeling en Medezeggenschap', *Sinzheimer cahiers* ,9, Sdu Publishers, The Hague.

Kam, C.A. de, W. van Drimmelen and N. van Hulst (1995), *Loonvorming en Loonpolitiek in Nederland*, Wolters-Noordhoff, Groningen.

Katz, H.C. (1993), 'The Decentralization of Collective Bargaining: a Literature Review and Comparative Analysis', *Industrial and Labor Relations Review*, 47(1), 3-22.

Koene, A.M. and H. Slomp (1991), *Medezeggenschap van Werknemers op Ondernemingsniveau: Een Onderzoek naar de Regels en hun Toepassing in zes Europese Landen*, Dutch Ministry of Social Affairs and Employment, VUGA Publishers, The Hague.

Korver, T. (1993), 'Labour market, Labour Contracts and Collective Bargaining', the Netherlands, in: J. Hartog and J. Theeuwes (eds.), *Labour Market Contracts and Institutions, a Cross-National Comparison*, Elseviers Science Publishers B.V., Amsterdam.

Layard, R., S. Nickell and R. Jackman (1991), *Unemployment, Macroeconomic Performance and the Labour Market*, Oxford University Press, Oxford.
Lever, M.H.C. and W.A. Marquering (1995), 'Effect Avv op Werkgelegenheid Blijkt Beperkt', *Economisch Statistische Berichten*, May 24, 484-488.
Lieshout, H. van (1996), *Beroepsonderwijs in Duitsland: een Analyse van het Duits Duale Stelsel van Beroepsonderwijs Vanuit Nederlands Perspectief*, Max Goote Knowledge Centre for Vocational Training and Adult Education, Amsterdam.
Münch, J. and T. Henzelmann (1993), *Systems and Procedures of Certification of Qualifications in the Federal Republic of Germany*, European Centre for the Development of Vocational Training (CEDEFOP), Berlin.
Niedenhoff, H.U. (1990), *Mitbestimmung in der Bundesrepublik Deutschland*, Deutscher Instituts-Verlag GmbH, Köln.
OECD (1991), *Employment Outlook 1991*, Paris.
——— (1994a), *The OECD Jobs Study, Evidence and Explanations, Part II, The Adjustment Potential of the Labour Market*, Paris.
——— (1994b), *Employment Outlook 1994*, Paris.
——— (1994c), *Vocational Training in Germany: Modernisation and Responsiveness*, Paris.
——— (1996a), *OECD Economic Surveys, Germany 1996*, Paris.
——— (1996b), *Employment Outlook 1996*, Paris.
——— (1996c), *Education at a Glance, OECD Indicators*, Paris.
Oulton, N. and H. Steedman (1992), 'The British System of Youth Training: a Comparison With Germany', National Institute of Economic and Social Research, NIESR Report Series no. 10.
Owen Smith, E. (1994), *The German Economy*, Routledge, London and New York.
Paqué, K.H. (1993), 'Germany: Living with Tight Corporatism', in J. Hartog and J. Theeuwes (eds.), *Labour Market Contracts and Institutions, a Cross-National Comparison*, Elseviers Science Publishers B.V., Amsterdam, 9-29.
Römkens, L. and K. Visser (1994), *Beroepsonderwijs en Scholing in Nederland*, European Centre for the Development of Vocational Training (CEDEFOP), Berlin.
Sanders, P. (1995), 'De Europese Vennootschap en de Europese Ondernemingsraad', *TVVS*, 3, 57-61.
Schilstra, K. and E. Smit (1996), 'Drie Scenario's voor de Belangenbehartiging van Werknemers', *Sociaal Maandblad Arbeid*, 51, 2, 116-127.
Schuit, M. (1995), 'Coordinatie en Decentralisatie als Basis voor het Nederlandse Loonvormingsproces', *Tijdschrift voor Politieke Economie*, 18, 2, 94-103.
Second Chamber of the States General, 1993-1994, *Bepalingen Inzake Arbeids- en Rusttijden*, no. 23646, Sdu Publishers, The Hague.
——— (1996a), *Wijziging van de Wet op de Ondernemingsraden*, no. 24 953, Sdu Publishers, The Hague, 1995-1996.
——— (1996b), *Wijziging van de Wet op de Ondernemingsraden en Titel 7.10 (Arbeidsovereenkomst van het Nieuw Burgerlijk Wetboek)*, no. 24 615, Sdu Publishers, The Hague, 1995-1996.
SER (1991), *Voorbeeldreglement Ondernemingsraden voor Grote en Kleine Ondernemingen*, Social and Economic Council, Dienst Bestuurszaken en Voorlichting, The Hague.

Slomp, H. (1995), *Between Bargaining and Politics, an Introduction to European Labor Relations*, Katholic University Nijmegen, Department of Political Science, Nijmegen.

Soskice, D. (1990), 'Wage Determination: the Changing Role of Institutions in Advanced Industrialized Countries', *Oxford Review of Economic Policy*, 6(4), 36-61.

——— (1994), 'Reconciling Markets and Institutions: the German Apprenticeship System', in L.M. Lynch (ed.), *Training and the Private Sector, International Comparisons*, National Bureau of Economic Research, NBER Comparative labor market series, The University of Chigago Press, Chigago, 25-60

Steedman, H. (1993), 'The Economics of Youth Training in Germany', *The Economic Journal*, 103, September, 1279-1291.

Streeck, W. (1984), 'Co-determination, the Fourth Decade', in B. Wilpert and A. Sorge (eds.), *International Perspectives on Organizational Democracy*, John Wiley and Sons, Chichester.

SZW (1996), *De Nederlandse Verzorgingsstaat in Internationaal en Economisch Perspectief*, Dutch Ministry of Social Affairs and Employment, The Hague.

Tessaring, M. (1993), 'Das Duale System der Berufsausbildung in Deutschland: Attraktivität und Beschäftigungsperspektiven, ein Beitrag zur Gegenwärtigen Diskussion', *Mitteilungen aus der Arbeitsmarkt und Berufsforschung*, 26(2), 131-161.

Teulings, A.W.M. (1987), *A Political Bargaining Theory of Co-determination: an Empirical Test for the Dutch System of Organizational Democracy*, University of Amsterdam, Institute of Sociology, Sociology of Organizations Research Unit, Amsterdam.

Teulings, C.N. (1996), *De Plaats van de Vakbeweging in de Toekomst*, Welboom, Scientific Publications Series, The Hague.

Turner, L. (1992), *Democracy at Work: Changing World Markets and the Future of Labor Unions*, Cornell University Press, Ithaca.

——— (1993), 'Prospects for Worker Participation in Management in the Single Market', in L. Ulman, B. Eichengreen and W.T. Dickens (eds.), *Labour and an Integrated Europe*, The Brookings Institutions, Washington D.C.

Tyrväinen, T. (1994), 'Real Wage Resistance and Unemployment, Multivariate Analysis of Cointegrating Relations in 10 OECD Economies', *The OECD Jobs Study*, working paper series, forthcoming.

Vanwersch, I., W. Zeijlstra, K. de Graaf and B. Westerbeek-van Eerten (1993), 'Het WORdt Anders, Overheid onder de WOR', FNV, *Documentatie en Advies*, 15.

Verdonk, O. and G. Wiggers (1994), *Loonvorming in Duitsland*, CPB Netherlands Bureau for Economic Policy Analysis, Internal Report, no. 94/II/17.

Visser, J. (1995), 'Kwaliteit voor de Vakbeweging, naar Aanleiding van de Publikatie van De Vakbeweging na de Welvaartsstaat', *Sociaal Maandblad Arbeid*, 50(6), 371-380.

Vogels, E.H.W.M. (1994), *De Onderkant van de Arbeidsmarkt, een Overzicht van de Wettelijke Minimum(jeugd)lonen, Laagste CAO-lonen en Loon- en Arbeidsvoorwaardenstelsels in Europees Perspectief*, Dutch Ministry of Social Affairs and Employment, Working Document no. 1.

Vries, I. de and F. Heere (1993), *Kosten en Baten van het Leerlingwezen bij Bedrijven*, OSA Organization for Labour Market Research, December.

Wijngaert, R. van de (1994), *Trade Unions and Collective Bargaining in the Netherlands*, Thesis, Tinbergen Institute, Amsterdam.

Winkelmann, R. (1994), 'Training, Earnings and Mobility in Germany', Centre for Economic Policy Research, CEPR Discussion Paper no. 982.

Chapter 10 Corporate Governance

Amsterdam Stock Exchange (1994), 'De Bestrijding van Misbruik van Voorwetenschap', *Beursthema*, 1.

Bakker, R. and G.J.C. Schlaghecke (1995), 'ABP Ziet Rol Als Rentmeester van Bedrijfsleven', *Het Financieele Dagblad*, November 2, 13.

Barentsen, W. (1995), 'Onze Mensen Bouwen aan een Kathedraal', *Het Financieele Dagblad*, September 19, 11.

Baums, T. (1996), 'Vollmachtstimmrecht der Banken – Ja oder Nein?', *Die Aktiengesellschaft*, 41, 11-26.

Baums, T. and C. Fraune (1995), 'Institutionelle Anleger und Publikumsgesellschaft: Eine Empirische Untersuchung', *Die Aktiengesellschaft*, 40, 97-112.

Beckman, H. (1993), 'Europees Jaarrekeningenrecht: Werkelijkheid of Fictie', *Accountant-Adviseur*, 1/2, 30-37.

Bishop, M. (1994), 'Corporate Governance', *The Economist*, January 29.

Blair, M.M. (1995), *Ownership and Control: Rethinking Corporate Governance for the Twenty-First Century*, The Brookings Institution, Washington.

Bloemsma, M.P. (1973), 'Beschermingsconstructies', *Tijdschrift voor Vennootschappen, Verenigingen en Stichtingen*, 225-229.

Boot, A.W.A. (1994), *De Financiering van het Bedrijfsleven: Tussen StructuurRegime en Financiële Sector*, Amsterdam University Press, Amsterdam.

——— (1995), 'Naar een Dynamischer Structuurregime', *De Naamloze Vennootschap*, 73, 280-284.

Borio, C.E.V. (1990), 'Leverage and Financing of Non-Financial Companies: an International Perspective', *BIS Economic Papers*, no. 27.

Bundesverband Deutscher Banken (1995), 'Macht der Banken', Daten Fakten, Argumente, *mimeo*, Köln.

Cantrijn, A.L.R., A.A. Jeunink and M.R. Kabir (1993), 'Beschermingsconstructies en de Rol van de Aandeelhouder', *NIBE katern* no. 24.

Carlin, W. and D. Soskice (1997), 'Shocks to the System: the German Political Economy under Stress', *National Institute Economic Review*, 1, 57-76.

CEPS (1995), 'Corporate Governance in Europe', Center for European Policy Studies, Working Party Report no. 12.

Charkham, J.P. (1994), *Keeping Good Company, a Study of Corporate Governance in five Countries*, Clarendon Press, Oxford.

Çorporate Governance Committee (1996), *Corporate Governance in Nederland, Een Aanzet tot Verandering en een Uitnodiging tot Discussie*, Secretariat Corporate Governance, Amsterdam.

Crist, W.D. (1995), 'The Corporate Governance Impact of US Pension Funds as Large Global Investors', *De Naamloze Vennootschap* 73, 257-264.

CS First Boston (1993), 'The Remaking of Europe, Employment and the Hidden Debt', Economics Research report.

Damme, E. van (1994), 'Banking: a Survey of Recent Microeconomic Theory', *Oxford Review of Economic Policy* 10, 14-33.

Deutsche Bundesbank (1994), 'Entwicklung und Bedeutung der Geldanlage in Investmentzertifikaten', *Monatsbericht*, 46 Jahrgang, no. 10.

Edwards, J.S.S. and K. Fischer (1994), *Banks, Finance and Investment in Germany*, Cambridge University Press, Cambridge.

Fisher, A. (1995), 'Cracks Around the Edges', *Financial Times*, February 27.

Franks, J.R. and C.P. Mayer (1993), 'Capital Markets and Corporate Control, a Study of France, Germany and the UK', *Economic Policy*, 3, 1-12.

——— (1995), 'Ownership and Control ', in H. Siebert (ed.), *Trends in Business Organization: Do Participation and Cooperation Increase Competitiveness?*, J.C.B. Mohr, Tübingen, 171-195.

——— (1996), 'Hostile Takeovers and the Correction of Managerial Failure', *Journal of Financial Economics*, 40, 163-181.

Frederikslust, R.A.I. van and A.J.T. van Veldhuizen (1996), 'Bescherming en Concurrentie in Europees Perspectief', *mimeo*, Rotterdam School of Management, Erasmus University Rotterdam.

Frijns, J.M.G., J. Mensonides and R.J. Schreurs (1995), 'Institutionele Beleggers en Corporate Governance', *De Naamloze Vennootschap*, 73, 265-270.

Fukao, M. (1995), *Financial Integration, Corporate Governance and the Performance of Multinational Companies*, The Brookings Institution, Washington D.C.

Gelauff, G.M.M. and C. den Broeder (1996): 'Governance of Stakeholder Relationships: the German and Dutch Experience', CPB Netherlands Bureau for Economic Policy Analysis, Research Memorandum no. 127.

Gerum, E., H. Steinemann and W. Fees (1988), *Der Mitbestimmte Aufsichtsrat, eine Empirische Untersuchung*, Poeschel Verlag, Stuttgart.

Gilson, R.J., (1995), *Corporate Governance and Economic Efficiency: When do Institutions Matter?*, *mimeo*, Stanford University.

Gorton, G., and F.A. Schmid (1996), 'Universal Banking and the Performance of German Firms', *mimeo*, Wharton School, University of Pennsylvania.

Goudzwaard, M.A. (1994), 'Affaires Maken Duitse Commissarissen Alerter', *Het Financieele Dagblad*, September 15.

Grinten, W.C.L. van der (1990), 'Structuurregeling als Beschermingsconstructie', in K. Geenks, W.C.L. van der Grinten, R.P Voogd, A.G. van Solinge, H.J.M.N. Honée, P.J. Dortmund, J.H.V. Struijck and J.A.W. Stevens, *Beschermingsconstructies*, Kluwer, Deventer.

Hart, O. (1995), *Firms, Contracts, and Financial Structure*, Clarendon Press, Oxford.

Hellwig, M. (1995), 'Comment on Julian Franks and Colin Mayer "Ownership and control"', in H. Siebert (ed.), *Trends in Business Organization: Do Participation and Cooperation Increase Competitiveness?*, J.C.B. Mohr, Tübingen, 196-199.

Honée, H.J.M.N. (1986), *Contacten Tussen Commissarissen en Ondernemingsraad*, Kluwer, Deventer.

Jacobs, M.T. (1991), *Short-term America, The Causes and Cures of Our Business Myopia*, Harvard Business School Press, Harvard.

Jenkinson, T., and C. Mayer (1992), 'The Assessment: Corporate Governance and Corporate Control', *Oxford Review of Economic Policy*, 8, 1-10.

Jong, H.W. de (1991), 'The Takeover Market in Europe: Control Structures and the Performance of Large Companies Compared', *Review of Industrial Organization*, 6, 1-18.

Kaar, R.H. van het (1995), 'Ondernemingsraad en Vertrouwenscommissaris, Structuurregeling en Medezeggenschap', *Sinzheimer cahiers*, 9, Sdu Publishers, The Hague.

Karpoff, J.M., Malatesta P.H. and R.A. Walkling (1996), 'Corporate Governance and Shareholder Initiatives: Empirical Evidence', *Journal of Financial Economics*, 42, 365-395.

Knoop, J. van der (1991), *Tussen Toeschouwen en Meesturen: de Rol van Commissarissen in en Tussen Grote Vennootschappen*, Thesis Publishers, Amsterdam.

Koene, A.M., and H. Slomp (1991), *Medezeggenschap van Werknemers op Ondernemingsniveau, Een Onderzoek Naar de Regels en Hun Toepassing in Zes Europese Landen*, Dutch Ministry of Social affairs and Employment, VUGA uitgeverij B.V., The Hague.

Kümpel, S. (1995), *Bank und Kapitalmarktrecht*, Verlag Dr. Otto Schmidt, Köln.

Lane, C. (1992), 'European Business Systems, Britain and Germany Compared', in R. Whitley (ed.), European Business Systems, *Firms and Markets in their National Contexts*, Sage Publications, London.

Ligtenberg, L. (1997), 'Walt Disney Belaagd om Hoge Bonussen', *NRC Handelsblad*, February 26.

Milgrom, P. and J. Roberts (1992), *Economics, Organization and Management*, Prentice Hall, New Jersey.

Moerland, P.W. (1995), 'Alternative Disciplinary Mechanisms in Different Corporate Systems', *Journal of Economic Behaviour and Organization*, 26, 17-34.

Monks, R.A.G, and N. Minow (1995), *Corporate Governance*, Blackwell, Oxford.

Monopolkommission (1994), *Mehr Wettbewerb auf Allen Märkten*, Nomos Verlagsgesellschaft, Baden-Baden.

Nickell, S.J. (1995), *The Performance of Companies: The Relationship Between the External Environment, Management Strategies and Corporate Performance*, Blackwell, Oxford.

Nobes, C. (1992), 'International Classification of Financial Reporting', in C. Nobes and R. Parker (eds.), *Comparative International Accounting*, 3rd e., 38-51.

OECD (1995a), *Economic Survey of Germany*, Paris.

——— (1995b), *National Systems for Financing Innovation*, Paris.

——— (1996), *Economic Survey of the United States*, Paris.

Offeren, D. van (1992), 'Onvergelijkbaarheden', *Financieel Economisch Magazine*, November 28, 20-21.

Porter, M.E. (1992), 'Capital Choices: Changing the Way America Invests in Industry', Council on Competitiveness, Research Report.

Pound, J. (1995), 'The Promise of the Governed Corporation' *Harvard Business Review*, March-April, 89-98.

Prowse, S. (1994), 'Corporate Governance in an International Perspective: A Study of Corporate Control Mechanisms among Large Firms in the United States, the United Kingdom and Germany.', *BIS Economic Papers*, no. 41.

Rietkerk, G. (1992), 'Structuurregeling aan Heroverweging Toe', *Economisch Statistische Berichten*, 124-127.

Schilling, F. (1994), 'Der Aufsichtsrat Ist für die Katz', *Frankfurter Allgemeine Zeitung*, August 27, 11.

Schleifer, A. and R.W. Vishny (1989), 'Management Entrenchment: the Case of Manager-specific Investments', *Journal of Financial Economics*, 25, 123-139.

Schneider-Lenné, E.R. (1992), 'Corporate Control in Germany', *Oxford Review of Eonomic Policy*, 8, 11-23.

——— (1995), *Die Rolle der Institutionellen Anleger in Aufsichtsräten*, paper presented at the conference 'Aufsicht und Rat', Frankfurt am Main, February 15.

Scholtens, L.J.R. (1996), *Ontwikkeling en Structuur van Financiële Systemen, Theoretisch Kader en Empirische Bevindingen*, Financiële Monetaire Studies, Wolters-Noordhoff, Groningen.

Schröder, U. (1995), 'The Changing Role of German Banks in Corporate Governance', Deutsche Bank Research, paper presented at a Centre for Economic Policy Research (CEPR) workshop, Milano, June 16.

Seibert, U. (1997), 'Kontrolle und Transparenz im Unternehmensbereich (KonTraG), Der Referenten-Entwurf zur Aktienrechtsnovelle', *Zeitschrift für Wirtschafts- und Bankrecht*, WM Wertpapier Mitteilungen, 51, Heft 1, 1-48

Slagter, W.J. (1993), 'Naar Nieuwe Machtsverhoudingen in de Nederlandse Vennootschap', *TVVS*, 8, 194-197.

——— (1994), 'Institutional Investors and Corporate Governance in the Netherlands' in T. Baums, R.M. Buxbaum and K.J. Hopt (eds.), *Institutional Investors and Corporate Governance*, Walter de Gruyter, Berlin, 329-345.

Statistisches Bundesamt (1994), *Statistisches Jahrbuch für die Bundesrepublik Deutschland 1994*, Metzler Poeschel, Stuttgart.

Stiglitz J.E. (1985), 'Credit Markets and the Control of Capital', *Journal of Money Credit and Banking*, 17, 133-152.

——— (1991), 'The Invisible Hand and Modern Welfare Economics', in D. Vines and A.A. Stevenson (eds.), *Information, Strategy and Public Policy*, Basil Blackwell, Oxford, 12-50.

Streeck W. (1984), 'Co-determination, the Fourth Decade', in B. Wilpert and A. Sorge (eds.), *International Perspectives on Organisational Democracy*, John Wiley and Sons, Chichester.

Swank, J., L. de Haan and F.J. Veldkamp (1989), *Financiële Balansen van Gezinnen en Bedrijven in Nederland, 1982-1987*, De Nederlandsche Bank, Monetaire Monografieën, no. 10.

Tamminga, M. (1995), 'Na Bedrijfsdebâcle Kan de Commissaris op Claims Rekenen', *NRC Handelsblad*, December 12, 19.

——— (1996), 'Bank-Verzekeraar ING Schuwt het Financiële Spektakel Niet', *NRC Handelsblad*, February 2, 13.

Vijver, J.J. de (1980), 'Proxy Solicitation', in B. Baardman, M.M. Mendel and M.J.G.C. Raaijmakers (eds.), *Jurist in Bedrijf: Opstellen van Bedrijfsjuristen bij het 50-Jarig Bestaan van het Nederlands Genootschap van Bedrijfsjuristen*, Kluwer, Deventer.

Voogd, R.P. (1989), *Statutaire Beschermingsmiddelen bij Beursvennootschappen, Monografieën Vanwege het van de Heijden-Instituut 32*, Kluwer, Deventer.

Waard, M. de, (1996), 'Wet Moet Finanzplatz Helpen', *NRC Handelsblad*, November 28.

Yafeh, Y., and O. Yosha (1995), *Large Shareholders and Banks: Who Monitors and How?*, Centre for Economic Policy Research, CEPR Discussion Paper no. 1178.

Zwiebel, J. (1995), 'Block Investment and Partial Benefits of Corporate Control', *Review of Economic Studies*, 62, 161-185.

Chapter 11 Science and Technology Policy

Abbott, A. and Q. Schiermeier, (1996), 'German Plans may Increase Competition', *Nature*, 374.

Acs, Z.J. and L. Preston (1997), 'Small and Medium-Sized Enterprises, Technology, and Gobalization: Introduction to a Special Issue on Small and Medium-Sized Enterprises in the Global Economy', *Small Business Economics*, 9, 1-6.

Archibugi, D. and M. Pianta (1992), *The Technological Specialization of Advanced Countries*, Kluwer Academic Publishers, Dordrecht.

Arrow, K. (1962), 'Economic Welfare and the Allocation of Resources for Invention', in R. Nelson (ed.), *The Rate and Direction of Inventive Activity: Economic and Social Factors*, Princeton University Press, New York.

Audretsch, D.B. (1995), 'International Diffusion of Technological Knowledge', Discussion Paper FS IV, 95-8.

BMBF (1996), *Bundesbericht Forschung*, German Ministry of Education, Science, Research and Technology, Bonn.

——— (1997a), 'Hochschulen für das 21. Jahrhundert', Internet Pages BMBF, www.bmbf.de, PD26.02.1997, retrieved June 1997.

——— (1997b), 'Innovationen durch mehr Flexibilität und Wettbewerb', Internet Pages BMBF, www.bmbf.de, PD11.07.1997, retrieved June 1997.

Brooks, H. (1994), 'The Relationship Between Science and Technology', *Research Policy*, 23, 477-486.

Carlin, W. and D. Soskice (1997), 'Shocks to the System: the German Political Economy under Stress', *National Institute Economic Review*, 1, 57-76.

CBS (1996), *Kennis en Economie 1996*, CBS Statistics Netherlands, Voorburg/Heerlen.

Cobbenhagen, J. (1990), 'Innoveren: Strategieën en Modellen', in J. den Hertog and F. van Eijnatten (eds.), *Management van Technologische Vernieuwing*, Van Gorcum, Assen.

Coe, D. and E. Helpman (1995), 'International R&D Spill-overs', *European Economic Review*, 39, 859-887.

Cohen, W.M. and D.A. Levinthal (1989), 'Innovation and Learning: the Two Faces of R&D', *Economic Journal*, 99, 569-596.

Dasgupta, P. (1987), 'The Economic Theory of Technology Policy: an Introduction' in P. Dasgupta and P. Stoneman (eds.), *Economic Policy and Technological Performance'*, Cambridge University Press, Cambridge, 7-23.

Dasgupta, P. and P.A. David (1987), 'Information disclosure and the economics of science and technology', in G. Feiwel (ed.), *Kenneth Arrow and the Ascent of Economic Theory*, MacMillan, New York.

——— (1994), 'Toward a New Economics of Science', *Research Policy*, 23, 487-521.

David, P.A. (1986), 'Technology Diffusion, Public Policy and Industrial Competitiveness', in R. Landau and N. Rosenberg (eds.), *The Positive Sum Strategy: Harnessing Technology for Economic Growth*, National Academy Press, Washington.

DFG (1997), General Information on Deutsche Forschungsgemeinschaft, DFG Internet Pages, www.dfg.de, retrieved May 1997.

Dijk, Th.W.P. van (1994), *The Limits of Patent Protection: Essays on the Economics of Intellectual Property Rights*, University Press Maastricht.

Eaton, J. and S. Kortum (1996), 'Trade in Ideas: Patenting and Productivity in the OECD', *Journal of International Economics*, 40, 251-278.

EZ/OCW/LNV (1995), *Kennis in Beweging: over Kennis en Kunde in de Nederlandse Economie*, Dutch Ministry of Economic Affairs, Dutch Ministry of Education, Culture and Science, Dutch Ministry of Agriculture, The Hague.

EZ (1996), *Rijksbegroting 1997, Economische Zaken*, Second Chamber of the States General, vergaderjaar 1996-1997, 25000 hoofdstuk XIII, no. 1.

FAZ (1997), 'Rüttgers: Deutschland soll Beste Forschungslandschaft der Welt Werden', *Frankfurther Algemeine Zeitung*, June 18.

FhG (1995), *Jahresbericht 1994*, München.

——— (1996), *Annual Report 1995*, Fraunhofer Gesellschaft Internet Pages, www.fhg.de, retrieved June 1997.

Frackmann, E. and E. de Weert (1993), 'Higher Education Policy in Germany', in L. Goedegebuure, F. Kaiser, P. Maassen, L. Meek, F. van Vugt and E. de Weert (eds.), *Higher Education Policy: an International Comparative Perspective*, Pergamon Press, Oxford.

Frederiks, M. and D.F. Westerheijden (1996), 'Kwaliteit van Hoger Onderwijs en Nationaal Concurrentievermogen', Centrum voor Studies van het Hoger Onderwijs Beleid, Twente University, Series Studies van het Hoger Onderwijsbeleid, no. 206.

Geroski, P.A. (1991), *Market Dynamics and Entry*, Blackwell, Oxford.

——— (1995), 'Markets for Technology: Knowledge, Innovation and Appropriability', in P. Stoneman (ed.), *Handbook of the Economics of Innovation and Technological Change*, Blackwell, Oxford, 90-131.

Goedegebuure, L., F. Kaiser, P. Maassen and E. de Weert (1993), 'Higher Education Policy in the Netherlands', in L. Goedegebuure, F. Kaiser, P. Maassen, L. Meek, F. van Vugt and E. de Weert (eds.), *Higher education Policy: an International Comparative Perspective*, Pergamon Press, Oxford.

Grossman, G.M. and E. Helpman (1991), *Innovation and Growth in the Global Economy*, MIT Press, Cambridge.

ISI (1997), 'Delphi II Geht in die Zweite Runde', Internet Pages of the Fraunhofer Institut Systemtechnik und Innovationsforschung, www.isi.fhg.de, retrieved January 1997.

Jacobs, D. (1996), *Het Kennisoffensief*, Samson Bedrijfsinformatie, Alphen aan den Rijn.

Kamien, M.I. and N.L. Schwartz (1982), *Market Structure and Innovation*, Cambridge University Press, Cambridge.

Klemperer, P. (1990), 'How Broad Should the Scope of Patent Protection Be?', *RAND Journal of Economics*, 20, 265-290.

Kline, S.J. (1985), 'Innovation is Not a Linear Process', *Research Management*, 36-45.

Klodt, H. (1996), 'The German Innovation System: Conceptions, Institutions and Economic Efficiency', Kiel Working Papers no. 775, November.

Klundert, Th. van de (1997), *Groei en Instituties: Over de Oorzaken van Economische Ontwikkeling*, Tilburg University Press, Tilburg.

Lee, Y.S. (1996), 'Technology Transfer and the Research University: a Search for the Boundaries of University-Industry Collaboration', *Research Policy*, 25, 843-863.

Levin, R.C., A.K. Klevorick, R.R. Nelson and S.G. Winter (1987), 'Appropriating the Returns from Industrial Research and Development', *Brookings Papers on Economic Activity*, 3, 783-820.

Lundvall, B.A. (ed.) (1992), *National Systems of Innovation: Towards a Theory of Innovation and Interactive Learning*, Pinter, London.

Matutes, C., P. Regibeau and K. Rockett (1993), Optimal Patent Design and Diffusion of Innovations', *mimeo*, Northwestern University.

Metcalfe, S. (1995), 'The Economic Foundations of Technology Policy: Equilibrium and Evolutionary Perspectives', in P. Stoneman (ed.), *Handbook of the Economics of Innovation and Technological Change*, Blackwell, Oxford, 409-512.

Minne, B. (1992), 'Technologie en Economie: de Nederlandse Positie', CPB Netherlands Bureau for Economic Policy Analysis, Research Memorandum no. 94.

Mowery, D. (1995), 'The Practice of Technology Policy', in P. Stoneman (ed.), *Handbook of the Economics of Innovation and Technological Change*, Blackwell, Oxford, 513-557.

Nelson, R. (ed.) (1993), *National Innovation Systems,* Oxford University Press, Oxford.

Nelson, R. and P.M. Romer (1996), 'Science, Economic Growth, and Public Policy', in B. Smith and C. Barfield (eds.), *Technology, R&D and the Economy*, Brookings Institution and the American Enterprise Institute.

Nickell, S.J. (1996), 'Competition and Corporate Performance', *Journal of Political Economy*, 104, 724-746.

NOWT (1994), *Wetenschaps en Technologie Indicatoren 1994*, Nederlands Observatorium van Wetenschap en Technologie: CWTS, Centrum voor Wetenschaps en Technologie Studies, Leiden University, MERIT, Maastricht Economic Research Institute on Innovation and Technology.

——— (1996), *Wetenschaps en Technologie Indicatoren 1996*, Nederlands Observatorium van Wetenschap en Technologie: CWTS, Centrum voor Wetenschaps en Technologie Studies, Leiden University, MERIT, Maastricht Economic Research Institute on Innovation and Technology.

OCV (1996), *A Vital Knowledge System: Dutch Research with a View to the Future*, Foresight Steering Committee, Amsterdam.

OCW (1993), *Onderwijs en Onderzoek in Cijfers*, Dutch Ministry of Education, Culture and Science, Zoetermeer.

——— (1996a), *Report of the NWO Evaluation Committee*, Dutch Ministry of Education, Culture and Science, Zoetermeer.

——— (1996b), *Wetenschapsbudget 1997*, Dutch Ministry of Education, Culture and Science, Zoetermeer.

OECD (1992), *Technology and the Economy*, Paris.

Reinhard, M. and H. Schmalholz (1996), *Technologietransfer in Deutschland: Stand und Reformbedarf,* Duncker & Humbolt, Berlin.

Reinganum, J.F. (1989), 'The Timing of Innovation: Research, Development, and Diffusion,' in R. Schmalensee and R.D. Willig (eds.), *Handbook of Industrial Organization*, Elsevier Science Publishers, Amsterdam.

Rosenberg, N. and R.R. Nelson (1994), 'American Universities and Technical Advance in Industry', *Research Policy*, 23, 323-348.

Solow, R.M. (1957), 'Technical Change and the Aggregate Production Function', *Review of Economics and Statistics*, 39, 312-320.

Stephan, P.E. (1996), 'The Economics of Science', *Journal of Economic Literature*, XXXIV, 1199-1235.

Stoneman, P. (1995), 'Introduction', in P. Stoneman (ed.), *Handbook of the Economics of Innovation and Technological Change*, Blackwell, Oxford, 1-13.

Stoneman, P. and P. Diederen (1994), 'Technology Diffusion and Public Policy', *The Economic Journal*, 104, 918-930.

Stoneman, P. and J. Vickers (1988), 'The Assessment: the Economics of Technology Policy', *Oxford Review of Economic Policy*, 4, i-xvi.

TNO (1996), *Jaarverslag 1995*, Netherlands Organisation for Applied Scientific Research, Delft.

VSNU (1997), Internet pages, www.vsnu.nl, Association of Universities in the Netherlands, May 1997.

Chapter 12 Regulation and Competition Policies

Armstrong, M., S. Cowan and J. Vickers (1994), *Regulatory Reform: Economic Analysis and British Experience*, MIT Press, Cambridge, Mass.

Bain, J.S. (1956), *Barriers to New Competition*, Harvard University Press, Cambridge, Mass.

Baumol, W.J., J.C.Panzar and R.D. Willig (1982), *Contestable Markets and the Theory of Industry Structure*, Harcourt, New York.

Bergeijk, P.A.G. van and R.C.G. Haffner (1996), *Privatization, deregulation and the Macroeconomy - Measurement, Modelling and Policy*, Edward Elgar, Cheltenham.

Bishop, M., J. Kay, and C. Mayer (1995), *The Regulatory Challenge*, Oxford University Press, Oxford.

CEPS (1996), *Towards a single market in utilities - Report of the CEPS working party on utilities*, Centre for European Policy Studies, Working Party Report no. 14.

Comanor, W.S. (1990), 'United States Antitrust Policy: Issues and Institutions', in A. Jacquemin *et al.* (eds.), *Competition Policy in Europe and North America: Economic Issues and institutions*, Harwood Academic Publishers, Chur, 43-72.

CPB (1992), *Nederland in Drievoud*, CPB Netherlands Bureau for Economic Policy Analysis, Sdu Publishers, The Hague.

Geelhoed (1993), 'Deregulering, Herregulering en zelfregulering', in Ph. Eijlander, P.C. Gilhuis en J.A.F. Peters (eds.), *Overheid en Zelfregulering*, W.E.J. Tjeenk Willink B.V., 33-51.

Høj, J., T. Kato and D. Pilat (1995), 'Deregulation and Privatization in the Service Sector', *OECD Economic Studies*, no. 25, 1995/II, 37-74.

Jenkinson, T. and C. Mayer (1996), 'The Assessment: Contracts and Competition', *Oxford Review of Economic Policy*, 12(4), 1-10.

Kahn, A. (1988), *Economics of Regulation: Principles and Institutions*, MIT Press, Cambridge.

Kamien, M. and N. Schwartz (1982), *Market Structure and Innovation*, Cambridge University Press, Cambridge.

Kantzenbach, E. (1990), 'Competition Policy in West Germany: a Comparison with the Antitrust Policy of the United States', in A. Jacquemin *et al.* (eds.), *Competition Policy in Europe and North America: Economic Issues and Institutions*, Harwood Academic Publishers, Chur, 189-205.

Koedijk, K. and J.J.M. Kremers (1996), 'Market Opening, Regulation and Growth in Europe', Ocfeb Research Centre for Economic Policy, Research Memorandum no. 9607, Erasmus University Rotterdam.

Laffont and Tirole (1993), *A Theory of Incentives in Procurement and Regulation*, MIT Press, Cambridge.

Mankiw, N.G. and M.D. Whinston (1986), 'Free Entry and Social Inefficiency', *RAND Journal of Economics*, 17(1), 48-58.

Monopolkommission (1996), *Wettbewerbspolitik in Zeiten des Umbruchs - Elftes Hauptgutachten der Monopolkommission* (summary), July 4.

Mueller, D.C. (1996), 'Lessons from the United States' Antitrust History', *International Journal of Industrial Organization*, 14, 415-445.

NERA (1992), *The Identification and Control of Market Dominance - A Report by NERA for the Dutch Ministry of Economic Affairs*, National Economic Research Associates, London, May.

Nickell, S.J. (1996), 'Competition and Corporate Performance', *Journal of Political Economy*, 104(4), 724-746.

Norman, P. (1997), 'Bonn Plans Cartel Law Change', *Financial Times*, April 28.

OECD (1992), *Privatization, Regulatory Reform and Competition Policy*, Paris.

——— (1993), *Economic Surveys, the Netherlands*, Paris.

——— (1995), *Competition policy in OECD Countries*, 1992-1993, Paris.

——— (1996), *Economic surveys, Germany*, Paris.

Peeperkorn, L. (1987), 'Mededingingsbeleid op Klompen', *Tijdschrift voor Politieke Economie*, 10, 57-75.

Rooy, Y.M.C.T. van (1992), 'Het Einde van het Kartelparadijs', *Economisch Statistische Berichten*, September 23, 908-912.

Schelling, T. (1960), *The Strategy of Conflict*, Harvard University Press, Cambridge, Mass.

Schumpeter, J.A. (1943), *Capitalism, Socialism and Democracy*, Harper & Row, New York.

Stoffers, M.J. (1995), 'Marktwerking en Performance in de Nederlandse en Duitse Bouw', CPB Netherlands Bureau for Economic Policy Analysis, Internal Note 95/III/8.

Sutton, J. (1992), *Sunk Costs and Market Structure*, MIT Press, Cambridge, Mass.

Tirole, J. (1989), *The Theory of Industrial Organization*, MIT Press, Cambridge, Mass.

Uitermark, P.J. (1990), *Economische Mededinging en Algemeen Belang: een Onderzoek naar de Economisch-Theoretische Fundering van de Mededingingspolitiek*, Wolters-Noordhoff, Groningen.

Vickers, J. and G. Yarrow (1988), *Privatization: An Economic Analysis*, MIT Press, Cambridge, Mass.

Welt, die (1996), *Wettbewerb in Freiheit*, July 11.

Williamson, O.E. (1975), Markets and Hierarchies, Analysis and Antitrust Implications, MacMillan, New York.

Chapter 13 Electricity and Gas Markets

Armstrong, M., S. Cowan and J. Vickers (1994), *Regulatory Reform: Economic Analysis and British Experience*, MIT Press, Massachusetts.

Beesly, M.E. (ed.) (1995), *Utility Regulation: Challenge and Response; The State of Britain's Regulatory Régime*, Institute of Economic Affairs in association with the London Business School, Bourne Press, Dorset.

Berg, S.V. and J. Tschirhart (1988), *Natural Monopoly Regulation: Principles and Practice*, Cambridge University Press, Cambridge.

Bundesregierung (1997), 'Soziale Flankierung des Anpassungsprozesses im Deutschen Steinkohlebergbau', *Sozialpolitische Umschau*, 105.

CPB (1997), *Economie en Fysieke Omgeving: Beleidsopgaven en Oplossingsrichtingen 1995-2020*, CPB Netherlands Bureau for Economic Policy Analysis, Sdu Publishers, The Hague, forthcoming.

FAZ (1996), 'Wettbewerb auf den Energiemärkten Angestrebt', *Frankfurter Algemeine Zeitung*, May 2.

Financial Times (1997), 'Electricity Competition Warning', June 10.

Gilbert, R.J., E.P. Kahn and D.M. Newbery (1996), 'Introduction: International Comparisons of Electricity Regulation', in R.J. Gilbert and E.P. Kahn (eds.), *International Comparisons of Electricity Regulation*, Cambridge University Press, Cambridge.

Green, R. and D.M. Newbery (1997), 'Competition in the Electricity Industry in England and Wales', *Oxford Review of Economic Policy*, 13(1), 27-46.

Helm, D. and T. Jenkinson (1997), 'The Assessment: Introducing Competition into Regulated Industries', *Oxford Review of Economic Policy*, 13(1), 1-14.

Huygen, A.E.H. and J.J.M. Theeuwes (1996), 'Vrije Elektriciteitsmarkt Vergt Onafhankelijk Netbeheer', *Economische Statistische Berichten*, May 22, 468-472.

Joskow, P.L. (1989), 'Regulatory Failure, Regulatory Reform, and Structural Change in the Electrical Power Industry', in M.N. Baily and C. Winston (eds.), *Brookings Papers on Economic Activity*, Brookings Institution, Washingtion, D.C.

Joskow, P.L. and R. Schmalensee (1983), *Markets for Power - An anlysis of Electric Utility Deregulation*, MIT Press, Cambridge.

Künneke R.W., M.J. Arentsen, A.M.P. Manders, A.E. Steenge and M.H. Voogd (1996), *Marktwerking in de Energiesector: Een Onderzoek naar de Mogelijkheden tot Introductie van Marktwerking in de Nederlandse Energiesector*, Twente University, Dutch Ministry of Economic Affairs, reeks Beleidsstudies Energie, 12.

Littlechild, S. (1994), 'Competition, Monopoly and Regulation in the Electricity Industry', in M.A. Einhorn (ed.), *From Regulation to Competition: New Frontiers in Electricity Markets*, Kluwer Academic Publishers Group, Dordrecht.

London Economics (1996), *Single Market Review 1996: Infrastructure Development Single Energy Market, Report to the European Commission*, London Economics in association with EWI, NTUA, AUPEC, London.

McKinsey & Company, Inc. (1996), *Capital productivity*, Washington, D.C., June.

Newbery, D.M. and R. Green (1996), 'Regulation, Public Ownership and Privatisation of the English Electricity Industry', in R.J. Gilbert and E.P. Kahn (eds.), *International Comparisons of Electricity Regulation*, Cambridge University Press, Cambridge.

NRC Handelsblad (1997), 'SEP: Fusie in Produktie van Stroom Bedreigd', May 17.

OECD (1995), *OECD Environmental Data, compendium 1995*, Paris.

——— (1997), 'The Economy Wide Effects of Regulatory Reform', ECO/GEN(96)15, Paris, *mimeo*.

OECD/IEA (1994a), *Energy Balances 1991-1992*, Paris.

——— (1994b), *Electricity Supply Industry: Structure, Ownership and Regulation in OECD Countries*, Paris.
——— (1995), *Energy Balances 1993-1994*, Paris.
——— (1996a), *Energy Prices and Taxes, fourth quarter 1995*, Paris.
——— (1996b), *Energy Prices and Taxes, first quarter 1996*, Paris.
Ruff, L.E. (1994), 'Comptitive Electricity Markets: The Theory and Its Application', in M.A. Einhorn (ed.), *From Regulation to Competition: New Frontiers in Electricity Markets*, Kluwer Academic Publishers Group, Dordrecht.
Spottiswoode, C. (1995), 'Developing Competition: Regulatory Initiatives', in M.E. Beesly (ed.), *Utility Regulation: Challenge and Response. The State of Britain's Regulatory Régime*, Institute of Economic Affairs in association with the London Business School, Bourne Press, Dorset.
Vickers, J. and G. Yarrow (1994), 'The British Electricity Experiment', in M.A. Einhorn (ed.), *From Regulation to Competition: New Frontiers in Electricity Markets*, Kluwer Academic Publishers Group, Dordrecht.
Yarrow, G. (1994), 'Privatisation, Restructuring and Regulatory Reform in Electricity Supply', in M. Bishop, J. Kay and C. Mayer, (eds.), *Privatization and Economic Performance*, Oxford University Press, Oxford.

Chapter 14 Health Care

Aaron, H.J. (1996), *The Problem that Won't Go Away*, Brookings Institution, Washington DC.
Arrow, K.J. (1963), 'Uncertainty and the Welfare Economics of Medical Care,' *American Economic Review*, LIII(5), December.
Bundesministerium für Gesundheit (1995), 'Daten des Gesundheitswesen', German Ministry of Health, Nomos Verlaggesellschaft, Baden-Baden.
CBS (1995), *Statistisch zakboek*, CBS Statistics Netherlands, Voorburg/Heerlen.
COTG (1994), 'Jaarverslag,' Central Agency Healthcare Tariffs, Utrecht.
Cutler, D.M. (1996), 'Public Policy for Health Care,' NBER Working Paper no. 5591, Cambridge, Mass.
Enthoven, A.C. (1988), *Theory and Practice of Managed Competition in Health Care Finance*, Elsevier Science, New York.
Fuchs, V.R. (1996), 'Economics, Values, and Health Care Reform,' *American Economic Review*, 86(1), March.
Galjaard-Middel, I. (1996), 'National Health Service,' CPB Netherlands Bureau for Economic Policy Analysis, Internal Note, 96/II/20, September.
Hellerstein, J.K. (1994), *Post-Patent Prescription Pharmaceuticals*, Harvard University Ph.D. Dissertation.
McKinsey (1996), *Health Care Productivity*, McKinsey & Company, Los Angeles.
Melker, R.A. de (1997), 'The Family Doctor,' in F.T. Schrijvers (ed.), *Health and Health Care in the Netherlands*, De Tijdstroom, Utrecht.
Newhouse, J.P. (1986), 'Capitation and Medicare,' Rand Report: R-3455-HCFA, The RAND Corporation.
——— (1993), *Free for All?: Lessons from the RAND Health Insurance Experiment*, Harvard University Press, Cambridge, Mass.

——— (1996), 'Reimbursing Health Plans and Health Providers: Efficiency in Production Versus Selection,' *Journal of Economic Literature*, XXXIV.

OECD (1996), *Health Data 1996*, Paris.

——— (1995), 'Healthcare Reform: The Will to Change,' *Health Policy Studies*, no.5, Paris.

RIVM (1993), *Volksgezondheid Toekomst Verkenning*, National Institute of Public Health and the Environment, SDU Publishers, the Hague.

Sachverständigenrat (1988), *Medizinische und Ökonomische Orientierung, Vorschlagen für die Konzertierte Aktion im Gesundheitswesen*, Jahresgutachten, Nomos Verlagsgesellschaft, Baden-Baden.

Schut, F.T. (1995), *Competition in the Dutch Health Care Sector*, Erasmus University Rotterdam.

Statistisches Bundesamt (1995), 'Grunddaten der Krankenhäuser und Vorsorge- oder Rehabilitationseinrichtungen,' Fachserie 12, Reihe 6.1, 1993, Metzler-Poeschel, Stuttgart.

VWS (1996), Jaaroverzicht Zorg, Dutch Ministry of Health, Welfare, and Sport, SdU Publishers, The Hague.

White, J. (1995), *Competing Solutions - American Health Care Proposals and International Experience*, The Brookings Insitutions, Washington D.C.

Chapter 15 Concluding Remarks

CPB (1992), *Scanning the Future: a Long Term Scenario Study of the World Economy 1990-2015*, CPB Netherlands Bureau of Economic Policy Analysis, Sdu Publishers, The Hague.

List of Figures

List of Tables

List of Boxes

List of Acknowledgements

It is hardly possible to thank all people who in one way or the other contributed to this study. Many CPB collegues performed exploratory research in the first phase of the project, provided data, informed about institutional arrangements and gave stimulating comments on various drafts. Two internal workshops also proved very useful in that respect. From outside CPB, researchers gave valuable advise and comments, staff members of ministries provided insight on relevant policy issues, and representatives from companies gave valuable views on the impact of institutions on daily practice. In particular we would like to thank:

Ark, dr. B. van
Breyer, prof.dr.
Broesterhuizen, drs. E.A.A.M.
Boot, prof.dr. A.W.A.
Börsch-Supam, prof.dr. A.
Bos, drs. M.
Damme, prof.dr. E.E.C.
Davis, prof.dr. P.
Delsen, dr. L.
Diederen, P.
DSM NV, Geleen
Duysters, dr. G.
Ekkers, dr. C.L.
Fremdling, prof.dr. R.
Frijns, dr. J.M.G.
Garretsen, prof.dr. H.
Geelhoed, mr. L.A.
Gent, drs. C. van
Groot, drs. J.C. de
Haan, prof.dr. J. de
Hebborn, A. dipl. Kfm.
Hoogovens NV, Velsen
Jong, mr. I.M. de
Jong, prof.dr. H.W. de
Kaar, dr. R.H. van het
Klodt, dr. H.
Koning, dr. J. de
Koopman, drs. G.J.
Koopmans, dr. C.C.
Klundert, prof.dr. Th.C.M.J. van de
Licht, dr. G.
Lieshout, dr. H. van
Lindlar, dr. L.
Lubbers, prof.dr. R.F.M.
Merrienboer, drs. E. van
Pötzsch, dr. T.
Reulig, dr. J.
Riphahn, dr. R.
Schaaij, mr. J.P.
Scheremet, dr. W.
Scherer, prof.dr. F.M.
Schlote, W.M.,
Scholtens, dr. L.J.R.
Schröder, dr. U.
Schut, dr. F.T.
Segaar, drs. P.F.
Siemens NV, Zoetermeer
Sinderen, prof.dr. J. van
Soete, prof.dr. L.
Spoorendonk, drs. P.A.R.
Sprangers, dr. L.
Steen, drs. J. van

Stoppelaar, drs. R.
Theeuwes, prof.dr. J.J.M.
Verspagen, dr. B.
Vries, mr. K.G. de
Walter, prof.dr. N.
Waasdorp, drs. P.M.
Wennekers, drs. A.R.M.
Westerhout, dr. E.W.M.T.
Wijnheijmer, drs. L.

Staff members of the German and Dutch Bureaus of Statistics, and of the directorate for Gas an Electricity Policy, directorate Economic Structure, and the directorate Technology Policy of the Dutch Ministry of Economic Affairs.